OSWALD'S TALE

OSWALD'S TALE

AN AMERICAN MYSTERY

NORMAN MAILER

RANDOM HOUSE   NEW YORK

To Norris, my wife,
for this book and for the other seven
that have been written through these warm years,
these warm twenty years we have been together.

AN APPRECIATION

to Larry Schiller, my skilled and wily colleague in interview and investigation, for the six months we labored side by side in Minsk and
Moscow, and then again in Dallas, feeling as close as family (and
occasionally as contentious); and to Judith McNally, my incomparable assistant, whose virtues are so numerous it would weigh upon
one's own self-regard to list them—yes, to Schiller and McNally, a full
and unconditional appreciation. Without them, there might have
been no tale to tell.

REPRESENTATIVE BOGGS. Why did your son defect to Russia?

MARGUERITE OSWALD. I cannot answer that yes or no sir. I am going to go through the whole story or it is no good. And that is what I have been doing for this Commission all day long—giving a story.

REPRESENTATIVE BOGGS. Suppose you just make it very brief.

MARGUERITE OSWALD. I cannot make it brief. I will say I am unable to make it brief. This is my life and my son's life going down in history.

—from Marguerite Oswald's
Warren Commission testimony,
February 10, 1964

CONTENTS

Volume One: Oswald in Minsk with Marina

Volume Two: Oswald in America

A NOTE ON STYLE

The definite and indefinite articles are not employed in Russian. Nor is the verb "to be." One would not say, "The man is in the room," but rather: "Man in room." (Which is why those Russians who do not command much English invariably sound brusque.) On the other hand, a construction like "Man in room" does tend to make you aware of the man and the room both.

One was tempted, therefore, to dispense with articles and the verb "to be" during the first half of this book, for it would have given an overpowering Russian flavor to the prose. A full effort in that direction would, however, have tortured the English language beyond repair, and so only a suggestion of this difference is present. Let me, then, wish you good reading and happy accommodation to small liberties taken with King's English.

Volume One

OSWALD IN MINSK
WITH MARINA

—◄◦►—

PART I

THE ADVENTURES
OF VALYA

1

Volchuk

When Valya was three years old, she fell on a hot stove and burned her face and was ill for a whole year, all that year from three to four. Her mother died soon after, and her father was left with seven children.

When they buried her mother, Valya's father said, "Now, look at her and remember her." He put them all around the coffin and told them again, "Try to remember your mother." There they were, all seven children, dressed in black. Valya's dress had an ornament like a small cross. She remembers that, and how all her brothers and sisters cried. Their mother had died giving birth to her eighth baby.

She passed away at a hospital fifty kilometers from where they lived, and when her mother felt she was at her last, she asked somebody to call Guri, her husband, and tell him that she wished to say a few words. So, she lay in bed waiting, her eyes on the door, and when she saw that door open, she was so weak she could only say, "Guri, please take care of our children," and then she died. She couldn't live a moment longer. Of course, she still comes back to Valya in her dreams.

While Valya was only the fifth child in this family, she was the second sister, so when her oldest sister left home a couple of years later, Valya had to take care of the house. It was a good family all the same, and they were kindhearted, and approximately everybody was equal. When Valya was seven, she could already bake bread in a stove where you had to use a flat wooden spade to insert your loaf of dough, and everybody was happy when she made her bread because it was tasty.

Her father was a switchman and worked on the Smolenskaya section of the Soviet rail system at a town called Pridneprovsk.

Since his children had no older woman to help them now, Guri married again. And his children were not upset by this new wife but loved her, for she was a nice person, and they even called her Mama. She was very kind to them, even if she was not healthy and had been married twice already; but her only child, from her second marriage, had died and now this was a third marriage, and Guri and this new wife did not have children together.

It is possible the stepmother married Valya's father so she wouldn't have to stay on a collective farm but could live with a man who did not need a wife to work outside. Sometimes Valya wondered why he did marry her, because she was sick a lot, even hospitalized; but though she did not help so much as hoped, these children needed her to feel like a family, and so they waited each time for her to return from her sickness. She did care for Guri's children. Sometimes when Valya's father went to Smolensk or to Vitebsk and returned with something special to eat, he would say to his new wife, "You see, there are so many children and they are so young, so I can only bring back this small thing for you," and the wife said yes, but when he left, she usually divided it all, and never kept it for herself. She lived with them for years before she died and they all grew up with her, and Valya's father lived on beyond that, and did not pass away until he was eighty-seven years old. Even when life was not easy, they always had their father.

Valya was very shy. Always upset about her cheek. One side of her face remained scarred from that burn when she was three. The medical cures in those days had been wrong. They used to put on some type of bandage that would dry out, so when they took it away from her skin, it left a mark. Besides, this treatment was painful, very painful. Valya remembers crying through the whole year. She even heard some people say, "Maybe it would be better if she died, because if a girl has a face like this, she does not have happiness." It made her a quiet person, she feels, who kept everything unhappy inside. She never was emotional. She went through things and never screamed at anybody, just felt unhappy inside.

Children, however, were never cruel to her in school. Valya had four brothers, so it was not easy for children to insult her. Her brothers and sisters were all healthy, and so they had a special feeling for Valya. They pitied her because she'd been sick for that entire year and they saw her suffering. Her father even said, "You know, when you were a child I spent more time with you than with all my others. I was always keeping you in my hands for that whole year, you cried so much." Valya grew up believing that this scar on her cheek had taken away her beauty as a woman. She had a nice body, she had nice teeth, but because of her cheek she did not consider herself attractive. And yet there were always men around her. It was strange. She didn't know why she attracted men, but she did. Even when she was already married and was traveling from Arkhangelsk to Minsk to join her husband, at a time when it was difficult to buy train tickets and she was standing in line for hours to get one, there was a captain standing behind her and they talked for three or four hours while in line. This captain said, "I don't know if you're married or not, but if you can marry me, then we'll register, and you'll be my wife." And she thought, "He says this even though I have such a problem with my cheek!" And she was maybe twenty-three or twenty-four years old. He was very serious. But she said, "I'm going to my husband; I'm married."

Perhaps, she would say, it was because people knew she could make a good home. All this time she was growing up, her interest was housekeeping. She made everything clean; she kept Guri's house spotless. It was a cottage with two rooms, one for his seven children and one for Guri and his wife. There was no kitchen, but in her father's room there was a stove and she cooked meals there. On holidays, like New Year's, they put their decorated tree in the other room, where seven kids slept on three beds.

By every railway station was a small house, usually in a field near the railroad tracks, and its first floor was an office, but the top floor was given to whichever station man lived there with his family. So now, whenever she passes a small railroad station, she feels sad. Her childhood had not been easy, but somehow she likes to remember it and enjoy it, and so this sadness is equal to a recollection of nice moments in life. She enjoys such sadness.

In high school she studied German as a second language, but students were always told that fascism was a totalitarian regime and they were in a democracy of socialism, and, of course, she never saw a German until they arrived in a large group soon after the war began, in June of 1941. She remembers that the fields were ripening and Germans were already in Smolensk. They came so quickly. Everywhere, Russian troops were retreating, leaving behind many tanks, retreating. Germans kept coming. They were masters of this place. First there were planes, and then Germans showed up themselves, but first there were airplanes high and low, bombarding them. Bridges, their railway station, burned villages. These planes came for a week, then tanks. They occupied everything. The Germans brought their laws, and didn't allow anyone to leave home and walk even a few kilometers without some special pass.

They would kill you. Germans were hanging people on trees. Valya saw that: young partisans on trees. She can see it to this day: There was an alley, and down this alley were young people hanging. Sometimes, on one tree, two people. Everyone in their village went down to look. They were all in horror, but they went to look, back then when she was sixteen and the Germans had overrun all this country she knew.

Her father had been working at the railway station, and the Germans passed through and kept him working. And he did. He had to earn a living. But they were very cruel in other places, and burned many villages. So, all the Russians who were working for the Germans in these villages were worried. They might be punished later. Certainly her father worried. He didn't say anything; but everyone worried about her father being punished, and they talked about it among themselves, and later they would wonder whether Stalin would do something in time to come. Her family always felt marked. Yet, she was never a collaborator, never. She'd always lived honestly in her life. Besides, those Germans beat her father.

Valya still remembers. Their family had a cow but no fodder. And when trains would pass, hay was sometimes left on the station platform, swept out from boxcars. Her father would gather such remains. And one time, some Germans coming by on a train decided he looked Jewish because he had black hair and a black beard and black eyes and was wearing a hat. There were three Germans and they pounded his face and he lost some teeth. Something was always wrong with his teeth after that.

When he managed to get back home that night, he cursed in a way Valya could not repeat. He said the strongest swear words, *Iob ikh mat*. Very strong. She could not say it aloud. It meant doing something sexual to your mother. All of Guri's life, he remembered that beating. He had to stay home for two weeks. Later, he was afraid, but he went out again to pick up hay on the station platform because their cows needed it, and he always worried about being beaten again, but then, they were all afraid.

Later, the Germans took her father and her brothers and two of her uncles away. While they didn't burn the railroad station, they smashed every window. And these Germans raped a lot of women, but not her stepmother, because she was not seductive enough, and none of her sisters or herself, because they were children. Then they tried to burn her house, but they lit it quickly and moved on, and Valya had some water she had been using for washing, so she poured enough on to stop their fire. Neighbors screamed at her and said if any Germans saw it, they'd burn other houses. It was very difficult. They were all standing in their yard, and these Germans had killed their dog, and all the villages around their station were burned.

Her father and her brothers had to stay a year and a half in the German prison camp, right until the end of war. It was fortunate that she could even see them. She and her younger sister and her stepmother would walk. It was thirty-five kilometers away, and they were allowed sometimes to bring food. Because there was a lot of snow, the family had killed their pigs and hid them. That way, her stepmother could boil meat and take it to her brothers and her father. In fact, they sacrificed their own food, though their men, in turn, insisted on giving back a portion. All the same, on their return, they would have to beg on the country roads. They were always hungry all this while that she was fifteen and sixteen, no shoes, no dresses. Once she heard her father talking to her stepmother, and he said, "My daughters are growing up without anything to put on. Take my suit; maybe you can alter it into a dress."

And once, in fact, when Valya was fifteen and her sister fourteen, they were dressed in such old clothes that some Germans called them *matki*, which is a rude word, like "old bags."

One day in June of 1944, with no warning, many Germans came and took every person her age and put them on a train, loaded them into a boxcar, closed it, and transported them away. All the girls were crying. It happened around noon, and they were rounded up and brought to the railway station. They told them not even to bother changing clothes, just took them along in whatever they were wearing, and she learned later that her father couldn't find her when he came back from camp, and fell to his knees and wept, but there she was, in a boxcar, jammed in with so many other girls, and no toilet. They had to pull up a plank and make a hole in their floor.

It was a long train, and they had been picked up from a place where they had been working with shovels; they had to climb up into the boxcar without even the kind of plank that cows go up.

"They just pushed us in there and closed the door. These Germans didn't scream at anybody, didn't beat us, but they were very strict. People were in there already from other places; they kept collecting people at each station. Later, after more stops, it was jammed." She would never forget what she saw on this train to Germany. "No painter could make that picture. On all faces, only fear, as if life had ended, horror had followed. It was dark inside. And then we had to make that hole in the floor of the train." She doesn't remember what tool they used; maybe there was already a little hole and they widened it with their fingers.

Valya never saw even one town and doesn't remember anything about Poland except that she was told, yes, you are crossing Poland. And then they came to a transit camp, where they were told to line up and take off their clothes, and their teeth were checked as if they were horses, and every other part of their bodies, and they were given injections, all in a line naked, both men and women. It was very uncomfortable; they didn't know what was going to happen next; they were all standing there nude without really knowing what was to come. She didn't feel ashamed, because everyone else was also without clothes, but it was uncomfortable. To this day Valya thinks the injections given them on that day kept her from getting pregnant later.

Then they were given back their clothes, and this time they were on that train for a week, with just a little food, a spoonful of soup, and room to sit down on the floor, which was better than when this train first went from Byelorussia to Poland. But everyone still had a bad expression, as if they were going to be executed. Even now Valya can't stop crying when she remembers.

Eventually they arrived at Frankfurt am Main and stayed in a camp with wooden houses and heard that Germans burned a lot of people in giant stoves, but all these girls she was with were young and were going to be put to work, not killed, although anyone was in trouble who looked a little like a Jew.

In camp, their beds were made of wood, no blankets, no pillows, and by preference they slept outside in warm weather. A little later, they were given wooden shoes with hide inside and jackets that bore a special signature, OST, so everyone would know they had come from the east.

Every morning at seven they would walk downhill from camp to take a train to Frankfurt am Main, where they would work all day, and not return until late at night. She was in this camp for nine months. Valya never saw anyone get shot, although a few young girls died of disease, malnutrition. But there came a day, in April 1945, when a train didn't come to pick them up for their job and they were forced to go to work on foot. Now they could see that American planes had come over the night before in a bombing raid, and Valya saw a railroad track standing straight up in the air. She was afraid to return to camp for fear of another air raid, so she stayed alone in Frankfurt while a friend started back, but not too many minutes had gone by when she thought, "What am I going to do here alone?" and so she ran to catch her friend. At camp, people said they were going to be evacuated, and everyone was afraid. Would they be put into stoves and burned?

People started to escape and, with others, Valya went down a hill so steep they had to slide down parts of it. They also had to cross a valley beyond this hill, and a small forest, and a couple of houses, and a German, who came along with their group, showed them how to hide in a storage bin below ground, and there they stayed for ten days with no light, until the war was over.

Valya heard that it had all been craziness up above while she was below earth. When she came out ten days later she didn't even know that the war had ended, but this German had saved her group, since their camp had been destroyed in a battle between Germans and Americans. It was then that she saw Americans for the first time in her life. There were a lot of Negroes. She remembers that they looked nice; they looked happy and alive, and so well built. They were proud they had liberated people. It was the first time she had seen smiles in a year. Valya thinks that even when she dies, she'll remember this day and how it was when she came out into the light and it was as if her life had started again.

Valya remembers one American soldier who came up to her, offered his canteen, and gave her a big piece of chocolate. It was the first time in Valya's life that she tasted chocolate, and there was wine in his canteen. So there she was, never drank alcohol before either, and suddenly she didn't feel well. There, full of happiness, she still had to throw up.

The American officers said, "If you don't want to return to Russia, you can stay here; we'll try to help you with jobs." But Valya felt she couldn't stay on the American side. She loved her father and missed him a lot. So those of her friends who also wanted to go home were sent to a transit camp—Russian Reevaluation Camp—and there they were mixed in with thousands of people in Frankfurt an der Oder in this Russian camp where they waited. By now it was June again, and she worked in nearby fields, separating good grass from bad for cows, then milked cows, then was put to work in a small butter factory and was promoted and even put in charge because she worked so well. Here in the butter factory she met a man she loved very much, but he was only there for two months. He was tall and very shy, a modest person, a very good person, and you could hardly say they were dating, but they would meet each night after work and kiss. He never even touched her breasts. He proposed to her and said, "When we are back in Russia, we'll marry." And she had a dream that she was kissing him and kissing him and couldn't stop, but when she told this dream to her girlfriends, they said, "Listen, it means you will never see him again." It turned out to be true, because the Russian Army needed him, and she didn't even have a chance to say goodbye. She cried then. She loved him so much, because she had never seen such tenderness in her life. He had been close to her for two months and never asked her once what happened to her face. He treated her as if something very special were true of her, whereas when she met the man not long after who would actually become her husband, he asked her on their second meeting why her cheek was the way it was.

She married this second man, but she always felt more comfortable with the first one. She never saw him again, even though they wrote letters back and forth. Even when she was married to her husband she wrote letters, but then she stopped. For in spite of her face, this second man had married her, so she felt grateful. She was afraid to lose him. Therefore, she stopped writing.

Later, the first man wrote to her that he was married to a schoolteacher and that they went to theatre a lot and to cinema, and added, "I knew you only for two months, but my heart belongs to you." And even though she didn't have anything sexual with him, she loved that man very much and believes that if he's alive now, he still loves her.

After he was gone, she kept working at this small place they called a butter factory, and a soldier who was assigned to a hospital nearby would come to her dairy to take food to the man who would become her future husband. Valya finally asked: "For whom do you take all this?" He said, "There is one lieutenant who is sick and I give it to him." She said, "Okay, give him my best regards and tell him we want him to be healthy." She said it just to be nice to someone who was ill. But when the soldier came back, he said, "This lieutenant, he sends you best regards too," and it turned out later that her husband-to-be had been told: "You know, there's one girl who works there, she's so kind and nice, she even gave food to me." Soon enough that lieutenant was put in charge of the whole butter factory, and he turned out to be tall and as strict as a German. Then one evening every other dairy girl decided to go to the movies, but Valya—she doesn't remember why—stayed home. Perhaps she was depressed. She saw somebody walk by in a leather jacket—even now she has this leather jacket—and he looked at her and said, "Why didn't you go out?" Then he recognized her and said, "Okay, let's introduce ourselves to each other," and as people of his rank usually did, he invited her to his office, and she went there and they talked. He said, "Let me hear your story." She told him everything. Then a friend of his came by who could play the piano, so this officer said to her, "Do you dance?" and since there was nobody around, he invited her, and then he said, "Thank you for your regards." It was then Valya understood that this was the sick man to whom she had sent all that food.

He was married. That is, he had been married in 1939, but his wife sent him only one letter in four years and then she divorced him in order to marry a pilot. This tall man told his story, and then said he had never had any children with that wife. He showed her a picture. His former wife was very attractive.

This officer was fifteen years older than Valya, and very severe, but he was nice when he danced. It was just that by the second evening, he asked her about her face, and she was offended and cried all night once she was alone. Only later did she tell him she was upset about it, upset because he certainly didn't know her, but already he was kissing her and asking her questions.

He was very intelligent, very cultured. After they were married, she discovered he actually had great tact and it was not possible not to love him, but it was a different type of love than she had had before. First love is first love. This man that she would marry was tall, slender and handsome, and not only elegant and intelligent on their first evening but remained so all their life. He always behaved in a calm, neat manner, very elegant. At the end of their life together, just a few years ago, when he was very sick and had a high temperature, he was so neat that when an ambulance came for him, he said, "Valya, do you think I can go without a tie?" She did not know whether to laugh or to weep.

They stayed together through most of that following year in Germany, nine months. They met in August of 1945 and were married in May of 1946, and Ilya—that was his name, Ilya Prusakov—courted her in a proper way. He protected her and treated her with great tenderness. She never thought they would marry. He treated her very nicely as a person, and she liked him, but he was often sick. He had gotten some kind of disease during his campaigns. Once in this period he was taken to a hospital and she couldn't even find the place—it was that difficult for her to visit; but when he came back, he said, "You know, you did so much for me when I was in trouble that I'll always take care of you. I'd marry you if you'd agree, but I know you're so young—I can't propose marriage to you because there's such a big difference in our ages. Maybe later on you'll find someone else and I'll be jealous. So I'd like to propose to you and to marry you, but it's up to you to decide."

Of course, he had a very serious inflammation in one of his bones, and after that he had another illness where he ran a high fever and had to go to another hospital, but he sent out word. He asked Valya to bring him chicken broth. It was not possible to buy a chicken, so Valya found a Polish woman who spoke German and took her to another town to find one, and Valya brought it back and made some soup. Then Ilya asked her to bring tea, and he wanted it to be of a certain temperature because he felt more comfortable with warm liquid, so she ran with it to him because she was afraid his tea would turn cold. Then there were other things she did: She repaired his clothes, and was happy to do it. She wanted to do it. He said that even if she didn't want to marry him, he would always take care of her. He said, "I'll always help you; I'll train you and teach you to be a typist. I'd always like you to be near me." But, in fact, she agreed to marry him. She had expected he would propose.

It also turned out that this fine officer, Ilya, had suffered several serious war wounds. Not only had his leg been badly injured by machine gun bullets, but he had been near some explosion that had left him with a condition called *khontuzheniy*. It meant he'd been close to some explosion, and his brain had suffered a shock. Concussion.

Meanwhile, the butter factory was closed, and because Ilya wished to keep Valya near him, he arranged to give her a job, and she cooked for Russian soldiers and officers.

She was so full of energy and so sweet and happy and so much on the move that Ilya began to call her *volchuk,* which is a toy like a top, brightly painted and always moving, very funny, very gay, very energetic, always moving. She, in turn, called him Ilichka. When they decided to register their relationship and be married, he went to Potsdam. She didn't even have a nice dress, but he bought her a beautiful one, with embroidery, and she remembers that they went by train from Berlin, and Valya was very happy because now she knew she was going to be married, since he had told his relatives.

Back in Russia, they moved in with his people in Arkhangelsk. That was more difficult. Arkhangelsk was all the way north of Finland. Now they were no longer just two, but part of a large family, way up in the far north. Ilya did not change when they got there; never in his life did he offend her or insult her personally, and she soon loved him so much that when he would come home from work, she would look at him with such admiration that his mother would say, "Don't show that much happiness. Don't look at him so much that evil comes." Yes, it was dangerous to let the devil know how happy you were.

All the same, thirteen years of living with the Prusakov family were to follow. Of course, that was not a surprise. Before they registered their marriage, Ilya had said, "Valya, I want to tell you that I'll never leave my mother." So Valya was prepared to share her life with his family instead of her own, and she knew that his mother had a very large influence on him. Ilya's first wife had been a woman he brought back from a holiday in a health resort, and his mother, Tatiana, had not been happy about it. In his mother's opinion, when a man goes to the Crimea on vacation, meets a woman and marries her, it's a bad idea, and very uncultured. You don't know this person; you have fun for a few weeks, then you marry; such a woman is tricky—she trapped him into marriage. Ilya's mother said it was not a serious decision. Just passion, not marriage, and his mother had been right. It didn't last through a bad war.

When Ilya came back with Valya, however, Tatiana accepted her. So did all of Ilya's sisters, more or less. Everybody, however, was surprised. Ilya was such an attractive and educated man and he had married a woman who had a problem with a burn mark on her face. Everyone said, "Couldn't he find someone who's his match?" And, of course, they talked about it. But Ilya did like young women, and she was young.

In the beginning, Valya couldn't get used to such an educated family as these Prusakovs. She was, after all, from a village. Later on she would learn, but at first it was not easy to do what was expected. There were so many new persons that she felt a little bit closed. Still, she was always trying to learn, and Ilya's mother, Tatiana, taught her a lot.

Tatiana was a very good cook. Since Valya was always around her, she learned to be better in the kitchen than Ilya's sisters. It helped that Ilya never made excuses about Valya; he said, "This is the woman I love"—that was it. He had brought her from Germany. If you don't love a woman, you don't take her home with you.

In their first years together, Valya wanted to have children, and every month she would cry, and Ilya would always say, "Don't worry." Now, she wonders if he was ever truly upset about it. When he was old, he even said to her: "Maybe it's good we didn't have children: Look around. Nowadays, children are not really good."

Of course, there were always lots of people around. In Arkhangelsk, they lived in Tatiana's apartment, which had three rooms. First thing Tatiana said was, "I have five daughters. Now, you'll be my sixth." That pleased Valya so much that she fell in love with Ilya for a second time, because she realized he had a happy family life already, and so if he had chosen her, that meant he really loved her. It wasn't as if he just needed her. Besides, his family lived together with love like Valya's family, but in a different way, more grace. More cultural. So she could love him more, because he changed her life for the better.

But she didn't have much freedom. Everyone's eyes were always on her, and she remembers that once when they were in bed, she even cried because she did not feel alone with him.

One night, they brought out an album of photographs, and Valya had to think how different it was from her family, where they'd never had anything like that, so poor. So she was embarrassed when they sat around their big table and his mother asked, "Now, tell me your stories, tell me about yourself." Fortunately, Ilya's mother then said, "You know, Ilyusha's first wife was brought up by a step-mother." Valya got upset, so she touched her husband's foot under the table, and he touched back, which she understood to mean,

"Don't tell her," and she didn't. But later on her mother-in-law asked, "Why do you always talk about your father? Why do you never tell me anything about your mother?" So she confessed. She, too, was brought up by a stepmother.

In this Prusakov family in Arkhangelsk were Ilya's sister Klavdia and her two children, Marina and Petya, conceived from separate fathers. There was also another sister, Musya, and still another, Lyuba, who lived with them, but the center of this household was Marina, Klavdia's daughter, who was five years old and very pretty and very bright. She had large beautiful blue eyes, and her grandmother more than admired her. You could say that Tatiana was completely in love with her. Marina was not exactly spoiled, but she was *izbalovanaya,* which is a little nicer than spoiled, for it means somebody who may have been loved too much. There was certainly a tendency to deal with Marina more leniently than a strict parent might accept. But she was a child you could like, and in school Marina got very high marks, and all her family was for Marina.

There was no father around, however, only a stepfather, named Alexander Medvedev, and at first he treated Marina very well, even after his first child with Klavdia, Petya, was born.

As for Marina's natural father, Valya was never sure what happened to him. He had disappeared in 1941, before Marina was born. Ilya never explained. He just said that Marina's missing father was a nice man, and Klavdia's sister Musya said she met him one time, and he was attractive, very attractive eyes, an engineer, whose name was Nikolaev. Nikolaev and Ilya had worked together building a small new city where before there had only been water and marsh, but now it exists, Severodvinsk, about fifty kilometers north of Arkhangelsk.

As for Nikolaev, Valya thinks maybe they didn't tell her any more about him because the Prusakov family did not want to disgrace themselves. Perhaps Nikolaev had been married to another woman and just made a baby with Klavdia and left. On the other hand, this all happened in Stalin's time. So Nikolaev could have been deported. Valya remembers how when she was a child Stalin once said: "We have started to live better and we have more fun." There had been a man in the crowd who heard this slogan and he added, "Yes, so much fun that you could cry." He was taken to prison for that. It was a terrible time. So, people had the habit of not talking. In any event, Ilya always said that Nikolaev was a good man.

Of course, Valya did not know much about such things. She lived at home and took care of things for her mother-in-law. Neither then nor later did she go to Ilya's office. He had a job in MVD—Ministry of Internal Affairs—and he would always be in MVD; he never left. Nor did she know exactly what kind of work he did, whether he was an office manager or a production manager. She knew there were people who worked in factories and camps who'd been sentenced for things they did. Ilya never worked directly with such people; he was more like someone who controlled production. He dealt with people who were managing factories. He didn't have the highest position, but he did have responsibilities in his job, and she would say he was happy with that. Certainly he never discussed anything negative with her.

Despite all those years in Arkhangelsk with Ilya's family, it was still a good life, because at least Valya and her husband had a separate room. They could make no noise, but still, one could live like that even if she couldn't look forward to summer, because Ilya didn't like to hunt for mushrooms. Mosquitoes were terrible in Arkhangelsk in summer, so you couldn't say you were going out with your husband to search for mushrooms and get to be alone out there in fields full of grass.

Arkhangelsk, in this period, was not yet a big city and didn't have many roads. Most were mud, or made of logs, but their Dvina River was deep, and oceangoing ships could come in from the White Sea. Still, it was much too cold. Ilya had some kind of arthritis in his back and needed to live in a warmer climate. In 1951, therefore, they moved to Minsk, first Ilya, then a month later Valya joined him, and at first they had to share a kitchen with a strange family and only had one room, although later, because of his job, they would live better. But again, Valya did not know exactly what kind of work he did, because of his being in this special Ministry controlling production under both Military and Security. In fact, Ilya's office was now in that same big building where KGB was located; MVD and KGB were both in a large yellow structure, five stories high, with columns in front—a government building, classical, with small doors, Valya remarked, for so large a place.

Ilya was, of course, a member of the Communist Party, but he and Valya never talked much about it, and he never asked her to join. In fact, he never said a word about it. While he was not what you could call devoted, he was responsible, and he was loyal; he paid fees regularly and did what he had to do; on everything he was responsible. If all Communists had been like Ilya, then it would be a different world, because Ilya was very honest. Valya never met anyone more so than him.

Valya had to like Minsk. It had been destroyed twice during the Great Patriotic War—once when the Germans came in and once when the Germans retreated back into Poland three years later. Ninety percent of Minsk had been leveled by all that. All the same, a decision was taken after the war to rebuild not in a different location, which would have been easier, but right over the ruins. That was in 1945. By the time Valya and Ilya moved there in 1951, Minsk's town center had been rebuilt in a new style. The city didn't look at all like it used to. Minsk had been a very large township of numberless small wooden houses all leaning against one another. Now it was stately. It had five- and six-story buildings with lots of yellow stone, like in Leningrad, and broad avenues, with good apartment houses that looked as if they'd been built a hundred years ago. Now, in 1951, it was a clean city, free of ruins, and food was everywhere: black caviar, red caviar, many different types of sausages and cheeses. She and Ilya didn't have a lot of money, but enough, and they lived near the center, which had been very well built by German prisoners before they had gone back to their country. Even Ilya's mother, who didn't want to leave Arkhangelsk, because she had a good apartment with three rooms and didn't pay a lot for it, was impressed when she came to Minsk. After she'd been there for a couple of months, she said, "Oh, here I feel as if I am in heaven," and at about this time, they were able to move into two rooms, and went on that way for years, with Tatiana, Valya, and Ilya all living in one small apartment, sharing a kitchen with a neighbor who had three children and worked as a prosecutor. They got along with them well, and in fact, their neighbors were upset when they moved, and said, "We'll never meet such nice people again." Of course, their toilet was in the yard, and one had to go out there when it was zero and worse, but then Valya felt strong. Since childhood, she had been used to going about without shoes, yet now at night Ilya would wake up too and say, "Wear your shoes." She was used to going barefoot in snow as a child, so it did not seem necessary to put on shoes to walk thirty meters to a toilet in their apartment-house yard.

In this period, between 1955 and 1960, Valya knew that this production which Ilya oversaw was done with prisoners. Her husband never said anything to her, but sometimes when fellow officers came over for dinner and drinks, she would hear them talking, and she knew there was a plan to be fulfilled: People should work well, and deliver production according to plan. But they never discussed it as husband and wife.

Valya could keep secrets. If you told her not to say something, she wouldn't. Once Ilya was on a business trip and telephoned her and said that one of his colleagues would come over to their apartment, and she should give him a key to his safe.

Shortly afterward, somebody knocked at her door and a man in civilian clothes entered and asked if he could have that key. She said to herself, "Maybe someone listened to my telephone conversation." So she asked, "Can you show me your I.D.?" And not until he did would she give him the key.

Later, he told Ilya, "You have such a wife! She demanded my I.D.!" Valya didn't know what kind of secrets Ilya had in his safe, but if he told her to do something, she did it properly.

Valya's only trip to Leningrad occurred when Marina was eleven or twelve. Klavdia lived in Leningrad then with her husband, Alexander Medvedev, in one room with three children, and when Valya and Ilya and Tatiana arrived, it was difficult, all eight people in one room, a huge family for so small a space, even worse because Alexander Medvedev also had a mother who did not take to Klavdia, and didn't like her son to be married to a woman who had a child by another man. This mother of Medvedev was a very intelligent woman, but mean and fat, a witch. So Marina's situation was now different, and she was no longer at the center of her family.

At this time, before Klavdia died, Medvedev did treat Marina and her mother properly, but still there were difficulties. Klavdia had an advanced case of rheumatism, and Ilya once told Valya: "You can see how sick she is." Besides, Alexander's attitude toward Marina had changed as his own two children with Klavdia grew older. Alexander now punished Marina a lot, and matters did get worse once Klavdia died, just before Marina turned sixteen.

Two years later, Marina wrote to Valya and Ilya in Minsk to tell them that it was very difficult for her to stay any longer with her stepfather, and asked if she could come to live with them.

Such a request was not too welcome for Valya. She was tired of her relatives. She didn't show it, but for all these years somebody in Ilya's family had always been living with them. Tatiana even died in their home. In her last ten months, Valya had taken care of her so well that before she went, she said to Valya, "I have survived only because of you, Valya." Ilya was in effect the father of his family, and that was fine, except that Valya felt he could give time to his wife only when they went to bed.

Still, when Marina arrived at the train station, Valya saw that she had only one suitcase, and pitied her. The girl seemed so happy to be able to move to Minsk. She was shy and, for a while, very obedient. Just a sweet eighteen-year-old. Marina had a natural color to her lips and never used lipstick. She was attractive even if she was afraid to smile—one of her front teeth was a little in front of the other. It would all have been nice if Valya didn't have to share her life with one more relative again.

Of course, Marina didn't know much about housework. If Valya asked her to do something, Marina would try it, but she couldn't cook. She did wash her own clothes, and hardly knew how to do that properly. Then, when Marina got a place in a hospital pharmacy, for which kind of work she'd been trained in Leningrad, she was usually tired when she came back from her job, so she didn't really have house duties. She was free to go to movies, to parties, to plays. Valya, after all, did not go out to work, so she was responsible for the apartment. Sometimes Marina washed floors, and sometimes she washed dishes, and certainly when she was eating alone, she never left dirty plates for Valya. And she had her job. People were needed in pharmacy work, and Marina liked her occupation. She told Valya and Ilya, "I'll cure you," because at that time she had access to medicine.

The only trouble Valya could foresee might yet be with dates, although Marina was usually critical of them. If a boy said something wrong or bought something cheap, that was goodbye! She told Valya that she stopped seeing a man she had dated in Leningrad because he bought her cheap sweets. Of course, being that critical was an unusual matter for someone in her position. Girls like Marina, with no more than a vocational education, were not considered to be as outstanding as girls who went to an Institute or to Universities. So girls like Marina were not usually dated for serious relationships by the best young men in the best schools. But Marina only liked people who were educated.

Valya never saw her go out with an average man. She had lots of boyfriends, students at an Institute or at the University of Minsk, and she went to their parties with her best friend, Larissa, and spent all her earnings for clothes. After all, Ilya and Valya were not going to take a part of her salary for food. Sometimes, if Marina wanted money for theatre or movies, she would make her own clothes.

She was very industrious. She liked to sew, do embroidery, and she cut up Valya's old fur coats to make hats for herself.

She also read a lot, particularly Theodore Dreiser. Marina loved Dreiser, who was very popular at this time, but then, there were hundreds of books in their apartment, because Ilya had purchased complete sets of works by famous Russian authors, and Valya would read Chekhov and Tolstoy and Dostoyevsky, Turgenev, Pushkin, Gogol, Lermontov. Marina, however, chose Dreiser. Writers like Chekhov she was always having to get through in school.

Taken on the whole, it was all right having Marina there. Valya never minded that she did not contribute to their living, because Marina had been so poor when she arrived that she didn't even have underwear, and her salary was small. She needed every-thing—shoes, stockings, clothes from her head to her feet—and Valya pitied her, for Marina had had a very difficult destiny. Marina even told Valya that she loved her. Loved her a lot. Marina said Valya was the first woman to treat her decently and give her all this freedom, and in turn, Valya loved and pitied her.

Ilya was much more strict. He worried till Marina came back at night from a date. Not everything went smoothly between them, either, for Marina had a quick tongue. On the other hand, there was one young man with very good manners that Ilya liked, a young medical student named Sasha, and Ilya even had coffee with him. And, of course, there wasn't really all that much friction with Ilya, because Marina didn't come home late all that often. Not when he was home. Marina saved her late nights for those times when Ilya was away on a business trip and Valya was alone. Marina had told Valya that in Leningrad her stepfather, Medvedev, didn't allow her back into his apartment if she was late. She would have to sleep on the outside staircase. Valya cried when she heard that.

Valya always wondered why, after Klavdia died and her stepfa-ther mistreated her, Marina never asked any of her aunts or Ilya to take her in. "Why did she stay on in Leningrad so long—two more years?"

Yet, Marina was full of envy when she finally arrived. She said, "Oh, what a paradise you two have here." Valya never understood these remarks, because there wasn't anybody to work for Valya. If it was as good as Marina described it, Valya was the one who worked hard to create it.

Still, there was no real problem with Marina. Her room was always neat and there was never any difficulty with their bathroom, which was inside now, and in turn, Valya would never say a word to her when she did come home late, because she trusted her to be a nice girl. For that matter, Marina shared her secrets. So Valya now knew which boyfriend she liked and those about whom she felt most critical.

Because of such knowledge, Valya pitied Sasha when Marina didn't treat him well. Valya just couldn't see people being handled so rudely. After all, Sasha came every time with flowers, and was so nice to Marina. And how Marina treated him!

In fact, he was so much in love with Marina that Ilya and Valya had even started to call him "son-in-law," but one day, feeling sorry for him, Valya told him that if you're going to marry Marina, you have to understand that she had a very difficult time in Leningrad. Sasha said, "I don't want to hear anything about that."

Marina came home about this time, overheard part of their conversation, took Valya into the kitchen to tell her how upset she was, then came out and said to Sasha, "I don't want to see you anymore."

It depressed Valya, but then you could say that Marina, living with her stepfather, Medvedev, had gotten used to being the boss of herself, anyway. No one could influence her, Valya decided, because Marina was accustomed to taking serious decisions without a mother, without a father. Valya knew, for example, that Marina was smoking. In Leningrad, somebody had introduced her to cigarettes that came in a pretty box. They were slender and slim and feminine. Valya knew she was smoking, because a neighbor saw Marina doing it in a restaurant and told Valya. It was fortunate Uncle Ilya was away in another city on business. And Valya had a toothache that time, so she said to Marina, "I took medicine; it doesn't help. I'm hurting. Give me one of your cigarettes." Marina was flabbergasted. She said, "I don't have any." Valya said, "Come on, don't lie to me. Go get it from your purse."

Marina said, "Did you check my things?" And Valya said, "I know you're smoking, so give me for my toothache. You know, nicotine, painkiller." After Marina passed one to her, Valya said, "You better stop doing it. If you don't quit, I'm going to tell Uncle Ilya."

But she wouldn't quit, Valya knew. Marina liked smoking. It was Western, adventurous. Like Italian cinema. Marina loved Fellini films so much.

Those movies certainly gave her ideas. Once, Marina even told Valya that in her opinion, Ilya was not for her; officers were always marrying educated women. Valya still remembers; it hurt so deeply.

Valya had been faithful to her husband, but Marina didn't understand why. She wanted Valya to have an affair. She even urged her. Since Valya couldn't have a baby with Ilya, why didn't Valya make a baby with someone else? "Why should you suffer because of him?" And Marina said that if Valya had a man over, she, Marina, could even sit at the entrance and watch to see if Ilya was coming. "You could have your affair, and then you could have a baby." To which Valya said, "No, I couldn't. If Ilya found out, he would kill me." Of course, Ilya was sometimes very strict with Marina. And Marina didn't like that. No one could offend her without being paid back. Once Valya and Marina were marinating cucumbers and needed leaves from a berry bush to flavor them, so they went to a theatre where there were many flowers outside, and a berry bush, and they started to pick leaves. There was a woman in charge of this park who began to scold them and said, "How do you dare? Don't you know why we put bushes and flowers around? Don't you know that we want to look beautiful so all of our city can enjoy it? And you come here and destroy such beauty?" But Marina said, "You know what we're going to do? Pickle cucumbers. Come visit us and you will have some cucumbers too. What are *you* doing, after all? We're not doing anything wrong." If it were not for Marina, maybe Valya would have been fined, but Marina could always stand by her decisions and feel that whatever she did was right.

One night in March of 1961, Ilya was away on a business trip and Marina went to a dance at the Trade Union Palace and then came back later that night and woke up Valya and whispered to her that she'd been dancing, and then she said, "Valya, get up. Show how cultured you are, because I have brought home an American. I brought you an American. Make a good cup of coffee." Marina was happy and said, "I would like for you to act educated."

Of course, Valya got scared. She almost shivered in bed. If Marina had come through the door with an American ten years earlier, back in Stalin's day, they'd all be in prison. Now, in 1961, there was a big difference in feeling—they had gone from Stalin to Khrushchev—and so Valya remembers that she was not very worried and she got up and made coffee for the American, who was nice, very nice, and dressed very neatly. His name was Alik because, as she learned later, nobody could say Lee—it sounded like Li, that is, Chinese—and so it was a while before she learned his full American name was Lee Harvey Oswald.

2
_____

Zyatouk

Sasha Piskalev, seventeen years old in the summer of 1958, could not pass his exams at Minsk Medical Institute the first time he tried. It was a serious blow. From childhood, Sasha had dreamed of becoming a doctor. He had been an ailing child, so he always loved and respected people in white gowns, and liked how they came and cured him and cured other people. Any person who could bring sick people over into a healthy state had to be very important. So, after he failed his exams, he obtained a job at Professor Bondarin's laboratory and served there as an assistant. Bondarin treated him well. Although Sasha was very young, this esteemed professor always called him by both his first name and by his father's first name, Nikolai, addressing him as Sanich, a nice way of speaking to somebody who's young, using the patronymic, Sasha Nikolaivich, by way of the short form, Sanich. And, by 1960, Sasha succeeded in becoming a medical student at the evening faculty while still working days with Professor Bondarin.

He also became friends with Professor Bondarin's nephew, Konstantin Bondarin. Kostya had finished high school while Sasha was working, and together they had passed their University exams. Kostya also had a friend named Yuri Merezhinsky, an only son of high-ranking scientists. Sasha didn't really have much time to run around with elite children in their easy life—he had to work, after all, and go to the University—but they took classes together and sometimes did go out afterward.

About this time, Sasha met Marina, and it started. She was a month or two older, and more experienced, and he was fascinated. Soon enough, he was crazy about her. They went to the movies, he played piano for her, and they listened to symphonic music. Tchaikovsky was their favorite. A month after they started going out, she introduced him to her relatives, and he was invited to meet her aunt and uncle, who had a three-room apartment near the opera house, and Valya fed them tea and cakes. At that time, Sasha admired Marina a good deal, but they didn't talk about marriage, although her relatives soon began to call him *zyatouk*, which is a warm word for son-in-law, a nice word. It's not that they were engaged, but it was supposed that they would be. And Sasha worked and studied well because he had Marina in his life.

He lived from one date to another. It made his work and study easy. And when he visited her home, Marina's aunt would put out sandwiches and cakes and either watch TV with them or leave them alone, so they would have a chance to sit there and kiss. Nothing more. This aunt looked like a very simple person, but such appearances were deceiving, because she read a lot, and inside her, Sasha thought, was contained much more than how she looked.

While Sasha was dating Marina, his medical school friends Yuri and Kostya went out with different girls all the time. Sasha thinks they were laughing at him for being serious; they mocked him sometimes, and maybe they tried to tease Marina. But he felt they were envious because he had the prettiest girl. He doesn't believe they ever teased her unpleasantly, because Marina had a strong character, and if anybody ever expressed himself in an unpleasant manner to her face, she would reply, "You are not needed yourself!" Nor did he feel that they wanted to take Marina away from him. They could see he was deeply in love, and they, of course, were not in love with anybody. For that matter, he very seldom invited Marina along with his friends, because he didn't really want to be with them. Maybe he was even a little afraid to take her around them.

When he would go out with Yuri and Kostya he would drink, but not get drunk, and he would talk a little about Marina, but not in a harmful way. Never. What she told him, he would keep in his heart. It was just that he liked to praise her, because he was so much in love.

He had met Marina at one of these parties for Medical Institute students, and he had invited her to dance once, and then again, and then he asked if he could accompany her home. She was a very good dancer and he was not, but she could make you feel better than usual when dancing. Which was rare for him. He wasn't the kind of person who is interested in ballrooms. He had learned how to dance by himself; nobody taught him. So, during their first few minutes he was somewhat awkward, but then she began to lead him, and it was as if she breathed a little more life into him. They could feel comfortable together. He was on the short side, but even when she was wearing her high heels, he was taller.

He had met Marina in the summer of 1960, when he turned nineteen, and no other girl interested him. They dated once a week, and would take walks together and discuss where they wanted to go next time, to which opera or theatre or concert or ballet. *The Nutcracker* was their favorite.

They paid for everything half and half. She understood that he was a student, and she was already working. So one time he would buy the tickets, and then she would next time. He remembers that tickets in those days cost about a ruble or a ruble fifty, and they could have sat up in the students' gallery, in cheaper seats, but usually chose parterre. That was expensive. Two rubles was an average worker's pay for an entire day.

He was charmed by her behavior. She was different from other girls. Even her manners were different, and the way she dressed with taste. The apartment where she lived with her aunt and uncle had high ceilings and large rooms and a decent foyer. He remembers he was shy when he came to her apartment, but then Aunt Valya came out and invited him into the living room, and it was easy to talk to her. She was very sociable.

When he finally proposed to Marina, she said, "Let's wait a bit." But he was ready to get married. He was working at night as an orderly in the emergency ward and was earning about 150 rubles a month, more than a doctor—which is why he couldn't date Marina every night; he was working too hard, and doing it in order to be able to have a nice time with Marina and later set up housekeeping. They could have rented an apartment somewhere. Valya said that they could live with her, but he wanted to get his own place.

Usually, he would come home with Marina after a movie or a concert and stay about fifteen, twenty minutes before he left. He remembers that Valya's husband, Ilya, seemed terrifying to him when first they met. He was tall, lean; he had a long nose. Colonel Prusakov. Yet, when he opened his mouth to talk, he was a kind person. However, in that first moment, Sasha felt small, and a little afraid. After all, he knew where the Colonel worked, and Sasha was afraid of the Organs. He thought KGB and MVD were both called the Organs, but then KGB and MVD were mixed up in his mind. And this Uncle Ilya was so tall and gaunt. Perhaps he understood Sasha's fear, however, for when he started to talk, he was easy, and did not speak in a prosecutorial tone but in a normal, human voice. Sasha had a feeling that they treated Marina very well. Of course, Ilya wasn't around much, but their home was not without his presence.

When Sasha would come by to take Marina somewhere in the evening, Valya would say, "Sasha, no later than eleven o'clock." They were just like parents. In fact, at first he thought they were her mother and father.

On the other hand, he had very little understanding of Ilya's occupation. How could a young man understand what went on in the Organs? He knew it was something to be afraid of, and Ilya was high up; there were stars on his epaulets. So at first, Sasha was not only scared of Ilya but, as a result, he was a little intimidated by Marina. Afterward, when he came to know Ilya better, he could see Marina without fear. In truth, he didn't want to know what Ilya did—didn't care whether he was a warden of prisoners or an administrator of a factory.

He did ask Marina once, and she said, "It's better not to know." In those days, to someone like himself, KGB and MVD were one and the same: a big, dark spot.

Sometimes Marina would try to tell him something about her past, but he would stop her. He was not interested. Then her aunt tried to tell him, but Sasha did not consider it dignified to engage in such conversations. Now, he thinks Aunt Valya wanted him to know the story of Marina's past because she was afraid that if somebody else told him, it could prove hurtful.

He does recall that he came to Marina's home after she did not show up for a date, and Valya made tea, and they talked, and were very much aware that Marina was not there. Valya began to speak of Leningrad and the conditions of life then for Marina, and Sasha said, "You know, I am not interested. For the future, I want to have her as my wife. So I am not interested in what is past."

Then Marina came in, and Valya said: "I told Sasha about you." And Marina, as if she had been expecting this, was very cool to Sasha. After that, it was as if she were trying to escape him. He believes she was afraid of his reaction. He went to her pharmacy, he called her at home, but she avoided him. She liked flowers and his mother had a large garden, so he kept trying to bring her bouquets well into autumn. But she wouldn't see him. He would wait for Marina outside her pharmacy, and finally he caught her coming home from work, and she agreed to let him walk with her. It was cold, a winter night, and they went to a small park near the opera house, and she told him she had had a very difficult life, told him she was nobody, no good—"I'm not what you think I am. I'm not an angel. I'm no good for you." Then she said, "You must get out of my life."

He felt Marina wanted to humiliate herself in front of him, so he repeated, "I am not interested in your past; I am only interested in our present and in our future." Now, he wonders if maybe she just wanted to get rid of him, although he doesn't think she was dating anyone he knew. When she tried to tell him about Leningrad, however, she grew very emotional; she cried. He, however, kept saying, "You are here for me, and you will be. I don't want to know what happened to you before. You are now my life and we're going to be happy all our lives."

She became quiet. Later that night they kissed each other, and she said, "I don't deserve you. I'm bad." But he told her, "I love you exactly how you are."

That was it. They were together again. He went home. His mother was very strict, and he had to be home by a certain time, but on warmer nights, sometimes she would walk him all the way to his home, and then he would come back with her, and that way they could enjoy an hour or two, walking back and forth.

This happiness, which began in the summer of 1960, had continued for Sasha, but for its one interruption, until March of 1961, when the Medical Institute had a large students' party at the Trade Union Palace. He invited Marina, of course, and Kostya Bondarin was there, and Yuri Merezhinsky, and as he recalls, Yuri brought Alik, an American. Just about the time that everybody was dancing, this American, Alik, invited Marina to do the same. Then, Sasha also danced with Marina—for that matter, many men had invited Marina to dance—Sasha didn't pay any great attention. She was dancing, that's all. But over the next couple of weeks, Marina became distant. When he called, Valya said she was not in. And when he went down to her pharmacy, she tried to avoid him again. So he knew that something was wrong. As they say in Minsk, "There was a black cat running between us." Soon enough, he learned that he had a tragedy in his love affair. It was over. His life, and his dreams, vanished. Even now, it is painful.

He waves his hand gently, as if the residue of this old sorrow, more than thirty years old, could overflow again. "It's okay," he says. "We stopped dating each other, and in a month or two, somebody told me, 'Sasha, did you hear that Marina's going to marry that American?' "

She was still in his heart. Whenever he had to go to her pharmacy for medicine, he would follow her with his eyes when she passed. He didn't have tears, but it was as if a cat were inside his soul, scratching with its paws.

3

White Nights

Now that Marina is in her early fifties, she remembers her grandmother as snobby. She doesn't know from what kind of roots Tatiana came, maybe peasant stock like practically everyone else, but Grandmother was snobby. Maybe she had married a little bit better than her peasant relatives. Her husband was a sea captain, and she was a strong woman. Marina can picture her grandmother even better than she remembers her mother. Her grandmother always smelled good to her, clean and crisp. She was very Victorian, very opinionated. And here was Marina, born from a woman who wasn't married, Tatiana's own daughter Klavdia, yet her grandmother never disowned mother or child.

They all lived in Arkhangelsk. Marina wonders if it's as lovely a wooden city as she remembers. But, of course, to a child, even birch trees smell good after a rain. When you are a child, you are closer to earth, so you are near to all those smells of flowers and herbs, and Marina remembers playing in a park on the day she met her stepfather, Alexander Medvedev. He came and said, "Hello, I'm your father." She remembers it was just after the war ended in 1945, and she can still recall how happy people were and how happy she was.

Yet, after this war she would have nightmares. And she remembers that her grandmother's household was so strict. When she was five years old, she hated to go by herself to the bathroom, because God could see everything. "I was embarrassed. If I'm going to tee-tee—and God sees it—that's not proper to do, you know?" When people used profanity, she would try to close her ears. She never could bring herself to repeat ugly words; it burned her ears.

Grandmother was religious. For Marina, when she was young, everything good was with Grandmother, and everything outside was devil's work. Komsomol and the Communist Party—garbage.

Her grandmother used to say, "You know, if I want to keep an icon in my house, there will be an icon. Come and arrest me."

With her grandma, it was always what is best for Marina. Her grandma would tell her fairy tales and point out the moral. Grandma would teach her not to lie. "Maybe that's what keeps me going," says Marina now. "Not that I am always truthful, but I am not comfortable in lying—you can catch me like that. I betray myself very quickly."

When Marina would disobey her grandmother, she would be kept indoors for several days, and her mother never dared to interfere.

Marina can no longer remember when she learned that her stepfather was not really her father, but she did not find out from her mother. A girlfriend had overheard Klavdia talking about it to her mother, so Marina came home and confronted Klavdia with what she had just learned, but her mother's only answer was: "I don't want to talk about it. Later." Marina says: "I guess we think that later on a child will understand, but I felt hurt, and I rebelled against my mother. I punished her. I loved her, but I made her suffer deliberately. I was testing her: How far can I push to see if she loves me? My mother said, 'When you grow up, I'll explain to you everything, but now you're just too young to know.' I thought what she had done was sloppy, even dirty."

After her mother died, Marina found some papers. Her mother had been looking for Nikolaev. It was after Stalin died and amnesty was given to former prisoners. So her mother had been fill-

ing out papers, looking for Marina's real father. Marina remembers that when her mother was close to dying, she still wanted to
punish her. Klavdia was in a hospital, and Marina would bring her
cruel messages from Alexander's mother, Yevdokia. This mother-
in-law didn't like Klavdia. Some messages would even say that
Alexander was fooling around—which he never did. His mother
was lying, but Marina didn't know—she thought Yevdokia had
proof. Of course, she also knew it was going to hurt her mother.
Marina would say, "Well, Papa is probably seeing someone health-
ier." Her mother started crying. Then she said, "Don't worry,
Marina, it won't be long. We'll find out who really loved us."
That's what she said. "Between love and hate," says Marina, "is a
thin line. I didn't hate my mother; I wanted all her love. I didn't
want to share her. That's how possessive I was of my mother, let's
put it that way. Yevdokia was cruel. She was evil enough to know
that I would be a good messenger for her cruel words. You know
how teenagers are."

After her mother's death, Marina wouldn't live by her stepfather's rules about curfew. She felt he wanted a new woman in his
apartment and Marina was in the way. She doesn't know if this was
true, but that's how she felt. If she came home late at night, her
stepfather would lock her out. He grieved over her mother so
much, however, that Marina doesn't think her stepfather was
really a mean person. She looks at him differently today. "Now
that I'm fifty-two, I walk in my mother's shoes. After my mother
died, it haunted me. That remark I made to her in the hospital.
She was always lovey-dovey with my stepfather, and I was jealous."
She had overheard too many intimacies between her stepfather
and her mother. When she would hear the bedsprings squeak, she
would put pillows over her head. She couldn't think of her
mother as a woman until she had her own children. Until then,
she didn't think women were supposed to have such needs. It was
such innocence. How could her mother allow that to happen
when other people were present in a room, even though the room
was dark? Marina wasn't embarrassed for herself; it was that her
grandmother was sleeping there, and Marina had to think, "What
if she heard?" Since they all lived in one room, Marina thought it
was awful, and she was embarrassed for her mother. Just like dogs;
couldn't wait. It wasn't that frequent, but . . .

In later years, when her mother was sick, she could overhear
her stepfather's mother, Yevdokia, saying, "Why did you have to

marry that woman? You could have got a healthy woman. Why do you bother to cater to this one?" And all the while Marina was thinking that if her mother had married Alexander in order to give her child a name, she had not succeeded so well. She was still Marina Prusakova. Alexander had never adopted her. That was another blow.

After her mother died, she had nobody to come home to. She might be free, but she felt like a slave. She didn't know what to do with freedom.

She had a neighbor, a girlfriend who had a bad reputation, and Marina knew it. She liked this girl anyway. Her name was Irina, and she had an illegitimate daughter and worked to support her child. Irina's man had not wanted to marry her. He had said he wasn't sure the child was his. Irina was a young girl and she had given him all her heart, so when this man saw that Irina's baby daughter did look exactly like him, he changed his mind and was ready for marriage, but Irina said, "No thanks. Not after I went through all that embarrassment." So when everybody told Marina, "Don't talk to this girl, she's no good," she and Irina would meet anyway, not in their neighborhood, but away, and they would talk. She found out about another side of Irina, who said, "Yes, I work from nine to five, but at night I dress up and sleep with men. They are doctors and lawyers, and they pay. I slice myself up for the whole world because that's how I can get what is best for my daughter, I love her that much." And Marina thought to herself, "A dedicated mother." She was almost seventeen then, and Klavdia had died a year ago.

Now, it was April, two months away from the White Nights, when even at midnight it is still close to twilight, and Marina came back from an outing with other kids on the outskirts of the city. A telegram was there; her grandmother's funeral was taking place, and Marina didn't have money to buy a ticket to go to Minsk for her burial. That was a stab to her heart. Everything she loved was gone with Klavdia and now, a year later, it was gone again with her grandmother, and she thought about Irina, who sacrificed her reputation for her daughter's sake.

One time when she was out with Irina, it was late. Marina knew that Alexander would lock her out if she was not home by eleven, but Irina said, "I met some guys who just came in from Vitebsk, a soccer team. They brought some fresh fruit. Let's go there and have a drink." Marina said she'd have no place to sleep because her door would be locked, but one of the soccer people over-heard, and told her, "We have a room, everything will be all right, don't worry." So she thought she would just sit up with some of the players and go home by morning. You cannot sleep on a landing all the time.

But as soon as she undressed and lay down in a bedroom by her-self, her door opened and a guy came in, strictly naked, and jumped on her. She fought with him, even if he was a soccer player, and finally she jumped out of bed and stood by an open window. It was moonlight outside and she was standing, trembling by a large fourth-floor window, and she said, "One step closer and I jump." At that moment she really thought she would jump through the window rather than submit to that man. And maybe she screamed. Because other soccer players walked in and dragged him out. She was shaking badly, but they said, "Don't worry, nothing's going to happen."

On nights when she got back only five or ten minutes late, Alexander would open the door for her, but any more than that—well, she didn't want to have to listen to all their crap. Maybe she slept on the landing ten times. She had to hope no cleaning lady would see her; it would even be embarrassing for her family that they were treating her so badly. On such nights she would just sit on the stairs; she couldn't sleep. Or she would go to stay with Irina.

It was a lazy summer until Irina's mother talked to her in hard words. This mother ran a pawnshop and sometimes, since she was not working, Marina would spend a day with her, and young boys might come and pawn things and flirt, and maybe she would make a date with them and go out to a restaurant and get a meal, and then come back to Irina's house and sleep with Irina in her bed. This went on—she doesn't know, a month? Two weeks? Two months? Whatever. One day, Irina's mother took Marina into her kitchen and said, "My husband died during the war and I was left with two children. I had to work to support them. I don't mind giv-ing you shelter for a little while; I know you have hardship at home. But to continue this way, to eat at my home and take advan-tage of me—no, go find some work. You're welcome here, but not for freeloading." Marina turned red; it was true. She apologized—and she never stayed there again.

It was a dose of strong medicine, but this woman really did her a favor. Because it happened after Marina had been thrown out of pharmacy school. She hadn't been attending classes. Plus, she felt sick. She supposed it was a vitamin deficiency or something. She had shingles; she still has scars from those big boils all over her head and body. She had to go to a clinic called Place for Curing of Contagious and Venereal Diseases, and she used to wait in line for her medicine and hear everyone whispering, "So young!" and Marina realized they thought she had VD. Actually, she had to take lamp treatments and glucose and vitamin shots. She was terribly undernourished. And she never had VD, of course not, but it was painful that people thought so.

Over a year before that, before most of the trouble with her stepfather, there had been one boy she actually fell in love with. She was sixteen and visiting Minsk just for the summer, two years before she went there to live; she met a boy named Vladimir Kruglov. Since every window was open in Valya's apartment because of the heat, Marina could hear Kruglov playing a guitar upstairs. Marina heard from Valya that Vladimir, who was a student at Leningrad University, was lonesome in Minsk. He was older than her, but since he was always playing his guitar, Marina thought he was serenading her. She fell in love.

One night she and Vladimir got tickets for a movie, and when they came out, it was pouring rain, and Vladimir said, "I have a friend who lives near here," so they went to that apartment and dried themselves with towels and sat together and that became the first time she was kissed. First time in her life. She started crying. She was only sixteen, and Vladimir Kruglov said, "What is this trouble?" and she said, "Volodya, I've never been kissed before." He said, "If I had known that, I never would have done it. Who could know that you would have such a reaction?" But she was in love, so she stayed there for a little while, although she was scared to death; and early next morning, like five o'clock, she went for a walk and a little later she told herself she would never wash her face again because it was her first kiss and she had to keep it forever.

After that summer, when she went back to Leningrad, things were not so fine. At that time, she was still studying at pharmacy school, but little by little, her stepfather began to isolate her. At table, they began to give her scraps. She had a little money from her grandmother, a small pension divided among her younger brother, her younger sister, and herself, but now, if she was hungry and bought dinner for herself two or three days in a row, her money was gone. She was having to find ways to make out. After such a bad winter in Leningrad, a lot started to happen. A fine spring followed, and a wild summer. She still remembers one night when her boyfriend, Eddie—a man twice her age—got off a boat with her and it was early morning. People were still cleaning the streets; the sun was shining; everything sparkled. She and Eddie were both in a good mood because the White Nights had been beautiful and their boat had gone out to the Gulf of Finland. Music had been playing all night, and you could dance and maybe smooch a little.

As they passed the market, Eddie said, "I want to buy you flowers," and he picked up a bunch, and they went skipping through wet puddles. Their city was so cheerful. But all of a sudden, she saw her stepfather walking toward her, and she had to run into the nearest entry of an apartment house.

She told Eddie that if her papa had seen her, what would he think? He would not know it was the next thing to innocent. With Eddie it was play and caressing, petting, never any more than that. But she was ashamed of what her stepfather would think. He would probably believe she was a streetwalker. All those flowers, and out with a man so early that morning.

So she tried to go home and sleep, but Alexander came in and said, "Still in bed? Get up!" Then he said, "Get out of here!" And called her a whore. Then she was sure he had seen her. He said, "I do not want you in this apartment. Get out of my life." And she said, "No, you cannot throw me out." And he said, "You have relatives in Minsk. Just go." Marina said, "I don't want to leave. I'm going to complain to the city militia that you are cruel and rude and sending me away against my will." He said, "Okay, see your militia, and I'll tell you who your real father was."

At that moment, he stopped himself and went out the door. That was it. She never did learn any more about her real father.

All this while, she kept seeing Eddie, who worked for a film studio in Leningrad, Eddie, from Soviet Georgia, who was dark and had a mustache. She liked him. She did not see him every day, and she had other boyfriends. But there was nothing big going on. She was very choosy.

Of course, she also had rough dates who would take her out for dinner, but at the end, she would manage to avoid them—so far. She just felt lucky to have a meal. Even excited. It was like you were balancing the meal against future trouble. You eat first, then you hold the man off afterward—a hard way to earn a meal. But she was so hungry, and yet was still a virgin. And she was still thinking of a white prince, a red carpet and flowers. It didn't happen. It was always a roughneck.

Eddie's last name was Dzhuganian, and he was very nice. She went over to his apartment one day to leave him a note, but when she asked for him, someone said, "Is that a man with a little boy?" So she found out that he was married and living in Leningrad with his wife. And she didn't know what he did to excuse himself— maybe he told his wife that he was shooting a movie all night long. Maybe he was free this summer because he had sent his wife and boy out to a *dacha* and so he owned summer for himself. He was playing with her, and she wrote him an angry letter, and wouldn't see him.

After that, she certainly felt too lazy to work. That was when she was staying with Irina, who took her out one night on a double date with a client, an Afghani, who tricked Marina into coming up to his hotel room. He said he was going right out again; would she come with him just for a minute and a bite to eat while he changed clothes. Then, he raped her. He took her by force, and that was how she lost her virginity. Afterward, he said, "I didn't know you were a virgin. I want my money back." That was how she found out he had paid Irina in advance. After this Afghani had put her out of his room, Irina said, "Well, what do you expect? Do you think you can go around with me forever, and eat, and do nothing for it?" And then Irina's mother spoke to her as well.

She felt she was a fallen woman. Yet, that summer she also met some boys who invited her on picnics, and they spent time tramping through forests outside Leningrad, a big group with musicians and a fire. They would sing through the White Nights. Some of these musicians would hire prostitutes, but she stayed with the nice naive kids. One night, there was even a wild orgy at one end of this picnic, but she just sat and talked with the nice kids, and when morning came, everyone went for a swim—just a little kissing, that's all. She spent an entire weekend like that, Saturday and Sunday, and when she came home she found herself thinking about her grandmother and how she was dead, and she had not even been writing to Tatiana before she died because she had felt so guilty about how she was living, but she had been receiving money from her pension and hadn't written to thank her. Even in a letter, she couldn't face Tatiana. She had failed her. It was horrible. She felt like a prostitute because she had been taking meals from men on dates. Now, out of stupidity, she had lost her virginity to that Afghani, and she didn't have a job; she didn't want to have a job— she wanted a good time. It was not what she wanted her grand-mother to see. She wasn't worthy of her love. Now Grandmother was gone, and she couldn't even go to her funeral. She looked at herself in a mirror and asked, "What has become of me?"

So, when Irina's mother shamed her for not bringing anything in, she decided that she must put herself together again. She found a job in a school cafeteria. She would clean tables and sweep floors after recess. One day, three or four boys came run-ning in who hadn't yet eaten, but she was still sweeping. They looked at her—they were younger than her, just kids, but wearing good uniforms, spoiled kids from elite parents—and they said, "What a pretty girl. And, look, she has a broom in her hand." That howled through her mind. Here were these boys making fun of her. She wasn't born to sweep floors. So, she switched to work in another school, and the principal there, a Mr. Nieman, liked her and took an interest in her and got her a job in a pharmacy, and she was enrolled again in a night school for pharmacists. She couldn't believe how much had happened to her all in one spring and summer, but now was the time to live quietly, and for her last winter in Leningrad, now that she was working and back in school, she saw a good deal of a family named Tarussin and their boy, Oleg, who was an exceptionally gentle young person. She thinks she would have made a good wife to Oleg Tarussin, except that she liked his parents more than she liked him. Of course, she did like him, and very much, although not in a way where you could feel crazy about the fellow. But his parents loved her. She was the daughter they had never had. For the first time since her mother's death, she felt loved again and time went by half peacefully com-pared to the summer before. Yet, when she graduated from phar-macy school, she wondered whether to go to Minsk. It would be too easy to marry Oleg Tarussin, and she did not think she could stay in Leningrad, not when memories were sharp knives. Besides, she was still seeing Eddie and he told her to go. She fell in love too easily, he said, and he feared she would get herself into real trou-ble if she remained. Soon after, another soccer player tried to rape her, and she didn't get home until nine in the morning. She bor-rowed the ten additional rubles she needed for train fare, packed a bag, and left to go live with Valya and Ilya. It was true, she had decided. Leningrad was not the right place for her.

PART II

OSWALD IN MOSCOW

1

King's English

From Oswald's diary[1]:

> **October 16, 1959**
> **Arrive from Helsinki by train; am met by Intourist Representative and**
> **taken in car to Hotel Berlin. Register as student on a five-day Deluxe**
> **tourist ticket. Meet my Intourist guide Rimma Shirakova. (I explain to**
> **her I wish to apply for Russian citizenship.)**

Rimma loved to speak English. Rusty now, she could say, but she would conduct, if you will, every word of this interview in English, and she could tell the gentlemen who were speaking to her now that back then, for the Soviet people, 1957 had been an exciting year. After much preparation, Moscow had opened at that time a festival to establish human relations between foreigners and Russians in Moscow. It was the greatest event for changing life in the Soviet, she explained. Rimma was twenty in 1957, a student at Moscow Foreign Languages Institute, and she met a number of new people and spoke to foreigners and taught English to children.

Freedom was very great in that year, you see. There were so many young foreigners and young Russians all together. Foreigners heard about it and wanted to come for visits. So, in 1959, Intourist was started to arrange all the work for tours and visas, and Intourist took on many guides, which is how Rimma would say she got into it.

First of all, new employees took courses on how to become good at their work. That was connected to studying relevant material that guides should use. For example, Rimma took examinations on how to show their Kremlin Treasury. That was in June of 1959, and those who passed were offered a job in July; most of them were her fellow students at their Foreign Languages Institute.

In September, most of these people, to use King's English, were sacked. Only those like herself, who showed excellent retention of facts, were accepted for permanent work.

Come autumn and winter of 1959, there were few tourists, but in general, through 1959, there had been a good number of Americans, and a big business exhibition came and went in August. Rimma had worked with seventeen "boys." That was how they introduced themselves: "boys." They were governors from seventeen Southern states of America, seventeen big boys, all of them with cameras. And Russian people in those days had a picture of Americans never being without their cameras.

Rimma was slender then and had blond hair and was good-looking. Besides English, Rimma spoke Arabic, and one time she worked with a high delegation from the United Arab Republic. They were pleased with her, high ministers, very high level, all of them, and they kept telling her how she was very good.

At the end of this United Arab Republic tour, she took them one evening to see the Bolshoi, and their evening ended at eleven, time for Rimma to go home. Time for those Arabs, too! But suddenly they began asking where they could go next. She was shocked. "What do you mean?" she said. "Evening is over. You go to bed." But they began saying maybe there were some restaurants (some late restaurants with women). She began to reprimand them: "How bad of you. You have shown me pictures of your wives, your children, you have such wonderful wives, and now you want to go somewhere with women—shame on you!" They might be high ministers from Arab countries—still, she scolded them and said, "We have nothing like this. What do you think of my country and of me?"

Next day, next morning, none of them spoke to her. Didn't even say good morning to her. Her boss scolded her. "How could you dare? Do you know what kind of people you deal with?" What could she say? Was it in her character to say yes to such matters? She was young and she was blond and she could have been very good-looking but for a small growth like an eraser tip of a pencil on one side of her nose, what you call in English a wen!

Now, as part of her regular work, each morning she would report to Central Administration in the National. There, at that hotel, guides would be given a list of tourists coming to Moscow.

One day in October of 1959, October 16, Rimma was given the name of a man she was now assigned to take around in Moscow for five days. When she met him, however, she was surprised. He had not only arrived by Deluxe class—but he was taking his whole tour Deluxe. Only rich people travel in such a class. The most wealthy! How many can come alone Deluxe to Moscow for five days? So, she was expecting quite another kind of fellow, some gentleman who would be like an equal maybe to her governors of seventeen Southern states, and they had not even been Deluxe. Only first class. Deluxe was two rooms to yourself, a suite. Naturally, she was expecting a middle-aged man who would be impressive. A *dandy*!

When she went, however, to the assigned section of the Berlin Hotel lobby to meet him, there was only a boy, slender, of medium height, wearing a dark blue three-quarter autumn overcoat of inexpensive material and military boots with thick soles. Ordinary boots. From her point of view, someone traveling Deluxe should not look like this, certainly not! And this boy was pale, very pale. She would say he looked gloomy and nervous—yes, nervous, very nervous. He wasn't calm.

She introduced herself and gave a preview of the program. Intourist had group plans for people on excursions, but now there was only Rimma and this Deluxe boy, who was to have everything private. So she offered him a sightseeing tour. He spoke quietly, but at first it could have been a closed door between them. He didn't seem to know a single word in Russian, so Rimma spoke to him in English, about obtaining tickets to this or that theatre, and she went down a list of what to tour with him, but he showed no interest in excursions. This first morning they went in a Volvo with a driver on a sightseeing tour around Moscow, and made stops. Their last one was Red Square, but the initiative for all of one hour and a half had been Rimma's. He did not interrupt any of her tour stories; he asked no questions. Such an odd Deluxe tourist.

Then, their morning tour was over and he returned to the Berlin Hotel and had his mid-day meal alone. Rimma just said she'd see him a little later. She was planning to take him to the Kremlin that afternoon. There was something about him, something maybe unusual, but he was nice. He was polite and getting more natural.

Rimma was an only child, a native Muscovite, proud of it. She was born in Moscow, and her mother had been born there in

1904, even her grandfather, so on. So maybe she looked forward to showing this boy her city. Maybe to Tretyakov next day and she could describe the paintings there. But that afternoon, this first day, he began speaking about himself. They did not go to the Kremlin after all. He wanted to talk.

Naturally, she didn't go to his suite: She would never do that. It wasn't allowed. So they went out. It was warm, and they sat on a bench, and he repeated, "If you don't mind, I don't want to go on a tour." Now, this was not against their rules; it was allowed, but it wasn't considered a good idea.

Anyway, he began to say a few words about himself, that he was from Texas, had served as a U.S. Marine, and had decided to go and see this country, Russia. He had read, he told Rimma, that Soviet people lived good, useful, and very peaceful lives.

Now, in those days, Rimma was a great patriot, a very great one, she would say, so she was quite sure she agreed with him. She told him, Certainly ours is the best country, and you were right to come. She also felt that he was trying to get closer to her, because she was someone he could exchange information with. Not serious information, just talk about life. She was very enthusiastic that he liked her country, but she had never expected him to speak like this.

He started talking about how war was very bad because innocent people got killed, and as he talked he became more friendly, and she understood that he wanted to tell her so many things from his point of view.

Then he said that his real idea was that he didn't want to return to the United States. There was no sense in his going back, he told her. He had already settled that in his mind. He was going to stay here. He gave reasons. To her, they sounded like good ones. He said that his mother had remarried and had another husband, practically had another family, so his mother was not interested in him. Nobody was interested in him there. And when he had served in the Far East, he had seen so much suffering, so many deaths, for which he blamed the United States. His country fomented unjust wars, he said, in which he did not want to take part. He gave her an impression that he had actually been in combat, fighting for his country, definitely gave her this impression, and he was sympathetic and believable to her. She thought he was quite right. It was certainly very strange that there was an American like this, but she was sure he was quite right. So she told him she shared his opinion, that there should not be unjust wars—certainly, it was unnatural to kill people. He said again he wanted to stay here. This was a proper country from his political point of view.

Rimma was surprised. Even shocked. It was not a simple situation. Not routine at all. Nobody in training had ever spoken about something like this. So she helped him to write a letter to Supreme Soviet and she had it delivered. Nobody asked her to; it was her young wish to help him. But later, when she spoke to her boss, a woman, and told this story, her boss was not happy. Her chief said, "What have you done? He came as a tourist. Let him be a tourist."

Rimma was a little upset because she felt her chief was taking the easiest way. That was bureaucracy. For sure. But Rimma knew her people. In general, most people were slow. They did not want to be energetic. They would say, "My job is not a wolf, it won't run away into the forest, so why should I hurry?" That was one prevailing attitude. But Rimma was also sure that her chief would get in touch with someone above her and they would know what to do.

> I explain to her [Rimma] I wish to apply for Russian citizenship. She is flabbergasted, but agrees to help. She checks with her boss, main office Intourist, then helps me address a letter to Supreme Soviet asking for citizenship.

2

The Idiot

Alexander Simchenko was the boss of OVIR, the Passport and Visa Office. Decades later, still speaking some English, he would say to the Oswald interviewers, "I can tell you very honestly that everybody at that time who was working for Intourist was under observation and control by our KGB. If they asked, 'What is your impression of so-and-so?' concerning someone we were taking around, it was not possible to say, 'I don't care to speak about it.' Even if you liked a tourist, you had to give your professional opinion. When some KGB officer would call, he would, to identify himself, give you his first name and patronymic, but not his family name. He might say 'This is Gennady Petrovich. We want to know about so-and-so.' "

Alexander, of course, understood. At that time, they were taught that a majority of foreigners are spies. So you had to understand certain requirements of his position. But as far as Alexander can tell, not of a single person on whom he reported could you say that he told something inaccurate. He would tell Gennady Petrovich exactly how he accepted and reacted to each person. He reported verbally.

Alexander was a Party member then, but he could also confess now that he had been afraid to become one, although he recognized that it was necessary for his future. He had been afraid, because he thought he would have to say on his application that his father had been a Czarist officer in World War I. While his father never joined the White Army after the Bolshevik Revolution and did move with his family back to the countryside where he was born and did help to organize a collective farm there, he was still arrested. In 1930. Although he was subsequently released, it was still frightening to Alexander. So, in his fourth year at Foreign Languages Institute, when one of his officers said, "You have to become a Party member," Alexander asked his father how to fill out the forms. His father replied, "By the time you were born in 1925, I was a peasant. Put me down as a peasant, therefore, not an officer." All the same, Alexander felt he was walking a knife-edge. It was just a few years after Stalin. Yet, his father was right. He was accepted, and entered a post-graduate course at Moscow University in the Faculty of Philology. Having money troubles when he finished, he read how Intourist was receiving its first group of foreign tourists, so he applied early and became its thirteenth interpreter. Now, by October 1959, he was director at the USA/Canada Department of OVIR, and had about thirty people under him.

Alexander had acquired some experience concerning persons from other countries who wanted to apply for Soviet citizenship. Ninety-nine percent of them were disturbed. He remembered a call from a militia-man in Red Square, who told him, "There's an American lady distributing leaflets here in front of Lenin's tomb," and he said, "Okay, bring her to my office. Also, bring her leaflets." Printed in Russian was: "Dear Soviet Citizens: Help me to receive Soviet citizenship." Alexander told her, "You have to apply to our Embassy in Washington for something like this," and she said, "I did, and they said, 'Go to Russia, and Intourist will help you.' " So Alexander told her that Intourist was responsible only for tourists who were acting as tourists. Others were always told to go back and apply again to the Embassy of the Soviet Union in their own country. When they still insisted on trying to get it done in Russia, his only answer was, "Go to the Presidium of our Supreme Congress," which Presidium happened to be in an adjoining building, and so they would walk over there, and someone would receive them and say, "Go back to Intourist." At the Russian Embassy in Washington, they kept saying, "Travel to Moscow on a tourist trip. Intourist will help you."

Of course, Alexander would often hear from KGB of such cases. Still, he had never met anyone from KGB; it was always a voice on his phone. If it wasn't Gennady Petrovich, it was someone who would get on and say, "I don't know you, but Gennady Petrovich recommended I call and speak to you . . ." Then they would proceed. He just listened, and tried to be helpful.

The first time Alexander came across Lee Harvey Oswald's name was when he received a call that a young American was trying to receive Soviet citizenship. When Alexander heard his first name was Lee, he thought, "Chinese, maybe he's Chinese by birth." But then he thought, "Oswald—that's not Chinese, not Oswald." So he wasn't too surprised when this young person came in accompanied by two pretty young ladies from Intourist, named Rimma and Rosa. He seemed an average young American.

He was very cute, he was smiling, a person who tried to be very appealing, and he was, yes, very appealing. Smiling. He came in wearing a short black parka and no hat and a knitted turtleneck sweater, and he was wearing a silver chain with his name on it, and a ring with a stone. He was an unusual case, and Alexander was afraid to speak to him for too long, just talked to him a little and told him nicely to go away. He certainly wasn't in a mood to call somebody higher up and ask them to help, because they would only say, "Why?"

Years later, for instance, when the President of McDonald's hamburgers first came to Moscow, he told Alexander he'd like to introduce McDonald's to all of the Soviet Union, and Alexander made a call to City Council's catering department, and they said, "What? What you are doing? You want to leave your job? Why are you introducing *this*?" That was why, in unorthodox cases, Alexander was reluctant to call anybody.

He did ask Oswald how he received his name Lee, and the young man replied, "Maybe it's my grandparents. Maybe it's Irish." But then, thinking there might be Spanish in this name Oswald, like Osvaldo, Alexander said, "*¿Habla español?*" and Oswald said, "No, no, no, no." He said he wanted to stay in the Soviet Union because he felt very sympathetic to Alexander's country; he had read Lenin, Stalin, newspapers, magazines, etc. Alexander thought his knowledge might be superficial; maybe he had read some books, but still, nothing deep. So, Alexander replied, "You know, we're not able to do anything here." At that time, it was difficult to extend a tour; everything had to be worked out in advance through a travel agency. Intourist couldn't sell to you on the spot. Alexander knew many cases where persons wanted to prolong their stay but couldn't find a way to buy new vouchers for food, entertainment, theatre, ballet, visits, trips, no way to connect at the last minute with an appropriate bureau to get vouchers. Besides, Alexander knew that if a high official were interested in having this tourist Oswald stay on, the high official would begin to take a few steps. Since Lee Oswald had been sent routinely to him, that meant nobody was interested. Alexander took it for granted that KGB knew more about Oswald than Alexander did and that it was not his business.

Still, it was most unusual, and Oswald was very cute, very appealing, yes, smiling, charming, very quiet—yes, yes, yes, cute, cute like a teenager. And he had no hat, nothing, very poor clothes. Alexander and his two Intourist girls agreed: We ought to buy him a hat. He is not going to be accepted, so let's at least somebody take care of him. Keep him warm.

Alexander also thought Oswald was like an actor in some way, because he was a little different with each person, yes. Like a mama's child, used to his mother doing everything for him.

Next morning, Rimma was asked by this boy, "Do you think I'll be allowed to stay?" and Rimma told him she didn't know. "As for me," she said, "I'll do everything I can to help you." She felt much closer to him now. He had become to her like a relative. It wasn't romantic on her side, although she felt there might be something on his side, because he certainly seemed sure she would only do good for him. He was sweet and natural, and maybe back then when she was young she was a little more coquettish. A little bit. She couldn't say she liked him very much: He wasn't her type.

Maybe it was a small amount romantic, but certainly they did not kiss each other. She was like a sister to him, you see. He was in such a difficult position in his life; he needed someone. And who was there to rely on but herself? So, they were friendly, very friendly, and she was upset also, and uneasy. She had thought official response would be quicker. That there'd be more interest. But nothing happened on this second day.

The next morning was Sunday, the third day of his visit, and his birthday, October 18. By his passport she knew he was now twenty, but he looked younger. She gave him a gift. She bought a book by Dostoyevsky—*The Idiot*—for him. And they visited Lenin's tomb in Red Square. No special reaction. He was waiting for news, but Sunday had no news. Ditto, Monday. Absence of new information. Still, there were reports to file.

After he had told her of his desire to stay, she reported each afternoon to the proper people. It was very important, you see, for his fate. But she was surprised. They did not seem to pay much serious attention to his case.

Today, thinking of herself as a source of information to her superiors concerning Oswald, she wonders what value a young girl could bring who had never had such an experience before. At least, she was sincere. But it's difficult to say what KGB thought.

Sunday and Monday he was saying maybe he could tell them some secret things. He had served in his armed forces and he had something to tell. Rimma went to her boss and reported that Oswald was now prepared to offer matters of interest. He knew about airplanes; he mentioned something about devices. He said he'd like to meet some authorities. Her boss said, "Oh, go and have another tour," and Rimma had a feeling that maybe people from Internal Security had come around already to take a quiet look at him. Not to talk to him, just to keep a little watch on him.

On Tuesday night, however, they told her that he wouldn't be allowed to stay; he would be refused. She could not give him such bad news then. She waited until the next morning, which was the last day of his visa.

He was shocked. Very depressed, very tense. She tried to calm him, but now it was as if he were dead. He spent a whole morning with her. So depressed. She did talk him into a trip for that afternoon.

After taking her big meal at lunchtime, she waited for him downstairs; usually he was punctual—nine sharp was always nine sharp for him; ditto for 2:00 P.M. Now, this afternoon, they had their car and driver waiting, and it was very difficult with cars; you had to reserve carefully in advance. So, by two-thirty she was so worried that she went upstairs to his room without permission.

The floor lady at the elevator landing said, "He's still in his room, because I don't have his key."

Rimma said, "Come with me." They began knocking. Nobody answered. His door was locked from the inside, and so the floor lady couldn't put her extra key in. They called someone from Internal Security, and a locksmith from their hotel crew joined them, but the locksmith had difficulty opening the door, and finally pushed it open with such a bang that both men fell into the living room. They saw nobody. Rimma, behind them, saw nothing. Then these two men went on to the left and into Oswald's bathroom. Rimma doesn't know where they found him, whether in the tub or on the bathroom floor; she couldn't see from where she was in the hall, and she did not want to. Then they came out and said, "Get an ambulance." Rimma went down to call, and soon after, a policeman told her that he had cut his wrists. He had said "cut his wrists," but she didn't know if it was one or two. "Old Italian method," he said. Rimma was scared certainly, but also glad. From a moral point of view, she thought it was good that she had come in time. When they brought him out on a stretcher she saw that he was dressed. His clothes were dry. He was lying unconscious on this stretcher and she sat next to him in the ambulance. Up front was a man driving, and another fellow who had helped carry his stretcher. She was alone with him in back, and he looked so weak and thin. His cheeks were hollow; his face was bluish. He looked like a person about to die. If he did, there might be a bad situation for her country, a scandal between U.S. and USSR. Tourists come, and now this one's dead, so other tourists might be afraid to visit. What with serious distrust between two great nations, Americans might think that Soviet officials had tortured him.

Their trip took a while because they had been assigned to Botkin Hospital, which for Rimma was one of the best in Moscow. It was not near the Berlin Hotel, but it had very good doctors, with a special department for diplomats, also for foreigners. When they arrived, however, they were taken to a locked-door facility for Russians. Mental ward.

At Reception, they had put him on a stretcher with wheels, and injected him. After surgery, when he opened his eyes, he couldn't understand at first where he was, but then she began speaking to him, and said, "Everything is all right. We are in the right ward. Don't worry." And she patted his hair. She was very gentle. He looked at her but did not smile. Since they had already stitched everything, there was a bandage on his left arm near his wrist. Right arm, nothing. Just his left wrist. She stayed with him from arrival at four in the afternoon until maybe ten o'clock. He asked her not to go, and so she stayed. For six hours.

He had been put in a room with Russians, and Rimma told them he was a good American, but she did not mention that he had tried suicide. She merely said she was from Intourist, and he was American and ill—no further details. She told him to be calm. He asked if she would come and she said she would. Tomorrow morning. Certainly.

Oct. 21
Evening 6:00
Receive word I must leave country at 8:00 PM tonight as visa expires. I am shocked! My dreams! I retire to my room. I have $100 left. I have waited for two years to be accepted. My fondest dreams are shattered because of a petty official, because of bad planning. I planned too much!

7:00 P.M.
I decide to end it. Soak wrist in cold water to numb the pain. Then slash my left wrist. Then plunge wrist into bathtub of hot water. I think, "when Rimma comes at 8 to find me dead it will be a great shock." Somewhere a violin plays as I watch my life whirl away. I think to myself, "how easy to die," and "a sweet death to violins." About 8:00 Rimma finds me unconscious (bathtub water a rich red color). She screams (I remember that) and runs for help. Ambulance comes, am taken to hospital where five stitches are put in my wrist. Poor Rimma stays at my side as interpreter (my Russian is still very bad), far into the night. I tell her, "go home." My mood is bad, but she stays. She is my "friend." She has a strong will. Only at this moment I notice she is pretty.

The Moscow doctor did not want her name used, but she could state unqualifiedly that she had been on duty at Botkin Hospital when Oswald arrived at 4:00 P.M., October 21. Not at night. Four o'clock. Now she is almost seventy but, unlike most Russians of her generation, looks younger than her age. One would take her for fifty-five, and well preserved, a short heavy woman, rather handsome, but stolid and sure of herself. She repeats that she does not want publicity and does remember that day well.

It was never a serious wound, she says. Not much more than a scratch. His cut was on the lower part of his left arm, and he was up walking around very soon. Not one day did he stay in bed, not one day. When she came to examine him, he was lively, talked to other people in his ward, was only able to communicate in very bad Russian, but was very communicative.

Given such good condition, he would not have been allowed to stay if he had been a Russian. In and out the same day for such a case. His cut was hardly more than a scratch; it never reached his vein.

As for one's psychiatric examination, you ask your patient about his family background and other history. Then you go on to his reason: Why did he want to commit suicide? You try to see what kind of mood he's in. In his mind, is there still something dark? Or is he coming back to life? People either feel grateful for having been saved or are annoyed. Important to distinguish. With him, you didn't really have to ask such questions because it was not really an attempt. Clearly, he wanted to demonstrate something. Wanted to stay in Moscow. He even said, "I am afraid to go back." But never said why.

She nods at another psychiatrist's report at Reception. It is written by a Dr. Mikhailova and states that this patient regrets his attempt and now wants to go home. But that was Reception. A couple of hours later, he doesn't want to go back. It is not uncommon to have shifting reactions after arrival.

A report by still another doctor states: "Has very definite desire to stay in Soviet Union. No psychosomatic disturbances and is not dangerous."

Reception reported that the cut was three centimeters, not quite an inch and a quarter long. Surgery stated it was five centimeters, and took four stitches. Agreement in any case that his cut is not deep.

He had not asked Rimma to bring back anything from his room, but she did look around there next day and saw that he had a dark green sweater and two shirts, no more. Maybe he washed one each night. Certainly he always combed his hair and shined his one pair of shoes.

She also brought over the book she had bought for his birthday, *The Idiot.* Maybe she had made a forecast for this Lee. Since his name didn't sound Russian at all, he now called himself Alik—her suggestion.

He was in that same ward where she had left him, sitting up, quite all right. His roommates soon told her, "Everything is okay; don't worry. We'll take care of Alik; he's a good guy." And again she spent a whole day with him and did not go to her office—everything would be taken care of without her.

She was pleased; Alik was so happy to see her that he even blushed, and she believed that now Soviet authorities would change their opinion and do something. Because they should. They would not allow him to die.

When Alexander received this news about Oswald, his reaction was terrible. Very terrible. Strong. If this young man feels that he is not able to return, Alexander thought, maybe someone is following him back there in the States, etc., etc. Oswald had not said that, but he did give such an impression. That he was afraid to go back.

Next day when she came to his mental ward and they asked who it was, she said *svaie,* which means "people who are close" or "family," and that struck her as funny. What kind of family was this, all cuckoo, and now she had become one with cuckoo people. She explained to Alik that she didn't think he was crazy, he was even normal, but they did have to examine and study him. And, for that matter, she thought to herself that some psychiatrists might be from KGB. She did not exclude such thoughts.

Rosa, Rimma, and Richard Snyder

Oct. 22
I am alone with Rimma amongst the mentally ill. She encourages me and scolds me. She says she will get me transferred to another section . . . (not for insane) where food is good.

Oct. 23
Transferred to ordinary ward. (Airy, good food.) But nurses are suspicious of me. (They know.)

Oct. 23 Afternoon.
I am visited by Rosa Agafonova of the hotel tourist office, who asks about my health. Very beautiful, excellent English, very merry and kind. She makes me very glad to be alive.

Rosa, at twenty-eight, was not only pretty but had the chief position of Senior Interpreter at Berlin Hotel's bureau of Intourist. So she did not often go out with groups or individuals. She was there to oversee visas, passports, train tickets, theatre tickets, excursions, escorts, and special occasions. Her visit to Oswald was in this last category. While her hotel staff at Intourist were careful not to talk about the American who tried to commit suicide, still, a couple of days after his attempt, her boss said to her, "Take one of our cars, go to a restaurant, get some fruit, take Rimma, and visit Lee Oswald at Botkin Hospital."

Rosa remembers he was wearing hospital clothes and had a bandage on his arm, but she didn't think he could have cut his veins very deeply, because he looked well. They joked a little. She didn't want to touch upon a delicate subject, so they just had a general conversation. Maybe the visit took thirty minutes, and she left with Rimma. The Intourist car was waiting for her.

Oct. 25.
Hospital routine. Rimma visits me in afternoon.

Oct. 26.
Afternoon. Rimma visits.

Oct. 27.
Stitches are taken out by doctor with "dull" scissors.

Wed. Oct. 28.
Leave hospital in Intourist car with Rimma for Hotel Berlin. Later, I change hotel to Metropole. Rimma notified me that [the] passport and registration office wishes to see me about my future.

Later, Rimma and car pick me up and we enter the office to find four officials waiting for me (all unknown to me). They ask how my arm is, I say OK; they ask, Do you want to go to your homeland? I say no, I want Soviet citizenship. They say they will see about that . . . They make notes. "What papers do you have to show who and what you are?" I give them my discharge papers from the Marine Corps. They say, "Wait for our answer." I ask, "How long?" "Not soon."

Later, Rimma comes to check on me. I feel insulted, and insult her.

October 29
Hotel room 214, Metropole Hotel.
I wait. I worry. I eat once, stay next to phone. Worry. I keep fully dressed.

October 31
I make my decision. Getting passport at 12 o'clock, I meet and talk with Rimma for a few minutes. She says: "Stay in your room and eat well." I don't tell her about what I am about to do since I know she would not approve. After she leaves, I wait a few minutes and then I catch a taxi. "American Embassy," I say. Twelve-thirty I arrive American Embassy. I walk, say to the receptionist, "I would like to see the Consul." She points to a large ledger and says, "If you are a tourist, please register." I take out my American passport and lay it on the desk. "I've come to dissolve my American citizenship," I say matter-of-factly. She rises and enters the office of Richard Snyder, American Head Consul in Moscow at that time. He invites me to sit down. He finishes a letter he is typing and then asks what he can do for me. I tell him I've decided to take Soviet citizenship, and would like to legally dissolve my U.S. citizenship. His assistant (now Head Consul) McVickar looks up from his work.

Snyder takes down personal information, asks questions. Snyder warns me not to take any steps before the Soviets accept me, says I am a fool, and says the dissolution papers will take time in preparing. (In other words, refuses to allow me at that time to dissolve U.S. citizenship.) I state: "My mind is made up. From this date forward, I consider myself no citizen of the USA." I spend forty minutes at the Embassy before Snyder says, "Now, unless you wish to expound on your Marxist beliefs, you can go." "I wish to dissolve U.S. citizenship." "Not today," he says in effect.

I leave Embassy, elated at the showdown, return to my Hotel. I feel now my energies are not spent in vain. I am sure Russians will accept me after this sign of my faith in them.

From testimony before the Warren Commission, June 9, 1964:

MR. COLEMAN. Why didn't you provide him with an affidavit at that time?

MR. SNYDER. . . . it didn't seem to me the sensible thing to do . . . it is sort of axiomatic, I think, in the consular service that when a man, a citizen, comes in and asks to renounce his citizenship, you don't whip out a piece of paper and have him sign it. This is a very serious step, of course, an irrevocable step, really, and if nothing else you attempt to . . . make sure that the person knows what he is doing. You explain, for one thing, what the meaning of the act is; and, secondly, again speaking for myself—I cannot speak for the Foreign Service in this—provide a little breather, if possible make the man leave your office and come back to it at a later time, just to make sure—for what value there is in making sure—that the man's action is not something completely off the top of his head.[1]

Oct. 31. 2 o'clock
A knock. A reporter by the name of Goldstene wants an interview. I'm flabbergasted. "How did you find out?" "The Embassy called us," he said. I send him away. I sit and realize this is one way to bring pressure on me by notifying my relations in the U.S. through the newspapers. They would say, "It's for the public record."

A half hour later, another reporter, Miss Mosby, comes. I answer a few quick questions after refusing an interview. I am surprised at the interest. I refuse all calls without finding out [first] who it's from. I feel nonplussed because of the attention.

MR. COLEMAN. Mr. Snyder, could you tell the Commission what the Petrulli case was?

MR. SNYDER. Yes. The Petrulli case I remember quite well.

Mr. Petrulli was an American citizen who . . . did apply for Soviet citizenship while in Moscow [and] was interviewed by me to renounce his American citizenship. I did not, in accordance with the thinking I outlined to you earlier—I did not accept his renunciation the first time he came in, but did accept it when he subsequently appeared, and insisted that is what he wanted to do.

The case had a . . . rather rapid denouement, when the Soviet authorities, after having looked him over for a number of weeks, decided that they did not want him as a citizen or resident of the Soviet Union . . . we subsequently learned . . . that Mr. Petrulli had been discharged from the Armed Forces . . . [with] a 100-percent mental disability [and] the head of the consular section of the Soviet Foreign Ministry called me into the Foreign Ministry one day and said [that] Mr. Petrulli has overstayed his visa in the Soviet Union . . . and "We request that you take steps to see that he leaves the country immediately."

I told the Soviet official that to the best of my knowledge Mr. Petrulli was not then an American citizen, he having executed a renunciation of citizenship before me.

The Soviet official said in effect, "As far as we are concerned, he came here on an American passport, and we ask that you get him out of here."

Well, [the State Department decided] that Mr. Petrulli's renunciation was null and void because he was not competent . . . and we shipped him home.

The Petrulli case, as I say, was very much in my mind when Mr. Oswald showed up.[2]

November 1
More reporters. Three phone calls from brother and mother. Now I feel slightly exhilarated, not so lonely.

REPRESENTATIVE FORD. Was [Oswald] satisfied or dissatisfied with the result of his conference with you?

MR. SNYDER. I think he was dissatisfied, if anything . . . It is quite possible that this was to be his big moment on the stage of history as far as he was concerned. He may have contemplated this for some time . . . as he said—and thus my refusal at that time may have been a hurdle which he was totally unprepared for . . .[3]

4

What's My News?

He still didn't know whether he could remain in the country. They were deliberating. To Rimma, his situation began to seem bad. He had no money. At the Metropole Hotel, it was no longer Deluxe for him like at the Berlin Hotel, but still, he had a good room. Only now it was cold. Not winter, not yet snow, but cold outside. No tour, no sightseeing, no money for food, and who should pay for his hotel?

She went to Rosa, and both of them talked about the poor condition of his clothing to Alexander, who approved a purchase in GUM department store of one good hat. Lee Harvey Oswald liked it very much and tried to hug Rimma and Rosa and kiss them. He was very happy. Affectionate, yes, yes, emotional. And Alexander had no fear of buying this hat, because, certainly, he would report it.

From Tachikawa airbase in Japan, a telegram was sent on November 9 to Lee Oswald c/o the American Embassy in Moscow. Its author was Sgt. John E. Pic:

> PLEASE RECONSIDER YOUR INTENTIONS.
> CONTACT ME IF POSSIBLE.   LOVE
>   JOHN[1]

John McVickar, of the American Embassy in Moscow, wrote a note for the Oswald file.

> Nov. 9, 1959
>
> I took a typed copy of the message from Pic (Oswald's half-brother) down to the Metropole Hotel today to deliver to Oswald. I went directly to the room (233) and knocked several times, but no one answered. The cleaning lady told me that he was in the room and only came out to go to the toilet. . . . I decided not to leave the message, but to have it sent by registered mail. On the way out I phoned from downstairs, but no answer.   McV[2]

Nov. 2–15
Days of utter loneliness. I refuse all reporters, phone calls. I remain in
my room. I am racked with dysentery.

Now, at the Metropole, Rimma would go up to his room. She could. She had been given new rules, as if it were a new case. She was assigned to taking full care of him. He was no longer a tourist. They took it as something very serious, and so did he. Why were they not solving this problem? He was very nervous. He told her that all his money had gone for his tour Deluxe. He had done it purposely. If he was on a tour alone, more attention would be given to him than in a group, and that way he could fulfill his plan.

Rimma's relationship with Lee became a good deal closer. He was very much like a relative now—but not a brother, not a boyfriend, in between. He wanted to kiss her and was ready to try, but she didn't want that. She never kissed him at all, not ever. It was considered, as the English would say, not good form to behave like that. People who did could lose their jobs. Of course, for her, as a person, she could certainly kiss him if she wished it that much, but, you see, she did not. Certainly not. She had a boyfriend, a young engineer, graduate of Moscow Power Institute, whom she would see once a week. A loving fellow. Moreover, with Alik it was a situation where it was impossible to be light-minded. The consequences of improper behavior could not be simple. A Russian writer said once, "It's better to die than to kiss without love," and good girls were of that same opinion. If she didn't love him and didn't want close relations, then she should not kiss. So she patted him on his hand. Enough. Her psychology.

Besides, she had to send reports to her chief and be factual, always factual. So how could she kiss? Was she to report that? She would say Alik was okay, he wanted to be accepted into their Soviet Union; she tried to give a good impression of him, but factual. Sometimes she wrote her report daily, sometimes weekly; it depended on how much information she received. They didn't ask her to tell them every day but absolutely when she felt she should. Very difficult days.

However, she must say: She enjoyed her Intourist job immensely, an adventurous job and patriotic, and connected with protecting her government and her country. She considered herself as doing a very important job that her country needed. So, when she gave her impression of Oswald to her chief, it was to enable them to make an educated decision on what to do. KGB needed intelligent reports. They had to know as many aspects as possible of how this specific person was different from other people, and Alik was different from others. Although she did not think he was a spy from American intelligence, she had never met a spy. So, despite her personal impressions, she had to be careful. Nowadays, if she were working in Intourist, she could analyze him, but in those days, they simply said to her, "Did he meet people in your presence?" They never asked her opinion if he was sincere. She would have told them he was; he is frank and wants to stay. But she wasn't asked. And, of course, KGB, not Intourist, would make that final decision. Besides, she didn't know what he did after dinner. Between nine and five, yes, but not after dinner.

> **November 15**
> I decide to give an interview. I have Miss Mosby's card so I call her. She drives right over. I give my story, allow pictures. Later, story is distorted, sent without my permission, that is: before I ever saw and OKed her story. Again, I feel slightly better because of the attention.

> **November 16**
> A Russian official comes to my room, asks how I am. Notified me I can remain in USSR until some solution is found with what to do with me. It is comforting news for me.

Priscilla Johnson McMillan, later to write *Marina and Lee,* would encounter Oswald that day, and he would give her an interview as well:

I had just returned from a visit to the United States and, on November 16, I went to the consular office of the American Embassy, as the American reporters did, to pick up my mail. John McVickar welcomed me back with these words: "Oh, by the way, there's a young American in your hotel trying to defect. He won't talk to any of *us,* but maybe he'll talk to you because you're a woman."

McVickar turned out to be right. At the Hotel Metropole I stopped by Oswald's room, which was on the second floor, the floor below my own. I knocked, and the young man inside opened the door . . . To my surprise, he readily agreed to be interviewed and said he would come to my room at eight or nine o'clock that evening. Good as his word, he appeared, wearing a dark gray suit, a white shirt with a dark tie, and a sweater-vest of tan cashmere. He looked familiar to me, like a lot of college boys in the East during the 1950s. The only difference was his voice—he had a slight Southern drawl.

He settled in an armchair, I brought him tea from a little burner I kept on the floor, [and he] spoke quietly, unemphatically, and only rarely betrayed by a gesture or a slight change of tone that what he was saying at the moment meant anything special to him . . .

During our conversation Lee returned again and again to what he called the embassy's "illegal" treatment of him . . . Once he became a Soviet citizen, he said, he would allow "my government," the Soviet government, to handle it for him.

Lee's tone was level, almost expressionless, and while I realized that his words were bitter, somehow . . . he did not seem like a fully grown man to me, for the blinding fact, the one that obliterated nearly every other fact about him, was his youth. He looked about seventeen. Proudly, as a boy might, he told me about his only expedition into Moscow alone. He had walked four blocks to Detsky Mir, the children's department store, and bought himself an ice cream cone. I could scarcely believe my ears. Here he was, coming to live in this country forever, and he had so far dared venture into only four blocks of it.

I was astounded by his lack of curiosity and the utter absence of any joy or spirit of adventure in him. And yet I respected him. Here was this lonely, frightened boy taking on the bureaucracy of the second most powerful nation on earth, and doing it single-handedly. . . .

"I believe what I am doing is right," he said. He also said that he had talked to me because he wanted to give the American people "something to think about."[3]

Now, days started to go by and still they didn't give an answer. Rimma spent every working day with him. Very long intolerable days. He was upset, he didn't know what to do, and she didn't even try to teach him to speak Russian a little because, from a psychological point of view, it was not a time to learn; to her mind, he was in his room too much, thinking and thinking. She didn't even know whether he was reading her gift—*The Idiot*. Maybe he had been a little shocked at such a title; could wonder if was personal, yes. And maybe Dostoyevsky was difficult for him, very difficult. He was interested in nothing but his own fate. Very self-centered.

Sometimes he would still say that all people are brothers and sisters, and the Soviets wanted more good for our world than America. But Rimma felt he had come to such ideas without knowing many facts. Very superficial. Not natural. Not deep.

She never said this to him, however, because it would be too easy to hurt his feelings. He knew that too. He would never insult her, she knew, because she could say something back that would show him to be a person who thinks too much of himself and shouldn't behave as he does. You should know the kind of person you are, she was ready to tell him if he got at all unpleasant—you are just nothing.

"What's my news?" he kept asking her. Always this same question. And she had a feeling that maybe he was going to ask her to marry him. But he didn't. Maybe he knew she wouldn't agree. However, he hinted many times, said how good and how happy he felt being with her. When she went to her chief and asked about his situation, one question they would always ask her is, "What can he do for a living?" Unfortunately, he could do nothing.

Finally, since he had no money, her boss told Rimma they should move him from his present good room to something smaller. They found such a cubbyhole, very small, very modest. His life was going from Deluxe down. Down and down. Which means up. Higher floor, smaller room.

Rimma couldn't even eat with him. In those days, even if her salary was 100 rubles a month because of her excellent marks, meals at a hotel were too expensive. She went to reasonable places. Then, because they couldn't afford to give him restaurant meals at his hotel any longer, higher-ups said, "Special meal." Poorer quality. Of course, he wasn't always gloomy. Sometimes he was certainly romantic, and would tell jokes, but mostly she had to try to cheer him up. He would say that if he was allowed to stay in her country, he would live in Moscow. Of course, if he married her, it would be easier for him to do that. But she never discussed this with him, and didn't think he was just pretending that he loved her; she thought his feelings were sincere. But he wasn't sleeping well. He was thinking of his situation. Always. His Russian didn't get much better, either—no, no.

November 17 to December 30
I have bought myself two self-teaching Russian language books. I force
myself to study eight hours a day. I sit in my room and read and memo-
rize words. All meals I take in my room. Rimma arranged that. It is very
cold on the streets so I rarely go outside at all for this month and a half.
I see no one, speak to no one, except every now and then Rimma, who
calls the Ministry about me. Have they forgotten? During December, I
paid no money to the Hotel but Rimma told the Hotel I was expecting
a lot of money from the USA. I have $28 left. This month I was called
to the passport office and met three new officials who asked me the
same questions I answered a month before. They appear not to know
me at all.

All this time, no company for him. Maybe at night, when she wasn't there, somebody could visit. Rimma can't say for a fact; maybe in the evenings he began to try to find more people. Sometimes he said to her that he spoke with some Russians, so he must have met some people. Maybe it was on his floor.

If he had had more funds, it is possible his behavior would have been a bit different, but he had no warm clothes and no money. It was snowing, he didn't know Moscow, didn't know Russian. It was all: "How do you pronounce this word?" "What is Russian for that?"

Most of the time, he was in a bad mood. And it was difficult to get to his room, which was somewhere on top, you see. No rooms for foreigners there. A floor for employees who worked in the Metropole Hotel, Russians. He was there from the point of view of economy, and maybe for surveillance. "That could be a reason, I don't deny it. Maybe." She doesn't know, because girls in Intourist never talked about a room being prepared. They did not talk like that; they did not exercise their head to think that way.

One day, finally, late in December of 1959, just before New Year's, they called Rimma into Intourist's main office and told her they were sending Oswald to Minsk. When she informed him, he was so disappointed he even cried at first, with tears, yes, he wanted Moscow not Minsk, but he was also happy he was allowed to stay, relieved and happy. Of course he was happy. He was shining. He did not hide it. But he was still upset he had to go to Minsk.

He had no idea where it was. Had never heard of it. Rimma told him it was a good city, which was true. She often took foreigners to Minsk in a railroad coach on trips. She liked its newest hotel, their

Hotel Minsk. People in Minsk, she told him, are much better than in many other places. But he was depressed. He wanted her to accompany him on his all-night railroad trip from Moscow to Minsk, but by now he understood that everything was not so simple as he had thought before—everything was more serious than he had thought. In America, when he took this decision to go to Russia, he must have been like a child, but then in these days he grew up, you see. So now, he understood that even if Rimma wanted, she couldn't leave her job and go with him. He understood it was impossible. He knew it was a very serious place here.

December 31
New Year's Eve, I spend in the company of Rosa Agafonova at the Hotel Berlin. She has the duty. I sit with her until past midnight. She gave me a small Boratin clown.

January 5
I go to Red Cross in Moscow for money [and] receive 5,000 rubles, a huge sum!! Later in Minsk, I am to earn 700 rubles a month at the factory.[4]

January 7
I leave Moscow by train for Minsk, Byelorussia. My hotel bill was 2,200 rubles and the train ticket to Minsk 150 rubles, so I have a lot of money and hope. I wrote my mother and brother letters in which I said, "I do not wish to ever contact you again. I am beginning a new life and I don't want *any part* of the old."

Rimma remembered that on this day he left for Minsk, it was snowing when she said goodbye to him. He was crying and she was crying.

But she did not write to him. It was understood that an Intourist girl was not to write letters to tourists she had guided, and Rimma could not violate such a principle.

REPRESENTATIVE FORD. If you had known that Oswald was in Minsk, what would your reaction have been?

MR. SNYDER. Serves him right.

REPRESENTATIVE FORD. Why do you say that?

MR. SNYDER. You have never been in Minsk . . . Provincial towns in the Soviet Union are a very large step below the capital and the capital, believe me, is a fairly good-sized step down from any American populated place.

But the difference between large cities and minor cities, and between minor cities and villages, is a tremendous step backward in time. And to live in Minsk, or in any other provincial city in the Soviet Union, is a pretty grim experience to someone who has lived in our society . . .

REPRESENTATIVE FORD. Have you ever been in Minsk?

MR. SNYDER. I spent about an hour walking around Minsk, between trains, one time.[5]

PART III

OSWALD'S WORK,
OSWALD'S SWEETHEART

1

Igor

How Igor Ivanovich Guzmin looked when young would be hard to decide in 1993, because his presence spoke of what he was now—a retired general from KGB Counterintelligence, a big man and old, with a red complexion and a large face that could have belonged to an Irish police chief in New York, impressive from his sharp nose up, with pale blue eyes ready to blaze with rectitude, but he looked corrupt from the mouth down—he kept a spare tire around his chin, a bloated police chief's neck.

Guzmin, Igor Ivanovich, born in 1922, had worked in Minsk for the KGB from 1946 to 1977, and had first been dispatched there by Moscow Center to undertake a "strengthening of cadres," and in Minsk he had remained for more than half of his fifty years in service. Having walked in as Deputy Chief in Counterintelligence, Minsk, he became Deputy Chief of Branch, and was finally promoted to Chief of Department in Byelorussia. While his arrival came more than a year after the Nazi occupation of Minsk had ended, he could inform his interviewers that one out of every four persons in that republic had died in combat, or in German concentration camps, or *under other circumstances*. He said no more. His point was that rebuilding had been done in Minsk under difficult conditions. There was not only physical disruption, but a population compromised by collaboration. Certainly, all standing policemen, local army, village headmen—all the persons installed by Germans—had to be seen as collaborators or fascist agents. His State Security office had, therefore, to cleanse everything that you could call an obstruction to reconstruction. Many people didn't want to take responsibility for their collaborative actions with the Nazis and so had gone underground, which gave the Organs a further task of freeing society from their concealed presence. It was a good deal of work. They weren't finished dealing with all of that until 1953.

Igor Ivanovich does not, however, recall an episode in any of their security tasks that had been remotely similar to the problems initiated by Oswald's arrival. Repatriates might be scattered around Ukraine and Byelorussia, but they were Byelorussians, whereas Oswald had been sent here to Minsk as a political immigrant for permanent residence. Of course, foreign agents had been dispatched to Minsk before, members of British or American or German intelligence, sent by air, smuggled across borders—in one manner or another, implanted. Much local KGB work had been concerned with exposing, arresting, and putting such people on trial. Four American agents had been dropped by parachute into Byelorussia in 1951 alone, but Oswald was obviously different and special.

On Oswald's arrival in Minsk in January of 1960, some reports from Intourist Moscow guides and officials had already come to Igor Ivanovich's office, so he was furnished with materials on why this young American had been allowed to stay in Soviet territory. It was a small dossier, however. Oswald was being sent to Minsk for permanent residence, and other branches of the local government would take care of settling him in. Igor's function would be to find out whether Oswald, Lee Harvey, was who he claimed to be. So the most significant document was the one which stated that it had been decided at highest levels to grant Oswald permission to stay after his suicide attempt, even though his attempt may have been staged. There was then, as could be expected, a directive from Moscow Center: Start investigation of this person.

Igor Ivanovich Guzmin had a man in his department who would serve as the developer on this case, that is, would, on a daily basis, conduct their inquiry—an intelligent, efficient man named Stepan Vasilyevich Gregorieff. Igor Ivanovich Guzmin's reasons for choosing him were as follows: Stepan Vasilyevich was pure Byelorussian, born in the Mogilev region, and knew local ways of life, habits, and such specifics very well. Even more important was his professionalism. He had handled interrogations of captive German spies and British spies; he had been specifically adept at locating and then defining suspect people who had stayed in the West after 1945 but, for various reasons, had now repatriated themselves, and had to be checked. Stepan also knew a little English, and where he would lack fluency, an English-speaking deputy could assist in the translation of documents—as, for example, any letters Oswald might receive from America.

Besides, Stepan's professionalism was known. He was approved right away. Stepan was seen, after all, as a serious person, cool-minded, with steady character and patience, who liked to develop questions down to their essence. "The work of our officers has no limit on its hours, and Stepan Vasilyevich was able to work a day and a night, as much as work required, never capricious, a good fellow officer. Besides," said Igor, "I knew him well. We lived in the same apartment house and I knew his wife and children, so his domestic side was spoken for." Stepan would report directly to Igor, who would communicate with the Chief of Counterintelligence in Byelorussia, and that officer, in turn, would report to the head of Moscow Center. It could be said, then, that there were only three steps in this chain of command before it reached the apex in Moscow.

Igor Ivanovich would add that there was a reason for such extreme attention and arch-secrecy concerning Lee Harvey Oswald. Preliminary analysis in Minsk had already suggested opposing hypotheses. There was, for example, Oswald's service as a Marine to account for. Among people in Counterintelligence, it was taken for granted that CIA and FBI would recruit some of their cadre from Marines. Oswald had also told some of their Moscow sources that he had experience in electronics and radar. Such knowledge was not alien to those serving in intelligence.

Their next variant was that he had a pro-Communist attitude, was Marxist. Yet, closer examination disclosed that he was not proficient in Marxist-Leninist theory. That elicited considerable suspicion.

It was still another matter to make certain that the Americans had not schooled him in Russian and he was concealing his knowledge. That was difficult to determine, but could be examined by observing closely how he proceeded to acquire more language proficiency. So, that would also become a task for any person teaching him Russian. The monitor would have to be able to determine whether Oswald was jumping from lesson to lesson with suspicious progress, or, taking the contrary case, was he experiencing real difficulty? That was certainly a question to clarify.

Now came another variant: Lately, KGB had been testing another country's legal channels to ascertain how difficult it would be to insert their agents into that nation. Igor now had to consider a possibility in reverse: Had some American intelligence service sent Lee Harvey Oswald here to check out their Soviet legal channels? Was he a test case to determine how moles might be implanted for special tasks?

Yet, in addition to all this, looking at it in human terms, Oswald was also being accepted as a potential immigrant. It was considered desirable, therefore, to create good conditions for him so that he would not be disillusioned about life in the Soviet Union. By 1960, Minsk did have a living standard that might not disappoint him about Communist society. Besides, for their own purposes, the Organs needed a city as big as Minsk, with many people circulating in the streets. Watching a person was thereby facilitated.

Be it said, their investigation was deeply prepared. They had a complex and double goal: not to miss anything suspicious in Lee Harvey Oswald's behavior, yet not to limit his personal freedom. They also were most interested to talk to him personally, but given their ultimate objective—to discover whether he was or was not a spy—they had to abandon this possibility. Direct contact would disrupt their attempt to elicit objective answers through more delicate methods of investigation.

2

Developer

Stepan Vasilyevich received his notice of Oswald's arrival in Minsk just two days before the man was on their doorstep.

Details of where he had served while in the U.S. armed services were also minimal. Instead came information of when he had arrived in Moscow, how he had behaved after slashing his wrist, how insistent he was on remaining in the Soviet Union.

In Minsk they had a special postal channel by which they corresponded with Moscow Center, and Stepan did receive word that Oswald had served with the U.S. Marine Corps in Japan, but he felt he did not have to pay too much attention to this matter. Obviously, Military Counterintelligence had already looked into it and was not requesting more.

On the other hand, Oswald was certainly special: "As we could see by materials received from those doctors who treated him in Botkin Hospital, it was clear," said Stepan, "that since his intentions to reside in our country could not be altered, Oswald, if once again refused residence in the USSR, could, given such a strong will, repeat his suicide attempt." Of course, it was equally possible that Oswald's insistent desire to remain was connected to some special American task—but what kind of task? He had gone into the U.S. Marines when he was seventeen. Now, suddenly, he was angry at the whole American way of life. Very suspicious. It was possible he represented some new phenomenon in American intelligence methods.

In their work, if they studied a person with the intention of eventually unmasking him, then they were not supposed to take any actions that might alert their target. Stepan was in accord with Igor's decision to make no attempt to debrief Oswald formally about his service in U.S. Marines. It was more important to discover whether he was or was not an agent. There was certainly no urgency to obtain minor military information that the Soviet military, without doubt, already possessed. And if there was useful information he might be able to offer, that would have to be sacrificed in order not to make him suspicious.

This much understood in advance, Stepan prepared to develop his case.

3

Alyosha

In 1960, Stellina—named after Stalin—was manager of Intourist's Service Bureau at Hotel Minsk, and two translators worked under her. She was, at that time, already married and had a one-year-old daughter, and her husband was a teacher at Minsk's Foreign Languages Institute. Stellina herself spoke English and German, also Byelorussian, and for that matter Czech and Polish and even some Yiddish. She had grown up next to Jewish neighbors.

Before 1959, there had been no Intourist in Minsk, so she was actually the first organizer of their Service Bureau. Hotel Minsk, where she worked, was new, and had been built, in fact, because Khrushchev, during a visit, remarked that Minsk lacked a good hotel. Before it opened, Stellina and two other officials, her hotel manager and the Secretary of the Ministry of Minsk Hotels, had been sent to Moscow for training. That was when she was instructed how Intourist people in Stellina's position did not have definite working hours but rather must be ready to serve an unlimited day. When there were large numbers of tourists, she would even be on call at night, although in slack periods she could take back time for herself. So, if some tourist group came in suddenly from Brest or Finland, a person might call her at home and say, "Stellina Ivanovna, please, can you come and help?" She would quit everything and run over.

There was one case she would remember all her life. A couple arrived in a car, some Canadian who had brought along his girlfriend from Hungary, a model, and they wanted to stay in one room. The hotel administrator said, "You are not married and you will have to take separate rooms." But this Canadian's young lady did not agree. She was very angry. Her Canadian agreed to Intourist's terms because he did not wish any scandal, but his Hungarian was furious. So, when he was given his suite and this Hungarian model was put into a single bedroom, she opened her door, pushed her bed in front of it, took off all her clothes, lay nude on top of the bed covers, lit a cigarette, and started to scream as loudly as possible. If you please, Intourist didn't need any scandal, so Stellina was asked to come over immediately from her apartment—the potential problems in this situation were numerous. Many people from Finland were staying in the hotel at that time, and these Finns drank—in fact, they drank so much that they never had any complexes. They would even wander into their hotel corridor entirely naked. So, with this Hungarian girl lying there also nude and a lot of men from Finland on the same floor, some of them with their clothes off already and walking around, Stellina certainly had to talk to her. But this Hungarian model said, "Who are you?" Stellina said, "Please, *put on your clothes*. You are a woman. You cannot behave this way." The Hungarian model answered, *"Blyat!"* which translates in this case to "whore." Stellina remembers that she was also called "Russian piece of pig." There was this Hungarian lying nude in front of men and calling Stellina a whore. Then the girl said, "Don't you dare close my door. If my boyfriend doesn't take me into his suite, these Finns can come and make love to me here, all of them."

Who could deal with such a problem? Even her Canadian couldn't quiet her down. Stellina had that couple removed from the hotel.

It was different with Americans. At that time, relationships were not warm between these two countries, but some admiration existed. Stellina had been brought up to be a good host to people, and besides, she had been in an orphanage during their Great Patriotic War, and remembered how afterward a lot of humanitarian help was received from America—nuts, sugar, chocolate, beds—imagine, beds!—and clothes. So, for her, America was a country that had been nice to her. When Lee arrived, her attitude toward him, therefore, was sincere, not formal, not bureaucratic, and she could see that he felt it and knew there was no danger from her. Besides, he had arrived in Minsk on January 7, and that was Stellina's birthday. So! It was an auspicious meeting—on her birthday, a white kitten comes.

Stepan says that no one accompanied Lee Harvey Oswald from Moscow. At the railroad station in Minsk, he was met by two women from the Byelorussian Red Cross, who took him to his hotel. Stepan did not even know the names of these women. Nor had there been any concern that Oswald was traveling alone. So, the Organs were not concerned that he might try to escape from his train. Since Oswald wanted to stay in the Soviet Union so much, why would he run away? But if one was to suppose the Americans had sent him so he could escape and become illegal, it would be a most primitive and stupid act for him to get off at some midway stop. Security forces would find him quickly. That much, their CIA had to know from their own experience. The Organs could even catch people dropped from planes at night.

Stepan doesn't have information about how he traveled, whether by first or second class, but what is certain is that from the moment he arrived, surveillance commenced. At the railroad station. In this first minute he came to Minsk.

January 8
I meet the city mayor, Comrade Sharapov, who welcomes me to Minsk, promises a rent-free apartment "soon" and warns me about uncultured persons who sometimes insult foreigners.

FROM KGB OBSERVATION
PERFORMED FROM 08:00 TO 23:00 ON JANUARY 9, 1960

At 10 o'clock Lee Harvey entered lobby of Hotel Minsk, came up to hotel administrator, and started talking to him about something. After that he went up to lobby on fourth floor, took a seat, and began a conversation with an interpreter by name Tanya who was joined by another hotel worker.

After talking to them for about 40 minutes Lee Harvey returned to his room 453.

At 11:40 Lee Harvey left hotel and hurried down Sverdlov Street toward butcher store. In there he walked around, looking briefly at displayed products, after which he left and headed down Kirov Street toward intersection of Train Station Square, stopped, looked at photo display window of Byelorussia train station technical cabinet, then came up to Raduga Restaurant, stopped there for a minute, then went to grocery store on Kirov Street. While entering this store, he paid attention to people entering after him. He walked around this store, left it without buying anything, and went straight to a bookstore, where he walked along its sections without stopping anywhere, then left and walked fast. He was back at his hotel by 12:25.

At 16:40 Lee Harvey left his hotel room and went down to Hotel Minsk restaurant. There he took seat at vacant table, and waited for waitress. (Observation at this restaurant was not done because there were very few people in there.)

He left restaurant in about 45 minutes and went up to his room. He did not leave his room until 11:00 P.M. and observation was terminated until next day morning.

January 10
The day to myself. I walk through the city. Very nice.

FROM KGB OBSERVATION
PERFORMED FROM 08:00 TILL 24:00 ON JANUARY 10, 1960

At 11 o'clock Lee Harvey left Hotel Minsk and went to GUM. There he came up to electrical department, asked a salesperson some question, then took money out of his pocket and went to a cashier of this department. He did not pay for anything but just put money back into his pocket and started pacing first floor of department store up and down looking at different goods. Then he went back to electrical department, paid 2 rubles, 25 kopeks for electrical plug, put it into his pocket and went up to second floor. There he spent some time in department of ready-made clothes, looked through available suits, then left GUM store walking fast. He was back at his hotel by 11:25.

At 12:45 he came out of his hotel room and went to restaurant. He took seat at vacant table and began to eat. (No observations were made during this meal because no other people were in there.)

At 13:35 Lee Harvey left restaurant and went back to his room.

At 18:10 he left his room and went to restaurant. He took vacant table, had his meal, left restaurant at 18:45, and took elevator to fourth floor where he went to his room.

He did not leave his room up to 24:00 after which time no observation was made until morning.

Since Stellina was short, she saw Oswald as tall. He seemed unhappy to her, a bird who'd fallen out of its nest. Usually, foreigners dressed very well, but he didn't, and always seemed to be wearing his one suit.

They gave him a single room of the kind offered to Soviet citizens. Nothing special. That was probably because he was going to be living here permanently. It made Stellina feel as if Oswald were entrusted to her, but then, she saw herself as a solid kind of person. He needed her. He was absolutely helpless about going out. Since she had a motherly feeling for him, she chose to show him around town by herself.

He was a lost soul. You had to nudge to get him to do anything. She lived only two houses away from her hotel, so that was easy. She wanted to make him feel good. In fact, she soon began to call him Alyosha, because such a name was very respected. There were monuments looking like obelisks erected to those Russian soldiers who had freed Bulgaria, and Bulgarians used to call such obelisks Alyosha. There was even a song about it. Actually, Stellina had not been thinking about that other Alyosha, who was in *The Brothers Karamazov,* and laughed when she was reminded. She certainly didn't think her Alyosha was saintly, but they did have a kind of family relationship. Since her pregnancy, Stellina had remained heavy, and she thought he must have seen her as an older person, for while she was only twenty-eight, he may have thought she was a nice middle-aged married woman. He certainly seemed to recognize that anything he wanted to accomplish in this city right away would have to be done through her. So after a while he just started coming over on his own. While he would tell her a few things about himself, she saw him as secretive, a very secretive young man. She does remember saying to him on this first or second day, "You have to have a plan. How do you expect to live?" He said he wanted to study, and asked what kinds of Universities and Institutes were in Minsk. He'd prefer something in humanities, not something technical. Since she was a graduate of Minsk's Foreign Languages Institute, she knew people and suggested that maybe he apply there. Such an idea interested him. But a couple of days later, he came and said, "I have a job at that radio factory on Red Street." Krasnaya Ulitsa was its name—Red Street in English.

January 11

I visit Minsk Radio Factory where I shall work. There, I meet Argentinian immigrant Alexander Ziger, born a Polish Jew, immigrated to Argentina 1938, and back to Polish homeland (now part of Byelorussia) in 1955. Speaks English with an American accent. He worked for an American company in Argentina. He is head of the department, a qualified engineer in late 40s, mild-mannered, likable. He seems to want to tell me something.

FROM KGB CHRONOLOGY

13.01.60   In accordance with order N6 (12.01.60) Oswald was taken on as regulator, 1st grade, in experimental shop at Minsk radio plant.

FROM KGB OBSERVATION
PERFORMED FROM 08:00 TILL 24:00 ON JANUARY 13, 1960

At 8 o'clock there was placed an observation upon exit from Radio Plant where Lee Harvey is now working.

At 16:25 Lee Harvey left radio plant and went down Krasnaya and Zakharova Street toward trolley-bus stop, where he got on trolley bus, route N2, and without talking to anybody got to Volodarskogo stop, got off trolley bus and went to hotel. It was 17:00 when Lee Harvey entered hotel. He went straight to his room . . .

At 21:55 Lee Harvey left his hotel room and went down to restaurant, where he took a seat at vacant table, ordered his meal through a waitress, had his dinner, then paid, and was back in his room by 22:25.

He did not leave his room. At 24:00, observation was stopped till next morning.

According to Igor Ivanovich, KGB had done nothing directly about choosing Oswald's place of work or where he would live. Such matters were overseen by the Council of Ministers. So, the Organs were not even consulted. It was policy. No matter how carefully Igor's people might work at placing him, a hint of their efforts could still reach Oswald and spoil their case. Now, however, that he had been given a job as a fitter-trainee at Gorizont (Horizon) and was able to use radio equipment and communication devices, it could be said that it did not hurt their purposes. If he was a specially trained agent, it would be possible to observe in a factory environment what level of expertise he had in handling radio equipment under different conditions. At that time, Horizon factory in Minsk was not under high security, at least not in Oswald's shop. However, this radio factory did, at times, cooperate with secret Soviet organizations, so it would be possible to observe whether Oswald made attempts to penetrate into such special networks.

It was a large factory, occupying perhaps as much as a quarter of a mile by an eighth of a mile, and inside its gates was a sprawl of streets, sheds, and three- and four-story factory buildings that had gone up in different years, a multitude of buildings, alleys, vans, trucks, and company streets not unreminiscent of an old-fashioned and somewhat run-down movie studio.

January 13–16
I work as a "checker," metalworker; pay, 700 rubles a month, work very easy. I am learning Russian quickly. Now everyone is very friendly and kind. I meet many young Russian workers my own age. They have varied personalities. All wish to know about me, even offer to hold a mass meeting so I can speak. I refuse politely.

Oswald at His Bench

By her early twenties, Katya had worked at the Horizon radio plant for six years. Born on a collective farm, she still didn't feel like a city girl. So, she was very quiet, but still she was pretty, if very slim and very shy, and she never spoke to Oswald, just observed him. Now, she's heavier, a mother, and braver, but she was timid then. Year after year, she had worked hard, wearing Horizon's white gown and a kerchief for her hair so it didn't get into any apparatus, the gown and kerchief both provided by the factory. When Alik came down her aisle, he didn't surprise Katya, just a young guy who looked like her own people, nothing special.

Except one matter. This American complained always that he was cold. In their shop it was warm, but he said he always felt cold outside. People laughed at him when he talked. His Russian was so bad people laughed, not mocking, but friendly. He would try to pronounce words, get them wrong. They would laugh.

Sonya, who worked near Katya, was also good-looking when she was young, even if she did have to go to work at Horizon in 1952, when she was sixteen. Her mother had five children and a difficult financial situation, so she left to find a job. But by 1960 Sonya was assigned to Horizon's experimental shop, which showed that she knew what she was doing.

Her first recollection of Lee Harvey Oswald is that on the day he came, men from her shop surrounded him in a circle and started asking questions. "You have cows in America? You have pigs in America?" He couldn't understand their words, so they showed him with sign language, made animal sounds, and he laughed.

What she remembers is that Lee Oswald was a very narrow-boned person with a strong neck, a foreigner, so nobody had any type of emotions against him—just a foreigner, he was treated that way.

Stanislav Shushkevich had seen some Americans before, but this type seemed already shaped in a Soviet way. He was wearing a Russian soldier's fur hat and it was so tidy, such a typical gray fur, and he was wearing it so comfortably.

It was sometime in February of 1960 and Shushkevich had recently finished post-graduate work at his University, and high officials at Horizon assumed that he knew English well, although actually he found it easier to deal with written material than to converse. So, two days after Oswald first came to Horizon, Comrade Libezin, the Communist Party Secretary at the plant, a big man, both by virtue of his personal size and the importance of his position, came up to say that Shushkevich was being given a Party errand: Teach this man our Russian language. Up to now, any meetings Shushkevich had had with Americans were at scientific conventions and symposia. This would be the first time he would have a direct relation. So, it was something of an entertainment for him, and he remembers many details. Shushkevich was not a member of the Party, but even so, he had been trained and educated to understand that Americans always represented a small but concrete danger: You could give away certain types of important information without any such intention. On the other hand, he had been assigned officially by a Party directive to teach this man Russian, so he could be in contact with an American without producing any problems for his private life. Stanislav was excited.

What reduced potential problems even more was that he was instructed to work with another Russian, who also spoke English. The Party obviously didn't want Shushkevich and Oswald to be alone. After all, Shushkevich was a senior engineer who had developed a certain number of new devices and only happened to be working at Horizon in order to fulfill requirements for his thesis. You had to have practical experience in an industrial enterprise before you could get a doctorate.

In any event, lessons took place in a second-floor room after work, and Oswald would come to visit him from another building in their factory compound. Shushkevich's first instructions from Libezin had been, "Don't discuss anything about his life before he came here." As a result, they never entered into personal conversation. Shushkevich just worked on verbs, and occasionally tried to teach this American colloquial Russian.

Oswald seemed not at all tense or unfriendly. He was not suspicious, but reserved, and never expressed gratitude for his lessons. Which hardly mattered. Shushkevich didn't like him. Having been brought up with old beliefs, he thought no person could be worse than a traitor. A man untrue to one side would always betray the other. It was an official assignment, however, and he took care not to let Oswald read his private opinion.

In any case, nothing Oswald did was about to change Shushke-vich's view. The American seemed to show no imagination, no emotion, no smile. Their lessons proceeded without great enthusiasm, and Oswald found Russian difficult.

He did get to a point where he could achieve understanding if Shushkevich spoke slowly, used gestures, wrote words on pieces of paper, and sometimes brought out a dictionary. Actually, he wished to have more of a conversation with him in English, but their relation had to remain one-sided. It never occurred to Shushkevich to worry whether Oswald might learn technical secrets from him. He would apologize, but he did consider himself smart, and he did not believe Oswald could get information from him.

Never for a moment did any personal feeling develop. Oswald was always very clean and very neat, and while most people would be embarrassed to wear a soldier's fur hat, Oswald knew how to put it on his head. Maybe he shaped it in some fashion, but it did make him look like a gentleman.

Finally, Shushkevich was annoyed by the fellow. Oswald was being given a good salary, but he didn't seem to work as hard as other people who received less money, and Shushkevich remembers turning to one of his assistants and saying, "Listen, we've a lot to do today and need to speed up. Why not give this stuff to our American and let him help?" but his assistant replied, "No sense. It will not be well done."

That is about all he can recollect, says Stanislav Shushkevich, now Chairman of the Supreme Soviet in the Republic of Belarus, formerly called Byelorussia.

Stellina did start to teach him a little Russian, for which he did not pay her a single kopeck. She would instruct him while she took her daughter for walks in her stroller out by Minsk's big athletic stadium, a couple of kilometers away. He liked children and enjoyed playing with her child, but he was a very complex person, very impressionable. To the point of tears sometimes; other times wholly closed, without emotion. Yet, he would call her Ma, even if she was only seven or eight years older than him.

When he first started work, he used to come back from the factory too tired to do anything, just destroyed. He wouldn't even go upstairs to his room, just come into her office, flop into her one armchair, and say, "Ma, I've gotten so tired I don't even have the strength to go and take my key and open my door."

She would tell him, "Well, you came to this society to build socialism, so you don't have to feel tired; you should feel proud."

He'd say, "First I need some food and rest and then maybe I can build socialism." And he showed his shoes, which were poor and worn out. He said, "Listen, it's cold outside. My shoes, they're cold too." Another girl from Intourist happened to be there, and he said, "You want me to give you a gift? These shoes are my gift so you will know what kind of worn-out shoes Americans wear," but the girl said, "We don't need gifts like that. We've been wearing worn-out clothes all our lives. It's nothing new for us."

5

Echoes from a Ghetto

Max Prokhorchik's parents were buried alive in the Jewish ghetto of Minsk during World War II when Max was four, and so he was raised by an uncle who was a Russian, not a Jew, who became Max's uncle by marrying Max's mother's sister. Max himself never heard much about the ghetto in which he was born; it was not something he wanted to know; it still hurts. When his relatives tried to tell him, he would say, "I don't want to hear." Still, everybody in Minsk knew. What is left of that ghetto is one short crooked street that slopes down a hill. It still has old wooden buildings, and at the bottom is a very small park, perhaps twenty by thirty feet in area, with a sizable hollow at the center that was left when all the bodies buried in this place were removed.

In 1941 a hundred Jews, maybe more, were machine-gunned and then interred there. People could see the earth still moving even as dirt was being shoveled on top, a phenomenon caused by victims struggling beneath. But, slowly, such life diminished. The earth lay there with no movement.

Max was rescued from the ghetto by this Russian uncle, who had become a partisan, but then he was killed soon after by the Germans. His widow, Max's mother's sister, had still another sister also killed by Germans, and subsequently her husband, who was also Russian and not Jewish, stole into Minsk to marry Max's aunt. In that manner, this family stayed together. By winter of 1942, however, they had to leave Minsk and fled into an outlying forest, where they stayed until 1944, coming back only in the last few days that the Germans were still there. Max's people had not been informed correctly. They thought that Soviet troops had already returned and Minsk was free. Instead, they came in exactly before the siege was lifted. A dangerous time. Germans were bombing what was left of the city, and so were the Soviets. As Max's family came in by foot, bombs were falling.

It was late in June. They found the sister of Max's real father and she now looked like a bandit chief, a very tough woman who had obtained false Russian documents to protect herself from revealing a Jewish identity, and after they all embraced, Max and his family were so tired this first night that they slept on bare ground, never moving while bombs fell on all the ruins around them.

After two days of bombing, three Soviet tanks came into Minsk at nine in the morning, and it suddenly became very quiet. A horrible quiet. Everyone expected something terrible. They thought at first it was German tanks. Suddenly, boys began to shout. But the Soviet soldiers remained inside. They were very careful. The gun on their lead tank was still moving slowly from side to side as these vehicles moved on. Then, everybody saw trucks and columns of tanks following. Soldiers in these tanks threw bread to children whenever they encountered a group waving at them.

There was not a great deal of noise, however, when Minsk was liberated. The real front was already far to the west of Minsk, which had been under siege for weeks before it surrendered.

Max felt nothing on seeing German prisoners. Of all that period when they were rebuilding Minsk with these Germans, he remembers little. What he does recall is that he was hungry. In those days, there was never enough. It was not until later, early in the Fifties, that there was finally enough food for all. He was seventeen, and he went to work in a factory producing purses and suits, and there he stayed until he was taken into the Red Army.

Recruited in 1956, he served for three and a half years as a foot soldier in Mongolia. When he got out, he started to work at Horizon. He had had some vocational experience in the service, so his job in the experimental shop was not unfamiliar.

Two days after he went to work, he encountered Lee Oswald. Max recalls this date as late in January, when he knew nobody. He had been given a workplace and instruments and he knew what to do, so he calibrated everything on his punch-press, and chose proper diameters. At lunchtime he felt free to go out and have a smoke. It was accepted practice among workers that if somebody left his bench, you had to wait until he came back and gave approval before you could start working with his machine. But when Max returned, all his settings had been changed and the special piece he had been working on was dismounted. It was Max's first job, and he wanted to show his foreman that he was skilled. A man who worked near this machine pointed Oswald out: "He's the one." And Oswald was standing with his back to Max. So Max touched his shoulder and said, "What are you doing?" This fellow started to speak some un-Russian language, and Max was shocked and surprised. He couldn't understand what was going on. Then this fellow turned and tried to move Max away—not a push, just to move him, but his expression was angry. Maybe it was a bad day for him, also. He made this gesture as if to say, "Move aside," and that made Max even angrier. He took this guy by his lapels, which is, as they say, "taking him by his breasts," and pushed him into a column. Then everybody surrounded them and pulled them apart and Horizon's Party Secretary, Libezin, came over screaming and took Max upstairs to see his shop manager. Libezin explained that this fellow he took by the breasts had come from America.

Then they brought Oswald up, introduced him, and said that Max should apologize. They were polite about it, but they said, "He's a new person here; he doesn't know our rules, so apologize. You started it." Max didn't want to.

Meanwhile, this fellow just sat there as if he didn't care, didn't understand. Max said, "I will apologize, but I won't shake hands. It will take time to do that." Max was very angry. They told him, "You are equal. He's American, you're Russian, you're both workers." But Max said, "He did something wrong to me and he should pay for it." Perhaps if Oswald had spoken Russian, they could have talked about it. But here they were steering Max into a strange situation. So he compromised by standing up, putting his hand on his chest, and bowing his head, not his body—he bowed his head. Because Oswald didn't understand this language, he thought Max had apologized, and he remained silent, and then he left with Libezin. That was all Max had to do with Oswald for quite a while.

· · ·

Stellina knew she was not supposed to have that much private contact with foreigners. So she asked another interpreter, Tanya, to go out with him. Tanya did speak English, and Stellina suggested that Alyosha invite Tanya to a film.

However, it proved complicated. While Tanya was happy-go-lucky and nice, though not particularly well educated—certainly not a girl from the *intelligentsia,* who might look down her nose at Oswald; in fact she lived with her mother, who was a janitor—still, you could not say that their first meetings ran smooth. Alyosha invited Tanya to see a movie, but there were two theatres in the same large courtyard, and he had gone to one and she was waiting near another. Next day, he came to Stellina and said, "Ma, what kind of girls are you introducing to me? She deceived me; she didn't come." In her turn, Tanya said, "He didn't show up." Next day, they agreed to meet at the Summer Theatre, but this time it turned out that Minsk had two such cinemas, identically named, but at opposite ends of town. So it happened again. He was boiling. "Ma, is she mocking me?"

That was all finally worked out, and they started going around together. A couple of weeks later, he came to Stellina and said, "What kind of woman did you give me? I tried to kiss her, and she said, 'No kissing. First, we'll get married, then kiss.' "

From KGB Observation
Performed from 07:00 to 23:00 on January 30, 1960

At 7:30 Lee Harvey left hotel, went to Volodarskogo stop, got on trolley bus, route N1, and without talking to anybody went to Pobedy Square, got off and went down Zakharova and Krasnaya Street to his work. He was at work by 7:45.

At 14:05 Lee Harvey left Horizon factory and walked fast to Pobedy Square, got on coming trolley bus N2, bought ticket and without talking to anybody went to Volodarskogo, got off trolley bus and was at Hotel Minsk by 14:20 . . .

At 17:55 Lee Harvey went down to lobby, went to hairdresser, had his hair cut, and went back to his room.

He did not leave his room until 23:00. Observation stopped at this point until next morning.

Stellina remembers that before too many weeks had gone by, Aloysha seemed to have found an English-speaking friend, a medical student named Titovets, who certainly spoke English very well, and this fellow would come over to the hotel often, and they would go out together. So Alyosha began to be a little more at ease. It wasn't like the first few days, when he was, as they say, "not on his own plate." Then, a week or two later, Stellina saw Alyosha once with another friend, a nice-looking blond-haired fellow named Pavel Golovachev. In Minsk, a number of people, including Stellina, had heard about Pavel Golovachev because his father was a famous Air Force General. Now, he and Alyosha were friends.

Of course, there was great interest in Alyosha as an American, a real American, and unmarried. Young women even came to the hotel and said, How do we get to meet this guy?

6

Twice a Hero

The work of Stepan Vasilyevich on Oswald was always studied critically by Igor. A developer could fail to see something in time, so Igor could not be satisfied only with what Stepan reported, but looked to give specific directions.

Igor did want to point out that he had a large number of other matters to oversee, and so it is important to understand that while he kept watch on each project, each developer had to *live* in his case, accumulate every fact, make evaluations, and then come up with proposals for action that would *develop* his viewpoint. Stepan, therefore, was leading the case.

"Now, of course, mistakes were made," Igor said. "Sometimes our actions were not commenced in time, and some of Oswald's actions were not prevented; nothing, obviously, can be perfect."

One early instance—and it still stands out in Igor's memory—is that Stepan did not take steps to screen Oswald away from one eighteen-year-old at the radio factory who happened to be the only son of an Air Force General who was also a twice-decorated Hero of the Soviet Union, a very high award. But his son, Pavel, was considered to be of "dissident nature" and was dealing in petty activities on the black market. So they were afraid of what a qualified agent could do with young Golovachev—maybe even recruit him over to Western thinking.

Libezin, the big man in charge of proper ideological environment, came walking down Pavel's aisle and said, "Anyone here speak a little English?" Pavel happened to be the one who did. He was not asking for it, he could have said that he did not know English, but he nodded. Libezin took him to meet Oswald at his worktable, and there they were, shaking hands.

Pavel had studied English from fifth to tenth grade and, of course, it wasn't much. His first reaction to Oswald was that he looked like an extraterrestrial who had all of a sudden ended up in their factory. "Well," said Pavel to himself, "if it is not Lucifer, it is a man. That will be proved by time, but there is nothing repellent about him."

Besides, in that period, Khrushchev had started a campaign for peace and friendship. Society was opening up. You had to keep in mind the specifics of that time. So, there was Pavel, on the second day after this introduction, standing with a pocket dictionary and Lee Oswald next to him with another dictionary. Of course, not knowing that their association would be important someday, Pavel did not keep notes. But then, for many years after, he wanted to forget all of it, the whole goddamn thing, you understand? He really did not keep it in his memory. Now, he doesn't remember too much, and he doesn't want to make up stories. He could spin a tale about how he and Lee Oswald went to pick up girls, but that was not the case.

It was more like he took Oswald around the shop and helped him communicate with other workers when a job had to be explained. At first, however, this American's vocabulary was minimal. Pavel had to explain a word like "falling" by taking a box of matches and dropping it from his hand. That way, he taught Lee a song, "Falling Leaves."

A few workers were hostile to Oswald, but just a few. There was one, Viktor, a *zhlob*, medium-sized guy, real strong. And Viktor always used to say, "Those American imperialists—if I had a machine gun, I would shoot them." A real *zhlob*. Viktor had a clear image of his enemy, and he once picked a fight with Lee, although it was broken up immediately. Pavel's recollection is that Lee was not pugnacious. Maybe he had such qualities hidden inside him, but he was not very big in the bones.

Of course, if Viktor had gone further, Pavel would have gotten in between. It was the very least he could do. While he would not call Oswald a "friend," it is only because that word in Russian is so holy that not only can you give up your last shirt, but you are ready to die for a friend. If you think in this way, obviously you don't have a lot of friends. In fact, you are lucky to have one. All others are "pals." In that sense, Lee was his pal. Maybe more, but still not his friend.

In fact, for a long time Pavel did not see a great deal of Lee other than at work. He did not go for walks with him or hang around with him. Pavel had had to take a job at Horizon in order to earn enough of a new reputation to enter his Institute. Pavel had been kicked out of Komsomol. So, when he left Moscow to go to Minsk, his last school had written such a résumé that he'd even be lucky to get into prison with it.

He could say therefore that for a long time he only saw Lee at work. Once in a while they would meet at lunch, or at the home of some Argentinians named Ziger. But that was all. Since the physical distance between their tables was not much more than five meters, they never did have much desire to meet after closing. After all, they were able to talk to each other through the working hours of each day. If Oswald went out at night, it was to his own places. A cat who walked by himself.

One night that winter, not two weeks after he met Lee, a stranger came up to Pavel on his way home from work. There, right outside his apartment entrance, this stranger showed an identification card from KGB.

Pavel said, "Can we go up to my apartment and talk? It's winter."

The stranger said, "Let's talk here."

It was too cold, however. Pavel was frozen. So he convinced the man to come upstairs.

They conversed in Pavel's room. His visitor took out about five pictures, and started off by saying, "Do you know this fellow?" He went through each one of these five pictures, and Pavel said, "No. I don't know any of them. Who are they?" And received for a reply: "They are state criminals." At which point his visitor looked at him hard, as if maybe he really did know them well.

Pavel said, "I don't want you to waste your time. I have never met these men in my life. It's strange you ask me these questions."

Then the man from KGB brought out a photograph of Oswald and said, "You know, you took on a relationship with this American guy so easily, but we would like to tell you that your Motherland now asks that you give us some information so that we know what kind of person he is. We need your help." Pavel didn't feel anything like a patriot, but knew for sure they would get cooperation. It was a demand. People senior to himself became nervous if they saw a KGB card in a man's hand. It was not that Pavel felt any kind of obligation to his Motherland; he was eighteen, and scared to death. That was, Pavel would say, a strong substitute for obligation: being scared to death.

Pavel never looked at a clock during this interview, but it must have taken an hour. A lot of questions went by. The KGB man kept going around and around for quite a while before he touched their main subject. Then he explained, "Oswald is from another country, a hostile country." It could not be more clear what he was saying. He must have been twice as old as Pavel, short, compact, sharp eyes—one Byelorussian who didn't show any feelings or emotions, just a small trim fellow with a smooth round face, a long thin pointed nose, and small dark eyes as sharp as his nose. He would depend on that nose. It seemed to sniff out everything inexact that Pavel was saying.

He didn't threaten Pavel, however, just stated, "From time to time, I'd like to meet with you. My name is Stepan Vasilyevich."

From Igor: "We can say it now—there were surveillants assigned to be Oswald's tails, and certain people were assigned to work with him, to become his associates and friends. We were especially careful to check if he was looking for personal contact with another agent. We were interested to see whether there were any signs of a prearranged meeting."

According to Igor's plan, various hypotheses were going to be tested in order to find out if Oswald was looking for secrets of a military, political, or economic variety, and also they would look to learn if he had developed any means of communication with foreign intelligence by radio, mail channels, or messenger. KGB would also attempt to find out if he had any means of cryptography to use for secret writing. Igor Ivanovich himself was ready to study Oswald's letters, should he send any, in order to make certain there was no chemical writing between the lines. Later, when Oswald bought a radio, they checked that equipment, and they were always alert for signs of his ability to communicate through special codes.

Nothing showed up that was suspicious in the first two months, but if Oswald was an American intelligence agent, he certainly would not make quick moves. Sometimes a man who is not an agent will do things that arouse suspicion; that happens often; but not even unfounded suspicions were stirred by Oswald. Studying him with close attention, they began to have a feeling that he was at the least semi-lazy; and very frugal; he didn't drink, didn't smoke, went to theatre and cinema within his budget, and had an income of 70 rubles a month in new money for salary and an increment of another 70 rubles a month from the Red Cross, or 140 rubles in all. This was, after all, 1400 rubles a month by the old measure, and so a good amount. Stepan, for example, was only earning 80 rubles in new money, and that was enough for him to get by. There was, for example, no telephone in Oswald's apartment, and KGB never received information that he wanted one. On those occasions when he wished to make a call, he went outside to a pay phone. It would be better if he had wanted his own instrument, but they couldn't install it for him, could they?

FROM KGB REPORT: 18 FEBRUARY 1960

> By means of personal observation and in conversation, "L" did not notice that OSWALD aroused suspicion in his behavior. He was not particularly interested in his work, and often made comments such as, "Why should I saw away at this metal with this saw, I'm not going to become an engineer. My real dream is to learn foreign languages and learn them well." (He did not say which ones in particular.) He is reserved in conversation, answers questions briefly, self-possessed manner.
>
> Once, according to "L," he and OSWALD were reading President EISENHOWER's speech in *Pravda*. In this speech, EISENHOWER attempted to demonstrate technical backwardness of Soviet Union compared to United States. OSWALD answered that EISENHOWER was lying, that USSR is not technically less advanced than U.S.
>
> OSWALD almost never talked about life in his country, or how he got here. Sometimes during a lunch break he will exchange two or three words with young people, girls and boys, and will compare life in USSR and U.S. But in those situations as well he speaks positively about position of workers in USSR.

. . .

By other reports, however, Oswald soon proved to be one Humpty Dumpty worker. He did not treat his job well. Igor could see that he showed no interest, and his behavior and attitude caused complaints from other workers.

Since Igor and Stepan were not satisfied by this image of him as lightweight, they deliberated whether his psyche was entirely normal. On the other hand, they were aware it could all be a pretense. Once again, they worked on two opposed hypotheses: Either Oswald was part of a foreign intelligence plan, or he was not but had some psychological difficulty. They began to study situations where Lee Harvey Oswald, if he were a spy, might expose himself.

For example, now that he had established contact with Pavel Golavachev, Igor and his people would watch Oswald with Golavachev to see whether the American would try to use him as a trampoline, so to speak, to gain access up to Pavel's father, a General who knew large secrets.

"You know," Pavel said to his interviewers thirty years later, "we have class struggle and class hatred, but we also have normal envies. People are envious." People were always telling him, "Oh, I would like to have had your father. I would have become Napoleon. I could have turned the earth around if I had had a father like yours!" Even at school, when they were all having fun and were all equally guilty of breaking some rule, Pavel would be blamed. He offered this as background for talking about his father. The war damaged a little bit of the General's nervous system. Honestly speaking, his father liked his children; but honestly speaking, he was also a bit of a despot. A true military person: He wanted everything done punctually and properly, whereas Pavel was born, he would say, a democrat.

During the Great Patriotic War, his father had been a Captain, a fighter-pilot with his one-seat plane, a Cobra, and most of his missions gave cover to bomber planes, but when Pavel read logs of his father's flights, he saw that four or five times his father had chosen to go out just to enjoy "free hunting."

A pilot was recommended for his first gold star as Hero of the Soviet Union if he shot down fifteen German planes. To get your second award, to be decorated Twice a Hero of the Soviet Union, you had to perform some extreme kind of heroic deed, something extra-dimensional. For example, one Captain, when he saw that one of his men had to make an emergency landing in a field, managed to bring his plane down alongside his buddy's crippled vehicle, and then he held off some German infantry long enough to carry the wounded pilot back to his plane and take off. For this he received Twice a Hero of the Soviet Union.

Pavel's father had been winning an aerial fight, at eleven thousand feet, but ran out of ammunition. Still, he succeeded in downing his opponent's plane by chopping up its tail with his propeller. Then, damaged himself, he managed to get back safely. That brought him a second gold star.

His father had become a Party member. It was necessary as a patriotic duty during World War II, but afterward, Pavel never knew whether his father felt disillusioned by the Party or was proud of it. He never talked of this. Of course, there were not many family conversations on such matters. Given their one-party system, one did not quit membership in the Party. One might as well quit everything and go straight up to heaven.

On the other hand, his father told Pavel to join Komsomol. You lived with wolves, you howled like a wolf. So Pavel's father was not a dissident, and did not want Pavel to be one. But there was never any political activity indoors. His parents' attitude was: Read for yourself—don't talk about it.

While his father did not like to give him pocket money, he never restricted expenses for technical hobbies. So, Pavel built airplane models and ship models, and his father would purchase anything good for his technical development. He certainly never felt deprived of his father's love, or his mother's.

Still, his father, being a military man, had his family moving all the time. In ten years, Pavel changed schools eleven times. He was in Monino, then Riga, then Tukums; then to the Kolski peninsula, and in Allakurti, Monino, Allakurti again, then Moscow by spring of 1957. In ten years, eleven schools. Upon completion of the tenth grade, he moved away from his family and came back to Minsk. Ever since, he had been on his own.

To his father's unspoken disappointment, he had not been interested in a military career. In 1956, during the Hungarian Revolution, TV showed Russian bodies cut into parts by Hungarians. But two years afterward, in 1958, in Moscow there lived on the same floor of their apartment house another General, whose son had served in Hungary, and this young officer told Pavel how he was driving a tank during the uprising and, having been surrounded by a Hungarian crowd, had to move his tank quickly to get out, and later had the guts of people on his treads. When this young officer came back to Moscow, he was exactly the same color as a white bird, a dove. He was not a close friend, but he changed Pavel's life for sure.

Pavel did have discussions with his father about a military career, because at one high school he had taken first place in a shooting competition, and his father, naturally proud, wanted him to go on into the Air Force, but in his family nobody forced you to do things, and what settled matters for Pavel even more than the tank treads was that there was a good apartment in Minsk open to him. His father, as one of the Byelorussian republic's national heroes—and there were only four Byelorussian-born soldiers who had become Twice a Hero of the Soviet Union—had been given his own cottage as a special honor; Pavel's parents had then exchanged that house for an apartment just off the grand circle of Victory Square, a gracious four rooms in a building designed for the Minsk elite. The ceilings were high.

When Pavel went to live there, it was occupied already by his mother's sister, who of course remained with her two sons. But there was ample space for Pavel.

He was interested in radio technology, and so work at Horizon was closest to his interests. Still, he found the factory kind of primitive. Real knowledge could only be obtained at a higher engineering school. He did want a more advanced technical education. While a well-qualified worker would earn higher wages than a person with an advanced degree (which to Pavel was a typical disproportion of their Soviet system), still, one's education could extend one's horizons.

Pavel had seen a French film, *The Wages of Fear*, about an engineer arriving in a far-off village where people were afraid of spirits. This engineer was supposed to set up an explosion for a dam. But everybody was afraid to lay in the dynamite, because of angry spirits. So this engineer had to do it all by himself.

Pavel wanted to be such an engineer, a man who could do things not only on paper but with his hands. He was working hard. He had three semesters where he not only had to do his factory work but was attending Minsk's Polytechnic Institute; seven factory hours each day, six days a week, and an academic program four nights a week. So, when it came to sex, he had to wait for summer. At that time, he and friends his age would be sent out on agricultural assignments and could be free of parents. Sex came not in the backseat of an American automobile, remarked Pavel, but out in a field while picking mushrooms. Of course, in those days, he still had golden hair and a wonderful apartment, one full room to himself, but working so hard, he did not see much of girls, especially not in winter, not on the kind of cold night when a fellow like Stepan, his KGB man, would be waiting for him.

It was a wild country, and you never knew how your parents would react. Peter the Great once tied a peasant to a bear and threw both into a pool. Everyone stood around and laughed. Pavel was tempted to tell his father about his KGB visitor, but decided not to. Pavel's father could be as impulsive as Peter the Great.

March 16
I receive a small flat, one room, kitchen, bath, near the factory, with splendid view . . . of the river, almost rent-free. 6 rubles a month. It is a Russian's dream.

It was an exceptional move, thought Stellina, to give him an apartment. His factory, like every other industrial enterprise and plant, had people on a waiting list, so how did you jump to the head? This waiting list included veterans of wars, invalids, families with many children, and also took into account how many years you worked at Horizon.

Then, after he moved, Stellina hardly heard from him. In fact, there was no word for more than a year, not until April 1961.

For example, Stellina didn't find out about his wife until then. Alyosha came to visit her one full year later, and said, "Ma, I'm getting married," and she said, "How can that be? You don't know Russian well enough. How can you communicate to this person? Does she know English?"

Alyosha smiled and said: "Two phrases: 'Switch off the light,' and, 'Kiss me, please.' "

Igor stated that Oswald received his place through factory decisions; nothing to do with the Organs. Of course, it was not easy to find apartments, but since this was an American seeking political asylum, the highest authorities decided to give him very good conditions. It was felt that Soviet institutions should show humanity to him.

There had also been a directive from Moscow Center to Minsk KGB to "point Oswald in the right direction." What did that mean?

Igor replied, "When we check out a person, whether it is for suspicion of espionage or anti-Soviet dissident activity, we never put aside our capability to make a person of him, so to speak. Certainly, when Oswald came here to get knowledge about Communism and our socialist way of life, this side of the problem also had to be considered. Because, if indeed he came here to participate in improving socialism, then we had to direct him in this matter. That's why Lee was given an extra monthly allowance from Red Cross, equal to his salary, and an apartment and a job. It was to enable him to find his place in our socialist regime. We did not wish to think only in negative terms. Give him some real possibilities to go in the right direction."

His lack of desire to work did, however, cause suspicions. "Labor is necessary for us, and absence of such a desire would take away his credibility that he was interested in our country," said Igor.

All the while that Oswald remained at his hotel, he never invited Pavel there. Their most memorable personal contact in such early days was when Oswald received his apartment in the middle of March, and Pavel and a couple of other fellows helped him move in some furniture. An interpreter from Intourist named Tanya came along. Pavel was not particularly surprised that Lee was given an apartment with a balcony and a beautiful view. "Below the waist," as they say, they had given it to him, but that had nothing to do with Pavel. After all, his own living conditions were far more satisfactory.

Oswald's kitchen was small, and his living room was not five meters by three. You couldn't get much more than a bed in there. A factory bed. For that matter, his table and chairs were also provided by his factory. Of course, he didn't pay much. A rent so low, judged Pavel, that it was symbolic. And he did have a small balcony, with one of Minsk's finest views. Four stories below and across Kalinina Street were lovely green banks. The Svisloch River, a meandering stream appropriate to a fine park, so nice and tranquil a river it deserved to have swans in it, ran along the bank of Kalinina Street. Thereby, Oswald's apartment house was elegant, even grand from the exterior; it had high columns on its facade, framing the balconies, and was situated, like Pavel's apartment, in your very best part of town. It just wasn't much inside.

Parties at the Zigers'

Pavel, as he said, would not go out often that year, but Lee did bring him over to meet some Argentinians that he knew named Ziger.

Pavel enjoyed visiting their apartment. The Zigers treated you with coffee, and would offer a glass of wine in a most gracious manner. On a tray. They did not behave like Russians. The atmosphere was relaxed. Besides mother and father, there were two daughters and their boyfriends and other young people. A joyful and interesting atmosphere, although the first time that Pavel tasted table wine at the Zigers' it was so dry that every Russian there was twisting his mouth. In Minsk, most wine was sweet.

Later that summer, Ziger's daughters used to sunbathe in their bikinis on the balcony of their apartment, which shocked their neighbors. It was a scandal throughout the entire building. The Zigers were not only foreign but Jewish, thereby doubly scandalous.

According to Pavel, Lee never went out seriously with either of the daughters, but then, the Ziger girls weren't his type. Anita was too big, too wide-boned, and the older Ziger daughter, who might have been a right match for Lee, was already married. Eleanora was her name. In Pavel's opinion, Lee liked girls who were micro-miniature, full of air and grace. Later, there would be Ella, then Marina, both thin and delicate, elegant girls.

For a time at the Zigers' parties, Lee seemed to have some interest in Albina, a big girl, always around the Zigers, but then Pavel recalled that when they were all young, back in 1960, Albina was not huge as she is now, nor was her hair colored to its present wild-orange; no, she was tall and slender and blond, with a powerful young bosom, so she was attractive to many.

Now, Albina and her family had had a hard time in the war and were poor afterward, with many hardships, but by the late Fifties life had bettered itself a little, and Albina was working in Minsk's Central Post Office, which is where she met Anita Ziger. Young people, said Albina, always mocked Anita for her way of dressing. She wore high-heeled shoes and slacks, and being Argentinian, Anita looked like she could do a tango, which she could.

Albina had met Don Alejandro Ziger and his wife first, then Anita, through her post office. These Zigers received parcels from

Argentina, and Albina was there to help them process such items through postal customs, postal declarations, other bureaucratic procedures. She must have done it well, because the Zigers invited her to visit them and gave Albina their address, even said, Come visit this Sunday. But Albina didn't go. She didn't have enough money to buy them a proper gift. In Russia, you come with something when you are invited, but she was too embarrassed to buy a cheap present. So she didn't go.

When Anita came again to the post office, she invited Albina to see a movie. They went to a German film, just two of them alone, and Albina was uncomfortable because Anita was much better dressed than herself, yet Anita was also a merry person, with jokes, lots of jokes. Afterward, she invited Albina to her parents' apartment, and it was nothing unusual. Like a common apartment that everybody had, one room. At that time, it was still very difficult with housing. So, there was one bed in the only room, and one in the hall, and that's where Anita slept, in Ziger's hallway. Nothing special. Ziger's second daughter, Eleanora, didn't live with them at that time. She was married and stayed in a town, Petrovsk, where, Albina thinks, her husband's relatives treated her badly. So, Don Alejandro managed to get a two-room apartment and visited Petrovsk and took Eleanora back with him. She never returned to her husband. She got her divorce while remaining in Minsk, a slender good-looking woman with a nice voice.

This new apartment was decorated differently from Russian apartments. "Latino-American interior," said Albina. "Their bed was big. They brought such a bed from South America, because Russians don't produce big beds for people. Very beautiful bed." At that time, there was a shortage of everything, and these Zigers were very practical people. They also brought their mattress from Latin America, and it, too, was beautiful, with bright threads and embroidered roses, other flowers, everything. They also knitted sweaters, and sold them to Russians they knew. They had come with very big trunks made of natural leather, and they cut up those trunks and sold pieces of leather to shoemakers. Don Alejandro was a man of resources.

In their apartment was a brown piano, and Anita could play everything—"Moonlight Sonata," "Barcarole," Vivaldi, Tchaikovsky, and a lot of Latino-American melodies, tangos included. Also, the Zigers had a combination radio set with gramophone. This was Albina's first time in a home that had so much music, records, life, vitality, such fun. Albina decided there was another person in her, some other human being inside who was curious about the world outside, and she decided she would like to travel and communicate with people.

These Zigers had friends who were also immigrants from Argentina, and at parties they would go into recollections of fine shops in Buenos Aires and lovely streets they used to walk on. How they missed their country! Since Anita Ziger went to a musical college in Minsk and would bring friends from there, the family's parties were always musical and filled with such interesting people. One of them turned out to be Lee Harvey Oswald, whom everybody called Alik. Don Alejandro had invited Alik over from that radio factory where they both worked, and Albina got to like this Alik more and more. He was alone, he was a young man, and by March he had a nice apartment. When he took her to see it, she was even a little bit upset, because she herself never had anything like that in her life. So, he had a lot to feel spoiled about, and maybe that was why, at his job, he was never enthusiastic. But then he did tell her once, "All those girls like me. When I cross the yard, they are all sitting around, saying, 'Alik, Alik.' "

Albina wouldn't admit whether it was more difficult to have said no to him than to other men, but she certainly could admit that Alik had not liked being refused. When she did say no to him in his apartment, he had clicked his fingers and said, "Dammit!" In English. "Dammit!" She knew that word. It was not anger he expressed so much as being upset. He touched her and said, "Oh, stupid, you don't know your happiness," which is a Russian expression—"Stupid, you don't know what happiness is."

Maybe she didn't, because she certainly lost him later. And not even to women. She felt as if she lost him to a man. Not as in a romance, but because this man could offer him other parties, other people. Or maybe it was because he could speak English so well.

It was her friend Ernst Titovets—if he was a friend. She had gone to high school with Ernst, who was also called Erich, and it was through her, Albina, that Erich met Alik. That was because she had known Titovets since he was fifteen, and sometimes in school they would even share desks together.

She had always thought Erich was a little strange, and nothing about him was fun, but he was all right. Some students used to speak of him as *manerniy*—full of mannerisms. So, nobody liked him much, but then he always wanted to show people he was better. And he certainly was interested in English. Of course, everyone should know such a language, because half of the world spoke it. To be an intelligent person with a cultural background you had to be able to speak at least one other foreign language, but Titovets always wanted to impress people that he was not average, and so he always did things by himself. He didn't chase young women; he was mostly involved in his hobbies; he played chess, he was interested in music, and he was going to medical school about the time Albina introduced Erich Titovets to Alik. In those years, when the Zigers were a very bright part of her life, Albina would feel sorry that she had made such an introduction, because Alik used to come to their house often and he spent a lot of time with her, but now Ernst had captured him, and took him to other places. Finally, one year later, Ernst even brought him to a place where Alik met his future wife, and then Albina's love was over forever, vanished.

She remembers right after she met Alik in January, she was walking with Anita and other Argentinian friends and then, not far from Victory Square, they suddenly ran into Erich. He came up to her and said, "Hi, what are you doing, how is your life, who are these people?" That was because he could hear these Argentinians speaking a foreign language, Spanish, and Albina said she didn't speak it but just listened, and then he said, "Oh, who's that person? It's an American, isn't it? Can you introduce me to him?" She said, "Why do you want that?" And he said, "You know I'm very much interested in some practice for English. My English teacher, I go to him and ask questions, but it isn't always convenient for him." So she said, "Excuse me, I have to ask other people first if they want to be introduced. I don't feel like I could do it here in front of everybody just like that."

So then Anita, very happy, so open, had to say, "Who is this young man?" And Albina said, "A man who's going to be a doctor wants me to introduce . . ."

Anita said, "Okay, invite him to one of our parties and we'll dance and we'll talk." They were without fear at the Zigers' home. Maybe that's why later they had such a problem getting an exit visa back to Argentina. They always said what they thought. And sometimes they spoke badly about Soviet life.

May 1
May Day came as my first holiday. All factories, etc., closed. Spectacular military parade. All workers paraded past reviewing stand waving flags

and pictures of Mr. K., etc. I followed the American custom of marking holiday by sleeping in in the morning. At night I visit with the Zigers' daughters at a party thrown by them [and] about forty people came, many of Argentine origin. We dance, play around, and drink until 2 A.M. when party breaks up. Eleanora Ziger, oldest daughter, 26, formerly married, now divorced, a talented singer. Anita Ziger, 20, very gay, not so attractive, but we hit it off. Her boyfriend Alfred is a Hungarian chap, silent, brooding, not at all like Anita. Ziger advised me to go back to USA. It's the first voice of opposition I have heard. I respect Ziger, he has seen the world. He says many things, and relates many things I do not know about the USSR. I begin to feel uneasy inside, it's true!

FROM KGB OBSERVATION
PERFORMED FROM 07:00 ON MAY 1, 1960, TILL 01:50 ON MAY 2, 1960

At 10:00 Lee Harvey came out of house N4 on Kalinina Street, came to Pobedy Square where he spent 25 minutes looking at passing parade. After this he went to Kalinina Street and began walking up and down embankment of Svisloch River. Returned home by 11:00.

From 11:00 to 13:00 he came out onto balcony of his apartment more than once. At 13:35 Lee Harvey left his house, got on trolley bus N2 at Pobedy Square, went to Central Square, was last to get off bus, went down Engelsa, Marksa and Lenina Streets to bakery store on Prospekt Stalina.

There he bought 200 gr. of vanilla cookies, then went to café <Vesna>, had cup of coffee with patty at self-service section and hurried toward movie theatre Central. Having looked through billboards he bought newspaper <*Banner of Youth*>, visited bakery for second time, left it immediately, and took trolley bus N1 to Pobedy Square and was home by 14:20.

At 16:50 Lee Harvey left his house and came to house N14 on Krasnaya Street. (Residence of immigrant from Argentina—Ziger.)

At 1:40 Lee Harvey together with other men and women, among whom there were daughters of Ziger, came home. Observation was stopped at this point till morning.

In Love with Ella

Pavel had begun to notice that Lee and a girl named Ella Germann would spend time together at Horizon. Lee was often at her worktable, and many times they were together at lunch. Lee never spoke about his friendship with Ella, but then, Lee was not one to go out of his way to show feelings. For that matter, he wouldn't even say he had been to bed with a girl. There was one, for example, huge as a horse, Magda. She was easy to get. Some people said her husband made her that way. When men were on the late shift, some would even have a dispute whose turn it was to have a poke. She weighed 120 kilograms—264 pounds. She was called Our Horse, Our Refrigerator.

Pavel doesn't think Lee did anything with Magda, but he could tell you that Oswald wasn't dropping on his knees in front of Ella, either. Still, when two people get together five times a week, that becomes suspicious. Pavel thought Ella was interesting in her way, but she was Jewish. Pavel wanted to explain that he was not an anti-Semite, it was just that she, personally, was not his type.

EXTRA PAGE (not included in formal diary)[1]

June.

Ella Germann—a silky black-haired Jewish beauty with fine dark eyes, skin as white as snow, a beautiful smile and good but unpredictable nature. Her only fault was that at 24 she was still a virgin due entirely to her own desire. I met her when she came to work at my factory. I noticed her and perhaps fell in love with her the first moment I saw her.

Now, at fifty-five, Ella is soft-spoken and very careful in her choice of words. She has a high crown of dark hair turning gray, and delicate aquiline features.

She would say that her childhood is not of interest, because she had been very timid as a child. She always did as she was told to do and stayed at home a lot. And even when she was an adolescent, her friends told her that she consisted of nothing but complexes. So, it might be, she suggested, that she was of no interest to the interviewers' project.

Her recollection is that she was four years old when the war started. She was living in Mogilev, a small place, with her grandparents. The first time their town was bombed she was so frightened that all memories from that time are lost. Her grandmother, however, told Ella what happened.

This grandmother was very strong. At her job she cut huge pieces of meat from cattle, and the child was in awe of her strength. When German planes started to bomb overhead, Ella just "jumped into her," as it was put, and hugged her neck and stayed there through an entire day. Nobody could remove Ella. It was as if the grandmother had to "wear" her all day long. Other children cried, other children talked, but Ella was quiet. Some parents even remarked, "Look! The child doesn't express emotion." They thought Ella was strong, but she realizes now she had a great shock.

Ella's family happened to be Jewish, but she knew nothing about it. Her grandmother was born in a very religious family and told her about a *talis* and a *yarmulke,* but she had never seen either.

Unlike her grandmother, who took care of her, Ella's mother had her own life. She was single at that time, since Ella's father was dead, and she wanted to arrange her life in a proper way; she was a very good singer but unable to make her career. Ella's mother would work all day at other jobs and then at night would often be out with her girlfriend at a movie or going to one club or another; in fact, she was always busy and did not pay a great deal of attention to her children. She was very pretty and full of presence, yet she did not become the singer and actress everyone expected. Finally, in order to make a living, she had to work in a chorus, and such difficulties went on through Ella's childhood.

At one point, she remembers, her mother was fired from a job and stayed home and wept for several days. She had two children to support, and two parents. Ella's grandfather was ill, but he used to go and buy something from somebody for one price, then move to a marketplace and try to sell it for more.

Of course, children are children, Ella would say, and they really cannot accept too many tragic events. While now she can see it was a miserable life, at that time she never felt unhappy. In her school, other children were no richer, all were equal, and she had friends and a lot of happy moments. They sang and had games. Besides, theatre was always present in their family. They knew some actors and actresses, and discussed their performances, and there was never a year in Ella's life when she did not go to theatre. Her mother remained mysterious, however. Even when Ella was six-

teen or seventeen, she did not know her mother's private life.
Since her mother was beautiful, however, and very emotional and
romantic, she kept waiting for someone who would be up to her
standards, "the prince in her life." Maybe that was why she never
married again. Or was it that when men came to visit, they saw two
children plus two grandparents in one room, and it frightened
them out of such a desire.

As Ella grew up, she liked to dance waltzes, but then her favorite
soon became the fox-trot. She did hear of this American band
leader, Glenn Miller, and then saw Mr. Miller and his orchestra in
a film called, in Russia, *Serenade of Sunny Valley* (which might also
translate into *Sun Valley Serenade*). She remembers that one U.S.
film she liked was *Twelve Angry Men,* because she was able to compare the jury systems in both countries. After that, she no longer
trusted what she was being told about America—that rich people
were only a small group and most people were poor. She remembers that people in those days would whisper that even the unemployed in America had a level of life equal to Russians who were
working. On the other hand, she did believe that the United
States government could start a war.

Of course, she was not really interested in technology or politics. When she and her girlfriend went to see a movie, such a program would usually start with ten minutes of news showing Soviet
achievements in agriculture and industry, then they would see pictures of demonstrations and unemployment in capitalist countries. She and her girlfriend would usually come in one quarter of
an hour late, which was when the real movie would begin.

She loved all of Deanna Durbin's films—a beautiful woman,
beautiful stories, nice clothes, nice furniture. She was much more
attracted by this side of life than politics, but then, at fourteen, she
already understood that something in politics was wrong. She
remembers walking along a street with a girlfriend and saying, "I
think that Stalin doesn't understand what's going on in our country because he is receiving false reports." This was a close friend of
hers and they could share such a thought. She couldn't say it at
home, but her closest friend agreed. They saw already how small
bosses lied to bigger bosses, always showing the best side of everything in their work, and so people on a higher level must also be
doing that with Stalin.

Not many of her girlfriends were political. Dates with boys interested them more. It left Ella a little apart, but that was all right.

She started to go out with young men very late—she was nineteen before she had her first date. It caused her no difficulty. Ella considered herself a person who was not envious. Maybe not a hundred percent not-envious, but mostly. And she liked girlfriends who were advanced beyond her, because they came to her and spoke of their experiences. She could learn about life through them, because they needed somebody with whom to share stories. One of her friends once said, "Listen, I like one young man, and I want to meet him, but it's difficult. Could you do it with me? We'll walk past where he lives and maybe we'll see him." So, Ella immediately put on her coat and went along, because she had begun to understand how important it was for her friend to meet this young man. And never once did the thought occur to Ella, "Maybe he will like me." No, she just wanted her friend to have her chance.

At that time, her mother was still a temple of perfection to Ella, and interested most in herself. Ella pities her now. Her mother never had a normal life. Now, Ella lives with her daughter and her grandchild and is a teacher and worries whether she has time for them. Teachers are always a little bit crazy, Ella would say. They not only give so much to other people's children, but when they come home, they have notebooks to check and don't have time for their own sons and daughters. Still, Ella cooked for her children, washed for them, worked for them as her grandmother had cooked for her.

All the same, there was a time when she thought she might be an actress like her mother, and Ella performed a lot in a public theatre, but finally decided she wanted to go to a University.

She failed her entrance exam, however. She couldn't get a high enough rating in the Byelorussian language. All her other marks were very good, but she couldn't sit and wait another year to pass Byelorussian, so in September, along with a good many other girls and boys who didn't get into Minsk University, she went around to a few factories, and was taken on at Horizon as a trainee. All the while, she still kept trying to enter Minsk University. But, for two years, she couldn't. Now that Stalin had died, bribery was prevalent. People in the University Entrance Commission even told her that they were given lists of people who should be accepted. If your name wasn't on such a list and you did well, they might insert false marks to create mistakes for you. All she knows is that after two years of study, her Byelorussian was good, yet she kept receiving 2's, a very low mark.

Once, when she took part in a poetry reading competition, one of her judges spoke of giving Ella the highest prize, but then, as she learned later, she was rejected because she was not Byelorussian, not "national cadre." Therefore, she couldn't represent Minsk in a national competition; being Jewish was looked upon as belonging to a separate nation. It didn't matter if you were Jewish and a Communist or Jewish Orthodox—you were part of another nation and could not represent Byelorussia. That did not build her confidence.

In her factory, however, it depended more on who was your boss. If you happened to be working under some person who hated Jews, you could have problems, but it didn't mean everyone was anti-Semitic; and with a good boss, you could have quite a nice life and job. So, she didn't have factory problems.

When she finally started dating, you couldn't even say it was true dating. A boy might get tickets to the opera and take her, but often, before she would accept, he would have to talk to her for a whole month about going out with him. She thinks her development was very slow.

By the time she met Lee, she was already twenty-three and had dated many young men. She would go out with someone a couple of times but then realize she didn't feel anything toward this person, so why continue? On the other hand, it was boring to sit home. Sometimes she would even go out on a date without any feeling that it could be the right man for her.

Meanwhile, she was still determined to get some higher education. What helped was that the Byelorussian Minister of Education had just developed a new law: If you worked in a factory plant for two years, you were put on a list ahead of others who were applying.

So, Ella not only got into Minsk University but had a scholarship, and could quit factory work. Two years later, however, she received a bad mark on an exam and they took away that scholarship. She had to move, therefore, from day study to night school, and resumed her job at Horizon. In fact, they welcomed her back. Ella was already well known because of her participation in amateur concerts. Indeed, the person in charge of personnel told her he was going to put her into a good department that assembled radios.

When she came in on her first morning, she remembers being introduced to Lee. All that week he kept looking at her during lunch break. She knew that if she went up to him and asked for a favor, he would like that even if lots of girls wanted to be his friend. She noticed that when he would walk along the factory aisles, many girls would cry: "Hello, Alik, hi!" as if he were of special importance.

Now, in her night school classes, she was working on some English text and had to translate a number of pages by a certain date, so it was not wholly a pretext to get him to help her. There was some real need. While this would not characterize her in a positive fashion, she would say, she sometimes did use men to do small things for her. For instance, there was an engineer she did not like particularly, but she was not good at drawing certain kinds of wiring schemes, so she asked him to help, even though she had no intention of dating him. For Lee, however, she did not have negative feelings. Since the American seemed to find her attractive, why not ask him to help translate her assignment? In fact when she did ask, he smiled, and they agreed to meet in a smaller workroom that afternoon. She assumed there wouldn't be anyone else there, although as it turned out, a few workers were still present. She and Lee sat down at a small table where a radio was playing music.

Lee spread out her pages and turned off the sound without asking whether anyone wanted to listen. But Max Prokhorchik was also working there, and he became indignant. He came up and turned the radio back on. Lee turned it off; Max turned it on. Then Lee turned it off, and said, "Russian pig!" Whereupon Max stalked off.

It was unpleasant for Ella. In front of several people, Lee had turned off their radio just because she had to study, but on the other hand, a well-brought-up person would have done exactly what Lee did. At that moment, Ella could say that she was on Lee's side. All the same, he did not seem too bright at first. His Russian was poor and he took everything as a joke. He laughed a lot. So they laughed a lot, too much maybe. Yet, as she saw more of him, it became interesting to talk about his country.

Before long, he was inviting her to see movies. They went often for walks and to parks and sat on a bench. He would tease her, "You know, I am a rich bridegroom. I have an apartment."

It was exceptional to be dating an American, and she was curious. Besides, he did not create problems. He was not aggressive. That was understood as their basis for going out together. Some men had been nasty, but he wasn't. And, of course, he didn't have financial problems; he even hinted to her that he had high connections. He had met the Chairman of the City Council, Sharapov. "If we need something," Lee said, "for our future, I can go to the mayor. We can get what we need." So Lee did seem a confident person to her, and merry. He had a sense of humor and they still kept laughing a lot. In those days, friends used to call her *khakhatushka,* a person who enjoys life, and so she and Lee did not have difficult or deep conversations, just talked like young people. She liked to tease him. Not in a bad sense, just to challenge him a little.

During all this time, they dated approximately twice a week, but had lunch together at their cafeteria every day. And they usually sat alone; other people respected their privacy and did not try to join their table.

She never felt: "Oh, I wish we'd go out with other people." She liked being alone with him. It was her way of dating. She had always had such relations with men. So, she hardly knew anything about his friends or who else he saw.

Once, at the theatre, a man named Erich Titovets came up and started to talk to Lee. This Erich didn't even put his eyes on her. It was as if she were furniture. He and Lee spoke together while she stood nearby, and she had time to notice that Erich was in his twenties, and blond and well built and handsome. High cheekbones. Erich looked like an American model in magazines, and Lee could have been Russian, as if he were trying to understand what Erich said. Of course, Erich spoke a kind of English you heard at school, a language of culture—precise, almost too fancy. And Lee spoke casually.

Erich was impressive. Erich was the first young man she had met who could speak English without being a student at the Foreign Languages Institute, and when she remarked on that to Lee afterward, he said, "I would like to talk in Russian the way Erich expresses himself in English."

Nonetheless, she couldn't say she took to Lee's friend. It is not easy to like someone for whom you do not exist. And Lee never talked about him. It was obvious that Lee was a person with compartments in his life. So, it was hard to trust him altogether.

She believes Lee knew that she was Jewish, maybe from their very first meeting, but she remembers that he only mentioned it once. That was when he realized she was not exactly jumping into marriage with him. Such a question never got to yes or no for many months, but he did tell her, "I know you are Jewish and people, you

know, don't like Jewish people, but I myself don't care about that."
It was his way of saying, "It wouldn't stop me from marrying you."

Before Lee, a few men had already proposed. There had been
one she liked, a Captain, who went off to do his service in Kam-
chatka, but Ella felt indecisive and didn't go with him; and there
had been another boyfriend she dated for a year, and he, too, had
asked her to marry him. So, Lee was hardly first in this kind of
relationship, and besides, if Lee was in love with her, she was not
in love with him. Rather, she felt it was all right to have nice feelings for someone in a good way, feeling that he was, underneath
everything, very lonely here. And so she pitied him enough to feel
that if she rejected him, he would be even lonelier. Therefore, she
didn't stop dating him. But she knew she didn't like him in such a
way that one goes on to get married.

Lee told Ella once that she knew more about him than any other
person ever had, and so she was surprised when she found out years
later that he had a mother still living—he had told her he didn't.
Also, he told her that he never wanted to go back to America.

Once, after they first started going out, he was quite upset. It
was when news came to Minsk that an American U-2 had been
shot down over Soviet territory, and its pilot, Francis Gary Powers,
had been captured. Lee asked her, "What do you think, Ella? Can
it damage me because I'm American?" She told him not to worry
personally, because "no one can say you are responsible." She
tried to calm him down and talked to him nicely. She wasn't really
sure, but she did want to support him. It was their most emotional
moment yet.

Lee told Ella that when he lived in Moscow he was afraid of
Americans more than Russians. In fact, he told her, the Soviet
authorities had sent him to Minsk because he would be safe there.
He even said: "Here in Minsk I'm invisible. But when I came to
Moscow, I was really outstanding." Americans had been very interested in him, he told her, and had been hunting him and wanted
to kill him. She thought maybe he had offered some information
to obtain a Soviet citizenship, information Americans didn't want
given out. He said, "If I go back to America, they'll kill me."

It made him more interesting, but she didn't believe it was real.
She just thought they were passing remarks; he was not that brave.
She recalls an episode when they were coming down a street that
led to her house, and a young girl ran up and said, "I've just been
attacked, they took my bag, help me!" Well, most Soviet men

would have run off to try to catch the thief, but Lee just consoled the girl, and Ella said, "Well, we probably won't get her bag—such thieves don't wait around." Lee even asked if they could take another street.

They did continue on a different route and everything was fine, except the girl took it very hard. She had, after all, lost her pocketbook. Later, thinking about it, Ella decided maybe he was a bit of a coward. Or maybe, if it was as he had said, that Americans in Moscow wanted to kill him, maybe he thought that here, too, somebody was looking to provoke him. So, he was staying out of trouble. He certainly didn't talk about political matters. Once she even went so far as to ask why many people in America wanted war, and he answered, "Americans don't really understand what war is because there was no combat on their territory." She told him, "I know what it is, and I don't like it." He just said, "Yes, yes, you are right. I know how much you suffered."

Otherwise, they did chat about many matters. But there were also moments on summer evenings when they just sat on a bench and enjoyed a silence as if he were a Russian man. She felt he reacted to everything with understanding, but was very reserved. Even though they dated for many months, maybe eight months, it was still too short a period for her to comprehend his nature. He never showed much. He was always even, kindhearted, smiling, nice, without ups or downs. Only twice, in fact, did they have a quarrel. Of course, she was also easygoing. People even said to her, "You laugh so quickly. If I show you my finger, you start to laugh. So easy you are."

It is possible she did laugh too easily. When she read his diary all these thirty and more years later, she could not believe how distorted was his sense of time. He had had them meeting after the summer of 1960 when, in fact, they had known each other back in May of 1960, when the American U-2 was shot down, and they talked about Gary Powers. How little she had known of Lee, and how little, obviously, he had known of her.

From KGB Observation
Performed from 12:00 till 24:00 Saturday, July 2, 1960

> At 14:30 Lee Harvey left his work and went for lunch to café-automat, situated on Pobedy Square. Had his meal, was home at 15:00.
>
> At 16:00 he left apartment house, got on trolley bus N1 at Ploshchad Pobedy and went till Central Square without paying

his fare. He got off bus through back door and went to newspaper store N1 at Marksa Street.

There he bought some newspaper and went to grocery store N13 at Prospekt Stalina. He did not buy anything, left store, went to GUM. Took a look at goods at plastics department and without buying anything left store and went to florist shop, then to bakery and then to café <Vesna>. Left café in 5 minutes, got on trolley bus N1 to Komsomolskaya stop, got off at Ploshchad Pobedy and was back home at 16:50.

At 20:20 Lee Harvey left his house and walked fast to Opera Theatre. There he started walking up and down near main entrance. After 10 minutes he headed for square, there at central alley he met with unknown woman by nickname <Dora>. They greeted each other by shaking hands and started talking. Having talked for about 3 minutes they parted without saying goodbye to each other. <Dora> went to apartment house N22 at Lavsko-Naberezhnaya Street while Lee Harvey stayed in square. After 20 minutes <Dora> came back, told him something, and both went to Circus building holding hands.

They looked at photo display window after which walked along Prospekt Stalina for about 35 minutes talking to each other about something.

At 21:45 Lee Harvey and <Dora> went to Circus Theatre. Lee Harvey showed tickets and they took their seats in row 10 and began watching American feature film <*Lili*>. At 23:45 after movie was over they went slowly to house N22 at Lavsko-Naberezhnaya Street, stopped there, talked for about 15 minutes after which they parted. <Dora> went inside her house (she is being identified) while Lee Harvey went home and was there by 24:00. Observation stopped here until next morning.

Dora proved to be Ella.

June–July
summer months of green beauty, pine forests, very deep. I enjoy many
Sundays in the environs of Minsk with the Zigers, who have a car,
"Moskvich" . . .

Later that summer, Pavel went boating once with Oswald. Lee liked the water, but as far as working the oars, this was one American who didn't mind, Pavel decided, if somebody else did it. Pavel, for example.

FROM KGB OBSERVATION
PERFORMED FROM 8:00 TILL 23:00 SUNDAY, JULY 3, 1960

At 10:35 Lee Harvey left his house, got on trolley bus N6 at Ploshchad Pobedy stop, bought ticket and got off at Komsomolskaya stop through back door. He went straight to bakery shop, bought himself a piece of cake and glass of coffee, ate it all up and left. Outside he looked around, went to movie theatre Centralny, bought newspaper *Banner of Youth* at paper stand, browsed it through and turned back. At corner of Prospekt Stalina and Komsomolskaya Street he stopped, looked through newspaper again, crushed it and threw it away in trash bin. After that he went to GUM, looked at goods in household department, left store, bought some paper at newspaper store N1 and returned home.

At 13:30 Lee Harvey left his house for second time and walked slowly to stationery store at Gorky Street where he bought portable radio and returned home. In 30 minutes Lee Harvey left his house again, got on trolley bus N1 at Ploshchad Pobedy stop, got off at Komsomolskaya stop through back door and came to GUM to records department. There he took 20 minutes looking through lists of records, didn't buy anything, left store and went to electrical goods store N71. There Lee Harvey bought a couple of records, after which got on tram N7 at Ploshchad Svobody stop and without talking to anybody got to Opera and Ballet Theatre stop, got off tram, visited stationery and consumer goods stores. 15:45 walked home.

Lee Harvey did not leave his house until 23:00. Observation was stopped at this point.

The interviewers did obtain one service report, filed by Tanya, of Minsk Intourist, on July 8, 1960.

SERVICE REPORT
July 8, 1960

As a result of their meetings, source has established good relations with Lee Harvey. He sees source as someone with whom he can spend his time pleasantly. Has not exhibited any interest in source's biography, with exception of her age. Lee Harvey is quite happy with his apartment and conveniences which it contains. It is still undecorated, but entirely suitable for a bachelor. While she was at Lee Harvey's place, he managed to ask her in conversation, "Why aren't you interested in my impressions of Soviet Union?" Source replied: "I think you will share those impressions with me . . ." And Lee Harvey's answer followed. He began to share his impressions. His narrative was composed of enthusiastic responses to Soviet reality. Having paid attention to two pairs of boots that he had acquired, source asked with surprise: "What do you need boots for?" He said, "I love everything Russian; I want to look like a Russian."

While sharing impressions of his acquaintances, he showed source several photographs, in which he was photographed in company of friends, an Argentinian and his wife. At same time, he informed her that he had yet another friend, who was also an engineer, a Russian fellow, who worked at radio factory. Lee Harvey's general development, his range of interest, seems rather limited to our source. He has a poor conception of art, music, painting, to say nothing of Marxist-Leninist theory. He is trying to enroll in Foreign Languages Institute and intends, in addition to English, to study German on an independent basis.

In Lee Harvey's behavior, a striving to become acquainted with girls, primarily blondes who have a command of English, has been noted, as well as a kind of calculatedness which borders on stinginess. For instance, he is capable of going on a date with a girl, but then going to a restaurant alone, considering that it is cheaper to go alone. He has arranged many meetings with source, since he can go to source's place of work, or call. Source is inclined to think that Lee Harvey has recently cooled down in his courting of her, since his demands that "he deserves a kiss after six months of dating" have not been satisfied. He pretended to be hurt or offended and after that began to visit source less frequently.

That summer, Oswald made improvements in his apartment. Small ones, bit by bit. For example, he got a cheap case for his records and he bought a turntable.

When he learned that Pavel knew a lot about shortwave radios, he asked if Pavel could make him one. With local radios, you only received Soviet news. Pavel told him he could put together such an apparatus, but it wouldn't look nice—all of its parts would be exposed—so Oswald then laid out his money and bought himself a shortwave radio that looked as pretty as a lady's purse. It had only two frequencies, high and medium, but on MF, 257 meters, the Voice of America was transmitted. Since it was all in English, they didn't even bother to jam it.

People talked about Oswald as if he might be a spy, but Pavel remembers Lee Oswald coming to him with a simple Soviet camera and he wasn't able to put film into it. Pavel had to show him how. Once, Oswald bought a radio set and tried to insert its batteries, but even in trying to do that much, he ripped a few wires loose. To take another example, Oswald liked to listen to the Voice of America, but he didn't know how to make adjustments for it on his radio set so it came in clearer. Pavel, using a penknife, had to play with one part and move it a little in order for Lee to be able to listen. Pavel assumed that if Oswald were James Bond, he would have arrived in the Soviet Union able to take care of such small details.

FROM KGB CHRONOLOGY

4.IX.60   Oswald saw *The Wind* in Letny movie house.

4.IX.60   Oswald visited a party for youth in Officers' House.

6.IX.60   Oswald saw *Babetta Is Going to War* in Mir movie house.

7.IX.60   Oswald saw *A Partisan's Spark* in Pobeda movie house.

8.IX.60   Oswald saw *Babetta Is Going to War* for second time in Mir movie house.

9.IX.60   Oswald saw *The Commander of the Detachment* in Letny movie house.

From September 4 to September 9 he saw five movies, one of them twice, and all but one were war movies. He had bought a single-barrel shotgun in August, and joined a hunting club organized by Horizon. But it was not until September 10, filled by now, one may assume, with images of himself as a participant in war movies, that he finally went out with a hunting club.

By now, Stepan had given his team of observers a code name for Oswald. It was Likhoi. That sounded like Lee Harvey, but the word meant valiant, or dashing. It was KGB humor. Likhoi never seemed to do anything but go to work, walk around, and shop.

FROM KGB OBSERVATION
FROM 13:00 TILL 15:20 ON SEPTEMBER 10, 1960

At 14:30 Likhoi left work and walked quickly home.

At 14:55 he left home carrying hunting rifle in cover, and grocery bag partly filled, and came back to entrance of radio factory.

There Likhoi came to group of 7 men, some of them also having rifles, and started talking with them.

After about 15 minutes, Likhoi and other men got into parked car no. BO 18–89 and at 15:20 left city via Storozhevskaya St. and Dolginovsky Trakt.

Upon agreement with head of department, surveillance of Likhoi is canceled at this point until September 17, 1960.

Leonid Stepanovich Tzagiko, a lathe operator all his life, became interested in hunting around 1955. Each year, after August 15, they could go out for fowl, then in September, ducks, partridge, waterfowl. By October, they started looking for fox. Wolves you could hunt all year round, but wild boar only with a special license, since such game was usually reserved for high Communist Party members.

At that time, maybe there were fifty people in his hunting club. There was a chairman, who collected dues and obtained licenses for elk and, on occasion, even wild boar, although you had to pay a lot for that, about 150 rubles.

In early 1960, when Lee Oswald came to work at the experimental shop, Tzagiko met him on the first day. It was almost a celebration. Everybody came up to the American immediately to get to know him. Then, at breaks, Oswald would often sit with his feet on a table, and once one of them said, "Why are you sitting like that?" and he said, "I am on strike. I am striking." He was just joking. They decided that Americans put their feet up on a table. That's what they do.

Now, at Horizon, they had what they called sections—people played basketball, soccer, volleyball, and on Sundays, some would go on hunting trips. It wasn't that important whether they'd kill; it was to get out into nature. So when Oswald asked one of the metalworkers if they would take him along, he said, "Of course." They didn't bring much to eat and didn't carry any vodka or brandy, because they were reasonably serious about coming back with something. They walked a lot on foot, passed through collective farms, fields, and villages, sparsely forested areas.

They were hunting for rabbit that day. There was no snow as yet, so they had to flush the rabbits with their feet. Walking single file, Oswald was next to last, Tzagiko was last, and Oswald was holding his gun crooked in his arm. Then, a rabbit practically jumped out from under his foot, and he went, "Aooaoh!" and shot into the air. Tzagiko said, "God, Oswald, you're going to kill me with that gun!" And Oswald said, "Your rabbit scared me." Later, he had another try, and missed again.

The fact that he was a bad shot and could not fix his radio tended to alert Igor and Stepan. How was it that a former Marine with a Sharpshooter rating back in his U.S. Marine Corps—yes, KGB had information that he was not a bad shot—could miss his targets so?

Certainly, when the Organs were informed that Oswald had bought a gun for hunting, and so would have opportunities to travel as part of a hunting party to an area where there were also military objects, they were on guard. Hunters were prohibited from walking into forbidden areas in specified regions; they weren't even allowed to approach certain fences. If Oswald was an agent, he might have special equipment and use it to record nuclear activities or military broadcasts—with the right technology, you could collect a lot of information.

Reports came in, but were puzzling. He had been such a bad shot. If they had had any inkling that he would later be suspected of carrying out a crime of high magnitude—of highest magnitude!—they would have studied his marksmanship in a more detailed manner. As it was, however, what with everything else involving him, they made no special attempt to find out whether he was an excellent shot trying to create the impression he was a bad shot or had been naturally incompetent that day.

> **August–September**
> As my Russian improves, I become increasingly conscious of just what sort of society I live in. Mass gymnastics, compulsory after-work meeting, usually political information meeting. Compulsory attendance at lectures, and the sending of the entire shop collective (except me) to pick potatoes on Sunday in a state collective farm. "A patriotic duty" to bring in the harvest. The opinions of the workers (unvoiced) is that it's a great pain in the neck. They don't seem to be especially enthusiastic about any of the "collective" duties, a natural feeling . . .
>
> **October**
> The coming of fall, my dread of a new Russian winter, mellowed in splendid golds and reds of fall in Byelorussia. Plums, peaches, apricots

and cherries abound for these last fall weeks. I have a healthy brown color and am stuffed with fresh fruit, at other times of the year unobtainable.

October 18
My twenty-first birthday sees Tanya, Pavel, Ella and a small party at my place. Ella [is] a very attractive Russian Jew I've been going walking with lately. [She] works at the radio factory also. Tanya and Ella are jealous of each other. It brings a warm feeling to me. Both are at my place for the first time. Ella and Pavel both give ashtrays (I don't smoke). We have a laugh.

9

Ella and Lee

After Ella had known him for a half year, he actually invited her to his apartment, and Pavel was there with a girl named Tanya from Intourist. Then a girl named Inna Tachina arrived. Pavel had disappeared for a short period of time, and when he came back, this girl was with him. And he said, "Okay, Lee, dance! Look who I've brought for you. Inna!"

Ella was shocked. At her factory all these months, Lee had never dated anyone but herself. So, she didn't know he was seeing other women. She assumed he did—she understood that—but then, by the manner in which Inna's arrival was announced, it was clear that Lee dated her in another way. That hurt Ella. By October, Lee was already hinting that they were going to have a serious relationship, but if it was so serious, what was he doing with this girl?

It started a quarrel. Ella was very emotional, very angry, and when she left the party, Lee had to walk out with her. She told him, "Listen, if you wanted to have a nice time with Inna, I was not needed. I would have felt more comfortable staying home." He said, "Inna was brought by Pavel. You saw I was with you all evening, and now I'm leaving Inna and Pavel behind." He persuaded her. He said, "Look, I left all my guests. I'm walking you to work at the plant." She was on night shift then and had come to his party before going to her job. "That ought to prove you are a most special person to me."

Afterward, Inna was often mentioned by Ella. She would tease him: "So there's another woman in your life?" and he would answer, "Don't you understand that you are my true love? She's just passion." Ella's attitude was, "Well, if I don't want to, this young man still needs some kind of physiology. If he gets it elsewhere, that's normal." She certainly had never loved anyone so much as to be possessive about everything they did, including their physical relationship. That was not as important as real love to her.

On the other hand, it had been Pavel who had brought over Inna Tachina, and Ella didn't really like Pavel. There had been a little trouble at Horizon, which left Pavel with a bad reputation. He had been in a tuning process in another part of their factory along with several girls doing an equal job. Occasionally, workers who tuned radios would come across one that was very difficult to adjust; it didn't receive well and sometimes was dead. Such an inert radio was called a "coffin," and it took a good deal of time to get one to sound better. When your salary and your bonus depended on how many radios you could tune in a day, substandard sets pulled your level down. One evening, a girl working at Pavel's station realized that she had left a set on her table at quitting time that was almost ready, yet now it was dead. And all the while Pavel kept delivering a good number of well-adjusted radios. So they suspected that Pavel, when he came to work on the day shift, might exchange his device, a complete coffin, for hers. He wouldn't do it to another man, these girls felt, because men are more precise. A man would remember what he had tuned yesterday. But girls forget. Their minds were not really on such a subject. So it was easier to fool girls, Ella felt.

This got to be a bad story. There was a big meeting, and a group came to check Pavel's behavior. His father, the General, was even present, and with tears in his eyes said at this meeting, "Please, forgive him. Please, people, don't spoil his biography. He will never do it again."

So, of course, after this, Ella's estimate of Pavel was not high. If he had had a large family and had been really poor, she could understand—you could justify such an act for your children; but Pavel was robbing poor girls who made less than him. So he was not, in her opinion, a decent man, and now he had come with

Inna, and said, "It's a girl for you, Lee." Ella also had some feeling that maybe Pavel didn't approve of her because she was Jewish. She had been told that in his private circle, among military people in Russia, there was more anti-Semitism than among civilian people.

> November finds the approach of winter now. A growing loneliness overtakes me. In spite of my conquest of Inna Tachina,[1] a girl from Riga, studying at the Music Conservatory in Minsk. After an affair which lasts a few weeks, we part.

> EXTRA PAGE (not included in formal diary)

> Inna Tachina . . . I met her in 1960 at the Zigers', her family (who sent her to Minsk) apparently well off. Inna likes fancy clothes, well-made shoes and underthings. In October 1960 we begin to get very close culminating in intercourse on October 21. She was a virgin and very interesting. We met in such fashion on 4 or 5 occasions ending November 4, 1960. Upon completion of her last year at Minsk Conservatory she left Minsk for Riga.

10

Zdradstvy

Sometime that fall, Albina realized that a problem had developed for the Zigers. They suddenly became very suspicious of everybody. They even acted as if somebody were reporting on them. Here is how it began. They had a cousin in Vilnius, in Lithuania, who wanted to visit them in Byelorussia, but Ziger's cousin didn't have permission to go to Minsk. So the Zigers took their car, a Moskvich, and drove to Vilnius in order to bring their cousin back to Minsk. But on this return trip, some highway police demanded their documents, and their cousin did not have the necessary papers. So, they lost a day at a provincial police office taking care of that. Not to mention how much worse it could have been. It left the Zigers very angry. How did these police know to stop them? Somebody among their friends had probably told somebody else that they were going to Vilnius to get their cousin. Albina noticed that they stopped inviting Ernst to their place, and after a while stopped inviting a good many other people, too. Ernst was not even surprised at what had happened, but then, he was not much interested in the Zigers. To be introduced to Alik had been his goal, and that had certainly been achieved, Albina could see, exactly because she was not seeing much of either of them now.

Their first need in this Oswald case, Igor remarked, was, of course, to find people who knew English. "While Oswald had some increasing capacity in Russian, we had to connect him to people who could exchange intimate conversations with him in English. After all, how can you develop a person under suspicion without knowing his language? So people were taken on who could speak to Oswald in his native tongue."

There had been a need to find a person who knew English well enough to go out with Oswald socially, be friends with him, and have insight into some of his thoughts. "And we also were ready to look for people at our Minsk Institute of Foreign Languages." So, those students who were studying English attracted Service attention. "You would have to assume," said Igor, "that Foreign Institute girls were in a position to inform us how Oswald was behaving. Counterintelligence monitored this entire process and was kept informed." Titovets, of course, had helped Lee make and widen his contacts with women there and had also recorded tapes while the two men were alone, in order, as he told Oswald, to be able to study his accent in English and so improve his own colloquial abilities.

TRANSCRIPT FROM TELEVISION PROGRAM:
Frontline, "Who Was Lee Harvey Oswald?" broadcast on PBS stations, November 1993

NARRATOR: (VO)	<u>He became fast friends with Ernst Titovets . . . Titovets made tape recordings of Oswald to study his Southern accent.</u>
OSWALD: (VO)	The door of Henry's lunch counter opened and two men walked in. They sat down at the counter. "What's yours?" George asked them.
TITOVETS:	I gave him . . . pieces to read and these happened to be Shakespeare, from *Othello*, Ernest Hemingway—

OSWALD: (VO)	They sat at the counter and read the menu. From the other end of the counter Nick Adams watched them.
NARRATOR:	<u>Titovets also interviewed Oswald in mock dialogue. This is the first time these tapes have been heard publicly. In one interview Lee played the part of a killer.</u>
TITOVETS: (VO)	Would you tell us about your last killing?
OSWALD: (VO)	Well, it was a young girl under a bridge. She came in carrying a loaf of bread and I just cut her throat from ear to ear.
TITOVETS: (VO)	What for?
OSWALD: (VO)	Well, I wanted the loaf of bread, of course.
TITOVETS: (VO)	Okay. (*pause*) And what do you think, take to be your, your most, most famous killing in your life?
OSWALD: (VO)	Well, the time I killed eight men on the Bowery, on the sidewalk. They were all standing there, loafing around, and I didn't like their faces so I just shot them all with a machine gun. It was very famous; all the newspapers carried the story. (*laughter*)
TITOVETS:	We were just having a great time and, actually, we were laughing our heads off.

Igor would not exclude the possibility that Oswald's English-speaking tapes had been gone over carefully to determine whether his Southern accent was bona fide; his Russian-speaking tapes were also studied to explore any possibility that he was concealing a better knowledge of their language than he pretended to have.

Stepan added: "It's important that information from a source can be double-checked. We always tried to combine surveillance with reports from human sources, plus what we could learn from other technical possibilities. That way, trust in our human sources can be built. However," he went on, "to create an artificial situation, to set up an experiment to determine whether a person gives ground for suspicion, is risky. The person might show interest by accident or out of curiosity, and that would still pique Counter-intelligence's concerns. Thereby, we could lead ourselves astray."

Stepan considered it fortunate that he had an opportunity to study Oswald in a natural manner. "If, for example, it had become known to us that Likhoi was taking steps to meet a scientist in a certain field, then we might have arranged such a meeting." But Oswald made no such efforts. So, they studied the incidents that arose naturally, monitored them thoroughly, and generally found little that was suspicious. He never made attempts to make special acquaintances or to penetrate some secret military object; he didn't exhibit such desires. Not yet, at any rate.

> **November 15**
> **In November I make the acquaintance of four girls rooming in the Foreign Languages dormitory in Room 212. Nell is very interesting, so are Tomka, Tomis, and Alla. I usually go to the Institute dormitory with a friend of mine who speaks English very well. Erich Titovets is in the fourth year at the Medical Institute. Very bright fellow. At the dormitory, we six sit and talk for hours in English.**

As Pavel saw it, maybe some girls at Foreign Languages Institute were more available, sexually speaking. Their psychology was different. They dealt with other languages, had to think a little in a different culture, and so wanted to explore more. They could see foreign films. In general, these woman were more relaxed—they smoked, they drank, they read literature. Erich Maria Remarque was very popular, and Hemingway wrote about women being free before marriage in *The Sun Also Rises*. So maybe they were trying to take on such an image. Some of them.

Inna Pasenko, not to be confused with Oswald's friend Inna Tachina, was in her first year at Foreign Languages Institute, and she was mad about English. Anytime she heard somebody speaking, she was happy just to stand and listen. (She was also mad about swimming and was, at that time, champion of Byelorussian swimming in freestyle and butterfly.)

On a given Saturday, she went with her friend Galya to the Philharmonic Society, and during the first concert break, they heard two men conversing in English. One of them was dark-haired and dressed in a gray jacket, the other was in a dark suit, the first, Oswald, as she learned later, and the second, Erich Titovets. Inna went to Titovets and said, "Excuse me—am I right or wrong: You, sir, are just Russian speaking English, and you are a real Englishman or—I don't know—American?" And Erich said, "We are both British," and Oswald said, "No, no, no, don't believe him." It was obvious he didn't want to be mixed up in this "we." He had his own identity. Inna said, "Don't tell me lies," and Erich said, "No, no, we are both"—but she could hear his accent, because phonetics was her favorite subject. She even did a Ph.D. in English Phonetics later.

They all started speaking, and Inna said, "Let's meet after this concert," which they did, and walked from Philharmonic to Victory Square, near the Foreign Languages Institute. Her house was just five minutes' walk away. She gave her telephone number, and Erich said, "Certainly we will phone you and we will come and see you." And she and Galya were excited at the fact that they had spoken in English for half an hour. Galya roomed at her Institute dormitory, but Inna lived in her father's apartment, where she and her mother and her entire family still dwell at present.

Next day, Sunday, Erich phoned and asked if they could come around, and Inna arranged for Galya to be there as well. She had one difficulty, however. Inna's father was a high Party figure, and a Colonel. A very patriotic man. He would not have put up with anyone from abroad being in his house. Even listening to a radio caused suspicion. But her mother was at home, not her father, so Erich and Lee came over that afternoon, and Galya joined them.

On introduction, Lee happened to say *zdradstvy* to Inna's mother instead of *zdradstvuytye* and her mother took Inna into her kitchen and said, "Where do you find such rude boys, who don't even know how to address grown-ups?" and Inna said, "Mother, he's not a Russian; he's an American." Her mother became pale, then said, "Take him away because Father will be home soon." But Inna said, "Mama, no, that will not do. We will stay on the first floor. We will not make noise. We will look through our dictionary and listen to some music." And her mother said, "All right, but only for a little while before Father comes home."

And so they did listen to music and had tea and spoke a good deal. She remembers that she asked how he had come here and he said that he had chosen Minsk because it was a nice city. At first he wanted to go to Leningrad but then decided otherwise. "It's quieter here, the climate is better. I wanted Minsk." When they asked where his apartment was located, he said it was also off Victory Square, and added, "Why don't you come to see my apartment? I've got a lot of English books." Galya and Inna said, Yes, of course. And managed to get their visitors to leave before Inna's father came back.

Lee had wanted Inna to visit alone, but her upbringing was such that she could not go to anyone's place in that manner. She said, "I'll bring Galya," and he agreed, and so they went a few days later.

She remembers they had walked over before dark, and she still recalls her excitement. She had thought, "Here I am coming to a place that will be full of English books"—indeed, that was her main reason for seeing him, since he didn't produce any other sort of vital impression on her. She was expecting to find Hemingway and Faulkner in his bookcase, or something forbidden, some knowledge that wasn't easily obtainable, but she remembers so well that when he opened the door and they entered, there was just a small kitchen plus a small room to their left, and in a corner of this second room was a little—you couldn't call it a bookcase, but a few planks of wood. Its lowest level had some newspapers, the next shelf was empty, and the top level held Karl Marx and Lenin, both in English. That was all. His bed almost filled the room, a military bed of iron covered with a gray blanket that had white stripes. Since the girls were just standing there, they finally sat down on his bed, and he made tea. He did have good tea, that she remembers, and he put it on a little stool in front of his bed.

After a while, she asked, pointing to Marx and Lenin, "Is this what you read?" and he said, "I find it really interesting, don't you?" She said, "We studied all this in Russian—why should we read it in English?" and he said, "Well, I haven't read it before, and I find it very interesting."

He was neat. She recalls there was no mess scattered around. He was wearing gray slacks and a blue tie and a striped shirt, and he was so pleased with the apartment, said he paid only 7 rubles for it. She, of course, was less impressed, because her family lived in a large, fine apartment, with three rooms for four people.

All the same, their visit did impress her. For the first time in her life she had seen a real American, and Inna was fascinated with all these variations in accent between American English and British English. This American, in turn, was paying a lot of attention to Inna. Even Galya said as much later. Inna, however, had no real interest in the man. She was fascinated but not attracted, and when he complained that he was lonely and didn't have anything to do, Inna said, "Let's go to my place once again," but he replied, "Your father's too strict." She remembers him adding, "No, no more at your house." Then he said to Galya, "I'd like to visit your Foreign Languages Institute." That pleased Inna, because she would now have more practice in English.

Taking him to Galya's dormitory, while it would certainly be seen as bringing back a prize, would also present a problem. At that time, you had to produce your identity card, and this was true even for Institute students who didn't live in the dormitory. It was certainly not routine. Girls who studied at Foreign Languages Institute were treated like young ladies in a convent. Their ideological upbringing was very important. After all, they were being introduced to Western literature and movies, and were allowed to listen to foreign broadcasts.

In this case, however, Galya got Oswald into her dormitory by telling him: "Be quiet. Be silent." She told her doorman that he was a relative. Galya was taking a chance. If she had been caught, she would have been deprived of her monthly stipend for a period. She took him in safely, however, and after that it was almost routine.

Inna recalls one occasion: There was Oswald with six girls, the center of attention in that dormitory room. He was sitting at a table with a couple of girls close to him and they were all playing a game. He would open the dark brown English book they offered him, *Miller's English Dictionary,* and pick a word at random, then somebody would offer a translation. Whoever was the girl sitting next to him would check it, and there was a lot of laughter while they played their dictionary game. He had a little Southern accent, and one girl, to everyone's amusement, even corrected his pronunciation.

Over the next month, he would visit often, and sometimes they would want him to go home, but he would stay. Several girls were scared that someone would catch him, so they kept their door locked. And they didn't make noise. Their laughter was not loud, more smiles than laughter. Her recollection was that he seemed glad to be accepted. She also felt that part of his interest in being there all the time was to get away from Erich. Her guess is that maybe Oswald wanted to make his own set of friends.

In any event, he was not wholly at ease, even though he was the center of attention. Of course, it was a special kind of interest. Girls would say, "Oh, we haven't seen *him* for three days," and Inna knew whom they meant. They were not only afraid to mention his name but reluctant to be alone with Lee—what if someone reported that one of them was alone with a foreigner? That was their first consideration. It was not that he was the sort of fellow one had to be afraid of—if anything, he was timid with women. The only girl who was at all adventurous was Nellya Korbinka, whom Inna did not know very well.

Soon enough, as Inna saw it, the Institute girls grew tired of Lee. They had become used to him, and would pay hardly any attention to him as a man. At this point, he had nothing new to say. He would talk about his family and tell jokes, but they were stupid stories. There was not much discussion. He did tell Inna how much he respected his mother, but Inna suspects that because she respected her own parents so much, he was ready to speak warmly of his mother.

Then, after a while, Oswald dropped out of sight. It was not noticed that much. Some girls used to gossip that his only reason for coming to the Institute was because no one else wanted to date him.

EXTRA PAGE (not included in formal diary)

Nellya Korbinka.[1] Large, 5 ft., 11 inches, 150 lbs., built proportionately, large upright breasts, hips wide and lovely but very pleasingly proportioned, from a village near the Polish border, of strictly Russian peasant stock. Gentle, kind, womanly, and understanding, passionate in heart, stubborn in both. She combined all the best womanly features with the kind, sizable Russian heart. I met her through one of her roommates, Tomka. Nell and Tomka together with three other girls lived in a room at the Foreign Languages Institute Dormitory in Minsk near the Victory Circle. I began to notice Nell seriously only after I parted ways with Inna Tachina.[2]

11

Razbitoye Karito

Whenever Lee wanted to talk about their future plans, Ella would try to avoid that topic. To discuss such a subject might mean she was getting ready to marry him. Her reluctance to show interest may have upset him, but he was not aggressive. Yet, even so, he became a little more pushy.

He said, "Do you want to know why I came here?" But she never asked him many questions. She was afraid he would think of her as someone who was trying to get information from him. It was part of how she grew up: Women didn't ask questions. It was considered bad style. So, he started to give information. And he also got a little pushy.

They might commence with a light conversation, nice and full of humor. They would see a movie and discuss every joke afterward. It was fun. They would talk nonsense. Once, they got into a discussion of how frogs talk. She insisted a frog says "qua." In Russian, a frog always says "qua." And his answer: "No, a frog says 'frok.' " It was funny.

But later, he began to discuss serious matters. For example, he didn't want to live in Minsk. It was, he said, a provincial city. He had lived in New Orleans; that was big. He asked her to share a dream. He said, "Maybe I will move to another socialist country. For example, Czechoslovakia." He said, "Shall we go to live in Prague?"

He was a very proud man. He didn't want to be rejected by Ella. She believes that's why he never asked directly. He would say, "How do you do things here? In America we have an engagement ring, a silver ring that's exchanged for a golden ring. But how do you do it here?" Perhaps he was waiting for her to ask, "Why are you interested in how marriages are made in Russia?" but he never said directly, "I would like you to be my wife."

One time, he showed his Russian residence papers, and he said, "Soon I have to make a decision. You're the one who's going to influence it. Do you want to live in Prague? Because if you do, then I won't take Soviet citizenship. But if you want to live here, tell me if you want that, and I'll take it—this all depends on you." And in December he showed her that his papers terminated on January 4, next year, just a few weeks away. He had to make a decision what to do with his life before 1961 was four days old.

But that was a big question for her: Why had he come here, and why did he now want to move? He told her, "You don't understand. In our country, we travel, we change places—you don't understand." But she didn't trust him. Besides, Lee was not really to her taste. She liked men with bigger shoulders.

FROM KGB OBSERVATION
PERFORMED FROM 08:00 TO 24:00 ON DECEMBER 23, 1960

At 11:30 Likhoi left his house, came to bus stop Ploshchad Pobedy, got on bus N5, reached stop Komsomolskaya, got off and entered GUM. At haberdashery department, he bought safety razors, then tried on hat at hat department, but didn't buy it and entered bakery department. There he had glass of coffee with cake, and went out toward Glavpochtamt. On his way he visited a number of industrial goods stores, then came to Glavpochtamt, came to Soyuzpechat kiosk, looked at papers but didn't buy, came out and got on trolley N3, reached Tsentralnaya Ploshchad. At square, Likhoi got on trolley N1, reached Ploshchad Pobedy, got off and entered café-automat, had lunch, came out and stopped off at home at 12:45 . . .

At 20:45 object left home and came east to house N22, apt. 2 at Lavsko-Naberezhnaya St. After 10 minutes he left place together with contact "Dora" and they together, talking about something, were walking along embankment of Svisloch River, and at 21:15 came to apartment of object.

At 23:10 Likhoi and "Dora" came out of his apartment and slowly walked along embankment of Svisloch River, talking with each other. On the way Likhoi was periodically taking "Dora's" hand and embracing her. At 23:40 they came to house N22 at Lavsko-Naberezhnaya Street, where they said goodbye and parted. "Dora" walked into said house and Likhoi came home at 23:55, and at that point surveillance was stopped until morning.

When he kissed her, he was not unpleasant—he was nice. But because Ella was not in love with him, she was not excited. All the same, he never scared her as a man. In that aspect, he was perfect. He was so tender. She was never scared. Yet, all those months she went with him, from May to January, she did not trust him. Some people told her that he was an American spy. And she thought, "Maybe he wants to marry me so he can stay in this country. When he says he loves me, he doesn't love me at all."

She never thought to herself, "Maybe I'll go to Prague and it'll work. Or, if it doesn't work, I'll get a divorce." For Ella, marriage was something you did for life. You loved a person and you trusted him. Because if you didn't, how could you go to a new world?

Finally, he became very pushy. He said, "You have to make up your mind if you're going to marry me," and when she asked for time to think it over—he said, "No, I have to decide by January 4." That made her feel more mistrustful. She told him, "I like you, too, but I need time to think." She was not a person to offend people who were nice to her.

They had another quarrel, however, concerning New Year's Eve. He had invited her to a party for that night, and so she turned down an invitation that came to her for another gathering. Then, at the very last moment, he told her that his evening was not going to take place. Now they were without anywhere to go that night for New Year's Eve.

There was an expression, *razbitoye karito.* It meant they were ready to eat, but only had a broken plate. Ella got very angry that they didn't have a proper situation; she said, "You let me down." She had never spoken to him like that before, except, perhaps, concerning Inna Tachina. That time he had been cool, but now he, too, became agitated. Finally he said, "You are playing a game with our situation. Oh, you are an actress!" It was equal to saying that her emotions were not sincere. They walked away from one another.

Since Ella wasn't going to any party now, she began to help her mother. Some of their family was coming over for a small New Year's Eve party, so they cleaned house and cooked, and then, as was common in Russia, they napped for a little while around 8:00 P.M. in order to be able to stay up all night. At 11:00 P.M., guests would begin to come, but on this night, at a little after nine, she heard their doorbell ring. She was sleepy when she opened her door. Lee was standing there wearing that Russian hat she had never liked, but he was proud of it, and was standing up straight with his hands behind his back. He said, "You know, Ella, Christmas is one of our dearest holidays in America, and your New Year's is like our Christmas. That's why I came to you. This is one day when I feel very lonely and I come to you." He added, "We have a tradition in America; we usually bring gifts," and he gave her a big box of chocolates decorated with a little candy statuette. She took his gift and said, "Wait a second. I want to put this away." She went in to her mother and said, "My boyfriend from America brought me this gift. Can we invite him?" Her mother said, "Yes, of course."

So she came back and said, "Listen, would you care to spend an evening with my family?" and he was happy about that.

When he came back around eleven, he was wearing his gray suit with a tie and was very neatly dressed. Her mother's brothers soon followed, with their wives. They had served in the Russian Navy and they came with guitars. It was a musical family. Not all had fine voices, but when they were in chorus, it sounded good enough. Everybody sang songs, and they did a step-dance up and down their outside stairs, a Western type of step, which was very popular in the Russian Navy, a Western sort of dance, and her mother's brothers did it, dancing upstairs, then downstairs, difficult steps, but they were good at it, and so it made for a creative atmosphere. And her mother danced to gypsy songs. Lee and Ella only watched. She was embarrassed to do anything in her own home because these others were so good.

Before Lee left, hours later, he told her of his impressions. He liked such an atmosphere, liked how everyone sat around eating and drinking and dancing, and then at midnight they had all taken champagne. They didn't kiss, because that was not a Russian tradition. But after midnight, through the early hours of morning, they would not only sit and eat but go outside, make snowballs, throw them at each other, run around a little, then go back in and eat again. Everyone got tipsy—in fact, she had never seen Lee Oswald as tipsy as he was this night. Friends came, and she introduced him to her friends and relatives, and they sat around the family table and proposed toasts to last year—"Goodbye, last year, you are leaving." Everybody talked to him, and he was treated as if he were a Russian person who had joined their family party. Her relatives were a little curious about him, but didn't reveal any special attitude, and her mother was also casual; of course, her attitude was, If Ella dates a man, it doesn't mean she's going to marry him.

> **January 1**
> New Year's Eve I spend at home of Ella Germann. I think I'm in love with her. She has refused my more dishonorable advances; we drink and eat in the presence of her family in a very hospitable atmosphere. Later I go home drunk and happy. Passing the river homeward, I decide to propose to Ella.

Next day, her mother, who had never interfered with her personal life, said to her, "Ella, it's up to you—you make your own choice. But I want to tell you something: In 1939 you could be taken to prison just because you were born in Poland." Those were her mother's words. It gave her pause.

January 2

After a pleasant hand-in-hand walk to the local cinema, we come home. Standing on the doorstep, I propose. She hesitates, then refuses. My love is real but she has none for me. Her reason, besides lack of love— I'm an American and someday might be arrested simply because of that example of Polish intervention in the 1920s that led to the arrest of all people of Polish origin in the Soviet Union. "You understand the world situation, there is too much against you and you don't even know it." I am stunned. She snickers at my awkwardness in turning to go. (I'm too stunned to think!) I realize she was never serious with me but only exploited my being an American in order to get the envy of other girls, who consider me different from the Russian boys. I am miserable.

On the night when they had their final conversation about whether he should or should not apply for Soviet citizenship, she finally said, "Alik, you're probably wasting your time with me. At this point, I can't agree to marry you. So, don't get Soviet citizenship. Maybe we should break up altogether because it might be harder afterward." He answered very nicely: "I understand that I should stop drinking. But the wine is tasty and I want to continue this pleasure for a while."

That, however, as she recalls it, was the last time they met. Ella agreed to see him once more, but he didn't show up. Afterward, he just ignored her in the shop.

Igor would say that his service looked at this matter from a human point of view. "He didn't go out and slash anything because he was refused," said Igor, "and he didn't seem to bear grudges. Of course, for a certain period of time he was upset, but it didn't manifest itself in his behavior. He didn't quit work, for instance, or get sick; he didn't start carousing—none of that." If he had undertaken any risky errands at this point—say, asking one person to convey something to someone else—that would have put Counterintelligence on guard. But none of that.

. . .

On the eleventh of January, after they had broken up and everyone knew it, Ella flew to Leningrad for ten days of vacation. There was all sorts of talk about her at Horizon: They had stopped seeing each other, people said, and she had gone to Leningrad to get an abortion. Ella thought, "As if I couldn't have had one in Minsk!" Fairy tales!

Still, everybody believed that because she was going out with an American, they had had sex. No American, they would say to her, would date you for so long without it. These men have whorehouses in America, and they always need sex. So when she and Lee stopped seeing each other, Ella had a bad reputation. Yet it was so strange, because he had always been afraid to offend her by being too physical. He was sensitive—yes, he was sensitive.

January 3
I am miserable about Ella. I love her, but what can I do? It is the state of fear which is always in the Soviet Union.

January 4
One year after I receive the Residence document, I am called into the Passport Office and asked if I want citizenship (Russian). I say no—simply extend my residential passport, [they] agree, and my documents are extended until January 4, 1962.

EXTRA PAGE (not included in formal diary)

Nellya, at first, does not seem to warrant attention since she is rather plain looking and frighteningly large, but I felt at once that she was kind and her passions were proportional to her size, a fact to be found out only after a great deal of research. After a light affair lasting into January and even February, we continued to remain on friendly but conventional terms throughout 1961 up till May when after being married, we no longer met.

This extra page is our only concrete evidence of his sexual life in Minsk before he meets Marina two and a half months later, on March 17, 1961. For the first fourteen months of his stay in Minsk, Inna Tachina and Nellya seem to be the only women with whom he went to bed.

Whether he was ever with men during this period is a matter that the KGB was not ready to discuss except by indirection, but then Stepan and Igor's separate references were often contradictory, as indeed they might be, since one was interviewed in Minsk and the other in Moscow, and more than thirty years had gone by.

In response to a question about bisexuality, Igor Ivanovich said that Lee was not a clean man, and he did not refuse any situations that offered themselves to him. He had sexual contacts when he could find them, which was not often.

According to Stepan, however, Oswald didn't exhibit any deviations. That was Stepan's forthright statement. Before his marriage to Marina, they had observed that Oswald would "meet with a girl sometimes and take her home, and God knows what they did there. Sometimes he took her only to the nearest tram stop." In that respect he led a normal, ordinary life, at least as they understood it by Soviet ways. If he was attracted to a lot of girls, that just meant he had what it takes—he was a guy. Otherwise, girls would have rejected him. "Besides, a homosexual reveals himself in his behavior," said Stepan, "and in his interests, in his voice. Usually a homosexual has a thin voice, something feminine to it, and then, such a fellow is only interested in women in a formal way, but his eyes start blazing when he sees a man, especially—excuse me for saying it— when his butt is big. He is constantly showing up at public toilets, and often they perform their acts there. So a homosexual has certain constant, distinctive traits which can be used to flush him out, and we didn't observe such traits in Oswald. I spent all this time thinking about traits because, before this, I had a case involving a homosexual and I knew a thing or two about such matters."

PART IV

MARINA'S FRIENDS, MARINA'S LOVES

1

Yanina and Sonya

At work, there were people who were not without love for Marina. Yanina Sabela had been in the pharmacy at Third Clinical Hospital on Lenin Street for ten years when Marina moved from Leningrad to Minsk, and Yanina saw her as a very attractive girl, with a rich internal world, and well brought up. Strong-willed, yet quite open. Yanina had entered the pharmacy in Third Clinical Hospital when she was very young and so the difference in age between them was just a few years—Yanina was twenty-four and Marina eighteen—but all the same, Marina was very professional, and Yanina saw her as sophisticated despite her age. As for herself, Yanina felt she lacked a lot of social knowledge, like how to introduce yourself to people—there were gaps in her development. She'd been brought up in a provincial place in the Mogilev region of Byelorussia, but Marina, being from Leningrad, had had a different development. Even schoolchildren from Leningrad seemed to know more than people from anywhere else. There were so many museums in that city. All the same, Yanina was close friends with Marina and they shared a lot.

Later, after Marina had been working in their pharmacy for about six months, she and Yanina spent a weekend together out of Minsk with friends; perfectly all right—girls slept together in the same bed, so nothing wrong there—and they got close; they talked a lot. Yanina remembers hearing about how Marina's stepfather used to scream at her. If he called her a prostitute, she was not; she was a normal nice person. Yanina could understand such situations because her father had also been very strict and sometimes screamed dirty words at his children, but Yanina just ignored such tirades. You know, among Russian men in small provincial places, you hear nasty rude words; so such accusations didn't impress Yanina. She knew Marina better.

. . .

Sonya was born in Zabolat, a village 150 kilometers from Minsk, and her father was in charge of a farm; her mother had been a milk-girl on that farm. Of eight children, Sonya was born first, and her family, being Byelorussian, had her baptized, but then, in these villages people were always being baptized in an Orthodox church, and sometimes even with a ceremony. What it really meant was that guests were invited to your house afterward and you laid out a special table of food and then neighbors and relatives were invited to celebrate. A Party member wouldn't show up unless he or she was also your relative. Actually, they didn't pay too much attention to whether there had been an actual baptism or not. Main idea: If a baby is born, let everybody come and celebrate.

In her late adolescence, after her secondary technical education, Sonya got an assignment to the pharmacy at Third Clinical Hospital, in Minsk. It was there that she met Marina, and Sonya recalls that Marina always dressed a little better than others. She was receiving a salary no larger than anyone else's, but Marina's aunt provided her with food, and Marina certainly spent her money on clothes. All the same, she was kind, not greedy. She had a ruble, okay, someone wants to borrow money, she would give it—she was not greedy. If you asked her, she wouldn't think, "Oh, maybe I'll need it later." She would just offer it. She was straight: She would tell you the truth to your face rather than whispering it behind your back. She was even not afraid to talk directly to people above her. She would just say, "I need this for my job."

Pharmacy work was from nine until four, and there were about fifteen girls on duty, assigned to different specialities. Sonya, for example, would do everything that needed high sterilization; Marina dealt mostly with eye prescriptions; but each could do another's job if there was a need for that in a given day. Marina was a good worker, very good on such matters.

Neighbors

Ilya had a fellow officer in MVD, Mikhail Kuzmich, a doctor, who lived across the hall from Ilya and Valya, and when it came to singing arias at parties, there were not many who had a better voice. Misha Kuzmich was full of energy as a young man. He received splendid marks in medical school. When not yet twenty years old he was already a military doctor and was sent to the Western front in the Great Patriotic War.

Afterward, he was both a professor and an academician—a little of everything, he said. Since he was speaking loudly to his interviewers, Misha's wife, a full-faced, good-looking blond lady named Ludmila, also a doctor, began to tease him gently. "He is being so lively," she said, "because Misha thinks that when he raises his voice, you will be able to understand Russian."

Ludmila is the older sister of Larissa, who was Marina's dear friend when Marina and Larissa were young adolescents and Marina would come to Minsk for visits. These sisters, Ludmila and Larissa, had a father who had been repressed in 1937. He was arrested on Ludmila's birthday, the second of February. Once, years later, she received a postcard on that date from Yalta, sent by her brother to congratulate her. He added, however: "I remember everything connected with this date." So did Ludmila. It had left her open to other people's feelings.

Sometimes when she visits her brother, she asks to read her old letters. He has kept a large album of such correspondence, with snapshots, and when she goes through the book that concerns 1937, she begins to cry. At that time she had three older brothers. She was a fourth child, born after the three boys, who would all love her dearly, and while Ludmila's parents usually celebrated everyone's birthday, hers was considered special. On the second of February, guests came—children, then grown-up people—and they were all waiting for her father to come back from work on this day in 1937, but he did not arrive. At night, there was a knock on the door, her mother opened it, and here was her father under arrest, accompanied by men from the militia. Her father apologized in front of everybody for having to make such an entrance.

At that time he was in charge of a huge meat factory in the far east, a very high position. Nonetheless, these militia-men began their search while everyone was still present—moved furniture at will, opened drawers. Their guests disappeared.

In prison, her father was not tortured, but neither was it easy. He may have been mistreated less than others since he was a well-known person, yet they would still put him on his knees in a corner and he would have to remain there through a night, or they would throw tobacco dust in his eyes. Nonetheless, it was not equal to that severe attitude with which they dealt with other people in this same prison. Mostly petty humiliation.

It developed that some people still respected him. So, a message was delivered to her mother at one o'clock one night, to tell her to visit the prison. Her husband had a message to give. His note said: "In a few days they are going to take me to my meat factory, where they want to prove I've committed certain acts, and I need the following documents to defend myself . . ." He had been accused of sending out a boxcar load of spoiled meat.

Fifteen months after his arrest, they not only allowed him to go home, but put him back on his job and he worked hard for many years, and then Marina's friend Larissa was born in 1941, fourteen years after Ludmila, and the war with Germany began.

Despite his high position, her father was not a Party member, although he knew what was going on. Ludmila remembers that whenever he heard a piece of propaganda on their radio which he found impossible to listen to, he would say to her, "Hi, darling—get me our potato masher." It was his way of saying, "If we could only smash such nonsense to bits!" He hated the war, but then, Ludmila's father was so much in love with his three boys that on the day war commenced, he began to cry, and said to her, "I'm going to lose my sons." He had become established again as an influential man, and so was able to keep his youngest boy, who had just graduated from high school, out of induction, but that son went voluntarily, and in four months was killed in combat. When the notice arrived, Ludmila's mother was so upset that she didn't tell her husband. Whenever she could contain her grief no longer, she would go over to her neighbors in order to weep so that at home she could behave as if nothing had happened. But Ludmila's father grew worried: Why for four months had there been not one letter? Yuzik was this son's name, and Ludmila's father went to his Party Secretary at work and started to complain: "Why are there no letters?" And that Party Secretary replied, "What do you mean, no letters? Don't you know about Yuzik?"

Her father came home and had a heart attack, and in four months he died. Then another brother was sent to the front and was killed too. Ludmila's mother had now lost two sons and a husband. Two sons and a husband lost within a year and a half. Difficult years.

More than four decades ago in Minsk, when Misha, then age twenty-nine, had already become an expert in radiology, he was asked to come in at two in the morning to the office of the Deputy Minister of Health. Stalin did not sleep at night; ergo, there was a rule that government offices also stayed open and only ceased working in accordance with when Stalin went to bed. So, 2:00 A.M. was not an unusual hour to be asked to appear. Misha had no idea why he had been summoned, but once he arrived, he soon encountered a special expression. It went: "There is an opinion that exists that you should . . ." Whichever official you were seeing would then state the details of this opinion that existed. Of course, you never knew who was behind such a suggestion. It might even be a Minister of the Republic, but in any case the particular high official that you are talking to only says, "There is an opinion that exists . . ." It is as if your entire country has come to the conclusion that they must adopt this opinion. All you can be certain of is that it has come from persons higher than yourself. In this case, the opinion that existed was as follows: "We wish you to become the head of our Medical Department in Ministry of Internal Affairs, Byelorussia." Which meant, of course, that Misha would now be moved over to MVD.

He was, as far as he was concerned, too young for such a job. It needed someone with more experience in organizing matters. So Misha tried to tell the Deputy Minister that he didn't want such an assignment; he was a doctor and wished to remain one. He didn't want to be a boss. The Deputy Minister said to him, "We'll give you an apartment." Misha said, "I'm not asking for an apartment. My wife and myself, we have a room, fifteen square meters, downtown." But this Deputy Minister of Health said, "You're a young family. You're going to have children."

When Misha still didn't agree to take this job, the Deputy Minister said, "Dr. Kuzmich, why don't you want to be promoted? We're promoting you." Misha repeated: He just wanted to follow his profession, be a doctor. The Deputy Minister said, "Since you are a very independent person, you can organize your life so you can do both, organization *and* research." He spent forty minutes trying to talk Misha into it.

Now, sitting next to this Deputy Minister was a man in charge of all personnel, and at last, he was told: "Try to see who is available for this job. If there's anybody in Byelorussia better suited than Misha, I'll offer it to him. If no one is better, don't even come back to me. Misha will be appointed."

After the interview, Misha took the personnel man aside and said, "Try to find somebody," but he replied, "I've looked through all my lists already; I'm not going through that again. It's easier for me to draw up the papers. You're going to be appointed tomorrow." Thereby was Misha drafted into MVD, and by 1953, he was working with Ilya Prusakov.

Misha could inform the interviewers that Prusakov was the department head in charge of furniture production by prisoners, which meant being able to coordinate the availability of work gangs in the local gulags with the arrival of materials, and that was a real task, considering how timber came from one part of Russia, paper from another, and he had to bring in these materials on schedule so that every day when his workers came on, the necessary materials would be there for them—paint, timber, glue. To have it all in place was an achievement.

Since Misha and Ilya had what amounted to equal rank in MVD, it was not extraordinary that they ended up living in apartments approximately equal in floor space and situated across the hall from each other. In addition to his being a neighbor, however, Misha liked Ilya; he considered him a special person. How to put it?—he was not like others. One could respect him. Ilya never talked too much, knew his value, was tall, thin, dignified, educated. Not snobbish, but very intelligent. He had a long fine nose. Knew his value. Misha would say that Ilya was proud of his job, and never late for it, a professional officer. In his Army career, he had won many medals, and not just for good behavior, no, Ilya had bona fide combat medals, an Order of Lenin, a Red Star Order, which is very high; he had even been nominated to be a Hero of the Soviet Union for participating in a major assault on the Scree River. Indeed, at Ilya's funeral in 1989, his Combat Red Banner had been carried in on a pillow. It was a Soviet custom for the last rites of a military man who had been awarded a fine medal.

Ilya in person, however, never put his medals on his jacket. And he was ready to contest the decisions of his bosses if he felt they did not obey proper principles.

Of course, there was no question who was boss of his household. Misha could give one good example: On a hot summer day, after they'd finished work and were on their way home, Misha had said to Ilya, "Let's go and buy a watermelon," but Ilya replied, "Oh, Valya will buy it." Since Valya didn't work at a job, he wasn't about to tote a watermelon home.

Of course, there were sides to his friend that Misha never came to know too well. At this period of time in their Ministry of Internal Affairs, most bosses were simple people; having returned with decorations after the Great Patriotic War, they were given high positions. But Ilya was not only well educated; he even had a copper plate on which was engraved ENGINEER PRUSAKOV. Before the Revolution, many people used a professional title and put it up on their door, but when Ilya did that, people didn't like it. They mocked him behind his back, until he obtained a sense of the general feeling and took his nameplate off his door.

Living across the hall, Ludmila saw Valya frequently, and she could see that her neighbor did not have an easy life. She took care not only of Ilya but of his sister Lyuba, who also lived with them, as did Ilya's mother, and those relatives acted just a little superior. Valya was not a person to complain to her neighbors, but Ludmila did hear about it—her apartment was that rare place where Valya could be open about unhappy matters.

What offended Valya most was that she was treated like a *dom-rabotnitza,* a woman you hire to keep your house in order. Most often, Ilya was not tender with her, or warm, and it was clear that Valya suffered. Years later, it changed. When his mother died and Marina left, Ilya realized then how much older he was than Valya; in his last ten years, he became very ill, and then they were a good deal closer. He came to realize how important this woman was to him and how she took such fine care of him, went to such lengths to buy food that was especially good for him.

All the same, all through those earlier years, Valya took pains to keep herself in good form; she even looked secure and self-confident; she was, in fact, confident that her family was not going to fall apart. She was never afraid Ilya would leave her for anyone else.

At that time, in the early Fifties, there was no TV, so generally, their two families would gather by a round table in the evening and Misha would read books aloud. Tatiana was often present. She usually wore dark clothes and was always decently dressed, a very religious person who went regularly to church and kept an icon in her room. Ilya might be a Party member, but he never objected to that, because this icon was just for her room, her private domain.

Tatiana's funeral took place at her church, a special service. Valya organized everything, and of course, Ilya was there, and Tatiana's daughters Lyuba and Musya. Tatiana had been friendly with a young priest, with whom she had a deep spiritual relation; when she was dying, she invited him to her home for a talk. Nothing happened to anyone because of this. In fact, Ludmila and Misha also went to this church on this day, and were not afraid to enter. But Ludmila cannot remember anyone else being buried in such a fashion.

All of Ilya's friends from the Ministry of Internal Affairs came— everybody, in fact, but the highest bosses. There must have been thirty people at this funeral. No one cried or showed emotion. Maybe they couldn't believe they were there in church.

After Tatiana's death, slowly but definitely, Valya came to be in charge of everything. When Ilya gave parties, they were good parties, with exceptionally good food cooked by Valya; she was certainly his hostess. But Valya did confess once to Ludmila that while there were very nice people at her gatherings, she could never get quite the same nice people who came to Ludmila's parties, as, for example, the Minister of Culture of Byelorussia. More or less, she had the same guests each time; Valya would even end up wearing her one best dress every time—maybe try to put a new flower on it.

All the same, it was a smooth and even life until Marina arrived to stay with them permanently late in 1959. New problems came with her.

Larissa

Ludmila's sister, Larissa, fourteen years younger than Ludmila, is now a lovely, even voluptuous, woman. Her manners are formal, but she smiles a good deal, and it offers a hint of that state of bliss in which she claims to have lived when young. In that time, due to great crowding at home, because Larissa's mother and her mother's sister and that sister's husband all lived in one room nine square meters in size, it was decided that Larissa should stay with Ludmila and her husband, Misha, and she adored them both.

In those years of early adolescence, Larissa wanted to become a doctor. She wanted to emulate Ludmila. She did well in school, but then in the ninth grade discovered that she could not look at blood. So, she could never go into a dissecting room or a morgue. After that, she even gave the Medical Institute a wide berth. There were corpses in that building.

In adolescence she dated a lot of boys and had some favorites, but essentially they were all part of a group, and one boy, Misha Smolsky, not to be confused with Ludmila's husband, Misha Kuzmich, happened to be the soul of their company, one in a million. Misha Smolsky was interested in Western culture. Everything he wore was elegant yet never flashy. It was a beautiful group; they knew how to spend their time tastefully. A lot of dancing went on, and in fact they formed a dancing group called Minchanka, which means "a female inhabitant of Minsk." She even traveled to other republics with her group. Larissa was slim then, very slim.

Now, Larissa knew Marina for a long time. She first knew her as a thirteen-year-old schoolgirl who came from Leningrad to Minsk to visit her grandmother in 1954, and that was at a time when Valya and Ilya dwelt across the hall.

Larissa admired Marina. At thirteen, she was so beautiful, and so curious. And very bright. You looked at her and you were attracted. So, they were friends. At that time, embroidery was popular and they did a lot of that, and took walks together or went to movies. And when Marina went back to Leningrad to live again with her mother and stepfather, Larissa found it hard to part.

Then Marina came again for a summer visit in 1957, and she had become more practical. She had matured. Larissa was still starry-eyed, but Marina, being now sixteen, knew a thing or two about real life. Her mother was dead, and Larissa could see by the expression in Marina's eyes that events had left another imprint.

Then, in 1959, Marina came to live permanently with Valya and Ilya. There she was again, on the same floor, and both girls were now enthusiasts about opera and never missed a premiere in Minsk. "Our standard of living was different in those days," said Larissa. "What we had wasn't the worst: We could buy smoked salmon and all sorts of fish, and clothes of some variety were available in stores. In that period we had attractive imported shoes, pretty clothes, and good craftsmen were about.

"As for sex education—none in those days, none at all. Parents never spoke to one, and you were never taught anything in school—God forbid, no!" Although Ludmila was a doctor, she explained no more to Larissa than that there were physical changes in a woman around early adolescence. There was no talk about sexual life. By tradition, girls were brought up to believe that marriage was not sex but security. So, they were raised in a very romantic way: "Fall in love with a man, kiss him, but you'll never know what's really going on—then a child comes. That's about how it was," said Larissa.

Marina knew more, but after all, she was from Leningrad. Even so, they never discussed sex. If they talked about a boyfriend, it was whether he was good at kissing. They might also decide questions of behavior—did he bring flowers? Did he rise to his feet when you entered a room? If he didn't, Larissa would not pay attention to the fellow, no matter how good-looking he might be. She thinks one reason Marina was attracted to Misha Smolsky's group is that they all had such good manners. Having come from Leningrad, Marina was more culturally sophisticated than the pharmacy girls she worked with, and so life was probably more interesting for her among Larissa and her friends. Yet, their desire to meet men with good intellect was also accompanied by how such an intelligent person dressed: Did he wear nice white shirts? Did his shoes shine brightly?

On New Year's Eve, Larissa went with Marina to give their welcome to 1960 at Misha Smolsky's *dacha,* all the way out on Kryzhovka Street, and when they walked in, Marina said, "Guys, no dirty jokes, please! She's a very modest girl." Marina treated her as if she were the only source of clear cold water, at least it seems that way to Larissa now. She was naive, and maybe Marina saw how when Larissa loved someone, her love was sincere. All she can say

is that this New Year's celebration was full of life and filled with literate, erudite young people. Larissa will remember it always.

Misha had come to his family's *dacha* early and fixed the place
nicely—put up a little Christmas tree, had a table of food laid out.
Everything was wonderful. Their jokes were witty, and their
records were both Russian and Western. Since they were all good
dancers, they did fox-trots, tangos, and waltzes, even a Charleston.

There were six girls and maybe a few more boys and everyone
was dancing with everyone else. It wasn't as if people had favorites
that night; Larissa felt it more as a collective. They all slept over—
chastely, of course—girls with girls, boys with boys; but on the next
evening, on the first of January, when she and Marina came back
by train from Misha's family *dacha*, Marina did talk a little about a
Jewish fellow she liked, Leonid Gelfant, who had been at the party
and was twenty-three years old and, even so, seemed to like her.
Larissa thought he was awfully old for their age.

Larissa remembers that Valya felt herself responsible for Marina
and certainly didn't want her getting mixed up with any wrong
people. So, whenever Marina was planning to go somewhere,
Aunt Valya would always ask, "Is Lyalya going along?" Because if
Larissa was with her, it meant everything would be all right. Larissa
is not sure how to say it exactly, but she had had no experience
with men and wasn't looking for any. To her, morality was important and all the rest was terrible. One was supposed to be honest
when one got married, a virgin.

4

Misha

In telling about himself, Misha Smolsky, elegant when young and
now saddled with bad teeth, wants to state that he belongs at present with high conviction to his minority in Byelorussia, who are
called Lithuanian Tatars. Smolsky's roots, which he is devoted to
studying, go back to a very old fifteenth-century family, very old
roots. His grandparents were noble people and had their own
heraldry.

In his day, Misha was educated like other Soviet people, which means being obedient, not asking a lot of questions. Actually, he and his friends spent their time thinking about girls; it was very dangerous to discuss politics during those late Fifties and Sixties. When they were twenty years old, all they talked about was where to drink, whom to date.

While he came from a large family, his father was in construction and had a good financial situation. So, Misha always had money for good clothing. When he was young, his hair was very blond, his Slavonic blood was strong, and he could say that the late Fifties and early Sixties was a period when he loved everybody and everybody loved him.

He was introduced to Marina through his friend Vladimir Kruglov at the time when Marina was a little bit in love with that guy. Once, they even went to Leningrad together—Kruglov, Marina, and himself. She was returning to her stepfather's home after her summer vacation, and Misha can say that he, personally, was overcome by Leningrad: "Can you conceive of it? You keep walking and there are buildings, buildings, buildings—you are caught in a stone forest. Then you go through an arch and suddenly you see this space, an unimaginable space—it is so large that you can't even think after seeing so many narrow streets. The people who built this are very great."

In that period, he wouldn't characterize Marina as being popular. She was certainly attractive enough and some young men were drawn to her, but that didn't mean she had a long line of people paying court. What was most striking about her was that she came from Leningrad. In those days, Minsk was a joke.

Misha used to go to movies with her, and they went out on riverboat trips where they could dance, and listen to Bach, Prokofiev, and Elvis Presley. In those days, Misha wore narrow trousers and shoes with high platforms—as a protest, perhaps. And he was a fan of serious jazz—of Armstrong, Sidney Becket, Goodman, Bing Crosby, Frank Sinatra.

He wouldn't say his group had the highest morals. But he and Marina were great friends and they didn't gossip about each other; they were higher than gossiping about each other. Real friends, very funny, nice company. Yet, because of that difficult relationship with her stepfather in Leningrad, he thought she was a most unhappy person.

Leonid

Leonid Gelfant was only sixteen when he finished high school and began to work on architectural jobs in Minsk. In fact, he has by now been thirty-three years in his profession, and his work is everywhere—but always as a part of his Minsk group.

At sixteen, he was not open at all, but closed, very shy. Still, he was goal-oriented and knew what his profession would be. Never interested in sports or tourism, he was brought up in a conservative family of doctors, and did like literature and opera. While his family was not religious and followed no Jewish traditions except for those holidays represented by certain kinds of food, his father had graduated from Hebrew school and could speak a bit of Hebrew and Yiddish. Yet, at this period of time, educated people were not brought up to acquire religion. His family did congratulate him for his thirteenth birthday, but no bar mitzvah took place.

He was friends with Misha Smolsky, who was always sparkling with energy. And during a New Year's party in 1960, he met Marina at Misha Smolsky's family's *dacha*. He was twenty-three years old and not thinking of marriage. He didn't even date a lot of girls; he was still shy. Of this party, he only remembers a few details.

He sees a room with a stove. It's cold outdoors, but inside is cozy because there's a fire in that stove. Next, he remembers seeing this same stove, but now a girl has arrived. It is Marina, a slender girl with large, luminous eyes, standing near that stove. It is all he remembers. Perhaps there were fifteen people at this party.

Marina had a way of looking at you. It was simple, yet it attracted. Something in her was unprotected. It gave a special charm. She had trembling lips and, for that matter, her nose was a little blue because she was always cold—she was one person who always felt cold—and a specific odor came off her, which she found embarrassing. When a person does pharmacy work, one's clothes and hair keep some whiff of medicine clinging to them, and she hated that. But Gelfant, personally, did not mind. Somehow, that seemed something good about her. It attracted him. Perhaps he was also drawn to her because she didn't have her own home, or a father or mother.

Gelfant, in comparison, had a close family. His father had been completely devoted to his home life and children, an attractive man, very charming, full of tact. In turn, Gelfant considers himself also a devoted man, who would like to live, perhaps, like his father. So, Marina and he were in different environmental and emotional situations, and had different goals. When they met, it was an agreeable surprise, but it was never something he saw as his future. Call it a New Year's adventure. On New Year's Eve, you always expect a miracle. Since she produced on him an impression of a person who needs protection, she inspired his desire to help her, to be tender with her.

Their relationship—which he never calls an affair—went on about six months, but it was not continuous. There were times when they wouldn't see each other for a couple of months. Perhaps on five occasions they had an intimacy—not more than that. And, indeed, he would not have wanted anything to develop with greater speed. It was a modest relationship, then.

6

Inessa

At the beginning of 1959, Inessa was already working. She had finished Construction Technical Secondary School, and lived with her parents and her brother and sister. Her father was an engineer at the Ministry of Construction, Byelorussia, and her mother stayed mostly at home, a housewife, but Inessa would say that her family had a cultural circle of friends and certainly did live at a high intellectual level.

She doesn't recall how she first met Marina, but it may have been in a cafeteria, probably in 1960. She remembers, however, her first impression: very bright lips with no makeup—just naturally bright lips; so Inessa found her attractive. A person can't become a friend in so short a period as two years, since it usually takes much longer to share all your difficulties, but nonetheless, Inessa felt close. Marina was like a sister to her. They visited at each other's homes; they went shopping together; and sometimes Marina would be invited to dinner, or to her parents' gatherings, which had become one of the traditions of Inessa's family in those days, for on such evenings art was always being discussed, and politics as well, and Marina would do her best to try to fit in. The very fact that Marina felt out of place only made Inessa feel closer to her, and out of such closeness, Marina began to tell Inessa some of what could be called "the dark secrets in her life." Marina did tell certain things that Inessa wasn't going to talk about now. However, she could say that it was "like a cry of the soul. A very bad negative experience."

Because of such a sharing of intimate secrets, Inessa could say that Marina remained special to her.

7

Kostya

A neat, spare man with a boxer's broken nose, he is in excellent shape and looks as much like a coach as a doctor, but there he is in his office at a clinic, cautiously ready, Dr. Konstantin Bondarin, and our interviewers are present because a New Year's Eve party welcoming 1961 (on the same evening that Lee Oswald was at Ella's home) took place at the apartment where Bondarin lived, at the age of seventeen, with his grandmother. Sasha Piskalev was also present at this party, and with him came Marina. At the time, Kostya's grandmother was in a hospital and so an opportunity had presented itself to celebrate New Year's with an intimate group. There were eight of them present—Sasha, Marina, Anatoly Shpanko, a girl for Shpanko, a girl for Konstantin himself, and one other couple whose names he no longer remembers, but they were friends of Anatoly Shpanko, a fellow medical student. For music, they played tapes, mostly Elvis Presley, and earlier in the evening, a lot of dancing and drinking went on, until about 2:00 A.M., when Kostya and Marina disappeared into a bedroom. Before they could get very far with any project, Sasha started knocking on the door.

Konstantin even had to step out and calm him down. He was tough enough for that—he liked to box—but then, there was no question of getting into a fight. Sasha was not such a type. Still, given that interruption, Marina was no longer in any kind of mood. They made a date, therefore, to have another meeting tomorrow, New Year's Day, at a bridge near the railroad station.

Since Sasha stayed over and awakened with a hangover, he and Konstantin talked next morning about Marina. She was a beautiful woman, Sasha said, and he was devoted to her, but Kostya could see that Sasha had an uneasy feeling about last night and was hurt that Kostya had been alone with her. Sasha even tried to ask what had happened, but Kostya said, "Nothing. You drank too much, and imagined a lot of things."

That evening, carrying a bottle of champagne, he met Marina at the bridge, and took her to a friend's apartment. He could not use his own place because Anatoly Shpanko, who shared a room with him, was still there with his guests, so Konstantin used his friend's abode. All this friend had to know was that he needed three hours.

In general, it was clear that Marina had prepared for their meeting. It even started off with light kisses and tenderness when he met her at seven that night by the station. At his friend's apartment, they played music and drank champagne. He had known while dancing with her last night that there was nothing in his way. And he was ready, although, of course, there was no question of going directly from door to bed. In Russia, women didn't do that. They needed psychological preparation. So, there was the sort of conversation where you talk about a lot of things at once—easy talk. Now, it's difficult for him to remember anything concrete, but it was flirty on his part. He would praise her, and compare her with agreeable examples. As far as he remembers, he didn't try to talk about her private life. They did touch on Sasha, and she said that she didn't feel much for him; but all the same, she really wouldn't want him to know about these relations. He could see that she was still interested in Sasha to a certain extent. As a candidate for marriage, anyway. That manifested itself afterward, when she started going out with Anatoly Shpanko, then maybe with Yuri Merezhinsky. At that point, it seems to Kostya, she was striving to get married.

It never occurred to Kostya that there was for himself a possibility of falling in love with Marina. Not by tomorrow, certainly. Falling in love could only occur as the result of a long-term relationship. And then there was another fact: She was Sasha's girl-friend. So, he didn't really know how long he was going to see her.

He did, however, spend a long time seducing her on this evening. Maybe so long as an hour and twenty minutes, or even more. They knew how it was supposed to turn out, so they didn't hurry; he paid no attention to time. He was certain it would end positively.

Kostya was only seventeen, and somewhat scared. He could sense that she was a woman with experience, so he didn't know whether she would like him, and therefore, to a certain extent, he felt a little afraid. Now, thirty years later, he could laugh. "When you have a very young man who is overexcited and a bit uneasy, he's like a rabbit. That could certainly cause a woman to react negatively." She did try to calm him down, to make it clear that everything would be okay so that he wouldn't be so nervous, and maybe that is why their prelude lasted so long. He had wanted to sleep with her right away, but his own lack of self-confidence held him back. Champagne helped, however, to dull his fear, and in general, he was still certain everything would turn out fine. Finally, they dimmed all lights. She waited for him to take her clothes off, and that happened rather fast. Right away, they were scattered all over. And his clothes came off quickly, too.

Why did a man have sex with a lot of different women if it wasn't to bring new experience into his life? So, in this sense, since Konstantin had very little experience, Marina gave him a lot to recall. It was from the extravagance of her behavior and her expression in bed. They had sex a second time, and he needed no help for that. She didn't do oral sex, but she really liked to be kissed, and when you kiss a young woman whose skin is soft, really very soft, you get excited. And by kissing her body, by just kissing her everywhere, you could bring her to a state of ecstasy. That's how sexually exuberant she was—or so he thought. He had been to bed with a few women before, but this was his first exciting time, his first real one, the first time with a young woman. Usually, it had been with women much older than himself. He was amazed because of her apparent excitement when he started to kiss her all over.

Still, she seemed to understand that when it came to these matters, he was still a youth. She wasn't entirely happy with him. Despite all her exuberance while they were doing it, it seemed to him (and it certainly turned out that way) that he didn't satisfy her all that much. She was further away from him when they parted than when they began.

At that time, he didn't have even an idea that women could have orgasms. She wasn't shy, and she dressed herself in front of him, and now he would certainly have been happy to continue their relationship, but when he went up to her and tried to caress her, she said, "No, no, no—don't take it too fast." And he understood that something didn't sit well with her, that it would not go any further. This haste with which she got ready to go home put him on his guard, and she only allowed him to see her as far as the bridge where they had met on this early New Year's night.

8

Yuri Merezhinsky

"My story will be very boring," Yuri says, "not interesting."

He is a handsome man of about fifty and may once have been as good-looking as a movie star. But now, he is ravaged by illness and his shoulders are hunched. To meet his interviewers, he has come from a hospital several hundred kilometers away, and has been drinking all day; at night, he is still drinking with the harsh pride of a Russian who measures his prowess by the slugs of vodka he can continue to mix with powerful emotions.

Speaking Russian combined with English, he proceeds to his narration, proud, aggressive, contemptuous of any specific reality he has to relate.

"My story will be very boring, not interesting. My parents and I lived in a building called House of Scientists near Minsk railway station, and I can tell you this should be called 'Story of Children Who Come from Cream of Society.' My father was a great scientist; he became part of our Soviet scientific history. My mother, the same—Honorable Scientist of Byelorussian Republic. Immediately after Gagarin was launched into space on *Sputnik,* my mother was interviewed, my father was interviewed, *I* was interviewed.

"I will tell you long story about myself. When I was small, I played football in an apartment. It was apartment of First Secretary of Communist Party of Byelorussia, and football was possible because their rooms were so big. My mother was part of governmental delegation to United Nations, together with Khrushchev.

"As for me, I liked Elvis Presley. Not important," said Yuri, "whether rock or jazz. Important was that something came to us from Western countries." Personally, he liked Ella Fitzgerald, and Louis Armstrong—but Elvis Presley even more. Most of what they heard was tape-recorded, although he and his friends listened to radio, too—BBC, Voice of America. He was very much interested in clothes then, was always well dressed.

"During that time, I was a student at our Medical Institute and there was a custom for prominent people to give a lecture after a visit to another country. So, my mother prepared one for our Trade Union Palace, and everything was demonstrated with slides. It was a large hall, maybe five hundred people, and someone came up to me then—Lee Oswald. Just introduced himself as Alik Oswald. Said he had come from America, and he started to speak English. At that time my English was good."

After Yuri's mother's lecture, they went upstairs to a ballroom, where a dance had started, and Alik got interested in Marina. "She was a very attractive, impressive person, effective. She—how you say?—attracted people. She looked right; she was not gray. She looked—the word we use is *effektnaya*—a powerful effect upon people. This evening she had to look like very best, like she never looked before. I knew her before. I knew her after. But she never looked so attractive as this evening. It was like from God—it was high, very high."

INTERVIEWER: Was she wearing lipstick?

YURI MEREZHINSKY: She painted her lips all of the time.

INT: All the time?

YM: Yes.

INT: That's interesting, because the word we get is that she never used lipstick.

YM: She was very attractive. Effective.

INT: How long had you known her then?

YM: It doesn't matter—one day, two days, a year—I knew her long enough to know who was who. She was a woman, not a girl. Not a young woman. She was older. We were tired of her in sex.

INT: Tired of her in sex? We? Let's be precise here.

YM: I don't know about other people. I can talk only about myself. I never went with her to bed. But I could sleep with her even on a staircase.

INT: You say you had her any way you wanted?

YM: Yes, sure.

INT: Your friends had her?

YM: Sure.

INT: For certain?

YM: Sure.

INT: I ask because, in her biography, she told the writer, Priscilla Johnson McMillan, that she was a virgin when she was married.

YM: I already told you Marina was not very precise in her biography.

INT: I wanted to be sure.

YM: She was sent out from Leningrad in twenty-four hours for prostitution with a foreigner, and she came to Minsk.

INT: For prostitution? Literally?

YM: With a foreigner. Then she came to Minsk. Because she had an uncle here. She was lucky.

INT: She was in such a jam?

YM: We call it 101 Kilometers—which means being sent very far away. From Leningrad.

INT: This is a matter we would like to clear up.

YM: System now is different.

INT: Who told you she was a prostitute in Leningrad?

YM: You ask a question which I consider very intimate.

INT: Let me ask it in a different way.

YM: No, it was right question to ask. She came here with four other people who were sent out of Leningrad together. She was in group. Two young men, two women. And her uncle worked for Ministry of Internal Affairs, MVD, that's why she was privileged to come to Minsk and not 101 Kilometers. What it means, 101 Kilometers, you have to cut trees in forest.

INT: A labor camp?

YM: Job for prostitutes and people who don't work. You were sent out of big cities to work, hard labor. At that time, anybody could be accused of any type of prostitution. She was seen regularly in Hotel Leningrad, and they told her to leave immediately because of foreigners. She was seen with foreigners and was asked to leave.

One of her friends was in Minsk too. A man taller than me, bigger than me. He had a nickname, *Gon-don-chick*, from the condom, wide condom. He bought condoms cheap—four kopecks for one—and he bought brushes with which you clean your clothes. Then he made four holes in each condom and he took hair from his brushes and put this hair into holes in each condom, and then he put another condom over this one with hair. And he sold it to prostitutes, and many people bought it. For big money. That's why they called him Condom-chick, because he made women happy, yes. At that time, you even had condoms with mustaches. So, that was his nickname. Condom-chick, *Gon-don-chick*. A large profit, of course. He was very popular with women.

Now, said Yuri, there was a problem—he and his group, he would say, were fed up with Marina. They didn't know how to get rid of her. She was good at sex, but when a woman is always with her legs spread, sometimes you resent it. She never worried about anything like reputation.

It was asked how she could conceal her reputation. After she met Lee at this dance, how did she manage that?

Yuri: "You know, we are now three men here in this room, okay? Then a woman comes. Then a fourth fellow comes who is getting interested in some woman. You don't tell this new guy, 'Man, you know, I fucked her in different positions so many times . . .' You don't pass this information. Sasha was the only one who was not her lover. Sasha was ready to marry her. He was in love up to his ears. Everybody fucked her but Sasha."

Marina, he told them, had access in her pharmacy to grain alcohol. Yuri didn't want to boast, but he could say that, as a man, he satisfied all women, and Marina brought him bottles, big bottles of alcohol, from her pharmacy.

Asked about Lee, Yuri said he wanted to explain. "We are one team, and we are ten people, and we have one, two, three, ten women, and they are all very beautiful. They are always just between us, touching us. And everybody on our team is fucking these women. At one o'clock she's fucking one, then another one—we all know it. It is not a secret. And we are tired of these women. We are bored by them."

So why did Lee become serious about her?

Yuri replied: "Every woman has her own raisin."

Kostya Bondarin told Anatoly Shpanko about his experience with Marina. He doesn't know when she and Anatoly first had a rendezvous, but it was not more than a few weeks later. Afterward, Kostya would introduce her to Yuri Merezhinsky.

He knows Yuri would say that he slept with her, but Kostya is not sure it happened. The fact is that Anatoly Shpanko did have intimate contact with her. That much Kostya knows for sure. Tolya was a serious man and, unlike Yuri, would never talk to others about an affair. Yuri, after all, was the same age as Kostya, seventeen, and so he would have been more likely to say, "Well, I got fucked, I really got fucked," but in this situation, Kostya didn't believe him. Tolya and Marina really had it for each other, and he doesn't believe she would have allowed Yurka to get into the middle of that.

Later, Kostya did hear that Marina was forcibly expelled from Leningrad by the authorities for allegedly having relations with some Georgian, an unpleasant incident in a hotel. Now, he can't remember if he heard it from Sasha or Yuri, but he did hear this story at that time, that much he remembers well. It was very simple in those days—once the authorities came down on you, you had twenty-four hours to collect your things, then you were out. Of course, Marina's uncle did work for MVD in Minsk and had helped her to hush it up. At least, that's what people were saying. It could all be grossly exaggerated. Easily, it could be exaggerated.

Anatoly

Anatoly Shpanko is a big lumbering man with large features who seems dazed—or is it preoccupied?—by the responsibility of his work. He is a doctor in southern Belarus near the Ukrainian border, and he deals with victims of Chernobyl—clouds of radiation passed over the bordering area of Belarus after that disaster. For this, or for other causes, he is drinking at ten in the morning and sings Russian songs to his interviewers in a heavy, slightly toneless voice, a bemused smile on his face.

His childhood was happier than events in these days. He had been very proud of his father, who drove trains in Siberia and, later, in Byelorussia. When Anatoly was still a kid, his father would take him along in the locomotive cab and let him pull the train-whistle and keep his hand on the engine throttle.

Years later, after high school, Anatoly and two of his friends wanted to become medical students and live in Minsk. So, they took exams there. In advance, they decided that if even one of them failed to pass, all three would go back to Gomel. And that is exactly what happened: One did get a bad mark; all three went home. Anatoly had a good test, but they had an agreement, so he observed it, and being out of high school, he was taken into the Soviet Army and served for three years—'57, '58, and '59. In his last months, he was stationed not far from Minsk and was allowed to take his exams again for entrance to Minsk Medical Institute, whereupon he received fives in all three exams, excellent marks, best marks.

His first memory of Marina is of a very, very pleasant woman, and he still remembers her this way. He would like to say that she never insulted him and he never insulted her. He usually treats women with great respect, but when a representative of the female sex is rude—and some can be very outspoken—he will just look at her and leave. With no notice. He can say that he likes kind-hearted women and modest girls.

He was serious in his studies—super-serious, he could say—and he hardly ever wore a tie. He lived then in a small room, and he can tell you that in all of a week he allowed himself only two hours for walking. All his other free time was spent in study. It was easy in those days to rent a room—not an apartment, but many families in those days had a single room to offer—so he lived with a couple who had no children. In his second year, however, he lived in a private house near his Medical Institute—Konstantin's house, in fact—and his time became more relaxed. He could socialize much more.

He didn't date one girl but a number. At that time, women were not conservative—if you went out with a girl, she didn't tell you, "Don't go to a movie with any other girl." But then, his relations with women were always individual. Not like a system where he had to be the exact same man with everybody. He might go to a movie with one, and it was understood—no kissing; then, another movie with another girl—lots of kissing. You could be found anywhere between petting and absolute; he didn't have a system.

At his Medical Institute there were more girls than men, so male students usually had a large choice, but it was a tradition that students usually found their marriages inside the Institute. However, it was virtually excluded that you could have sex and live together while students. Especially for him. He was an officer in Komsomol. You could be accused at Komsomol meetings if you lived in such a way. They didn't have a cult of Stalin any longer, but they certainly had their cult concerning Komsomol, and Anatoly was *komsorg*. That means he was in charge of half of his Komsomol organization. He was Secretary of the *potok*. If you had a thousand students, the *potok* made up a group of five hundred, and if you were their leader, that meant you could expect to receive some special appointment later. Upon graduation, students were usually assigned to miserable places far out in the USSR, but people who were high in Komsomol could choose first. You might even be asked, "Where do you want to go?" When they came to him, however, he said, "Where is there need for a doctor?"

As far as women go, he would say that if you lived openly with a woman, you could be discussed endlessly. So, you did things underground. Who would want to be some main topic of discussion at a Komsomol meeting criticizing improper sexual behavior? One's biological need to have sex had to be satisfied, but you did it underground. Nobody had to know whom you were seeing that way.

Now, Marina was one of the first girls he met. His opening year of medical school had been so tough for him that he had hardly dated in 1959. But in the following year, Marina was one of the first, yes.

Speaking of Marina, he cannot say anything bad: She was just a simple girl, very simple, ordinary, positive. And he just treated her like a woman. All he can remember is that there was nothing negative from his side to her and nothing negative from her side to his.

Priscilla Johnson McMillan's book, *Marina and Lee,* amplifies this spare account from Marina's point of view:

> . . . She consented to be Sasha's date for New Year's, but she promised herself that she would dance with anyone who came along . . . That evening she found herself in the arms of Anatoly Shpanko, a lanky fellow with unruly, dark blond hair and a wide, appealing smile. Tolya, as she soon called him, was a twenty-six-year-old medical student who had already served his term in the army. He was whimsical, yet deferential, to Marina, and from the moment of their first kiss—they were standing in a dimly lit courtyard, with snow swirling all around them and a lantern creaking in the doorway—she was deliriously in love with him. "He was a rare person," Marina recalls. "He was honest in everything he did."
>
> There was only one drawback. Attracted as she was to Anatoly, Marina did not think he was handsome. Nor did she like the way he dressed. He simply did not fit the image she had created for herself of a girl who goes out only with handsome men. Not wanting to be made fun of, fearful that her friends might think less of her, she steered Anatoly along back streets when they were together as surreptitiously as if they were engaged in a clandestine affair. But she forgot her calculations when he kissed her. His kisses made Marina's head spin. Finally he proposed, but there were obstacles. Anatoly had two or three more years in medical school, no money and, even more important, no apartment. Marina consulted Valya and Ilya. "No, my dear," Ilya said. "Let him finish the institute first. He can talk about getting married then."[1]

Anatoly does remember kissing in a dimly lit courtyard, but there was no snow coming down. The snow was already there. He remembers nothing special—it was routine, nothing special. You remember details when something was not ordinary.

Being told that Marina did remember his kisses, he said, "She appreciated it, I think, ha, ha, ha." Then he added, "I am trying to be honest. I don't want to invent. I am sorry if I can't be helpful."

When asked why Marina singled him out as being "a rare person . . . honest in everything he did," he replied, "I think maybe she got this information from some of my friends. She didn't get it out of my behavior, but something she heard from other people." He would add, "That's why everybody wanted me to be Secretary of Komsomol, because many of them were younger and had not been in the Soviet Army." So when he would say, "This is fair," people would often accept it. When asked if he was considered by most people to be honest, he replied, "Even today." Asked about how he dressed in those days, he said, "I never worried about clothes. If someone said, 'I don't like this way you're dressed,' I'd say, 'Okay, buy what you want me to wear and I'll wear it.'" He would not get dressed up just to please a woman. His opinion: A woman should like a man's soul, not some clothes he is wearing. "We have a saying here that you greet a person by how they are dressed, but by the time you say goodbye, you respect a person for how they are."

As he recalls, nobody told him anything negative about Marina. Nobody ever said to him that Marina had some history in Leningrad. "People knowing me, like I am, never passed on rumors. You can't come close to me this way." He would tell them, " 'You want to talk about this person? Bring that person here and then say it, but don't talk to me alone without this person.' It was my rule."

Besides, they didn't have sex. He would say they didn't achieve such a desire. He has no recollection of proposing to her, and if she gave as her reason for rejecting him that he didn't have his own apartment, he would say that was not exactly true. Because he had an aunt in Minsk who did have a house with land, and on this plot was another small house that was empty. So, if he had really wanted to marry, he could have lived with his wife in that small house, although while still dating he would not bring a girl there, because he would never do such a thing to his aunt. It would be an insult.

When asked if he was more moral than others, he said, "In those days—our Khrushchev era—there were young men like me, but not many, not many." As for a wife, he wanted a woman who was simple, average, very human. Marina would have fit his idea of whom to marry. If he did propose to her once and was turned down, he thinks he would have joked about it later.

He finds it hard to believe that on a night in March of 1961, at a long-forgotten dance, some Trade Union dance, Marina told him to meet her at ten o'clock outside the Trade Union Palace.

He cannot see a possibility of that. He would not have waited more than five minutes for a girl. Maybe he'd give it another five minutes, but never more. When that much time has passed, he leaves—that's it. Maybe he could have gone earlier, and popped out to look for her at ten, but to him it doesn't make sense. At that time, he thought many girls were in love with him. He was not being egotistical, either. Minsk Medical Institute was a very high, privileged educational college, so women were attracted to students there.

When told that, according to Marina, they had a fight that night and he said, "I have to talk to you," and she said, "I can't talk now, can't you see? Go away," he would only say that he has no recollection of her speaking to him disrespectfully, but maybe it is true she walked out of his life and into another life—this man she would marry. So his response now would be, "Ah, she was lucky; she married her man and she is happy now. She was not waiting for me. She found another man, so that's good for her."

Of course, he is amazed that such a small love can create such a large interest. Even now, he is surprised; he is even shocked that interviewers from America have come to ask about a girl who didn't marry him. In response to a hint of explanation, he asks, "Her husband is accused of killing somebody?" Then he adds, "Don't forget to tell me, because I'm nervous. I'm nervous about who was killed."

His interviewers assured him it would not affect his present life and that they would tell him later. With his agreement, they would like to go on with their interview.

They reminded him that he phoned Marina and asked to see her, but she told him that she was now having a serious relationship. He recalled that they had only spoken once more and that was when they met on the street and she said that she might be going to America. He had joked, "Come on, take me with you." And, to the interviewers, he added, "I can joke like that. With my character, I can say, 'Good, you have a good life. Take me with you.'"

Sasha said: "You know, even now, I admire her. If you notice, I respect women in general, and my principle is always that you should pet a woman along the fur and not against it. And you should love a woman."

Yet, how does he feel about how it all ended? "Now, I can see she looked at me as just a young boy. I think if she had waited for me and had been patient enough, her life would be much happier than it was after she left for America. Because everything I wanted to devote to her, I have since devoted to my family. I think maybe now, deep in her heart, she is a very unhappy person. But if you see her, give her best regards from Sasha, and tell her that I'm not offended or insulted, although I had some unpleasant moments.

"I understood some of what she felt when I was dating her, but now it's proved that she never shared my feelings, and this is the most difficult part. But at that time I was young. I suppose the best way for her was to marry a foreigner, and go to another country."

After they broke up, he was very depressed. He didn't study well. It was a hard time. But step by step—and it took a year and a half—he came out of it. Then he was introduced to his wife, and he has been happy all his life with her. So he could thank the interviewers for having been to see him. They had brought a little bit of entertainment into his provincial life, he said.

PART V

COURTSHIP
AND MARRIAGE

1

Alik

March 17
I and Erich went to a trade union dance, boring, but the last hour I was introduced to a girl with a French hairdo and red dress with white slippers. I dance with her, and ask to show her home. I do, along with five other admirers . . . we like each other right away. She gives me her phone number and departs home with a not-so-new friend in a taxi. I walk home.

MR. RANKIN. Where did you meet him? . . .

MARINA OSWALD.[1] In the Palace of Trade Unions.

MR. RANKIN. What kind of place is that? . . .

MARINA OSWALD. Sometimes they do have meetings there. Sometimes it is also rented by some institutes . . . for parties . . . I had gone there with my friends from the Medical Institute and one of them introduced me to Lee.

MR. RANKIN. What was his name?

MARINA OSWALD. Yuri Merezhinsky . . .

MR. RANKIN. Did you know that Lee Oswald was an American [and] did that make any difference?

MARINA OSWALD. It was more interesting, of course. You don't meet Americans very often.[2]

From a narrative on her life prepared by Marina for the FBI:

Anatoly was quite ugly (and in this I think he has something in common with Mel Ferrer). But I was embarrassed to appear with him in public—silly girl. I was afraid that my friends would say, "What an ugly boyfriend Marina has." For that reason we would talk on the telephone for two or three hours at a time and it was very, very interesting to talk with him . . . He loved his mother very much and talked about her very tenderly. I liked that. I no longer had a mother, and it was very agreeable to see how this big, fully grown man acted like an innocent little child toward his mother. Not everyone can do this so straightforwardly . . .

Anatoly wanted to marry me but I refused, since he was still a student, and . . . to wait five years until he finished seemed too long for a young girl . . .

One day Sasha invited me to a social evening at the Medical Institute, and I knew that Anatoly would be there, too. You see what a frivolous girl I was. Sasha forced me to promise that I would be there and gave me an invitation. Anatoly told me that if I came with Sasha he would not want to see me again, and that we wouldn't be friends any longer. But I thought I could arrange things somehow so as not to offend either of them . . .

Something detained me at work, and I got home quite late; then I took two hours to get dressed and sat a long time in front of the mirror, then I lost my courage completely and was tired of dressing, so I put on an ordinary house dress. But my uncle . . . started laughing at me: "Was it worth while standing in front of a mirror so long?" And finally something dragged me to that evening, even against my will. I can say this quite sincerely—I felt something quite unusual that evening but did not pay attention to it. To my amazement Sasha was waiting for me. He was standing out in the cold without an overcoat. He ran out every ten minutes to look and see if perhaps I had showed up . . . At the dance I tried to catch sight of Anatoly but I was told that he saw me with Sasha and left—which upset me very much.

Sasha was with his friends from the Institute. One of his friends introduced me to Lee, calling him Alik . . . and when Lee invited me to dance, and we started to talk, I decided he was from one of the Baltic countries, since he talked with an accent. But later that same evening I found out that Lee was an American . . .

I liked Lee immediately. He was very polite and attentive, and I felt that he liked me too . . . Later, when we were married, Lee told me that he noticed me as soon as I came into the dance hall. Don't think that I have an especially high opinion of myself or am anything unusual, but I can say that . . . I had just come in from the cold [and] by then [other] girls were already tired, whereas I had just taken off my overcoat— so that I had a fresh look . . . I remember having on my favorite dress made of red Chinese brocade (Lee liked this dress afterwards), and my hair was done à la Brigitte Bardot. That evening I even liked myself. You see how I am boasting, but I am writing what I felt . . .

Later . . . we all went in a group to the house of the Yuri whose mother had been in the United States . . . I remember that she quarreled a little with Alik, since Alik . . . spoke very favorably about his country and very interestingly. I was very pleased that he was trying to show the best side of his country. Later, when I asked him if he liked America, he said that he liked it, but not everything in it; for instance, unemployment, discrimination, the fact that it is very difficult and expensive to get educated, the high cost of doctors when one is ill. But he said very proudly that in America the apartments are prettier and not so crowded, and that the stores have things for every taste provided one has money. He also said that in America there is more democracy and that every person can say what he wants in the press, on the radio, or on TV . . .

That evening Sasha and Alik took me home. We were alone in the street for a few moments, when Lee asked when and where he could see me. I told him that perhaps I would come again to the dances at the place where we met but did not make any precise promise. But then, a week later, I went again with a friend to a dance—Lee was there. That evening he came home with me, and I introduced him to my Aunt. My Aunt liked his modesty and politeness, also the fact that he was very neat. She told me with a laugh that only an American was lacking in my collection.[3]

In those months before she met Alik and was having several romances at once, she had been scared. Still, she was able to feel power over men. Of course, it was easy to fall in love, and she was looking for love. In love with love. When you're eighteen, hormones do your thinking. You are a proud young deer, and you meet and fall in love with different people because you are looking. One attracts you because he knows how to open the door, a gallant. Another, because he loves you dearly. She wanted a man to be romantic and a good provider, to be excellent, nice, and love her. But then there was always Anatoly. He made her head spin. With just one kiss. What you learn is that nobody is there to give you everything you need.

She didn't want to talk about her experiences. Catherine the Great had lots of lovers and was considered okay; that did not mean Marina had lots—she was not saying that. She just didn't want to talk about sex. Everybody was looking for bad; then they trash you. It wasn't that she'd done something she was ashamed of, nothing horribly wrong, but she knew when she first came to Minsk that maybe she needed advice. Because she was not that experienced. Maybe men thought she was something that she was not.

She talked to her friend Misha Smolsky, who had never laid a finger on her. They were friendly, just friends. He said, "Come on, I won't touch you. You're not Anita Ekberg." That said it all. He told her: "Marina, there's a guy spreading gossip around that you're sleeping with him. Is it true or not?" She told him, "Misha, I'm asking you what can I do if I have nothing to hide? I cannot defend myself door to door if a guy is lying."

So Misha said, "I cannot punch him in the nose, because it is not my business"—meaning she was not his girl—"but I'm going to tell him it is baloney."

She did not know why Merezhinsky—if that was the guy, Yuri Merezhinsky—talked about her that way. Maybe it was because he was always drunk and liked to make a fuss. Maybe it was rejection. Was this the person that Misha was talking about? She felt humiliated in front of all the world.

Now her reputation felt like ugly clothing, smelly, that she was condemned to wear. Lee Harvey Oswald, for example. This Alik had tried to be intimate with her when she saw him again at the Trade Union Palace eight days later, Saturday night. That night she took him back alone to meet Valya, since Ilya was away.

He had wanted her to make a bed so he could sleep over. He pretended it was too late for buses, so maybe he could sleep somewhere there? He must have assumed she was a floozy. She sent him home. He could walk home, she told him. But she was not really angry. After all, on that first night, when she was wearing her red dress, she insisted on everybody going over to a bar to have champagne. Maybe Lee assumed she was a type who has to drink, but her only concern was to see Anatoly and prove to him that he was going to talk to her whether she came with Sasha or not. Anatoly, however, ignored her, just as he had told her he would. So her group went back to the Trade Union Palace, and she spent that Friday night dancing with Lee. He was a teaser, kind of. "In America," he would say, "they dance this way," and would bring her closer to him. Then, he would dip. She could see it was his way to get closer. But not by grabbing, no, little by little.

All that while, she was thinking, "How am I going to prove to Anatoly that he can't just brush me away like I am nothing?" Moreover, she was feeling pity for Sasha. He was the victim of her strategy. So, when Anatoly acted like he'd never seen her in his life, it kind of freed her of an obsession with him, for this night, anyway.

She began to flirt with everybody, including Lee. He must have thought she was some floozy! Which may be why he expected so much more than he got eight days later, when she took him home to meet Valya. He even said, "You have so many fellows, I thought you were some kind of . . . you know . . ." And then, she'd been wearing her red dress. Maybe she stood out.

Now, looking all that long way back, she would say that Lee had intrigued her. He looked deeper into life. If he had been a dumb Vanya, just another dumb worker, she would never have gone on a date with him. She would say she respects factory workers very much—"but you are not going to date Vanya. Because what are you going to talk about with such men? They pinch girls openly—nothing but vulgarity. So, you stay away. No factory workers, thank you. You try to associate with a class ahead of yourself. Even if you come from the middle of nowhere." It wasn't her desire to go backward. Lee did work in a factory, but he also looked deeper into life. It certainly wasn't just his interest in politics. Her grandmother had told her about politics: Do not touch—then you won't stink. All the same, once you grow up, even if you don't want to belong to political groups, you do become interested in how things happen, and Lee was part of a group of her friends who were interested in how this world was working.

After the night when she made him walk home, he made a date for one week later. But a few days later, Aunt Valya said, "Guess what? Your American called." He could not make it. He was sick, and stuck in some hospital way out at one end of Minsk. Marina was not too concerned. Even when he rang to tell Valya that he was ill, she had been out with Anatoly. She liked Lee, but she certainly didn't consider him a serious date. He was something maybe for one free evening.

Now, his ear was infected badly enough for him to be in a hospital. He had had infected ears from childhood, he told her later, and a mastoid operation when a boy.

Valya said, "Why don't you visit him? He has nobody here from home and this is Russian Easter." Valya said, "I know for a fact that over in America they celebrate Easter. It'll be nice and touching." Valya put some cakes together on a plate and said to Marina, "Show him that Russians have some heart."

But when she finally got to this hospital—such a long trip by streetcar—he was glad to see her. He hadn't expected a visit. What a low opinion he must have had of her! But he was so happy she had brought him canned apricots. He told her it was his favorite dessert. Intuition must have let her know.

It was sad, however. He did look ill and his smile was pale. Physically, she couldn't say she liked him now. A little later that visit, he kissed her (after asking permission), and she didn't take to this first kiss, either. There was negative feeling. Like a warning to stop. Stop right there. She asked herself: "Do I want this to continue?" She had never thought of it before, but that first kiss could tell you a lot. Did she really want to know him more? Maybe no. Yet, her mind remained curious. And he was so gentle. She remembers that his kiss wasn't just a peck, thank you for coming—no, it showed expectations. But he didn't smell like a Russian. He didn't even smell like he was in the hospital. His skin had some funny odor. There could be a lot of scents on top, but underneath was some basic scent. Kissing him gave her that negative response. He did not smell like fresh air and sunshine.

Later, she would come to accept this scent of his body. Still there, but she accepted it. If you love a man, you accept.

It was funny. After work, every day she would go to visit him. She could get in when no one else could. Visiting days were Sundays only, but she was wearing her white uniform from the pharmacy at Third Clinical, so, no problem.

She did not love him yet, but she certainly felt sorry for him. He was so alone. She could understand that. Loneliness is an everyday companion to a lot of people, but it is certainly not your good companion. And Valya was so sorry for him.

While he was still in the hospital, he told Marina that he wanted to be engaged to her and she should not see anyone else. "I promised, but I did not take this seriously." She did not love Lee— not yet; she just felt sorry for him. Still, he was an American. You weren't going to say no if an American said you should be engaged; not right away, in any case.

On the day he got out of Fourth Clinical Hospital, Valya had him over for dinner with Ilya.

She liked how Alik could handle himself with her uncle. Very dignified. He told Ilya he had come to live forever in Russia. He intended to work hard. Ilya said, well, if that was so, then he, Ilya, would be ready to help him organize his life. And Marina could see that Valya was thinking, yes, they could have a little guidance over him, because Alik didn't have anyone in Minsk, and they would treat him well.

He charmed Valya. He was very tender. He kissed Valya on her good cheek after dinner and said, "Thank you, this meal was great." Well, it was, but he also said it nicely.

After dinner, Ilya said: "Take care of this girl. She has plenty of breezes in her brain." Wasn't that awful? She was a serious person. She would have liked to have breezes in her brain—she certainly wanted to have fun—but she was always feeling responsible, or examining her conscience. She could never say, "Just wash it off!"— she never did. Maybe, from Ilya's point of view, it was because she liked one guy this week, another guy the following week; but Marina would have told him, "I'm still looking. I meet somebody, and he's an idiot. He takes me out to dinner and wants me to pay for it. Or, he's always clearing his throat because he's an opera singer. All evening long, that's what my opera singer did." Yes, she had known one; she had gone on a date with him. "He had a nice cashmere coat and scarf." When they went to a restaurant that he chose, she thought, "Well, maybe he'll show some culture here," but he ate his dinner and said, "I forgot my wallet." Then he said, "Pay for it. I'll give you some tickets for my opera." When she got to that, he turned out to be Soldier 29, back somewhere in the chorus—a real Enrico Caruso! Of course, she had to drop him.

No, she did not want to talk about her courtship with Alik. It was not that remarkable. All courtships are the same: Put your best foot forward. The trouble with courtship is that you never know the other person until you get married and live the first twenty-four hours with him.

Still, she was ready to talk to others about this courtship with Alik. And her girlfriends, especially Larissa, encouraged Marina. As Larissa saw it, this American boyfriend would distinguish Marina from other girls. Besides, he had an apartment. When Alik invited Marina to visit his place on the night after his dinner at Ilya and Valya's, Marina came with Sasha, Yuri, and Larissa. Safety in numbers. But Larissa talked about him positively afterward. He had such good manners.

2
_____

A Little Bit of Conquering

Sasha recalls that night at Alik's place. The American lived in a grand building, but his apartment did not look cozy. It was what they call *kazyono,* that is, bureaucratic, lacking in home atmosphere.

Alik spoke good Russian. An accent, and his pronunciation was off, but he could speak. He put on Tchaikovsky's First Symphony, and as they listened, Alik told his life story. He'd been in his armed forces, served in Asia, didn't like war, didn't wish to be a part of war. So, he had decided to come to the Soviet Union for residence, and Moscow had sent him to Minsk. Now he worked at Horizon radio factory, "as an engineer." They had a bottle of Russian champagne. Sasha liked him—thought he was cool, very balanced, no unneeded emotion. Oswald didn't smoke, but enjoyed others inhaling their cigarettes—or so it seemed to Sasha. However, his apartment did look poor. "Iron dirt," as they called it. And his table was *neobtyosoniy,* not polished properly. His chairs were ordinary, and his bookcase was put together out of a few boards.

He had many records, however, long-playing records, all classics. Maybe they spent an hour and a half there. It must have been ten o'clock when they left. And Sasha said to Marina, "Let me see you off because tomorrow morning early, I have to go to my job and you, too, have to wake up early."

At this point, Sasha indicated that he wanted the interviewers to turn off the tape. He then told this story: When he arrived at his home, there was a car waiting outside which took him to the offices of KGB, where they played for him a recording of what he and others had been saying at Lee's party. They did not explain why they were doing this, nor did they go into other details. They told him merely that they wanted him to report in whenever they asked him.

All this took place in a basement room of the KGB building, on Lenin Street, and he had been brought there in a car. He was allowed to walk home, a good few kilometers. When he arrived, his mother scolded him for hanging out with his kind of friends, too upper-class, too well established, members of the *intelligentsia*— Yuri, particularly, and Kostya Bondarin. She told him, "Look, you come from simple peasant folk. You shouldn't be around people like that. You're going to get into trouble."

To his interviewers, he now said that after he stopped seeing Marina because she was going with Lee, he also stopped seeing Yuri and Kostya Bondarin, who, he assumes, were also called in. It was as if none of them wished to see the others in order not to have to report on one another. You could say that they shared a new language in which there was no need to have a conversation.

Neither Igor nor Stepan would admit to more than some early concern about Lee and Marina. When that romance developed quickly into marriage, it could be said, Igor admitted, that they did lose some sleep, and felt somewhat at fault that no steps had been taken to keep this courtship of Oswald and Marina Prusakova from flourishing.

When asked what such steps might have entailed, Igor's response was deliberative, even delicate. There were girls, he suggested, some of them attractive, certainly, certainly, who at one stage or another could be called upon by the Organs. Perhaps one of them might have diverted Oswald. They also could have attracted Marina perhaps to some other person, some very attractive man qualified for such activity. They didn't do that, however. It was a large move, after all. So that gave Lee and Marina a possibility to begin. Then came a wedding, with almost no warning. More problems to deal with. Would there now be any leak of information to Oswald through Marina? That was a possibility which could happen by way of her uncle, Lieutenant-Colonel Prusakov of MVD. To ensure themselves against such an outcome, they were obliged somewhat later to make personal contact with Ilya Prusakov.

That period, therefore, offered considerable stress, and it was a fact—Stepan didn't always sleep too well. Nor Igor.

Close to three years later, Marina wrote her account of these early days with Lee:

> Lee had a lot of classical records, and he loved to listen to them when we were alone. He did not like noisy company and rather preferred to be alone with me. I remember one of these evenings when we drank tea with pastry and kisses. Then (please excuse my vulgarity, due to youth) this tea was very tasty. I never again drank such tea or ate such pastry—ha ha! Lee told me that he wanted us to get married and stay here forever. He had a small darling apartment . . . with a separate entrance—quite enough for two, especially if they were young. I told him that I would become his wife (since I had already fallen in love with him) but that we should wait several months because it was a little embarrassing in front of our friends to get married so quickly. But Lee agreed to wait only until the first of May [and] planted some flowers on the balcony in honor of my agreeing to marry him.[1]

> **March 18–31**
> **We walk. I talk a little about myself. She talks a lot about herself. Her name is Marina N. Prusakova.**

> **April 1–30**
> **We are going steady and I decide I must have her. She puts me off and so on April 15 I propose. She accepts.**

All right, once Lee had gotten out of the hospital, they had started dating, she would tell her interviewers thirty years later. She didn't see him every night; she certainly kept seeing Anatoly until she finally accepted Lee's proposal. Then, no more of Anatoly.

It was not just that Lee was neat and polite. When people were clean, that was very attractive to her. She did like people who bathed and people who could think cleanly. She would admit it: She liked starch. Starch was in Lee's shirts, and that made her feel free: She could walk out from seeing him anytime she wished. So she had thought. So, she kept seeing Anatoly. Although not to the point of intercourse.

"Ah, well," she said to her interviewers, "number one, in Russia, you don't have that many opportunities to be in somebody's . . . inside. It was winter when I met Anatoly. So, mostly it was just kissing. And he was a good kisser. Put it that way." She never felt she was what you call a "sexual person." More like sensuous. Going to the very end in sex was not her goal. She wasn't looking for climax. "It's the part before that interested me." But with Anatoly, for the very first time, she had wanted to go further. Only, it never happened.

On the other hand, Lee certainly wanted to sleep with her. Sometimes they would go to his apartment, and things would get to the point of no return. Once, he threw her out, said: "Okay! Stay, or get out!" She got out. But he wasn't rough. What she liked about Lee, and about Anatoly as well, was the prelude, talking. It wasn't just physical—grab, kiss, here we go. You talk, and gradually you warm up to it. "I think that was what I liked with Lee prior to marriage. A little bit of conquering."

So, he might be gentle, but he was also a bit aggressive when it came to sex. "Why do you think we got married?" she would ask. She shook her head. "Well," she said to her interlocutors, "dear President Ford told everybody that Lee was impotent and that's the thing which is not true   People like that become President. I am sorry. I have no respect for Mr. Ford."

From an FBI report on an interview with Marina Oswald on December 1, 1963:

MARINA advised [that] her uncle and aunt did not disapprove of OSWALD and, in fact, were glad that she had reduced the number of her boy friends to almost one. They offered no objections to OSWALD and told her it was her decision to make . . . Permission for the marriage was granted [by the registrar] in seven days, and it was thereafter necessary to only wait three more days to fulfill the required ten-day waiting period. They were certified as married by the registrar on April 30, 1961, [and] her aunt and uncle had a reception for them in their apartment. Their mutual friends were invited.

She advised she was not interviewed by any official and that the only documentation necessary for this marriage was registration of intent and the certification of the marriage ten days later . . .[2]

From Marina's narrative: . . . It was one of the happiest days in my life. Alik, too, I think, was very happy that we were allowed to get married. He only calmed down on the day of our marriage; before that he went every day to ZAGS [the marriage bureau] to find out if we were to get permission. Only after our wedding did he finally believe that what we wanted had really happened . . . I remember that [on our wedding day] Lee bought me some early narcissi, and we went to the ZAGS with our friends. We came back on foot; the sun was shining; it was a warm Sunday, and everything was beautiful.[3]

3
_____

The Wedding Night

One day, about a year after Lee moved from the Hotel Minsk to his apartment, Stellina heard that he had gotten married. A floor lady at the hotel said: "Did you know? That American married a Russian girl. One of ours." But she added: "A woman who is spoiled goods. A Leningrad sidewalk prostitute." That rumor had spread around Minsk. Stellina remembered that he had told her the girl had said: "Switch off the light and kiss me, please." A respectable decent young lady wouldn't talk that way. Respectable young ladies, if they knew any English, would know more than such a phrase. Russian girls were brought up, said Stellina, to take no initiative with men. Sex was friendship and caring, part of the big relationship. Many women were not even told about female orgasm. What for?

"Turn off the light and kiss me" was unheard of. Enough! She didn't want to meet this young woman.

. . .

First, her aunt and uncle had thought she was going out with too many men. Now that she had it down to two, and wanted to get married, Ilya had to say: "Don't be in a hurry. What are you getting yourself into? You should know this man better. Such a short period of time."

On their marriage day, however, Ilya was nice. He said to Marina, "Maybe you are ready. Love each other. Now that you are married, you should live a peaceful life. Don't put shame on yourself. Just live so that people see you have a beautiful life."

At their pharmacy, Sonya first heard about Oswald when Marina started to say, "I was introduced to this American, Alik—Alka, I call him." Then Sonya heard a little later that they began to see each other. So when Marina came to them and said that Alka had proposed marriage, the girls thought, well, Marina's uncle has such a high position and we're just small people. If he, in his high position, allows them to marry, who are we to decide no? When the girls did remark that he was a foreigner, Marina said, "He's not going to America."

Not one of the pharmacy girls was invited to her wedding, but then, it wasn't a big party, just her uncle and aunt—not a regular wedding in a restaurant where many people were asked to come. Just close relatives, close friends.

During the period when Yuri Merezhinsky was friendly with Lee, Konstantin Bondarin noticed that whenever he was returning home from an evening at which Lee was present, a man was always following him. So, he stopped having contact with the American.

It was precisely for that reason that Kostya didn't take part in Marina's wedding. "Yuri and I talked about it. I said to Yuri: 'We're being grazed.'" There was a special word, *pasut,* which was used when you were clearly under surveillance. You were sheep and you had a shepherd watching you.

As for Marina, Kostya would say that she had a goal in mind and Lee was Victim Number One.

A victim, after all, is someone who is used as a means. That Marina wanted to get married was obvious to every man who ever had anything to do with her, but Tolya Shpanko would have been the most appropriate for her.

. . .

Inessa didn't recall when she heard the name Alik for the first time, but there was a period when Marina seemed to disappear for a while and Inessa didn't see her. So, Inessa was surprised to discover that she was getting married to an American.

Marina never told Inessa anything in absolute detail, but she did share some of her feelings. It gave Inessa a sense that Marina had dirt upon her, that it was creeping, maybe, toward her soul but hadn't managed yet to sully it.

"You can be soiled on the outside, that's my feeling, but in your soul remain honest and decent. No, those are the wrong words. How can I say it? Well, she's dear to me, and I saw something in her," said Inessa.

"She was confessing; she spoke with a great deal of pain, with a very great deal of pain, believe me. I am afraid of seeming self-assured, but it seems to me that she needed me. She approached the subject gradually. She would talk and talk and then afterward she did get more specific. It was before she got married that she told me all that. She felt entirely alone, as if nobody needed her."

Inessa knew that, right before her marriage, Marina was worried that on their wedding night Lee would find out about her past. As she spoke with Inessa, she told her that she did know what to do with herself so that he wouldn't find out. It was difficult to talk on this subject because it involved physical and medical matters, but afterward, Marina said everything was okay and Lee had thought she was a virgin. Something she did medically—yes, she did it.

Inessa said, "Of course, it shocked me, but I didn't judge her." Inessa hadn't known how she had managed something like that, but Marina told her that she was in a pharmacy, after all, and there were one or two substances—when you put them in, you could give yourself strain and tension down there. When the bridegroom consummated the first night, you would have pain. You didn't have to take acting lessons. Blood was not necessarily present, but the experience was uncomfortable enough to convince any new husband. "This is what I remember Marina telling me."

After her wedding, Marina told Inessa that all had gone well and she was happy. This was not because he was such a great hero in bed, but because she had succeeded in convincing him she was a virgin.

After marriage, Marina became a good and decent wife, Inessa said. It changed her. She had always wanted to have her own home and now she had achieved that. Somehow, Marina settled down.

INTERVIEWER: One person responded to a question by saying: You're right, she wasn't a virgin on her wedding night. She was worried that Lee would find out, and she went to the pharmacy and got something. She was protecting her marriage.

MARINA: Okay.

INT: That's exactly what was said.

M: Okay. It's true. So? So you are a sex pervert to spend five days to get somebody to talk about subject like this . . . I mean, isn't it enough?

INT: I'm telling you what happened in the course of the interviews. Pavel told us about an incident that happened at the radio factory, when guys came up to Lee and kidded him, and said: "Well, was your wife a virgin or not? How much blood was on the sheet?" We could never find out what Lee's answer was.

M: I don't know.

INT: Nobody seems to remember how he answered that question. So we don't know whether that was something which bothered him. It's of value to know whether every time he had a disagreement with you, every time he had an argument with you . . .

M: Your guess is as good as mine.

INT: We're not interested in the sex by itself but in what knowledge he had of your past. How did it affect him? Your girlfriend said you were concerned about your marriage. She said it with a lot of emotion and feeling. That you were doing it to protect your marriage.

M: At least I was serious about that.

INT: Exactly right. That helped us understand that you were serious about the marriage.

M: I wanted to have a family. I was damn serious about that.

INT: Let me get it out, so we don't have to feel anybody is hiding anything. Inessa told us in this same interview, in kindness, with great love and affection for you, that you, Marina, carried a great burden from Leningrad. And about how difficult your life was in Leningrad and with your stepfather, and that you had to live a life which you were not proud of.

M: It wasn't by choice.

INT: Inessa explained how you felt very bad and were very much worried that you had had this life in Leningrad, and that you had to resort to things to survive, to eat, to find a place to sleep . . .

M: I never once in my life was paid money.

INT: I'm sure you weren't.

M: I was looking for love in some wrong places and sometimes I had to pay for that. I actually was raped by a foreigner.

INT: What?

M: I mean, I was trapped in a room. He locked the door. And you know how they have those *dezhurnayas* that sit over there in the hallways of hotels holding keys for people who are out? I couldn't scream. I thought, what would this woman think of me? So I fought this man. He finally threw me against him. He said, "Well if I knew you were a virgin, I would not have touched you." . . . Lee didn't ask me, but on my wedding night, I pretended. I was terrified, I said to myself, When night comes, what am I going to do? I mean, what? It's a clean-cut life from now on. I want to be serious, and I was terrified. But Lee did not ask me.

INT: He never asked whether you were a virgin?

M: He did thank me for it. So I thought, "Oh my God. I flew over that . . . now I'm holy again."

INT: Right.

M: All my life that's all I wanted to be . . . And then Lee came from the factory and told me about how guys there talk, and he laughed and he said how barbaric and awful. And I said, "Don't you talk about us. I don't want to be discussed." And once, now I recall, we had an argument and he kind of mumbled: "Yeah, little virgin." And I said, "Yes, I am." I said, "Prove it that I'm not." And he dropped the subject.

April 3'
After a seven-day delay at the Marriage Bureau because of my unusual passport, they allow us to register as man and wife. Two of Marina's girlfriends act as bridesmaids. We are married at her aunt's home. We have a dinner reception for about twenty friends and neighbors, who wish us happiness (in spite of my origin), which was in general rather disquieting to any Russian since foreigners are very rare in the Soviet Union, even tourists. After an evening of eating and drinking in which Uncle Wooser started a fight and a fuse blew on an overloaded circuit, we take our leave and walk fifteen minutes to our home. We lived near each other. At midnight we went home.

Honeymooners

Marina would say now that her main reason for getting married was to find someone to belong to, and to have a family. Marriage was holy. One entered it for life. So, of course, she wanted to come to her marriage with purity. Of course. In Russia it was a tradition that a man married a virgin, but with Americans she didn't know how to read their feelings. Americans were a novelty. Maybe they wouldn't care as much.

She could say this much again: Lee did like to laugh about how barbaric it was in peasant villages. Showing bloody sheets!

She remembers that in Leningrad, when she was fourteen years old, she would dream of getting married. Some white prince would come. No dirt, nothing. So, when she became—what would you call it?—a witness to life's reality, she was not prepared. Probably, she said, it's that way for every little girl.

After they were legally married at the license bureau, ZAGS, and a stamp was put on her passport, she happened to notice Alik's date of birth. It was 1939. She realized then that he had been lying when he told her he was twenty-four. He was only twenty-one. She said, "If I knew, I wouldn't have married you." It was only a joke, but he said to her that he had worried whether she would take him seriously. After all, she had said that Sasha was only twenty and she was not about to marry babies.

For their wedding, Valya had prepared a feast: crab salad, salami, black caviar, red caviar, pâté. And then she had stuffed a fish with its own cooked meat, kept the skin whole and put all the fish meat back inside, but now, no bones. Not one. It looked like a real fish again. And yet you could slice it. Such a special effort.

Marina had already begged her aunt not to go through any Russian tradition of saying, *"Gor'ko, gor'ko."* But as they sat around their table eating, somebody pretended to be choking on too much pepper, and so everybody started crying out: *"Gor'ko"*—which means bitter—and Marina turned red. In obedience to such custom, they now made her kiss Lee over and over every time somebody said, *"Gor'ko."* Later, she danced with everyone, and then Erich Titovets and Pavel and Alik sang "Chattanooga Choo-Choo." Next morning, Valya walked right into their apartment and dropped a plate on the floor with enough noise to wake up ghosts. Then she said to Alik, "Russian custom."

At her wedding, Marina had been embarrassed by Aunt Musya's husband, Vanya, who got drunk. (Lee called him Wooser!) As usual, he couldn't handle liquor. A Vanya! He crowed like a rooster, screaming away at the wedding party. Marina was embarrassed. "I thought, my new husband will ask himself: 'What kind of family did you just marry into?' It was very uncomfortable."

That night, when they went back to his apartment, they discovered that Valya and Larissa had placed flowers all around their bed. Her nightgown was on a pillow.

They didn't have a honeymoon. They just spent two days in bed getting accustomed to each other—what would you want her to tell? They were new. They couldn't analyze everything. Talk a little, observe a little—bit by bit you go on; you don't make any big issue. Little by little. When you read romantic books, it's not enough; you want more. But sex was not romance. More like soiled clothes.

One thing: Lee was not bashful. He could walk around their apartment naked. As if it were nothing. That was surprising to her—that a man could be so comfortable before he got dressed. But she never said anything about it. For Minsk, however, he was some exhibitionist. She had just never experienced this American way. Lee was not even embarrassed to get up and go to the bathroom while leaving the door open. That was unusual. Marina was trying to find out what was expected of her. She did not know what her man wanted, so she had to learn.

Guys at Lee's factory, she soon found out, were always talking about sex. Quite a big topic over there. That was why Marina never wanted to date factory boys—their mentality. When Alik would laugh at what they said, she would say, "Don't tell them about our lovemaking. Don't you dare."

Alik's first experience with sex had not only been with a Japanese girl, but he also said that he'd never had an American girl. Just Japanese and Russian girls. Marina wondered whether he felt that he was missing something. Maybe he should have had a girl from his own country first? No, Marina didn't know what to expect during these first few days of marriage. She could say that she kind of lived in euphoria. Finally married, you know! And she had married an American. She had that stupid apartment she'd always dreamed about. God was smiling on her. Finally! A year or two before, she had been with Larissa and they'd been walking past this same apartment house. It was such a beautiful place from outside, with its high balconies between high white columns. Marina had pointed up to one and said, "I'd like to have that," said it before she ever met Lee, even said to Larissa, "Do you know anybody who lives here?" Larissa said no.

May 6, 1961
Found us thinking about our future. Despite the fact I married Marina
to hurt Ella, I found myself in love with Marina.

Maybe a week after their marriage, Aunt Valya said, "Let me see your pampered, manicured hand," and all Marina could show were Polish fingers: Her nails were broken from cleaning stone walls on her balcony and washing their floor. For that one moment, she had said to herself, "Is this what married life is about? Broken nails? Oh my God!"

But for the first couple of days, since that was all they had off from their jobs and couldn't have a honeymoon, they would stay in bed and not get up until late afternoon. A honeymoon was sexual; you explored. Marina felt as if now she was free to do what she wanted to do. She didn't think about their problems in sex, and she didn't want to talk about that, really. You expected fireworks, and it didn't happen, and you thought maybe it's supposed to come later. It never did. That was all right. But she didn't know if what little was happening to her was all that was supposed to happen, and so in bed everything was a problem. She didn't know what to do, and Lee was always eager-beaver. Later on, when Marina was tired or in a bad mood, she didn't avoid him, just told him, "No, I don't want to make love to you, because I feel used one more time. What for? Something there for you, maybe, but nothing for me." Even if that was kind of insulting to him, he would try to handle it. "Come on," he would say, "you know I love you." He would play that he was a little boy and make jokes. Sometimes she would give in. She thinks he really liked sex, but she resents talking about it. "Nobody asks Jacqueline Kennedy what Jack Kennedy was like in bed." And here she has to discuss such private things as what it was like to have a person inside you. There is nothing dirty about sex unless you let people watch—then it's degrading. But she would say that no matter what their difficulties, people ask if Lee was a homosexual and she would say she never had any sense with Lee that he'd be partial to a man, never. Maybe he could be gay somewhere else, but not around her.

Lee liked to stand in front of his mirror and admire himself, that was true. "How unbashful he was," said Marina. "He would admire himself. He was not tall, but he was well proportioned. He had beautiful legs. And he knew I liked them, so he would flirt. 'Don't you think I have gorgeous legs?' he would say. Just begging for compliments. Kind of a joking relationship. Private, but of the sort people do have." Her understanding: He really liked women. That was her interpretation.

When told how Lee went for months without trying to seduce Ella, never forcing her, Marina asked if it was possible that Ella was embarrassed to talk. "You know, I'm holier right now than I was then, know what I mean?" And then she thought, "Maybe he liked her so well that if she didn't want him that bad, he wouldn't push."

Lee did tell her, and with a lot of admiration, about that beautiful Japanese girl who had been the first woman he knew. Marina was left with an image of a lovely Oriental blossom whom Lee still longed for. It made her jealous. Of course. There in his mind was a lovely woman. Was that to influence her? So that she would pay more attention to all kinds of sex? And learn new ways? She wanted to compete when Lee—always with great admiration—described all the sexual things this Japanese girl did to him, this unknown beauty.

5

Early Married Days

Valya thought Marina now a *dama,* not a girl but a young woman. When you get your position in society in Russia, you're a *dama.* Once, after she was married, Marina said to Valya, "My husband may do factory work, but I never see him dirty. He comes back from his job as if he's an engineer."

Valya wanted Marina and Lee's apartment to be just as neat as he looked, so she often came to help. Once, Valya even went over to wash their balcony, a hard job and dirty, a long job, and she had been at it for three hours when Alik came home from Horizon to have lunch. Marina was cooking, and put food on the table for him, but did not invite Valya to sit down. Later, she said to Marina, "I'm not hungry or poor, but it's a tradition when you clean up for people to be offered something. Yet, there are some who sit and eat and don't offer anything, okay, please!" Marina must have told Alik, because after that, whenever Valya visited, Alik was all over her saying, "Valya, do you want this? Would you like that?" Maybe they had been looking for an hour alone that day, but still, after you wash their balcony, you shouldn't be treated like a servant.

From Marina's narrative: May was our honeymoon month . . . Of course we were both working but we had evenings after 5 o'clock and Sundays entirely to ourselves. We ate in restaurants, in the first place because I did not have time to cook dinner . . . and in the second place because I did not know how to cook properly . . .

He and I loved classical music. We had many Tchaikovsky records, as he was Lee's favorite composer, and also Grieg, Liszt, Rimsky-Korsakov, Schumann. Lee's favorite opera was the Queen of Spades. In Russia, a film was made of this opera, a beautiful film. Lee went to it four or five times and at home I even came to be jealous of this opera. After work he would immediately start playing the record, not once but several times. [Also] we often went to the opera, theatre, the conservatory or the circus . . . and many of my friends envied the way we lived. Lee was very anxious to have a child and very grieved when the honeymoon was over and there was no sign of a baby.[1]

They wanted her to be pregnant right away. For the first month, nothing happened, and Lee and Valya were equally disappointed. Valya even said, "We were hoping you would have a child, but you're probably going to be like your uncle, won't be able to." Said it after one month! Lee wanted to have a boy. He was going to call him David. Their boy, he assured Marina, would someday be President of the United States. And then, whenever Marina would go to the bathroom, at least when her period was approaching, he wouldn't let her shut that door. He wanted to know for sure whether she was having a period. When she asked him why he didn't trust her, Alik said, "Well, you work in a hospital. If you don't want to have a child, you could have an abortion. So I want to know." It didn't hurt her feelings; she wanted a child too: She thought he was being stupid, but she brushed it off. She even said, "Well, leave the door open"—took it like a joke. She said, "Lee, I want a child as much as you. I'm not going to do anything foolish." So, it was not such a big deal. It wasn't like he stood there and said, "You must pee-pee in front of me"—no, it was more gentle. After all, late spring had come, and her mood was, "I'm going to have a child and I'm going to have a family right here," and she wanted them to be as young and happy as they could be.

> **May**
>
> **The transition of changing full love for Ella to Marina was very painful, especially as I saw Ella almost every day at the factory, but as the days and weeks went by I adjusted more and more to my wife mentally . . . She is madly in love with me from the very start—boat rides on Lake Minsk, walks through the park, evening at home or at Aunt Valya's place mark May.**

During the first weeks of their marriage, Lee would meet her at the pharmacy entrance and walk her home, and when evening came, Alik would go out on their balcony and look at sights far off with his binoculars. At night, he would wash the breakfast dishes, and on days when they had hot water, he would do their laundry. When Marina would climb up their entryway from Kalinina Street, she could hear him singing "Volga Boatmen" from four flights down. He wouldn't be one for a choir, but he could sing with zest. A pleasant voice. And he was washing his own work clothes. He just didn't want her near his dirty things.

One day, he was hammering a piece of furniture together and hit himself on his finger. She knew it hurt—would you believe it?—she was physically hurt for him. She really went all the way. She felt their souls touching in his pain. Of course, he also liked to be pampered. He had been like a little boy when she put that bandage on his finger.

She soon learned that he didn't enjoy his job. He claimed that they resented him and his privileges. But she didn't know how true it might be. Lee played with people. That she soon learned. Maybe he even played with her.

A few weeks after they were married, some letters arrived from America and in one was a picture of Marguerite Oswald. She was in a white nursing outfit, just sitting in a chair. "That's my mother," he told Marina. He studied the picture and said, "She's gained some weight. As I remember her, she wasn't that plump." That was it. Marina said, "You told me your mother was dead." He said, "Well, I don't want to talk about my mother."

She did not know how to accept that. He had said he was an orphan. Now, she thought to herself, "Stupid me! There I was believing late at night that it was a sign and God sent me an orphan like myself."

> *From Marina's narrative:* Sometime in the middle of June we were out on Lake Minsk . . . lying in the sun and swimming. That was a wonderful day [and] Lee told me that he was sure that . . . we would have a baby. I did not believe it, but a week later we were eating in a café and I fainted. I think this was the first sign . . . It was a great joy for us and for my aunt . . . but the doctors told me that I might lose the baby since I have Rh negative blood. Lee was very upset by this, but when he had his own blood checked, it turned out that he was also Rh negative. Only a very small percentage have Rh negative blood, and this very unusual coincidence—in which husband and wife were both Rh negative—pleased us very much.[2]

Good signs are important. They enable you to forgive. You could call Rh negative fundamental. Maybe God had chosen Lee for a certain girl from Leningrad.

> **June**
> **A continuation of May except that we draw closer and closer now and I think very little now of Ella . . .**

6

Back to America

After she became pregnant, Lee showed her Dr. Spock's book one night. She didn't know whether he had owned it all this time or asked his mother to send it. But every day he translated passages for her until Lee, courtesy of Dr. Spock, was informing Marina how their embryo would develop. He was very proud. He played doctor with her, and she felt him come closer. His Russian even got better. He was making progress.

He had a habit she liked. He could always put everything else aside. Nobody could push him when he was reading. His spelling was horrible, but that could be forgiven. Russian—it's a hard language. Many Russians do not spell it well. And he did not know grammar. But for speaking, yes. He applied himself. He would stumble only occasionally. His vocabulary was not large, but his pronunciation was good.

However, she was pregnant—"an entirely different language." Sometimes she felt distant from him. Then, with each week of pregnancy, more and more. Maybe such a condition was normal. "You still love me," he would say. "It's just a chemical imbalance." But she felt a little distaste for him. Now that she had got to know her husband better, Marina decided that he was stingy. They had an apartment that she wanted to fix up, and he kept putting a stop to that. "No," he would say. "We have everything we need." Well, sure, but she wanted some feminine touches, and there he was in charge of all their money.

She didn't like that. She gave him what she earned at work and now she didn't have money of her own. It wasn't like they each had their own little drawer. He had it all.

Before they married, she felt there was no need for either one of them to control the other, but then, she didn't know much. She thought she could be her own person and so had no idea that he was going to tell her what to do. Now, she would bristle when he took a domineering attitude. During courtship, she had been in control; since marriage, the rules were being changed. All the same, there were still lots of times when she would be pleasantly surprised. They would listen to an hour of classical music on their radio, and he would know which composer was playing. Very often they would start a game: She would say it was one composer, he would say another; many times he was right. That was great. He could recognize whether a piece was by Bach or Chopin or Wagner.

Also, Lee taught her to play gin rummy. Her grandmother would not allow cards in their house in Arkhangelsk. Card games were there to please the devil. So Marina had never been interested, but now she played gin rummy with Lee. He beat her, usually. He would enjoy winning: "See, I won again!"—it was important for him. But nothing to her. Somebody had to lose.

Sometimes she would get a glimpse—if only for a little while—
of what was in him. Then he would lift his shield again. He was
embarrassed to show vulnerability. Only in intimate moments
could he be himself, this little boy who wanted attention. Then he
would pretend that he didn't need anything. "He would isolate
himself," said Marina, "and play games with people. Treat them
like they were not people."

Once, on a day when everyone was supposed to vote for some
Presidium or something, election workers started knocking on
their door at 7:00 A.M. Lee told them to go away—it was too early.
They came back again, and Lee wouldn't open up. He kept
yelling, "This is a free country." He gave them lectures while they
stood outside. She doesn't remember whether she went to vote,
but Lee kept telling her that the Soviet constitution said it was a
free country. They were not supposed to drag you out to vote. So
she received a speech on politics early that day. Of course, she had
never studied that stupid Soviet constitution. That is, she had
studied, had even passed her exam, but now she couldn't recall
any of it. So, he had to teach her about her own system, and told
her how they were not practicing their constitution properly.

He also liked her to be at home when he arrived. If she came in
even ten minutes after him, he'd be upset. "Where were you?"
he'd ask. "How come you're late?" She thinks maybe that's how his
control over her began. Lee's factory hours were always the same,
and hers too, but sometimes she might stop by a store, so how
could you know who would come home first?

Pregnant, she was now very sensitive to odor. Their walls
seemed to smell; even her balcony seemed rank when she opened
its door. She was always sniffing somebody else's cooking. Nor
could she eat. And then there was Lee. If you boiled him in water,
he would still have his special body odor. So, by the second month
of pregnancy, when he started being not so nice, she began to
look for fights. And she had second thoughts—had she made a
mistake? Maybe she didn't love this man.

Soon enough, she learned that Lee not only had a mother but a
brother, with a wife and children. All of a sudden, Lee was part of
a family—he kept getting more correspondence. Since she didn't
read English, she could not know what these letters were about,
but then, one Sunday morning, she found out. Lee woke up and
said, "If I have a chance to go to America, would you go with me?"

"You're joking," she said.

He said, "No, it's a possibility. I don't know for sure, but would you go with me?"

That gave her a feeling that he truly loved her. And she said, "I don't know. I'm kind of scared." She took a breath, and added, "Okay. I'll go."

It wasn't that short a conversation—maybe it took an hour, maybe it took three days—but by its end, she said okay. He said, "I told them at the American Embassy that I was giving up my passport. So maybe they won't allow me to go back. There might be complications. I'll have to write a lot of letters. And my mother will help. Will you go?" When she finally said yes, he said, "I don't want you to tell Aunt Valya or any of your relatives. And nobody at work. Not yet. Because maybe it won't go through."

Marina did not believe it could happen. Later, when she had to fill out her own applications, she still didn't believe it. Her dream of marrying a foreigner had not included leaving her country. It was just finding a man who had an apartment. She didn't want to huddle in somebody else's corner. That was the largest thing about marriage: your own apartment. To meet and marry a foreigner was, in addition, flattering to her, and adventurous. Sometimes she dreamed, Boy, wouldn't it be great to work in Czechoslovakia for a couple of years? Or East Germany? Buy a sporty coat, look nice. Having married an American, she could tell the girls at work: "See what I got? You just have your Russian nothing." They answered: "Isn't your husband a worker?" She told them: "It doesn't matter. He's still a foreigner. He's Oswald, not Vanya."

But now it was scary. Going to America! It gets scarier if you don't tell your relatives and keep it to yourself at work. Then in July, Alik said he might have to take an illegal trip to Moscow in order to visit the American Embassy. She wondered if the KGB would come for her then, or would they call her in from work?—she didn't know how the KGB got in touch with you.

What Marina also did not know was that her husband had been in correspondence through half the winter with American officials in Moscow. More than a month before he even met her, back in early February 1961, he had already sent a letter to the Embassy, requesting the return of that same passport he had left on Richard Snyder's desk in late October 1959. Snyder had mailed an answer back to Minsk, suggesting that Oswald take a trip to

Moscow so they could discuss the matter. They had been in communication since. Oswald was to tell his wife many a lie over their years together, but no single deceit may have been as large as his decision not to inform Marina or Valya or Ilya before the marriage that in his heart he was already on his way back to America.

PART VI

A COMMENCEMENT OF
THE LONG VOYAGE
HOME

—◀◯▶—

1

Remarks from the Author

Up to this point, nearly all of Oswald's acquaintances have been Russian, but as his focus of interest moves from Soviet friends, girl-friends, and workers to American government officials, so do the bureaucracies of the U.S. and the USSR consume a larger part of his attention.

So be it. This is, after all, a book that depends upon the small revelation of separate points of view. We are, in effect, studying an *object* (to use the KGB's word for a person under scrutiny) as he tumbles through the prisms of a kaleidoscope. It is as if by such means we hope to penetrate into the psychology of Lee Harvey Oswald.

Given the variety of interpretations that surround him, he has continued to exist among us as a barely visible protagonist in a set of opposed scenarios that range from Mark Lane's—ready to open the case—to Gerald Posner's—eager to close it. We cannot even begin to list the near-to-numberless practitioners of the art of investigative writing who have been fitting Oswald into one or another species of plot.

Perhaps it would be more felicitous to ask: What kind of man was Oswald? Can we feel compassion for his troubles, or will we end by seeing him as a disgorgement from the errors of the cosmos, a monster?

In this regard, it may as well be stated here that in the effort to find his kernel of human reality, certain liberties have been taken. Even as one stains a slide in order to separate the features of its contents more clearly, so Oswald's letters and writings have been corrected here for spelling and punctuation. Oswald was dyslexic, and his orthography is so bad at times that the man is not revealed but concealed—in the worst of his letters he seems stupid and illiterate. Considering that he was still in his very early twenties, it is, however, not wholly inaccurate to speak of him as a young intellectual. In this regard, it may be worth taking a look at the Appendix, pp. i–xiv in the back matter. That he had no extraordinary reach of mind as an intellectual is also apparent, even with corrected orthography, but since we are giving him every benefit in this direction in order better to perceive the workings of his mind, let us also recognize how prodigiously crippling is dyslexia to a man who would have a good polemical style. Indeed, it is as intimately crippling as arthritic fingers on a violinist. (The Appendix to this book also contains a short essay on the disabilities attendant on dyslexia written by Dr. Howard Rome of the Mayo Clinic for the Warren Commission.)

It may well take the rest of these pages to decide, all the same, whether such a method of approach—to search for the nature of the man before we decide on the plot—is of use for finding out how Kennedy was shot and why. Until then, we will keep asking who was behind it and which conspiracy was operative. It is virtually not assimilable to our reason that a small lonely man felled a giant in the midst of his limousines, his legions, his throng, and his security. If such a non-entity destroyed the leader of the most powerful nation on earth, then a world of disproportion engulfs us, and we live in a universe that is absurd. So the question reduces itself to some degree: If we should decide that Oswald killed Kennedy by himself, let us at least try to comprehend whether he was an assassin with a vision or a killer without one. We must not only look at Oswald from many points of view—first Russian and soon American—but even try to perceive him through bureaucratic lenses. All too often, that is all we will have. Let us recognize, however, that it makes some difference to our commonweal, each and every time, whether an act of murder is visionless and mindless or is a cry of wrath that rises from a skewed heart maddened by its own vision of injustice.

We have come at least to the philosophical crux of our inquiry: It would state that the sudden death of a man as large in his possibilities as John Fitzgerald Kennedy is more tolerable if we can perceive his killer as tragic rather than absurd.

That is because absurdity corrodes our species. The mounting ordure of a post-modern media fling (where everything is equal to everything else) is all the ground we need for such an assertion.

Correspondence

On February 13, the American Embassy received a letter from Lee Harvey Oswald whose contents would prove startling to both State Department and KGB officials. Postmarked Minsk, February 5, 1961, it had taken eight days to reach Richard Snyder in Moscow.

While it is all but impossible that Igor and Stepan had not intercepted such a communication from their prize defector in Minsk, they volunteered no information about what had been their reaction. Given, however, what they have imparted about their attitudes governing this case, they must certainly have decided to wait and study further developments.

But here is Oswald's letter:

> Dear Sirs:
>
> . . . I am . . . asking that you consider my request for the return of my American passport.
>
> I desire to return to the United States, that is if we could come to some agreement concerning the dropping of any legal proceedings against me. If so, then I would be free to ask the Russian authorities to allow me to leave. If I could show them my American passport, I am of the opinion they would give me an exit visa.
>
> They have at no time insisted that I take Russian citizenship. I am living here with non-permanent type papers for a foreigner.
>
> I cannot leave Minsk without permission, therefore I am writing rather than calling in person.
>
> I hope that in recalling the responsibility I have to America that you remember yours in doing everything you can to help me since I am an American citizen.
>
> Sincerely,
> /s/ Lee Harvey Oswald[1]

In response, the American Embassy in Moscow waited until February 28 and then, by air pouch, asked for an Instruction from the Department of State:

. . . an invitation from the Embassy may facilitate his traveling to Moscow. The Embassy would as a last resort, if the Department found no objection and provided the Embassy were reasonably sure that Oswald had not committed an expatriating action, return his American passport to him by mail for what help this may be in facilitating his application for a Soviet exit visa.

The Embassy would like to be informed whether Oswald is subject to prosecution on any grounds should he enter the jurisdiction of the United States and, if so, whether there is any objection in communicating this to him.

> For the Ambassador
> Edward L. Freers
> Minister Counselor[2]

Richard Snyder followed this with an answer to Oswald on the same day, February 28:

Dear Mr. Oswald:

We have received your recent letter concerning your desire to return to the United States . . .

Inasmuch as the question of your present American citizenship status can be finally determined only on the basis of a personal interview, we suggest that you plan to appear at the Embassy at your convenience. The consular section of the Embassy is open from 9:00 A.M. to 6:00 P.M. . . .[3]

It is worth including at this point an exchange between Gerald Ford, of the Warren Commission, and Richard Snyder:

REPRESENTATIVE FORD. [Your answer] took 15 days to get out of the American Embassy.

MR. SNYDER. You must remember that in my eyes, as the officer on the spot, Mr. Oswald had no claim to prior action from the Embassy among other cases. And although the consular officer attempts to be as impersonal as he can about these things, as a matter of fact it is very difficult to be entirely impersonal.

Mr. Oswald had no claim to any unusual attentions of mine, I must say.[4]

In turn, Oswald seemed in no rush, either. On March 12, only five days before he would first meet Marina at the Trade Union

Palace dance, did he reply to Snyder's letter of February 28, and we can assume from the tone of his answer that he expects the KGB to also be reading what he writes and so is choosing language that will irritate them as little as possible under the circumstances.

Dear Sirs,

In reply to your recent letter, I find it inconvenient to come to Moscow for the sole purpose of an interview.

In my last letter, I believe I stated that I cannot leave the city of Minsk without permission.

I believe there exists in the United States also a law in regards to resident foreigners from socialist countries traveling between cities.

I do not think it would be appropriate for me to request to leave Minsk in order to visit the American Embassy. In any event, the granting of permission is a long drawn-out affair, and I find that there is a hesitation on the part of local officials to even start the process.

I have no intention of abusing my position here, and I am sure you would not want me to.

I see no reason for any preliminary inquiries not to be put in the form of a questionnaire and sent to me. I understand that personal interviews undoubtedly make the work of the Embassy staff lighter than written correspondence, however, in some cases, other means must be employed.

Sincerely,
Lee Oswald[5]

If Oswald's last paragraph was, at the least, sardonic, Snyder's reply on March 24 was dry.

Dear Mr. Oswald:

. . . As stated in our previous letter, a final determination of your present American citizenship status can only be made on the basis of a personal interview . . .

We suggest that you inform us in advance of any intention to visit the Embassy so as to be assured of an appointment without delay. You may, however, drop in at any time during normal office hours. You may wish to present this letter to the authorities in Minsk in connection with an application for permission to travel to Moscow . . .[6]

Bureaucratic Soundings

Now the State Department is having to contend with technical questions. Just what is Oswald's status? If he has not renounced his citizenship, then what are the circumstances under which his passport is to be returned? Can it be mailed to Minsk? A serious matter. The document could be intercepted and replaced with a counterfeit passport. Certainly, the KGB labs are as well equipped for that as the CIA and FBI labs.

In any event, State sends an Instruction on March 27 to the American Embassy in Moscow:

> . . . if you are fully satisfied that [Oswald] has not expatriated himself in any manner, you are authorized to amend his United States passport to be valid for his direct return to the United States and effect its delivery to him by mail under proper safeguards.
>
> The Department is not in a position to advise Mr. Oswald whether upon his desired return to the United States he may be amenable to prosecution for any possible offenses committed in violation of the laws of the United States or the laws of any of its States . . .[1]

Four days later, on March 31, the bureaucratic security of being "not in a position to advise Mr. Oswald" is obliged to encounter a cogent reason why he should be allowed to come back to the United States. A confidential inter-office memo is sent from one State Department official, named Hickey, to another, named White:

> . . . it is believed that whatever risk might be involved in transmitting the passport by mail . . . would be more than offset by the opportunity provided the United States to obtain information from Mr. Oswald concerning his activities in the Soviet Union. For the best interests of the United States, therefore, and as the possession of a passport might facilitate his obtention of an exit visa it is believed that we should do everything within our power to facilitate Oswald's entry into the United States.[2]

This will become a subtext in much of the correspondence to come. Since each side was ideologically buried under large misrepresentations of the other, both sides were starved for a little real knowledge about conditions in the daily existence of their opponent. The State Department will end with a voluminous file of caveats, precedents, loopholes, directives, waivers, and sanctions, but under them all is another theme: Oswald is useful. The intelligence to be gained from him about Soviet life is a factor powerful enough to take him through some bureaucratic locks and gates. Yet, in the interim, what locks, what gates!

A letter from Oswald dated only "May 1961" arrives at the Embassy on May 25. If it has taken more than a month for him to reply to Snyder, we can remind ourselves that this period all but covers the first month of his marriage to Marina.

Dear Sirs,

In regards to your letter of March 24. I understand the reasons for the necessity of a personal interview at the Embassy, however, I wish to make it clear that I am asking not only for the right to return to the United States, but also for full guarantees that I shall not, under any circumstances, be persecuted for any act pertaining to this case. I made that clear in my first letter, although nothing has been said, even vaguely, concerning this in my correspondence with the Embassy. Unless you honestly think that this condition can be met, I see no reason for a continuance of our correspondence. Instead, I shall endeavor to use my relatives in the United States to see about getting something done in Washington.

As for coming to Moscow, this would have to be on my own initiative and I do not care to take the risk of getting into an awkward situation unless I think it worthwhile. Also, since my last letter I have gotten married.

My wife is Russian, born in Leningrad, she has no parents living and is quite willing to leave the Soviet Union with me and live in the United States.

I would not leave here without my wife so arrangements would have to be made for her to leave at the same time as I do . . .

So with the extra complication I suggest you do some checking up before advising me further.

I believe I have spoken frankly in this letter. I hope you do the same in your next letter.

Sincerely Yours,
Lee Harvey Oswald[3]

We know nothing specifically about the State Department's reaction to this "extra complication," but we can certainly suppose that they are feeling Oswald's presence. Another turn of the screw.

4

Return to Moscow

It is becoming obvious, given the slow pace of his correspondence with Snyder and the non-appearance of his passport by mail, that he will probably have to risk an unauthorized trip to Moscow to visit the American Embassy. But what a gamble!

In an interrogatory that J. Lee Rankin sent from the Warren Commission to Abram Chayes of the State Department in May 1964, the situation is assessed long after the risk was taken:

QUESTION 1
Your file reflects the fact that Lee Harvey Oswald believed that he could not travel from Minsk to Moscow for the purpose of discussing his return to the United States with American officials without first obtaining the permission of Soviet officials in Minsk . . . do you have any information or observations regarding the practicality of such travel by Soviet citizens or persons in Oswald's status?

ANSWER
It is impossible to generalize in this area. We understand from interrogations of former residents in the Soviet Union who were considered "stateless" by Soviet authorities that they were not permitted to leave the town where they resided

without permission of the police. In requesting such permission they were required to fill out a questionnaire giving the reason for travel, length of stay, addresses of individuals to be visited, etc.

Notwithstanding these requirements, we know that at least one "stateless" person often travelled without permission of the authorities and stated that police stationed at railroad stations usually spotchecked the identification papers of every tenth traveler, but that it was an easy matter to avoid such checks. Finally, she stated that persons who were caught evading the registration requirements were returned to their home towns by the police and sentenced to short jail terms and fined. These sentences were more severe for repeated violations.[1]

It is a species of Russian roulette. If one traveler in ten is given a spot-check, then the odds are 9 to 1 in Oswald's favor. Since he has to return to Minsk as well, such odds reduce to 9 to 2. Of course, if there are six chambers in a revolver and only one bullet is placed in the cylinder, the odds are 5 to 1 that you will pull the trigger and still be alive, but it is a fair surmise that if one were to perform such an act, the chance of sudden death, at least as measured by one's anxiety, would have to seem equal to survival.

Say as much for the trip to Moscow. All through Marina's early pregnancy in June and into the onset of summer, Oswald is living with the anxiety that he must dare to take that trip. It can improve neither his mood nor his confidence that the man he will have to face at the Embassy is bound to be Richard Snyder.

July
I decide to take my two-week vacation and travel to Moscow (without police permission) to the American Embassy to see about getting my U.S. passport back and make arrangements for my wife to enter the U.S. with me.

Earlier, back in the winter of 1960–61, Oswald wanted to visit Moscow on a bus with other factory workers but had been quietly refused. That is, his fellow workers left without discussing their plans with him. "It was our opinion then," said Igor, "that he should not be one of a group from Horizon radio factory." Igor could list his reservations: What, after all, did Oswald plan to do in

Moscow? Perhaps he had a safe place to visit where he could receive equipment or instructions or make a radio transmission. Maybe he would visit a drop and leave something. Since the KGB in Minsk could hardly afford the disbursement necessary to send proper people to Moscow for surveillance on Oswald and Moscow Center might not be pleased at inroads on their budget, Minsk KGB decided they had to block his trip.

When Oswald did go to Moscow during his vacation in July of 1961 and visited the American Embassy to discuss returning to America, that raised no suspicions. After all, they knew by now, Igor would point out, that he didn't like it here, so from a political point of view, there was no reason to keep him. Despite all those favorable conditions Soviet institutions had created for him, he still didn't want Soviet citizenship. Okay. Let him go to America. KGB would not interfere with his illegal trip to Moscow, since they knew his intentions through his correspondence. If there had been no idea where he was going or with what purpose, they would have taken measures. But Oswald's goal was evident.

In Moscow in July, he was, as it turned out, under surveillance after all, but it could be said that he didn't do anything to evoke suspicion, Igor said.

July 8
I fly by plane from Minsk at 11:20. Two hours and twenty minutes later, after taking a tearful and anxious parting from my wife, I arrive in Moscow . . . From the airfield I arrive in the center of the city, make my way through heavy traffic. I don't come in sight of the Embassy until 3 in the afternoon. It's Saturday—what if they are closed? Entering, I find the offices empty but manage to contact Snyder on the phone (since all Embassy personnel live in the same building). He comes down to greet me, shakes my hand. After the interview, he advises me to come in first thing Monday.

5

French Champagne

Lee was so afraid of being arrested for trying to get to Moscow that he kept analyzing his situation, said Marina. He used to write down each item he thought about so that he could cover all possible points.

In July, having made his final decision, he still did not even know if he could enter the American Embassy without being stopped by Russian guards. She would ask herself later whether he was more worried about the Soviets not letting him leave or about the Americans locking him up for giving secrets away. Marina was frightened, too. She expected him to be caught for traveling without a permit.

All the same, nothing could stop him. He had said to her, "One more winter in Russia and I am going to die."

So much was happening at once. On the same day, July 8, that he left for Moscow, there was a call for her at the pharmacy. A voice said, "Marina, this is Leonya." A voice from her past. "What are you doing tonight?" asked the voice. It belonged to Leonid Gelfant, her elegant friend, the young architect whom she had seen maybe a total of six times before she met Lee. She asked, "Why are you calling? You know I'm married." He said, "It's Saturday; I thought I'd call." She said, "It happens that my husband's away. And I'm not doing anything. I'm just going to go home from work, take a shower, be at home." He said, "Would you have dinner with me? I have some French champagne." Then, he added that he was staying for a few days at a friend's fine apartment while the friend was away and it would be nice to see her in such an environment.

She fixed herself up, and they saw a movie. Then, they went to his friend's apartment. She had decided she was going to test some waters. Maybe she didn't love Lee. Maybe one reason for seeing Leonid Gelfant is that she was afraid of going to America. So, maybe she was wondering if this old boyfriend was still a possibility: She liked Leonid, he was Jewish, he had wonderful manners. Maybe if he loved her enough, she would divorce Lee. By the end of the evening, however, she had to tell the man that it was still too early for him to get married.

She felt dirty. So full of shame. She ran home. How, she kept asking herself, could I have betrayed Lee? When she reached her own apartment, she nearly threw up. There she was on her knees in their bathroom. Even now she does not like to recall that day, "although time, the bitter medicine, is the best medicine," she said to her interviewers.

Leonid could admit it, he was not really all that concerned that Marina was married. More important was that she was charming on this occasion, warm and tender, and they had nothing negative between them, no bad memories to keep. And they certainly didn't talk about continuing this situation. Indeed, he thought that might harm her. After all he, personally, was not interested in going with her, and so he did not ask personal questions, and didn't learn that she was pregnant. When she became sad—not at all untypical of her—this was his usual Marina. Leonid didn't feel that she thought she had made a mistake.

Reminded of her parting remark that it might be still too early for him to marry, he replied that since she now had a sexual relationship with Lee, she was perhaps more experienced than himself. However, she hadn't said anything insulting. Indeed, he didn't feel she treated him unkindly. He was very green in those days and had just started his own sex life. She was a great help.

He never rushed into sex with women. He liked to meet them emotionally, so to speak. He even went to the Caucasus with one woman and still didn't have sex. He had remained very romantic and was looking for his princess, that person who could satisfy his intellectual point of view and his emotional point of view, Mrs. Right for Mr. Right. That was why Marina could never stay in his life.

Traveler's Qualms

AIR POUCH   OFFICIAL USE ONLY

Foreign Service Dispatch   July 11, 1961
FROM: Amembassy, Moscow   Dept. No. 29
TO: The Department of State, Washington
SUBJECT: Citizenship and Passports: Lee Harvey Oswald

Lee Harvey OSWALD appeared at the Embassy on July 8 on his own initiative in connection with his desire to return to the United States with his wife.

Oswald . . . was questioned at length concerning his activities since entering the Soviet Union. No evidence was revealed of any act on his part which might have caused loss of American citizenship. He exhibited Soviet internal "stateless" passport . . . No. 311479 . . . which is *prima facie* evidence that he is regarded by the Soviet authorities as not possessing Soviet citizenship. Oswald stated that despite the wording of the statement which he handed to the Embassy on October 31, 1959 . . . he never in fact actually applied for Soviet citizenship . . .

Oswald stated that he has never been called upon to make any statements for radio or press or to address audiences since his arrival in the Soviet Union and that he has made no statements at any time of any exploitable nature concerning his original decision to reside in the Soviet Union . . . When queried about a statement which he had made to the interviewing officer on October 31, 1959, to the effect that he would willingly make available to the Soviet Union such information as he had acquired as a radar operator in the Marine Corps, Oswald stated that he was never in fact subjected to any questioning or briefing by the Soviet authorities concerning his life or experience prior to entering the Soviet Union, and never provided such information to any Soviet organ. He stated that he doubted in fact that he would have given such information if requested despite his statements made at the Embassy.

Oswald indicated some anxiety as to whether, should he return to the United States, he would face possible lengthy imprisonment for his act of remaining in the Soviet Union. Oswald was told informally that the Embassy did not perceive, on the basis of information in its possession, on what grounds he might be subject to conviction leading to punishment of such severity as he apparently had in mind. It was clearly stated to him, however, that the Embassy could give him no [complete] assurance . . . Oswald said he understood this. He had simply felt that in his own interest he could not go back to the United States if it meant returning to a number of years in prison, and had delayed approaching the Soviet authorities . . . until he "had this end of the thing straightened out."

Oswald was married on April 30, 1961, to Marina Niko-laevna PRUSAKOVA, a dental technician. He is attempting to arrange for his wife to join him in Moscow so that she can appear at the Embassy for a visa interview in the next day or two.

Oswald intends to institute an application for an exit visa immediately upon his return to Minsk within the next few days. His American passport was returned to him for this purpose after having been amended to be valid for direct return to the United States only . . . it was felt that there was little prospect that Oswald could accomplish anything with the Soviet officials concerned unless he displayed his American passport . . .

Twenty months of the realities of life in the Soviet Union have clearly had a maturing effect on Oswald. He stated frankly that he had learned a hard lesson the hard way and that he had been completely relieved of his illusions about the Soviet Union at the same time that he acquired a new understanding and appreciation of the United States and the meaning of freedom. Much of the arrogance and bravado which characterized him on his first visit to the Embassy appears to have left him . . .[1]

July 9
Receive passport, call Marina to Moscow also.

July 14
I and Marina return to Minsk.

July 15
Marina, at work, is shocked to find out [that] everyone knows she entered the U.S. Embassy. They were called at her place of work by some [Soviet] officials in Moscow. The bosses hold a meeting and give her a strong browbeating, the first of many indoctrinations.

TO: American Embassy, Moscow
July 15, 1961

Dear Sirs,

As per your instructions I am writing to inform you of the process and progress of our visas.

We have approached the local "OVIR" office and the results are not discouraging. However there have been some unusual and crude attempts on my wife at her place of work. While we were still in Moscow, the foremen at her place of work were notified that she and I went into the Embassy for the purpose of visas. Then there followed the usual "enemy of the people" meeting, in which, in her absence, she was condemned and her friends at work warned against speaking with her. However, these tactics are quite useless, and my wife stood up well, without getting into trouble.

We are continuing the process and will keep you informed as to the overall picture.

Sincerely yours,
Lee H. Oswald[2]

FROM KGB TRANSCRIPTS
FOR OBJECT: OLH-2658
FOR PERIOD: 17 JULY 1961

[In these transcripts, OLH (Oswald, Lee Harvey) has been changed to LHO. Marina was always referred to as WIFE. Stepan underlined those speeches he considered pertinent to his needs, whereas any comments that appear in italics as stage directions were made by the KGB transcriber. That worthy was making his (or her) observations through a peephole in a rented room adjacent to the Oswalds' apartment.]

LHO: I can't tell you what to do. Do what you want to do. If you want, you can go with me.

WIFE: I don't want to.

LHO: Why?

WIFE: I'm simply afraid.

LHO: Of course you're afraid.

WIFE: I don't know America, I only know Russia . . . You can go back to your own people . . . I don't know how things will be there. <u>Where will you find work?</u>

LHO: I'll find everything, everything. I'll do everything. That's my job.

WIFE: How will they treat me there?

(*radio drowns out conversation; impossible to get in entirety*)

FROM KGB TRANSCRIPTS
FOR OBJECT: OLH-2658
FOR PERIOD: 19 JULY 1961

WIFE: All you know how to do is torture . . .

(*LHO goes out; yells something from the kitchen*)

WIFE: Go find yourself a girl who knows how to cook . . . I work, I don't have time to prepare cutlets for you. You don't want soup, you don't want kasha, just tasty tidbits, please!

LHO: I can go eat at a restaurant.

WIFE: Go to hell! When are you ever going to leave me alone? I'll probably never live to see the day when you leave me alone.

LHO: But you don't know how to do anything.

WIFE: Leave me alone!

   She bumped into Misha Smolsky once on the street, and he asked her how she was doing with her man, and she answered, "Very difficult." Misha said, "If it is difficult, why did you jump into it?" She said, "No, he's not a bad guy, but food is very difficult." At that time, in shops there was a lot to buy, but what do people in Minsk eat, after all?—potatoes, pork fat, pickled cucumbers, pickled cabbage, beef, pork, mutton, turkey, goose. She wasn't able to buy food he would like. For instance, Alik would say, "I want to have corn," and any corn they grew around there was for livestock. So she said to Misha Smolsky, "Let's say we have cultural difficulties."

FROM KGB TRANSCRIPTS
FOR OBJECT: OLH-2658
FOR PERIOD: 21 JULY 1961

LHO: Well, why are you crying? (*pause*) I told you crying won't do any good.

(*Wife cries*)

You know, I never said that I was a very good person.

(*Wife cries and LHO calms her down*)

WIFE: (*through tears*) <u>Why did I get married?</u> You tricked me.

LHO: . . . You shouldn't cry. I understand, you don't understand yourself why.

WIFE: (*through tears*) My friends don't recognize me.

LHO: Well? I've also lost weight, right?

WIFE: (*cries*) <u>Why did I get married?</u>

LHO: Well, what am I supposed to do? Is it my fault that you have a lot of work? I mean, you don't ever cook, but other women cook. And I don't say anything about it. I don't yell. You never do anything and you don't want to do the wash. What do you do? The only thing you ever talk about is how tired you are at work.

WIFE: I didn't get any rest.

LHO: Well, what can I do?

(*pause*)

WIFE: Everything was so good, but lately everything has gotten bad, nothing's right. You can't please <u>a man like you.</u>

(*they are silent*)

Later that night

LHO: Well, what? This is ridiculous!

WIFE: I want to sleep, don't bother me! . . . <u>You're so crude!</u> I'm tired, I swear, I'm tired.

LHO: And what did you do that you're so tired? <u>You didn't do anything. You didn't cook anything.</u>

WIFE: The cafeteria's good enough.

LHO: And who's going to wash the shirts, the socks?

WIFE: Everything's already washed, go and take a look. You'll leave and then you'll be unhappy alone, you'll see. So get off my back. What is it you want from me, anyway, what? For God's sake, just don't torture me. Soon enough you won't have me, and that's all there is to it.

(*pause*)

WIFE: You're laughing, but you'll cry later . . . (*pause*) I don't want to now. I'm tired.

LHO: What did you do that you're tired?

WIFE: Don't throw things around . . .

LHO: What can I do? (*mocks Wife*) "I don't want to!" Well, what can I say! We're going to be here four or five months anyway.

WIFE: I'll be here. Let the baby stay by itself.

LHO: Are you crazy!? (*yells*) You should be ashamed! A child without a father! You should be ashamed! (*laughs*) <u>You're still my wife, you're going!</u> And if I leave, I'll send you an invitation.

WIFE: You'll leave on your own.

LHO: You should be ashamed! You don't believe yourself what you're saying . . .

WIFE: I'm not going to promise. If I don't go then that's it.

LHO: You're my wife, you're going.

WIFE: No.

LHO: Why?

WIFE: I know why.

LHO: Well, why? You don't know yourself. There, you see. Do you know how many foreigners live there?

WIFE: <u>They won't take me there, and they won't create the conditions for me, they won't create them. The American Embassy won't look after me.</u>

LHO: <u>Why do you think that? I mean, I wrote that I was obligating myself.</u> [Note in left margin: "Obviously, he is obligating himself to provide her with everything she needs in United States."] You understand that you're my wife and that you're going with me. <u>When I arrived here it was difficult for me too.</u>

WIFE: That is an entirely different matter.

LHO: <u>But I'm obligating myself! I'll do everything.</u>

(*pause*)

WIFE: You won't convince me.

(*pause*)

LHO: You're just stubborn.

WIFE: And you're always yelling. (*radio drowns out conversation*)

When Inessa met Lee Oswald, he seemed not exactly unfriendly, but very suspicious about things. They exchanged a few words and then he sat down in a chair and became completely occupied with some comic books his brother had sent him from America. Inessa spent her time chatting with Marina.

After a few more visits, however, Alik's suspicions began fading away. Before long, Inessa was eating with them in their kitchen. Indeed, she even liked it that he hadn't become open right away but had waited and observed. She thinks she probably wouldn't have believed him if, immediately, he had been too friendly. In fact, she liked him as a husband for Marina. He did all the man's work around their apartment without needing reminders. Which is not too often true of Russian men.

What she wasn't so comfortable with was that all of a sudden he would announce what he liked about the Soviet Union and what he didn't like, and he would do it in the open—never whispering. And there were other little things. She really couldn't say that she approved of him entirely, even if they were only small things. He would carry on if dinner wasn't cooked on time, and in her opinion, Marina didn't fit into his American standards of what a wife should be. When they had fights, Inessa saw them as children, one more stubborn than the other. She liked them both and was comfortable with both, and—maybe she was just lucky—in her presence they never had any really big arguments. She does remember that Marina would get irritated when Alik would read his American comic books and begin to laugh loudly. On the other hand, Marina thought he was too pedantic and told Inessa that she was dissatisfied with his mind.

He also had bad habits. Like a worker or a crude soldier. He was always spoiling the air with gases. That was shocking, and he did it as naturally as drinking water.

All the same, Inessa always felt that Alik was more calm than Marina. Outside of those gases, he was very organized. He liked perfection in everything, and Marina used to complain about this trait. Taken all together, Inessa never really thought that Marina was deeply in love with him. She thinks Alik loved her more.

FROM KGB TRANSCRIPTS
FOR OBJECT: OLH-2658
FOR PERIOD: 24 JULY 1961

21:20

WIFE: Alik! Look, I forgot to iron the bedsheets—there's one lying over there. Alik! Look how warm my ears are.

(*they joke around; they laugh*)

LHO: Not bad songs they're singing.

WIFE: There's some festival going on. Everyone's going to Moscow and people can say what they want. Before, you couldn't say anything: not on the street, not on the streetcar, not on the trolley. When Stalin was alive there was a microphone in every house and you couldn't say anything. Nowadays it's a different matter.

LHO: Yes, yes, my sister.

FROM KGB TRANSCRIPTS
FOR OBJECT: OLH-2658
FOR PERIOD: 26 JULY 1961

LHO: So, there was a meeting?

WIFE: Yes, there was a meeting.

LHO: Where?

WIFE: In our clinic.

(*pause*)

You see, they would have been satisfied if I had said, no, I'm not going, I won't leave [my] Motherland. Never tell them any truth. Really, I shouldn't have said anything at all. I should have said that my position was such that I don't know what to do.

LHO: And what did they say?

WIFE: They said that I was rude . . . So, I said, I don't need a good reference, I don't care . . . <u>I'll go with a bad reference if necessary.</u> I told them that I wasn't such a criminal. I told them that I love pharmacy girls a lot as girlfriends and that I'm not a bad friend and that I would give everything for the girls because they're simple, good girls. (*pause*) I came right out with it. If you don't like me, I don't like you—no skin off my back.

LHO: And you . . . (*doesn't finish his sentence*)

WIFE: . . . They're going to kick me out . . . They said people like you don't belong in Komsomol, that you should be expelled. I said that was fine, I'm very happy . . . Why don't you want to [be a member of Komsomol?] They asked me a million times. Well, because I don't like it, because it's boring. And why didn't you say so earlier? Because I didn't want people to think I was different . . . I said a lot of things I probably shouldn't have, but I couldn't hold back. [They asked] what do you think of Komsomol? I answer Komsomol is Komsomol. (*pause*) Actually, I'm an anti-Soviet element. Let's make it easier for them.

(*pause*)

And then, you know, he asks me what's your relationship to this man you went to Moscow with? And someone else says that it's her husband.

LHO: (*laughs*)

WIFE: And who is your husband, what sort of person is he? I say you better ask MVD. And why MVD if we can ask you? And I say, because I might not tell you . . .

LHO: They know the most important thing is that I want to leave.

WIFE: He longs for his homeland, I told them, everyone longs for their homeland. But didn't you try to convince him to stay here? No, I say. Then . . . I say, I don't think it'll be better there, not because I'm looking for something better. I'm just going with my husband. It's possible it'll be worse there . . . I say, you know, I haven't been there and you haven't been there, so how can we express an opinion? . . .

(*pause*)

I said that I wouldn't leave my husband. He's a good person and I'm satisfied with him . . . he's more dear to me than their opinion . . . I behaved rudely, very rudely. I said, what are you going to do, confront people who gave me good references and yell at them? . . . I ask that you not persecute them . . . Better to reprimand me . . .

"We respect you, we love you," they said. "You won't have friends like us there," they say. And I say, "I don't want to have friends like that. I see how much you love me."

LHO: Don't worry, everything will be fine . . .

(*pause*)

WIFE: <u>The most important thing now is leaving.</u>

LHO: I know that—we're leaving, no need for scandals . . .

(*pause*)

WIFE: Don't look for truth, you'll never find it anyway. I was told that by my mother . . .

LHO: Everything will be fine.

WIFE: You think so?

(*pause*)

WIFE: Why do I feel sad? My husband isn't throwing me out of the house.

LHO: I love you.

WIFE: That's what you say now, but afterward you'll say that you don't love me.

LHO: Your husband loves you . . .

Marina's friend Sonya was, of course, a member of Komsomol. That was practically automatic. They have a saying: You are born, go to school, become a Pioneer, become Komsomol. Like everyone else.

According to Sonya, it was not so big a matter, however, to be excluded from Komsomol. You can ignore it. If Marina had changed her mind and decided to stay in the Soviet Union, it wouldn't have been a bad mark in her life. It was not like being excluded from the Communist Party—that's serious. But Komsomol—you're a young person. Everybody thinks maybe you made a mistake, you slipped a little bit. Marina's main worry, Sonya thinks, was whether she was making a right decision or a wrong one about going to America. Komsomol was not so important. After all, Komsomol had a rule that whenever you go to a foreign country, you are not a member anymore. You give it up. This organization did not want members in another country. Could cause international trouble.

From KGB Transcripts
For Object: OLH-2658
For Period: 29 July 1961

(*LHO kisses her*)

LHO: Come here, lie down.

(*quiet*)

19:40

WIFE: My God, your pants are so wrinkled.

LHO: It's been a while since you ironed them.

WIFE: Four days ago.

LHO: A week.

WIFE: So? You could wear them for a week [but] you lie around in them.

LHO: Take it easy . . .

WIFE: You're so wicked! (*squeals*) It's true what they say about men not having any brains until they're thirty. (*laughs*) Ay! . . . (*laughter*) What did you do?

(*they go to bed*)

LHO: Don't touch me, damn you.

WIFE: No, damn you. In a minute I'm going to cut off a particular place. Oy, mama.

(*they laugh*)

(*they talk about pregnancy; Wife tells about conversation with her doctor*)

WIFE: When the baby first starts moving, it'll be exactly half of my term. Give or take one or two days. Why does it seem to me that everything smells—my clothes, pillow, blanket? I look so horrible. We all look horrible in last months [of pregnancy]. And if I'm dying, who will save me? I have narrow hipbones.

LHO: Me.

WIFE: The medical profession won't help, but you will.

LHO: Be a composed lady. You're a lady. The very first day you became a lady. Good night. That's all.

(*they are silent*)

23:00

Tamara Alexandrovna, who was den mother to their pharmacy and knew everything about every girl's personal life, was approached: Marina asked, "Tamara, would you go to America with your husband or not?" She and Yanina and others discussed it. Many of them were newly married—so Marina would hear advice of this sort: "Listen, I know my husband," one girl would say, "and with my husband I'll go to America. Do you know your husband well enough to go there? That's your question." They told her: You should analyze your situation. You work in a socialist country; you're going to a capitalist country. They have their culture, their habits. Can you cope with it? If you think you are able, okay, but it's your decision. Yanina knew she didn't want to take responsibility for giving more advice than that, but maybe Marina had already made her own decision.

When Komsomol excluded her, nobody thought about that for too long. What else could Komsomol do? And who cared? It was no big deal to be kicked out. The only reason people belonged was because you couldn't *not* belong to it.

Valya was the only relative, said Inessa, who would visit Marina once she admitted that she was trying to go to America with Lee. None of Ilya's sisters ever did, nor did Ilya. Valya was the only person who visited.

As for her situation at work, there, too, were problems, Inessa recalls. After Komsomol tried to talk her out of it, they spoke of whether Lee might be an American spy. She told them to mind their own business. Maybe her hard days in Leningrad had left an imprint, but she could carry herself with a certain authority; she wouldn't let anybody lower her self-esteem.

Still, Komsomol kept her from getting a raise. She was not promoted and her feelings were definitely hurt.

If she had been in Marina's situation, Inessa believes she would not have wanted to stay in Russia any longer, either. The system hadn't been fair with her.

On the Observation of Intimate Moments

Pavel always felt there was something in Marina's face that was like Erich's expression—calculating. But Pavel would rather say that he wasn't prepared for Marina. He didn't even meet her until the wedding, and then he didn't take to her at first.

Maybe Pavel saw her twenty times altogether, and he looked at her as a friend's wife, nothing more. Whatever she was as a woman did not interest him. He had no hate for her; he just looked at her as a sheet for his friend's bed. That was an expression he had learned at Horizon. His factory, maybe because there were so many Jews in it, was considered to be the most humorous plant in Minsk. Certainly, tractor factories and military factories were nothing like that, but then, Jews who wanted to work in such places couldn't get in.

Pavel never saw Lee become very angry with Marina, but Oswald didn't like it at all when his new wife lit a cigarette. So, whenever Pavel and Marina were out on the balcony together, Pavel used to hold one in his hand for her. That was to make it look as if Pavel were smoking, not her. He could say she inhaled as lightly and delicately as a yogi.

Soon after Lee and Marina were married, Pavel was getting ready to visit his parents in Khabarovsk, and Stepan had a meeting with him. "Tell Oswald," said Stepan, "that your father works on big deals as Air Force General. See if he will be interested."

The next time, when Stepan asked for Oswald's response, Pavel said, "He just didn't react at all."

Oswald had, in fact, ignored Pavel's remark, but Marina said, "Oh! Why are you saying that to him?" And Pavel knew then that she understood a game was being played and that Pavel was a cog. He didn't know if she was very quick or whether this news about his father had just been more interesting to her than to Lee.

All the same, Pavel would say that he was not an active informant for the Organs. He never gave a written report, he never signed anything, and he did his best to be minimal with his Organ bosses when he did have to report. Pavel even told Lee not to talk too much with *anyone*. Then he added, "I'm telling you this, but *other* people might not." He couldn't allow himself to get more specific than that.

During all of this year and more, Pavel had to have meetings with Stepan, usually on the street or in a park. Now, Pavel thinks it might have been better if he had told his father about his situation, because he knew that sooner or later KGB would approach his father. Pavel could hear some lowly officer from KGB, some Lieutenant or Captain, saying, "So, General, what do you think of your son?"

Pavel didn't have any patriotism; he just felt like filth. That was why he warned Oswald about it. He knew there was someone else, another source of information, closer and more reliable, that KGB was using for Oswald, but this other source wouldn't confess it to Lee.

The interviewers could not find out when Lee's apartment had first been wired. The earliest transcripts they would receive from the KGB were dated mid-July, which was just after Oswald returned from his trip to the American Embassy. The question, however, remained open. Had Oswald's apartment been bugged in early March of 1960, prior to his moving in, or at some other period before July 1961? It is also possible, since the daily labor consequent upon bugging was an expensive item in their budget, that the local KGB, having close human sources in place, did not install equipment until those four days in July when both Oswald and his wife were in Moscow.

In conversations with his interviewers, Igor did say that after Likhoi was married, it became crucial to learn all they could about Marina's character. Was she a type of person to obtain secrets from her uncle and pass them on to Oswald?

When installing a bug, the Organs would often rent a room in an apartment above or next door to their target. That was usually not too difficult, since people always had rooms for rent in a larger apartment. In Oswald's case, conversations were transcribed from a chamber above his apartment, and later, such equipment was moved to a room next door. If the Organs had been able to rent an entire apartment above Lee rather than a single room, they would have bugged the bathroom, kitchen, and balcony—all three. But they did not have that kind of access.

As for being able to observe people visually, that was no longer difficult by 1961. A hole less than a two hundred fiftieth of an inch, less, that is, than one tenth of a millimeter, was made and a special lens inserted, a most useful tool thirty years ago—an early use of fiber optics. At that time, it was their "greatest weapon," because it provided a good deal of information.

For example, knowledge started to come in to Igor and Stepan that Marina had a low opinion of Lee as a partner. Still, their relationship was interesting. They got married and now they were going to have a child. Was their reason love, or was it Oswald's desire for better cover? This was one question Counterintelligence had to determine. If, in the course of going back to his native country, Oswald all of a sudden divorced his family and left without them, that would put the Organs on guard. Was it that he had completed his work and was now running away? But no—this man wanted his wife to go with him. That caused many suppositions to fall away. Studying the character of Oswald's marriage reduced anxieties for Igor and Stepan.

FROM KGB TRANSCRIPT
FOR PERIOD: 26 JULY 1961

9:50 P.M.	(*LHO goes into the kitchen; comes back*)
10:10 P.M.	(*they go to bed*)
10:15 P.M.	(*intimate conversation*)
10:30 P.M.	(*quiet; they are sleeping*)
11:00 P.M.	(*surveillance ends*)

Stepan was asked if it was KGB policy to discontinue bugging at 11:00 P.M., since people usually went to bed then. He replied that this type of measure could be conducted around the clock or for only a few hours. A matter of operative expediency.

Nor was there a set policy about recording intimate moments. Usually, a KGB transcriber would state that such an action had occurred, but would not give details. It goes without saying that each developer had the major responsibility for such decisions. It depended on what he was looking to analyze. Stepan, for one, preferred to avoid this sort of thing. "But assume I am CIA or FBI and I am trying to recruit a Soviet engineer. I would have to look for compromising materials on him, first and foremost sexual things. Working as an analyst on such a case, I give this order: 'Take down everything in the most detailed manner possible. All sexual processes. Take photographs. So on.' Everything depends on which goal is being pursued."

In Lee Harvey Oswald's case, sexual details were not necessary. "If he and Marina said something of interest, let our transcriber take it down, but if Oswald and Marina are just making love, a person listening or looking through our device would write no more than 'intimate, tender moments.' " In fact, Stepan did not relish these personal occasions. Why irritate higher-ups who have to read it? But if something said is significant, well, his transcribers wouldn't miss that—it goes without saying. If, for example, subjects start, during lovemaking, to speak about important matters, that would be mentioned. Stepan recalls nothing significant, however, being noted during Oswald's case.

All the same, they had to take some note of it. "The process of surveillance has to consider our target in all spheres. Afterward, we can decide that the sexual aspects of this person are not interesting. But first we have to receive a total volume of information so we can select what we need." The FBI and KGB both do it that way, Stepan pointed out. In Oswald's case, the sexual part could have been a factor. "It was important to know whether this person got married because he is in love or whether he is using it as a cover. His sexual relations could also indicate if he is an agent looking for information. Everything has to be considered."

Alik and Marina were sure the Organs were bugging them. "Yeah," says Marina now, thinking about it. "We'd become like two kids. Nothing or nobody is going to stop us. I was his ally all the way through. Just for the damn principle of it." Once, when all lights were off in their apartment, they examined their electricity meter with a flashlight. The needle was still moving. That was when Lee said, "They bug our apartment." Maybe he was just playing some game with her, making it dramatic. But if they wanted to talk, they did go out to their balcony or turned on their radio. Especially so they wouldn't jeopardize any persons they were talking about— Pavel or the Zigers or whoever, Valya, Ilya, whoever. Still, it did not become part of her life. If she wanted to talk to Lee, she did not always go out on that balcony. Because, really, there was nothing to hide. The most horrible thing, you would expect, was that maybe somebody was recording them in bed. Yet, and it sounds stupid, they weren't all that concerned about it—isn't that funny? But if they wanted to discuss something about their upcoming trip to America, they would go out to the balcony. Maybe she was just blocking out everything about this "intimacy part," but as she remembers, she didn't mind all that much if someone was listening. Maybe it was because they didn't make love as frequently in those months of pregnancy.

Pavel knew that Lee's apartment was wired. He couldn't say exactly how he knew; probably, it was intuition reinforced by experience. Stepan, after all, knew certain things about Lee he could have learned only by such methods, and hints of such knowledge came out when he met with Pavel to give instructions on what questions to ask next. So, Oswald's apartment had to be bugged.

Not his balcony, however. Pavel calculated that it would be difficult to disguise a microphone out on a naked balcony. Moreover, cars would be passing, and there would be wind and interference from birds. From detective stories, you would have believed that the Organs had enough technology to put a miniature microphone in a button on a shirt, but that is very expensive.

All the same, they were always there. Or so it felt. Pavel, when talking to Lee, would not allow himself to get curious. He didn't want to gain any information he would have to divulge or else not be serving his Motherland.

8

Doing the Floor

When speaking to the interviewers, Stepan always put his emphasis on the more efficient aspects of security activities. He did not dwell on lapses. Whatever impediments might hinder good transcription were not going to be discussed by him. Reviewing those particular transcripts that the KGB did provide, it is, however, hard to suppose that we are in the presence of advanced technology. As was often indicated by their transcriber, the sound was poor and Oswald's radio was usually on. Indeed, he often had to yell above it for Marina to hear. Since it was summer, there were frequent visits to their balcony, and from there nothing could be heard, while the sounds of running water are what is picked up most often from the kitchen.

Add to this that there might be unprofessional fatigue visiting that KGB auditor in the next room, even periods, conceivably, of dozing off: One is left for the most part with a portrait of two young married people who argue with each other so fiercely and—for all we can make out—so pointlessly that an impulse arises to compose a one-act play—*Newlyweds*.

INTERVIEWER: Did you ever fight over washing the floors?

MARINA: No.

INTERVIEWER: Would he ever complain about the floors?

MARINA: I don't remember . . . but I don't think so.

INTERVIEWER: Did you ever argue about cleaning the house?

MARINA: We probably argued about even the cats scratching the roof.

FROM KGB TRANSCRIPT
FOR OBJECT: OLH-2658
FOR PERIOD: 3 AUG. 1961

18:24 (*they enter room*)

WIFE: (*yells*) I'm tired of everything! And what about you? Can't you wash? I suppose you want me to wash floors every day?

LHO: Yes, wash these floors every day!

WIFE: You don't do anything and I'm supposed to spend all day cleaning up. A decent man would help. Remember you used to say: I'll help! You did wash once, and now you talk about it endlessly, and I wash our clothes every time and it doesn't count for anything . . .

LHO: You have to make something to eat!

WIFE: (*yells*) I can't. I'm not going to cook.

LHO: You could make cutlets, put on water for tea. I mean, I bought everything, everything.

WIFE: I won't.

LHO: You haven't done anything.

WIFE: Well, what have you done for me?

LHO: Silence!

WIFE: <u>I'm not going to live with you.</u>

LHO: Thank God!

WIFE: Take a look at yourself! A tidy man! You're twenty times dirtier than I am. Look at your pillow; you sleep on it once and it's already dirty.

LHO: You never do anything!

WIFE: That's right, I just carouse. I carouse with my health.

LHO: You don't do anything.

WIFE: Have you ever cleaned up in this apartment—just once? I've done it twenty-one times. You'll do it and then talk about it all day.

LHO: This house has to be cleaned every day. There's dirt in our kitchen, dirt everywhere. What good is that? You sleep until ten in the morning and you don't do anything. You could be cleaning up during that time.

WIFE: I need my sleep. <u>If you don't like it, you can go to your America.</u>

LHO: (*calmly*) Please, thank you.

WIFE: You're always finding fault; nothing's enough, everything's bad.

LHO: You're ridiculous. Lazy and crude.

WIFE: I want you to feel what it's like to be me for one day. (*after a silence, she begins to cry*)

LHO: Well, what's the problem?

WIFE: Get out! I'm not your housekeeper. Give me proper conditions . . .

LHO: Don't cry. I'm just saying that you don't want to do anything.

WIFE: So? I never washed our floors?

LHO: You're not a good housewife, no, not a good housewife.

WIFE: You should have married a good one . . .

(*they're silent*)

WIFE: . . . If you don't like it, you can go to your America.

LHO: I've told you for a long time that you don't do anything.

WIFE: I wash floors every day.

LHO: It's dirty.

WIFE: What's dirty to you is clean to me. I washed floors yesterday and you walk around in shoes.

LHO: There's dirt and dust because you open our balcony doors.

WIFE: (*yells*) It was closed all day. You don't understand anything.

LHO: <u>Don't cry.</u>

WIFE: Don't you see that I dust each morning?

LHO: You don't clean up over there on our table.

WIFE: Yeah, yeah, I dirty it up. I washed it twice and you never even washed it once.

LHO: Calm your nerves.

WIFE: Just say: "Marina, it has to be done." Don't yell; it's hurtful . . . Alka, do you hate me when you yell at me?

LHO: Yes.

WIFE: Yes?

LHO: Yes.

WIFE: . . . Why are you afraid of people? What scared you?

LHO: (*yells angrily*) Shut up, shut up . . . You stand there and blab.

WIFE: <u>You're afraid of everybody!</u> . . .

LHO: Shut up!

WIFE: Are you afraid that they'll steal everything from you, a pot of gold that you have? (*laughing*) At times like this you could kill me. You have to have some kind of strong will.

LHO: How about some potatoes?

WIFE: They're not ready yet, what can I do?

22:37 (*they go into the kitchen*)

22:40 (*Wife makes LHO wash his feet*)

23:00 (*it's quiet in the room; no conversation*)

It was painful for Yuri Merezhinsky to see this marriage. Alik had a good apartment, quite acceptable if you were a single man. No matter if Yuri's English was good or bad, he was going to tell interviewers everything in English. He had talent for English and he could say that he was there in this apartment before, and after. Before marriage, bright. After marriage, gray.

He remembers Marina in her living room, and she is bent over. Like a crab. She washes her floor. Her ass is higher than her shoulders, like a crab.

Yuri is drunk, but he is not out of command of his drinking. He will go on drinking. He will go on telling them what he can. No longer fluent in English, he will say. Once was.

The interviewers tried to talk to him about Lee and Marina's wedding. He said: "Nobody who fucked Marina was invited to wedding. If Alik knew she was fucking around, he would never marry. But then, in every family, man is equal to head and woman is equal to neck—neck turns head whichever way it wants." He, Yuri, could say that he was fucking Marina.

Before marriage?

Before marriage, after marriage. No question. Everybody knows.

In sex, when together, he and Marina—no problem, Yuri would say. They didn't have any—how do you say?—prejudice; they were not ashamed. Tried to satisfy each other—that's it.

He does not remember his conversations with Marina. "We talked nonsense. She was happy with me, otherwise why would she visit? She was not interested in relationship, just sex."

How was Alik in bed, he did not know. That could be described only by a woman. But on outside, Alik was never aggressive. Yuri would give examples. Once, in Oswald's bachelor days, somebody grabbed Alik by his shirt. There, right on the street. Yuri saved him. Alik could not defend himself. Couldn't even hit somebody. Yuri would defend him many times. On the street, people came up to them and said, "Give me something to drink. Put a bottle on my table." They knew Lee had money. In those days, you could buy alcohol until midnight. So, they would come and say, "Alik, buy a drink, put something on our table." Alik wouldn't say yes or no. Yuri would respond. Alik couldn't even raise his hand to defend himself, but Yuri hit this guy who was asking. Straight in his face. At that time, Yuri could say, he was good fighter. Russian word for wimp is *sleeznyak,* a jelly. Not true for Oswald, said Yuri. Lee was not one to round off a sharp corner, but he was not *sleeznyak.* It's just that Yuri was boss of situation such as this. Even now he was not afraid to meet and talk to interviewers. At that time, he was stronger. Because he was young. Strong, but that does not matter. If you don't have brains, it don't matter how strong— consider yourself an invalid. But he had brains and he was strong.

Behind his shoulders, behind his back, were his mother and his father. KGB and MVD were somewhere far away. Nobody could scare him then. He could hit anybody in their face. But Alik could not afford it. Different situation for Alik.

He could say that his parents were against this friendship with Lee. They said, "He's a foreigner. We would prefer that you don't have meetings with him." They said it could damage their careers. And they were worried about Yuri's future, too. His mother might be friends with Khrushchev, but she did not consider herself untouchable. Yuri disagreed. His mother and father worried a lot, but they were so high that they, in fact, *were* untouchable. His behavior could damage his life, not theirs.

After Alik's marriage, changes in this American were like a difference between earth and sky. After marriage, Oswald was *zabitiy,* which means somebody beats you, beats you, beats you, until you are beaten down. *Zabitiy.* There's Marina in middle of her new apartment washing the floor, washing with her ass high like a very low peasant woman. This is how Yuri remembers her after marriage. She turns to Alik and says, "Get out of here; you disturb my washing."

But, Yuri was asked, if they both changed so much, what kept them together? "Who," Yuri replied, "was kept, and who was keeping? This is your question. Answer is that this relationship was saved because she wanted to go to America. But what kind of marriage? They had one fold-up bed. Who can fuck in fold-up bed? No family life inside. No love. It all depends on your woman. If she wanted, she would not have such a bed. She would change it. Such things rely on your wife. Before marriage, Alik's apartment was bright. After, gray. What else can be said?" said Yuri.

FROM KGB TRANSCRIPTS
FOR OBJECT: OLH-2658
FOR PERIOD: 11 AUGUST 1961

LHO: If you don't love me, then how can you live with me? I give and will give you every opportunity . . . What do you want? One minute you say you want to leave, next minute you don't want to leave.

WIFE: <u>Sometimes I'm just afraid of going with you</u> . . . I don't want to try to prove to you that everything here is great, and everything there is bad. But . . . <u>if here I don't have anything and won't have anything, it's home.</u>

LHO: You'll never have anything here, but over there you'll have your husband and everything.

WIFE: . . . What will I do there? I'll sit at home the whole time and that's it.

LHO: . . . <u>But you're going to live with me there. You'll have everything.</u>

WIFE: I'm not looking for material advantages. Money doesn't interest me. It's not important. Most important thing is how you treat me.

LHO: Ah, well, then everything is in order.

WIFE: <u>I don't have any guarantee that you won't abandon me there.</u> Then what do I do? . . .

LHO: If you don't love me, then don't go.

WIFE: No, I'm afraid you're abandoning me . . . You're leaving, after all.

LHO: I'm leaving?!

WIFE: See, you're already yelling, and what will it be like later? . . .

LHO: . . . What do you have here? One room. Is that so much? One room, and even that isn't yours.

WIFE: We live here, it's ours.

LHO: You think it's mine? I don't sense that it's my own . . . I don't get any feeling it's mine.

(*pause*)

WIFE: You torture me . . .

LHO: I hate it when you're the way you are now. I say one thing and you say another.

(*pause*)

WIFE: Sleep peacefully.

LHO: How can I sleep peacefully if I don't know what you think? With you, everything depends on your mood. We have to decide one way or the other once and for all . . .

WIFE: Idiot, you don't understand anything. (*mimics him*) Property, property.

LHO: You don't understand this concept of property. You don't know yourself what you want. <u>I want to live there because the standard of living is high.</u>

WIFE: And did you think that you would come here and you wouldn't have to work and you'd just live? <u>Why didn't you study? You could study, you're just lazy.</u>

LHO: You don't understand anything. People leave this country by the millions. Here are crude people . . .

WIFE: <u>You look at us through dark glasses.</u>

LHO: What dark glasses? That's not true.

WIFE: I, for instance, don't say bad things about America. It's just not decent . . . You have to be a real pig to say bad things about a country which you don't know. And I don't do that.

LHO: Maybe, but there you'll be living with your husband. <u>The standard of living there is high.</u>

WIFE: You don't get it. It's not my home. I won't hear sound of Russian being spoken . . .

LHO: . . . If you want to go, then go. If not, then don't . . .

WIFE: I won't go . . . I'm afraid . . . Even now when Erich comes over and you speak English, I can't take it . . .

LHO: Oy, you're talking like an old village woman . . .

WIFE: . . . We'll never understand each other . . .

LHO: If you want to, you'll go!

WIFE: Don't yell.

LHO: You're the one who's forcing me to yell. I'm not being coarse with you. You've gotten indecent and bad.

WIFE: You're the one . . .

LHO: No, I was decent and good when I met you. But there was a lot in you that was indecent.

WIFE: I don't see it that way. I didn't even kiss Sasha. No one called me indecent. I didn't act like other girls. I didn't have a mother to put me on the right path. Once a week, I was very wicked.

LHO: I understand.

WIFE: You just have to be moderate in all things. If only I had known!

LHO: This last month you've changed entirely. No tenderness, nothing. If it weren't for your being pregnant . . . (*doesn't finish his sentence*) I can't yell at you in the presence of other people, but you're always saying things about me around other people . . . And then you tell fairy tales about how I'm going away, how I'm leaving you, that everything's my fault. <u>But even so I want you to be with me.</u> I understand that you are the way you are and that you can't be any different than you are. (*pause*) Why do you make yourself out to be so wronged? The most wretched girl in the world! You're talking nonsense.

WIFE: To hell with you!

LHO: Ah, you don't respect me.

WIFE: Alik, we already fought enough. And now you're at it again.

LHO: You weren't this way before.

WIFE: Neither were you.

23:35 (*quiet; they're asleep*)

Marina would say that Alik truly loved Aunt Valya and knew it would be cruel for Valya and Ilya when they went to America, but he had said, "Don't tell your relatives. Not yet."

Of course, her uncle found out. Informed by the Organs. Because of his position.

At Valya's, for dinner, Ilya said, "What is this about leaving Russia?" At his office, Ilya had received a call: "Guess what? Your niece is on her way to America." What a slap in his face! Marina had always been grateful for nice people, and now she had been put in a position where she had to lie to her family. It felt unclean. She had betrayed them.

Sometimes Marina would wonder if Lee thought it would be harder for Americans to arrest him if he came home with a wife and a child. Maybe his mother had told him to bring his Russian along. Since his mother wrote letters to him in English, how could Marina know? She would apologize to Americans, but she did not really like their language. It was much less beautiful to her than Russian.

9

The Queen of Spades

July 15–August 20
We have found out which blanks and certificates are necessary to apply for a visa—they number about twenty papers: birth certificates, photos, affidavits, etc. On August 20th, we give the papers out. They say it will be three and a half months before we know whether they'll let us go or not. In the meantime, Marina has had to make four different meetings at the place of work held by her bosses at the direction of "someone" by phone. Young Communist League [Komsomol] headquarters also called about her and she had to go see them for one and a half hours. The purpose (expressed) is to dissuade her from going to the USA. Net effect: makes her more stubborn about wanting to go. Marina is pregnant; we only hope the visas come through soon.

August 21–September 21
I make expected trips to the passport and visa office, also to Ministry of Foreign Affairs in Minsk, also to Ministry of Internal Affairs, all of which have a say in the granting of a visa . . .

On September 10, he writes a letter to his older brother, Robert, with whom he has been corresponding since he decided to go back to America.

Dear Robert,

Well, apparently I was too optimistic in my last letter . . .

The Russians are holding me up and are giving me some trouble about the visas, so for now I can only wait. In general, for an ordinary Russian, it's impossible to leave the USSR simply because he wants to. However, I and my wife have the possibility because of the fact I am still an American citizen and have the U.S. passport . . .

Robert Lee sounds like he is growing into a fine boy and Cathy is . . . already four years old. It hardly seems possible. I remember when Mother phoned me to say she was born, August 21 or 22. [My outfit was] getting ready to leave for Japan . . . A lot has changed since then!! . . .

Keep writing.

Your brother,
Lee

Enclosed are some views of Minsk.[1]

TO: The American Embassy
Moscow USSR
Oct. 4, 1961

Dear Sirs:

I am hereby requesting the Offices of the American Embassy and the Ambassador of the United States, Mr. Thompson, to act upon my case in regards to my application to the Soviet authorities for an exit visa.

This application was made on July 20, 1961, and although three months have already elapsed, I have not received this visa . . .

I believe there is justification for an official inquiry, directed to the department of "Internal Affairs, Prospekt Stalin 15, Minsk," and the offices of the "address and passport office," Ulitsa Moscova, Colonel Petrakof, Director.

Also, I believe it is doubly important for an official inquiry, since there have been systematic and concerted attempts to intimidate my wife into withdrawing her application for a visa. I have notified the Embassy with regard to these incidents by the local authorities in regard to my wife. These incidents had resulted in my wife's being hospitalized . . . on September 22, 1961, for serious exhaustion . . .

I think it is within the lawful right, and in the interest of, the United States government, and the American Embassy, Moscow, to look into this case on my behalf.

Yours very truly,
Lee H. Oswald[2]

He has instincts on how to set one bureaucracy upon another. Since he can be certain that his letter to the American Embassy will be read first by the "local authorities," he is allowing them to contemplate the consequences of a complaint by the State Department. Of course, if he is engaging in a war of nerves, it can be said that Marina is one of the first to suffer, and soon she decides to visit an aunt in Kharkhov during her three-week vacation from the pharmacy.

Oct. 14

Dear Marina,

I was very glad to receive your letter today. I was also glad to learn that everything is all right with you at Aunt Polina's.

I hope you dress well because it is already very cold here.

While you are in Kharkhov, of course I am very lonesome, but I see Erich often and I also go to the movies . . .

Weather here is cold and wind is cold too.

I eat at the automat after work or at the factory dining room.

Well, enough for the present! Please write! (I received your telegram also on Tuesday.)

I kiss you,
Alik[3]

His letter of October 14 may not be as cold as the weather but it is certainly lukewarm. On October 18, however, he sees his favorite opera *The Queen of Spades,* and Pushkin and Tchaikovsky succeed in bringing him back to love. He even jots down some Russian fragments of one aria. In the translation offered by the Warren Commission, the words come forth in impassioned bursts:

Act 2 "Queen of Spades"

I love you, love you immeasurably. I cannot imagine life without you. I am ready right now to perform a heroic deed of unprecedented prowess for your sake . . . I am ready to conceal my feelings to please you . . . I am ready to do anything for your sake . . . not only to be a husband but a servant . . . I would like to be your friend and keep on being one for always . . . But what is the matter with me, how little you trust me . . . I am sad with your sadness and I weep with your tears. Oh, I am tormented with this—passionately to you with all my soul I repeat: Oh, my dear! I love you.[4]

Oct. 18, 1961

Dear Marina,

Today I received presents from you. Thanks a lot. They are very, very nice and I shall always remember this day.

Well, are you returning soon? I will be glad to see you again—I will love you so!!

Well, again, thanks for the presents. You selected so well the records and books and frames which I will always hold.

So long,
Your husband,
Alik[5]

Larissa thinks that out of everyone Alik knew, she was probably that person to whom he related best. In fact, when Marina left to visit her aunt in Kharkhov, she asked Larissa to stop by and take care of Alik a little.

She too recalls that Marina always said she would get married either to a Jew or to a foreigner. One could not eliminate one's past, but perhaps the difficulties of such a past were less hard to live with when you were married to a foreigner. No matter what had happened, she loved Marina, loved her so much it is difficult to convey it. Marina was so good, so attentive, and she had an out-standing knowledge of literature. They had read so many books together when they were young; Marina was literally interested in everything. Larissa also understood why Marina liked Jews and wanted to marry one. She had seen how, among Jews, a woman was always respected. If, in a few Russian families, you could also find such agreeable treatment of women, it was only among the highest levels of the *intelligentsia,* like her sister Ludmila and Misha. "Today," said Larissa, "perhaps our level of culture and refinement in Minsk has been raised somewhat among our working class, but Marina lived here nearly thirty years ago. And it is possible that her contact with foreigners in Leningrad had given her a new perspective on how women could be treated."

When Larissa first met Alik, however, she was puzzled why Marina had chosen him. He seemed a little colorless. Then, she spent some time with him and realized he could change in personality with different people. If you were educated, he sensed that immediately; if you were a worker, he approached more simply.

Of course, Lee was an enigmatic person. Once, Larissa said to Marina in jest, "Is he an American spy?" and Marina just smiled. But when Marina left for Kharkhov and told Larissa to make sure to visit him while she was gone, Larissa would go by sometimes to ring his doorbell and there would be occasions when Lee did not answer for the longest time. Yet she knew he was there. From the street, she had seen a light in the windows. Then, he would come to his door and ask who it was, and only when Larissa identified herself would he open up. She always joked about that. "Are you hiding something in there? Are you broadcasting?" He would smile.

She liked him well enough, but he was strange. Company might be at Lee and Marina's apartment for an evening, yet at ten o'clock he would say, "I'm tired, I feel like sleeping." That was not accepted behavior in Minsk. He would get up, and the others would also get up, but he would say, "Lyalya, stay a little longer with us." After everyone else had left, she and Marina would still be talking. Then, he would say, "Now, we'll take you home," and he and Marina would put on their coats and walk Larissa back. But she must say that in company, he always showed respect for Marina; he was devoted. If Lee nagged her to clean up their house better, Larissa never heard that. Besides, their apartment was clean. Everything was clean. Marina went around wiping up with a rag all the time. She was an exceptional mother and a wonderful wife. Lee wanted her to use a brush rather than a rag when she washed dishes, but that was their only other difference.

She thinks he was jealous of his wife because she stood out physically and was so lively and interesting. Of course, he was possessive. It would even bother him if Marina went for a walk alone.

Oct. 22, 1961

My dearest girl!

Today I received your postcard; thank you, dear, only I do not like your talk that you have a feeling that you will lose me. You will never lose me and that's all!

Today also I received a letter from Mother. She sent me several books. She also tells me that you should learn to speak English.

I wrote back and told her that you do not want to . . . I sent her regards from you.

You can't tell when you will return. Tell me as early as you can. The weather is here cold and rainy.

And our personal affairs: I went, but they say, "No answer yet."

But that's all right. You will be home soon again. It will be so good to be with you. I am glad that the baby is so active; that's good.

Well, so long, write,
Your husband,
Alik[6]

While in Kharkhov, Marina could not stop thinking of Valya and of Ilya. They had been trying to persuade her. They did not want her to go to America. Valya even told her that it would be very bad for Ilya. Marina, however, wasn't sure this was so. Times were changing, and she was only Ilya's niece. Now, with Nikita

Khrushchev, young people were believing in freedom: It was not 1945; it was not Stalin. They weren't going to prosecute Ilya just because his niece went to America. Of course, they might not promote him in his job. Valya told her that Ilya had worked honestly all his life toward his pension. Maybe he would even be denied that. Valya said, "God forbid, what if they send us to Siberia?"

Ilya's sister Aunt Lyuba was also disturbed. After all, she was working at MVD as a bookkeeper. Her job might be in jeopardy as well. Yet Valya never scolded Marina—she just opened her cards and spread them out. "You know," she said, "you hold our lives in your hands. Maybe it is a *kapriz* to go to America." Marina walked back from such conversations with a heavy burden. What was she to do? She wasn't ungracious or ungrateful, but they were putting a heavy decision on her shoulders. It was not a *kapriz*, she decided. She was not capricious.

So, yes, thinking about it now in Kharkhov, she would take a chance. Valya and Ilya would be all right. She was not going to destroy her family. Yet even Aunt Polina, in Kharkhov, was advising her not to go to America. Polina said: "Stay in Russia for the good of all." When Marina would go for a walk with Polina's son, she was so upset in her movements that he became concerned she might fall down. He was a lovely young boy, and he loved her, and he said, "Marina, don't pay attention to my mother. Do what's right in your heart."

She went back to work after these three weeks in Kharkhov, but things got worse.

November 2
Marina arrives back radiant, with several jars of preserves for me from her aunt in Kharkhov.

PART VII

FATHERHOOD AND MOTHERHOOD

1

Cruel but Wise

In the later months of Marina's pregnancy, Lee became careful. Dr. Spock's book said: Don't make love once a certain month is reached—now, she can't remember which month. And Lee was protective, very protective of their unborn baby, and tender, very tender; he measured her stomach and he petted it.

She wasn't showing anything for a long time. Just a little belly. Once he asked, "Are you sure you're pregnant?" He was afraid their baby might be too small. But he was excited when he heard the heartbeat for the first time—a nice quiet moment. He loved to lay his ear on her stomach and listen.

All through their marriage, she would say, little by little, maybe their sex got better. Only one thing she would never allow—"what do you call it?—when people kiss feet—fetish?" She never heard about anything like that until she read of it. She would never allow men that, but Lee was not perverted in such a way. He was nice. When her feet felt wooden in the last months of pregnancy, Lee would massage them. And later, he was very kind about a few stretch marks she had after June was born. He would look at their baby and say, "Your mama did all this for you," and he would stroke those stretch marks and kiss them. But, of course, they were never that bad. She never got that big.

Now, at night, in their small apartment, as winter came on, he would write in a notebook. Since they were going to America, he had started a journal, and for a couple of nights he wrote so much that she finally asked him if he was a spy. Up to then, she had tried to respect his privacy. She didn't believe marriage was a place where you have to smother each other. People must have their own lives. But she was curious. So she asked him what he was writing, and he told her it was his memories of Russian life. She said, "Are you sure you're not a spy?" He said, "What if I were?" He stared at her. He said, "What would you do if I am?" She really didn't know. She started thinking about it. When he saw how worried she looked, he said, "Don't worry. I was joking. I'm not a spy." So she trusted him. Still, she could see how he might be a spy. Who could love the Soviet Union? She didn't. No admiration there at all. Why, she even smoked Belamor cigarettes. Her private protest. She could explain: Belamorski Canal had been built by political prisoners, whose bones were buried in the canal banks, and later, when they named a cigarette Belamor, people saw it as a symbolic memento of all the bones that were buried during Stalin's period. "A great economic achievement—so many bones were buried there. Our system was such that you have to read between the lines. People knew what was happening even if they could not tell. We felt solidarity with people buried near Belamorski Canal. Even now, people won't switch, even now. Belamor is not just a cigarette. If you buy it, you're saying, 'Thank you, brother. You died. I'm with you.' So, Russians laugh when they smoke Belamor. They say, 'My God, everything built in Russia is on the bones, you know?' "

Lee kept writing in his notebooks. Sometimes he would ask her what a Russian word meant. It wasn't that he wrote a lot of pages. As she remembers, it was a small notebook and maybe he would write in it twice a week, or sometimes for three days in a row, sometimes not for three weeks. Over many months, it must have come to fifty pages.

She felt an outcast at work, however. When she walked into a room, others became quiet, like maybe they had been talking about her. She wasn't invited to have lunch with them anymore.

November 1, 1961

Dear Sirs:

. . . In regards to I and my wife's application for exit visas, we have still not been granted exit visas and still have not received any answer to our application, although I have repeatedly gone to the officials in Minsk . . . They have failed to produce any results and are continuing to try to hinder my wife in relation to her application.

In the future I shall keep the Embassy informed as to our progress . . .[1]

He keeps tweaking the KGB with his letters to his brother:

November 1, 1961

Dear Robert,

   . . . We heard over the radio today that the present Russian government has decided to remove Stalin's body from the hall on Red Square. This is big news here and it's very funny for me . . . when I listen to the radio or to some of the political commissars we have here, I always think of George Orwell's book *1984* in which "doublethink" is the way of life also.

   In any case, everything over here is very interesting, and the people are generally simple and nice . . .

   Well, that's about all the news from Minsk.

Your brother,
Lee[2]

November–December
Now we are becoming annoyed about the delay. Marina is beginning to waver about going to the U.S. Probably from the strain of her being pregnant. Still, we quarrel and so things are not too bright, especially with the approach of the hard Russian winter.

She had not wanted to marry a Russian boy, because it was accepted that with 99 percent of them, you would end up being beaten by your man—slapped or struck, anyway. Now, all of a sudden, here she was married to a foreigner who was beginning to control her physically.

In Russia, women would always tell you, "After your honeymoon, don't let your husband dominate. What goes on in the beginning is how it will be later." So, she and Lee both stood their ground. They would argue and slam doors. But there came a day when he hit her. She was so ashamed. She left Lee and went to her aunt. She doesn't remember what their fight was about, but she thought, "I'm not going to take it." She left. Lee had slapped her with an open hand on her cheek, and she went and knocked on Valya's door—it was late at night. Her aunt asked, "Who is it?" and when Marina said, "Can I come in?" Valya said, "Are you alone?" Then Marina heard Uncle Ilya say, "Tell Marina to go back home." Her aunt stood up then to Ilya. She let Marina in. Her uncle said, "This is the first and last time you are coming here after you have a fight with your husband. Come here together once you patch everything up, but don't come here alone. If you want a marriage, solve your own problems. Don't visit this place every time you have something wrong." At the time, Marina thought he was cold-blooded, but now she would say he was right. Ilya had been cruel but wise.

When she went home the next day, Lee said it would never happen again, he was sorry, but she remembered how just before he got violent, he had turned very pale and his eyes had no expression, as if he were looking at her from very far away.

In Minsk, he hit her only three or four times. That is not what she found degrading in Russia. It was that KGB was always bugging whatever they did, and then the FBI got into their act in America. Now, she was having to dissect her life for interviewers one more time. So, who was worth it, and what for? Why did she have to explain herself to anybody? She didn't want to talk about Alik hitting her. Because that put him in a bad light. How could he defend himself from a crime she doesn't think he committed if people have mental pictures of him beating her?

FROM KGB REPORT

> During meeting on November 20, 1961, Mr. Prusakov, I. V., clarified that twice during this recent period he spoke with his niece Marina and her husband, Oswald, L. H. . . .
>
> As a relative of Oswald's wife, Prusakov expressed an opinion that Oswald's decision to return to America may turn out to be a mistake. Prusakov spoke to him of complications in international situation, also to a possibility he would be recruited into American army, problems of finding work in America, as well as some possibility of his arrest there. Oswald explained to Prusakov that he hardly thinks he will be called for military service, since he has already served his term . . . and concerning his possible arrest— he doesn't think Embassy employees would lie to him. Nevertheless, Oswald promised to weigh all these obstacles concerning his return to America.
>
> As Prusakov further explained, he also tried to convince his niece Marina that it was inexpedient to go to USA. A similar influence on Marina was undertaken by her Aunt Polina, living in Kharkhov. As a result of these conversations, Prusakov decided that Marina didn't feel like going. However, she was very concerned how she would carry on her further life, having a baby from Oswald.

Prusakov promised to continue to work on convincing Oswald and his wife to change their opinion about going to America. Prusakov didn't recall any suspicious moments in Oswald's behavior.

Nov. 23

Dear Mother,

Today we received your grand gift. I am very surprised you guessed my taste in color and fabric.

Here it is already cold so your wool stole will be very useful.

It is very nice to feel that you are so attentive to me, more so, even, than to Lee. I shall always remember your gift as a mark of our friendship.

I hope you won't be nervous for us. You shouldn't worry about us too much.

I have never seen you (except on a photograph) but I have a lot of affection for you already.

I hope you shall be well. I thank you again for the fine present. Marina

(I wrote it for her but the words are hers.—Lee)[3]

2

―――――――――

A Bomb Scare

In the chronology kept by KGB, Oswald, on December 6, "appealed to American Senator John Tower to help him to return to USA." Here follows a translation in English of the Russian translation of Oswald's letter in 1961.

FROM KGB MAIL SURVEILLANCE
   Senator John G. Tower
   Washington, D.C.
   of Senate Building

Lee Oswald
Minsk
Kalinina Street 4–24

Dear Senator Tower!

My name is Oswald. When I came to the Soviet Union, I presented documents that I was a citizen of the United States and that I had come to the Soviet Union temporarily. American Embassy in Moscow is familiar with my case.

Since July 1960 I have attempted unsuccessfully to obtain an exit visa to go to U.S. but Soviet authorities refuse to let me and my Soviet wife go . . .

I am a citizen of the United States (passport no. N1733242, 1959) and I ask you to help me, since Soviet authorities are detaining me against my will.

Respectfully,
Lee Oswald

Perhaps the time had come for KGB Counterintelligence, Byelorussia, to divest itself of a person who could easily create an international episode and was contributing very little at work, or so said a report on December 11, 1961, sent to the Minsk City Militia Department from the Plant Director and the Personnel Department Chief.

Lee Harvey Oswald . . . hired as regulator in experimental shop of this plant on January 13, 1960.

During his employment as regulator his performance was unsatisfactory. He does not display initiative for increasing his skill as a regulator.

Citizen Lee Harvey Oswald reacts in an oversensitive manner to remarks from the foreman, and is careless in his work. Citizen L. H. Oswald takes no part in the social life of our shop and keeps very much to himself.[1]

At Horizon, Katya, working down the aisle from Alik, had come to notice that he was becoming less and less of a worker. More and more often, he would sit with his feet on the table. When there was no table, he would put his feet on a chair. His fellow workers decided it was American culture.

They would say to him, "Alik, why do you come here and go to sleep? It's still morning." He would answer, "I made love a lot. That's why I'm sleeping now."

"Maybe he said it in joking," said Katya. "But it was not important for me."

Step by step, people stopped being curious about him. Once or twice, after Alik was called into the office for a reprimand, he would come back to his worktable and say, "I am going to write my memoirs—'How I Remember the Soviet Union.' "

Nobody reacted. Everybody thought: "What is he going to write if he can't even speak properly?" It was best to keep some distance from him. How could you know what is in his mind?

Dec. 14, 1961

Dear Robert,

Today I received your letter of November 29.

First of all, I can confirm [that] I did not receive any letter with "certain" questions. It's quite possible they destroyed it . . .

I hope you get our little package by Christmas. Marina worked on those table napkins for Vada for two weeks . . .

The housetops are covered with snow, but the pine trees stand out green. The river near our apartment house is frozen now. We have a very good view from our fourth floor windows.

Well, that's about all for now. Marina sends her love. Keep writing.

Lee[2]

After she filled out every paper, every one of so many needed for her to go to America, and all those weeks went by, and then all those months from August to December, a phone call came to her at last when she was at work. Marina was told to go over to the main government building on Lenin Street, where MVD and KGB were housed.

She came in from a side street and walked downstairs. There was only one man in the room; he "was gray-headed, he was authority." He was tall, but she doesn't remember his face. Just that he was in uniform. Nor does she recall whether he called her Marina or Mrs. Oswald; but he did say, "I'm here to talk to you about your papers. You're applying to go to the United States."

She told him that was correct. He said, "You don't have to be afraid. This is not an interrogation. I just want to talk to you to find out what is your reason for leaving this country. I want to ask a few questions. You know," he said, "you are not going to be arrested or anything. It's just normal procedures." Then he asked, "Is there any political reason? Do you have anything against this country? Do you disagree with something?"

She said, "No. My reason is that I'm married to an American. He's going home and I'm his wife. That's my only reason for going. That's all there is to it."

He said, "Is there any way I can persuade you not to leave? Because such an act will jeopardize the reputations of people you work with, and your relatives."

She picked up on this. She said, "My uncle had nothing to do with it. He didn't approve of my marriage. He agreed only because my husband told him he was not able to go back to America. So it was my uncle's understanding that I would not go. Now, my husband does have a chance to return, and," she added, "I'm not leaving for any political reason."

He chewed it over from this side and that; then, he closed his file on all his papers and said, "If that's what you think, I guess it's what you do."

As he opened his door for her, he said—and she remembers that here he did call her by her first name—"I'm not talking to you right now as an official, Marina. Look at my hair—I've been through the war. You're young, you could be my granddaughter. I'm strictly talking to you as a man. How do you know that your best circumstances are not right here? You cannot guarantee that your marriage will be all right. You're taking a large leap. If your marriage doesn't work, there's no easy way back. You'll be all alone. Think about that when you go home now. I'm talking to you like a grandfather, and this decision is yours."

She did think about it. As she walked home, she thought about it a lot. He had been a nice man. He had not switched to his mean side. He had talked to her as another human being. When she told Lee, word for word, what had happened, he said, "I don't think we're going to have any problems. The light looks green."

They had come a long way. Even when Lee had proposed, she hadn't thought that they would allow them to get married. So much had happened so quickly.

December 25,

Christmas Day, Tuesday

Marina is called to the Passport and Visa office. She is told we have been granted Soviet exit visas . . . It's great (I think)! New Year's we spend at the Zigers' and a dinner party at midnight attended by six other persons.

By now Igor and Stepan had come to their assessment of Oswald: He was a person you could call emotional. That had manifested itself in fights which arose between him and his wife, although such fights tended to be short-lived. On the other hand, Oswald was never involved in acts of public violence. In fact, the head of MVD militia delivered an official document to KGB saying that Oswald had never been observed in any form of hooliganism. In turn, when Marina was excluded from Komsomol, it was because she was regarded as ballast: She had entered grudgingly, without personal desire, and had taken no part in organizational life.

In addition, Oswald's hunting trips now offered no problem for Counterintelligence. He had gone on several occasions, and according to their sources, he was a poor hunter and came back with nothing. He never made attempts to isolate himself from his group, never tried to approach industrial sites in the forest, and never made suspicious movements. KGB questions on this matter, therefore, were put to rest; Oswald even went without his camera. If he had brought it along, they would have looked to determine whether he approached such installations in order to take pictures. But he didn't even bring it. Finally, he sold his gun on the second of January, 1962, approximately a year and a half after purchase, the gun bearing serial number 64621.

So, the Organs concluded that they might as well allow Oswald to return to America. A heavy stone would be removed from their workload. After all, Oswald could always try to kill himself again. Next time he might succeed. Then there would be propaganda of the ugliest sort.

So, at year's end, a decision was taken that enough material had accumulated to conclude Oswald was not a foreign intelligence agent. Of course, they would still keep him under surveillance. It is never possible to be altogether certain. Some spies are so careful that you can watch them for years and they don't make mistakes; finally, they make one mistake. It is not professional, therefore, to come to quick conclusions. Now that Oswald had decided to leave the Soviet Union, however, they decided, after analyzing all their material once more, that during the year and a half he had been in Minsk, there had been no evidence that he was an active agent of any intelligence service.

They did, however, have one scare. A thoroughgoing scare. Their observer, looking through the peephole in the apartment next door to Oswald, saw some suspicious activity. Was Oswald making a bomb? He seemed to be putting gunpowder and metal fragments into a small box. It could be said that was one overnight sensation for them: Khrushchev would be visiting Minsk in January!

The interviewers asked whether Oswald's apartment had been entered while he and Marina were at work, but the replies were not responsive. Stepan would only say that Oswald's device turned out to be some kind of toy. A species of firecracker, perhaps? He shrugged. It was nothing; it was nonsense. Oswald threw away this toy a day or two later. They had, said Stepan, been able to examine it in the apartment-house trash bin. Then, in January, before Khrushchev's visit, Oswald even sold his shotgun for 18 rubles, at the exact same store at which he had bought it. However, he caused a shock to surveillance when he got on a bus holding his gun; but then they observed that he was merely on his way to sell the weapon. Much ado about nothing.

If Oswald had chosen to remain in Minsk for five years, even ten, he would still have been kept under occasional surveillance; that goes without saying. One never drops one's guard altogether. But this toy bomb retained no large significance for them. Whereas last July, when he had gone to his Embassy in Moscow to get permission to go back to America—why, then they had certainly continued to monitor his activities. For if he had chosen not to follow through on his repatriation, they would have had to suppose that it had been a pretext to enable him to visit his Embassy and receive instructions.

Now, they had no good choice but to allow him to leave. To keep him inside the Soviet Union might yet require that they prove to world opinion that they had good reasons. If evidence of espionage had been there, they might have decided to put him in prison and conduct a formal interrogation. But no such material was available.

Back last summer, when Oswald first asked permission for an exit visa, therefore, Stepan did not have to take a lot of time to consider. This was a file he knew like the five fingers of his hand; you could wake him three hours past midnight, ask any question—Stepan could tell you everything about him. So, his answer was positive. Oswald could go. No objections. Likhoi had become a negative factor—no Communist principles, nor did he want to work or to study. For a while, they had thought he was adjusting himself. They had even made allowances. Not now. Let him go home. Good riddance.

Of course, Stepan would say, KGB was not the organization to give formal permission to leave. They could only say, No objections, and send such a paper over to OVIR, a branch of MVD which had its own protocol for visas. OVIR would send such papers on to Moscow. From there would come a final decision. That was why it had all gone on for months.

There will still be street surveillance of Oswald from time to time, and periodic transcriptions of his quarrels with Marina, but Stepan will not return often to our narrative, not until November of 1963, when incredible events will occur in Dallas and Stepan will be summoned to Moscow Center. That will be a memorable day in his life. Until then, he will work on other cases. Before we take temporary leave of him, however, it may be of interest to pay some attention to the daily matters of his life. He has had, after all, the sort of circumscribed existence that Flaubert might have enjoyed depicting.

3

The Good Boy, the Good Man

Stepan's parents were poor peasants who worked on a small collective farm in the Gomel region of Byelorussia, but Stepan, who started school at the age of seven, was always an excellent student.

Since he thought highly of his teachers, he began at an early age to dream about becoming an instructor himself. He was very good at math, and assiduous in his studies. Often, he would come to school before classes started, and if any pupils had been unable to do their homework, they came running to him.

Such desires continued in adolescence. He found his teachers to be among the most decent people he knew; they treated children well—at least those who studied. That influenced his decision. When he graduated from high school, he wanted to go to the Pedagogical Institute in Minsk. Yet, he couldn't stay there without financial help from his parents, and they were without that kind of money. So, he had to find a subject at this Institute that would provide him with a stipend large enough to live away from home. Therefore, he decided on journalism. That stipend was decent. But then, war broke out.

He was seventeen. In Byelorussia, adolescents born in 1923 and 1924 were not yet subject to conscription. Instead, they were given small-caliber rifles to use in case German paratroopers tried to land among them, and they were organized to drive livestock east to the Sorzh River, where green grass and wetlands abounded. In these marshes they lived and learned how to milk cows. Stepan still remembers the first German he saw, a pilot in a plane just overhead, and he and the other adolescents had to hide because, in those first days of war, Germans were chasing not only soldiers but civilians, and were even shooting down on livestock. Stepan remembers bullets hitting the ground—explosive bullets. Earth flew about. That was when he first experienced the terror of war.

His father was called up at the beginning, and immediately disappeared. There was no news until Stepan's mother received a letter from his father, who was now in a Soviet military hospital. A machine-gunner, he had been seriously wounded. His arm was crushed. Only after Byelorussia was liberated could he return home. And at home he stayed until he died, in 1960.

As for Stepan, he was allowed, once it became clear that the Germans would occupy all their territories, to leave the marsh and return to his village, where he lived, like the others, in all kinds of hardship until Byelorussia was liberated, in November 1943. Soon afterward, he was drafted. The war was at its height and there was no time for training. He, too, was assigned to a machine gun, number one in a four-man team, and in an unheated barn they taught him to use it, and sent him straight into the fighting at the front. Whenever you sat on duty, if there was a sound, you pulled your trigger. You didn't know whether you'd killed a German or not. Then you sat some more. You heard a whine, and a shell flew by—would it blow up right overhead? Once you knew that it was going to explode on someone else, you felt better. That's what his defense line was like.

He was wounded and spent three months in a military hospital, then went up again to take part in several battles, and wasn't demobilized until early 1947. When he returned to his parents' village, he had, of course, to decide where to go. Central Statistics Board in Minsk, he read, was organizing courses, so Stepan took along a few necessary documents, and was enrolled in the program. His math helped him.

Since his dream was still to be a teacher, he didn't wish to be in statistics, but there wasn't much he could do about it, and soon he received his first official job. It was in the Gomel region, as District Inspector for Central Statistics. Immediately, due to shortages of personnel, he was one of the top three men, not a bad position. Still, frankly speaking, it was not a job he wished to keep for life. Two years, however, after going to work there, he was invited to the Central Office of State Security, where a department head made an official offer: Would Stepan like to work for them? He replied that he didn't know whether he was qualified. Return answer: "You shouldn't think that we're going to hire you now. We'll send you away for training." That was in 1949, and he was sent to a school in Byelorussia.

Up to this point, Stepan Vasilyevich had had a most nebulous idea about the activities of State Security. But by way of his class work, which was based on the analysis of already documented KGB cases, he became very interested. As he puts it, "An other-worldly world began to open up." Some of it seemed equal to advanced mathematical propositions. He embarked on these studies with pleasure, and never thought again about being a teacher. Instead, he was immersed over the next two years in absorbing every bit of instruction he could employ in his practical work. He did have a high opinion of most of his teachers. Then he entered practical work.

By the time Oswald's case came along, he had already had ten years of working for State Security and a good performance record as a developer.

When asked to analyze himself, he would say that he's a modest person who has never tried to get ahead of others but he is, by nature, hard-working, assiduous, and inclined to analysis. That he can say about himself without reservation. During his time in KGB he was known for sticking with a case once he started. He never made hasty decisions; he thought things out, and tried to base conclusions on concrete materials, not speculation. In addition, he did not drink and did not smoke. He was—he says with a smile—"morally reliable." Then he laughs. "I was never particularly interested in girls. Most of my attention was devoted to work."

In 1953 he married. He and his wife have two children, a daughter and son. His son, he mentions, did not follow in his father's footsteps. If he had, it would not be permissible to tell you, but since he didn't, one can say so. His wife also worked all these years for the Central Committee of Komsomol as an instructor in a sewing workshop. While you could not let anyone know, particularly any girls you took out, that you were working in Counterintelligence, when he married his wife, it was different. He was able to tell her, but that was because he had been introduced to her by a co-worker in KGB who happened to come from her village. In such a situation, he could hardly keep it secret. For that matter, he did not want to. In 1953, they worked sometimes until two in the morning. What would a wife who did not know his occupation have thought if he returned home that late? Yet, to this day, his wife is aware of no more than that he is an operative. Same goes for his children. He's one person who can keep a secret.

When asked what his normal working day was like, he would say that in winter he usually got up early, a habit since childhood—never rose later than seven o'clock; shaved, washed, had his breakfast, and walked to his office. Living approximately three kilometers from Minsk KGB headquarters, he'd take a quiet street to Gorky Park, then up a hill and over Yanka Kupala to Lenin Prospekt. He usually walked home as well. Did that for exercise. His system. He would also arrive by eight-thirty instead of nine, and would then spread out all his necessary documents in order to organize his work for the day.

Stepan's office on the third floor was occupied in those years by himself and another officer. They each had their own table and their own safe. A normal working day would begin with documents; of course, there were always people to meet and conferences with superiors, sometimes staff meetings, but these only took place if really necessary, since they tended to distract people. It was considered better if Stepan approached his boss in private or, preferably, solved a problem himself. You couldn't bring up everything at a staff meeting, because you had to maintain security. That his office was shared with someone else did not, however, present exceptional difficulties. If you run a tight ship, joint occupation is not difficult. As soon as Stepan was finished using a document, he would put it in his safe. Nor did he have any curiosity about what his colleague might be working on. That was your rule. You're not allowed to ask questions, and it's not a matter to feel hurt or offended about. Each man had his own safe; each man was responsible for what was entrusted to him.

Toward the conclusion of his labors on Oswald's case, he can say that he was promoted. It was a natural matter. During his entire time of service, he never skipped a grade, and each promotion was achieved by honest hard work: Junior Operative Officer; Senior Operative Officer; then Assistant Director of Department. At that point, he was given his own office. Now, people came to see him in order to solve one or another problem, yet even so, his friend, who had started at the same time as himself and was working at the same level, was made Major, which was the appropriate rank for an Assistant Director of Department. Stepan, however, was not promoted. Six months went by. He did not feel comfortable drawing attention to himself, but finally he decided that he must. Sort of joking, he said to his friend that maybe he wasn't so good at his job, and his friend said, "Stepan Vasilyevich, I'm not going to waste time arguing with you. They didn't make you Major—well, find out why. You haven't done anything wrong." He went to Personnel politely, made inquiries, and his boss started to apologize. They had forgotten. Bureaucrats. Of course, no one could see his rank, because they didn't wear uniforms.

In his office, there was one large window that looked out on the courtyard, and that was much to Stepan's preference. As far as he was concerned, too much din came from the windows which had access to Lenin Prospekt. One minute a car screeched, the next minute someone yelled, a militia-man blew his whistle—it was distracting. He liked quiet.

As for his leisure during the working day? It could be summarized easily. On a normal day, they'd usually eat inside. At that time, they had what he calls a wonderful cafeteria. Also, there were gazebos in the KGB courtyard. Many of those who lived close by went home for lunch, but those who dwelt further away ate in this cafeteria, which offered beefsteak, cutlets, bottles of 20 percent cream for tea, and some kind of salad. Afterward, for their remaining half hour, some people would shop. Or sit in the courtyard. At that time, you could relax under a shade tree. At two o'clock, it was back to work.

There was no fixed routine on that. It wasn't as if one did one thing before lunch, then another afterward. There were no established parameters. You could be on your job until ten or twelve at night, or leave after a normal day, and things could come up in any file at any time, so a day at work might vary emotionally. It was rarely monotonous. There was always a question of which matters to solve first. His superior, for example, might give instructions, but after Stepan thought about it for a while, he could come to still another conclusion. So, he would go back and coordinate, in order not to disobey his commander's rules.

It was a creative process. A matter might be resolved in a month, or it might take a year—or years. You didn't look to find results in a given period—it didn't happen that way. Unforeseen circumstances usually arose. Who, for example, could have predicted Oswald's marriage to Marina? Sometimes a task cannot be resolved, no matter how hard you try.

Asked if one of his digressions from work was playing chess, he says: "Playing chess, checkers, or dominoes was not appropriate—only for loafers. It was different if you smoked in order to wind down a little—there was a place where people who needed their dose of nicotine could go." But he was not in that category. Whenever he felt tired—although generally he was full of energy and health—he would visit a co-worker, someone he was close to. They would talk for ten or fifteen minutes, then go back to their desks. And when he had a little time after lunch, he did like to play chess, but was hardly what you would call one of the strongest players, merely third class. He did it for pleasure. During summer, on lunch break, he would play volleyball. While not tall, he was good at defense, and his hook shot was pretty good. He relaxed that way.

KGB workers would often hang around after work. Some would stay to play chess and then justify it to their wives by saying it was necessary for work. But he almost never lied to his wife. And he never delayed that long; he didn't abuse his domestic privileges. Played a game, had a laugh, washed up, went home. Usually, when she knew he would be late, his wife timed her dishes to match his arrival. In fact, she wouldn't eat by herself, even if sometimes he came very late. To this day, such a tradition still stands. He comes home and says, "Why didn't you eat?" and she says, "I was waiting for you." "Why did you spend all that time waiting?" Her reply: "I can't do it alone."

Of course, whatever his wife cooked, he was happy to receive. He would come home and eat with gusto. Everything was fine, and he would get rid of stress that way. Leaving work, you see something interesting in a store, you go in, so on. Their domestic life was a little easier because his wife worked too. So, they put their children in a twenty-four-hour kindergarten for five days a week. Only during weekends did they see their kids. On Mondays, they brought them in to work. There was a bus waiting that took children of KGB personnel to the outskirts of Minsk, where there was a nice kindergarten located in a *dacha* that had once belonged to a former Minister. While it made things easy around their house, you could say that in terms of the children's upbringing, these weren't your best conditions. Still, kindergarten was strict, and his children did not turn out spoiled—that's good, too.

For entertainment, he would go to the theatre or cinema. He liked the Russian National Choir, and most sporting events. He was a big hockey fan and he often watched soccer, but Stepan couldn't stand boxing—it was face-bashing. He liked to read books so long as his vision was still good. Journals and the daily press as well—that goes without saying. It was part of his job. He saw many films as well: *Cossacks of the Don, Swineherder and Shepherd*—he liked upbeat films, but didn't go for dramatic situations; they affected his nervous system and got him upset. His passion, however, was fishing. He could say that he is ready to fish anywhere: lakes, rivers, any body of water, winter, summer, any wind or season.

Asked to criticize himself, Stepan would state that, as a person, "I feel I was really too tough with my children. I disciplined them a lot and I think maybe some children need more softness. I am too impatient with certain people. I like it that when people talk, they talk sense. Discreet and brief. But, you know, people are different. Some people want to express themselves more emotionally, and I was not patient. If somebody starts to blab and blab, I interrupt, I direct conversation to what I see as the essence of the matter. But one should be more patient. Not all people are like me.

"On the other hand, when I was devoting all my attention to work, I didn't always pay attention to important events. I would overlook a colleague's birthday. As for my wife's birthday, I would not forget. For decency's sake, you should make things pleasant, for your wife and for people around you, your co-workers, your family."

Asked one more time to give his opinion of Oswald's case, he says it proved to be "primitive—a basic case," because it did not involve anyone of extreme intelligence. Nor did it cost too much money. Oswald did not have a large circle of friends and was not erratic in his behavior. It wasn't as if one week he had three friends and by the following week had accumulated twenty so they had to increase their budget immediately to watch twenty people instead of three. No, this case was simple because it did not have variables, it did not fluctuate, and finally there wasn't much that really raised a lot of new questions.

4

On the Turn of the Year

FROM KGB TRANSCRIPTS
FOR OBJECT: OLH-2727
FOR PERIOD: 31 DEC. 61

LHO: You won't look good in this dress.

WIFE: Why?

LHO: It's too open.

WIFE: Where is it open? It's nice.

LHO: Doesn't go.

WIFE: Now, my shoes are a different matter! They don't go with this at all . . .

LHO: You really don't know how to dress, I swear!

WIFE: Buy me different shoes.

LHO: Those are nice shoes.

WIFE: That's true. But they're no good for winter. They're white. There are winter shoes and summer shoes.

(*LHO goes into the kitchen and comes right back*)

LHO: Are you going to put on a jacket?

WIFE: What jacket? I don't have any jackets. Do you think it'll make a difference [to the Zigers] if they see that it looks bad?

LHO: Yes!

WIFE: It's a simple dress.

LHO: No, it's not nice!

WIFE: Well, I can't put this one on. It's full of holes . . . I don't know what to wear.

LHO: Everything will be fine! Everything will be just wonderful.

WIFE: You know that no one needs me.

LHO: Jesus, what about Oswald? (*kisses her*) People are going to look at us and say, There's a handsome pair!

WIFE: Handsome! (*laughs*) In that case, I'll go in a skirt and sweater. You'll just have to be embarrassed. (*pause*) If there were something to wear, I would dress better than you, better than your Americans.

(*they laugh*)

WIFE: If I had been wearing these shoes when we first met, you wouldn't have danced with me.

(*they laugh*)

So much had happened to them in a year. We can wonder if at the Zigers' party that will welcome the arrival of 1962 they will recollect their previous New Year's Eve. Lee had spent it with Ella and her family; Marina had been with Sasha, then with Konstantin.

Jan. 2

Dear Mother,

Well, I have pretty good [hopes] we shall receive our visas about the middle of February, which means we may arrive in the U.S. about the 1st of March give or take a month or so.

I would like you to do something important for us. Get in touch with the Red Cross in Vernon and ask them to contact an organization called "International Rescue Committee" or any organizations which aid persons from abroad [to] get resettled. There are many such organizations.

We need $800.00 for two tickets from Moscow to New York and from N.Y. to Texas . . . You can tell the Red Cross . . . that both of us have now received Soviet exit visas to leave the Soviet Union . . .

We only need money for the tickets now.

Ask them to contact the American Embassy, Moscow, for information . . . I want you to try to get the money through some organization, and not try to collect it yourself, alone.

Do not, of course, take any loan, only a gift, and don't send your *own* money . . .

We received your Christmas card with photos. They were very good; both of us enjoyed them very much.

> Write soon,
> Love,
> Lee[1]

On receiving this a couple of weeks later, Marguerite Oswald proceeded to act upon it at once, and would remember every detail when she related the event to the Warren Commission two years later.

MARGUERITE OSWALD. So when I entered the Vernon Red Cross . . . I told the young lady, showed her the letter and showed her the paper . . .

She said, "What is your son doing in Russia?"

I said, "I don't know."

"You are his mother and you don't know what he is doing in Russia?"

I said, "Young lady, I said I do not know what he is doing in Russia."

"Well, I think anybody goes to Russia doesn't need any help to get back, they should stay over there."

So I said, "I am not interested in your personal opinion. I need help. Would you please contact, give me the address of the International Rescue Committee so I can continue to try to get money for my son to come home?"

She did not know of any address for the International Rescue Committee . . .

Now this young lady [in Vernon Red Cross] was very, very regalish. She didn't want to help anybody going to Russia. So when . . . I called her at her home and told her that I had the address from the State Department of the International Rescue Committee, and would she be so kind enough to come to the office and write the letter for me.

She said, "Well, Mrs. Oswald, I don't have a key."

This is on a Saturday morning and she is in the courthouse.

I said, "Do you mean to tell me you are in charge of the Red Cross and you don't have a key?"

"No, I don't."

"Well, young lady, you have delayed me 4 days and I don't like your attitude. I am going to ask you especially to make a point to come to the office and get this in the mail for me. It is very important."

So, reluctantly, after much persuasion, she came.

So she wrote the letter to the International Rescue Committee, and handed it to me, and I mailed the letter—I mailed the letter.[2]

5

Pen Pals

January 4
I am called to the [Soviet] Passport Office since my residential passport expires today. Since I now have a U.S. passport in my possession, I am given a totally new residential passport called "Passport for Foreigners" . . . [It's] good till July 5, 1962.

They are so confident they will be able to leave in a few weeks. He will have his new passport, she has her exit visa; his mother will convince some charitable American organization to give them a gift. Maybe they can even travel before their baby is born. When you push a wall and the wall begins to move, it is natural to be optimistic.

Shocks await them. Bureaucratic snags. Questions about his defection begin to circulate in inter-office memos at State. Concerns arise in the Department of Justice: Are they being asked to aid an American Communist and his Soviet wife? And who will guarantee support for Marina?

Letters circulate through January and early February 1962. Oswald will send three to the Embassy in Moscow before the month is out, and two to the International Rescue Committee. He writes seven letters to his mother in the next two months and four to Robert Oswald; he receives six letters from the American Embassy in the same two months. In Washington, over the preceding two years, inter-office memos concerning him have been passing back and forth at the State Department, more than ten in 1959 and early 1960, twenty or more in the last year. A certain division of opinion has developed at State on whether Oswald is to be helped in this repatriation project. It cannot be said that the arrogance he exhibits in his letters proves endearing to American officials, but who is to say that his tactics are not effective?

January 5, 1962

Dear Sirs:

. . . As I have already informed the Embassy, [Soviet] exit visas for myself and my wife have already been granted. I can have mine at any time, but it will be good for 45 days only. Since I and my wife wish to leave the USSR together, I shall delay requesting my visa until such time as documentation from the Ministry of Foreign Affairs of the USSR and the American Embassy is completed on my wife . . .

I would like to make arrangements for a loan from the Embassy or some organization for part of the plane fare. Please look into this and notify me.

Yours truly,
Lee H. Oswald[1]

Samuel G. Wise, who has replaced Richard Snyder, now replies to Oswald on January 15, 1962.

Dear Mr. Oswald:

. . . The petition which you filed to classify your wife's visa status has not yet been approved by the Immigration and Naturalization Service. Moreover, evidence required by law to show that your wife will not become a public charge in the United States has not been presented to the

Embassy. One possibility, in this regard, would be for your mother or some other close relative in the United States to file an affidavit of support in your wife's behalf. . . .

In view of these circumstances, you may wish to reconsider your decision to defer your departure until Mrs. Oswald's documentation is complete, particularly inasmuch as it may prove difficult to provide the necessary financial support evidence while you are still in the USSR. Please inform us of your intentions in this matter.

The question which you raise of a loan to defray part of your travel expenses to the United States can be discussed when you come to the Embassy . . .[2]

Oswald has to know that requesting a loan from the State Department will slow his progress. Yet, if the State Department is willing to lend him money, then it is probable they expect no prosecution against him.

January 16, 1962

Dear Sirs,

In reply to your informative letter of January 5 . . . I hope you will inform me of any other documents that are needed and not wait until the last minute . . .

You suggest that because of the documentation necessary I go to the United States alone.

I certainly will not consider going to the U.S. alone for any reason, particularly since it appears my passport will be confiscated upon my arrival in the United States.

I would like for all documentation to be completed at or by the Embassy in Moscow.

We have not had an easy time getting our exit visas from the Soviet authorities, as the Embassy well knows. I would not like this whole thing repeated because of a lack of this or that on anybody's part. I'm sure you understand.

Also, we will have a child in March, and although the Russian processing in this case will be to write in age, sex, and place of birth on my wife's travel passport (a process of four days in Moscow), I would like to know what you will require in this event.

Sincerely,
Lee H. Oswald.[3]

We may be encountering Oswald's profound anxiety about returning to America. To account for his zeal to go back with Marina—and never without her—let us provide him with more than one motive. The side of him that is always ready to calculate his situation would probably judge that it is safer not to go back alone. His wife and newborn child are bound to produce some sympathy for him in America.

This does not have to be, of course, his only consideration. If he and Marina are having their difficulties, he is even more miserable at the thought of living without her. And he does have to wonder whether she will love him enough to join him once he is far away. In any case, he will not leave without her.

Joseph B. Norbury, another Consul at the Embassy, replies on January 24:

> Dear Mr. Oswald:
> . . . Regarding the visa petition for your wife, we are attempting to get an early decision from the Immigration and Naturalization Service . . . You may be sure that this question will be fully explored. Meanwhile, I cannot urge you strongly enough to attempt to obtain a support affadavit from a close relative in the United States, in order to insure that your wife will be able to travel with you . . .[4]

State sends another Operations Memo, on January 26, to the Embassy.

> The petition, check and marriage certificate submitted by Mr. Oswald . . . were forwarded for approval to the Dallas District Office of the Immigration and Naturalization Service on October 6, 1961. No reply has been received to date . . . Pending the completion of that investigation, neither the approval of the petition nor the waiver of the 243(g) sanctions can be granted . . .[5]

We now have a new bureaucratic term to contend with: *the waiver of the 243(g) sanctions.* That will account for most of the delay of the next four months. Sanction 243(g) is designed to keep out immigrants departing from the Soviet Union, and so if it is not waived, then the Oswalds will have to go from the USSR to some sanction-free country, like Belgium. There, Marina can apply for a visa to the U.S. It could take an extra week, it could take a month, and the Oswalds have no money; the State Department, therefore, anticipates added expenses, and much added difficulty with Oswald. So, they do not tell him that the waiver of the 243(g) sanction has not only not been granted but, indeed, might not be. The State Department does not have jurisdiction over the Immigration and Naturalization Service, which is a branch of the Department of Justice. Communications between officials from each department will go on, therefore, for months, and Oswald will not be kept informed of this problem. All the same, he seems to sense that something is out of place:

January 23, 62

Dear Mother,

Please do me a big favor, go to the nearest office of the "Immigration and Naturalization offices" and file an "affidavit of support" on behalf of my wife, this is a technical point in regards to permission to enter the U.S. for Marina, and must be made in the U.S. You simply fill out a blank (there may be a charge of a few dollars) and that's all.

Please do this now, as they are actually waiting for this document in Moscow . . .

Thanks
Love Lee[6]

He then asks Robert to perform a scouting mission:

January 30, 1962

Dear Robert,

. . . You once said that you asked around about whether or not the U.S. government had any charges against me. You said at that time "No." Maybe you should ask around again. It's possible now that the government knows I'm coming, they'll have something waiting . . .

Your brother,
Lee[7]

On January 31, Joseph Norbury writes again to Oswald:

. . . Although the Embassy is making every effort to complete action on your wife's visa application as soon as possible, it seems highly unlikely that the visa can be issued in time to permit her to travel before your child is born. Most airlines will not accept passengers during the ninth month of pregnancy. Therefore, it would seem advisable for you to plan for the baby to be born before you leave for the United States.[8]

A week later, the waiver of sanctions is denied by J. W. Holland of the Travel Control Central Office in San Antonio.

Marguerite, meanwhile, is attempting to be creative in the art of raising money, and she is also being denied.

> February 1, 1962
> Dear Mrs. Oswald:
>   . . . Concerning your suggestion that you make your son's story public with an appeal for help, although the [State] Department is not in a position to advise you on this matter, it is not believed this would offer a solution to his problem.
> > Sincerely yours,
> > George H. Haselton,
> > Chief, Protection and Representation Division[9]

> Feb. 1, 1962
> Dear Mother,
>   . . . I don't know if giving the story to the newspapers is too good, maybe you'd better hold off for awhile about that. I'll tell you when . . .
>   . . . I want you to understand that although you can aid us in certain, small ways, this business about our coming to the U.S. is relatively simple. Don't make it more complicated than it is . . .
> > Lee[10]

Now at State they decide that there is only one way to disembarrass themselves of their most prominent petitioner. On February 6, Norbury writes to Oswald from the Embassy.

> . . . We are prepared to take your application for a loan. [However] the recipient must keep the Department of State informed of his address in the United States until such

time as he has liquidated his indebtedness. After repatriation, the recipient will not be furnished a passport for travel abroad until he has reimbursed the Government . . .[11]

Feb. 9, 1962

Dear Mother

Well, it won't be long now until the baby is born and until we shall be seeing you . . .

Also you can see about sending me some clippings or columns from the Ft. Worth papers for the month of Nov. 1959. I want to know just what was said about me in the Ft. Worth newspapers so I can be forewarned. If you don't have clippings yourself, you can always get back issues of newspapers . . . at their offices or the public library . . .

Love from us both,
Lee[12]

6

An Addition to the Family

February 15, dawn
Marina wakes me. It's her time. At 9 o'clock we arrive at the hospital. I leave her in care of nurses and leave to go to work. Ten o'clock Marina has a baby girl.

In the last month of pregnancy, her body would ache sometimes, or her legs, and Alik would rub them and say, " 'My poor, poor girl. You're hurting yourself just to give life to our baby,' "[1] and she felt at such times as if Alik really loved her.

She had often thought that she was going to lose the child; she kept fainting, all too often. Yet, narrow hips or not, the birth was quick; she was fortunate. Even those pharmacy girls who had turned away from her because she was going to America were supportive when it came to a matter of her pregnancy. They insisted that the baby be delivered at Third Clinical Hospital, and when

Marina said, "I don't agree," they said, "Marina, right here in Third Clinical by our pharmacy you'll be safest of all." They were very considerate, and so she agreed.

The night before, she and Alik had been visiting friends and had an evening she would call full of gaiety. Then, before dawn, it happened. Marina woke up at six and told Lee they had to go. It was almost funny. Lee was so frightened that it was humorous to watch his suffering. He acted as if he was the one—he kept hurrying her—and now, of course, since there wasn't anything terrible to feel in her early labor pains, she didn't even want to leave their apartment—Lee had to persuade her.

Finally, they went out at 9:00 A.M., and then they couldn't get a taxi. Not one to be found. Had to wedge themselves onto a crowded bus. She had never seen Lee looking so nervous. What with snow underfoot, every step felt slippery, but finally they did reach Third Clinical in safety. Lee had to turn around almost immediately and go to work. They wouldn't allow him to be with her. In Russia, the prevailing procedure was for women to stay in the hospital for ten days after a baby is born. It even took three days before you could talk your nurses into letting you out of bed, and in all that time, no one but hospital people are with your baby—no relatives or friends admitted, no infections from outside! Even the father is not given permission to enter the maternity ward. He can only visit the hospital lobby and leave gifts there for his beloved.

On that morning, June was born near ten o'clock, February 15, 1962, and Alik hadn't even reached his job before Marina's friends at the pharmacy were calling Horizon. So, when he came to his workbench, there were all his fellow workers congratulating him on a daughter. When he had wanted a son. He dropped off a letter to her that evening.

February 15, 1962

Dear Marina,

You and I did not expect a girl at all but I am very glad just the same. You are a stout fellow! How did you succeed in delivering so fast? . . . You are a stout fellow! And I will say that again!

If you need anything, tell me any of your wishes; you and I are completely ready for June Marina Oswald.

Alik[2]

In turn, her letter was waiting for him:

Dear Alik!

So you are a father now. It is even nice that we have a girl. The delivery went off very well and fast. June was born at 10 o'clock. They sewed up only four small outside cracks. I myself did not expect that everything would be so fast. Aunt Valya will probably come to see you this evening. She has been here already today. Do not bring anything today. And tomorrow bring only kefir and some dessert. I no longer can have chocolates. You already know the rest.

I kiss you,
Marina[3]

Notes went back and forth. Sometimes on scraps of paper. He was restricted to the hospital lobby, and she was up on Floor Three.

Dear!

How are you? There is no kefir. What do you need? Did you nurse the baby already? . . . Who called you up today?

I love you,
Alik[4]

She discovered that she wanted to see him. Very much. She managed it by sneaking down to her pharmacy on the first floor. She was breaking hospital rules. One more sin on her soul. Ha, ha.

Lee was very glad to have a daughter, he said, as if he had never had any dreams it would be a son. Then he said that a girl, first born, was probably better for the mother, but the next one ought to be, it would have to be, a son.

Feb. 18 '62

Dear Marina,

. . . Aunt Valya and Uncle Ilya visited me this morning. She will come to see you tomorrow at 2:00 o'clock. I told her what should be bought. Erich and I were at the Zigers yesterday until 24 o'clock . . .

What do you need? Can you walk? . . . Is June still red? When Aunt Valya comes tomorrow, give her the photographs . . .

Well, so long.

Your husband,
Alik

P.S. I will not come tomorrow. Is it all right?[5]

Marina was irritated. She wrote back: "You don't even see me for a night." Then he appeared late on the following evening, sneaking up from her pharmacy. He had a gift for traveling soundlessly. But she was feeling neglected. She recalls that he saw a lot of Erich that week. Of course, now, thirty years later, she can hardly remember Erich.

2/20/62

Hello, papa!

. . . Aleck, I did not think it was so difficult to nurse a baby. June eats through your cover. But the milk rises before each feeding time and should be drawn off. It is so painful that it would be better if I gave birth to one more baby. Dear Aleck, immediately, *this very day,* buy for me and send me a *breast pump,* . . . so that the rubber bulb is taut, not soft.

. . . Aleck, I became so awful looking that you would not recognize me. This is all because I worry about June not taking the breast. Also, they do not let you have enough sleep here—only from 2 A.M. to 5 A.M. I cannot imagine what I will do at home. Aleck, I also urgently need 1 ruble 20 kopecks. After all, I cannot walk around without a brassiere. Someone bought two for a woman here and she sold me one of them. I must pay her back. This is not for making myself beautiful, but to keep milk from getting stagnant. You all there do not even think about bringing me what I need. All you are doing is just asking what I need. . . . Oh, well, enough of this, I close.

/s/Marina[6]

Feb 21 '62

Dear Marina,

Today we received a very nice present for June from the factory; I know you will like it.

They bought: one summer blanket, 6 light diapers, 4 warm diapers, 2 chemises, 3 very good warm chemises, 4 (?) very nice suits and two toys (total 27 rubles) . . .

How is June eating?

I probably won't come tomorrow. All right?

I love you,
Alik[7]

February 23
Marina leaves hospital. I see June for first time.

At the entrance to Third Clinical, Marina was met by relatives and friends, a crowd. It was cold outside, and she and Alik were terrified that if June took even one breath of cold air she would be endangered. Later, when they reached their apartment, he wouldn't even let people come into the room where June was being kept until all chill was off their clothing; they had to stay in the kitchen until then. Lee was so excited he kept running around back and forth and couldn't talk, couldn't breathe; he was in more danger than their baby from the cold air.

On this first night home, Valya was having a birthday party at her home, and Marina sent Lee to congratulate her, but he did not come back as soon as he had promised. Marina waited. Their baby was crying and she did not know how to change diapers. It was okay at Third Clinical, where you practiced on a doll, but this was her live baby and she was scared to death to touch her. So she was crying and her baby was crying and her husband was not home. She ran across to this neighbor who had children and asked what to do—then everything became all right. Her neighbor showed her how to put a fresh diaper on June in the Russian manner, swaddling. She had been shown before, but now she knew.

It was late at night when Lee came home, and he was drunk. She had never seen him so drunk. He was loud, he was singing, he wanted to dance. He said, "They made me drink for our baby, for Aunt Valya, for Marina." He had been singing all the way home. He said, "Now I have my two girls." Yes, her poor American was not so used to Russian vodka. It was terribly funny to see him. He said so many silly things to her and to June. He swore on his love, and by his love, and was extremely happy, not at all rowdy—very obedient, in fact, sort of sheepish. Before long, he went straight to bed; he fell into it.

It may have been Valya's birthday, but Ilya would have other reasons to remember it. Stepan had had a conversation with him, and wrote a memo which he labeled TOP SECRET:

> Met agent of MVD "P" at meeting on 23.II.62. Said that he had recently spoken on two occasions with his niece, Marina, regarding her upcoming departure from the Soviet Union for the U.S. "P" explained to Marina necessity

of conducting herself in worthy manner and not taking part in any anti-Soviet propaganda or other hostile actions aimed at Soviet Union, so as not to cause any trouble for "P" and other relatives living in USSR. Marina promised "P" that she would not commit any acts in U.S. that would compromise "P" or her other relatives.

"P" will continue to have educational conversations and will have a talk with "Likhoi"[8] so that upon arrival in U.S. he will refrain from making any slanderous statements about USSR.

"P" explained that in conversation with Marina, expressing concern about her well-being, he inquired as to whether she had noticed anything suspicious in L.H. Oswald's behavior or actions which would show him to be a dubious personality. Marina stated to "P" that she had noticed nothing of that sort in Oswald's behavior.

During his meetings with her, "P" also asked Marina if she wasn't afraid that Oswald would be repressed by American authorities since he defected from United States. Marina is aware, having been told by Oswald, that in U.S. it is not considered to be a crime which would threaten him with arrest and that, supposedly, according to American laws, there is no basis for making Oswald answer for it after his return to U.S.

There may have been organizational tension present in such a meeting between an MVD Colonel and a KGB Captain. At one time, Misha Kuzmich, Ilya's neighbor, had been chief doctor in Minsk for both KGB and MVD. A line of patients from both organizations would form in his outer office as people waited for their turn. When a Colonel from MVD came in, however, he would approach Misha's nurse like a big boss, and she would take him right through. He was a Colonel and in uniform, after all. KGB guys were more modest. They didn't wear uniforms. So you couldn't determine their rank. They might be well dressed and elegant, but they would have to wait in line. KGB got upset, therefore, but could do nothing about it. They were too secretive to show who was of higher rank among their people. In fact, KGB was so unhappy that they eventually set up their own polyclinic, and even their own hospital, as a means of avoiding such annoyances.

There were other differences. KGB did surveillance and so did MVD; but the latter did it in a more primitive style. At MVD, there was a saying: "If you have enough strength, you don't need brains."

Of course, should a job concern internal security, they would cooperate. All the same, you would usually know who was from one organization and who from the other, because people in KGB had better manners and were more cultivated. Misha could say with some authority that a lot of people who spoke of being brought in by KGB had in fact been approached by MVD. Since both were located in the same building on Lenin Prospekt, you weren't going to separate one from another just by being summoned to that large yellow building, with its high white columns out front and its small doors.

7

"There Are Microbes in Your Mouth"

February 28
I go to register (as prescribed by law) the baby. I want her name to be June Marina Oswald. But those bureaucrats say her middle name must be the same as my first. A Russian custom supported by a law. I refuse to have her name written as "June Lee." They promise to call the City Ministry (city hall) and find out in this case, since I do have a U.S. passport.

His next entry is for February *29*, although 1962 is no leap year.

February 29
I am told that nobody knows what to do exactly but everybody agrees, "Go ahead and do it 'Po-Russki' [the Russian way]." Name: June Lee.

When Valya came to visit, Marina was ironing diapers. Since they were too dry, she held some water in her mouth and blew it out in a spray. Alik said, "What are you doing? There are microbes in your mouth." This meant to Valya that he cared about the baby. He actually took a plate and put a little water in it and showed

Marina how to do it with her fingers, lightly. Of course, Marina's family might be elegant to look at, but Valya knew by now—peasant stock. Rich peasant stock. Tatiana, for instance, had not been educated—she could barely read—but all the same, elegant.

Then, one day in early spring, when Marina and Alik had a terrible fight over at Valya's home, Alik said, "Stay in Russia if you want, but at least let me take my baby," whereupon Marina grabbed June and said, "You have no right to remove a child from her mother." Valya ran back and forth between them, and then told Marina that Alik was pale as a ghost standing by her window. Of course, they made up. Valya was the peacemaker. "Look what you've done to him," Valya kept saying.

After his marriage, Stellina heard nothing from Alyosha. No contact. After the baby's birth, however, serious problems began, because he did call. He said, "You know, Marina doesn't know how to cook; she doesn't clean up." He said, "You, Stellina, had a child and you still went to work. But I come home and bring her money and our clothes aren't washed, the house is dirty, the kid's crying, she doesn't have anything to eat for me . . ."

Stellina told him that was strange. You have to talk to her, she told him. Explain! With a child, a woman has to work. Your wife has to clean and cook. You should help, of course, but that's what she should do.

After this conversation, there was no word for a while, then he called again and said, "Ma, this situation is unbearable. Our child isn't taken care of. I leave for work hungry. I come back home hungry. We are constantly getting in fights." He began to cry.

Sometimes he would meet Stellina at night. She taught night school for workers, and on their way, as they were walking, he would be crying, out on the street, yes. Then he started to say that his wife was insisting they go to America. She would say there was no way he could earn any more money at his factory, and finally she insisted they go.

Let no one say that he did not have different sides to offer to different people. We can be certain that the State Department was hardly seeing Oswald in the same light as Stellina.

On March 9, Joseph Norbury, the American Consul at the Embassy, wrote to Oswald to inform him that the American Embassy was now authorized to advance him as much as $500 "to defray the cost of travel to an American port of entry," for his family and himself:

> . . . You will of course be expected to use the cheapest available mode of transportation [and] will be asked to sign a promissory note for the funds at the time you receive them . . .
>
> We have not yet received the approved visa petition for your wife [but] as soon as it is approved, you can submit your passport to the OVIR for your exit visa . . .[1]

Why had the American Embassy in Moscow not yet received approval of Marina's visa? Was there a problem still unsettled? Lee told Marina, "If they don't allow you to enter America, I will stay in Russia. I am not going alone." At that moment she would have supported him if he had told her they must go to the moon. They were really a family, she decided. Good days came back to their marriage.

Now, when Lee came home from work, he always had a nice smile no matter how bad his day had been. He might tell her about his troubles at work later, but once he opened their door, he would say, "Daddy's home," or, "Here I am." Would announce himself as if he were an actor bounding onstage. And she looked forward to that. "Girls, Daddy's here, everything's fine. *Devochki, ya doma.* Little girls, I'm home."

As soon as he came in, he would take off his dirty clothes, shower right away, and put on clean ones. Of course, they only had hot water three times a week, so on days there was none, he would not take a cold shower but just clean himself off. She did not have to boil water for him. Lee would help her with laundry as well and sometimes wash their dishes.

Meanwhile, the sanction was still in force. The next two communications speak for themselves. The first is from the American Consul, Joseph Norbury, in Moscow, to the State Department in Washington.

> March 15, 1962
> Decision needed soonest on re-consideration 243(g) waiver Marina OSWALD. Husband . . . telephones and writes Embassy frequently to find out reason delay. We deemed it unwise discuss 243(g) problem as long as waiver still possible, but find it increasingly awkward put Oswald off.[2]

The second is from Robert Owen, in the Office of Soviet Union Affairs in the State Department, to John Crump, the officer in the State Department's Visa Office handling Oswald's case, and it may be the most important single memo in the file.

March 16, 1962

VO Mr. John E. Crump
SOV Robert I. Owen

. . . SOV[3] believes it is in the interest of the U.S. to get Lee Harvey Oswald and his family out of the Soviet Union and on their way to this country as soon as possible. An unstable character, whose actions are entirely unpredictable, Oswald may well refuse to leave the USSR or subsequently attempt to return there if we should make it impossible for him to be accompanied from Moscow by his wife and child.

Such action on our part would also permit the Soviet Government to argue that although it had issued an exit visa to Mrs. Oswald to prevent the separation of a family, the United States Government had imposed a forced separation by refusing to issue her a visa. [Moreover, a] detour to a third country would require additional United States funds.

SOV recommends that INS be asked to reconsider on an urgent basis its decision regarding the 243(g) waiver for Mrs. Oswald . . . motivated in part by the fact that Oswald is using up his funds while awaiting documentation.[4]

Marina was still not sure she wanted to go. She was looking for advice. Some of the pharmacy girls tried to talk her out of it. She would say to them, "What am I going to do? I have a baby, and a baby should have its father." But they would say she was going to a foreign country with a man who was not such a balanced person. He wants to live here, gets married, gets her pregnant—then suddenly he wants to go back to America. Lots of uncertainty in him. Maybe her child needs a father, but he was moving his wife into a new country without knowing—can she cope with such a situation? After all, people were brought up here in a different way. He is taking his wife over there without even thinking ahead of how she will feel.

Second Thoughts

Along with everything else, Lee was having an exchange of letters with a Brigadier General in the Marine Corps.

                                        7 Mar 1962

Dear Mr. Oswald:

  . . . A review of your file at this Headquarters reflects . . . reliable information which indicated that you had renounced your United States citizenship with the intention of becoming a permanent citizen of the Union of Soviet Socialist Republics. The Commander, Marine Air Reserve Training, made responsible efforts to inform you of your right to appear before the review board in person [but in] the absence of reply from you concerning your rights, [the board] met on 8 August 1960 at which time a recommendation was submitted that you be separated from the Marine Corps Reserve as undesirable . . .

                    Sincerely,
                    R. McC. Tompkins,
                    Brigadier General U.S. Marine Corps[1]

One can feel the pressure of Oswald's hand upon each word he chooses to emphasize in his reply of March 22.

Dear Sirs:

  In reply to your notification of the granting of an *undesirable* discharge and your conveying of the process at which *it* was arrived:

  I would like to point out in direct opposition to your information that I have never taken steps to renounce my U.S. citizenship. Also that the United States State Department has no charges or complaints against me *whatsoever.*

  I refer you to the United States Embassy, Moscow, or the U.S. Department of State, Washington DC, for the verification of this fact.

  Also, I was [not] aware of the finding of the board of officers of 8 August 1960. I was notified by my mother, in December of 1961.

My request to the Secretary of the Navy, his referral to you, and your letter to me, did not say anything about a *review,* which is what I was trying to arrange.

You mention "reliable information" as the basis for the *undesirable* discharge. I have no *doubt* it was newspapers' speculation which formed your "reliable information."

Under U.S. law governing the use of passports and conduct abroad, I have a perfect right to reside in *any* country I wish *to* . . . therefore, you have no *legal,* or even moral, right to reverse my *honorable* discharge . . . into an *undesirable* discharge.

You may consider this letter a request by me for a full *review* of my case in the light of these facts, since by the time you *receive* this letter I shall have returned to the USA with my family, and shall be prepared to appear in person at a reasonable time and place in my area before a reviewing board of officers.[2]

On March 27 comes the last entry in his diary:

I receive a letter from a Mr. Phillips (employer of my mother) pledging to support my wife in case of need.

March 27, '62

Dear Mother,

. . . We should be in the States in May at the latest. *The Embassy* has *agreed to loan me $500.00* for the trip, and also they accepted my own affidavit of support so yours won't be necessary after all. However, *don't try to get that businessman friend of yours to cancel his affidavit; it may come in handy someday.* As you say, *my* trip here would make a good story about *me.* I've already thought about that for quite a while now. In fact, *I've already made 50 pages of longhand notes on the subject.*

Love xxx
Lee[3]

March 28

Dear Mother,

. . . You asked whether I'll be staying at your place or Robert's in Fort Worth. I don't think I'll be staying at

either but I will be visiting both. In any event, I'll want to
live on my own . . .[4]

April 12, 1962

Dear Robert,
. . . It looks like we'll be leaving the country in April or
May; only the American side is holding us up now. The
Embassy is as slow as the Russians were . . .
. . . Now that winter is gone, I really don't want to leave
until the beginning of fall since the spring and summer
here are so nice.

Your brother,
Lee[5]

Can he be thinking of his undesirable discharge and all the problems it could cause him when looking for a job? America may be
waiting for him like an angry relative whose eyes glare in the heat.

9

"His Impertinence Knows No Bounds"

From March 16 to May 4, there has been no change in the problem concerning the waiver.

INCOMING TELEGRAM DEPARTMENT OF STATE
May 4, 1962
FROM: Moscow
TO: Secretary of State
Decision needed soonest on re-consideration 243(#) [sic]
Oswald . . . We deemed it unwise discuss 243(g) problem as
long as waiver still possible, but find it increasingly awkward
put Oswald off.

THOMPSON[1]

Does Oswald have any idea how many people whom he dislikes,
and who in turn detest him, are now working for his cause? Tele-

grams are even being sent out from Moscow under Ambassador Thompson's name.

From a letter on May 8 by Joseph Norbury, to Robert I. Owen, in the Office of Soviet Union Affairs, Department of State:

> Dear Bob,
>   . . . You will also have noted our cable of May 4 on the OSWALD case. If the 243(g) waiver is not granted soon on this one, I think we should call the Oswalds in and send them on to Belgium. It is not that our hearts are breaking for Oswald. His impertinence knows no bounds. His latest letter contained an imperious demand that the State Department stop trying to get travel funds from his relatives in the U.S. . . . On the two or three recent occasions he has telephoned from Minsk, I have had to refer lamely to a still unsettled "problem" which is still holding up his wife's case . . .[2]

If, for months, State has been requesting Justice to waive the sanction, now . . . the Immigration and Naturalization Service of the Department of Justice finally relinquishes its punitive position in a letter on May 9 to Michael Cieplinski of the Bureau of Security and Consular Affairs at State.

> Dear Mr. Cieplinski:
>   . . . Your letter also states that the waiving of sanctions in behalf of Mrs. Oswald would be in the best interests of the United States.
>   In view of the strong representation made in your letter of March 27, 1962, you are hereby advised that the sanctions imposed pursuant to Section 243(g) of the Immigration and Nationality Act are hereby waived in behalf of Mrs. Oswald.
>   Sincerely yours,
>   Robert H. Robinson, Deputy Assoc. Commissioner
>   Travel Control[3]

It is well worth quoting from the most salient paragraph of Michael Cieplinski's letter of March 27:

> . . . if Mrs. Oswald is not issued a visa by the Embassy, the Soviet Government will be in a position to claim that it has done all it

can to prevent the separation of the family by issuing Mrs. Oswald the required exit permission, but that this [American] Government has refused to issue her a visa, thus preventing her from accompanying her husband and child . . .[4]

Finally, on May 10, Joseph B. Norbury can write to Oswald with positive news.

Dear Mr. Oswald:
I am pleased to inform you that the Embassy is now in a position to take final action on your wife's visa application. Therefore, you and your wife are invited to come to the Embassy at your convenience . . .
The Embassy has on file two copies of your wife's birth certificate and one copy of her marriage certificate. Therefore, she need bring only one more copy of her marriage certificate, three photographs, an X-ray, serological analysis and certification of smallpox inoculation.
As you were notified previously, three photographs of your daughter and a copy of her birth certificate will also be necessary for the Consular Report of Birth and the amendment to your passport . . .
Please notify the Embassy when to expect you.[5]

10

Farewell to Ella

It may be recalled that Max Prokhorchik was the fellow who had a fight with Oswald when the settings were changed on Max's drill. That had been back in the early days of January 1960, just after they both started to work at Horizon. Afterward, Max had been interested in Ella, since there was a sort of mystery about her. She had seen so much of that American. Later, Max and a fellow named Arkady went out in a threesome with Ella until she chose Max, and then soon after he proposed, and Ella's mother said, "Let it be. Let her be your wife." So they were married on May 4,

1962. A very small ceremony. Fifteen months had gone by since she stopped seeing Lee, and not once in all that time had Lee spoken to Ella. In fact, he now pretended not to know her. But one day, most suddenly, toward the end of May, he came up to her workbench just as Ella was getting ready to go home and have lunch with her new husband. Lee came in, walked straight up to her, and said, "Can we meet today? There's something I want to talk to you about."

Ella lost her head. If she'd been married a little longer she might have said yes, but she'd only been living with Max a couple of weeks, and he was so close to her that he was following her around, watching her every step, so she thought she probably couldn't, probably shouldn't, not after that fight between Max and Lee over two years ago. She shook her head. She said, "I just got married," and Lee said, "Did you marry somebody I know?" She looked at him and said, "Yes." He turned his back and walked out through the same door by which he had walked in. Some days later, someone told her that he had left for America. If only she had known he was going away.

She remembers that Lee certainly seemed to want to tell her something, but once he turned away, she didn't have time to react. And she didn't feel like running after him.

She thinks Lee must have seen her with Max. In the weeks before their marriage, she and Max had always been together. Lee would have seen that not only did she leave Horizon with Max each evening, but she would walk to work with him each morning. Lee certainly wouldn't like the idea that she had married Max.

Ella was very surprised, however, that Lee was going back to America. She even started to contradict people about it. Someone would say, "Do you know Lee Oswald is in America?" and she'd answer, "No, I can just bet it's not America he's going to." She was so sure of herself that she was very surprised later to find out she was wrong.

11

Leave-taking

FROM KGB TRANSCRIPT

FOR OBJECT: OLH-2983

FOR PERIOD: 19 MAY 1962

LHO: How could you! You were off from work somewhere for three hours.

(*baby is crying*)

WIFE: <u>You idiot! I'm not going anywhere with you.</u> You can take the baby and go. Take her and go.

LHO: Shut up. Take your baby.

(*baby is crying*)

WIFE: Leave me alone. Do whatever you want, I'm not going with you. You never do anything to help me out. Go, feed the baby. You can kill me, but I'm not going to get milk. I'm just going to sit here and watch. You'll <u>create these scandals until two in the morning.</u> I don't just take off from work somewhere—I have to sleep at that clinic. These doctors seem to make a point of not waiting for me.

   (*cries*)

   What, I have to run home [from my clinic]?

LHO: Exactly.

(*they go into kitchen*)

12:50   (*they come back in*)

WIFE: (*sobbing*) <u>Out of my sight, you dog! You scoundrel!</u> Don't look at me that way—nobody is afraid of you. <u>Go to hell, you bastard!</u>

LHO: You're very good.

WIFE: <u>You can go to your America without me, and I hope you die on the way.</u>

(*LHO leaves*)

(*quiet in the apartment*)

That dialogue was in the afternoon. By evening of the same day, Pavel has arrived, and then a man and woman come to visit. Given the nature of their conversation, they have to be Mr. and Mrs. Ziger, and so they appear here with their names rather than—as in the documents—Unidentified Man 3 and Unidentified Woman 2. Having taken this much liberty with our KGB transcript, "Wife" will now be changed to Marina, and "LHO" can appear as Lee.

21:30

MRS. ZIGER: We knocked and knocked!

MARINA: We were on our balcony; we didn't hear anything.

MRS. ZIGER: Where's your daughter? Let's hope she stays healthy. She has her mother's eyes—they're big.

LEE: She has her mother's eyes, lips, nose. She got everything from her mother, nothing from me.

MRS. ZIGER: Next time you'll have a son.

LEE: We already received all our papers. <u>We're probably leaving on Tuesday</u> . . .

MRS. ZIGER: How are you going? By boat or plane?

LEE: From Moscow either by train or by plane. It depends on what sort of visa they give us . . .

(*they all talk at same time; can't understand anything*)

MRS. ZIGER: When she grows up, she won't even know where she was born. Maybe June'll come to visit sometime.

MR. ZIGER: Visiting is another matter. She just shouldn't come here to stay.

LEE: Have you put on tea?

MRS. ZIGER: Don't worry about us, we're fine.

LEE: Are there any glasses?

MARINA: We have two glasses. There's also my small cup. He already packed everything.

LEE: Our entire fortune. An empty room.

MRS. ZIGER: . . . You're happy, of course?

LEE: We're happy.

MRS. ZIGER: Marinochka, you must be?

MARINA: I'm not all that happy, of course . . .

MRS. ZIGER: [The baby] will be blond; she's going to be pretty.

LEE: She's going to have a good life; she'll have everything . . .

(*they're all talking at once; difficult to make out*)

(*Pavel arrives and all three men move to kitchen*)

MRS. ZIGER: Marinochka, you don't know how much I envy you, you're so healthy.

MARINA: I'll arrive [in America] with my daughter, I don't know, maybe it'll be difficult, maybe he won't find work.

MRS. ZIGER: Why won't he find work? . . . You'll get settled, everything will be fine, you'll have lots of everything, you'll have freedom.

MARINA: We'll have money, freedom.

MRS. ZIGER: God, how I hate living in this city. You don't have a lot of linen. Do you have a chest? God, and we have so much junk! How much we brought! And how much we gave away! There was our dresser, our bed, our cheval glass, oaken, huge. And dishes! We sold them all.

MARINA: At first you probably didn't have all that?

MRS. ZIGER: Yes, I remember it as if it were yesterday. He was twenty-one, and I was twenty-four; I was older than him.

MARINA: You look like you're younger . . .

MRS. ZIGER: How are you set for money?

MARINA: We saved . . . Because we're both that way.

MRS. ZIGER: How much does it cost?

MARINA: One ticket costs 440 new rubles. For two.

MRS. ZIGER: Didn't your aunt help you a little?

MARINA: No.

MRS. ZIGER: Thank God you're going. It's fate, you met your beloved American . . .

MARINA: I'll tell you one thing, he helps me.

MRS. ZIGER: Most important thing is that he doesn't have any other women.

MARINA: Who knows, maybe I won't always be good for him. I wouldn't say that I'm really good.

MRS. ZIGER: You have a good soul.

MARINA: At first he was unhappy that she was a girl and not a boy, but now he doesn't mind.

MRS. ZIGER: Oh, not at all, he'll love her.

MARINA: He loves her now.

(*they talk about baby, about fact that some husbands are bad, drink or treat their wives badly*)

MRS. ZIGER: Maybe you'll want to come for a visit here sometime . . .

MARINA: It's easier to live there. He'll be making more money than he makes here. What can he do here? You work and work and you make chicken feed.

MRS. ZIGER: . . . It's amazing that your aunt didn't help you—she could at least have bought you a present.

MARINA: What are you talking about! She didn't even buy diapers for June. He and she alone make thousands. They could at least have bought something. I'm not asking for expensive presents, maybe a little hat for 40 kopecks. Now, the pharmacy girls helped—one of them would bring over diapers, another would bring something else. Every little bit helps.

MRS. ZIGER: Did you already say goodbye to your aunt?

MARINA: Not yet.

MRS. ZIGER: When did you tell her?

MARINA: I think they got my letter day before yesterday . . . I told her that I was leaving. "Are you crazy! You're going to leave after all."

MRS. ZIGER: I'm following my husband. Wherever needle goes, thread follows . . .

(*they talk about what Marina will wear for her trip; they talk about furniture: how much, more or less, they'll get for it; then they talk about her baby*)

MARINA: Alik, come over here; she's sleeping.

22:40 (*Lee, Pavel, and Mr. Ziger come in from kitchen*)

MRS. ZIGER: So, Alik, are you going to miss us?

LEE: Of course, we'll miss you.

(*everyone's yelling; can't make out what; Pavel is taking pictures*)

(*they all talk at same time; can't make anything out*)

MRS. ZIGER: You have to promise to teach this baby Russian.

LEE: I promise.

MRS. ZIGER: It's good to know Russian; it never hurts. Isn't it good you can understand?

(*guys talk about radio; women talk about their problems; can't understand anything*)

PAVEL: <u>Customs won't look.</u>

MARINA: They don't look at everything, anyway—they do it selectively.

MRS. ZIGER: <u>When we arrived in Odessa,</u> there was an enormous warehouse; everyone had brought 7 or 8 chests. We brought a piano, a stroller, four enormous chests full of everything—everyone brought half a train car of things. And the Ukrainian women say: "Look at all the stuff they brought with them, and they say that people there are dying of hunger." And my girls came wearing thin high heels: "Look at those heels!" We were crestfallen, you can't imagine . . . Things here have changed so much during this last five years!

PAVEL: For worse?

MRS. ZIGER: For better. Let's hope so. I'm tired of living and suffering in a country like Russia, the biggest and richest country.

PAVEL: In the final analysis, the number of bombs in every country isn't all that terrible. When there are enough bombs, no one will start a war.

MR. ZIGER: You'd have to be crazy.

PAVEL: They say that we're arming because Americans want war. Americans had their bomb before we did; why didn't they attack then? They don't want war. No one wants war.

MR. ZIGER: I don't know whether there'll be a war or not.

PAVEL: There can't be two systems for very long.

MR. ZIGER: If Marxism is really right, then capitalism is dying, expiring, so there'll only be one system. If it's not right, then Communism won't last very long. Communism has changed when you compare it to Communism that was described by Engels and Marx.

(*static; nothing audible*)

MRS. ZIGER: Goodbye.

MR. ZIGER: We'll still see each other before you go.

23:10 (*Mr. and Mrs. Ziger leave*)

There was something she had never told anyone before. It seemed irrelevant. Yet, before they left Russia, Lee took her out on the balcony and asked her to try—before she quit her job at the pharmacy; he said, Try to get some narcotics and bring them home. When she told him she couldn't obtain such items legally—you have to sign for everything—he said, "Can't you steal it?" She wouldn't. She couldn't and she wouldn't.

But to this day, she has no idea why he wanted narcotics. He didn't say morphine or amphetamines, just "narcotics." It wasn't as if he was drug-addicted; why, he couldn't even take much alcohol. Maybe he wanted to sell drugs in Minsk so he could come home to America with more money. But she didn't understand. He was scared to death even to smuggle his writing papers out. He spent a lot of time worrying about where to put those mysterious pages. He would bring up such a concern now and again on the balcony.

FROM KGB TRANSCRIPT

FOR OBJECT: OLH-2983

FOR PERIOD: 20 MAY 1962

LEE: . . . You won't say anything. You'll answer their questions, you [won't] talk. You're going to sit there and keep your mouth shut, got it?

MARINA: If there's trouble, you'll have to deal with it.

LEE: That's all there is to it. It's my responsibility. You just sit tight . . . [At the American Embassy] you should say: No, I'm not a member of a trade union. I've never been in any Soviet organization.

MARINA: So do they persecute you for that in America? <u>Why should I go to a country like that?</u>

LEE: Just say it.

MARINA: I haven't left yet and the trouble's already starting, and wait till I get [to America]—aha, you're a Russian! You're a member of a trade union!

LEE: Shut up, your brains are ugly.

MARINA: . . . I'm a Soviet girl, I'm not about to be afraid of anything. If I'm a member of my trade union, I'm a member and I'm not going to hide!

LEE: Idiot!

MARINA: I haven't got anything to fear.

LEE: <u>Fool!</u> [Just] say you are a pharmacist . . .

MARINA: Well, I won't go to a country where they persecute a person for every word. [bracketed in left margin]

LEE: (*idiotic laughter*)

MARINA: <u>You smug ass!</u> You'll burst like a soap bubble.

LEE: You already burst a long time ago . . .

MARINA: . . . Honest people don't hide anything, but you're a deceiver. You're always deceiving, you deceive everyone.

10:05 (*Lee leaves*)

13:20 (*Sonya arrives; they talk about Marina's baby*)

SONYA: . . . You don't have a lot of things, just suitcases, right?

MARINA: Just suitcases.

SONYA: That's it?

MARINA: I have to wash my floor before we leave.

SONYA: Why should you? Let them do it.

MARINA: It has to be polished.

SONYA: It's not essential. You can get by with just washing it . . .

Finally, after a year of deciding to leave, and getting ready to leave, after their letters have been written and all their permissions granted, all possessions sold and packed, they are still a day and a half away from departing but will leave the apartment now to spend their last night and last day in Minsk at Pavel's place. Next day, on the eve of their departure, Stepan interviewed Ilya Prusakov once more.

FROM KGB REPORT

On 21 of May 1962 I conducted an interview with "Nalim's" uncle, Prusakov, I. V., who informed me that on 20th of May he was visited at his apartment by his niece, Marina, and "Nalim." In their conversation, "Nalim" told Prusakov of their intention to leave for Moscow . . . on the 22nd of May in order to fill out all necessary documents and then go to America.

As a result of this, Prusakov and his wife, being Marina's relatives, gave Marina and "Nalim" several pieces of advice. In particular, Prusakov, expressing concern for his own well-being, asked Marina and "Nalim" not to take part in any actions hostile to the Soviet Union after arrival in the United States. Prusakov reminded "Nalim" that he was provided for and always well treated by Soviet people. "Nalim" assured Prusakov that they would not undertake any actions harmful to the Soviet Union. At the same time, "Nalim" explained that in order to avoid possible meetings and interviews with correspondents, he had decided to go straight to his brother's residence without stopping in New York.

Before her departure for Moscow, Marina is supposed to visit Prusakov's apartment again. Considering that fact, a recommendation was made to Prusakov that he have a conversation with her, which would help to prevent Marina and "Nalim" from taking part in anti-Soviet propaganda abroad. Prusakov's attention was brought to an understanding that this interview not evoke any suspicion on the part of Marina and "Nalim."

Dear Robert,

. . . This will be the last letter you get from us from the USSR.

In case you hear about our coming or the newspapers hear about it (I hope they won't), I want to warn you not to make any comments whatsoever about me. None at all!! I know what was said about me when I left the U.S. as Mother sent me some clippings from the newspapers, however, I realize that it was just the shock of the news which made you say all those things. However, I'll just remind you again not to make any statements or comments if you are approached by the newspapers between now and the time we actually arrive in the U.S.

Hope to see you soon. Love to the family.

Your brother,
Lee[1]

Friends came with flowers to say goodbye, and Marina knew she was leaving Mother Russia, leaving her friends and family behind. So, in a way, it was like a funeral. After all, at a funeral, you see a person for the last time. So, she thought, "Here I am leaving and my relatives might as well be dead." She had done them so dirty. She didn't think Valya and Ilya would come, and they didn't. Only some friends.

As the train began to pull out of Minsk, the Ziger family and Pavel began to wave, and all the others who had come to say good-bye (except Erich—he didn't come), and now they were on their way to Moscow.

They would stay in Moscow for ten days, time enough to pick up their last papers and fill out their last questionnaires, and then they would depart again from Moscow by train to pass through Minsk once more (but in the middle of the night), and in fact, on that occasion, right there, indeed, in the early hours of the morning, way over there in the dark of Minsk station, where no lights could reach, Marina saw her aunt clinging to her uncle, just like two birds nesting, and Marina said to herself, "She made him come." Then their train went on into the night, into Poland and, later, into Germany and the Netherlands. Several days would be spent on that train. But that was later. While they were still in Moscow, Lee and Marina and baby June visited for an evening with Marina's friends Yuri Belyankin and his wife, Galina.

The next day, Galina visited the American Embassy with Marina. "To be honest," said Yuri Belyankin to his interviewers, "my hair stood on end when Galya told me she had been inside there. After all, I was working at an ideological agency, Central Television, and it was not that I was really afraid—the Iron Curtain had already opened a crack—but it wasn't something that would help me to get promoted, either."

In the event, Galina, once she was inside, sat in the visitors' lobby and spent her time looking at American magazines. For Lee and Marina there was, however, a small episode. Jack Matlack, the Embassy officer interviewing Marina for her visa, told Oswald, positioned most authoritatively beside her, that applicants for visas had to be seen alone. Oswald protested. His wife knew no English. Matlack assured the husband that he knew Russian. Oswald did not move. Matlack then picked up a few papers on his desk related to other work and began to peruse them. After five minutes, Oswald asked when the interview with Marina would commence and was told it would begin as soon as he left the room, whereupon Oswald stalked off.

Matlack was impressed with the differences in this couple. Marina was humble and drab, a young Soviet girl from the provinces finding herself in a foreign government office, whereas Oswald seemed as much of a peacock as young Napoleon.

When Matlack began to interview Marina, he soon decided that she was lying about membership in Komsomol, for she denied having any. Matlack knew this was highly unlikely and wrote as much in his report, indicating that in his opinion the applicant was not telling the truth, but then, since membership in Komsomol would not be grounds for denying her visa, he proceeded, in due course, after questioning was done, to grant it.

Let us recall the transcribed KGB dialogue taken in the Oswalds' apartment on May 20, just a few days earlier:

MARINA: No, you can kill me, but I'm not going to do things the way you do . . .

LEE: How ridiculous!

MARINA: No point in arguing . . .

LEE: Shut up, fool! . . . You won't say anything. You'll answer their questions, you [won't] talk. You're going to sit there and keep your mouth shut, got it?

MARINA: If there's trouble, you'll have to deal with it.

LEE: That's all there is to it. It's my responsibility. You just sit tight . . . [At the American Embassy] you should say: "No, I'm not a member of a trade union. I've never been in any Soviet organization."

MARINA: . . . If I'm a member of my trade union, I'm a member and I'm not going to hide!

LEE: Idiot!

As it turns out, the irony is bifurcated. He is right; she is right. Either method works. All those passionate fights over issues that are not really going to be contested.

On the last night before the Oswalds left, they had dinner again at Yuri's mother's apartment, and Alik kept rocking June until Yuri's mother said, "Go sit with the others," and Lee said, "No, no, Sofia Leontievna, I like to keep my baby," whereupon she said, "I've already rocked three babies; don't worry." So he gave June up, but he was very jealous. Yuri added, "He was kind of a male mother—that is: man; mother."

There are no photographs of that night, Yuri told the interviewers, because Soviet cinematographers had a silly tradition in those days. When they switched over to moviemaking, they threw away all their still cameras. It was a point of view. They were great filmmakers, and did not wish to be connected any longer to working with stills. It was only later, when he started to make documentaries about people like Shostakovich, that he understood one could make beautiful use of still cameras in cinematography.

Galina remembers that Marina was very nervous on her visit to the American Embassy. Galina brought along apples for them to eat en route, and at the Embassy gates, before they went in, there was a big arch with two militia-men, Russians, big ones, standing in front. Galina's paper bag of fruit began to fall apart, and these militia-men actually helped her pick up the apples. Somehow, in this confusion, although she didn't have documents to get inside the American Embassy, she did walk in with Lee and Marina—plus the apples. It had not been her intention to deceive anyone, but now she was inside.

Galina became the only person to see them off from Moscow. The Oswald family left in the afternoon, and Galina remembers this parting well. She and Marina began to cry; they cried terribly; it was only now that they realized they were separating forever. Marina had an ordinary little ring on her finger, a bright imitation pearl—she didn't have any real jewelry—but she put it on Galina's finger and said, "I don't have anything to give to you, but you must at least have this." Unfortunately, Galina lost it a few years later.

From America, Marina wrote a letter to them. Galina did not write back. Yuri now says, "I'll tell you honestly, I didn't allow her. Marina asked in her letter what she should send us, and I was afraid to reply. I was still at Central Television."

They left Moscow by train on May 30, 1962, and traveled through Poland, Germany, and Holland. In Holland they boarded the SS *Maasdam* for the U.S., and arrived in New York on June 13, 1962.[2]

Page thirty-one of the FBI Report on the Investigation of the Assassination of President Kennedy states:

An FBI investigation of Oswald had been instituted on May 31, 1962, so that the FBI would be notified of his re-entry by Immigration authorities. The purpose of this investigation was to determine if Oswald had been recruited by a Soviet intelligence service.[3]

PART VIII

IN THE ANTEROOM
OF HISTORY

—◁○▷—

1

Across the Briny Deep

On the ship, Oswald does some writing. He has all the free stationery he needs, courtesy of the Holland-America Line, and he sets down answers for himself in expectation of his first press conference in America. He is living with the possibilities. Should he be forthright and therefore unforgettable? Or should he be diplomatic, hypocritical, wise? He is a man of parts, and the art of political life is to manipulate the manipulators. He poses himself eight questions, and all but the fifth reply, which turns into a detailed exegesis of an old wire-service interview in Moscow, are worth repeating. With the exception of Question 6, the column on the left represents his candid reactions and the one on the right presents Oswald's notion of viable public relations.

Q. 1 *Why did you go to the USSR?*

I went as a mark of disgust and protest against American political policies in foreign countries, my personal sign of discontent and horror at the misguided line of reasoning of the U.S. Government and people.	I went as a citizen of the U.S. (as a tourist) residing in a foreign country which I have a perfect right to do. I went there to see the land, the people and how their system works.

Q. 2A *What about those letters?*

I made several letters in which I expressed the above feeling to the American Embassy when, in October 1959, I went there to legally liquidate my	I made no letters deriding the U.S.! In correspondence with the U.S. Embassy, I made no anti-American statements. Any criticism I might have

American citizenship and was refused this legal right.

had was of policies, not our government.

Q. 2B *Did you make statements against the U.S. there?*

Yes.

No.

Q. 3 *Did you break any laws by residing or taking work in the USSR?*

I did, in that I took an oath of allegiance to the USSR.

Under U.S. law, a person may lose the protection of the U.S. by voting or serving in the armed forces of a foreign state or taking an oath of allegiance to that state. I did none of those.

Q. 4 *Isn't all work in the USSR considered state work?*

Yes, of course, and in that respect I also broke a U.S. law in accepting work under a foreign state.

No. Technically, only plants working directly for the state, usually defense plants, [do state work]. Other plants are owned by the workers who work in them . . .

Q. 6 *Why did you remain in the USSR so long if you only wanted a look?*

I resided in the USSR from October 16, 1959, to spring of 1962, a period of two and a half years. I did so because I was living quite comfortably. I had plenty of money, an apartment rent-free, lots of girls, etc. Why should I leave all that?

I resided in the USSR quietly until February 1961 when I wrote the Embassy stating that I would like to go back. (My passport was at the Embassy for safekeeping.) They invited me to Moscow for this purpose [where] the Embassy immediately gave me back my passport and advised me how to get an exit visa from the Russians for myself and my Russian wife. This long and arduous process took months, from July 1961 to May 1962 . . . That's why I was there so long, not out of desire.[1]

Q. 7 *Are you a Communist?*

Yes, basically. No, of course not.
Although I hate the USSR and
the Socialist system, I still
think Marxism can work under
different circumstances.

Q. 7A *Have you ever known a Communist?*

Not in the USA. I have never even known a
Communist outside of the
ones in the USSR—but you
can't help that.

Q. 8 *What are the outstanding differences between the USSR and the USA?*

None, except that in the Freedom of speech, travel,
USA the living standard is a outspoken opposition to
little higher; freedoms are unpopular policies, freedom
about the same; medical aid to believe in God.
and the educational system
is better in the USSR than
in the USA.

NEWSPAPERS: Thank you, sir, you are a *real* patriot!![2]

On sails the SS *Maasdam* to America.

We cannot be certain whether an early draft of his political beliefs was also composed in the ten days he was on the steamship. The creed is written on Holland-America letterhead, but then, he could have written it later with stationery he took ashore. Still, his return passage would have been a natural time for such an effort. He has studied Marx and Lenin, he is not unfamiliar with the notion that great political leaders often compose their immortal tracts in exile or in prison or, for that matter, in transit in the tourist salon of an inexpensive steamship. In this manner, one is ready to assume, he prepared himself for America. He will return with the essence of a political philosophy for people ready to receive his message. If his mission to be an important figure in the Soviet Union has not been a striking success, perhaps it has armed him to come back to America with an even deeper sense of apocalyptic purpose: He will improve the nature of both societies.

. . . To a person knowing both systems and their functional accessories, there can be no mediation between the systems as they exist today and that person.

He must be opposed to their basic foundations and representatives . . .

True democracy can be practiced only at the local level. While the centralized state, administrative, political, or supervisory functions remain, there can be no real democracy, [which should be] a loose confederation of communities at a national level without any centralized state whatsoever.

In equal division, with safeguards against coalitions of communities, there can be democracy—not in the centralized state delegating authority, but in numerous equal communities practicing and developing democracy at the local level . . .

I intend to put forward just such an alternative . . . what is needed is a practical and constructive group of persons desiring peace but steadfastly opposed to the revival of the forces who have led millions of people to death and destruction in a dozen wars and now, at this moment, lead the world into unsurpassed danger . . .

But how many of you have tried to find out the truth behind the Cold War clichés?

I have lived under both systems. I have *sought* the answers, and although it would be very easy to dupe myself into believing one system is better than the other, I know they are not.[3]

So he comes back to America with the foundation laid in his mind for future activities. He will establish a political movement of the purest principles, the highest principles.

Homecoming

REPRESENTATIVE FORD. When he did return, after having borrowed money from the Federal Government, did he ever ask you for any help and assistance in repaying the loan?

ROBERT OSWALD. On his arrival in New York City, I believe the date to be June 13, back in 1962, my wife received a telephone call from Special Services Welfare Center located at New York City stating that Lee and his family were present and that they needed funds to reach their destination, Fort Worth, Tex., and the lady that talked to my wife put it to the extent they were unable to help them and if some member of the family was going to help them, they had better do so then. My wife didn't know anything else to say but of course that we would, and this is what I wanted her to say. She called me at my office that day [and] I wired the money to the welfare bureau in New York, care of Lee Harvey Oswald.

REPRESENTATIVE FORD. And that was the money that they, Marina and Lee, used to get to Fort Worth.

ROBERT OSWALD. That is correct, sir.

REPRESENTATIVE FORD. Did Lee ever repay you for that?

ROBERT OSWALD. Yes, sir; he did. He had actually spent a little over $100 for the plane tickets and, of course, we met him at Dallas, Love Field, on their arrival there. The next day, even though I insisted he keep it, he returned what he had left from the $200 and he said he would pay me back as soon as he was able to and I told him not to worry about that, but just to take his time [and] he repaid this $10–$20 a week from his paycheck.[1]

From Marina's narrative: . . . I remember that we took a short rest in Atlanta for several minutes while the airplane was being readied for its further flight. We went out to take a breath of fresh air. And people were eyeing us askance. I cannot boast about the way we were dressed. And even June was dressed in Russian style. In Russia, children's . . . arms and legs are wrapped in diapers . . . the result being that they look something like an Egyptian mummy. I am looking at myself now with different eyes and think what a comical sight we must have been then.

In Dallas we were met by Robert and his family. I was very ashamed of how sloppy we looked. We were both very tired from the trip and didn't have anything very good to wear anyway, not to speak of the way my hair must have looked. I am afraid that Robert also was ashamed of having such a relative as myself. But they are very good people and did not say anything to me; quite to the contrary, they helped me get used to the new country. Their very delicate approach to me and to our whole family immediately gave me a very good impression of Americans [even if] I felt quite out of place . . .[2]

REPRESENTATIVE BOGGS. Was the relationship between your family and your wife and Mrs. Oswald . . . pleasant?

ROBERT OSWALD. Yes, sir. I would describe it as very pleasant . . . my wife and I both were just tickled to death, so to speak, for an opportunity to be with somebody like Marina and to show her things she had never seen before.[3]

From Marina's narrative: I remember that Robert suggested that I exchange my dress for shorts, since it is very warm in Texas in the summer. This was a revolution for me. Up until then I had only seen in the movies how American girls simply walk around the streets in shorts . . .

Robert showed me the American stores and I was delighted that everything was so simple, and that there were so many things which I had only dreamed of . . . I immediately liked the many neon advertisements. Perhaps Americans are used to them and pay no attention to them. But for me they were unusual—these gay, many-colored lights in the windows and advertisements made me feel good . . .[4]

MR. JENNER. . . . what did you observe, and if in contrast, by way of contrast, in his physical appearance and demeanor as against the last time you had seen him, in 1959?

ROBERT OSWALD. His appearance had changed to the extent that he had lost a considerable amount of hair [and he] appeared the first couple of days upon his return, June 14, 1962, to be rather tense and anxious . . .

MR. JENNER. Did he make any comments when you met him at Love Field, and did you ride in with him from Love Field to your home?

ROBERT OSWALD. Yes, sir. We were in my personal car, my wife and my children were with me. We met him and his wife and his baby. He seemed, perhaps the word is, disappointed, when there were no newspaper reporters around. He did comment on this . . . I believe his comment was something [like,] "What, no photographers or anything?"

I said, "No, I have been able to keep it quiet."

MR. JENNER. And where was that remark made?

ROBERT OSWALD. At Love Field, as they came through the gate . . .

MR. JENNER. Having in mind the changes in physical appearance, and also the course of events since the day of his arrival at Love Field to the present time, have you formed an opinion, Mr. Oswald, as to whether your brother may have undergone some treatment of some kind in Russia that affected his mind?

ROBERT OSWALD. Yes, sir. Since Lee's death on November 24th, I have formed an opinion in that respect.

MR. JENNER. What is that opinion?

ROBERT OSWALD. . . . perhaps something in the nature of shock treatments or something along that line had been given to him in Russia . . .[5]

Let us move from the fraternal to the maternal:

MARGUERITE OSWALD. . . . I was on a case in Crowell, Texas . . . And I was taking care of a very elderly woman whose daughter lived in Fort Worth, Texas.

So I was not able to leave and meet Lee.

Robert, his brother, met him and Lee went to Robert's home.

Approximately about a week later—I could not stand it anymore—I . . . took 3 days off and went to Fort Worth to see Lee and Marina.

Marina is a beautiful girl. And I said to Lee, "Marina, she doesn't look Russian. She is beautiful."

He says, "Of course not. That is why I married her, because she looks like an American girl."

I asked where he had met her, and he said . . . at a social function, a community function.

I said, "You know, Lee, I am getting ready"—I was getting ready—"to write a book on your so-called defection." . . .

He said, "Mother, you are not going to write a book."

I said, "Lee, don't tell me what to do . . . It has nothing to do with you and Marina. It is my life, because of your defection."

He said, "Mother, I tell you you are not to write the book. They could kill her and her family." . . .

While I was in Robert's home, Lee was immediately out job-hunting. And I felt very bad about that, because . . . I thought he should have at least a week or two before he would look for work.

But I want you to know that immediately Lee was out looking for work.

And this is the time that Lee had gone to the public stenographer, made the statement that he was writing a book . . . I, myself, gave him the $10 that he gave the public stenographer.[6]

MRS. BATES. I think it was around 10 o'clock or 11 o'clock in the morning, on the 18th of June, 1962 . . . He just walked in . . . He said, "First, I want to find out what your prices are and see if I can afford it." So I gave him my price . . . I said it was either 2 and a half an hour or a dollar a page [and] he brought out this large manila envelope, legal size—oh, I think it was 10 by 14 or something—one of those large ones. And he said . . . that he had notes that he had smuggled out of Russia. And I looked up at him kind of surprised. I said, "Have you been to Russia?"

He said, "Yes, ma'am. I just got back." And that he had smuggled these notes out of Russia under his clothes, next to his skin . . .

And that he wanted to have them typed by a professional typist. He said, "Some of them are typed on a little portable, some of them are handwritten in ink, some of them in pencil."

He said, "I'll have to sit right here and help you with them because some of them are in Russian and some of them are in English." So we agreed that I would do it—but I hadn't seen them yet . . .

MR. JENNER. Had you reached a conclusion as to the rate?

MRS. BATES. Well, I immediately lowered it to $2 an hour. I was anxious to get on it.

MR. JENNER. Why . . . ?

MRS. BATES. Well, anybody that had just come back from Russia and had notes, I would like to have seen them. And . . . he looked like a high school kid to me when he first came in. I thought he was just a kid . . .

MR. JENNER. Now, give me your best recollection of everything that was said on that occasion . . .

MRS. BATES. . . . I asked him how come he had gone to Russia. I said, "It can't be very easy. How did you arrange it? Why did you want to go?" . . . He wasn't very talkative. And whenever I did get him to talk, I had to drag it out of him . . .

He said that the State Department had finally agreed to let him go over, but they would not be responsible for him . . . in case he got in trouble or anything.

So, he went. And that's all I got out of him . . .

And then we got busy and he opened this large package and he brought out his notes. And, as I said, they were on scraps of paper not even this big, some of them [indicating with finger] and some of them large pieces of paper, some of them were typed, some of them handwritten in ink and pencil. And he said that he had had to just do it when he could. And it was about the living conditions and the working conditions in Russia . . .

MR. JENNER. Did he say when he had prepared these notes? . . .

MRS. BATES. They were all done in Russia. And he smuggled them out of Russia. And he said that the whole time until they got over the border, [he and his wife] were scared to death . . .

MR. JENNER. Did he imply that Marina was aware that he had these notes?

MRS. BATES. He didn't say. He just mentioned his wife once or twice in the 3 days he was up there . . .

MR. JENNER. Did he spend substantially all day with you?

MRS. BATES. No, it was 8 hours altogether in the 3 days. . . . I spent 8 hours typing 10 pages, single-spaced.

MR. JENNER. Which would indicate to me, as a lawyer, that you were having some trouble interpreting these notes?

MRS. BATES. . . . A lot of it was scribbled . . . he just had to . . . muffle the tone of the typewriter . . . so people wouldn't know that he was—what he was doing . . . he said [his wife] would cover or watch for him . . . I tell you [those notes] were fascinating to read. "Inside Russia"—was what it was . . .

MR. JENNER. Did you type all of his notes?

MRS. BATES. No; not even a third of them.

MR. JENNER. Tell me that circumstance.

MRS. BATES. Well, on the 20th he came up and he was—uh—quite nervous. Um—the other 2 days he'd sit right there at my desk and—uh—if I needed to ask him anything, why, I would. But, this day, he was walking up and down and looking over my shoulder and wanting to know where I was—and, finally, I finished the 10th page. He said, "Now, Pauline, you told me what your charges were." He said, "This is 8 hours you've worked and 10 pages. I have $10 and no more money. I can't let you go on."

And that's when I asked him if I couldn't go on and type the rest of them. I told him I'd do it for nothing, or if he got the money, why, he could pay me.

And he said, "No, I don't work that way. I've got $10." And he pulled a $10 bill out of his pocket and walked out.

MR. JENNER. Were you in possession of these notes from day to day or did he take them back with him at night?

MRS. BATES. Oh, he took them with him. He never left anything. And he never left the office until he had picked up what I had typed—even the carbon paper.

MR. JENNER. Even the carbon paper?

MRS. BATES. Oh, yes, he took the carbon paper . . . he had the deadest eyes I ever saw.[7]

Had he begun to mistrust Pauline Bates and her interest? If he was feeling paranoid, his suspicions would hardly have been relieved when in the following week the FBI asked him to come by their office for an interview.

From an FBI report:

> Character: Internal Security—Russia
> Reference: Report of Special Agent JOHN W. FAIN, Dallas, Texas, 7/6/62

. . . OSWALD stated that no attempt was made by the Soviets at any time to "brainwash" him. OSWALD stated that he never at any time gave the Soviets any information which would be used in a detrimental way against the United States. He stated that the Soviets never . . . sought any such information from him. OSWALD denied that he at any time while in Russia had offered to reveal to the Soviets any information he had acquired as a radar operator in the U.S. Marines.

. . . OSWALD stated that in the event he is contacted by Soviet Intelligence under suspicious circumstances or otherwise, he will promptly communicate with the FBI. He stated that he holds no brief for the Russians or the Russian system. [However] OSWALD declined to answer the question as to why he made the trip to Russia in the first place. In a show of temper, he stated he did not care to "relive the past."

During most of the interview, OSWALD exhibited an impatient and arrogant attitude. OSWALD finally stated that Soviet officials had asked him upon his arrival why he had come to Russia. OSWALD stated that he told them, "I came because I wanted to." OSWALD added that he went to Russia to "see the country."

OSWALD advised that newspaper reports which have appeared in the public press from time to time are highly exaggerated and untrue. He stated that the newspaper reports had pictured him as out of sympathy with the United States and had made him look attractive to the Russians. OSWALD stated that by reason of such newspaper reports he had received better treatment by the Soviets than he otherwise would have received.[8]

In 1964 when Robert Oswald appeared before the Warren Commission, he was asked a few questions by Allen Dulles, the former Director of the CIA.

MR. DULLES. How did you know that the FBI had talked with Lee?

ROBERT OSWALD. . . . I was aware that they had called my house and requested Lee to come down to their office in Fort Worth and talk with them.

MR. DULLES. Did he report to you on that conversation at all? The details of it?

ROBERT OSWALD. A very small detail of it, sir.

MR. JENNER. What details?

ROBERT OSWALD. I asked him when I returned home from work that afternoon how did it go. He said, "Just fine." He said they asked him at the end whether or not he was an agent for the United States Government. His reply was, "Don't you know?"[9]

3

A Visit to the Organs

Marina did not tell anyone, but Dallas and Fort Worth were disappointing. She was not impressed with Texas. She had thought it would be like the movie *Oklahoma!*, which she had seen in Minsk, and that had been full of cowboys and the West, but here it was not like that. The residential area was all right because the grass was mowed, and no matter how poor the house, it was at least big enough for a family—but she did not like the two cities Dallas and Fort Worth. They had no harmony. They were disorganized. One tall building and three short ones, then an empty lot. Never anything beautiful or old. She did not know if the city was dying or growing up. No, she was not impressed. The only thing she really liked was the smell of the mimosa trees.

She wrote a letter back to the girls at the pharmacy and said that the Russian language had been difficult for Alik and he had always been mispronouncing words, but now she was living in his shoes, mispronouncing American words. At her letter's end, she wrote, "Remember, I'm Marina. Don't let her get lost in history."

As Stepan would inform the interviewers in the fall of 1992, Likhoi's file was discontinued by the summer of 1962. In his actions, his behavior, in his way of life, there had been no indication that he was any kind of intelligence agent. Of course, the possibility still existed that he had been sent over to study USSR living conditions intimately. That information could then be used by American special services. Such a possibility could not be excluded, although there was no way to find that out. A person could always walk around, meet people, study everything, make mental notes. Then, on his return home, a report could be written telling about everything. One cannot do much about that. But as far as Oswald being an active agent—all indications were negative.

They could ask their own overseas agents in the First Directorate who were stationed in America to watch Oswald now that he was back in his own country, but it would be very difficult, very expensive. To put surveillance on him in the United States would suggest that they considered him highly important, but by the time he left Minsk, he was no longer looked upon as being in so serious a category. Nor would any Russian people who lived in Fort Worth be considered a potential source. Over there, KGB officers avoided the Russian community and American Communists and sympathizers. If a KGB agent working illegally in America sees an American Communist coming his way, he will go in the opposite direction. One does not want to stray into the FBI's field of surveillance. So, while there might have been some interest in following Oswald's activities on his return to America, any estimates of risk and cost made it not worthwhile.

On the other hand, they would never let Likhoi's file die. It would live on, even if new material, now that Oswald was in America, would have to come through other channels—by press, radio, or television. Personnel in the Soviet Embassy in Washington were watching all that happens in America and, of course, whatever came in would go to Moscow Center, because they would never exclude altogether the small possibility that Oswald had been a spy for America, and so skillful that he evaded discovery. So, they would monitor letters written back and forth between him and Soviet persons. In this context, Pavel's letter to America on September 15, 1962, two months after Oswald's return, may have presented considerable concern for the Organs. It was written in a form that was compatible with a sophisticated code, a system of special allusions capable of being comprehended only by agents who were working closely together.

Sept. 15, 1962

Hello, Lee and Marina!
I received your letter today after returning from work. I am answering it immediately as I am overflowing with joy . . .

The incident of the crocodiles about which you wrote me is rather amusing; I like it. It even somehow resembles an anecdote; such an unexpected event. Marina, you should not tell me that you are unable to fix the record player; we are not speaking of repairs, just a remodeling. It's too bad that there are no uniform standards in the world for the most important things. In Europe 50 cycles originated in Germany and in your hemisphere 60 cycles—[originated] in America. The easiest thing would be to buy a small motor which would resemble ours in construction and size and to put it into that box . . .

The speed of revolution may not coincide and then you will have to match diameters of bushings just the same. For the beginning, try to take off from the axle of the motor a small brass bushing . . .

So, if you take it off, the speed of the revolution of the disc will be diminished. I don't remember exactly the brand of your record player but if it is the most common its motor should be of this construction . . .

By the way, Marina, . . . the basic idea of Pogodin's play *A Man with a Rifle* is contained in the words "Now we do not have to fear a man with the rifle." This, as doctors say, is a quintessence . . . Goodbye, I am waiting for your letters.

Pavel[1]

In the fall of 1962, Pavel's mother came on a visit to Minsk and told him that the Organs had insisted she take him to their offices. His mother said that they not only called her but required that both she and her son come over with every letter he had received from Oswald. Pavel didn't understand why. He was sure KGB had copies. All the same, he took with him the two letters he'd already received from America. It was strange. The officer looked and said, "Oh, why did you bring these? We don't need them. We signed the Geneva Convention about freedom of letters and correspondence, and we don't need any of this." Then this officer handed them back. Perhaps it had been to check on whether they had missed one.

He didn't know how many times his father had been called in to talk to the Organs, but here in Minsk, with his mother, it was Pavel's first time in the building. And his mother said to him on the way over, "You're going to damage our whole family." She was his mother and he didn't want to fight with her, so he just listened while she told him how bad he had made everything for his father, his mother, and even his sister.

FROM KGB REPORT
10.13.62

. . . GOLOVACHEV's mother told me that [she and] her husband . . . were indignant at behavior of their son, and were very worried about his actions, and GOLOVACHEV's mother even decided to make a special trip to Minsk in order to obtain a clearer understanding of his actions and make appropriate suggestions . . .

Considering that in one of his letters to OSWALD, which GOLO-VACHEV brought, there was mention of [*Doctor Zhivago*], I inquired as to whether he had received [this book from Oswald and] GOLOVACHEV answered in the negative . . .

In answer to a question about how *Doctor Zhivago* had attracted his attention, GOLOVACHEV explained that he had wanted to familiarize himself with this book purely out of curiosity, in order to have some idea about that work. It was explained to GOLOVACHEV that it was a conclusion of prominent Soviet literary critics, writers, and other persons who had familiarized themselves with Pasternak's *Doctor Zhivago* that it contained slanders of Soviet reality and was not of artistic value. Therefore, GOLOVACHEV's acquaintance with the book *Doctor Zhivago* would not enrich his knowledge but, to the contrary, would lead him to have false notions about particular issues. MRS. GOLOVACHEV sharply criticized GOLOVACHEV's desire to read *Doctor Zhivago*, noting that no decent person would waste his time on such a book.

In further course of my conversation with GOLOVACHEV I reminded him of our earlier meetings, during which he had been given appropriate suggestions about his behavior with respect to OSWALD and . . . pointed out GOLOVACHEV's lack of discipline, which was manifested in his not appearing for an interview with an operative. These actions were seen as indicative of GOLOVACHEV's disregard for interests of state security. At the same time, I indicated to GOLOVACHEV that we were not entirely certain that he had not told OSWALD about his interviews with this operative. GOLOVACHEV urged us to believe him that he had not discussed any interviews or suggestions made to him concerning OSWALD.

Indignant at GOLOVACHEV P. P.'s display of indifference toward requests of this operative to meet with him, GOLOVACHEV's mother addressed the following words to him: "Is this how Soviet patriots behave? You should have gone yourself and told them about your friendship with an American." Agreeing with these arguments of his mother, GOLOVACHEV asked to be excused for his uncircumspect actions.

At the conclusion of our interview, I asked GOLOVACHEV to immediately inform us of any facts which might be of interest to the Organs of the KGB, including those persons who may try to contact him as a result of his friendship with OSWALD. GOLO-VACHEV stated that in the future he would act accordingly . . .

After GOLOVACHEV's departure, his mother, who shared with me her fears about her son's fate, expressed her regret that over four years he had been detached from his parents and was able to come under the influence of undesirable persons . . . MRS. GOLOVACHEV promised to spend more time on her son's [political training]. She intends to come to Minsk more often in order to find out how GOLOVACHEV P. P. is behaving. Moreover, in the future she is going to limit GOLOVACHEV P. P. financially, giving him only money to cover absolutely essential expenses. According to her, GOLOVACHEV P. P.'s father made him promise to subscribe to and regularly read youth newspapers and magazines. They will try to monitor GOLOVACHEV P. P.'s faithfulness in carrying out these instructions.

GOLOVACHEV P. P.'s mother also expressed her wish that representatives of the Organs periodically meet with her son, which, in her opinion, would have a positive educational effect on him. I explained to GOLOVACHEV's mother that this was not necessary and expressed my certainty that they were themselves capable of influencing their son in a correct direction, so that he would be worthy of his parents and would take an active part in building Communism in our country.

Stepan Vasilyevich Gregorieff

Stepan would not see Pavel again until the period immediately following Kennedy's assassination.

As for that event, and Stepan could recall the date as if it were etched on his retina—November 22, 1963—he can say that when he heard President Kennedy had been shot and Lee Harvey Oswald was the leading suspect, his immediate thought was: "It's impossible! This inconspicuous person who didn't evoke any suspicion on our part. He commits this crime? It cannot be! It cannot be!"

By the logic of our narrative, we have just come to the end of Volume One. It is obvious that whatever we have learned about Oswald in Russia is not enough to answer our basic question. For that we will have to follow his adventures in America. The changes in Oswald's life have already been large and abrupt, and now we will have to accompany him on future adventures in Fort Worth, Dallas, New Orleans, Mexico City, Dealey Plaza, and the Dallas city jail. Since we have gone from Russia to America with a minimum of ceremony, and have just taken a quick visit back, perhaps we can obtain a more satisfactory farewell by observing the reactions of Oswald's friends and acquaintances in Minsk after they encountered the news of Kennedy's assassination.

PART IX

SHOCK

1

Limbo

Katya remembers shock. For everybody at Horizon. She couldn't believe it had happened. He was just a young boy with a running nose. When it was cold, you could always see his running nose. And suddenly he killed this American President? Other men in her factory were stronger than him, much stronger. He was like that, small.

At Horizon, people did speak about it a little, but it was something that happened far away, and in a few days, representatives from the Organs came over and told them it was best not to talk about Oswald. Forget him. Best to forget him. Best for all.

Back in Moscow, when Yuri and Galina Belyankin heard that a man named Lee Harvey Oswald was suspected of killing Kennedy, they didn't pay any attention. They didn't know him as Lee. It was only a few days later, when *Izvestia* published a photograph of Jack Ruby shooting Oswald, that Yuri, taking his newspaper out of his mailbox downstairs, saw it, ran upstairs, came in on his mother and Galina, and said, "Girls, I think this is our acquaintance." And he recalls very clearly his mother crying out, "Alik, Alik, Alik."

As he puts it, "By a strange twist of fate, I went that night to shoot Mikoyan's departure for Kennedy's funeral," and he remembers, "My friend and I worked together, and we did Mikoyan's departure. It was late at night at Vnukovo Airport." As they were driving back, his friend said to him, "That was your last shot. Now, the Organs will pick you up."

At that time, Yuri's name was on a special security list. There were only a few cameramen allowed to go to Red Square for parades and other occasions where they could photograph people like Khrushchev. Yuri would say that no one in Russia would believe that

Kennedy could be killed without the cooperation of security forces—it's not possible.

After the assassination, Stellina's mother gathered together every last photograph that Lee had taken and tore them up. It was an awful time for Stellina, something terrible. She couldn't believe it. She sobbed. Her husband said, "See what happens? You shouldn't work in Intourist. Now our whole family's going to have to pay for it."

In fact, no one ever approached her. Not in thirty years did anyone, official or unofficial, ever ask her to talk about Lee Harvey Oswald. But in December 1963, she and her family were overcome by an immense fear that something terrible would happen, that she had gotten herself tangled up in some sort of horrible international affair. They didn't even stay around Minsk long enough to hear rumors and gossip about Oswald. "We have an expression in Russian," said Stellina. "When we are very much surprised, 'we even sit down.' So when my mother and I heard this news on our radio that John Kennedy was killed and Lee Harvey Oswald was involved, we sat there in our armchairs. We didn't move. I still remember that great fear. It captured me and my family. Then came further information that American witnesses to this assassination were in accidents and bad things happened to them. So my family lived for a long time in this great fear."

Although it was not easy for Stellina to leave, since she had spent her whole life in Minsk—was even there through the German occupation—she was afraid a lot of fingers would be pointed. People would say, "She was walking around with Oswald, she was friendly." If there had been any women in his life, he had done all that behind closed doors, but she had walked openly with him through public streets.

Only in 1977 did Stellina return to Minsk, and then only after she had buried her husband. She thought, "Well, you know, it's probably quiet. It's fourteen years." Besides, in 1976, her daughter had enrolled at Minsk University. But for all that interval, they had lived in Vitebsk, where she worked as a teacher. She tried during those years not to think about it and was afraid to ask herself the question, "Could my Alyosha have killed Kennedy?"

She had an answer: "I saw his goals. He was interested in women, he wanted to achieve everything easy, he didn't want to invest time or go through hardship. For example, he didn't want to study. I even went to the Institute of Foreign Languages and negotiated with their President and made certain efforts to help him, but he was never really serious, just wanted attention.

"In Czech there's a saying that you can find good in anything—you can even find good in a car crash, because at least you're somewhere in the newspapers. It's better to be spoken about badly than not be spoken about at all. I think even if he was told he had to kill President Kennedy, he would never stop to think what it would bring to the world, how it would influence his life and the future of his family—he would just say, 'Oh, I'll kill Kennedy and I'll achieve this attention.' "

Rimma had always known she could hurt his feelings and so she never did. "I could paint a portrait of him as someone who thinks too much of himself but doesn't work to become the person he wants to be. You should know what kind of person you are. The most important thing for Alik was that he wanted to become famous. Idea number one. He was fanatic about it, I think. Goal number one. Show that he was different from others, and you know, he achieved this goal."

Rimma felt that Alik was connected somehow with the crime, but never killed the American President. He was only somehow connected with it.

The permanent effect of knowing Lee Harvey Oswald, she would say, is that ever since 1963 she has been afraid to visit the United States. No longer is her motto *ad astra per aspera*—through adversity we reach the stars.

Sasha's impression of Lee Oswald is that he could never have assassinated Kennedy. He was a person who would not kill a fly. When Sasha heard about the event, his emotional reaction was: "It cannot be this man. It was some manipulation." He thought that because Oswald came from the Soviet Union, somebody in America used this fact and manipulated him, but Oswald was a decoy. Really, it was more interesting to talk about Marina.

Now, thirty years later, thinking of his life experiences, and how he has lost his hair and is almost bald, Sasha sees his own past differently. He thinks women can keep many secret lives, but at that time he was a blind kitten, blinded by love, and saw no black holes. But he would like to say: "If you see Marina, give her my regards. I have the best feelings for her, despite all the bad."

. . .

Albina thinks that maybe the Zigers did not play so nice a role in Alik's life. He'd been treated with curiosity and respect when he came to the Zigers' home, but he was always hearing negative thoughts promoted about Russia. She thinks that influenced Alik, even though he had an apartment, free medical services, privileges, and everything good. So, she thinks that had it not been for these Zigers, maybe he wouldn't have even thought about leaving her country. Maybe he would have stayed. She can't say that she thought he was a happy person, because he obviously had secrets and they were hidden, but all the same, when that assassination took place, she couldn't believe it was Alik. Even now, inside herself, she cannot believe it. She certainly wouldn't say whether she thought he was a spy, because she can't say—he was just an acquaintance. Didn't know him, really, because he was strange. They were still friends, but he never called her, and never told her he was going to get married. Didn't even invite her to his marriage, didn't stay in touch. That was strange for her. She wouldn't say, however, that she felt jilted. There's a song in Russia that says: "If your bridegroom goes to another bride, you never know who's lucky." She laughed. She had been thinking, actually, about another kind of life with him. She had an aunt in Crimea who lived in a warm place by the Black Sea, and she and Alik had talked about going there to live with her aunt so that they could lie in warm sun by the seaside with fresh fruit to eat. She believes if that had happened, he would never have gone to America, and would never have killed President Kennedy. And maybe they would have had a bigger apartment later on—you never know what will happen.

After the assassination, they were all worried at the pharmacy. "What will Marina do, being so lonely and with two children? How is she going to live financially; how will she manage?" They were certainly worried.

Pavel was offended when this Warren Commission presented Lee as an underdeveloped mentality. Very offended. Pavel didn't like the idea that somebody who was not stupid was being shown to the whole world as if he were.

What with the time difference between Dallas and Minsk—eight or nine hours!—Pavel happened to be out with young students at a large dancing party. He had been acting as the disk jockey. He had his tape recorder, and was putting on different kinds of music; then, suddenly, information came over their radio—Kennedy was killed. He listened to the Voice of America and it said that Lee Harvey Oswald, a person who lived in Dallas, was being arrested.

For years, Pavel kept collecting all kinds of different articles on this subject. He could never accept it as a fact. Reading more and more about it, however, he decided that one person could always make another do anything. You can break a person, and you can certainly change a person by force. In Pavel's opinion, Lee Harvey Oswald is not Kennedy's murderer but was somehow involved in a plot. Because, after all, Lee was no angel. He could be a part of somebody's plot.

After Lee was killed by Ruby, Pavel mailed a letter to Marina giving his condolences. Next morning, KGB was at his door. That was November 26, 1963. He was taken to their office by trolley bus. He was not so important a criminal that they were going to send a car. He remembers that he had on a Chinese blue coat, a scarf and cap, and both men who came for him were dressed in regular street clothes, but then KGB people only wear their uniforms when on parade, or in a coffin.

They went through a side entrance, up crazy stairs to the second floor, and from there he could look out a window and see a bookstore. He didn't know whether he'd ever get back to that street outside. Maybe it was the worst emotional moment in his life. His letter to Marina had sympathized with her feelings; now, he was a criminal. Only later did he understand that by writing such a letter he had truly scared the Organs. His letter might influence international relationships: Somebody in Russia was sorry for the wife of this man who had killed Kennedy.

They let him sit in a chair. They were very polite; they didn't beat him. They were KGB, after all. He was sitting in a room with a big table, and there were a lot of officers and bodyguards around, maybe seven people.

They started by telling him: "In our country, only representatives of the people can send sympathies. You are not a representative of our people. You have no right to express sympathy. That's one thing. You have lost your political vigilance. You have become politically short-sighted. If you don't want somebody to write the laws of our country on your back, if you want to see some sky again, then stop doing stupid things. Speaking of that, how are you related to Marina Oswald? Did you sleep with her?" They would ask him other questions, then go back to that: "Ever sleep with Marina?" For some reason that interested them. They might accuse him once more of losing vigilance, but that was only an excursion. Then they would come right back with something like, "Why did you write this kind of letter if you didn't sleep with her? Are you crazy?"

They went with him to the post office, and he had to fill out a document saying that he wanted his letter back. So, Marina never received his last communication to her. In fact, he thinks KGB already had it, but needed him to request it back in order to give formal proof that they were properly honoring the Geneva Convention.

Before they let him go, they told him not to speak on this subject. That became Pavel's largest reason for leaving Minsk and going to study at Tbilisi, in Georgia. Half of the radio factory knew, after all, that Lee Oswald was his friend, so how was it possible that he wouldn't talk about it if he stayed? In fact, one or two people actually said, "We hope you didn't mention our names while you were interrogated."

Soon after, KGB agents made that visit to Horizon when they told everybody to keep their mouths shut about Oswald. By then, Pavel was already in Tbilisi, but he heard that shop people were called in one by one, and the Organs had private conversations with them about respecting silence.

Now, in Tbilisi, relations with his father were not warm. Pavel had gone down there in December of 1963, and he didn't come back to Minsk until 1965. At first, he stayed in an apartment with his father while his mother went to a health resort. He was studying at Tbilisi University, and one day in the spring of 1964 he came home a little late and his father looked at him and said, "At your age, I was already flying an airplane." Pavel said, "I understand . . ."

He left and went to live at a student hostel, where they found a bed for him. He and his father never spoke again. Not even when his parents came to Minsk. Didn't speak.

Pavel's father died eight years later of cancer. So Pavel felt twice as bad. He was serving then in the Army Reserve at a camp about a hundred kilometers from Minsk, and when he received this news that his father was on his deathbed, he asked if he could visit him, and his officer said, "Tomorrow morning we'll consider your request." But Pavel's father died overnight. Then all these officers around him got to show their humanity. It was a weekend, and the officer in charge of their entire camp happened to be off fishing. To leave the camp, Pavel needed a special seal that only the officer in charge could provide, so they went out to where he was fishing and obtained his seal on the required papers. Pavel bought some flowers and went to his home, but his mother said, "It's too late."

Anatoly Shpanko would say that he never felt any sensation that anybody in KGB had invaded his privacy. He never had any experience that he was under surveillance, never.

Now, Anatoly is fifty-five, but he has never been interviewed by them. He would say that since his biography is clean, why would you report on him? Anatoly insisted that he did not know what had happened to Marina. He did not know her history. When told her husband's name and that Oswald was alleged to have killed President Kennedy, only to be himself killed two days later, Anatoly replied, "Somebody kills somebody and then is killed in two days—it's very dubious if he really did it. There is somebody unaccused who is guilty. It's very negative to me."

As he remembers, there was, in November 1963, no information in Minsk that this man Lee Harvey Oswald had lived in their city for two years. He never saw any stories in his local paper. Nobody talked about it. He didn't know that was Marina's husband, absolutely not. Maybe some people knew but kept silent. Today is when he learns. First time. Asked if it is a shock, he replies: "Approximately."

Sasha came by one day to knock on the door of Ilya and Valya's apartment. There was no answer. He came another time, and even knocked a third time, and then some neighbor opened a door across the hall and said, "They don't live here anymore. They left this place." These neighbors said to Sasha that nobody knew where they had gone.

Ilya suffered a lot from that assassination. It didn't matter how many years he lived. All that had happened took life away from him. He suffered a lot because his life was in his career and now everything was in jeopardy and his situation took away some of his health. They didn't fire him, but they didn't promote him anymore. Ilya never talked much about the assassination except to say it was organized. Said that once. Killing Kennedy was organized. If they had used Alik, it was because he had been in the Soviet Union.

Everyone in his family was scared. How many people would find out that it was Ilya's niece who was involved in Kennedy's assassination?

At this time, he and Valya had an apartment with three rooms. They were only two people living in a three-room apartment. So, shortly after President Kennedy's assassination, everyone started to blame them, began to say they lived in too luxurious a place. That was not true. Just a nice apartment with a lot of books. There was even an article in one newspaper that Ilya was a Communist Party member and lived in a more privileged way than other people. Valya said, "My husband was very honest. So, when this one man from *Byelorussian Star,* a military paper, came to us and then wrote an article—'Look at these two people, they live in this luxurious apartment'—Ilya decided to move. Some of our neighbors said, 'Don't hurry. Wait. Something will change,' but Ilya said, 'No, I don't want my name to be used in this way; I don't want to know this type of shame,' " and so we moved to a two-room apartment."

On the other hand, five people were given the old three-room apartment. So, says Valya, maybe that was fair.

Ilya never showed what it cost—he still remained interested in painting and in books, his second hobby. He kept buying new sets of books and lining every wall of his apartment with them. You couldn't say he lost interest in literature.

Among Ilya Prusakov's collected sets of Russian authors in five to twenty volumes were Tolstoy, Petrov, Lermontov, Kuprin, Nekrasov, Adamov, Bunin, Ilya Ehrenburg, Chekhov, Alexei Tolstoy and Konstantin Simonov, Turgenev, Pushkin, Sholokhov, and Dostoyevsky. In collected sets translated into Russian were Jules Verne, Swift, Emily Dickinson, Romain Rolland, Zola, Dreiser, Balzac, Hugo, de Maupassant, Rabindranath Tagore, Sir Walter Scott, Robert Louis Stevenson, Heine, Feuchtwanger, Stendhal, Steinbeck, Boccaccio, Prosper Mérimée, Galsworthy, Proust, and Jack London.

Thirty years later, in 1992, Valya and Marina spoke on the phone. They cried, and Marina said, "I understand that you were very upset about Ilya and all that happened to him after I left, but you know, Ilya didn't die when I left—he was eighty years old at the end, and I became a widow with two children when I was twenty-two."

. . .

After Ilya's death, in 1989, Valya was going through his papers and discovered that he had a collection of nude pictures. Professional photographers had taken them; they were postcard size. Something he had bought. But she was philosophical about it. She said to herself, "Of course, every man has a secret life. That's why he's a man." And then, in her heart, she said to herself, "I allow him everything. I allow him to like young women."

When Kennedy was assassinated, Ella was waiting to be asked, "Come to our KGB office. Sit down and give us your information." But she was never approached.

Ella remarked that she could invent stories now: "It's very fashionable to say, 'I was abused by the Organs. They ruined my life.' It's very high style to have been approached by them and suffer." She says she could invent a story, but she'd rather tell the truth. She was not approached.

After the assassination she had worried that they would come, and she did live in fear—kept thinking they were going to ask her to come in—but nobody did. Now that she thinks about it, she would say she might have had friends who were approached. From what she's learned since, she believes Lee must have been watched constantly, and she thinks she must have been watched, too. But since there were only two of them, she thinks Pavel must have been more interesting, because Pavel brought people to meet Lee. She was always alone with him, so maybe she was of less interest.

As for whether Alik was guilty of assassination, she cannot believe that. "He was so gentle," she says.

Sometime around the end of March of 1962, Kostya's uncle, Professor Bondarin, told him that he was living the wrong kind of life in relation to women. Moreover, it was not considered proper that he had a pornography collection. His uncle told him, "If you don't want to be expelled, stop chasing skirts." And Kostya had to destroy all his French postcards and his diary. He was keeping a purple diary at this point, where he maintained a brief record of personal events whose references nobody but himself could understand— he had never written "Marina," for example, only "M."

When the assassination occurred, Kostya was summoned to KGB, and so too, he is certain, were his friends. They all went in different directions afterward, and didn't have anything to do with each other. This was years after Stalin's time, ten years later, but contact with the Organs evoked fear. They could take you somewhere. You might not return home.

His own family had suffered. In the Thirties. During the civil war, his grandfather had served as an officer in Tukhachevsky's army, so naturally, when they arrested that General in the late Thirties, this affected his grandfather as well. Kostya grew up hearing about interrogations conducted in Stalin's time.

So when Kostya walked through the front door of the building, his legs were weak. But, actually, it proved to be only a short conversation: What sort of relationship had he had with Alik, and had he corresponded with Alik and Marina? He was able to reply in the negative. They did not ask him whether he had ever slept with Marina. This man who was interrogating him sat down at a desk and Kostya stood. There was someone else present, also in civilian clothes, but Kostya didn't know whether he was taking notes or not—never dared to look in that direction.

The man questioning him wanted to know if Kostya possessed photographs of Alik and Marina. He had had a few, but by now they were ashes in his stove.

Because Yuri and Kostya and Sasha had been certain that there was official surveillance of Alik and Marina after those two made a decision to go to America, they stopped visiting them. But Erich didn't. He remained Oswald's friend. Could it be, the American interviewers now asked Kostya, that Titovets had had some special relation to Oswald? To which Kostya replied that Erich had managed to keep everything he wrote during that period. Everyone else had his papers confiscated or took pains to destroy them, so Kostya was surprised when Erich said, "You all ran. You hid like a bunch of cowards and threw everything overboard." But, Kostya asked, why was Erich so brave? One could only guess how he had been able to keep his papers.

In any case, it seems to Kostya that, in this period after the assassination, Erich should have been shaken like a pear tree. Yet, he got out of it; nothing really happened to him, even though he had had the closest relationship with Alik.

As for his present opinion of Oswald, Igor Ivanovich said, "Lee was the scum of society, a person spoiled from the cradle, so to say. Not serious. Inconstant. Something was probably wrong with his state of mind."

Igor Ivanovich was asked, "After the assassination, you must have felt bad?"

And he replied, "Bad? I felt horrible. In fact, it was the worst moment of my life."

When asked if KGB had interrogated any of their prime sources after the assassination, Igor Ivanovich suddenly became emotional. He looked as if he might burst into tears. He did not answer the question. Instead, he cried out: "Everybody blames me for this! It was as if I knew he would shoot." After a minute or two, he added, "We had no data. You could not find one single person from Minsk who would say, 'Yes, Oswald had these intentions to go back to America and cause all this trouble.' "

He and Stepan had tried to consider where they could have failed. Their inner fear: "What if the preparation of this action commenced in Minsk?" They were considering everything.

Then he added, "Quite frankly, we were not worried about public opinion in America. We worried about what Moscow would say once we sent them Oswald's file. Would they consider our job well done or poor? That was what we worried about."

When Stepan Vasilyevich heard the announcement on the radio, his second thoughts, after first saying to himself, "It's impossible!" were more complex. As more news arrived from various broadcasts, he came to a conclusion that Oswald could not have done it alone. Oswald had been sucked into it somehow. Because a single fact was being exploited—that Oswald had been in the Soviet Union. A convenient shield for certain people! "Their mass media started blaming everything on our Soviet Union. My opinion is that it was all sewn together with white threads. To cover their tracks in this crime."

When asked how long it took for word to come from Moscow that they wanted Oswald's file, Stepan's reply was that Moscow Center's request came late on that night of November 22. Igor Ivanovich was given an order, and he told Stepan to take Likhoi's file to Moscow. Gather it together and leave.

No preparations were necessary. Both men knew Oswald's materials well, and the file had been stored in the archives of their building. So, all Stepan had to do was take it out, put it in a sack, sign for it, and leave. He used a gray mailbag, the kind used for sending quantities of mail, and the file was not large enough to fill it.

Then, Stepan flew to Moscow on November 23, and arrived at Lyubertsy Airport, accompanied by another KGB man from Minsk, who was armed. It was not a regular flight, since Moscow wanted it quickly, but there were two seats open on a military plane.

When asked if he was very nervous, he said, "I don't think so. I didn't feel any guilt. I was pure as crystal. What could I be afraid of? Of course, it was a tragic situation. But being nervous, hands shaking, so forth—why? I was flying to our Center in Moscow with a clean conscience. I didn't have any excessive emotions or anything like that. I just thought about what sort of questions they would ask. And I had only one answer: Oswald did not have any undisclosed relation to our agency. What worried me more was whether official people would be there to meet me at Lyubertsy Airport because, otherwise, how would I get to Moscow on public transport?"

He did not have to worry. Official people greeted him right away, introduced themselves, showed their identification, and they all drove off. It was an overcast day, but no rain, no snow. Gray.

They went to the main building, to Lubyanka, drove directly into the edifice, and were received by higher-ups. Stepan thought it might be the Assistant Director of KGB. He didn't know these high officers personally. It was his first visit to Moscow Center, and this legendary building, Lubyanka, was full of labyrinths. He had to follow closely behind whoever was walking in front of him, down endless narrow halls. A thin red carpet ran the entire length of each long hall.

Later he would go to Lubyanka many times on business trips, so he was able to find his way along some of these halls, but he can't say he ever got it all down. You could go there and go there and still get lost. If he had to get out of that building on his own, he might lose his way. From the exterior, it was a large building of yellow stone, but inside it was strange, with these narrow corridors. In Minsk, their corridors were wide and you could walk more freely.

When he finally was led to the appropriate office, several people were waiting for him in a reasonably large room, but there wasn't anything on their table. He doesn't know if it was in their American Division or some other department, but Stepan merely said, "According to your instructions, our file on Oswald is now delivered." And they said, "Good, just leave it here."

Their first question came: "Did you attempt to recruit Oswald?" He said, "You can cut off my head, but not only did we not try to, this very thought did not even enter our minds. Read these documents. It's very clear in which direction we were working. In accordance with your instructions."

He looked at them and noticed that they practically sighed with relief. He wasn't worried about their believing him, because the documents made it clear what kind of work they had been doing. You couldn't falsify something like that. Of course, Stepan was somewhat disturbed, but he had no large fears. These documents made it clearly visible how they had been conducting their operation.

Afterward, when slanders concerning the Soviet Union kept circulating, he thought maybe Nikita Sergeivich Khrushchev would give these files to the American government. All these American rumors would then burst like a soap bubble. But it didn't happen.

On this day, at this meeting on November 23, 1963, they invited him to sit down; they were polite. He remembers he even tried to stand up, and they said, "Sit down, sit down," but there was nothing on their table, no tea. He doesn't recall whose picture was on the wall, maybe it had been Dzherzhinsky, but no flag—that, he would have noticed. And the room was brightly lit. The last thing they said was, "Leave this file. And thank you. Your mission is over. We'll organize a return ticket for you."

He took a regular night train back to Minsk with the same fellow he had taken off with. Before leaving, they strolled around Moscow and went shopping. He bought something for his children.

On his return trip, Stepan didn't have special thoughts. If Oswald had been CIA, he could not have done any more in Minsk than gather information in a contemplative way, not manifesting anything, not being an active agent. He could have studied Soviet life, and then disclosed such information later in America. Such a version could not be excluded. As much could be said for any foreigner who spent two years in the Soviet Union. "Besides, when Oswald came to Minsk in January 1960, Kennedy wasn't yet elected President. So, Oswald could not have been sent with such a goal in mind."

If Stepan had any troubled thoughts on his return trip, therefore, it was not over his own performance. He explored various scenarios, thoughts came into his head, various versions appeared, but in the end he said to himself, "Ach, it's time to go to bed. Americans cooked it up. Let them figure it out."

When he got home, which was Sunday morning, it was still Saturday night in Dallas, so Oswald would not be ambushed by Ruby

for another ten hours; about six in the afternoon on Sunday in
Minsk is when Stepan would receive that word. When he returned,
therefore, on Sunday morning around eight o'clock, the first thing
he did was go to his home to shave. Leaving in such a hurry for
Moscow, he had not taken his toilet kit. He washed, then had something to eat and went straight to work, where he reported to his
superiors. People, of course, were talking about it in the building.
Everyone was listening to radios. Even then, a lot of his colleagues
did not know he had worked on this case, but everyone's opinion
was stirred up. After all, it was a shadow on Minsk.

People who knew Oswald immediately said Alik couldn't have
done it. So said people who knew him.

Even many people who didn't have contact with the fellow didn't
believe it: We're getting along with America a little bit better, so now
all this business?

They didn't do further analysis. Their file was in Moscow; they
didn't have materials. Besides, what could they have analyzed any
further? When the file came back from Moscow some twenty-
seven years later, nothing had been removed or commented
upon; everything was there as he recalled it, certified and signed
by him. Stepan was asked why then had Igor Ivanovich reacted so
strongly as to say, "Everyone blames me," but Stepan indicated
that Igor was a more sensitive person than he was.

2

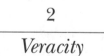

Veracity

The bulk of the interviews in Minsk had been completed, but the
interviewers still had one large problem. It was whether to give
any credence to Yuri Merezhinsky's account of his relations with
Marina. If she was anywhere near as promiscuous as he stated,
then all interpretations of her life with Lee Harvey Oswald would
be colored by such information: It would suggest a different subtext to her marriage than what had emerged from her account of
their difficulties.

Kostya Bondarin had, of course, been dubious of Yuri's claims, but then, he was only one witness. The real question must be whether Yuri was a liar of dramatic proportions or was telling some kind of truth—exaggerated, perhaps, by the intensity of his presentation, but still not unpossessed of its own veracity.

So, the interviewers went back to Yuri Merezhinsky one more time, which is to say that they asked him to come to Minsk from his sanatorium several hundred kilometers away and subject himself to an interview about his experiences after the assassination, to which he complied, and met them at his mother's apartment, had his vodka, and talked. Given his personal style, which consisted of dictating the content of the interview from his own point of view rather than responding particularly to most of the questions, he began by speaking of his parents:

Very important people, he would say. He waved a finger in warning. Let nothing in the air be ready to disagree! Very important people, he repeated, but all the same, obedient! When they received their big Soviet encyclopedia and an order followed years later to cut out certain pages because they were now historically incorrect, his father obeyed. Yuri's parents were not average people, but still, they were afraid. For example, his father kept a private diary, yet even his own pages were not truthful. They never mentioned that every day Yuri was asked to go over to KGB. It had been a nightmare.

This was when he started to understand life. Every day, he would tell you, he was called to come to KGB, a terrible nightmare.

"When was this?" his interviewers asked.

He waved his hand. "First they said, 'Confess, confess, are you an agent of Japan? Are you an agent of CIA?' " Instead of going to his Medical Institute for his daily lectures, he had to visit the Organs and spend his whole working day there. Each time, he had to register; then, he would sit in front of one person, Captain Andreyev. This Captain would sit with a newspaper in front of his face and pour so much hot coffee for Yuri that afterward Yuri could not stand coffee—he vomited when he saw it. For a long time.

They asked: Was this after Lee was accused of killing Kennedy?

"Yes," said Yuri.

The interviewers asked, "Earlier, when Lee Harvey Oswald married Marina, did the KGB bother you?"

He shook his head vigorously. His parents were high people, said Yuri. When he did something that KGB did not like, they would call his mother and say, "Your son got drunk," or, "He is making love with a certain girl, the wrong girl." His family was watched because they were high-ranked people.

After Kennedy's assassination, however, he was called directly to KGB. It happened in this manner: Every Institute has a resident officer from the Organs—in this case, Captain Andreyev, who invited him into his office and had a conversation with him there. All subsequent conversations, however, were in the main KGB building, on Lenin Street.

The first questions were: What kind of relationship did you have with Lee Oswald? What did you talk to him about? Was he a spy? Was he CIA? No one was taking notes, just two of them.

"Tête-à-tête," said Yuri.

After this first meeting, Yuri went home and told his parents, and they responded with fear. They didn't blame him; they started to discuss what protective measures could be taken. They wanted to use their friends.

Another interrogation from KGB was started on the following day. They called him at home and asked him to come over to their main building. He went alone. He bought a pack of cigarettes and walked in.

At the entrance was a booth with a window. There he gave his name and showed his passport, and Andreyev came down in civilian clothes and took him back to his office, where they sat at a table. He had to answer the exact same questions he had been asked at his Institute, and he thinks this new room may have been bugged, although, unlike yesterday, Andreyev now took notes. Their meeting consumed six or seven hours. Every day after that they met, except on Sundays. It was now Yuri's daily job to go to the main KGB building on Lenin Street.

He smoked cigarettes. There were always Prima cigarettes on Andreyev's table, and coffee. Sometimes when Yuri arrived, Andreyev did not even speak to him. Merely read his newspaper while Yuri sat before him. They would give him an hour for lunch. Then he had to come back. He didn't sign anything. They told him to, but he never signed one paper. Not one. His parents told him not to. This officer said, "You don't want to sign? Then don't. Any punishment will come through a court; they will decide how to treat you." Of course, at that time you didn't need a lot to be punished. He was asked if he had been a Japanese spy. He didn't know why they'd choose Japan, except that Oswald had been there. No Japanese in Minsk.

Since he went to this office every day except Sunday, he stopped going to his Institute. Education was no longer something that he worried about. And every day when he went home he told his parents what had happened, and every day they gave advice. They thought maybe some of his friends were also being questioned, but he didn't worry too much about that. When you spend your entire day at KGB, you don't think about your friends. He had even been warned not to talk to anybody.

These interrogations went on for a few months—same time, same man, same room. It was a big stone on his shoulder. The only picture in this office was a portrait of Felix Dzherzhinsky. Plus a safe, a table, chairs. That's it. Plus a window through which he could see the street. And every day he went with a feeling that this would be the day they would not let him leave. He had a signal to give his parents. He would make a point of coming home every day by a certain hour. If not . . .

His mother worked at the Academy of Sciences. She was doing secret work on space. So, there were KGB Colonels who worked in association with her. His mother was always trying to use such a connection to save him. During this period, his parents were worried much more about him than over their own careers. And his father kept telling him not to sign anything, because among such papers usually there is a special paper which states that you are not allowed to leave your city. Finally, his father told him: "Leave Minsk. Don't take any suitcases. Just go the way you are, in your own suit."

They gave him lots of money, several thousand rubles, and he went to the railroad train station and jumped on the night train to Moscow without a ticket and paid the conductor. In Moscow, he never lived for more than two days in any hotel; he changed his residence every two days. Yuri had many relatives in Moscow, and many good friends, but he never went to visit any of them. He had arrived with no more than what he was wearing on his back, and he never worried about growing a beard or dyeing his hair.

In Russia, said Yuri, all you needed for travel was your residence passport, so on each night that he went to a new hotel, he handed it over, and by morning he'd be given it back. Then, in forty-eight hours—no more—he would move.

For two months, he did that. He spent each day in museums or at the movies, and he enjoyed his time. He was free; he was not under arrest. He never called home; he never wrote a letter. He had fear inside him, of course. It was uncertainty. So, he only made new acquaintances. Because it was safer, he never took a single room. That would attract attention. It was better to share with strangers.

Then, on December 31, 1963, he decided to go back to Minsk. He still had a lot of money, but he was lonely and he wanted to have a good New Year's Eve. So, he bought an airplane ticket and flew to Minsk, took a taxi, came home. His parents were pleasantly surprised and happy.

They told him that his file was closed. His whole investigation was now closed and over. He thinks maybe some people in KGB, some ugly elements, thought they could make a career on his mother, his father, and himself. So, they had tried to damage his parents through him. But it had not worked. His parents were too strong.

In fact, it damaged Andreyev, the man who interrogated him, because his parents had gone to the highest people in Byelorussia.

Yuri saw Andreyev again, fifteen years later, on Lenin Street. Andreyev smiled at Yuri, came up to him and said, "How are you?" as if, after fifteen years, they were best friends meeting again. Yuri was so taken aback that he just turned away. He was trying not to spit into Andreyev's face. Andreyev even asked him to obtain medicine for him.

The interviewers were puzzled. Yuri's story had taken them around one turn too many. If the Organs had interrogated him all day long, six days a week, for months, what had they talked to him about? The interviewers encouraged him to tell his story again. In more depth.

Underneath all of this, Yuri said, was an undertext, a subtext. It concerned Komsomol. There were really two groups studying then at Minsk Medical Institute: First were those who had already done their military service and so were now high Komsomol members. The rest were like himself, who had come into Minsk Medical Institute from high school and so had been in severe competition to pass their entrance exams. For that reason, they knew how to study. So, people from that first group, who had done military service, were envious and tried to humiliate all these younger students.

For example: When they all went out in summer to work on a collective farm and bring in the potato crop, these high Komsomol members said that Yuri, Kostya Bondarin, and Sasha Piskalev had stolen a large piece of *salo*. That, he explained, was high-grade pork fat and very tasty if eaten with pickled cucumbers, bread, and vodka. A thin slice of *salo* coated your stomach. You could drink more.

Salo cost very little, but Komsomol acted as if such an act of petty theft, a prank, had been highly irresponsible. It was built up into a big moral issue—they said that Yuri and his friends were not only well educated, the cream of their country with the best chance for a future, but had been educated free of charge and with a stipend taken from the taxes of other people less well educated and so the future of such an elite group belongs to the country, not to themselves. Stealing one piece of fat brought moral damage to their Medical Institute: One piece of fat, five centimeters by ten centimeters by ten centimeters! It was small enough to shove into your pocket!

Yet, they were all three brought up before a Komsomol meeting at his Medical Institute, and all his personal feelings, said Yuri, were treated with contempt. "They mixed me up with dirt." And his friends Konstantin Bondarin and Sasha Piskalev were also mixed with such dirt.

It was all because Yuri's father was Vice-President of this Institute, and they wanted the dirt to reach up to his father. Ugly elements were opposed to his father and were using Komsomol members recently discharged from the Soviet Army, people whose highest entertainment was to get drunk in a hostel, get down on their knees to fart, and put a match to their ass—lightning! This was the very best entertainment in their life. This was their culture! All the Komsomol leaders at his Institute. These were his judges concerning that theft of *salo*!

Highly confused by this enrichment, the American interviewers went through Yuri's story again. If they understood what he was saying, on the second or third day after President Kennedy's assassination, he had been asked to come to Andreyev's office, and that had set off a process of going to the main office for two consecutive months, so it could only have been well after New Year's that he quit Minsk and went to Moscow. But then the interviewers pointed out that he had stayed in Moscow for two months, so it would have been something like three months after New Year's before he came home.

Now Yuri decided that the Organs had begun to interrogate him before Kennedy's assassination. Perhaps it had been in the

first days of August 1963, after he had been caught in the embarrassment of helping to steal a little pork fat. Then they interrogated him for a very long time, for two or three months, until
November, he would guess. Then, after the assassination, he had
gone to Moscow. In fact, he now remembers every detail of how
he left town. He was with friends, and they were all drunk, and he
was drunk, and they all went to Minsk railway station to see somebody else off on another train to another place. But since the next
train happened to be for Moscow, he got on. And he slept on the
third bench, the top rack in a third-class car, where mattresses and
pillows were kept.

It had been planned he should go away. His father knew how to
act in situations. His father had worked years ago for Stalin, and
when Stalin ate a meal, his father had been the man chosen to be
in charge of Stalin's food. So, if the Soviet leader took one piece
of meat, his father had to take two. Yuri's father's name was
Mikhail Fedorovich, and he had learned a lot in those years, so he
also knew how to run away from the Organs. His father had once
been on a business trip, but they had taken him off his train and
put him in a line of people waiting. He had asked, "What is this
line for?" and they said, "Here is where they take away your Party
membership."

His father said: "You didn't give me my Party membership and
you are not going to take it away."

That very same day, years ago, Mikhail Fedorovich left that line
and took his wife and son and went away to the Urals. Years later,
on another day when his father was working in his own office and
his mother happened to be standing next to him, some officers
came in and said to Yuri's mother, "Good news for your family.
Here are official papers proving that your husband was shot for
nothing back then." They didn't even know Mikhail Fedorovich
was the person next to her. Obviously, this Soviet system was like
some compartmental organism in which all kinds of different processes were happening at the same time. There was no core to the
system. Not really. Nothing really central. So, it was his father's
fear that if Yuri stayed in Minsk, he would be selected as a victim,
while if Yuri went away, they would, bureaucratically speaking,
soon be paralyzed. The big machine was so big that you could
exploit it.

So, he got to Moscow. Now that he was there, he could say that
when you were on the run, you didn't care whether your room-

mate for one night was *simpatico* or a *zhlob*. Main thing to consider: that your roommate should not be a danger to you. But Yuri was lucky. He only met good people. If someone asked him why he was there, he just said, "Vacation." He was a student. He was big, he looked respectable, so no one was interested. Of course, he had to say he was from Minsk because of his passport.

Nor was he afraid of being robbed. At each railway station, they had deposit boxes. For 15 kopecks a day, he would leave most of his money in a locker. While he was in Moscow, he stayed at the Peking, the Leningrad, the Ukraine, the Exhibition—everywhere. If you took a map of Moscow, he would live two days in one hotel, then he would take a taxi crosstown. He had no system—he would just go far away from his last hotel. In those days, you could get into any hotel—it was easy.

Nor were rates bad. At a restaurant, you could drink vodka and eat expensively or just take a side of cabbage. Of course, he didn't count his money; he had so many rubles he never looked at how much he spent. It was cheap. One meat pie cost 7 kopecks. For good meat and beer, 22 kopecks. Movies, 20 kopecks. Everything was kopecks, not rubles. If you had a buddy, you could go to a hotel dining room or a hotel canteen and eat bread together free of charge, then put mustard on bread, plus pepper, salt, then pour a glass of vodka, have more bread—it was a meal.

He had no close calls in Moscow, and he didn't worry about it, but he was homesick even if he was having a good time with girls. He had no problem there—he did not have to find his pennies in garbage. He never paid for a woman. He was young, good-looking, he knew how to talk. If he liked a woman, he invited her to a restaurant. Beautiful women were everywhere, plus shop girls. Then, he flew back to Minsk on New Year's to see his parents. At that time he could drink a whole case of vodka, six bottles. Today he can only drink two bottles of vodka, as he had done today. Two bottles before he came to this interview. Now, more vodka during his interview. In those days he and a buddy could drink their first bottle of vodka in fifteen minutes, the second in twenty, the third in thirty. Just a little more than an hour for three liters. Now, he can still drink a lot of booze, but not like then, no, *c'est dommage*.

What was to be made of his story? Toward the end of this interview, Yuri's mother, Lidia Semenovna, came into the room. She was small and frail and had the title of Honorable Scientist of the Republic of Belarus.

Lidia Semenovna did work on marrow chemistry and radio-biology, and she was proud of having traveled on scientific business trips to international congresses, even to America. When she came back to Minsk in 1961 from America, she had been asked to share her impressions about her visits to different American Universities. "A great many students from the Medical Institute wished me to speak." She even thinks it was those students who arranged to have her give a lecture at the Trade Union Palace.

She remembers that Oswald, as one member of her audience, came over afterward to say that he was an American, and that Yuri then asked if this American could come home with them. That's how Oswald happened to visit their apartment on March 17, 1961.

She didn't have a first impression of him—she was too busy talking to people after her lecture. He was just a young man, a boy really.

At that time her team did research on a nuclear reactor with cobalt sources. She had a large group under her, about thirty people, and her project was under closely held security, like all other subjects concerned with radiation. So, after Oswald appeared at her house, the Organs soon told her it was undesirable, even inadmissible, that he should come again. Such sentiments were also passed on to her husband, Professor Merezhinsky. Their house was not a place where any unknown foreigner should be able to come.

Now, the interviewers asked her about Yuri's extended trip to Moscow, and she immediately replied that he had gone in the fall of 1963. He had been ill, and he had stayed in a hospital there.

At this point, Yuri interrupted to say: "Mother, I ask you . . . the truthful way of life. Please. Forget that you are a Party member. Don't lie."

Mother: "Then I won't talk. I am saying how it was."

"Say the truth," said Yuri.

"I'll say the truth," said his mother. "There was an unpleasant story about an episode on a farm, an unpleasant story . . . Komsomol said three boys should be excluded from the Medical Institute."

It was not enough, Lidia Semenovna said, to justify this attempt to expel Yuri from his Medical Institute. But what has to be understood is that at this farm, Yuri had also been sick, with a constant temperature of 39 degrees centigrade. An inexplicable temperature. Equal to 102.2 Fahrenheit. Since their daughter already had

TB, the obvious question was whether Yuri now also had it. No doctor in Minsk Hospital, however, was ready to give a diagnosis. She and her husband were too high in medicine, and so these Minsk doctors did not wish to make a serious mistake. They told her it was better to go to the Tuberculosis Hospital at Second Moscow Institute. So, Yuri spent four months that fall in Moscow—the fall of 1963—and was given a leave from his Institute in Minsk. When he came back, in order to prevent more talk, Yuri's mother made her son a lab assistant at her own Institute.

After this exposition, mother and son argued in English and in Russian:

YURI: Mother, be truthful at least once in your life.

MOTHER: I'm saying only truth.

YURI: Throw away your Party card.

MOTHER: It has nothing to do with my Party card.

YURI: You have Party card in your brains. Why did I leave for Moscow? Because I was ill?

MOTHER: You *were* ill.

Lidia Semenovna would explain: This man Andreyev had, in fact, participated in a situation against Yuri to injure her husband. Yuri had been used. That was one more reason for Yuri to go to Moscow—so he wouldn't be expelled from his Medical Institute because of his trouble with that *salo* in the summer of 1963. Once he was in Moscow and medically excused from the Institute, Andreyev and his people couldn't hurt Yuri, and so they couldn't hurt her husband. This also coincided with the inflammation of Yuri's lungs. So, their move had logic. She could say that because Yuri was suffering this inflammation, it did help her to send him to Moscow, but she was also trying to find a doctor in Moscow who could help him.

She could explain further: Being a nuclear researcher, she had her own KGB people to inform her, a Colonel. She was close to her Colonel, because he would go abroad with her when she went to international congresses and so he always alerted her. Whenever trouble started, her KGB Colonel was telling her, "Lidia Semenovna, please keep in mind, don't let Yuri see this person. It is better if he does not." They told her about Oswald and how it was better

Yuri didn't meet with him. They talked to her about Yuri's relations with different women. They didn't advertise it, but she knew all about Marina and her bad biography in Leningrad. Marina was a beautiful girl, and Lidia Semenovna was worried that Yuri could have interest in her, because she had been warned that this relationship should be stopped.

When, in early fall of 1963, she heard that Yuri was going to be expelled from his Institute, a high retired KGB officer was called in, and a few days later told her, "Lidia Semenovna, don't do anything with these doctors here. Go to Moscow." And Yuri's mother used a slang expression, *motaite.* " 'Skip town,' they said. 'It's not advisable to deal with it here. Get out of town and take Yuri with you. *Smativat*—take off!' "

So, from Minsk she made a reservation at the Akademicheskaya Hotel in Moscow, a room for her son and herself in a hotel where academicians of all republics go. She made her reservation from Minsk and, once in Moscow, took him to a proper hospital, where he stayed for four months. By then, this problem with Andreyev was solved by itself.

YURI: Do you remember how I was living in Moscow?

MOTHER: I lived with you in Akademicheskaya Hotel.

YURI: Don't do this, Mother. Once in your life be honest. I can't stand it. I'll leave.

MOTHER: I told everything as it was.

YURI: Yes, of course, long live the Communist Party.

MOTHER: It has nothing to do with Stalin and the Party.

YURI: Lidia Semenovna, have you read a simple thing, *Gulag Archipelago?*

MOTHER: No, I didn't . . .

YURI: If you read an article about Gulag, you'll know better about Soviet reality, [but] you don't want to read it.

MOTHER: No, I don't want . . . Can't you understand that my position forced them to make me join the Party? They had a special direction for me.

YURI: Why does all the world hate Russians, Communist revolutionaries . . .

MOTHER: Okay, you hate me. So what can I do?

YURI: And you hate me. That's why I am telling.

MOTHER: Why would I hate you?

YURI: No. I know that she hates me.

MOTHER: You ought to be ashamed to say so! . . .

She was old, and he was ill. At fifty years of age, still handsome, he was bent over and coughing, curled around his glass of vodka like a leaf seared by heat. And she was in her seventies. Together they fought. Bitterly, and with the rage that only a mother and son can feel at the control each has the power to exercise on the other.

The interviewers could wonder if Yuri would ever forgive his mother for revealing that he was a liar on a prodigious scale and so virtually all of what he had told them about Marina and himself was doubtless not true. Ambiguous—since it seemed as if he had seen her to some little degree—but probably not true. Experience bore the same relation to his memory as facts to high romance.

3

The Most Degrading Moment in Her Life

If we are to take the reminiscences of Russians we have known about the state of their feelings in the aftermath of Jack Kennedy's death, can there be an ending to Volume One more appropriate than to inquire into Marina's state of mind?

She would say that the most humiliating thing that she ever experienced was on her walk from the police car to the police station after they told her that Lee had been arrested.

The police brought her out of the car, and she had to walk—she didn't know how far; it looked forever. Maybe it was some short distance; she does not recall. But, such shame—the most degrading, humiliating moment ever in her life. Just by going from car to building. Reporters were shouting, and it was nothing she could understand. She wished some earth would swallow her. She even believed that Lee had committed this crime, because she believed all American authorities. She blindly believed them. They had made an arrest, so what else could there be? She was from Russia—when that black wagon comes (*voron,* they called it in Russia—black crow), you are guilty. Automatically guilty. *Voron* is here! Then she walked through a tunnel filled with reporters. Jammed. She couldn't believe it. This nightmare had herself in it. Leading role! She was playing a sleepwalker.

All of a sudden, someone shouted to her in Russian: "Mrs. Oswald, did your husband kill America's President?" That Russian voice kind of woke her up. Fortunately. She was feeling as if she could have drifted out of everything forever. She was abandoned—wife of an assassin who had killed the President.

VOLUME TWO

OSWALD IN AMERICA

—◁○▷—

PART I

EARLY YEARS,
SOLDIER YEARS

1

On Becoming an Usher

One stimulus to the writing of this book was an offer from the Belarus KGB to allow a look into their files on Oswald. While the materials proved to be less comprehensive than promised, it was still the equivalent of an Oklahoma land-grab for an author to be able to move into a large and hitherto unrecorded part of Oswald's life. Moreover, the end of the Cold War encouraged Russian and Byelorussian acquaintances of Oswald to loosen habits of discretion formed under Stalin and preserved by Brezhnev. So, we were able to conduct interviews that gave us a reasonable portrait of Alik and Marina and their friends and detractors in Moscow and Minsk.

Then, an old hunger came alive. One wished to come to the end of an ongoing question: Did Oswald kill President Kennedy? And, if so, did he do it on his own or as part of a conspiracy? The only answer Minsk had provided was that one could not tell as yet—much too much of Oswald's life back in America still had to be explored. Moreover, no one in Minsk knew anything about his past.

Of course, the task in Russia had not been to look for such an answer. We are dealing, after all, with the greatest mountain of mystery in the twentieth century, a metaphor first employed when approaching KGB officers for interviews. Why are you here, they would ask; what do you expect to find in my country? And for reply one could only say that this was not a search for a smoking gun; no, it was more one's aim to come close enough to this period of Oswald's life to be able to set up a base camp on the slopes of such a mystery. To the degree that one could obtain a portrait of Oswald as he lived in Russia—a sense of him as seen through Russian eyes—one might be contributing to a future attempt by others to attain the summit. So, our venture might prove of real use. Oswald was forever being put on a bed of Procrustes to fit the dimensions of a plot; he had been portrayed as everything from a patsy to a CIA agent or a KGB agent. Our ability to stay afloat in such scenarios might be improved by coming to know Oswald a little better; we could then, at least, avoid plots he did not fit. Before we can understand a murderer—if he is one—we must discover his motive. But to find the motive, we do well to encounter the man. In Oswald's case, that could be no simple task. How many young men are as timid and bold as Lee Harvey Oswald?

If this metaphor of a base camp served to explain our presence to those KGB officers who did not look upon us with the bemused suspicion that we were representatives of some new exotic venture of the CIA, it also proved useful to us, first as a figure of speech and then as a metaphor that became real. Few who build a base camp have no ambitions to reach the summit.

The book concerning Oswald in Minsk is done, but questions remain. In perusing the first twelve volumes of the House Select Committee on Assassinations Hearings and the full twenty-six volumes of the Warren Commission Hearings and Exhibits, one's own interpretations began to assert themselves; one began to feel that one could do better than know Oswald, one might even *understand* him. To know a man, after all, is to do no more than predict what he will do next, even if you do not have a clue as to why he does it; but to understand a person is to comprehend his reasons for action. The conceit arose that one understood Oswald.

Hence this second volume. If it grew out of the first one, it will nonetheless be different in tone. "Oswald in Minsk" depended upon the integrity of the interviews, and they revealed a simple if surprising phenomenon—the memories of most of our subjects were clear even though thirty years had passed. After the assassination, they had been instructed by the KGB not to speak about Oswald or Marina, and indeed, they did not. So, their recall was often pristine; it had not been exposed to time so much as sealed against it.

In America, however, the key witnesses had been interviewed and, in turn, had read the testimonies of others, as well as endless newspaper accounts of the event, and they had discussed the assassination with friends, and witnessed elaborate reconstructions on television that sometimes involved their own evidence or ran counter to it. Now, at this late date, to interview hundreds of such

over-saturated witnesses would produce results that could hardly
be trustworthy. How would the witness distinguish between what
had been experienced then and what served his or her small personal legend now? That gap of three decades which had been an
asset in Minsk would prove a liability in America.

One came to the reluctant conclusion that the Warren Commission Hearings, in 1964, offered the best opportunity for studying Oswald's character. It is a point to underline. The Hearings
are a resource when it comes to understanding our protagonist
even if they are of little or no help in determining whether he was
part of a conspiracy. Of course, it should also be said that these
same twenty-six volumes are a much maligned and misunderstood
manifest of a prodigious work, compendious enough to bear comparison to the Encyclopedia Brittanica (had the Brittanica been
devoted to only one subject). On the other hand, the Hearings
and Exhibits are also—which is why the Commission is so despised—a singularly bland, slow-moving, even limp set of polite
inquiries that fail to pursue a thousand promising trails.

This is, however, to mistake the avowed purpose of the Warren
Commission for its actual achievement. It was so pedestrian an
investigation, so benignly void of the inquiring spark, that the
good motives of the Commissioners have long been under suspicion. For if the seven august men who presided were not trying to
blur every possibility but one—that Oswald was a twisted and
lonely killer—then one has to assume the opposite: These most
accomplished judges, lawyers, and high government officials
really did not know how to conduct an inquiry of this sort. As
inquiry, the Warren Commission's work resembles a dead whale
decomposing on a beach.

Yet, one does not have to view the work in this fashion. For two
generations of Americans, the Warren Commission's twenty-six
volumes of Hearings and Exhibits have become a species of Tal-
mudic text begging for commentary and further elucidation. To
the novelists and historians who may be writing on this subject a
hundred years from now, the twenty-six volumes will also be a
Comstock Lode of novelistic material, not of much use in solving
a mystery—so little is followed through to the end!—but certainly
to be honored for its short stories, historical vignettes, and vast
cast of characters, plus its methodical presentation of bureaucratic inquiries and reports that do make some attempt to cut
tracks through the wilderness surrounding Oswald's motives.

So, let us give due regard to the Warren Commission's twenty-six volumes. The work is rarely to be applauded for its acumen, but what a treasure trove it provides of American life in the midst of our century, what an air it insinuates of the workings of the American establishment under the stress of wishing both to reveal and to conceal the answer to a most momentous matter.

For that reason, perhaps, the Hearings, at their best, do provide passing insights into Oswald that accumulate in value. It is startling to discover, as one pans these government volumes for bits of gold, how much does gleam in the sludge. One could even make a career as a minimalist writer (of the second rank) by laying out many of the testimonies in two- and three-page narratives.

An attempt to come to grips with the full twenty-four years of Lee Harvey Oswald's life seems in order, then. We have an advantage, after all! What was previously the dry material of the Warren Commission Hearings takes on more life because of our knowledge of Oswald's behavior in Minsk. We have come to know him well enough to be able now to picture him in American scenes and situations that were formerly meaningless. He has changed from a name on the page to a man who quarrels with his wife in much the manner that one can quarrel with one's own mate. He is nearer to us. The situation is now not without its analogy to seeing an old acquaintance across the room at a party. By the expression on his face, we can have a good idea of what he is feeling. As we follow Oswald through our American sources, he is no longer Oswald-the-cipher but, to the contrary, Oswald-from-Minsk, that fellow we got to know a little, and how interesting it is to hear about him in a new environment. So it is that many of the transcripts have now become revealing because we have a better idea of whom we are observing. Indeed, there are a number of chapters in this second volume when there will be no more demand on the author than to serve as a literary usher who is there to guide each transcript to its proper placement on the page.

That will hardly prove to be the limit of his task. The second volume is also, as advertised, replete with speculation. How else can one deal with the leading actor? After all, Oswald was a secret agent. There is no doubt about that. The only matter unsettled is whether he was working for any service larger than the power centers in the privacy of his mind. At the least, we can be certain he was spying on the world in order to report to himself. For, by his own measure, he is one of the principalities of the universe. We may envision the proportions of Oswald's psychology better if we are ready to compare the human ego to architecture. If most egos are analogous to a peasant's hut, a trailer home, or a ranch house, a few resemble such separate and immense edifices as Mont-Saint-Michel, the Pentagon, or the World Trade Center. It helps our understanding of Oswald if we look for comprehension of his sense of certainty (as well as his mother's) in the ego-kingdom of mansions, palaces, and consummately ugly high-rises. To approach Oswald, we must deal with metaphor as often as with fact.

Let me propose, then, that a mystery of the immense dimensions of Oswald's case will, in the writing, create a form of its own somewhere between fiction and non-fiction. Technically, this book fits into the latter category—it is most certainly not fiction. The author did his best to make up no dialogue himself and attribute no private motives to his real characters unless he was careful to label all such as speculation. Still, it is a peculiar form of non-fiction, since not only interviews, documents, newspaper accounts, intelligence files, recorded dialogues, and letters are employed, but speculations as well. The author's musings become some of the operative instruments. Of course, speculation is often an invaluable resource of the novelist. The result can be seen, therefore, as a special species of non-fiction that can be put under the rubric of *mystery*. That is because all means of inquiry have to be available when one is steering one's way through a cloud— especially if there are arguments about the accuracy of the navigating instruments, which in this case are the facts. Because our facts will often be fogged in, let us at least look to agree on this much—that we, author and reader, are in collaboration to explore a mystery, our own largest American mystery, and move forward on that understanding into the excerpts, the transcripts, and the speculations of Volume Two. If we obtain nothing else, we can count on gaining a greater understanding of the dominant state of our political existence in these decades of the Cold War, for Oswald, willy-nilly, became one of the leading actors in this tragicomedy of superpowers who, with limited comprehension, lived in dread of each other.

Mama's Boy

Taking up service as a literary usher, the first guest to escort to her place has to be the mother of our protagonist:

MARGUERITE OSWALD. . . . Chief Justice Warren, I will start with Lee as a baby . . .

Lee was born October 18, 1939, in New Orleans, Louisiana . . . His father's name was Robert Edward Lee; he was named after General Lee . . .

Lee was born 2 months after the death of his father, who died from a heart attack, coronary thrombosis.

Lee was a very happy baby.

I stayed home with the children as long as I could, because I believe that a mother should be home with her children.

I don't want to get into my story, though.

Lee had a normal life as far as I, his mother, is concerned. He had a bicycle, he had everything that other children had.

Lee has wisdom without education. From a very small child— I have said this before, sir, and I have publicly stated this in 1959—Lee seemed to know the answers to things without schooling. That type child, in a way, is bored with schooling because he is a little advanced.

Lee used to climb on top of the roof with binoculars, looking at the stars. He was reading astrology. Lee knew about any and every animal there was. He studied animals. All of their feeding habits, sleeping habits . . . that is why he was at the Bronx Zoo when he was picked up for truancy—he loved animals.

Lee played Monopoly. Lee played chess . . . Lee read history books, books too deep for a child his age. At age 9 he was always instructed not to contact me at work unless it was an emergency, because my work came first—he called me at work and said, "Mother, Queen Elizabeth's baby has been born."

He broke the rule to let me know that Queen Elizabeth's baby had been born. Nine years old. That was important to him. He liked things of that sort . . .[1]

Robert E. Lee Oswald was Marguerite Claverie Oswald's second husband. Her first had been Edward John Pic, who lived with Marguerite in New Orleans long enough to father a child, Lee's half-brother, John Pic, who would join the Coast Guard in 1948, when Lee was nine years old.

By that year, however, Marguerite had already come to the end of two other marriages, the last being to Edwin A. Ekdahl. Between Pic and Ekdahl came the six-year interval, starting in 1933, when she was married to Robert E. Lee Oswald, and they soon had a son, Robert Lee Oswald, Lee's middle brother. Five years later, Robert E. Lee Oswald died while Marguerite was in her seventh month of pregnancy. Lee Harvey Oswald was born, therefore, fatherless.

So much for the natal and nuptial facts. The impact of Robert E. Lee Oswald's death was borne in isolation by Marguerite, and that was characteristic of her. She was proud of her Southern manners, which were self-acquired. The youngest sister in a large New Orleans working-class family, she had developed airs and aspirations in her adolescence, and even achieved a measure of gentility through her second marriage. After the death of Robert E. Lee Oswald, Marguerite was, however, reduced to penury. Her life became a journey through stunted little commercial enterprises—moves from low-paying jobs to business ventures so small that the heart of the profit was chewed out before she began. But we can leave these details to John Pic, Lee's oldest brother.

> **MR. PIC.** Well, while we lived on Bartholemew Street, my mother opened in the front room a little store called Oswald's Notion Shop. I think she sold spools of thread and needles and things like this.
>
> **MR. JENNER.** Did she sell any sweets or candy for children?
>
> **MR. PIC.** Yes, sir; I remember we used to go there and swipe it. [The store] was [in] the very front room . . . we had a dog and the dog's name was Sunshine . . .
>
> **MR. JENNER.** Was it a nice neighborhood? . . .
>
> **MR. PIC.** Well, digging back in my Sociology courses, I would say it was upper-lower class, if there is such a classification . . .
>
> **MR. JENNER.** Now, I ask you again to recall the circumstances under which you entered the Bethlehem Orphanage, you and your brother Robert?

MR. PIC. . . . . I think properly the notion store wasn't a booming business, and she had to go to work and since we were reminded we were orphans all the time, the right place to be would be in an orphan home . . .[2]

Marguerite had an older sister, Lillian Murret, who had five children, and Lillian would take Lee into her household for periods when he was two years old.

MRS. MURRET. . . . he was a very beautiful child . . . I would take him to town, and . . . he would have on one of these little sailor suits, and he really looked cute, and he would holler "Hi" to everybody, and people in town would stop me and say, "What an adorable child he is." [My children] liked him . . . I had 5 in 7 years, . . . had to get my own five children ready for school, and I didn't have any help on that and it kept me pretty busy, and that's why I guess it was that Lee started slipping out of the house in his nightclothes and going down the block and sitting down in somebody's kitchen. He could slip out like nobody's business. You could have everything locked in the house, and he would still get out. We lived in a basement house, and we had gates up and everything, but he would still get out.[3]

Lillian Murret's daughter Dorothy is more than ready to corroborate her mother's description.

MISS MURRET. . . . He had a certain manner about him that other children never had. I mean he was very refined, he really was, and extremely well-mannered . . . he was darling, and very outgoing and a very pretty child. He was adorable . . .[4]

Relations, however, between Marguerite and Lillian were frequently on edge.

MRS. MURRET. She was very independent . . . She didn't think she needed anyone at any time, . . . no matter how much anyone would try to help or how much they would try to do for her, she never thought that anyone was actually helping her . . . Sooner or later it seemed like she would just take one little word or something that she would think was wrong, and we would have these little differences.[5]

While his brothers, John Pic and Robert Oswald, were in Bethlehem Orphanage, Lee would, for thirteen months, go back and forth from the orphanage to the Murrets'. John Pic remembers his presence well.

MR. PIC. . . . Robert and I enjoyed Bethlehem. I mean we were all there with the kids with the same problems, same age groups, and everything. Things for myself became worse when Lee came there . . .

MR. JENNER. Tell us about it.

MR. PIC. At Bethlehem they had a ruling that if you had a younger brother or sister there and they had bowel movements in their pants the older brothers would clean them up, and they would yank me out of classes in school to go do this and, of course, this peeved me very much . . .

MR. JENNER. He was only [2 or] 3 years old?

MR. PIC. Yes; but I was 10 . . .[6]

In those difficult years, Marguerite met an electrical engineer, a Yankee from Boston described by John Pic as "Tall . . . over six feet. He had white hair, wore glasses. Very nice man." He proved to be one electrical engineer who had an eye for ladies with verve, and he and Marguerite traveled together on his business trips through Texas for months, and Lee went with them until he was old enough for school, at which point Mr. Ekdahl married Marguerite and bought a house in Benbrook, Texas, a suburb of Fort Worth.

Her economic situation now solved, she took John and Robert out of the orphanage and sent them to military school in Mississippi, at an academy called Chamberlain-Hunt. However, Marguerite's good life with Ekdahl began to deteriorate. Their disputes were many, and often over money; they would quarrel and separate, come together and fight once again. During one of these separations, in the summer of 1947, at a time when John Pic was home from Chamberlain-Hunt and closing up the store in which he worked that summer, Marguerite and Mr. Ekdahl "drove up and told me that they were going downtown to the Worth Hotel. This was one of their reunions."[7]

MR. PIC. . . . So, I went back and told Lee and Robert, and this seemed to really elate Lee, this made him really happy that they were getting back together. Mr. Ekdahl, while Robert and I were at the academy, would write us, he was a great one for writing poetry. He would send us a poem about ourselves or something, treated us real swell.

MR. JENNER. . . . did Lee like him? . . .

MR. PIC. Yes, sir; I think Lee found in him the father he never had. He had treated us real good and I am sure that Lee felt the same way . . .[8]

The marriage, however, proceeded to come further apart. Marguerite, as John would put it, had "strong suspicions."

MR. PIC. . . . Mr. Ekdahl was seeing another woman and [my mother] knew where the woman lived and everything.

So, one night [my friend] Sammy, my mother and I all piled into this young couple's car, went over to these apartments, and Sammy acted as a messenger, and knocked on the door and said, "Telegram" for this woman, whoever she was, I don't remember the name. When she opened the door, my mother pushed her way in, this woman was dressed in a nightgown negligee, Mr. Ekdahl was seated in the living room in his shirt sleeves and [my mother] made a big fuss about this. She's got him now and all this stuff . . .[9]

Lillian Murret goes into further detail:

MRS. MURRET. . . . his coat and tie and shirt was off, and he had his athletic shirt on [so Marguerite] questioned him about that, and he said he was there on business, which was absurd, because you know you don't disrobe yourself on business, so that's what started off the Ekdahl case, and then of course she wanted to get a divorce from him right away, you see, and that's why I say she's quick, you see, because I would not have gotten a divorce. I would have got a separation, because he was making a big salary, [but] she wanted a divorce [although] it seemed like he had connections [because] her pastor told her that if she would press this case against Ekdahl, that he would have a heart attack and that would make her a murderer, that she would be the cause of him dying, so he was in the hospital, I think, so she went to the hospital to see him, and I think they had a roar-up there . . .[10]

Came the trial:

MR. PIC. . . . I don't remember my testimony completely. I do remember that my mother had made the statement that if Mr. Ekdahl ever hit her again that she would send me in there to beat him up, something which I doubt that I could have done.

I was told by her that she was contesting the divorce so that he would still support her. She lost, he won. The divorce was granted. I was also told that there was a settlement of about $1,200 and she stated that just about all of this went to the lawyer . . .[11]

Ekdahl died soon after, and the family was in economic trouble again.

MR. PIC. . . . Robert and I were informed that we would not return to Chamberlain-Hunt in the fall. This, I think, was the first time that I actually recall any hostility towards my mother . . .

MR. JENNER. How did Robert react to that?

MR. PIC. He felt the same way, sir. He wanted to go back. But we were informed because of the monetary situation it would be impossible . . . I was 16 at this time. In September, Lee and Robert returned to school, and I went to work. I obtained a job at Everybody's Department Store which belonged to Leonard Bros. I was a shoe stock boy at the salary of $25 a week.

MR. JENNER. Did you pay some of that money to your mother?

MR. PIC. I think at least $15 out of every pay check . . .[12]

As soon as he is old enough, John joins the Coast Guard. Robert was going to school in Fort Worth and working. Marguerite was working, and Lee was alone.

MRS. MURRET. Yes; she told me that she had trained Lee to stay in the house; to stay close to home when she wasn't there; and even to run home from school . . . She said she thought it would be safer . . . than to have him outside playing when she wasn't there [so] he just got in the habit of staying alone like that . . . he was with himself so much.[13]

John Pic adds a telling detail, and not without malice:

MR. PIC. Also, Lee slept with my mother until I joined the service in 1950. This would make him approximately 10, well, almost 11 years old.

MR. JENNER. When you say slept with, you mean in the same bed?

MR. PIC. In the same bed, sir.[14]

3

Indian Summer, New York

In 1952 Marguerite sold her house, got into her car with Lee, and drove to New York, where John Pic was stationed in the Coast Guard:

MARGUERITE OSWALD. . . . I had no problem of selling my home and going there . . . the main thing was to be where I had family . . .

MR. RANKIN. And what date was that?

MARGUERITE OSWALD. That was exactly August 1952, because I wanted to get there in time for Lee's schooling . . . Robert joined the Marines in July of 1952. And that was my reason for going . . . So at this time I was living in my daughter-in-law's home and son. And we were not welcome, sir.[1]

John Pic had not known in advance that Marguerite was planning to live permanently in New York. He had thought it was just a visit, and so he could put her up. At this time, he and his wife lived in his mother-in-law's apartment in the Yorkville section of Manhattan. It was what John called "a freight-car type," one room after another, but there was space because his mother-in-law was away visiting her other daughter in Norfolk, Virginia.

MR. PIC. . . . They brought with them quite a bit of luggage, and their own TV set. On my way home from work I had to walk about 8 or 10 blocks after the subway, and Lee . . . decided to go up and meet me. We met in the street and I was real glad to see him and he was real glad to see me. We were real good friends. I think [in] a matter of a few days or so I took my leave. Lee and I visited some of the landmarks of New York, the Museum of Natural History, Polk's Hobby Shop on 5th Avenue. I took him on the Staten Island Ferry, and several other excursions we made.

MR. JENNER. Go ahead.

MR. PIC. Well, sir; it wasn't but a matter of days before I could sense they moved in to stay for good, and [my mother-in-law] was due back in a matter of a month or so.

During my leave I was under the impression that I may get out of the service in January of 1953, when my enlistment was up, so [my mother drove me] to several colleges . . . Fordham University, for one, and Brooklyn . . . I remember one conversation in the car that she reminded me that even though Margy was my wife, she wasn't quite as good as I was, and things like this. She didn't say too many good things about my wife. Well, naturally, I resented this, because I put my wife before my mother any day.

Things were pretty good during the time I was on leave but when I went back to work, I would come home and my wife would tell me about some little problem they would have. The first problem that I recollect was that there was no support for the grocery bill whatsoever. I don't think I was making more than $150 a month, and they were eating up quite a bit, and I just casually mentioned that and my mother got very much upset about it. So every night I got home . . . and my wife would have more to tell me about the little arguments . . . It seems that there was an argument about the TV set one day between my wife and my mother . . . According to my wife's statement my mother antagonized Lee [until he was very] hostile towards my wife and he pulled out a pocketknife and said that if she made any attempt to hit him that he would use it on her. At the same time Lee struck his mother. This perturbed my wife to no end. So, I came home that night, and . . . my wife told me this in private, sir. I went and asked my mother about it . . .

MR. JENNER. Was Lee present when you spoke with your mother? . . .

MR. PIC. I am getting to that, sir. So I approached Lee on this subject, and about the first couple of words out of my wife he became real hostile toward me . . . it perturbed my wife so much that she told them they are going to leave whether they liked it or not, and I think Lee had the hostility toward my wife right then and there, when they were getting thrown out of the house as they put it.

When I attempted to talk to Lee about this he ignored me, and I was never able to get to the kid again after that. He didn't care to hear anything I had to say to him. So in a matter of a few days they packed up and left, sir. They moved to the Bronx somewhere . . .[2]

Marguerite offers a variation on this episode:

MARGUERITE OSWALD. . . . it was not a kitchen knife—it was a little pocket knife, a child's knife, that Lee had. So she hit Lee. So Lee had the knife—now, I remember this distinctly, because I remember how awful I thought Marjory was about this. Lee had the knife in his hand. He was whittling, because John Edward whittled ships and taught Lee to whittle ships. He puts them in the glass, you know. And he was whittling when this incident occurred. And that is what it occurred about, because there was scraps of wood on the floor.

So when she attacked the child, he had the knife in hand. So she made the statement to my son that we had to leave, that Lee tried to use a knife on her.

Now, I say that is not true, gentlemen. You can be provoked into something. And because of the fact that he was whittling, and had the knife in his hand, they struggled.

He did not use the knife—he had an opportunity to use the knife.

But it wasn't a kitchen knife or a big knife. It was a little knife. So I will explain it that way, sir.

So immediately then I started to look for a place. I did find a place, I think off the Concourse . . . in the Bronx. And it was a basement apartment . . .[3]

A month or more later, Robert, taking his first leave as a Marine, came to visit Lee and Marguerite at their apartment in the Bronx, and John and Marjory were invited for a family dinner.

MR. PIC. . . . [Lee] sat in the front room watching TV and didn't join us whatsoever . . . Didn't speak to me or my wife.

MR. JENNER. That kind of put a pall on the visit, did it not?

MR. PIC. Yes, sir . . . Lee walked out and my mother informed us that he would probably go to the Bronx Zoo. We had Sunday dinner, and in the course of the conversation my mother informed me that Lee was having a truancy problem and that the school officials had suggested that he might need psychiatric aid to combat his truancy problem.

She informed me that Lee said that he would not see a head shrinker or nut doctor, and she wanted any suggestions or opinions from me as to how to get him to see him, and I told her just take him down there. That is all I could suggest.

MR. JENNER. What was her response to that?

MR. PIC. . . . He was definitely the boss . . . I mean if he decided to do something, regardless of what my mother said, he did it. She had no authority whatsoever with him. He had no respect for her at all.[4]

Soon enough, Marguerite and Lee were called into children's court. Eleven years later, testifying before the Warren Commission, Marguerite consults her notes:

MARGUERITE OSWALD. I have that information here.

Went to school in the neighborhood, Public School 117, which is a junior high school in the Bronx. It states here he attended 15 of 47 days. This is the place we were living that Lee was picked up by the truant officer in the Bronx Zoo.

I was informed of this at work, and I had to appear before a board, which I did.

Lee went back to school.

Then he was picked up again in the Bronx Zoo. And I had to appear before a board committee again.

Then the third time that Lee was picked up, we were—I never did get a subpoena, but we were told he had to appear at Children's Court . . . I did not think it was anything serious, because the Texas laws are not like the New York laws. In New York, if you are out of school one day you go to Children's Court. In Texas the children stay out of school for months at a time.[5]

Youth House

MR. CARRO. I forget whether he had just turned 13 or was still 12, but in New York State we have a law that requires each boy to attend school until at least 16, and this was a young man of tender age who had at this point taken it upon himself to just not bother to go . . .

The judge felt that since there was no father figure . . . this was not a salutary situation [and] he wanted to find out a little more about this boy before he made a decision, and consequently he asked for the study at the Youth House . . .[1]

MR. LIEBELER. Would you say that Oswald was more mentally disturbed than most of the boys that you had under your supervision at that time?

MR. CARRO. Not at all, actually. I have handled cases of boys who committed murders, burglaries, and I have had some extremely disturbed boys, and this was just initially a truancy situation, not one of real disruptive or acting out delinquent behavior. No; I would definitely not put him among [boys] who turned out to be mentally defective, mentally retarded, quite psychotic, and who really had . . . disturbances that were far, you know, greater in depth than those displayed by Oswald.

MR. LIEBELER. . . . would you say that it was just as much a function of the environment that he found himself in here in New York?

MR. CARRO. . . . in my mind there was an inability to adapt from the change of environment [but] you meet the situations. Either you meet them head on or you retreat from them.

Now he apparently had one or two incidents where he was taunted over his inability to speak the same way that the kids up here speak and to dress the same way [and] apparently he could not make that adaptation, and he felt that they didn't want any part of him and he didn't want any part of them . . .[2]

Youth House reports describe him as a non-participant in any of the floor activities. He reads whatever books are available and by 8:00 P.M. asks to be allowed to go to bed. A psychiatric social worker, Evelyn Strickman, who certainly writes well, takes an interest in him.

. . . What is really surprising is that this boy has not lost entirely his ability to communicate with other people because he has been leading such a detached, solitary existence for most of his life.

He told me that . . . his truancy is caused because he feels he would prefer to do other things which are more important. Questioning at first elicited, "Oh, just things," but what I finally learned from him is that he spends all of his time looking at television, leafing over various magazines or just sleeping . . . he feels almost as if there is a veil between him and other people through which they cannot reach him but he prefers this veil to remain intact. When I questioned whether it were painful or disturbing for him to [talk with] me today . . . he let me know that . . . he was not as disturbed in talking about his feelings as he thought he might be. This gave me an opening to inquire into his fantasy life and what I got was a complete rejection of any probing and a reminder that "this is my own business." I let him know that I respected this but there were some things I had to know. Suppose I asked him questions, and if he wanted, he would answer. He agreed to this and actually answered every question that I asked. He acknowledged fantasies about being all-powerful and being able to do anything he wanted. When I asked if this ever involved hurting or killing people, he said that it did sometimes but refused to elucidate on it. None of these fantasies, incidentally, ever involved his mother . . .

[He did confide] that the worst thing about Youth House was the fact that he had to be with other boys all the time, was disturbed about disrobing in front of them, taking showers with them, etc. . . . Actually if he could have his wish he would like to be out on his own and maybe join the service. He acknowledged the fact that in the service he would have to live very close to other people and obey orders and follow a routine which he finds extremely distasteful, but he said he would steel himself to that and make himself do it . . .[3]

There is a rather pleasant, appealing quality about this emotionally starved, affectionless youngster which grows as one speaks to him . . .[4] His face lighted up from its usual impassive expression when he talked about the three-month-old baby [at his brother's house] and admitted that he had found a good deal of enjoyment in playing with it.[5]

Concerning his home life with Marguerite in the Bronx apartment off the Grand Concourse, the interviewer noted: ". . . His mother had found work as an assistant manager in a women's wear shop and she is away again all day. He mostly makes his own meals . . ."[6]

Marguerite, however, soon lost this job.

MR. PIC. . . . she told me that they let her go because she didn't use an underarm deodorant. That was the reason she gave me, sir. She said she couldn't do nothing about it. She uses it but if it don't work what can she do about it?[7]

Some spiritual disruptions may even be strong enough to assert themselves through a deodorant. Marguerite has to be passing through still another bad time in her life.

MARGUERITE OSWALD. . . . I think conditions of this kind in our United States of America are deplorable. And I want that to go down in the record . . . I had to stand single file approximately a block and a half, sir, with Puerto Ricans and Negroes and everything, and people of my class, single file, until we got to the main part of this building . . . I had packages of gum and some candy for my son. And the gum wrappers were taken off the gum, and the candy wrappers were taken off.

And my pocketbook was emptied. Yes, sir, and I asked why. It was because the children in this home were such criminals, dope fiends, and had been in criminal offenses, that anybody entering this home had to be searched in case the parents were bringing cigarettes or narcotics or anything.

So that is why I was searched.

So I was escorted into a large room where there were parents talking with their children.

And Lee came out. He started to cry. He said, "Mother, I want to get out of here. There are children in here who have killed people, and smoke. I want to get out."

So then I realized—I had not realized until I went there what kind of place we had my child in.

We don't have these kinds of places in Texas or New Orleans, sir.[8]

The psychiatric social worker, Evelyn Strickman, is less charmed by the mother than by the son:

Mrs. O. is a smartly-dressed gray haired woman, very self-possessed and alert, and while making a superficial appearance of affability, I felt that essentially she was defensive, rigid, selfish, and very much of a snob.

One of the first things she wanted to know was why Lee was at Youth House because she had no clear understanding of the purpose of the institution. Before I even had a chance to explain to her, she went on to ask me if he had received a complete medical examination and in my answering in the affirmative, confided to me that she had noticed lately he had gotten very big "down there" and that while of course he was getting a little too big for her to look at him, she had been worried lest anything was the matter with his genitals . . .

Mrs. O., incidentally, bathed all her children herself until the time they were 11 or 12 and then said in an embarrassed manner that at that age they got a little too old for her to look at . . .

She went on to tell me that she had had him to a doctor six months ago for a head to toe examination and the doctor had examined the boy in her presence. He had apparently not examined the boy's genitals and Mrs. Oswald had insisted upon this so he asked her to step from the room. She said she wasn't gone but a few minutes when he called her back and said there was nothing the matter, and she somehow felt very dissatisfied with the examination . . . When I indicated we had found nothing the matter with his genitals, she then looked at once relieved and, I felt, a little disappointed.

Mrs. O. gave her current "analysis" of the reason for Lee's truancy—the upset in moving from Fort Worth. She went on to tell me . . . that she had found it very difficult to adjust to New York and is sorry she came here. She indicated that she has always been a manager of shops of one kind or another and made it a point never to mix with her help. She said they were always respectful to her at home but here in New York, employees talk back to her, etc., and she finds it extremely difficult to take, complaining of their arrogance. Furthermore, she feels that life moves at a much faster pace here; living conditions are unsatisfactory, etc. Later on in the interview after I had gained her confidence much more, she confided in me that she had come from Fort Worth because she thought that it might be better for Lee since he was suddenly left alone after Robert joined the Marines and she wants to be close to what family she had for his sake. With her eyes filled with tears at this point, she told me that she had come to New York to be close to her son, John. There had been an exchange of letters and long distance phone calls and apparently John and his wife were very anxious for her to come, but she said that when she got here, she found an extremely cold reception. Her daughter-in-law is only 17 and apparently went out of her way to let Mrs. O. know that she could not settle with John and herself permanently . . . She said she was made so uncomfortable, that she moved just as soon as she could to an extremely inadequate one-room basement apartment. The living conditions were extremely miserable and she felt that Lee was becoming very depressed but she could not help herself. Just as soon as she was able, and had found another job, she took a three-room apartment in the Bronx and said that Lee seemed to perk up considerably after that.[9]

Lee did perk up. He would go out in the morning and take the subway to the Bronx Zoo. We can enjoy the thought that Lee was happy with the animals. Wild beasts and little children are his natural companions. Nothing in the record tells us, however, which animal he happened to be studying at ten in the morning when a truant officer collared him long enough to ask a few questions.

Let us go back to Evelyn Strickman:

Near the end of the interview she confided in me [that her husband] died suddenly one morning at 6 A.M. of a heart attack [and] she had had a rupture with her husband's family at this time [because] she wanted him buried the same day. Her thought had been for herself and the baby she was carrying, since she felt she could do her husband no good by having a wake and a funeral, and she thought it would be just decent to get him out of the way as quickly as possible. His family had been completely aghast, said that they never saw anything as cold in their whole life, and had not spoken to her from that day to this. She had to rely upon her neighbors' help when Lee was born and she had never had anything to do with her husband's family since that time. She justified herself at great length to me, said that she did not feel it was cold but only sensible, and that her husband, when he used to joke with her, had always said, "Mag, if anything ever happens to me, just throw some dirt in my face and forget about it," and she felt she had acted according to his instructions.

When I offered that it must have been rather difficult for her to have to be both parents and bread-earner at the same time, she told me very proudly that she had never found it so. She said she was always a very independent, self-reliant person who had never wanted any help from anyone, had always had "high fulutent" ideas, which she felt she had to a large measure accomplished, and she always was able to pull herself up by her own bootstraps . . .[10]

She could. She did use her own bootstraps. At a certain point, enmeshed in the counseling that followed Lee's provisional discharge from Youth House, she made her move.

MR. CARRO. . . . the mother took off in January, without letting us know . . .[11] We don't have extra-state jurisdiction and we didn't even know where she had gone . . .[12]

5

Macho Teenage Marxist

What is insufficiently appreciated about manhood is that it is an achievement, not a gift of gender. To be bold, forthright, competitive, individual, courageous, and innovative does not come as a gratuity that is included with a male infant's penis and scrotum. No, such male qualities have to be earned through brave acts, the honoring of one's private code, and through fierce attachment to one's finest habits.

Of course, more than a few women would assert that the virtues listed above belong to the female sex as well. It is hardly the purpose of this book to jump—as Lillian Murret would put it—into a roar-up on such a matter; let it suffice that we are dealing with the psychological realities of the late Fifties, when some enormous majority of Americans still believed that men and women had highly separate roles and that the first obligation incumbent on a male was to behave like one. It is almost certain that Lee Oswald at fourteen and fifteen shared this point of view—how else can one account even in part for his dedicated reading of the Marine Corps manual, and his dreams, as we shall soon see, of daring deeds?

When we encounter him again, after the debacle of New York, he has changed to some degree from the terrified twelve- and thirteen-year-old who wept during his mother's visit to Youth House. Having passed though vats of shame and fear, he seems to take on strength as he enters into adolescence. New York has done something for him after all: Back in New Orleans, he is more ready for combat.

> MRS. MURRET. . . . Now, at the Beauregard School at that time, they had a very low standard, and I had no children going there and never did. My children went to Jesuit High and Loyola University, but they did have a very bad bunch of boys going to Beauregard and they were always having fights and ganging up on other boys, and I guess Lee wouldn't take anything, so he got in several scrapes like that . . .
>
> MR. JENNER. Did you have the impression that Lee Harvey was doing well in school, or what was your feeling along that line?
>
> MRS. MURRET. I think he was doing very poor work in school most of the time. Then he got to the point where he just didn't think he ought to have to go to school, and that seemed to be his whole attitude, and when I mentioned that to Marguerite, that seemed to be the beginning of our misunderstanding. She didn't think her child could do anything wrong, and I [couldn't] say that Lee ever showed that he liked school.[1]

Well, no, he wasn't about to like it. He had dyslexia. At that time, it had not been recognized in most schools as an affliction which so distorted your spelling that it was guaranteed to make a teacher think you were close to moronic. And then of course there were always students around to beat up on him in twos and threes. He didn't like school.

Still, it could not be said that he gave up all at once.

MRS. MURRET. . . . I remember one morning he came over to the house, and he said that he wanted to get on the ball team, but he didn't have any shoes and he didn't have a glove, so I said, "Well, Lee, we can fix you up," and I gave him a glove [and] Joyce's husband sent him a pair of shoes from Beaumont, a pair of baseball shoes, and I told Lee, I said, "Lee, when you need anything, just ask me for it, and if there's a way to get it for you, we will get it." So then he got on the team, I think, but he got off as quick as he got on. I don't know why. He never discussed that with us as to why that was, and we never found out.

. . . I don't think he was the type of boy who was too good an athlete.[2]

Not good in school, not special at sports, and no money to date girls . . .

MRS. MURRET. . . . Most of the boys had money, you know, and went out on the weekends with girls and so forth, but Lee couldn't afford those things, so he didn't mix, but he did like to visit the museums . . . and go to the park and do things like that, and you very seldom can get a teenager to do that kind of thing these days, not even then. They don't all like that type of life you know, but that's what he liked.[3]

[One time] we went to the store and we bought Lee a lot of clothes that we thought he might need so he would look presentable to go to school, you know, whatever a boy needs, and when we gave them to him, he said, "Well, why are you doing all this for me?" And we said, "Well, Lee, for one thing, we love you, and another thing we want you to look nice when you go to school, like the other children." So that was that.

MR. JENNER. Did he wear this clothing to school?

MRS. MURRET. Oh yes; he wore the clothing that we bought him [but] he was very independent. Like one time I remember asking him a question about something, and he said, "I don't need anything from anybody," and that's when I told him, I said, "Now listen, Lee, don't you get so independent that you don't think you don't need anyone, because we all need somebody at one time or another," . . .

MR. JENNER. Do you think that a little of this independence might have rubbed off from his mother? . . .

MRS. MURRET. Well, she was independent herself all right . . .[4]

Marguerite was doing her best. She might be living above a pool hall on Exchange Alley at the wrong end of the French Quarter, but even in a bad neighborhood you could maintain some modicum of style.

MRS. MURRET. . . . A lot of people would be surprised, because . . . it looks like a pretty rough section, but she had a real nice apartment . . . she fixed it up real nice . . .

Of course, they had these poolrooms and so forth in that section but I don't think that Lee ever went into those places, because he never was a boy that got into any trouble. For one thing, he never did go out . . . The average teenager who was going to school at Beauregard would have probably been in there shooting pool and things like that, but he didn't do that. His morals were very good. His character seemed to be good and he was very polite and refined. There was one thing he did: He walked very straight. He always did, and some people thought that was part of his attitude, that he was arrogant or something like that, but of course you can't please everybody.

MR. JENNER. But he did have a good opinion of himself, did he not?

MRS. MURRET. Oh, yes; he did.[5]

It is only fair to give Marguerite Oswald much of the credit for this:

MARGUERITE OSWALD. . . . Lee continued reading Robert's Marine Corps manual . . . He knew it by heart. I even said, "Boy, you are going to be a general if you ever get in the Marines."[6]

People with a good opinion of themselves tend to enjoy a double life. While living on Exchange Alley, he started to read Karl Marx as well as the Marine Corps manual. Life at school, however, was another matter. A schoolmate speaks:

MR. VOEBEL. . . . I don't exactly remember when I first saw him . . . but I really became acquainted with him when he had this fight . . . with a couple of boys . . . the Neumeyer boys, John and Mike [which] started on the school ground, and it sort of wandered down the street in the direction naturally in which I was going [and] it kept going on, across lawns and sidewalks, and people would run them off, and they would only run to the next place, and it continued that way from block to block, and as people would run them off one block, they would go on to the next.

MR. JENNER. That was fisticuffs; is that right?

MR. VOEBEL. Right.

MR. JENNER. Were they about the same age? . . .

MR. VOEBEL. I don't know; I guess so . . .

MR. JENNER. How about size?

MR. VOEBEL. I think John was a little smaller, a little shorter than Lee . . .

MR. JENNER. All right, what happened as this fight progressed down the street?

MR. VOEBEL. Well, I think Oswald was getting the best of John, and the little brother sticking by his big brother stepped in too, and then it was two against one, so with that Oswald just seemed to give one good punch to the little brother's jaw and his mouth started bleeding . . .

MR. JENNER. The little boy?

MR. VOEBEL. Yes, sir. Mike's mouth started bleeding, and when that happened the whole sympathy of the crowd turned against Oswald for some reason, which I didn't understand, because it was two against one, and Oswald had a right to defend himself. In a way, I felt that this boy got what he deserved, and in fact, later on I found out that this boy that got his mouth cut had been in the habit of biting his lip. Oswald might have hit him on the shoulder or something, and the boy might have bit his lip, and it might have looked like Oswald hit him in the mouth, but anyway, somebody else came out and ran everybody off then, and the whole sympathy of the crowd was against Lee at that time because he had punched little Mike in the mouth and made his mouth bleed . . . [then] a couple of days later we were coming out of school in the evening and Oswald, I think, was a little in front of me and I was a couple of paces behind him, and . . . some big guy, probably from a high school—he looked like a tremendous football player—punched Lee right square in the mouth, and . . . ran off.

MR. JENNER. He just swung one lick and ran?

MR. VOEBEL. Yes; that's what they call passing the post . . . That's when somebody walks up to you and punches you . . . I think this was sort of a revenge thing on the part of the Neumeyer boys, so that's when I felt sympathy toward Lee for something like this happening, and a couple of other boys and I . . . brought him back to the restroom and tried to fix him up, and that's when our friendship, or semi-friendship, you might say, began . . . I think he even lost a tooth from that . . .

MR. JENNER. Well, you had a mild friendship with him from that point on, would you say?

MR. VOEBEL. Right.

MR. JENNER. Tell me about that.

MR. VOEBEL. . . . sometimes I would stop off at Lee's and we would play darts and pool. Lee's the one who taught me . . . He lived over the top of the pool hall . . . on Exchange Alley . . .

MR. JENNER. Did you find him adept at playing pool?

MR. VOEBEL. You see, I had never played before and he showed me the fundamentals of the game, and after a couple of games I started beating him, and he would say, "Beginner's luck," so I don't think he was that good . . .

MR. JENNER. . . . was he a drinker?

MR. VOEBEL. Well, you see, we were only at the age of about fourteen or fifteen, and smoking and drinking just wasn't of interest to a lot of people of our age at that time . . .

MR. JENNER. All right, those are the things I am interested in . . . I'm trying to get a picture of this boy as he became a man . . .

MR. VOEBEL. Right. Now I want to make one thing clear. I liked Lee. I felt that we had a lot in common at that time. Now, if I met Lee Oswald, say, a year ago, I am not saying that I would still like him, but the things I remember about Lee when we were going to school together caused me to have this sort of friendship for him, and I think in a way I understood him better than most of the other kids . . . and if he had not changed at all, I probably would still have the same feeling for Lee Oswald, at least more so than for the Neumeyer brothers . . .

MR. JENNER. . . . Would you say there were other boys of the type of the Neumeyer brothers at Beauregard School? . . .

MR. VOEBEL. Oh, yes . . . it was almost impossible [not to get] involved in a fight sooner or later. You take me, I am not a fighter but I had to fight at that school.

MR. JENNER. You did?

MR. VOEBEL. Well, no; I will say this: I would back down from a fight a lot quicker than Lee would. Now, he wouldn't start any fights, but if you wanted to start one with him, he was going to make sure that he ended it, or you were really going to have one, because he wasn't going to take anything from anybody. I mean, people could call me names and I might just brush that off, but not Lee . . . You couldn't do that with Lee . . . he didn't take anything from anybody . . .[7]

MR. JENNER. And you also . . . had an interest in guns; is that right?

MR. VOEBEL. . . . we had guns around the house all the time . . .

MR. JENNER. Did Lee share your enthusiasm for collecting weapons? . . .

MR. VOEBEL. . . . I don't think Lee was interested in the history of any weapons. For example, he wanted a pistol . . . just to have one, not for any purposes of collecting them or anything . . .

MR. JENNER. Did Lee ever own a weapon?

MR. VOEBEL. . . . Not that I know of . . . he did own a plastic model of a .45 . . . and he showed that to me. I guess you want to know now about his plan for a robbery. Actually, I wasn't too impressed with the whole idea at first, [and] it really didn't bother me until he did shock me one day when he came up with a whole plan and everything that he needed for . . . stealing this pistol [from] a show window, on Rampart Street . . . It might have been a Smith & Wesson. I think it was an automatic, but I really didn't pay too much attention to it . . . The following week I was up at his house and he came out with a glasscutter and a box with this plastic pistol in it, and . . . he had a plan as to how he was going to try to get in and get this pistol.

MR. JENNER. You mean in the Rampart Street store?

MR. VOEBEL. Yes. Now, I don't remember if he was planning to use this plastic pistol in the robbery or not, or just . . . cut the glass and break it out . . . I don't think he was really sure even then how he wanted to do it [but] we walked over there to this store and we looked at this pistol in the window . . .

He said, "Well, what do you think?" and I . . . happened to notice this band around the window, a metal tape that they use for burglar alarms, and I got working on that idea in the hope that I could talk him out of trying it, . . . I said, "Well, I don't think that's a good idea, because if you cut that window, it might crack that tape, and the burglar alarm will go off," . . . and so [he] finally gave up the idea . . . I don't think he really wanted to go through with it, to tell you the truth . . . I think maybe he was just thinking along the lines that if he went through with it, that he would look big among the guys, you know . . .[8]

It was in this period that Oswald began to read Marxist literature. Just which books is somewhat in question. He would tell several people in Moscow and Minsk that his radical politics were first stirred by a pamphlet about the execution of the Rosenbergs handed to him in 1952 by an old lady outside a subway stop in New York, and he would also remark that he took out *Das Kapital* and *The Communist Manifesto* from his local library in New Orleans. On the other hand, he is reading *Das Kapital* seriously in Minsk, and his remarks suggest it is for the first time. In New Orleans, it is probably *The Communist Manifesto* that is giving him all the fire he needs for striking radical opinions at the age of sixteen.

William E. Wulf, a studious young man, contributes to such a picture. Oswald worked for a time at Pfisterer Dental Laboratory in New Orleans as a delivery boy and had made friends with another runner there named Palmer McBride, who was a member of the New Orleans Amateur Astronomy Association (a group of high school students), of which Wulf was president. Oswald was interested in astronomy, he informed McBride. After a preliminary phone call, Oswald and McBride dropped in one night around ten or eleven at Wulf's house.

MR. WULF. [I told him that] we were not very much interested in teaching some fledgling all this data we had already gone through over the years, and he would actually be hampered in belonging to the group, and I actually discouraged him from joining for that reason. This is all I can remember of the first contact, because it was kind of late . . .[9]

However, Oswald came over again with Palmer McBride, and this time began to expound on politics.

MR. WULF. . . . McBride had always told me that he wanted to get into the military service as a career, especially rocket engineering and rocketry—like we were all nuts on rocketry at the time—and I told him, I said, "This boy Oswald, if you are associated with him, could be construed as a security risk . . ."

MR. LIEBELER. What led you to make that statement to McBride?

MR. WULF. [Oswald] was reading some of my books in my library, and he started expounding the Communist doctrine and saying that he was highly interested in communism, that communism was the only way of life for the worker, et cetera, and then came out with the statement that he was looking for a Communist cell in town to join but he couldn't find any [and then] my father came in the room, heard what we were arguing on communism, and that this boy was loud-mouthed, boisterous, and my father asked him to leave the house and politely put him out of the house, and that is the last time I have seen or spoken with Oswald . . .[10]

On his sixteenth birthday, with a birth certificate forged with Marguerite's connivance, he tries to enlist in the Marine Corps and is rejected as too young. So, he has to undergo another year of memorizing that Marine Corps manual. How much he must have absorbed about the erection of pup tents and squad tents, care of one's weapon, close-order march, proper salute, disassembly of the .30 caliber machine gun, dress uniform, guerrilla tactics, traversing a three-rope bridge, aims and standards of the Marine Corps obstacle course and, of course, the procedure for firing the M-1 rifle from prone, standing, and sitting positions.

Marguerite moved from New Orleans back to Fort Worth in July of 1956, three months before Lee would be seventeen and so eligible to enlist. On October 3, 1956, just twenty-one days before he would sign up for the Marines on October 24, he put his *X* on a coupon from an advertisement found in a magazine: "I want more information about the Socialist Party." Then, he added a personal letter to the coupon:

Dear Sirs,
 . . . would like to know if there is a branch in my area, how to join, etc. I am a Marxist and have been studying my

Socialist principles for well over fifteen months. I am very
interested in your YPSL.[11]

John Pic had a short comment on why Lee had gone into the
Marines:

MR. PIC. He did it for the same reasons that I did it and Robert
did it, I assume, to get from out and under.

MR. JENNER. Out and under what?

MR. PIC. The yoke of oppression from my mother.[12]

In April 1960, during Oswald's first spring in Minsk, an FBI
agent named John W. Fain was making inquiries about Lee in Fort
Worth and here refers to an interview with a neighbor of Marguerite Oswald:

Mrs. TAYLOR stated that the subject was a student in Arlington Heights High School and was only about 16 or 17 years of
age when the OSWALDS moved to this address [and] that the
subject was a peculiar boy inasmuch as he read a great deal
and kept very much to himself . . . Mrs. TAYLOR stated that she
actually felt sorry for the subject inasmuch as it appeared to
her that he had few if any friends and no social life. She stated
she pitied the boy because . . . she has never seen anyone stay
at home more closely than did the subject. She stated that
Mrs. OSWALD . . . on occasion urged him to go out and seek employment but that he preferred to sit at home and read . . .[13]

MARGUERITE OSWALD. Yes, sir. [This] is a picture of Lee in Atsugi,
Japan, in 1958, showing his strength.

MR. RANKIN. That shows him in [his] Marine uniform also, does it?

MARGUERITE OSWALD. In his Marine uniform showing his muscles
to his mother.[14]

The Loose End

There can be little doubt that the Warren Commission came to the unvoiced conclusion that it might be all for the best if Oswald turned out to be homosexual. That would have the advantage of explaining much even if it explained nothing at all. The Warren Commission did have, after all, a lone killer as their desired objective, but there was no evidence of particular animus by Oswald toward Kennedy, and more than a few key witnesses testified to Oswald's positive utterances concerning JFK. So, a history of homosexuality located in Oswald's closet would prove helpful to them. In 1964, homosexuality was still seen as one of those omnibus infections of the spirit that could lead to God knows what further aberration.

Nonetheless, there is a real chance that Oswald had considerably more of a sexual career as a homosexual than as a heterosexual through his Marine Corps days and through his first year in Minsk. Paradoxically, it would help to explain the patience with which he wooed Ella and the haste with which he married Marina. Indeed, his young life is a study in one recurring theme—I am not yet a man and I must become one—which in the late Fifties and early Sixties became a compelling motif for many young men terrified by homosexual inclinations and ready to go to great lengths to combat and/or conceal them.

One must always read accounts of Oswald's behavior with double vision: Yes, he was serious—no, he was jesting; yes, he was gay—no, he was merely shy with women; yes, he was obsessed with violence—no, he had only a small and intermittent interest in such matters. Any attempt to put a thematic stamp on him will run into contradictions—his actions are not often predictable—but given the oppressive psychological climate of the Fifties, we have to entertain the possibility that one of the major obsessions in Oswald's life was manhood, attaining his manhood. If he was in part homosexual, then the force of such a preoccupation would have doubled and trebled.

From the affidavit of David Christie Murray, Jr.:

. . . Oswald did not often associate with his fellow Marines. Although I know of no general explanation for this, I per-

sonally stayed away from Oswald because I had heard a rumor
to the effect that he was homosexual . . .[1]

Much is said to this effect by another Marine, Daniel Patrick
Powers, a high school football and wrestling coach at the time of
his Warren Commission testimony. He must have seemed an ideal
soldier to the Commissioners. Powers was a big man physically,
and his testimony gives off an air of sincerity which powerful men
often possess when they know they can depend on their bodies
more than most.

> MR. POWERS. . . . he had a large homosexual tendency, as far as I
> was concerned, and . . . a lot of feminine characteristics as far as
> the other individuals of the group were concerned, and I think
> possibly he was an individual that would come to a point in his
> life that he would have to decide one way or the other.
>
> MR. JENNER. On what?
>
> MR. POWERS. On a homosexual or leading a normal life, and
> again, now, this is a personal opinion.
>   And I think this, more than any other factor, was the reason
> that he was on the outside of the group in Mississippi.
>   He was always an individual that was regarded as a meek per-
> son, one that you wouldn't have to worry about as far as the lead-
> ership was concerned, a challenge for leadership or anything . . .
>   He had the name of Ozzie Rabbit, as I recall . . .[2]

This question of whether he was or was not homosexual may
hinder our understanding of Oswald more than it helps. Why not
suppose instead that he had the kind of double nature which
would leave him miserable after gay activities and more certain
than ever that he was really heterosexual, whereas, conversely,
when with a woman a year or two later, he might feel more powerful homosexual inclinations than when he was with men. It may
have mattered less what he did than what he was tempted to do. In
any event, we can be reasonably certain of one matter: By the age
of seventeen and a half, he had not yet had a woman.
   We are advancing too quickly, however. Powers did not meet
Oswald until Lee had been in the Marines for almost half a year,
and so Powers' account skips over one of the most telling periods
in any soldier's life—his basic training—but then, the Warren

Commission was not about to delve too deeply into Oswald's military career. After all, what if Oswald turned out to be some spawn of military intelligence? Better not to open that door more than a crack.

Assassination by conspiracy was, however, not a likely topic for the Warren Commission—their emphasis was on family values. A bang-up job they did, and we can take the benefit of that, but no one could ever say that keen inquiry was the Warren Commission's prevailing passion. Their treatment of Oswald's Marine Corps days can only be termed slack. In *Legend*, his landmark work on CIA involvement with Oswald, Edward Jay Epstein gives us a richer portrait of Oswald's military service than do all the volumes of the Warren Commission, for he managed to uncover a dozen Marines who had known Oswald and not been interviewed.

All the same, there is not much anywhere about his boot camp in San Diego, just enough to let us know that Oswald had a hard time. The Marine Corps manual could hardly have prepared him for the reality. A trainee in Oswald's platoon named Sherman Cooley described it as "holy hell."[3] Of course, all basic training can be so described—it was just that the Marine Corps liked to pack two basic trainings into one. Oswald, according to Cooley, was soon being called *shit-bird*. He had trouble managing to qualify with his rifle, and that was horrific. The Marine Corps laid it out for you: Your ability with an M-1 was equal to your virility—there was no reason to be in the Marine Corps if virility was not the center of your focus.

From San Diego, Oswald went on to combat training at Camp Pendleton in California—full menu—infantry assaults in coordination with tanks, bayonet drill built around hand-to-hand combat, training for amphibious landings—it is a little painful to think of this mother's boy, over-loved and much neglected, Hamlet to Marguerite's much-mortified Gertrude, conceiving in his fantasies of great and noble Marine glory (to accompany his Marxism), now reduced to the spiritual rank of shit-bird. He had begun to toughen up in New Orleans, but hardly enough to be prepared for the kind of tests that the Corps would lay on him. He had to feel feminized by his failures. It must be repeated: In the mind-set of the 1950s, a century away from the prevailing concepts of the 1990s, to be weak among men was to perceive oneself as a woman, and that, by the male code of the times, was an intolerable condition for a man.

Such a set of values hardly helped Oswald to balance the opposites in himself. Hysterical and timid, he still has an ego ready to judge the world around him. The form it takes in his personality is to be cool, reserved, and sardonic whenever and wherever he can—his first nine months in the Marine Corps offer little opportunity for that. Powers describes how Lee, on the boat over to Japan (following aircraft and radar control school in Jacksonville, Florida, and at Keesler, in Biloxi, Mississippi), would play chess with him all day and virtually do a war dance of delight when he would win: " 'Look at that. I won. I beat you.' "[4]

On September 12, 1957, two years and one month before he will enter Russia, Oswald lands at Yokosuka, Japan, close to Tokyo. He and Powers have read *Leaves of Grass* on the troopship, and he gives the book to the big Marine.

At Atsugi airbase, thirty-five miles southwest of Tokyo, where he was now based in a two-story wooden barracks, Corporal Thomas Bagshaw was his roommate. Bagshaw, who was making a career in the Marines, told Epstein that Oswald was "very thin, almost frail, shy and quiet." At that time, he was five feet nine inches tall, and may not have weighed 135 pounds.

> [Bagshaw] also recalls feeling sorry for him when other Marines in the barracks began "picking on him." The rougher Marines in the barracks, who generally preferred spending their liberties carousing in Japanese bars and finding women, considered Oswald (who spent his early liberties in the television room of the barracks alone, watching *American Bandstand* and replays of football games) a natural object of derision. They called him Mrs. Oswald, threw him in the shower fully dressed and hassled him in every other conceivable way. Oswald would not fight back; he would just turn away from a provoker and ignore him.[5]

To this should be added a keen observation by another of Epstein's Marines, Jerry E. Pitts, who pointed out that there was an unspoken rite of passage for every new recruit, and the initiation took different forms.

> . . . [Pitts] explained that savvy Marines could breeze right through such treatment, laughing off the insults and swap-

ping them back. But Oswald was the exception. He seemed to take each insult seriously and responded with a quiet fury that he was incapable of converting into physical violence . . .

Pitts . . . remembers . . . "certain areas—such as indecent references to his mother—that really set Oswald off . . ."[6]

There is one sympathetic portrait of Oswald in this period. Gator Daniels, who had been an alligator wrestler in the Florida swamps, a huge man who had spent his first eighteen years fishing and trapping, described Lee as " 'simple folk, just like I was . . . we were a bunch of kids—never been away from home before—but Oswald came right out and admitted that he had never known a woman. . . . It was real unusual that a fellow would admit that. Like me, he was naïve about a lot of things, but he never was ashamed to admit it. . . . He was just a good egg,' Daniels remembers. 'He used to do me favors, like lending me money until payday . . . the sort of friend I could count on if I needed a pint of blood.' "[7]

Nonetheless, hazing continued, and one day Oswald discharged a pistol into the wall while a few Marines standing nearby were riding him mercilessly.

It is a complex account and well worth avoiding; the descriptions vary a good deal. One of the more sinister versions, as described by Edward Epstein, has a Marine, Pete Connor, insisting that "the derringer which Oswald was playing with as he sat on a bunk, discharged and sent a bullet seven inches above Connor's head to slam into a wall locker."[8] Since Connor, by his own admission, was one of the Marines ridiculing Oswald, a suspicion arises that the shot was no accident.

Then there is another episode, perhaps a couple of weeks later, when Oswald wounds himself with the same derringer. Oswald's outfit had been alerted that they were shipping out in a few days from Japan to parts unknown, and scuttlebutt had it that he nicked himself purposely to avoid going. By the record, Oswald grazed his upper left arm with a .22 caliber bullet from his mail-order derringer, and then said to the several witnesses who rushed in, "I believe I shot myself."

He could have faced an immediate court-martial, but his outfit was getting ready to ship out from Japan and the legal proceedings were put on hold. As soon as Oswald was discharged from the hospital, he was put on mess duty as an interim punishment. His outfit (MACS-1—Marine Air Control Squadron-1) left Atsugi on November 20, 1957, to embark on an old World War II LST that would wallow past Okinawa toward the Philippine archipelago. While their mission was as yet undetermined, the Marines heard talk of military intervention, possibly in Borneo. Meanwhile, MACS-1 never saw a coastline for a month. It was hot and monumentally boring in the South China Sea as they moved in convoy with thirty or more ships of the Seventh Fleet. Finally, after a hot and dreary Christmas at sea near the equator, they made camp at a place called Cubi Point off Subic Bay, set up a radar tent, and stood guard duty in the awareness that many of the Filipinos in the area might be hostile to them and friendly to the Hukbalahap—Communist guerrillas.

The football season now over, and the Far East Armed Services bowl games having all been played, his friend from early Marine training, Daniel Powers, rejoined MACS-1.

> **MR. JENNER.** Now, was the same group . . . still together at Cubi Point when you rejoined the squadron?
>
> **MR. POWERS.** [Of] the people in my particular group that originated in Jacksonville, the only [ones] left were Schrand, Oswald, and myself . . .
>
> **MR. JENNER.** And did an incident occur with respect to Mr. Schrand?
>
> **MR. POWERS.** [Schrand] was on guard duty one evening and he was shot to death. Now, I have never seen the official report or anything, but the scuttlebutt at that time was that he was shot underneath the right arm and it came up from underneath the left neck, and it was by a shotgun which we were authorized to carry while we were on guard duty . . . he was either leaning against the shotgun or was fooling with it, but he was shot anyway . . . we could never realize how a guy could have shot himself there other than he was leaning on it this way [indicating], and "boom," it went off.[9]

From an affidavit by Donald Peter Camarata: "I heard a rumor to the effect that Oswald had been in some way responsible for the death of Martin Schrand."[10]

Schrand and Powers and Oswald had traveled in the same car from aviation school in Florida to radar school in Biloxi, Mississippi, and all three had gone on together to Atsugi and then to Cubi Point. Epstein offers the account of another Marine, named Persons, who

> . . . heard an explosion, which he instantly knew was a shot-gun blast, and bloodcurdling screams from the area that Schrand was patrolling. "The screams were like some wild thing. . . . I knew I wasn't supposed to leave my post, no matter what happened, but I just said, 'Hell, the guy's in trouble,' and took off over there," he later recounted.
>
> About 50 yards away he found Schrand in a pool of blood, mortally wounded. His shotgun was about six feet away on the ground behind him . . . It was determined that Schrand had been shot under the right arm by his own shotgun. Suicide was ruled out because the barrel of the gun was longer than Schrand's arm and no object with which he could have pulled the trigger was found at the scene.
>
> At first . . . it was assumed that he had been attacked by a Filipino guerrilla and, in the scuffle, shot with his own weapon. But when no other evidence of infiltrators could be found, the death was ruled "accidental," on the assumption that the weapon had accidentally gone off when Schrand dropped it. The enlisted men, continuing to suspect that something more was involved in Schrand's death, grew increasingly nervous about guard duty.[11]

To this, Epstein adds the following note: "A number of Marines asserted that Oswald was on guard duty that night and was possibly involved in the Schrand incident," but adds, "After questioning nine officers and enlisted men who were at Cubi Point that night, I was unable to find any corroborating evidence . . ."[12]

There is an uneasy gap in scattered details. How can a man be in position to get killed by a shotgun blast that enters under his right arm and exits by his neck? An undeclared possibility is that someone was being forced to kneel and commit fellatio and so was in position to pick up the shotgun from where it had been placed on the ground at his feet.

There is no record whether Schrand, after all his travels with Oswald from Florida to Mississippi to California to Japan to Cubi Point in the Philippines, is to be characterized as his friend or his tormentor, but given Oswald's sexual reputation, there is no wonder that his name became vaguely attached to this event.

In World War II, it was not uncommon for many a combat veteran in the Philippines, hardened, mean-spirited, and never in doubt about his heterosexuality, to use Filipino boys while on guard duty and brag about it later. He was being serviced.

What was current practice in early 1945 on Luzon had probably not altered a great deal by early 1958; Schrand could have been killed by a Filipino.

If it was Oswald, however—and let us assume that the probability of that has to be small but not inconceivable—then what a sense he would have had thereafter of being forever an outlaw, an undiscovered and as yet unprosecuted criminal.

Of course, it is wholly questionable to base any serious interpretation on such an assumption: Other events, however, will soon occur which might also have a large and secret effect upon him.

MACS-1 would move from Cubi Point all the way over to Corregidor, and there Oswald would spend hours exploring the old tunnels and fortifications of World War II. Still assigned to mess duty for the illegal possession of his derringer, he seems to have found a sense of balance by comporting himself like a clown. Working breakfast in the mess, he exhibits his own method for scrambling dozens of eggs. A fellow Marine, George Wilkins, told Epstein: "Ozzie . . . [would] take a mess tray and slide it under the puddle of eggs [on the griddle] and flip them all at once. It was quite a sight."[13]

When his outfit returned to Atsugi in March, Oswald began drinking with other Marines. On return from a liberty, he would wake up his end of the barracks by shouting, "Save your confederate money, boys; the South will rise again!"[14] If only for this brief hour, he has come into union with American life: He is a Marine, and happy when shit-face drunk. Soon enough, according to Epstein, his drinking buddies

> . . . introduced him to the vast array of cheap bars near the base and the girls who worked in them. From neonrise to neonset the bars served as bargain-basement brothels for enlisted men from the base. And they cheered him on when he finally had his first sexual experience with a Japanese bar girl.[15]

Powers remarks that he was now "more aggressive, and outgoing in his manner . . . now he was Oswald the man rather than Oswald the rabbit."[16] Of course, Powers knew less about thesis and antithesis than did Oswald:

> *Epstein:* Several witnesses recall a wild place in Yamato pronounced "Negashaya," where men wore dresses and lipstick. One witness described the place as a "queer bar" and reported that he and Oswald once went there—at Oswald's suggestion—and took out two deaf-mute girls. "Oswald seemed to know his way around the place," the witness, who prefers not to be identified by name, recalls. "I don't remember that he knew anyone by name, but he was comfortable there."[17]

Part of Oswald's bravura may have come from a reasonably successful resolution of his court-martial for owning a derringer. He was found guilty on April 11, a month after they had come back from the Philippines, and he was sentenced to hard labor for twenty days, a $50 fine, and loss of his PFC stripe, but the judgment was not operative, and would be canceled in six months if he got into no more trouble.

That proved unworkable. He could flip three or four dozen eggs at once, but mess duty was still demeaning. He wanted to go back to the work for which he had been trained, which was to recognize on radar all incoming aircraft, friendly or hostile. In class at Keesler, he had finished seventh in proficiency in a training group of thirty enlisted men with high IQs. He liked the work; it was a job that required a security clearance. Oswald's erect posture and quiet voice, the frequently stiff-lipped set to his mouth, suggested a divinity student, and everything that was priestly in him must have resented the greasy routines of a military kitchen.

"Oswald finally took his resentment out on the man who had reassigned him to mess duty, Technical Sergeant Miguel Rodriguez . . . [who] saw Oswald at the Bluebird Café, a local hangout for Marines . . ."[18] and "in the course of complaining to Rodriguez about his mess duty, Oswald spilled a drink on him, Rodriguez shoved him away and Oswald then invited the sergeant outside to fight. When Rodriguez refused, Oswald called him yellow."[19]

Oswald, by general consensus, was no match for Rodriguez, but friends who were with the Marine sergeant talked him out of any visceral response. Rodriguez and his fellow Marine NCOs had recently been warned that there were too many fights in the local bars, and non-coms could be demoted if they were involved. So, Rodriguez held off long enough to file a complaint next day. At his summary court-martial, Oswald was judged guilty for using provocative language and given four weeks in the brig.

If the Marines prided themselves on basic training that could not be equaled by any other major branch of the military, their brigs were ready to compete with the punitive capacities of maximum-security prisons.

Epstein: Prisoners were not allowed to say a solitary word to one another. Except for sleeping and eating periods, [they] were made to stand at rigid attention during every moment they were not performing menial duties . . . when a prisoner had to use the toilet, he had to toe up to a red line and scream his request over and over again, until the turnkey was satisfied and granted permission.[20]

By the time he was released from the brig, Oswald, according to a fellow Marine, Joseph D. Macedo, was "cold, withdrawn and bitter. 'I've seen enough of a democratic society here . . .' Oswald said. 'When I get out I'm going to try something else . . .' "[21]

Somewhere around this time Oswald could have gotten in touch with, or been approached by, Japanese Communists. Atsugi airbase, given its high security clearances, its U-2 flights, and its warehousing of nuclear materials, was a focus for hostile espionage efforts in the Far East.

Epstein: Two lawyers for the Warren Commission, W. David Slawson and William T. Coleman, Jr., suggested in a report which was released under the Freedom of Information Act: that ". . . there is a possibility that Oswald came into contact with Communist agents at that time, i.e., during his tour of duty in the Philippines, Japan, and possibly Formosa. Japan, especially because the Communist Party was open and active there, would seem a likely spot for a contact to have been made. . . . Whether such contacts, if they occurred, amounted to anything more than some older Communist advising Oswald, who was then eighteen or nineteen years old, to go to

Russia and see the Communist world is unclear." The Warren Commission did not, however, pursue this in its final report.[22]

It may not be unfair to say that what the Warren Commission lawyers call a possibility is a probability. It certainly explains a good deal about Oswald's actions then and later.

Let us begin by noting that Oswald had learned to use a 35 mm camera, an Imperial Reflex, and was seen taking many a photograph of objects and buildings on the Atsugi base, including the radar antennae with which he worked.

Epstein: He frequently went to Tokyo or otherwise disappeared on his passes. One of Oswald's Marine friends recalls meeting him at a house in Tamato with a woman who was working there as a housekeeper for a naval officer. He was impressed at the time that Oswald had found a girlfriend who was not a bar girl or prostitute. In the house was also a handsome young Japanese man for whom Oswald had apparently bought a T-shirt from the PX on base. While the girls cooked sukiyaki on a hibachi grill, the men talked, but the Marine was unable to understand exactly what Oswald's relation was to the group.[23]

So far, it is a small matter. He takes photographs on base, and could be sharing a ménage-à-trois with a Japanese man and woman. He states to Joseph Macedo that he doesn't care to return to the United States. He will never forgive the Marine Corps for what those four weeks in the brig have done to his pride. On such a flimsy note, we can hardly bring in a case against him, merely a suspicion.

He forms, however, one relation that is virtually without explanation unless it is a quid pro quo between Oswald and a beautiful Japanese woman who is working at one of the best and most expensive nightclubs in Tokyo, the Queen Bee. Any hostess one chose for a night would cost more than Oswald could earn in a month. The Queen Bee was for officers, not enlisted men. Yet Oswald was seen going out with her often:

Epstein: "He was really crazy about her," observed [a Marine named] Stout, who met the woman with Oswald on several occasions in local bars around the base. Other Marines, less friendly to Oswald . . . were astonished that someone of her "class" would go out with Oswald at all.[24]

That the Queen Bee and similar places were marketplaces for the pursuit and purchase of pieces of military information seems to have been taken for granted. Epstein offers Marine Lieutenant Charles Rhodes, who

> recalls an incident at Atsugi when a girl he was friendly with informed him that she was sorry to hear that he was going on maneuvers to Formosa. Rhodes, an officer assigned to MACS-1 as an air controller, told her that she was misinformed—that there were no plans for the unit to go to Formosa. Ten days later Rhodes was officially informed of the maneuver.[25]

MACS-1 was indeed dispatched to Formosa in order to provide radar surveillance. The U.S. military expected a possible invasion of Taiwan and/or a serious naval battle with the Chinese Communists.

Once installed in their radar bubble on Formosa, however, the officers in command of Oswald's outfit discovered that their most crucial signals—the ones by which planes flying by could identify themselves as friendly—appeared to have been compromised:

> *Epstein:* The Communist Chinese seemed to know all the code signals, which, on one occasion, allowed them to penetrate air defenses and appear on the radar screens as "friends" rather than "foes." . . . [Lieutenant Rhodes] vividly recalls the Communist Chinese jets "breezing right through the IFF system." Someone with access to the [codes] . . . had apparently passed them along to the enemy. "We never knew how they got their planes through," Rhodes observed, "but they all had the signals . . . we really caught hell about that." . . .[26]
>
> One night, soon after they had arrived, Oswald was on guard duty at about midnight when Rhodes . . . suddenly heard "four or five" shots from the position Oswald was guarding. Drawing his .45 caliber pistol, he ran toward the clump of trees from which the gunfire emanated. There he found Oswald slumped against a tree, holding his M-1 rifle across his lap. "When I got to him, he was shaking and crying," Rhodes later recounted. "He said he had seen men in

the woods and that he challenged them and then started shooting. . . ." Rhodes put his arm around Oswald's shoulder and slowly walked him back to his tent. "He kept saying he just couldn't bear being on guard duty." . . .[27]

Rhodes reported the incident to his commanding officer, and almost immediately after that, on October 6, Oswald was returned to Japan on a military plane . . . Rhodes believed then, as he does today, that Oswald planned the shooting incident as a ploy to get himself sent back to Japan. "Oswald liked Japan and wanted to stay. . . . I know he didn't want to go to Formosa and I think he fired off his gun to get out of there. . . . There was nothing dumb about Oswald."[28]

It could have been calculated; it could have been honest panic. If he was giving or selling secrets to Japanese Communists, he might have been full of the fear of being found out. On guard duty in the dark in a strange land, it would not take a great deal of imagination to begin to feel that retribution was stealing up on him for his misdeeds.

Returned to Atsugi, with his outfit still in Taiwan, Oswald was soon transferred hundreds of miles south to an airbase at Iwakuni.

Epstein: Owen Dejanovich, a tall, lanky native of Chicago who went on to play professional football, immediately recognized Oswald . . . as someone he had gone to radar school with at Keesler Air Base and tried to renew the acquaintanceship. He quickly found that Oswald had grown enormously bitter since he had last known him.

"He kept referring to the Marines at the center as 'You Americans,' as if he were some sort of foreigner simply observing what we were doing," says Dejanovich. His tone was definitely accusatory. He spoke in slogans about "American imperialism" and "exploitation" . . .[29]

As Oswald would remark to reporters in Moscow in the fall of 1959, he had by October of 1958 decided to defect and become a citizen of the Soviet Union.

Of course, it is not quite so pat as that. Stationed in California for much of the intervening time, he would also think of going to Cuba and becoming one of Castro's lieutenants.

The Man Who Would Take Over the Team

After his thirteen-month stint in Japan, Oswald was given a thirty-day leave and spent it with his mother at her small apartment in Fort Worth. Robert Oswald, newly married, took Lee out hunting with .22s for squirrel and rabbit—by all accounts, an uneventful leave.

Then, he reported to another Marine Air Control Squadron, MACS-9, in California at Santa Ana, near San Diego, and worked in still one more fenced-off radar bubble.

> *Epstein:* . . . unlike Atsugi, where occasional enemy planes strayed into the allied Air Defense Identification Zone, causing alerts to be sounded and intercept paths plotted on the board, little happened in California to break the tedium . . .[1]

Oswald, however, was busy trying to learn Russian. As we know from every report of his early lack of proficiency in Moscow, the conversational levels he attained in America had to be rudimentary, but he did study while at Santa Ana, California. Two months after his arrival, he took a Marine Corps proficiency examination and scored a plus 4 in reading Russian (that is, he had four more answers right than wrong) was a plus 3 in the writing of Russian, but in comprehension of spoken language was minus 5—all in all, a mediocre performance. It only seemed to inspire him to study further with a Russian-English dictionary. He also subscribed to a newspaper printed in Russian and to *People's World,* which was put out by the Socialist Workers Party.

> *Epstein:* When astonished clerks in the mailroom reported the fact that Oswald was receiving this "leftist literature" to their operations officer, Captain Robert E. Block, he questioned Oswald [who] explained that he was only trying to indoctrinate himself in Russian theory in conformance with Marine Corps policy. Although not entirely convinced by Oswald's answer, Block did not press the matter.[2]

The lack of more serious inquiry by Captain Block and other Marine officers has been a cause of much suspicion after the fact.

The likelihood, however, if one is to guess, is that Oswald was not being taken too seriously. Known already as a clown, he may have been doing his best to fortify such impressions.

From the affidavit of Richard Dennis Call to the Warren Commission:

During this time . . . many members of the unit kidded him about being a Russian spy; Oswald seemed to enjoy this sort of remark. At that time I had a phonograph record of Russian classical pieces entitled, "Russian Fireworks." When I would play this record, Oswald would come over and say, "You called?" I had a chess set which contained red and white chessmen; Oswald always chose the red chessmen, making some remark to the effect that he preferred the "Red Army." In connection with this general joking about Oswald's interest in Russian, he was nicknamed "Oswaldskovich."[3]

From an affidavit to the Warren Commission from Mack Osborne:

I once asked Oswald why he did not go out in the evening like the other men. He replied that he was saving his money, [because] one day he would do something which would make him famous. In restrospect, it is my belief—although he said nothing to that effect—that he had his trip to Russia in mind when he made that statement . . .[4]

He rarely moves in one direction, however, without exploring another. Cuba also appeals to him, and he proceeds to talk about it with a Puerto Rican—Corporal Nelson Delgado.

MR. DELGADO. . . . we got along pretty well. He had trouble in one of the huts, and he got transferred to mine.

MR. LIEBELER. Do you know what trouble he had in the other hut?

MR. DELGADO. Well, the way I understand it, he wouldn't hold his own. Came time for cleanup, and general cleanliness of the barracks, he didn't want to participate, and he would be griping all the time. So the sergeant that was in charge of that hut asked to have him put out, you know. So consequently, they put him into my hut . . .

MR. LIEBELER. Did you ever notice that he responded better if he were asked to do something instead of ordered to do something?

MR. DELGADO. Right . . . that's what worked with him. I never called him Lee or Harvey or Oswald. It was always Oz.

MR. LIEBELER. Oz?

MR. DELGADO. Ozzie. I would say, "Oz, how about taking care of the bathrooms today?" Fine, he would do it. But as far as somebody from the outside saying, "All right, Oswald, I want you to take and police up that area"—"Why? Why do I have to do it? Why are you always telling me to do it?" Well, it was an order, and he actually had to do it, but he didn't understand it like that.[5]

Liebeler brings the conversation back to Cuba, and reminds Delgado that he and Oswald had spoken of going there to fight for Castro in future battles now that Fidel had entered Havana.

MR. DELGADO. . . . it just so happened that my leave coincided with the first of January, when Castro took over. So when I got back [Oswald] was the first one to see me, and he said, "Well, you took a leave and went there and helped them, and they all took over." It was a big joke . . . We are dreaming now, right? . . . I speak Spanish and he's got his ideas of how a government should be run . . . we could go over there and become officers and lead an expedition to some of these other islands and free them too . . .

MR. LIEBELER. That is what you and Oswald talked about?

MR. DELGADO. Right . . . how we would do away with Trujillo, and things like that, [but] he started making plans, he wanted to know, you know, how to get to Cuba . . . like how can a person in his category, an English person . . . be part of that revolution movement?

I told him, to begin with . . . the best way to be trusted is to know their language, know their customs, you know; so he started applying himself to Spanish, he started studying. He bought himself a dictionary, a Spanish-American dictionary. He would come to me and we would speak in Spanish. You know, not great sentences but enough. After a while he got to talk to me, you know, in Spanish.[6]

That project goes nowhere. As the American media become more and more critical of Castro and his growing ties with the USSR, Delgado develops some second thoughts about endangering his future years in the military by such a move, and draws away from Oswald.

During this period in California, there are other assessments of Oswald. To the degree that he is preparing to defect to Russia, he seems to become proficient at work. One of the officers in his control center gives him good marks on the job.

> **MR. DONOVAN.** . . . Sometimes he surveilled for unidentified aircraft. Sometimes he surveilled for aircraft in distress. Sometimes he made plots on the board. Sometimes he relayed information to other radar sites of the Air Force or Navy. And sometimes he swept the floor when we were cleaning up and getting ready to go home. I found him competent in all functions.
>
> Sometimes he was a little moody. But . . . in working with most people, as long as they do their job, if they are moody, that is their business . . . I have been on watch with him when an emergency arose, and in turning around and reporting it to the crew chief and to myself . . . he would tell you what the status of the emergency was . . . and what he thought the obvious action we should take . . . Then he waited for you to tell him what to do, and he did it, no matter what you told him.[7]

Sometimes, they played chess together.

> **MR. DONOVAN.** . . . as a matter of fact, he was a pretty good player. I won the base championship that year in chess. I know that on occasion he beat me. That was not a very big base. But he and I were comparable players.[8]

His relation with Lieutenant Donovan warmed up to the point where they would enter discussions during quiet times on duty.

> **MR. DONOVAN.** . . . His bond with me was that I was a recent graduate of the Foreign Service School, at least fairly well acquainted with situations throughout the world. And he would take great pride in his ability to mention not only the leader of a country, but five or six subordinates in that country who held positions of

prominence. He took great pride in talking to a passing officer coming in or out of the radar center, and in a most interested manner, ask him what he thought of a given situation, listen to that officer's explanation, and say, "Thank you very much."

As soon as we were alone again, he would say, "Do you agree with that?"

In many cases it was obvious that the officer had no more idea about that than he did about . . . polo matches in Australia.

And Oswald would then say, "Now, if men like that are leading us, there is something wrong—when I obviously have more intelligence and more knowledge than that man."

And I think his grave misunderstanding that I tried to help him with is that these men were Marine officers and supposed to be schooled in the field of warfare as the Marine Corps knows it, and not as international political analysts . . .[9]

Donovan also coached the squadron team in touch football. Oswald tried out for end.

MR. ELY. Was Oswald a proficient football player?

MR. DONOVAN. No; . . . I think the boy only weighed about 125, 130 pounds, as I remember. He had a slender build.

MR. ELY. Would you say, however, that he was normal in terms of speed and agility?

MR. DONOVAN. Oh, yes; he was fast enough.

MR. ELY. So would you characterize him as athletic, but too light to be a really good football player?

MR. DONOVAN. I don't think he would ever make first string high school in a good high school. [On the other hand] he often tried to make calls in the huddle—for better or for worse, again, I should say, a quarterback is in charge of the team and should make the calls. A quarterback did. And I don't know if [Oswald] quit or I kicked him off. But, at any rate, he stopped playing.[10]

If he will always pretend to be as cool as the injunctions of reason itself, his emotions, on the rare occasions that he permits them to show, suggest other states of feeling.

We obtain some insight from the testimony of Kerry Thornley, who was one of the brightest Marines on the base.

Thornley was neither bewildered nor particularly impressed by Oswald's presence, but then Thornley may have been Lee's equal as a maverick in the service, since he subscribed to I. F. Stone's newsletter. In those days, by leatherneck standards, that was a Red sheet right next to *The Worker.*

MR. THORNLEY. My first memory of him is that one afternoon he was sitting on a bucket out in front of a hut, with some other Marines. They were discussing religion. I entered the discussion. It was known already in the outfit that I was an atheist. Immediately somebody pointed out to me that Oswald was also an atheist . . .

MR. JENNER. What reaction did he have to that?

MR. THORNLEY. . . . he wasn't offended by this at all . . . he said to me with his little grin . . . "What do you think of communism?" And I replied that I didn't think too much of communism in a favorable sense, and he said, "Well, I think the best religion is communism." And I got the impression at the time that he said this in order to shock. He was playing to the galleries, I felt.

MR. JENNER. The boys who were sitting around?

MR. THORNLEY. Yes, sir . . . He was smirking as he said this and he said it very gently. He didn't seem to be a glass-eyed fanatic by any means.[11]

Soon enough, Albert Jenner becomes interested in Thornley's opinions on many a matter:

MR. JENNER. What habits did he have with respect to his person—was he neat, clean?

MR. THORNLEY. Extremely sloppy.

MR. JENNER. Extremely sloppy?

MR. THORNLEY. He was. This, I think, might not have been true of him in civilian life [but] it fitted into a general personality pattern of his: to do whatever was not wanted of him, a recalcitrant trend in his personality. [Oswald would] go out of his way to get into trouble, get some officer or staff sergeant mad at him. He would make wise remarks. He had a general bitter attitude toward the Corps. He used to pull his hat down over his eyes . . . and you got the impression he was doing this so he wouldn't have to look at anything around him.

MR. JENNER. . . . so he would not be assigned additional work or—

MR. THORNLEY. No . . . this was just an attempt, I think, on his part, to blot out the military . . . he made a comment to that effect at one time; that . . . he didn't like what he had to look at . . .

MR. JENNER. What about his powers of assimiliation of what he read, and his powers of critique?

MR. THORNLEY. . . . he was extremely intelligent. With what information he had at hand he could always do very well in an argument; he was quick. [For example] Oswald had argued previously that communism was a rational approach to life, a scientific approach to life . . . I challenged him to show me any shred of evidence to support the idea that history took place in the manner described by Engels and Marx . . . and he, after some attempt to give me a satisfactory answer, which he was unable to do, became aware of that and he admitted that there was no justification, logically, for the Communist theory of history, . . . but that Marxism was still, in his opinion, the best system for other reasons.

MR. JENNER. Best as against what?

MR. THORNLEY. As against, well, primarily as against religions . . . That first comment of his always sticks in my mind, about communism being the best religion. He did think of communism as, not as a religion in the strict sense, but as an overwhelming cultural outlook that, once applied to a country, would make it much better off than, say, the Roman Catholic Church cultural outlook or the Hindu cultural outlook or the Islamic cultural outlook, and he felt that, as I say, to get back to this argument, he felt there were enough other things about communism that justified it that one could accept the theory of history on faith.

MR. JENNER. What other things?

MR. THORNLEY. Well, for one thing, the idea he felt—as did Marx—that under capitalism workers are exploited, [but] that under the present Soviet system, for example, that the money was spent for the benefit of the people rather than going to the individual who happened to be running the enterprise . . .

MR. JENNER. Did you raise with him the price the individual had to pay . . . in terms of individual liberty as against the capitalistic or democratic system?

MR. THORNLEY. You couldn't say this to him. Because he would say: "How do you know?" . . . he would challenge it on the grounds that we were probably propagandized in this country and we had no knowledge of what was going on over there . . .

MR. JENNER. Did you have any impression at any time that he . . . might like to experience by way of personal investigation what was going on in Russia?

MR. THORNLEY. . . . It was the farthest thing from my mind. Although I certainly will say this: When he did go to Russia it did seem to me a much more likely alternative for Oswald than, say, joining the Communist Party in the United States.

MR. JENNER. Excuse me.

MR. THORNLEY. It seemed to fit his personality . . .

MR. JENNER. Would you elaborate, please?

MR. THORNLEY. Well, Oswald was not militant. At the time it didn't seem to me he was . . . at all a fighter, the kind of person who would glory in thinking of himself as marching along in a great crusade of some kind. He was the kind of person who would take a quiet . . . approach to something. For example, going to the Soviet Union would be a way he could experience what he thought were the benefits of communism without committing himself to storming the Bastille, so to speak.[12]

Thornley, however, is quick to explain that he doesn't pretend to understand Oswald past a certain point . . .

MR. THORNLEY. He was extremely unpredictable. He and I stopped speaking before I finally left the outfit [in June].

MR. JENNER. How did that arise?

MR. THORNLEY. It was a Saturday morning. We had been called out to march in a parade for [some] staff NCOs who were retiring from the Marine Corps. This was a common occurrence. Every now and then we had to give up our Saturday morning liberty to go march in one of these parades and everybody, of course, having just gotten up, . . . and having to look forward to a morning of standing out in the hot sun and marching around, was irritable . . . We were waiting at the moment, in a parking lot by the parade ground. Oswald and I happened to be sitting next to each other on a log [and he] turned to me and said something about the stupidity of the parade . . . how angry it made him, and I said, I believe my words were, "Well, comes the revolution you will change that."

At which time he looked at me like a betrayed Caesar and screamed definitely, "Not you, too, Thornley." And I remember his voice cracked as he said this. He was definitely disturbed at what I had said to him and I didn't really think I had said that much. He put his hands in his pockets and pulled his hat down over his eyes and walked away and went over and sat down someplace else alone, and I thought, well, you know, forget about it, and I never said anything to him again and he never said anything to me again.

MR. JENNER. You mean you never spoke to each other from that time on?

MR. THORNLEY. No; and shortly thereafter I left the outfit for overseas.[13]

It is possible that Oswald was engaged again on the periphery of espionage. Epstein makes a close calculation of what it cost Oswald to travel to Moscow[14] against what he had saved in the Marine Corps, and ends with the estimate that there was not enough money to account for the Deluxe arrangements Oswald purchased from Intourist. There seems a shortfall of at least five hundred dollars; the possibility can certainly not be ignored that he had made up the difference by selling information in Japan, and there is some indication that he was doing it again in Los Angeles.

Epstein: As Oswald's tour of duty neared completion, Delgado noticed a stack of "spotter" photographs showing front and profile views of a fighter plane among Oswald's papers. He realized that they had probably been used as a visual aid in training classes, and wondered why Oswald had them in his possession.

Oswald stuffed the photographs into a duffel bag with some other possessions and asked Delgado if he would bring the bag to the bus station in Los Angeles, put it in a locker, and bring him back the key. According to Delgado's recollection, Oswald gave him two dollars for doing this.[15]

This is hardly hanging evidence, but if Oswald did give away radar-spotting codes in Japan, he could also have taken up such activities again in California. Such a premise does help to explain his fears in Minsk when walking with Ella that he could be ambushed by hostile Americans. It also accounts for his fear of arrest on his return to America. He could certainly have defected to Russia without committing any acts of espionage in Japan or America, and we could still follow his motives—but not quite as well. It is his character rather than hard evidence which enables us to assume that he did play at the edges of espionage with Japanese Communists.

In any event, he shows considerable skill with his next moves. He applies to Albert Schweitzer College, in Switzerland, thereby freeing himself of the obligation to remain in America for two years on Marine Corps inactive reserve. On this college application, he lists Hemingway and Norman Vincent Peale as favorite authors, speaks of studying philosophy and psychology, and of becoming "a short story writer on contemporary American life"[16]—yes, he had enough material for that—and at the same time is arranging for an early hardship discharge from the Marines by instructing Marguerite on what steps she has to take. Having been injured on her job by a can of candy that fell off a shelf onto the bridge of her nose, she manages to obtain affidavits from her doctor, her lawyer, and two friends: The accident has incapacitated her, she claims; she needs her son back from the Marines to support her.

As soon, however, as he obtains this hardship discharge in September 1959, he will stop off in Fort Worth just long enough to tell Marguerite that he is in the import-export business and is shipping out. He stores most of his gear in her apartment, leaves her a hundred dollars, and from New Orleans, a few days later, writes to her with restraint worthy of Hemingway:

> I have booked passage on a ship to Europe. I would have had to sooner or later and I think it's best I go now. Just remember above all else that my values are different from Robert's or yours. It is difficult to tell you how I feel. Just remember this is what I must do. I did not tell you about my plans because you could hardly be expected to understand.[17]

Next day he embarks on the SS *Marion Lykes,* a freighter that carries passengers from New Orleans to Le Havre. There he lands on October 8. Then come London and Helsinki. On October 15, visa in hand, he leaves by overnight train for Moscow, where he arrives on the morning of October 16, and falls into the not inconsiderable company of Rimma, our Soviet guide from Intourist.

Endless debates have gone on about how he obtained his visa and whether his entrance into the Soviet world was routine or had been stage-managed in advance by the KGB. It is best to avoid such debates, and indeed, as our next chapter—a quick tour of Moscow and Minsk—will try to point out, it is almost irrelevant how he arrived.

Rather, let us note the reaction at MACS-9 in Santa Ana.

MR. DONOVAN. Shortly before I got out of the Marine Corps, which was mid-December 1959, we received word that he had showed up in Moscow. This necessitated a lot of change of aircraft call signs, codes, radio frequencies, radar frequencies.

He had the access to the location of all bases in the west coast area, all radio frequencies for all squadrons, all tactical signs, and the relative strength of all squadrons, number and type of aircraft in a squadron, who was the commanding officer, the authentication code of entering and exiting the ADIZ, which stands for Air Defense Identification Zone. He knew the range of our radar. He knew the range of our radio. And he knew the range of the surrounding units' radio and radar.

If you had asked me a month after I had left that area, I could not have told you any [codes] but our own. Had I wanted to record them I certainly could have done so secretly, and taken them with me. Unless he intentionally with malice aforethought wrote them down, I doubt if he would have been able to recall them a month later, either . . .

MR. ELY. Are authentication codes changed from time to time as a matter of course?

MR. DONOVAN. They are changed from time to time, that is right.

MR. ELY. Are they changed even if there is no specific incident that elicits the change?

MR. DONOVAN. They are methodically changed anyway.[18]

This may indeed be one reason that the KGB showed no quick interest in debriefing Oswald on military matters. Soon enough we will discuss whether they were concealing much or little from the interviewers who approached them for this book, but if, as the KGB would have known, all spotter codes would have been quickly changed on news of Oswald's defection, then, of course, they could afford to be patient with Oswald and study him.

One last word from the Marines; it is in the affidavit of Peter Francis Connor: ". . . He claimed to be named after Robert E. Lee, whom he characterized as the greatest man in history . . ."[19]

8

Return to Moscow and Minsk

For Americans, the most astonishing aspect of Oswald's defection was that he had been a Marine. Marines do not defect. They plant flags on Iwo Jima. Oswald had injured one of our Cold War certainties.

By contrast, the effect upon Moscow Center can better be described as a series of small but continuing disturbances.

Over the length of a six-month sojourn in Moscow and Minsk, the interviewers (Lawrence Schiller and Norman Mailer and their translator, Ludmila Peresvetova) had conversations with seventeen KGB officers. Some were active, most had retired, and of these seventeen men, there were five, including Igor and Stepan, who agreed to be interviewed in some depth. Within the limits of seeking to obtain answers from people who belong to what is, among other things, a closed club, the interviewers did acquire a reasonable amount of information. Whether these five officers were forthcoming or merely gulling the American visitors into acceptance of one more KGB legend can be debated, but if the interviewers, highly skeptical at first, ended by accepting the larger part of what was told to them, it is because an internal logic began to present itself.

For example, Oswald, by way of his Historic Diary, chooses eight o'clock in the evening as the hour at which he cuts his wrist, whereas Rimma, Rosa, the Botkin Hospital doctors, and a number of medical reports have him coming to Reception at around 4:00 P.M., subsequent to making his attempt an hour and a half earlier. Now it could, of course, have been possible for the Organs to coordinate some twenty witnesses and falsify their reports, but to what end? What conceivably could be gained? Which dire purpose concealed? It seemed safe to conclude that these hospital accounts were correct and that Oswald had, once again, misremembered, or was lying.

Obviously, not everything related by the KGB officers resolves itself so neatly. Moreover, there was a collective desire among them to remain anonymous. Of the five main KGB sources, none wished his name to be used. "Please don't," said one, "or all my peace in retirement will be lost. The media will come to me."

Their requests were honored. Igor and Stepan are pseudonyms, and three of the others will be gathered into one voice. Unlike Igor and Stepan, these three officers were outspoken—their own reputations, after all, were not connected to the case. Besides, they were of high rank and seemed to enjoy the curious nature of the inquiry. Their response to the interviewers was usually in direct relation to the intelligence of the queries. An etiquette soon developed: An incisive, well-placed question produced signally better results than an off-balance lunge. Lack of incisiveness was a cardinal sin. It must be kept in mind that what we perceive as the brute work of KGB interrogations—physical torture, gulags, overt intimidations in public places—were acts usually performed by MVD and were scorned by KGB as practices that lacked finesse, even as CIA officers would look askance at the more brutal activities of high-security prisons like Marion and Attica and feel no identification with security guards.

Under these conditions of collective anonymity, it was decided that one imaginary KGB officer named General Marov might as well become sole spokesman for these three separate KGB sources. While not all three were generals, they could still serve as a chorus of high-level KGB reflection on Oswald's sojourn in Russia.

General Marov, then. If one would look for a face to attach, let us assume he looks like the late William Paley, who directed affairs at CBS for decades. The KGB men of higher rank looked astonishingly like a good many Americans—William Phillips of *Partisan Review,* Irving Howe of *Dissent,* Ben Bradlee of *The Washington Post,* Henry Miller, William Faulkner; one looked very much like the editorial director of Random House, Jason Epstein, and there was even one officer who could have been mistaken in a dim room for Norman Mailer at the age of seventy. Thomas Wolfe once remarked that people in the same occupation tend to look alike in all countries—waiters, for example, or taxicab drivers. The corollary is that there may be profound similarities of character and function between American intellectuals, writers, and media chiefs—and high KGB officers. What wit resides in the cosmos!

Marov claimed not to know whether Oswald had given military information to the Japanese hostess at the Queen Bee in Tokyo. He did, however, say that if it were so, such information probably would have been available at Moscow Center late in 1959, when Oswald arrived.

"Such a contact," said Marov, "is, of course, precious. Any American in any form—military, merchant, scientist—any slight record of contact will be kept for years."

Oswald's defection would not, however, have excited good reactions in Moscow Center. "If any such information had come over from Japan in 1957 or 1958 and had given us any cause to value this man as a possible future agent, such value collapsed entirely," stated Marov, "in the moment Oswald declared that he wanted to remain here. The American community would know he had defected and his value would be zero as any kind of worker for us. Too tricky to play with. This," said Marov, "is an absolute fact."

The suicide attempt augmented their certainty. "That was a small disaster for the gentleman if he still clung to any ambitions to be trained as an agent. The KGB would never recruit such a man."

Then, said Marov, there was Oswald's adventure at the American Embassy. "He comes out of Botkin Hospital, visits his Embassy, and talks to the American official there in a loud, clear voice as if he is also speaking to any instruments, theirs or ours, that might be implanted in the wall. You know, my impression is that Oswald is not quite all right. A normal man would never come to such an Embassy and say, 'Okay, I'll give my secrets to the Russians.' What for? What is to be achieved by such declarations? After this, no KGB man could accept his information. It is not precious enough to risk discrediting our Soviet authorities. Whatever is given to the KGB must be done secretly, deeply, and with very strong precautions. We would never take a person who tried to commit suicide and wanted to defect. This is an abnormality."

In intelligence work, however, second thoughts do arise. If Oswald's suicide attempt was superficial, as the Organs could ascertain from the medical reports, then other suspicions were ready to follow. Had Oswald been given an unorthodox agenda by American intelligence? Had he been dispatched to the Soviet Union as a man programmed to appear irresponsible? "These were questions we had to pose to ourselves, because improbable as were his actions, nonetheless American intelligence could have sent him over as a probe, a monitor, to see how we would react to such a curious stimulus. It was an improbable hypothesis but not to be entirely discarded. Oswald might be something new under the sun."

Under such circumstances, they decided, therefore, not to react but to observe. They would, for example, not seek to debrief him overtly, for that would send too simple a signal to the Americans. KGB had numerous sources for obtaining military information in Japan—it was highly unlikely, therefore, that they would lose anything of value by not moving quickly with Oswald.

However, General Marov did not exclude the possibility that one of their people in Moscow might have had direct talks with Oswald, but never as an official representative of the Organs. It could have been some officer with a cover story—in the guise of a Soviet reporter, for example. "But certainly no official debriefing. This is not only my opinion but my information."

In the actual event, he remarked, three Soviet journalists had gone to interview Oswald on separate occasions. One of them could have been a bona fide journalist who was also serving as a source, but the other two had come from Moscow Center, and their stories never appeared in any newspaper. A well-employed game in his service, Marov remarked, was to have all three ask the same questions; you could compare the target's varying answers as part of your evaluation.

Since Oswald spent much of his time with an Intourist girl, Marov confirms that she, too, would have been coached on what to ask him.

"Since she was young herself, and did not know as much about military and electronic units as would an expert, she was programmed each day, every day, with the next set of questions. Her case officer might ask for information on certain points, until she would come to understand more and more which kind of questions to ask."

There was another option as well. If, in fact, a former Marine had become so deeply displeased with the capitalist system that he defected, then this might serve to demonstrate that life in America was not as agreeable as the U.S. media suggested. Since there was a special department for propaganda in Moscow Center, they too would have made an evaluation and that would have gone to the top of the Central Committee, up to Mikoyan.

Nonetheless, General Marov insisted that any differences between Counterintelligence and KGB's Propaganda Department would have been resolved without conflict. "The aim is to have an understanding. If two Generals sit together, we tend not to speak officially. One says, 'Look, what are we going to do with this guy Oswald?' 'Well, he's a mess.' 'Okay, agreed. Now, do we ship him back, or do we let him stay?—whichever we agree upon.' And, of course, we knew of Mikoyan's desire to keep him. That was a huge factor."

The proposition would have been seen as follows: On the side of taking him as a political immigrant for propaganda purposes, General Marov now said, in English: "Positive is that this young man has come to the paradise of working toilers, etcetera. But on our negative side—very hot coal in one's hand—very hot. Where do you throw it? You have to give him money, and some job, you have to watch him constantly, defend him from curious people. You have to decide whether he could become a source of future counterpropaganda against our Soviet Union because, of course, he could always go up to some Embassy or newspaper and start to tell stories about how bad it is in our provinces."

On the other hand, if you had to send him back to the States, that would also be negative. "After all, why did our country reject him? Our call in those years, successful or not, was to try to be very human, even in a high sense of the word. Under the circumstances, Minsk proved our viable compromise." Marov shrugged. His favorite proverb, after all, would tell you that "When a child has seven baby-sitters, it will lose an eye."

So Oswald was put in a bell-jar. His actions were studied, and the Organs knew their own kind of frustration when he proved to be a poor worker. If he had accommodated himself to the radio plant, their own activities could have focused on interesting alternatives: Either Oswald was sincere, or he was skillful enough to pretend to be sincere. Instead, he put his feet on the table.

We ought to know Oswald well enough by now to understand how demoralized he was by working in a radio factory. To labor collectively was the essence of anonymity. The finished product had more importance than his own person. He had not voyaged from the Marine Corps to the Soviet Union in order to become anonymous. If to work with no enthusiasm would attract more attention, then, indeed, he would put his feet on the table. He wishes to make his mark and keep making it. So, he dramatizes his presence by going to sleep.

The House Select Committee on Assassinations would later say of Oswald, "His return to the United States publicly testified to the utter failure of what had been the most important act of his life,"[1] but it is more likely that Oswald would still have been seeing himself as important in the scheme of things. Who else had manipulated the bureaucracies of the U.S. and the USSR to so much effect? He had done it, in fact, even better than he knew, for more than a few analysts in CIA believed it had all been stage-managed by Moscow Center because it would have been impossible for him to bring it off all by himself. It is staggering to recognize how mutually paranoid a view each superpower had in those days of the other. We can rely on this paranoia to affect a few actions in and around Oswald's life on his return to America.

But slowly. It happened slowly. CIA was as subtle, restrained, and as full of cautionary nuance as KGB when it came to dealing with their breakaway American.

Of course, that can hardly be said for Lee's mother, Marguerite Oswald.

9

Maternity House

Let us go back once again to April 1960, after Oswald had been in the Soviet Union no more than six months. At that time, the FBI agent John W. Fain was making his early inquiries in Texas:

... Mrs. OSWALD stated that she was very much shocked and surprised to learn later that he had gone to Moscow, Russia. She stated that she had no idea how he arrived there but that she does know he had saved up about $1600 from his services in the U.S. Marine Corps. She stated that he did not previously discuss with her any intention to go to Moscow, Russia. She also stated that he had never shown any proclivities for the ideologies of communism [but] subject was always a studious type of individual and that he read books that were considered "deep." [While Mrs. Oswald] felt that subject had a right as an individual to make his own decisions, however, she stated that she was very greatly surprised and disappointed that he had taken this action [and] since January 22, 1960, she had sent three different letters to her son but that all had been returned to her undelivered. She stated that she feared that he might have become stranded and in danger [so] she has had correspondence with her Congressman and with the U.S. State Department inasmuch as she has been very much alarmed for fear that something might have happened to subject.[1]

Indeed, a month before John Fain had come by to interview her, she had begun efforts to find out what had happened to Lee. She had written to her Texas congressman, Jim Wright, on March 6, 1960, and a day later to Christian Herter of the State Department:

Dear Sir:

In October 1959 my son (age 20 years) Lee Harvey Oswald (serial no. 1653230) went to Moscow, Russia, three days after his discharge from the Marine Corps . . .

I am very much concerned because I have no contact whatsoever with him now . . .

I am writing to you because I am under the impression that Lee is probably stranded and even if he now realizes he has made a mistake he would have no way of financing his way home. He probably needs help.

I also realize that my son might like Russia. That he might be working and be quite content. In that case, feeling very strongly that he has a right as an individual to make his own decisions, I would in no way want to hinder or influence him in any way.

If it is at all possible to give me any information concerning my son, I would indeed be very grateful.

Thanking you in advance for your kindness in this matter.

I remain
Sincerely,
Mrs. Marguerite Oswald[2]

Confidential memos will go back and forth between State and
the American Embassy in Moscow discussing whether the Embassy
is in a position to find out from the Soviets where Oswald is
located, but the inquiry falls between the cracks.

Bureaucracy is the only form of human organization that can
manage to pass a hot potato through a small crack. Ten and one
half months will go by before State will hear from Marguerite
Oswald again. That lady, however, has been gathering her forces.
The next time they hear from her, she is on their doorstep. At the
Warren Commission hearings, she will recall the occasion clearly:

MARGUERITE OSWALD. . . . I arrived at Washington 8 o'clock in the
morning. I took a train and borrowed money on an insurance
policy I have, [plus] I had a bank account of $36, which I drew
out and bought a pair of shoes. I have all that in proof, sir, the
date that I left for the train. I was 3 days and 2 nights on the
train, or 2 days and 3 nights. Anyhow, I took a coach and sat up.

I arrived at the station 8 o'clock in the morning and I called
the White House. A Negro man was on the switchboard, and he
said the offices were not open yet, they did not open until 9
o'clock. He asked if I would leave my number. I asked to speak
to the President. And he said the offices were not open yet. I
said, "Well, I have just arrived here from Fort Worth, Texas, and
I will call back at 9 o'clock."

So I called back at 9 o'clock. Everybody was just gracious to
me over the phone. Said that President Kennedy was in a conference, and they would be happy to take any message. I asked
to speak with Secretary Rusk and they connected me with that
office. And his young lady said he was in a conference, but anything she could do for me. I said, "Yes, I have come to town
about a son of mine who is lost in Russia. I do want to speak—I
would like personally to speak to Secretary Rusk." So she got off
the line a few minutes. Whether she gave him the message or
what I do not know. She came back and said, "Mrs. Oswald, Mr.

Rusk [said] that you talk to Mr. Boster who is special officer in charge of Soviet Union affairs,"—if I am correct. And Mr. Boster was on the line. I told him who I was. He said, "Yes, I am familiar with the case, Mrs. Oswald." He said, "Will an 11 o'clock appointment be all right with you?" This is 9 o'clock in the morning. So I said—this is quite an interesting story—I said, "Mr. Boster, that would be fine. But I would rather not talk with you." I didn't know who Mr. Boster was. I said, "I would rather talk with Secretary of State Rusk. However, if I am unsuccessful in talking with him, then I will keep my appointment with you."

So I asked Mr. Boster—I said, "Mr. Boster, would you please recommend a hotel that would be reasonable?" He said, "I don't know how reasonable, Mrs. Oswald, but I recommend the Washington Hotel. It will be near the State Department and convenient to you."

So I went to the Washington Hotel. [And] they asked me if I had a reservation. I said, "No, I didn't but Mr. Boster of the State Department recommended that I come here." So they fixed me up with a room. I took a bath and dressed. I went to the appointment [and] arrived at Mr. Boster's office at 10:30.

But before arriving at Mr. Boster's office, I stopped at a telephone in the corridor and I called Dean Rusk's office again because I didn't want to see Mr. Boster, and I asked to speak to Dean Rusk. And the young lady said, "Mrs. Oswald, talk to Mr. Boster. At least it is a start."

So then I entered around the corridor into Mr. Boster's office [and he] came out and said, "Mrs. Oswald, I am awfully glad you came early because we are going to have a terrible snow storm and we have orders to leave early in order to get home."

So he called [in two other men and] we were in conference. So I showed the papers like I am showing here. And I said, "Now, I know you are not going to answer me, gentlemen, but I am under the impression that my son is an agent." "Do you mean a Russian agent?" I said, "No, working for our Government, a U.S. agent. And I want to say this: That if he is, I don't appreciate it too much, because I am destitute, and just getting over a sickness," on that order.

I had the audacity to say that. I had gone through all of this without medical, without money, without compensation. I am a desperate woman. So I said that.

MR. RANKIN. What did they say to you?

MARGUERITE OSWALD. They did not answer that. I even said to them, "No, you won't tell me." So I didn't expect them to answer that.

THE CHAIRMAN. Did you mean that you were seeking money from them?

MARGUERITE OSWALD. No, sir . . . What I was saying was that I think that my son should be home with me, is really what I implied [but] I didn't come out and say I want my son home. I implied that if he was an agent, that I thought he needed to be home.

MR. RANKIN. Did you say anything about believing your son might know full well what he was doing in trying to defect to the Soviet Union, he might like it better there than he did here?

MARGUERITE OSWALD. I do not remember saying this . . . I said— because I remember this distinctly. I said, "Now, he has been exploited all through the paper as a defector. If he is a defec- tor"—because, as we stated before, I don't know he is an agent, sir—"and if he is a defector, that is his privilege as an individual."

And they said, "Mrs. Oswald, we want you to know that we feel the same way about it." That was their answer.[3]

Still, Marguerite was not about to give up the more interesting alternative. A little later on that day in 1964 when she testified before the Warren Commission about events early in 1961, she would add:

MARGUERITE OSWALD. . . . On January 21 was my trip to Washing- ton, 1961. Approximately 8 weeks later, on March 22, 1961, I received a letter from the State Department informing me . . . that my son wishes to return back to the United States—just 8 weeks after my trip to Washington.

Now, you want to know why I think my son is an agent. And I have been telling you all along.

Here is a very important thing why my son was an agent. . . . On April 30, 1961, he marries a Russian girl—approximately 5 weeks later.

Now, why does a man who wants to come back to the United States, [only] 5 weeks later [decide to] marry a Russian girl? Because I say—and I may be wrong—the U.S. Embassy has ordered him to marry this Russian girl. . . .

MR. RANKIN. Now, was there any time that Marina said anything to you to lead you to believe that she thought your son, Lee, married her because he was an agent?

MARGUERITE OSWALD. No, sir, no, sir. Not at any time at all.

MR. RANKIN. You think she loved him?

MARGUERITE OSWALD. I believe that Marina loved him in a way. But I believe that Marina wanted to come to America. I believe that Lee had talked America to her, and she wanted to come . . .

MR. RANKIN. I am not clear about this being ordered to marry her. You don't mean that your son didn't love her.

MARGUERITE OSWALD. Well, I could mean that—if he is an agent, and he has a girl friend, and it is to the benefit of the country that he marry this girl friend, and the Embassy helped him get this Russian girl out of Russia—let's face it, well, whether he loved her or not, he would take her to America if that would give him contact with Russians, yes, sir.

MR. RANKIN. Is that what you mean?

MARGUERITE OSWALD. I would say that.

MR. RANKIN. And you don't think it was because your son loved her, then?

MARGUERITE OSWALD. I do not know whether my son loved her or not. But I am telling you why he would do this in five weeks' time . . .

MR. RANKIN. . . . . I think it is a very serious thing to say about your son, that he would do a thing like that to a girl.

MARGUERITE OSWALD. No, sir, it is not a serious thing. I know a little about the CIA and so on, the U-2, Powers, and things that have been made public. They go through any extreme for their country. I do not think that would be serious for him to marry a Russian girl and bring her here, so he would have contact. I think that is all part of an agent's duty.

MR. RANKIN. You think your son was capable of doing that?

MARGUERITE OSWALD. Yes, sir, I think my son was an agent. I certainly do.[4]

PART II

CHARITY IN FORT WORTH

◂◦▸

1

Honeymoon

Robert Oswald and his wife, Vada, had two children; Lee and Marina had June. Robert's house was small. Marguerite Oswald, as we can recall, visited Lee and Marina on their second day home, and made an executive decision. She would give notice on her nursing job in Crowell, Texas, move to Fort Worth, rent an apartment, and Lee and Marina could live with her. In a matter of two or three weeks after Oswald's return, he was, therefore, back in his mother's domain. "Mr. Rankin," she tells her interlocutor at the Warren Commission, "we had no quarrels. This month was beautiful. Marina was very happy."

MARGUERITE OSWALD. . . . I had the car and the television and we went around.

As I say, they were free to come and go like they want. They would take long walks.

If you are not familiar with Fort Worth, Texas, from the Rotary Apartment to Leonard Brothers is approximately 3 miles, and they used to walk there, and they came home—Marina came home with a Cancan petticoat and some hose that Lee bought her with a few dollars that Robert and I had given him—he spent [it] on his wife.

So that was a very happy time . . .

MR. RANKIN. How did Marina treat you then?

MARGUERITE OSWALD. Fine. But then Marina was not satisfied with the things that I bought her.

As you see, the way I am properly dressed—I don't say I mean to be the height of fashion, but I have—before becoming a nurse I was in the business world, and I have been a manager in the merchandise field. So I do know clothes.

And I bought her some shorts. And she wanted short shorts, like the Americans . . .

And I bought her a little longer shorts.

And "I no like, Mama."

I said, "Marina, you are a married woman and it is proper for you to have a little longer shorts than the younger girls."

"No, Mama."

And I will stress this—that Marina was never too happy—"No, Mama, no nice, no, Mama, no this."

That was perfectly all right. I thought she didn't understand our ways. I didn't feel badly about it . . .[1]

"I didn't feel badly about it," Marguerite says, and probably she is lying.

As described by others, including her sons John and Robert, Marguerite is characterized as unfeeling, self-centered, keyed on money, a virago when she does not get her way. All this is true, doubtless, for those she does not really love. When it comes to Lee, however, she is ready to travel down the loneliest aisles of her heart to encounter his rebuffs, his surprises, his betrayals: She helps to get him out of the Marines on a hardship discharge and he spends but one night with her before going to Russia, and all without warning. Yet she continues to love him with a full operatic passion equal to all the unutterable arias of those who are talent-less at love, adores him as only a selfish woman who has lost out in various ways with three husbands can still love one child.

He, of course, whenever he returns to the stifling surround of a mother always ready to overtax his restricted capacity to love, is obliged to repel her. He and Marina stay with Marguerite for a few weeks; he finds work at a sheet-metal factory called Leslie Weld-ing, where he earns $50 a week and, other than disbursements for can-can petticoats for Marina, spends nothing on rent or for food. Marguerite is taking care of his family from her savings. She cooks his favorite dishes. Marina will comment on how much Lee, a finicky eater, will gobble down when Marguerite cooks. Free rent, all the food you can eat . . . and an exorbitant demand for love. He saves one week's pay, then another, and puts down a monthly rent of $59.50 in advance on a semi-detached little bungalow with a porch in a flat row of similar boxes on Mercedes Street, the leviathan warehouse of Montgomery Ward staring back at them from the end of the street. Then, he enlists Robert and moves out of Marguerite's apartment with no warning to his mother. While Robert waits outside in his car and Marina looks bewildered, Lee and Marguerite have a passionate shouting match, after which Lee takes off, leaving Marguerite in the doorway like a dark-eyed heroine in a silent film. She does not know where he is going. She even runs after the car. But let us take up the continuation from Priscilla Johnson McMillan's book *Marina and Lee:*

> *McMillan:* . . . his mother soon reappeared, wholly unchastened, on the steps of the house on Mercedes Street. No one quite knew how she got there, since both Lee and Robert had been at pains to conceal the address [but three days later, Marina] heard a knock on the door. She looked out and there, to her astonishment, stood "Mamochka," looking just as blithe and unconcerned as if the hysterical scene of parting had never occurred. Marguerite brought a high chair for the baby and silverware, dishes, and utensils for Marina and Lee. Marina welcomed her in, Marguerite played with the baby, and then left.[2]

> **MARINA OSWALD.** . . . I felt very sorry for her. [Lee and I] had a quarrel because he said to me, "Why did you open the door for her, I don't want her to come here anymore." . . . It seemed peculiar to me, and I didn't want to believe it but he did not love his mother, she was not quite a normal woman. Now, I know this for sure.

> **MR. RANKIN.** Did he tell you that at the time?

> **MARINA OSWALD.** . . . Lee did not want to talk to her. And, of course, for a mother, this is painful and I told him he should be more attentive to his mother but he did not change. I think one of the reasons for this is that she talked a great deal about how much she had done to enable Lee to return from Russia, and Lee felt that he had done . . . the greatest effort in that respect and didn't want to discuss it . . .[3]

From this point on, we will be using citations from *Marina and Lee* more than any other source but the Warren Commission. Mrs. McMillan interviewed Marina over a period of many months in the year following the assassination, and in a certain sense the author was even doing an approved biography, since her relation to Marina's material was exclusive. While one hardly agrees with McMillan's understanding of Lee Harvey Oswald (her approach to him was clinical) and while some of her material on Marina in Minsk is inaccurate due in the main to Marina's still trying at that time to protect many an uncovered base, nonetheless McMillan is an invaluable source for many insights into the home life of Mr. and Mrs. Lee Harvey Oswald, even if one does not have to come to the same interpretations as McMillan on many of Lee's actions and deeds. Since the opportunity was present, however, for Marina's latter-day interviewers to query her on the accuracy of McMillan's descriptions of personal scenes, one had the advantage of being able to choose only those excerpts from *Marina and Lee* which Marina, thirty years later, would accept, somewhat grudgingly, as more or less accurate. That seemed preferable to forcing Marina back into events where her memory of the past was virtually burned out or laid to waste by the depredations of thirty years of media investigation of her marriage.

At this juncture let us go back, however, to the Warren Commission. Marguerite's version of the same event Marina described for them is not nearly so unhappy.

MARGUERITE OSWALD. . . . I bought [a] highchair and brought it over there, and Lee was not at home. And Marina didn't know what a highchair was. I said, "How do they feed babies in Russia?" . . .

"We put baby on lap, Mama, and baby eat on lap . . ."

So approximately 2 or 3 days later I go over there and Lee says to me, "Now, Mother, I want you to understand right here and now—I want you to stop giving all these gifts to me and my wife. I want to give Marina whatever is necessary, the best I can do. I want you to keep your money and take care of yourself, because today or tomorrow you take sick, and you spend all your money on us, I will have to take care of you." Which makes very good sense.

But he strongly put me in my place about buying things for his wife that he himself could not buy.

MR. RANKIN. What did you say to that?

MARGUERITE OSWALD. I agreed with him. And I said—the shock of it—I realize what a mother-in-law I was in interfering. And, of course, that is the part that we mothers do unconsciously. We try to help out our children, and in a way we are interfering in their life. They would rather have their own way of doing things.

And I realize that I had interfered, and the boy wanted to take care of his wife. So no more was said about it . . .[4]

If relative peace could now be found with Marguerite, their abode was soon disturbed by another visit.

From Marina's narrative: . . . One day Lee came home from work and had not yet changed his clothes when some man knocked at the door. He turned out to be an FBI agent and asked Lee to come into a car, which he had parked across the street. There was one other man in the car. They talked for two hours, and I started getting angry at these uninvited guests, since it is no fun to heat up dinner several times. Lee came home very upset but tried not to show it . . .[5]

This is now the second time that the same man from the FBI, John W. Fain, has had a talk with Lee:

MR. STERN. What was Lee Harvey Oswald's demeanor in the course of this interview?

MR. FAIN. He was tense, kind of drawn up, and rigid. He is a wiry little fellow, kind of waspy.

MR. STERN. Did he answer all of your questions?

MR. FAIN. No, he didn't . . . he was a little insolent in his answers. He was the type of individual who apparently doesn't want to give out information about himself, and we asked him why he had made this trip to Russia, and he looked like it got under his skin, and he got white around the lips and tensed up, and I understood it to be a show of temper, and in a show of temper he stated he did not care to relive the past. He didn't want to go into that at all . . . We wanted to find out whether or not the Soviets had demanded anything of him in return for letting him come on over . . . he said, "No." . . . He downgraded it all the way through, and belittled himself. He said, "I was not that important . . ."

MR. MCCLOY. You felt he constituted no security risk to the United States? . . .

MR. FAIN. Well, I am suspicious of any Communist, obviously, and I think any Communist is a threat because I think they are atheistic, materialistic; I don't think they know what the truth is, [but the] checks we made were to the effect that he was not a . . . member of the Communist Party. [So] I closed it because my investigation was completed . . . The man had found a job, he was working, he was living in this duplex with his wife, and he was not a member of the Communist Party . . .

REPRESENTATIVE FORD. Do you have in this area, or did you have at that time in this area reliable confidential informants?

MR. FAIN. Yes, sir; yes, sir. Excellent informants.[6]

The American Communists, who were by the end of the 1950s as dangerous to the security of the United States as the last American buffalo, nonetheless stimulated an all-out FBI effort at penetration into their ranks. Many of the most active members of the American Communist Party were, by the early 1960s, FBI men working under cover, and they kept the Bureau very well informed about what was going on in every corner of the Party. Out in the field, therefore, wearing the badge, FBI Special Agents like John Fain, decent, God-fearing, right-thinking, and comfortably ignorant of Marxism, were able nonetheless to have the confidence that specific individuals were or were not members of the Party.

MARGUERITE OSWALD. . . . I said to Lee, "Lee, I want to know one thing. Why is it you decided to return back to the United States when you had a job in Russia, and as far as I know you seemed to be pretty well off . . ."

He said, "Mother, not even Marina knows why I have returned to the United States."

And that is all the information I ever got out of my son. "Not even Marina knows why I returned to the United States."[7]

Would Oswald have been ready to admit that he came back to America to find fame? He was looking for our most cherished asset, but then, America is the land where the value of fame is understood by all. From Oswald's point of view, he is one of the few world authorities on the separate and misunderstood characters of Communism and capitalism. His knowledge is unique. He comprehends the dire comedy of the Cold War—which is to say the near-fatal misperceptions and misinterpretations each nation has of the other.

A meeting, therefore, with John Fain, where he was obliged to declare that he had not amounted to much in the Soviet Union, had to leave him with more than a lingering depression.

2

In the China Closet

Putting together aluminum doors, louvers, and windows at Leslie Welding left Oswald no happier than he had been at the radio factory in Minsk, and probably he was obliged to work harder at Leslie. Once again it was not what he had been looking for. When it came to labor, his dream was of clean hands—dealing with nothing heavier than books and writing paper. Indeed, in the first week after he was back in America, he made a serious effort in that direction.

MR. LIEBELER. Would you tell us about your first contact with Lee Harvey Oswald?

MR. GREGORY. Yes, sir.

It was in the middle of June 1962. On that particular morning, I was in the office, my telephone rang, and the voice on the other end told me that my name was given to him by the Fort Worth Public Library. He knew I was teaching Russian at the library, that he was looking for a job as a translator or interpreter in the Russian and English languages, and that he would like for me to give him a letter testifying to that effect . . . so I suggested . . . that he might drop by my office and I would be glad to give him a test. He did. He came by the office about 11 o'clock that morning, and I gave him a short test by simply opening a book at random and asking him to read a paragraph or two and then translate it.

He did it very well, so I gave him a letter addressed to whom it may concern that in my opinion he was capable of being an interpreter or translator . . .

MR. LIEBELER. Did you and Mr. Oswald have lunch together that day?

MR. GREGORY. Yes, sir. It was about noontime when I gave him that test, and so I invited him to lunch, and during the lunch being naturally curious about the present day life in the Soviet Union, I was asking him questions, asked how the people lived there and so forth.[1]

Peter Paul Gregory was a petroleum engineer in his early sixties, a Russian born in Siberia who had come to America in 1923, and he was sufficiently intrigued by his visitor to pay a visit to the Oswalds on Mercedes Street. Depressed by their drab circumstances, he decided it was time to introduce the Oswalds to the Russian community in Dallas–Fort Worth. So, he set up a dinner party in mid-August, to which he invited his friend George Bouhe, an accountant born and raised in St. Petersburg and curious to meet Marina after hearing that she had grown up in Leningrad.

Bouhe was a bachelor, in his early sixties, and by general account was also bossy, fussy, opinionated, and powerfully fearful of complications. Before he even came to the dinner, he checked with a man named Max Clark, a lawyer at General Dynamics rumored to be on good terms with the inner councils of the FBI, and Clark gave Bouhe the reassurance he needed.

MR. CLARK. . . . I said, "As far as Oswald coming back here, you can be assured or bet that when he returned to the United States the FBI has got him tagged and is watching his movements or I would be very much surprised . . ." I said, "You know that they know exactly where he is in town," and I said, "I imagine they know who he is contacting because I know enough about the boys in the FBI; they would keep a record."[2]

Bouhe went to the dinner. Marina had her first social success in America on this occasion.

MR. LIEBELER. You also conversed with Marina in Russian, did you not?

MR. BOUHE. Oh, yes; she is very good, I must say, to my great amazement . . . I complimented her, because most of the displaced persons whom we met here who went through wars and mixtures and Germany and French speak a very, very broken, unpolished Russian, which I tried to perfect . . .

And she said, "My grandmother who raised me"—I don't know what period—"she was an educated woman. She went to—" and she gave me a school for noble girls. Something like—I don't know, are you a Dallas man?—perhaps Bryn Mawr.

MR. LIEBELER. Some prominent school?

MR. BOUHE. Yes. The grandmother was a graduate and she gave me the name, which is a top school. And when you come out of that school as a young girl, you are polished—Smolny Institute for Noble Girls.[3]

Did Marina steer him toward this misapprehension, or did he choose to believe it in order to justify his positive reaction to Marina? Positive evaluations are no trivial matter for a snob!

In any event, Bouhe began to focus on the Oswalds' lives. Appalled by the conditions in which this well-brought-up young waif and this American escapee from the Soviet system were now living, Bouhe organized a food-and-clothing rescue operation.

MR. BOUHE. . . . The sense of charity is very deep in me. Marina and the child, the latter sleeping on the floor, attracted me very much. As I repeated to the FBI and Secret Service many times, while they were not relatives of mine, I still felt that if I enjoy a good automobile and a good meal and if I know around the corner somebody's kid is sleeping on the floor, I will not digest that dinner so very good.

So being endowed with what I thought was boundless energy, when I saw the situation, I thought I would make an effort the first time to put them on their feet. I always thought that communism breeds among the down and out and the dissatisfied people . . . I thought that by, so to speak, putting a little meat on his bones, lift the kid into bed, get a little clothes for the kid, meanwhile assembling from all of the ladies some clothes for Marina, who was in rags, I thought I will make [Oswald] less bitter, which he was, and he will see, as I told him, that it can be done here if you apply yourself. And I added to him, "Lee, I am exceedingly uneasy from being a foreigner by birth, telling you, a native-born American, that you can lift yourself by your own boot-strap here and live a decent life because the opportunities are here if you just only take advantage of them." . . .

MR. LIEBELER. Did Oswald seem to appreciate your efforts?

MR. BOUHE. No; he passed a remark shortly after the second or third visit to their house when the ladies brought clothes to Marina and such—I even brought two shirts for him—not new, used, and this is where I saw him for the first time trying to show his displeasure over me.

He measured and he measured the shirts so many times, and those were not new shirts. Finally, I said, "Lee, this is go-to-work. Wear them 3 or 4 times, get them dirty, then throw them away." So finally he folded it up and gave it back to me. "I don't need any."

Then I understood that he objected that myself and a couple of others brought groceries to the kid and something for them when the icebox was empty.[4]

It is worth noting another comment from the rescue party.

MR. LIEBELER. Mr. Bouhe also bought a bed for the baby?

MRS. MELLER. . . . I think we bought her one dress, probably couple underwears, couple pairs, and stockings; something she is really need and certainly more groceries. Then one day when came with groceries like that Lee Harvey come from work and [he] was furious why we did all that and buy all that and he said, "I don't need"; he was in rage; "I don't need," he say.[5]

Marguerite Oswald provides our counterpoint:

MARGUERITE OSWALD. . . . Now, it has been stated in the paper that the Russian friends have gone into the home and [found] that there was no food in the house and no milk for the baby.

I say Marina nursed the baby.

. . . Maybe they didn't have at that particular time any milk in the box. Maybe Lee was going to bring groceries home. But I know they were not in destitute circumstances in that respect . . . I brought groceries and I brought a roll of scotch toweling . . . And the next day when I went by, the scotch toweling was in the kitchen, on a coat hanger, with a nail.

And I think that is real nice, a young couple that doesn't have any money, that they can use their imagination and put up the scotch toweling to use on a coat hanger. They are just starting married life in a new country. And they have no money. But here is the point. The Russian friends, who were established, and had cars and fine homes, could not see this Russian girl doing without. They are the ones that interfered. They are the ones that interfered . . . and within a short time, then, this Russian girl had a playpen, had a sewing machine, had a baby bed, and a Taylor Tot . . .

I say it is not necessary for a young couple to have a playpen for a baby. We have millions and millions of American couples in the United States that cannot afford playpens for the children. I, myself, have been in that position.

So I think those things were immaterial.

The point I am trying to bring out is that these Russian friends have interfered in their lives, and thought that the Russian girl should have more than necessary.

And my son could not supply those things at that particular time. He was just starting to work . . . it was in this period of time that all these things were accumulated from Russian friends.

And no man likes other people giving—interfering in his way of living, and giving all these things to his wife that he himself cannot supply. This is a human trait, I would say . . .[6]

3

Deep in the Heart of Texas

It was Oswald's misfortune that he landed in Fort Worth. He would have been better received in Austin. By 1962, a couple of hundred blacks and whites were rooming together at the Community of Faith and Light at the University of Texas. Radicalism, posed against the profound conservatism of most Texans, had real luster in the Southwest in those early years of the Sixties, and

Oswald might have found some friends; radicalism was even elegant in its stand against the rabid and raucous conservatism of Texans. It was raucous for a reason: People who had been poor but a generation ago were now wealthy. Like Arabs, they owed it to oil—which was like owing it to the devil. Brought up as good Christians, and for the most part still clinging to the fragments of a strict upbringing, a lot of newly rich Texans were uneasy with such quick-gotten gains. Of course, they were also greedy for more, and their anxiety about possessing such an un-Christian appetite made them search for justification of the way they lived. Anti-Communism satisfied that quest altogether. Americans in general, and Texans even more so, had profound faith in anti-Communism in the 1950s and early 1960s. Red-baiting solved just about every moral and spiritual problem at hand. Now, they could be good Christians without having to brood on the contradictions between washing the feet of the poor and gobbling up all the goodies in the bowl.

To be wholly opposed to Communism became all the philosophy that was needed by the power elite of Texas. We need not be surprised, therefore, if such a world-view trickled down to the prosperous middle class inhabiting all the suburbs within the spread of Dallas and Fort Worth. This was especially true of the local Russians (whom we may as well refer to as the émigrés). They are generally depicted as "generous, outgoing, and warm."

> *McMillan:* While they embraced wholeheartedly the American ethos of individualism and hard work, they had also kept the values they had brought over from Eastern Europe: the spirit of community, of sharing, of the responsibility of each for all.[1]

What comes across, however, in the Warren Commission testimony of the émigrés sounds more like fear, pride of possession, untrammeled patriotism, and a fair share of the human desire to control others. Oswald, sensitive as always to any attempt by outsiders to manage his life, saw how much of the émigrés' generosity depended on gaining power over Marina. To him, that was a declaration of war. As a husband, he knew how difficult it was to obtain any kind of power over her, and he was damned if these émigrés with—as he saw it—their dirty track record were going to seduce her allegiance by way of their gifts.

If it be asked, What was their "dirty track record"?—it was that many of them in the early years of the Second World War had, like Valya, been swept up by the German Army and taken to work in Poland and in Germany. The difference is that Valya went back to the Soviet Union with Ilya. They didn't. By the end of the war, they managed to make their way over to the Americans, and not all of them can be said to have had an absolutely clear conscience about wartime associations with the Germans. Dr. Johnson is always there to remind us that "patriotism is the last refuge of a scoundrel," and the émigrés certainly competed with one another in the size of their slavish adoration of America and American capitalism. The reasons may not be so mysterious: Certain native lands are more difficult to leave than others. Russia, for whatever myriad reasons, has a call upon its expatriates which even seems proof against the legitimate detestation many of the émigrés were holding for the Soviet system. If some of them had no record of collaboration with the Germans, if their conscience at defecting to America was relatively clear, their hearts were nonetheless pocked with unadmitted anguish at quitting their native land. Ergo, they did not wish to hear anything even remotely decent about Sovietism.

Shadowed by dubious conscience, it is hardly surprising that they soon came to detest Oswald. He had not only chosen to live in the Soviet Union but now, on his return, looked down upon them as traitors; the curl of his lip said as much, and they reacted to that as to effrontery.

MR. LIEBELER. Why did the Germans take you from Russia, do you know?

MRS. MELLER. . . . I stay in country and worked for Germans for piece of bread so I wouldn't die of hunger because Russia was in bad shape, and then that very place, hospital, was retreated back. I went with, or I had to stay and die of hunger. That way, I was brought piece by piece further deeper into Poland and Germany.[2]

ALEX KLEINLERER: I have always been very grateful to America. Americans have been very kind to me and I think a good deal of this country. It upset me when Oswald would say things against the United States. I did not argue with him because he appeared to me to be dangerous in his mind and I was frightened. I once said to him that unlike him, I had come to this country for freedom and not to look for trouble by criticizing the United States.[3]

MRS. FORD. . . . books like Karl Marx open in front of him, just lying there on the table, and he didn't even hide it when someone came in, and then someone else said there was a book laying there of How to Be a Spy, laying right open there.[4]

MR. JENNER. . . . it's your viewpoint that if any American goes to Russia with the intention of living there that we ought to leave them there?

MRS. DYMITRUK. That's right.

MR. JENNER. And not encourage him to return to the United States?

MRS. DYMITRUK. Not encourage—or if he ask to come back, just let him stay there.[5]

MRS. VOSHININ. . . . we were expecting, rather to hear from Oswald publicly some anti-Communist declaration, some, you know, reports, lectures, or a couple of articles in the newspapers, you know, we expected from him to behave like a person who got disappointed in Communism, came here sincerely— like people we know. For example, Eugene Lyons . . . So, his behavior after he came here, from what we heard about his behavior, was unnatural . . . Now, wouldn't that be natural for an intellectual person to get his living from lecturing against Communism?[6]

MR. RANKIN. Did he tell you why he did not like your Russian friends? . . .

MARINA OSWALD. Well, he thought they were fools for having left Russia; they were all traitors . . . he said they all only like money, and everything is measured by money. It seems to me that perhaps he was envious of them in the sense they were more prosperous than he was . . . he did not like to hear that . . .[7]

Was he beginning to realize that when it came to political values, he and Marina were facing each other across a divide? She loved middle-class values.

In Russia, he could not have sensed this so clearly. Despite every altercation between them, she had nonetheless committed herself to going to America; indeed, she disliked her Soviet system in much the way he had come to find it disappointing, dull in its privileges, corrupt, second-rate. Now, Marina's attraction to the values of the émigrés left him feeling betrayed.

It is a wholly unexpected turn for him. In Minsk, they had been able to see themselves as a married team—much in need of improvement, but a team. They were positively married, at least to some degree. They would go to America together with their beloved baby. They would manage despite all obstacles. She was following him. With every tug of fear for each relative she might compromise, still she would follow him. They shared important beliefs.

Now, with the Russian community charmed by her and taking to him not at all, now that Marina was enraptured by the dazzling if, to his eye, morally blind face of American commodities, he had to feel that she was turning against the project of his life—which was to give no quarter to the resplendent superiority of the moneyed enemy, but to stand proud, partisan, and a guerrilla fighter—if, for the most part, only in the privacy of his mind.

We must not leave Marguerite in exile. She has been relegated to the sidelines, but her keen nose informs her that demons of social opprobrium are gathering against her son.

Marguerite might not be wholly welcome, Marguerite might be jealous of the marriage and ready to drive her spike into the wedding tree—she was a mother-in-law—but then, she was also a mother; she would save the marriage. Not for too little had God given her god-like gifts as a sleuth. Just as she had been first to pick up the investigative trail when her husband Mr. Ekdahl had been acting oddly enough to suggest marital peccadilloes, so it did not take long for Marguerite to become suspicious of Marina. One day, going to visit her daughter-in-law on Mercedes Street, Marguerite discovered that she was not at home.

MARGUERITE OSWALD. . . . I sat in the car on Montgomery Ward's parking lot, where I could see the house, because I wanted to see who Marina was going to come home with . . .

I sat in the car all day long. She didn't show up.

Finally, I went home, had my supper, left my apartment, and on the way going back to the house Lee was leaving Montgomery Ward.

Now they did not have a phone. I am just assuming—this is not a fact—that Lee went to a telephone trying to locate his wife . . . He got in the car with me, and we had about a block to go. I entered the house with Lee and I said, "Lee, where is Marina?" Of course, I knew that she wasn't home because I had stayed in the car all day.

He said, "Oh, I guess she is out with some friends."

"Would you like me to fix your supper?"

"No, she will probably be home in time to fix my supper."

So I left. I am not going to interfere in their married life . . . Two days later, I went to the home and my son was reading, he read continuously—in the living room and Marina was in the bedroom. I could not see Marina. And I said to Lee, "Tell Marina I am here."

Marina made no appearance.

So I went into the bedroom, and she was nursing June with her head down. And I started to talk. And she still had her head down. And I came around to the front and I saw Marina with a black eye.

Now, gentlemen, I don't think any man should hit his wife, [but] I will say this. There may be times that a woman needs to have a black eye. I am not condoning the act. But I strongly am saying that this girl was not home. And this man was working. And I saw, myself, that this man came home and didn't have any food. This couple doesn't have a maid or anyone to give this working man food. And I think it was her duty to be home and have his supper ready.

This is a little thing, maybe. But to me it shows the character of what I am trying to bring out . . . I have worked in these very fine homes, and have seen very fine people fight. I have seen a gentleman strike his wife in front of me. We know this happens. It is not a nice thing to do. But it happens in our finest homes. I am not condoning the act. But I am telling you that there probably was reasons, we will say . . . [8]

That black eye was the first order of gossip in the Russian community:

MRS. MELLER. One of these times we came to Marina's house and husband was still not at home, she has a terrible blue spot over her eye and I said to her, "What's the matter?" Marina was shy little bit. She's shy little, a little bit in nature, I think, too. She said, "I have to get up during night and quiet baby and I hit the door and hit my head here," and it was very blue.[9]

MR. BOUHE. . . . she had a black eye. And not thinking about anything unfortunate, I said: "Well, did you run into a bathroom door?" Marina said, "Oh, no, he hit me."[10]

MR. LIEBELER. Did you ever see or hear of Marina making fun of Oswald in front of other people? . . .

MRS. HALL. Oh, yes; she would do it.

MR. LIEBELER. Can you think of any specific examples?

MRS. HALL. She was always complaining about him. He was not a man. He is afraid. I don't know, not complete, I guess, or something like that. Not complete man.[11]

MR. BOUHE. I . . . made a point of it never to be in Marina's house without somebody else being there.

MR. LIEBELER. Now, can you tell us why you took such care in this regard? . . .

MR. BOUHE. Because he was a peculiar guy and I am not a fighter. I am an expert fighter with the word but not with the muscles. And by his smirking appearances or other expressions on the face, [he] indicated that I am not welcome and I am persona non grata, because apparently he was jealous that I filled the icebox once . . .[12]

Here in these first three months in Fort Worth their marriage suffers grievously from these episodes, and what may be an irremediable set of blows—and he withdraws from her, turns into himself and the dank pit of the ugliest part of himself—that coward who had found no stature in the eyes of other men. Now, from time to time, he will indulge a crucially expensive portion of his rage by striking his wife.

4

The Well-born Friend

If there is any place where a narrative of Oswald's life is bound to take on the seductive ambiguity of a spy novel, it is with the entrance into Lee's affairs of Baron George De Mohrenschildt,[1] a tall, well-educated, powerful, handsome fifty-one-year-old with an incomparable biography.

> *McMillan:* . . . born in Mozyr, Belorussia, in 1911 . . . he was . . . fond of pointing out [that] he was . . . a mixture of Russian, Polish, Swedish, German, and Hungarian blood . . . the Mohrenschildts traced their ancestry back to the Baltic nobility at the time of Sweden's Queen Christina—the proudest nobility in all Russia. The men of the family had a right to be called "Baron," but such were their liberal opinions that neither George's father, Sergei von Mohrenschildt, nor his Uncle Ferdinand (first secretary of the czarist embassy in Washington, who married the daughter of William Gibbs McAdoo, Woodrow Wilson's son-in-law and Secretary of the Treasury), nor George himself, nor his older brother Dmitry, ever made use of the title.[2]

Gary Taylor, who had been married to De Mohrenschildt's daughter, Alexandra, offers a good description of the Baron:

> **MR. TAYLOR.** Uh—he is a rather overbearing personality; somewhat boisterous in nature and easily changeable moods—anywhere from extreme friendliness to downright dislike—just like turning on and off a light.
>
> **MR. JENNER.** What about his physical characteristics? . . .
>
> **MR. TAYLOR.** He's a large man, in height only about 6'2″ but he's a very powerfully built man, like a boxer . . . And he has a very big chest which makes him appear to be very much bigger than he actually is . . .
>
> **MR. JENNER.** All right. Give me a little more about the personality of George De Mohrenschildt . . .
>
> **MR. TAYLOR.** I would say that he has an inflammable personality. And he's very likable, when he wants to be . . .

MR. JENNER. Is he unconventional? . . .

MR. TAYLOR. Yes; oftentimes wearing merely bathing trunks, and things like this, that—for a man of his age, which is about 50 to 52—is a little unusual . . . In fact, during the time that I was married to his daughter, I have not known him to hold any kind of a position for which he received monetary remuneration. So, as a result, why, he could spend his time at his favorite sport, which is tennis. And this could be in 32-degree weather in the bathing shorts I mentioned [any] time during the week. They have always owned convertibles and they would ride in them in all kinds of weather with the top down. They are very active, outdoor sort of people . . .

MR. JENNER. Is [his wife] unconventional at times in her attire in the respects you have indicated in regards to him?

MR. TAYLOR. Yes; very similar.

MR. JENNER. She, likewise, wears a bathing suit out on the street, does she?

MR. TAYLOR. Yes, quite a bit. And usually a bikini.[3]

Inasmuch as Jeanne De Mohrenschildt was blond and agreeably overweight, she too had her impact on observers. The Warren Commission was, naturally, interested in her, but they were fascinated with De Mohrenschildt. His testimony would fill 118 pages of close print. Virtually half of this extended contribution was devoted to his biography, but then, so various were the details of his life that it was difficult not to wander afield:

MR. JENNER. . . . the records show [that your brother Dmitri] was naturalized November 22, 1926, in the U.S. District Court at New Haven, which is where Yale University is located . . . do those facts square with your recollection?

MR. DE MOHRENSCHILDT. Yes; approximately the right period. I remember he went to Yale with Rudy Vallee—they were roommates.[4]

When it came to name dropping, De Mohrenschildt had credentials. He was the only man in the world who had known both Jacqueline Kennedy when she was a child and Marina Oswald when she was a wife and a widow, and you could count on him to speak of that. He looked to the moment in conversation. Twitted by Warren Commission counsel Albert Jenner for arriving bare-chested at a formal dinner party—or so Jenner had already been told by a good number of witnesses—George was asked if he didn't have a taste for shocking people.

> **MR. DE MOHRENSCHILDT.** Well, it is . . . amusing to get people out of their boredom. Sometimes life is very boring.
>
> **MR. JENNER.** And get you out of your boredom, too?
>
> **MR. DE MOHRENSCHILDT.** Maybe my boredom also.[5]

He had, in fact, lived in so many countries, worked at so many occupations—cavalry officer in the Polish army, lingerie salesman in Belgium, moviemaker in New York, and petroleum engineer in Dallas—and had accumulated so many adventures and married so often (so cynically and so idealistically, sometimes for money, sometimes for love, having once been as wealthy as a gigolo who had hit on double-zero in matrimonial roulette, but reduced by 1962 to living on what Jeanne, his fourth and last wife, was making as a fashion designer at Nieman-Marcus) that boredom could eas-ily have been one of his afflictions: Too much experience can prove as dangerous to maintaining a lively interest in life as too little.

We will learn a good deal more about him, however, if we take a close look at his writings and his testimony. The two are separated by thirteen years: He gave his testimony to the Warren Commission in 1964 and wrote his manuscript about Oswald in 1977—it would be printed in the twelfth volume of the House Select Committee on Assassination Hearings—but we might start with the manu-script, for De Mohrenschildt gives an interesting description there of meeting the Oswalds. Having heard about the new arrivals from the other émigrés, he claims he was curious to know more, and so, sometime in the first or second week of September, he set out to visit them. A window now opens to banish the stale and unanimous verdicts of the other émigrés. Odd currents blow in.

> Someone gave me Lee's address and one afternoon a friend of mine, Colonel Lawrence Orlov, and myself drove to Fort Worth, some 30 miles from Dallas. We drove over the dreary sewage-smelling miles separating the two cities. Texas

does have lovely open spaces, but here they were degraded and polluted. After some searching, we found a shack on Mercedes Street in a semi-detached, slummy area, near Montgomery Ward.

I knocked and a tawdry but clean young woman opened the door . . . To Orlov she was beautiful notwithstanding bad teeth and mousy hair . . .[6]

Marina offered us some sherry and said that Lee would soon be home from work. We spoke a little, fooling around; she had a pretty good sense of humor but the opinions she expressed seemed trite to me. And then entered Lee Harvey Oswald who was to become so famous or infamous. He wore overalls and clean workingman's shoes. Only someone who never met Lee could have called him insignificant. "There is something outstanding about this man," I told myself. One could detect immediately a very sincere and forward man. Although he was average looking, with no outstanding features and of medium size, he showed in his conversation all the elements of concentration, thought, and toughness. This man had the courage of his convictions and did not hesitate to discuss them. I was glad to meet such a person and was carried away back to the days of my youth in Europe, where as students, we discussed world affairs and our own ideas over many beers and without caring about time.[7]

These positive evaluations continue:

Lee's English was perfect, refined, rather literary, deprived of any Southern accent. He sounded like a very educated American of indeterminate background.[8]

. . . it amazed me that he read such difficult writers like Gorky, Dostoyevsky, Gogol, Tolstoy, and Turgenev—in Russian . . . I taught Russian at all levels in a large university and I never saw such proficiency in the best senior students who constantly listened to Russian tapes and spoke to Russian friends.[9]

. . . both Lee and I were non-conformist, even revolutionary . . . but my long years of experience in Latin America, followed by my son's death and the ensuing sadness, made me commiserate with the fate of the poor and of the starving. As a younger man, I was career- and money-mad, a hustler . . .

But Lee was the same since his childhood, which made him such a beautiful and worthwhile person to me.[10]

. . . He was socially motivated, was a dreamer and a seeker of truth. But such people have a very hard time in life and that's why so many people considered him a failure and a loser.[11]

Very often people ask me with suspicion why I, a person with several university degrees and of fairly good financial and social standing—with friends among the rich of this world—became such a friend of that "unadjusted radical"— Lee Harvey Oswald? Well . . . I already spoke of his straightforward and relaxing personality, of his honesty or his desire to be liked and appreciated. And I believe it is a privilege of an older age not to give a damn what others think of you. I choose my friends just because they appeal to me. And Lee did.[12]

De Mohrenschildt's manuscript is titled *I'm a Patsy*. Jeanne De Mohrenschildt mailed it to the House Select Committee on Assassinations the day after her husband committed suicide in March 1977.

In 1964, when De Mohrenschildt testified before the Warren Commission, he did not speak in such favorable terms of Lee or of Marina:

MR. DE MOHRENSCHILDT. . . . I found her not particularly pretty, but a lost soul, living in the slums, not knowing one single word of English, with this rather unhealthy looking baby, horrible surroundings.[13]

. . . She is that type of a girl—very negligent, poor mother, very poor mother. Loved the child, but a poor mother that doesn't pay much attention. And what amazed us, you know, that she, having been a pharmacist in Russia, did not know anything about the good care of children, nothing . . .[14]

MR. JENNER. Do you recall making this statement . . . "Since we lived in Dallas permanently last year and before, we had the misfortune to have met Oswald, and especially his wife Marina, sometime last fall."

MR. DE MOHRENSCHILDT. Yes.

MR. JENNER. What do you mean by the misfortune to have met Oswald and especially his wife Marina?

MR. DE MOHRENSCHILDT. . . . it is not pleasant to have known the possible assassin of the President of the United States. And since he is dead, it doesn't matter. But we still know Marina. We had the misfortune of knowing her—it caused us no end of difficulty, from every point of view . . .[15] people like us should have been protected against even knowing people like Oswald. Maybe I am wrong in that respect . . .[16] He is just a kid for me, with whom I played around. Sometimes I was curious to see what went on in his head.

But I certainly would not call myself a friend of his.

MR. JENNER. Well, that may well be. But Marina, at least, expresses herself that way—that you "were the only one who remained our friend."

MR. DE MOHRENSCHILDT. . . . We were no friends, nothing. We just were too busy to be with them—period . . .[17] they were very miserable, lost, penniless, mixed up. So as much as they both annoyed me, I did not show it to them because it is like insulting a beggar—you see what I mean . . .[18] I did not take him seriously—that is all.

MR. JENNER. . . . Why didn't you? . . .

MR. DE MOHRENSCHILDT. Well, he was not sophisticated, you see. He was a semieducated hillbilly . . . All his opinions were crude . . .[19] His mind was of a man with exceedingly poor background, who read rather advanced books, and did not even understand the words in them . . . So how can you take seriously a person like that? You just laugh at him. But there was always an element of pity I had, and my wife had, for him. We realized that he was sort of a forlorn individual, groping for something . . .[20] I was not interested in listening to him because it was nothing, it was zero . . .[21] After we found out what was going on in that town of Minsk, what was the situation, what were the food prices, how they dressed, how they spent their evenings, which are things interesting to us, our interest waned. The rest of the time, the few times we saw Lee Oswald and Marina afterwards, was purely to give a gift or to take them to a party, because we thought they were dying of boredom, you see—which Marina was.[22]

While thirteen years separate us from the negative testimony in 1964 and De Mohrenschildt's handsome appraisals of 1977, the gap between these two sets of evaluations is, nonetheless, too great. What is going on?

Not in a Million Years

There is one place where De Mohrenschildt's reactions in 1964 and in 1977 do not conflict. It gives a clue.

Oswald had his own manuscript, a fifty-page work in longhand (the first ten pages of which were typed by Pauline Bates a couple of days after he came back to America). It is an ungainly text, dense in its material, but does offer a closely seen view of existence in the Soviet Union; at that time it would have been of some value to American intelligence: Oswald was offering a working-day perspective of life in Minsk that was percipient. (Indeed, a large part of his manuscript is printed in the Appendix.)

Soon enough, he was induced to show these pages to his new friend George.

Here is De Mohrenschildt's account in 1977 of how he spoke to Oswald about the manuscript in 1962:

> "Your story is simple and honest but it is very poorly written. It is deprived of any sensational revelations and it's really pointless. Personally I like it because I know Minsk, but how many people know where Minsk is? And why should they have interest in your experiences? Tell me!"
>
> "Not many," Lee agreed mildly.
>
> I did not say, not to offend him, that his grammar was poor and his syntax was abominable. And those long, pompous words . . .[1]

His remarks to the Warren Commission in 1964 give much the same estimate:

> **MR. DE MOHRENSCHILDT.** . . . It was just a description of life in a factory in Minsk. Not terribly badly written, not particularly well . . . I just glanced through. I realized that it is not fit for publication. You can see it right away . . .
>
> **MR. JENNER.** It is horrible grammar?
>
> **MR. DE MOHRENSCHILDT.** Horrible grammar.
>
> **MR. JENNER.** And horrible spelling.
>
> **MR. DE MOHRENSCHILDT.** Yes.[2]

Given the huge discrepancy in other places between his manuscript and his testimony, it is obvious that De Mohrenschildt was working from one agenda in 1964 and another in 1977. Yet, on this specific point concerning the value of Oswald's manuscript, his reactions are close to identical: It is the only place where there is agreement between testimony and manuscript. Even in 1977, De Mohrenschildt is still doing his best to shift attention away from the thought that he had any interest in Oswald's manuscript. Evidence of interest, after all, could suggest the possibility that he had had a task to perform, and one part of it was, precisely, to obtain Oswald's fifty pages long enough to have a copy made and passed on to the proper people. So, he was still debating in 1977— out of fear, presumably, of how much he had to tell—whether to reveal his covert connections. Yet, a few weeks later, most desperate for money, he was ready to be interviewed in depth by Edward Epstein, although not wholly ready—his suicide interrupted his confession. Most of what he had to tell was now lost.

It has to be understood that the Warren Commission in their own decorous fashion had been suspicious of George, and pursued the details of his biography with exceptional attention. There was so much, after all, to check up on.

Having arrived in New York just before the Second World War began, De Mohrenschildt soon went to work for his cousin, Baron Konstantine Von Maydell, on a documentary about the Polish resistance. Yet, not too long after the partition of Poland in 1939 between the Soviet Union and Germany, Maydell became a Nazi agent, or so he was later identified by the FBI. De Mohrenschildt, on his own declaration, was "collecting facts on people involved in pro-German activity" for another friend, Pierre Freyss, who was head of the Deuxième Bureau for French counterintelligence. De Mohrenschildt was almost certainly serving as a double agent in that period, but whether his primary allegiance was to the French or the Germans is another matter.

By the following year he tried to join the OSS, and his name pops up in the intelligence files of various countries over the next fifteen years, culminating finally in some serious connections with the CIA, most notably on geological surveys he did in Yugoslavia and West Africa to provide an overview of their oil resources. (Needless to say, it also involved much mapping of sensitive areas.) On his return from Yugoslavia in 1957, he was debriefed by J. Walton Moore of the Domestic Contacts Division of the CIA in Dallas.

It is amusing to observe how De Mohrenschildt, as he speaks to the Warren Commission, veers off from any suggestion that he might have sophistication in these matters:

MR. DE MOHRENSCHILDT. . . . [Before] we met the Oswalds . . . we talked about them to Max Clark, and again to Bouhe. And I asked Mr. Bouhe, "Do you think it is safe for us to help Oswald?" . . .

MR. JENNER. Why did you raise the question?

MR. DE MOHRENSCHILDT. I raised the question because he had been to Soviet Russia. He could be anything, you see. And he could be right there watched day and night by the FBI. I did not want to get involved, you see.[3]

During the fall of 1962, De Mohrenschildt was arranging the largest business transaction of his life—a search for oil reserves in Haiti that could make him a wealthy man—with the aid, that is, of "Papa Doc" Duvalier, President of Haiti. George was hardly looking to add any Soviet associations to his name. Not at this point. Papa Doc was perfectly capable of seeing that George's career, reduced to the line items of a dossier, showed an unmistakable profile: He had the classic background for a spy. Since these were the years when it was considered possible, even likely, that Castro, after his success at the Bay of Pigs, might make a move on the Dominican Republic or Haiti, it was a question whether the Baron, under the burden of his suspicious background, could arrange terms with a man as suspicious as Duvalier of infiltration by agents of Castro. So George needed the CIA to pass along a few hints that they were favorably inclined to him and to his project in Haiti.

Before George would agree to meet Oswald, therefore, he not only checked with Max Clark, as had George Bouhe, but had looked to establish the understanding he needed with the CIA:

MR. DE MOHRENSCHILDT. . . . I have the impression to have talked—to have asked about Lee Oswald with Mr. Moore, Walter Moore.

MR. JENNER. Who is Walter Moore?

MR. DE MOHRENSCHILDT. Walter Moore is the man who interviewed me on behalf of the Government after I came back from Yugoslavia—G. Walter Moore. He is a Government man—

either FBI or Central Intelligence. A very nice fellow, exceedingly intelligent, who is, as far as I know—some sort of FBI man in Dallas. Many people consider him head of FBI in Dallas. Now, I don't know. Who does—you see? But he is a Government man in some capacity. He interviewed me and took my deposition on my stay in Yugoslavia, what I thought about the political situation there. And we became quite friendly after that. We saw each other from time to time, had lunch . . . I just found him a very interesting person.[4]

De Mohrenschildt would have known that Moore was not FBI and not G. Walter but J. Walton. De Mohrenschildt was blurring his own relation to the CIA by projecting himself as an innocent. Since J. Walton Moore had debriefed him on Yugoslavia, De Mohrenschildt would have had to know that Moore was CIA. The FBI by its charter did not deal with foreign affairs and the CIA most certainly did! Of course, by 1964, De Mohrenschildt's game had been seriously skewed because of the assassination, and the CIA could wreck his project in Haiti if he now connected the Agency in any small way with Oswald.

Back in 1962, however, the CIA had had need of someone with real skills to debrief Oswald. Lee was an unknown quantity. Even as the KGB had contemplated the possibility that their Marine defector was some new kind of CIA agent, now the CIA could return the compliment. Was the KGB engaging in a novel ploy? Oswald could have been sent back from Russia for purposes of Soviet propaganda. A direct debriefing, if it turned out badly and Oswald found a newspaper that would not hush it up, could prove internationally embarrassing and, worse, would injure relations once more with J. Edgar Hoover: Oswald was now ostensibly under FBI jurisdiction. Technically speaking, the CIA was not supposed to go near him. Yet, the CIA needed to know what Oswald, after living in the Soviet Union for two and a half years, could tell them about life there. A debriefing in depth could fine-tune their knowledge. The need was real, but the operation, while small, had to be delicate. They would go in for an *unwitting debriefing*—even as Oswald had been debriefed in Moscow without formal declaration.

MR. JENNER. Did the Oswalds, either together or separately, come to your home frequently or several times and spend the day with you?

MR. DE MOHRENSCHILDT. I was trying to pin down how many times we saw them in all, and it is very hard, you know. I would say between 10 and 12 times, maybe more. It is very hard to say . . .

MR. JENNER. And [Oswald] was aware that you had approached [people] to have them out socially . . .

MR. DE MOHRENSCHILDT. Yes . . . I did ask some people to invite them because they were so lonesome . . .[5]

In the novel *Harlot's Ghost,* Hugh Montague, also known as Harlot, gives a lecture on the procedures employed to gain the confidence of a person who has been selected as a target for espionage. "Disinterested seduction," Harlot assures his CIA class, is the underlying mechanism. He then asks:

"Would any of you be familiar with the cardinal law of salesmanship?"

Rosen's hand shot up. "The customer doesn't buy the product until he accepts the salesman." . . .

"Perfect," said Harlot. "I, as the principal, am there to inspire the putative agent—my client—with one idea. It is that I am good for his needs. If my client is a lonely person with a pent-up desire to talk, what should be my calculated response, therefore?"

"Be there to listen," said several of us at once . . .

"Clear enough," said Harlot. "In doubt, always treat lonely people as if they are rich and old and very much your relative. Look to provide them with the little creature comfort that will fatten your share of the will. On the other hand, should the client prove to be a social climber who gnashes his teeth at the mention of every good party he was not invited to, then sympathy won't get you much. Action is needed. You have to bring this person to a gala gathering . . . However," added Harlot, "one has to keep a firm grasp on the intrinsic problem. An exceptional friendship is being forged. One is acting as generously as a guardian angel. That can arouse suspicion in a client [so] you, as the guardian angel, have to be ready to dissolve the client's distrust. It is reasonable to assume that the client, in some part of himself, knows what you are up to, but is amenable to your game. Now is the time to talk him into taking the first step [but] keep the transition modest . . . Reduce the drama. Request something minor . . . Warm the soup slowly . . . Now, ask for a bit more. Can your friend let you have a look at X report? You happen to know that this X report is sitting on his desk."[6]

Oswald, of course, was not being developed as an agent. It was much too early for anything like that. The immediate objective was to determine whether the KGB had turned him into their agent and, if not, to debrief him skillfully of his knowledge of Minsk and learn enough about his character to decide whether he could be of any use.

On the morning of March 29, 1977, Edward Epstein had just finished his first session with George De Mohrenschildt in Palm Beach. Using *Reader's Digest* funds, Epstein was paying $4,000 for four days with the Baron and was preparing to return after lunch to the house where George was staying for the afternoon interview. Abruptly, via the FBI, word arrived that in the interval between Epstein's first meeting and the projected second meeting, De Mohrenschildt had learned that an investigator from the House Select Committee on Assassinations wished to meet and talk to him. That, presumably, was the preface to subpoenaing him for new testimony. De Mohrenschildt could control his interview with Epstein to a considerable degree, but that would not be nearly as feasible with the House Select Committee on Assassinations. De Mohrenschildt promptly killed himself with a shotgun. For Epstein's literary purposes, the suicide was a catastrophe. He had already learned quite a bit and was anticipating that he would hear a good deal more. Back in Washington, among those Committee members who believed that elements in the CIA had been responsible for Kennedy's death, De Mohrenschildt's abrupt termination was assumed to be a murder.

In his book *Legend,* Epstein recounts what the dead man had already told him:

De Mohrenschildt had claimed that morning that he had been dealing with the CIA since the early 1950s. Although he had never been a paid employee of the CIA, he said that he had "on occasion done favors" for government officials who were connected to it. In turn, those same officials had helped him in his business contacts overseas. For example, he pointed to a contract awarded him in 1957 for a survey of the Yugoslav coast. He assumed his "connections" had arranged it for him, and he provided them with reports on the Yugoslav officials in whom they had expressed interest. Such connections were, as he put it, "at the crux" of oil exploration in underdeveloped countries.

In late 1961—De Mohrenschildt could not pinpoint the date—he had a lunchtime meeting in downtown Dallas with one of those connections, J. Walton Moore . . . [who] purposefully steered the discussion in a new direction, the city of Minsk, where, as Moore seemed to know even before he told him, De Mohrenschildt had spent his childhood. Moore then told him about an ex-American Marine who had worked in an electronics factory in Minsk for the past year and in whom there was "interest," since he was returning to the Dallas area. Although no specific requests were made by Moore, De Mohrenschildt gathered he would be appreciative to learn more about this unusual ex-Marine's activities in Minsk.

In the summer of 1962, De Mohrenschildt heard more about this defector. One of Moore's associates handed him the address of Lee Harvey Oswald in nearby Fort Worth and then suggested that De Mohrenschildt might like to meet him . . . [whereupon] De Mohrenschildt called Moore again . . . Some help from the U.S. Embassy in Haiti would be greatly appreciated by him, he suggested to Moore. Although he recognized that there was no quid pro quo, he hoped that he might receive the same sort of tacit assistance he had previously received in Yugoslavia. "I would never have contacted Oswald in a million years if Moore had not sanctioned it," he explained to me. "Too much was at stake."[7]

PART III

DARK DAYS IN DALLAS

1

Evenings in Dallas

George will speak of seeing Oswald as often as a dozen times from September 1962 to March 1963, but the testimony of his daughter, Alexandra, suggests a greater frequency. Of course, Alexandra's memory for dates is lamentable, as is Jeanne and George De Mohrenschildt's, and Marguerite's, and George Bouhe's, and just about all of the émigrés'. Marina's recollection of a date, given the set of shocks she was to pass through, was rarely of use. Yet, in the study of espionage, crime, and romance, accurate chronology is paramount, for it is our best guide to motive: A lover who takes a vow of fidelity before an act of adultery is hardly to be comprehended in the same light as one who takes the vow afterward. In the first case, the lover is treacherous; in the second, repentant.

The Warren Commission left much to look for in the style of inquiry, yet without their careful compiling of records on Oswald's wages and places of employment and residence, there might have been no chronology at all. By dint of FBI and Warren Commission research, however, we can know at least where Oswald lived, when he moved, and who some of his associates proved to be.

For the changes in his inner life, however, there are few chronological details. If not for public library records of withdrawal and return of books in New Orleans—no such files exist for Dallas or Fort Worth—we would not even have an idea of what he read or when.

Much the same can be said of the De Mohrenschildts' growing intimacy with the Oswalds. If George and Jeanne dropped in on numerous occasions, and helped them to move during various marital or economic crises, or arranged for others to assist them, the progress of the relationship as recounted in either the Baron's memoirs or testimony remains static. For example, his manuscript relates the following:

> . . . I told Lee that I had known Jacqueline Kennedy as a young girl, as well as her mother, father and all her relatives and how charming the whole family was. I especially liked "Black Jack" Bouvier, Jacquie's father, a delightful Casanova of the Wall Street.
>
> Lee was not jealous of the Kennedys' and Bouviers' wealth and did not envy their social positions, of that I was sure. To him wealth and society were big jokes, but he did not resent them.[1]

Let us employ the rough rule of thumb that the manuscript recaptures for us the tone De Mohrenschildt exhibited when visiting with Lee—gracious, cosmopolitan, and always ready to compliment his target for qualities of mind and character—whereas the Warren Commission testimony represents George's unspoken feelings while with Lee. All his concealed annoyance and boredom well up in that testimony. So many hours had to be spent, after all, developing a friendship with this unlikely companion. Yet, the Baron knows enough about Lee to touch his secret snobbery: Oswald would take it for granted that he was born to be in touch with people who knew the leaders of the world and their beautiful ladies. What a pity that we cannot place De Mohrenschildt's anecdotes about Jackie in chronological context, for it might underline the moment when Oswald began to trust De Mohrenschildt more than a little.

In any event, we can assume that after a month of accelerating friendship, the Baron has, by October 7, begun to take over Oswald's working career. For that we have Gary Taylor as witness. At the time of his testimony, he is already George's ex-son-in-law, so he may have had a jaundiced eye, but he does put it in this fashion:

> **MR. TAYLOR.** . . . It would be my guess that De Mohrenschildt encouraged him to move to Dallas, as he suggested a number of things to Lee—such as where to look for jobs. And it seems like whatever his suggestions were, Lee grabbed them and took them whether it was what time to go to bed or where to stay or to let Marina stay with us while he stayed at the YMCA.[2]

At that time, in October 1962, two years before Gary Taylor gave his testimony, he and De Mohrenschildt's daughter, Alexandra, had an apartment in Dallas, where they lived with a baby son who was June Oswald's age. George now approached Gary and Alexandra with the fine idea of bringing them together with Lee and Marina. On October 7, a Sunday when George and Jeanne were taking the thirty-mile trip from Dallas to Fort Worth to hear a Van Cliburn concert by Soviet pianists, they all arranged to meet later that afternoon at Oswald's house.

We can guess the state of Alexandra's feelings—she was not about to dismiss a rare invitation from a handsome and charming father, especially since she had grown up with an aunt, and had seen little of her father, for she had only been sixteen years old when she wed Gary, who was twenty. Now, in 1962, Gary was a frustrated young filmmaker working as a taxicab driver, and he and Alexandra had their difficulties—all the more reason for Alexandra to accept the overture from her father with its implicit promise of a little more intimacy.

Yet, when she arrived at the Oswalds' apartment on Mercedes Street about four on that Sunday afternoon, other people were present. A gathering (without refreshments) was in progress, with George Bouhe, Elena Hall and her husband, Jeanne and George De Mohrenschildt, and—not least—Marguerite Oswald.

One says *not least* automatically when referring to Marguerite, but in this case it does not necessarily apply:

MR. JENNER. Did you have an opportunity to form an impression of her? . . .

MR. TAYLOR. I just have a vague recollection of a somewhat plump woman who seemed to be—uh—out of place in the present crowd that was there that afternoon. And she didn't seem to be particularly interested in anything that went on—and I think that's what prompted her to leave.[3]

It is sad to relate that this is the next to last time Marguerite will see Lee alive.

MARGUERITE OSWALD. That was on a Sunday. I went there [two days later] on a Tuesday and the [house was vacant.] . . . So then I went to Robert's home, and Robert was at work. So I was all upset. They didn't tell me they were leaving. [Vada] said,

"Robert helped them to move, and they gave us the food in the refrigerator."[4]

How could Marguerite not be aware that the arrangements must have been made on that Sunday afternoon after she left?

> **MR. JENNER.** All right. What else was discussed?
>
> **MR. TAYLOR.** . . . Lee's job—which I believe he had just left the Friday before . . . He terminated his employment. I don't know if he was fired or how he became severed from it—and he wanted to move to Dallas . . . Marina came to stay in my home . . .
>
> **MR. JENNER.** Why?
>
> **MR. TAYLOR.** . . . Just to give her a place to live until he was able to find a job here in Dallas . . . Lee stayed in Fort Worth that night and . . . next day, moved their bigger belongings—more bulky ones other than clothing—to Mrs. Hall's garage and stored them there. And then he came to Dallas and—uh—took up residence at the YMCA here.[5]

Oswald had given his visitors an impression that he had been laid off his job, but in fact he had quit.

> **MR. BARGAS.** . . . he didn't give any indication [that] he was going to leave or anything like that.
>
> **MR. JENNER.** You expected him back the next day?
>
> **MR. BARGAS.** . . . he didn't call in and he didn't have a phone . . . so I never tried to get in contact with him . . .[6] as much as I can remember of the short time he was there . . . he was a good employee. I imagine if he pursued that trade, he might have come out to be a pretty good sheet metal man—I don't know.[7]

The assumption has to be that De Mohrenschildt had not only assured Lee that there would be a job for him in Dallas—but a serious end had been achieved. Now that Lee was separated from his wife, the relationship between the Baron and the defector could accelerate.

Mystery commences again. Lee and Marina will be staying in separate places for the rest of October and the first few days of

November—four weeks in all. She will camp out a few days with Gary and Alexandra Taylor in their small apartment in Dallas and then move over to Elena Hall's house in Fort Worth, where Lee will go out to visit June and Marina a couple of times a week, then ostensibly travel back to his room at the YMCA in Dallas, where everyone, including Marina, believes he is staying.

The difficulty, however, is that Lee was registered at the Y for but five days—from October 15 through October 19. In the previous week, and in the two weeks following October 19, no one knew or was ready to admit that he or she knew where Oswald lived. This gap is present despite the best efforts of the FBI and the Warren Commission to answer that question.

The source of his money is another enigma. He had, according to Robert, already paid back the $200 he had borrowed, and this had been accomplished on a salary of $50 a week over a period of twelve weeks while paying a rent of $59.50 a month. If no more than $20 a week was spent on food and all other necessities for the nine weeks they lived on Mercedes Street, the feat of paying back $200 to Robert is accountable, but there would be no other money on hand.

Alexandra Taylor has an erratic flash of memory on this matter:

ALEXANDRA GIBSON.[8] . . . I think my father lent them money, didn't he? I don't know . . . he had to have money to stay at the YMCA. He had to have money to get started, and I know who gave him money, George Bouhe did. . . .[9] he liked Mr. Bouhe very much and . . . I think he thought that Mr. Bouhe might be his key to getting a good job . . . I'd say George Bouhe was the one that stuck by him the most, more than my father, more than any of them . . .[10]

Either Bouhe or De Mohrenschildt or both may have been supporting him for a period. It is certainly true that De Mohrenschildt, by way of Anna Meller's husband, Teofil, managed to stimulate some job interviews at which Lee showed himself to be cleanly dressed, polite, and attentive (as reported later by the Texas Employment Commission). After three days, he got work he liked at a special printing plant called Jaggars-Chiles-Stovall. The firm had a considerable variety of photographic equipment and typefaces and so could develop an advertisement all the way from receiving the design to mailing the finished mats to the local newspapers.

MR. GRAEF. . . . I asked him where his last position was and he said, "The Marines," . . . I said, "Honorably discharged, of course," as a joke, and he said, "Oh, yes," and we went on with other facts of the interview.[11]

Oswald would be more interested in this job than any he had had before or would later find, and for a period he learned quickly and enjoyed the collateral advantages: With Jaggars-Chiles-Stovall's range of equipment, he was able to forge identity cards for himself. Moreover, his pay, with overtime, came to as much as $70 a week.

The questions still arise: What was Oswald doing each evening through October, and where in Dallas was he living? During those four days when Marina and June stayed with the Taylors, Lee visited twice, but according to Gary, "there was no personal communication between them."

MR. TAYLOR. . . . within one door of us was a big park where they could have taken walks and been alone together and talked—but this never happened . . . It was just like two friends meeting.[12]

Before the move from Fort Worth, Marina had been complaining to the émigrés that Oswald was showing no interest in her.

MR. DE MOHRENSCHILDT. She openly said that he didn't see her physically—right in front of him. She said, "He sleeps with me just once a month, and I never get any satisfaction out of it." A rather crude and completely straightforward thing to say in front of relative strangers, as we were.

MR. JENNER. Yes.

MR. DE MOHRENSCHILDT. I don't blame Lee for giving her a good whack on the eye.[13]

Marina had said as much to Elena Hall. Then, driving with Jeanne one day in the De Mohrenschildts' convertible, she had proceeded to comment on how attractive and muscular were the black men they passed on the street. Jeanne, despite her not-ordinary career as a ballet dancer in China and her flamboyance with a bikini, was shocked. She thought it highly improper for a married woman to speak in such fashion. Or so she presented it to the Warren Commission.

Marriages can trudge through weeks and months that are equal to sustained expeditions in the desert on the hump of a camel. Oswald had obviously withdrawn from Marina. The question that arises again, as it did while he was in the Marines and in that curious first year he spent in Minsk, when he never had a woman and was content to go on platonic dates with Ella Germann, is whether he was homosexual. If so, it has to be the closet drama of his life.

It is far from wholly improbable, however, to outline a scenario where Oswald lived for a week with some older man, had a spat, moved to the Y for a week, had a reconciliation, and went back to the man for a fortnight, all the while receiving money for his pains. No proof for such a scenario can be offered, but then, some explanation has to be found for those missing three weeks. Since our hypothesis is not anchored, however, let us levitate even higher. We can enjoy the kind of surprise one would find in a novel, and will assume, if only for a page, that George Bouhe is the secret lover:

> MR. BOUHE. . . . I had a desire, if I could, to put him on his feet economically so he could support his wife and child—I said, now those were my words, "Lee, you've now got a job, a lithographic job at $1.45 an hour as an apprentice. If you apply yourself"—those were my very words—"in a couple of years you'll have a skill that can be saleable any place."
>
> And he said, "You think so." And he didn't even say thank you.
>
> Then I added, "Well, I would like to hear how you get along," which is a standard statement I would ask anybody.
>
> And for 2 or 3—or possibly 5 days thereafter, he would call me at 6 o'clock, I guess when he finished his work and say, "I am doing fine. Bye."[14]

The description of George Bouhe by others as a "fussy, opinionated old bachelor" was the euphemism at that time for a late-middle-aged homosexual who had led a reasonable and useful life and had earned enough in the course of things to pay for a few pleasures. Someone as ungracious as Oswald could have been deemed equal to rough trade for a man as physically timid as Bouhe. And, indeed, according to Priscilla Johnson McMillan, Lee did use Bouhe's name as a reference, "going so far as to list Bouhe at a false address." As Bouhe would remark later to the same author, "He always got what he wanted . . ."[15]

There is an alternative scenario. It is that matters had advanced between Oswald and De Mohrenschildt; it was now judged by De Mohrenschildt and his handlers that Oswald was not working for the KGB, and serious undertakings that could employ Oswald as a provocateur against the Soviets were being examined. To force the imaginative possibilities, Oswald may even have been holed up in a safe house and only moved over to the Y for the week of October 15 to 19 to give credence to his cover story that he was staying there.

A career in spookdom does seem to take place too quickly, however, to be a viable hypothesis. He would have fit few acceptable categories for any examiners passing on him for some venture in covert action. It is easier at this point to think of him as trade for the closet rather than as a paid novice beginning contract work for the CIA.

2

Oswald's Kampf

One ought to list another possibility, and it may be the most viable, if the least novelistic. Oswald had been under scrutiny for years in the Marine Corps, the Soviet Union, and lately with the FBI and the émigré community, not to mention living under the acerbic criticisms of Marina. So, by this time, he may have wanted no more than to have a secret address, a secret name, and a place where no one could find him or observe him unless he chose to go out and visit others.

If it is uncomfortable to try to comprehend a man who might have been traveling on any one of these three tracks, let us recognize that this is likely to be our situation from now on.

> *McMillan:* Lee himself was reading a good deal, Hitler's *Mein Kampf,* and William L. Shirer's *Rise and Fall of the Third Reich.* He also reread . . . *1984* and *Animal Farm* . . . loaned to him by . . . George De Mohrenschildt.[1]

While chronology in relation to Oswald can, as advertised, rarely be depended upon, one can think of no moment in Oswald's life when he would have been more ready to read *Mein Kampf* and feel some identity with Hitler than in these weeks alone in Dallas working at a low-paying job while feeling within himself every presentiment that he was a man destined for greatness against all odds. So it is worth looking at a few of Hitler's remarks:

> I soon learned that there was always some kind of work to be had, but equally soon I found out how easy it was to lose it.
>
> The uncertainty of earning my daily bread soon seemed to me one of the darkest sides of my new life.[2] . . .
>
> I studied more or less all of the books I was able to obtain . . . and for the rest immersed myself in my own thoughts.
>
> I believe that those who knew me in those days took me for an eccentric.[3] . . .
>
> Five years in which I was forced to earn a living, first as a day laborer, then as a small painter, a truly meager living which never sufficed to appease even my daily hunger . . . I had but one pleasure, my books.
>
> At that time I read enormously and thoroughly. All the free time my work left me was employed in my studies. In this way I forged in a few years' time the foundations for a knowledge from which I still draw nourishment today.
>
> And even more than this:
>
> In this period there took shape within me a world picture and a philosophy which became the granite foundation of all my acts. In addition to what I then created, I have had to learn little; and I have had to alter nothing.[4]

> *It must never be forgotten that nothing that is really great in this world has ever been achieved by coalitions, but that it has always been the success of a single victor . . . Great, truly world-shaking revolutions of a spiritual nature are not even conceivable and realizable except as the titanic struggles of individual formations* . . . [Hitler's italics][5]

"Individual formations" are, of course, to be understood as a synonym for *one man*. It is possible that De Mohrenschildt, intrigued by the extreme contrast between Oswald's anarchism and his authoritarianism, could have suggested that he read *Mein Kampf.*

> **MR. VOSHININ.** . . . I was invited by George to go to the Bohemian Club. He will give a historical lecture . . .
>
> I was present on that occasion.
>
> And George discussed the question, you know, about the Vlasov army. That was an army composed of Russian—Soviet Russian prisoners . . . who wanted to fight the Communists. And . . . in between, he injected a lot of praise for such people as Himmler . . . He said, "After all, I came to the conclusion that Himmler wasn't a bad boy after all."
>
> You know, that's typically George.

> **MR. JENNER.** Do you think that this was sincere or do you think that he was just attempting to provoke shock?

> **MR. VOSHININ.** I think he was attempting to provoke shock. Especially [since] there were, at least, three Jewish people there present—Sam Ballen and Lev Aronson [and myself]. I saw that Lev Aronson . . . became red, terribly red in his face. I was afraid that the poor guy, you know, would have a stroke, you know. And George was looking into the face of Aronson and, you know, continued praising the Nazis and look what effect it has on Lev, who is a close friend of George. Of course, Lev was terribly bitter—and I understand, after that, Lev and him went to drink vodka the whole night. So, well—that's the type of person you have . . .[6]

Possessor of an eclecticism that made him delight in presenting himself as right-wing, left-wing, a moralist, an immoralist, an aristocrat, a nihilist, a snob, an atheist, a Republican, a Kennedy lover, a desegregationalist, an intimate of oil tycoons, a bohemian, and a socialite, plus a quondam Nazi apologist once a year, De Mohrenschildt could hardly have failed to see that there was a profound divide between Oswald's ideology and his character: Absolute freedom for all was the core of his political vision, yet he treated Marina as if he were a Nazi corporal shaping up a recruit.

Alex Kleinlerer is not our most unbiased émigré, but this moment does offer an image:

> . . . Oswald observed that the zipper on Marina's skirt was not completely closed. He called to her in a very angry and

commanding tone of voice . . . His exact words were, "Come here!" in the Russian language, and he uttered them the way you would call a dog with which you were displeased in order to inflict punishment on him . . . When she reached the doorway he rudely reprimanded her in a flat imperious voice about being careless in her dress and slapped her hard in the face twice. Marina still had the baby in her arms. Her face was red and tears came to her eyes. All this took place in my presence. I was very much embarrassed and angry but I had long been afraid of Oswald and I did not say anything.[7]

It is best, however, not to carry any analogy to Hitler too far. Oswald would have identified with the early struggles in Vienna, and would have been heartened by the fact that a plain ordinary-looking man with nothing better than a high school education had succeeded for a time in dominating half the world. He could certainly have accepted Hitler's way of reading and absorbing knowledge, he would have given assent to Hitler's belief in great individuals, and he would have applauded the following from *Mein Kampf:*

> . . . anyone who wants to cure this era, which is invariably sick and rotten, must first of all summon up the courage to make clear the causes of this disease [and then organize] those forces capable of becoming the vanguard fighters for a new philosophy of life.[8]

Oswald, however, would have found Hitler's most fundamental concept indigestible.

> . . . *For only those who . . . learn to know the cultural, economic, but above all, the political greatness of their own fatherland can and will achieve the inner pride in the privilege of being a member of such a people.* [Hitler's italics][9]

Oswald was a Marxist. To relax his grip on Marxism would have been equal to intellectual decomposition for himself. The concept of a fatherland was odious to him; can one conceive of his "feeling inner pride in the privilege" of being an American? He would hate concepts of race and historically destined folk. Hitler's success, however, was another matter—it probably lit a candle in the dungeon of Oswald's immense hopes for himself.

Sometime in the fall of 1962—the date is wholly unclear—De Mohrenschildt took Oswald to meet his friend Samuel Ballen with the possibility that Ballen would employ him in his corporation or send him to some promising place. The three men were together for two hours:

> MR. BALLEN. . . . during the entire course of the two hours [there were] general observations, general smirks, general slurs that were significant to me that he was equally a critic of the United States and of the USSR and that he was standing in his own mind as somewhat of a detached student and critical of both operations . . .
>
> . . . the one thing that greatly started to rub me the wrong way is, as I started to seriously think through possible industrial openings or possible people I could refer him to, and he could see I was really making an effort in this respect, he kept saying, and then he repeated himself a little too often on this, he said to me, "Now, don't you worry about me, I will get along. Don't you worry yourself about me." He said that often enough that gradually it became annoying and I just felt this is a hot potato that I don't think will fit in with any organization that I could refer him to.[10]

It was not corporate for Lee to suggest, "Don't worry about me." The corporation is built on the premise that it not only takes care of all its people but worries about them, because it is, after all, the largest factor in their lives. Not unlike the Soviet Union, one is tempted to say.

3

―――――――

"I Refused to Tell a Lie"

Back on October 7, we left Marina and June at the Taylors' house. By the next day, Jeanne De Mohrenschildt had arranged for Marina to receive some dental work. We can pick up an idea of how much Marina's presence annoyed Jeanne by the following:

MR. JENNER. You immediately noticed that she was ignorant, let me say?

MRS. DE MOHRENSCHILDT. In bringing up the child? . . . Absolutely . . .

MR. JENNER. The pacifier would fall on the floor, she would pick it up and stick it in the baby's mouth?

MRS. DE MOHRENSCHILDT. No; first she put it in her infected mouth and then in the baby's mouth . . . Pick it up off the floor. The floor was less germs than her infected teeth, but she was not aware of it. That is what didn't make . . . sense at all. After all, a pharmacist . . .[1]

Jeanne might be Russian by birth, but she had developed American notions of sanitation. Marina lived by other premises: She loved June so much that she would take it for granted that the adoration in her heart would imbue her saliva with cleansing powers. Perhaps she was right. Love plus infection might be more than equal to disinfectant that comes in a big company's bottles.

But, working together, the De Mohrenschildts and George Bouhe took steps to fix Marina's teeth. With the aid of Elena Hall, who lived and worked in Fort Worth as a dental assistant and made arrangements for them at Baylor University's dental clinic, Marina had six teeth extracted, and preparations for new ones commenced over a Monday and a Wednesday, October 8 and 10. Bouhe paid the $70 fee, and Jeanne was in charge of driving Marina to the appointments in Fort Worth, then bringing her back to the Taylors' in Dallas, a harrowing few days for Marina, it is safe to suppose.

Alexandra Taylor, being deputized on each occasion to take care of baby June, offers her sidelight:

ALEXANDRA GIBSON. . . . The minute Marina left, the child would start to cry . . . Every time I got near her she'd scream. She never slept . . .

MR. JENNER. Do you think she found it strange to have anyone speak to her in English as distinguished from Russian?

ALEXANDRA GIBSON. . . . I don't believe she had ever been with anybody but her parents and I think that might have had a lot to do with it, plus she was very spoiled, very catered to by her mother and her father.[2]

Following the dental work, it was agreed that Marina would move over with June to Elena Hall's place. An émigrée, Elena Hall spoke Russian, had a larger apartment, and was separated at this time from her husband, an American. The immediate result was that Lee was in Dallas and Marina was now back in Fort Worth. They were thirty miles apart and he could see her less frequently, but Kleinlerer was standing in for him as resident critic of Marina:

> I noticed that [she] did nothing to help Mrs. Hall in the house. Mrs. Hall often complained that Marina was lazy, that she slept until noon or thereabouts, and would not do anything . . . to help.[3]

Nonetheless, Elena Hall and Marina were able to collaborate on certain matters. On October 17, in the evening, the two women knocked on Alexandra Taylor's door in a state of excitement. An hour earlier, they had had June baptized at a Russian Orthodox church. Elena Hall was now the godmother. Since Marina was certain that Lee would object strenuously, she had done it "on the sly" and asked Alexandra not to tell him.[4]

Since Lee's twenty-third birthday was tomorrow, October 18, and they would not be together but thirty miles apart, Marina asked Alexandra if she could leave a small box of new clothes for him. (In those days, Oswald dropped by frequently at the Taylors'.) As soon as Marina returned to Fort Worth, however, she had a change of heart. When Lee called her that night, she told him about the baptism. When he came by the Taylors' apartment to pick up his gift the next day, he was cool. Alexandra remarked: ". . . said he didn't like the idea, but that was all."[5]

On October 18, Lee's birthday, Elena Hall got into a car crash that would put her in the hospital for eight days. About that, Alexandra said, "It was very shocking . . ."[6]

We can assume the émigrés were even more disturbed by the news, particularly when they learned of the baptism. The accident had to intensify everyone's fear of Oswald: Marina, with her deep if unfocused intuitions about magical matters, could hardly be free of the guilty assumption that she had helped to injure Elena Hall.

The immediate result was that Marina now lived alone in Elena's apartment in Fort Worth. Indeed, since Elena Hall went off to New York as soon as she was discharged from the hospital in order to be reunited with her husband, Marina would continue to dwell there alone for more than two weeks. Alex Kleinlerer, left to look after the apartment and make certain that it remained in some kind of order, gave his usual generous evaluation:

> On a good many of the occasions that I dropped by the Hall residence during my lunch hour, I found that Marina had not yet awakened. I would have to arouse her by ringing the door-bell and banging on the front door. I would find the household unkept, unwashed dishes in the sink or on the eating table, and hers and the baby's clothing strewn around the room. Marina would come to the door in a wrap-around, her hair dishevelled and her eyes heavy with the effect of many hours of sleep. She would make some excuses about sleeping late.[7]

This may have been the first period of real rest for Marina in years. Who can measure the exhaustions of her harsh adventures in Leningrad, Minsk, and Texas? Now, over the space of a week and three days, she had had six teeth taken out and her daughter baptized and had then been the prime mover—could it be?—behind a fearful accident. No wonder, then, if she overslept and was exhausted on awakening. There was a series of obsessions to encounter each night, including the bottomless question—"What do I do next with my existence?"

Paradoxically, her sexual life may have been stimulated. Curses that prove successful open the gates to libido. (Otherwise, there would be no warlocks.) In this period, while Elena was away, Lee came to visit for full weekends, and was full of himself.

> *McMillan:* "This is your house. I give it to you—all!" he would announce to Marina, sweeping his arm grandly around the entrance hall upon his arrival on a Friday. "Isn't this a fine house I bought you?"
>
> Marina remembers that he was "always running to the ice-box," a thing he never did at home when he was paying for the groceries himself, to fix a Coke or a sandwich. "A full ice-box!" he would exclaim delightedly before he pounced . . . And at night, he made love to Marina while watching . . . the bedroom television set, a distraction which helped slightly his problem of premature ejaculation. Afterwards, the two of them slept in separate bedrooms, a luxury which Lee said made him feel "like an aristocrat."[8]

By the twenty-sixth of October, he is searching for a place they can live in together, and finally chooses an apartment on Elsbeth Street in Dallas, a ground-floor lodging that has a back entrance as well as a front door. He will not have to call as much attention to himself when he comes in and when he goes out.

On November 4, Lee and Marina move into the Elsbeth Street place. Elena Hall, still in New York and distrustful of Lee, asks the reliable Kleinlerer to make certain that Mr. Oswald, in the course of removing his worldly goods from the Halls' garage, does not take anything belonging to her.

Lee inveigled Gary Taylor into contributing his taxi, then rented a U-Haul, and the two spent a good part of the day on the packing, the move, the unpacking, and the return of the trailer. Kleinlerer weighs in one last time:

> I supervised the placing of the Oswald goods and wearing apparel in the "U-Haul-It" trailer. There were several instances when I had to intervene when Oswald picked up some of Mrs. Hall's things . . . I could not say whether this was deliberate or inadvertent, except that there were several instances.[9]

Alexandra Taylor comes along with Gary for the last leg of the move and gives a telling description of the apartment on Elsbeth Street that the Oswalds would occupy for the next four months:

ALEXANDRA GIBSON. It was a hole. It was terrible, very dirty, very badly kept, really quite a slum . . . large, quite large, built very strangely, little rooms here and there, lots of doors, lots of windows. The floor had big bumps in it . . . you walked uphill, you know, to get from one side of the room to the other. It was not a nice place, no.

MR. JENNER. Was it a brick structure, wooden?

ALEXANDRA GIBSON. It was brick outside, dark red brick. It was a small apartment building, I think two stories, overrun with weeds and garbage and people.[10]

McMillan: On the first night in their new apartment, November 4, Marina stayed up till five in the morning, scrubbing everything in sight. Lee helped for a while. He cleaned the icebox, then left about ten in the evening. He had paid for a room at the "Y," he said, and he might as well use it. But since the YMCA has no record that he stayed there after October 19, it is likely he spent a final night in whatever rooming house he had been living in for the last two weeks.[11]

Or, spent the night with whomever he had been seeing. The answer to that we may never know—he could have quit the new apartment that night from no more than the cold fury of recognizing that she felt no joy in being back with him and instead was buried in cleansing powder. Or, indeed, having returned to her, he may have regretted giving up his other life, even if it had amounted to no more than loneliness and privacy. In any case, they are far from reconciled. In two more days they will have a terrible fight that begins with what Marina sees as a small matter, a conversation with Mrs. Tobias, the wife of the building superintendent.

> MRS. TOBIAS. . . . I said to him, "What nationality are you folks?" . . . He said, "Oh, we are Czech." . . . that's all I got out of him that [first] night . . . Well, the first time she came in, I said, "Your husband says you are Czech," and she began to shake her head . . . she was Russian . . . She said that in English, she said . . . "My husband told me if I said I was Russian, people would be mean to me," . . . and I said, "Nobody will be mean to you . . . you are always welcome to come into my house . . ."[12]

Lee was livid. Once again, she had disobeyed his instructions and, in effect, blown his cover. The quarrel grew, fed conceivably by the recognition that they were together again and miserable about that.

She could live with the émigrés from now on as far as he was concerned. To covet the possessions of others, and make up to them, was just one more form of whoring, he told her. He was using the most insulting single word for whore in Russian, and Marina was not only wounded but incensed—he, who raided Elena Hall's icebox and slept on her sheets, was calling her *blyat*. Half of her reason for marrying him had just been destroyed with that single word. She might just as well have wed a Russian who knew all the gossip about Leningrad. She was in such a state that she ran into the street.

Weeping, shaking, and with a hundred words of English, she succeeded in explaining to the attendant at the nearest gas station that she wished to call Anna Meller.

MRS. MELLER. Yes, yes, sir. It was in November, I think, on a certain Monday about 10 in the evening, she will call me and say that her husband beat her and she came from the apartment and reached the filling station and said the man—she did not have a penny of money, and the good soul helped her to dial my number and she's talking to me if she can come over my house. I was speechless because to this time I didn't even know they were in Dallas. To understand, sir, we went to Fort Worth two or three times to help Marina and then there was for certain period quiet . . . I came to my husband and I asked him if we can take Marina. He did not want to. We have one bedroom apartment and he said, "Do not have very much space." I, like a maniac woman, started to beg and said: "We have to help poor woman, she's on the street with baby. We could not leave her like that; we had our trouble and somebody helped us." My husband said, "Okay, let her come." She said to me she did not have a penny of money. I said, "Take a taxi and come here and we will pay the way." So about 11 or 10:40 she came over [to] our house . . . with baby on her hand, couple diapers and that was all; no coat, no money, nothing.[13]

George Bouhe brought several of the Russians together for a quick conference on the matter:

McMillan: "I don't want to advise or interfere," he told Marina . . . "I can't come between a husband and wife. If you leave him, of course we'll help. But if you say one thing now and then go back, next time no one will help."
"I'll never go back to that hell," Marina promised herself.[14]

She was now committed. She would stay away from Lee, and the émigrés, one way or another, would take care of her. If the speculation that George Bouhe had had a private relation with Lee is not entirely without foundation, then his extreme position on Marina's separation suggests that he was not only fussy, balding, and opinionated but—assuming things had turned out badly with Lee—vindictive.

Being the most physical man among them, George De Mohrenschildt is now deputized by the émigrés to talk to Oswald about the terms of the separation. It is agreed that Lee and Marina will meet at the De Mohrenschildts' apartment to see if they can resolve their difficulties. De Mohrenschildt suggests that Bouhe be present at the meeting, but he demurs: "If he sticks his fists in my ears it will suit neither my age nor my health."[15] Then he adds, "I am scared of this man. He is a lunatic," to which De Mohrenschildt replies, "Don't be scared. He is just as small as you are."[16]

The site and time are established. The meeting will be on November 11 in De Mohrenschildt's apartment. On that Sunday morning, June is left behind with Anna Meller, and Bouhe brings Marina over in his car, then leaves on the quick. Jeanne, Marina, and George wait for Lee, who comes in "obviously embarrassed to be having such a scene in front of the De Mohrenschildts."[17]

After an exchange of grievances which merely increases the heat between Lee and Marina, Jeanne suggests that they have a trial separation. George gives his account:

At that, Lee [shouted,] "You are not going to impose this indignity on me!" . . . He was incoherent and violent. We never saw him in this condition before.

"If you do this, you will never see June and Marina again. You are ridiculous," [Jeanne] said quietly. "There is a law here against abuse."

"By the time you calm down, I shall promise you will be in contact with baby June again," I interceded, knowing that Lee was afraid that someone would take the child away from him. And so he calmed down, promised to think the situation over, [and] assured us that there would be no more violence . . .[18]

Lee and Marina go into another room to talk. He wants her to come back; she speaks of divorce. He asks again whether she will come back; she tells him that she will only return to the Elsbeth Street apartment with the De Mohrenschildts, and will only stay long enough to pick up her clothes and leave.

MARINA OSWALD. . . . I simply wanted to show him, too, that I am not a toy. That a woman is a little more complicated. That you cannot trifle with her.

MR. RANKIN. Did you say anything at that time about how he should treat you if you returned?

MARINA OSWALD. Yes. I told him that if he did not change his character, then it would be impossible to continue living with him. Because if there should be quarrels continuously, it would be crippling for the children.

MR. RANKIN. What did he say to that?

MARINA OSWALD. Then he said that it would be—it was very hard for him. That he could not change. That I must accept him such as he was . . .[19]

An impasse. She will not accept him as he is. Finally, he agrees that she can move out. The four of them, two De Mohrenschildts and two Oswalds, drive over to Elsbeth Street with Lee sitting silently in the backseat of the convertible. But when they enter the apartment, Lee has a change of heart:

MR. DE MOHRENSCHILDT. . . . Lee said, "By God, you are not going to do it. I will tear all her dresses and I will break all the baby things."

And I got very mad this time. But Jeanne started explaining to him patiently that it is not going to help him any—"Do you love your wife?" He said yes. And she said, "If you want your wife back some time, you better behave."

I said, "If you don't behave, I will call the police."

I felt very nervous about the whole situation—interfering in other people's affairs, after all.

"Well," he said, "I will get even with you."

I said, "You will get even with me?" I got a little bit more mad and I said, "I am going to take Marina anyway."

So after a little while . . . I started carrying the things out of the house. And Lee did not interfere with me. Of course, he was small, you know, and he was a rather puny individual.

After a little while, he helped me carry the things out. He completely changed his mind.

MR. JENNER. He submitted to the inevitable?

MR. DE MOHRENSCHILDT. He submitted to the inevitable, and . . . we cleaned that house completely.

We have a big convertible car and it was loaded . . . And we drove very slowly all the way to the other part of the town, Lakeside, where the Mellers lived, and left her there.[20]

And there was Lee left alone in the half-empty apartment on Elsbeth Street. In his manuscript, De Mohrenschildt picks up on Lee's lonely state:

The next evening Lee was back with us, all alone. Again, he wanted to talk the situation over. He sat gloomily on our famous sofa and both of us tried to talk some sense.

"I heard of love accompanied by beating and torture," I said half-seriously. "Read Marquis de Sade or observe the life of the underworld—*l'amour crapule,* as they say in France. But your fights seem to be deprived of sex, which is terrible . . ."

"If you think you are fond of each other, cannot you do it without scratching, biting, and hitting?" Jeanne tried another reasoning.

Lee sat gloomily without saying a word . . .

Jeanne kept on talking about a nice temporary home for Marina and the baby and the good care both of them will have. Naturally, we did not mention the name of the Mellers.

"I promise you, Lee, that after a cooling off period, I shall give you the address and the telephone, so you can communicate with your child. Nobody should separate a child from her father."

Lee believed my promise because he knew that myself I had been a victim of a vindictive wife who prevented me from seeing my children . . .

That night, we separated rather sadly. "You may hate us, Lee, or maybe you will be grateful to us one day for enforcing this separation," I said. "But I don't see any other way out under the circumstances . . ."

Lee agreed but he was on the verge of tears. "Remember your promise. You will give me soon their address and the telephone."

We shook hands and Lee left.[21]

In fact, Marina and June were not staying at the Mellers' any longer but at the Fords', who had a larger house. Katya Ford, however, had some hard-edged ideas about Marina's real future:

MR. LIEBELER. Was there any conversation . . . about the possibility of a divorce? . . .

MRS. FORD. . . . she didn't want to go back . . . but she wasn't right for domestic help and I told her to stay with Lee, that is what I told her myself, and wait until she could be able to take care of herself . . .

MR. LIEBELER. What did she say about that?

MRS. FORD. . . . she didn't say anything.[22]

George Bouhe thought he had found a solution. He arranged for Marina to stay with still another émigrée, Valentina Ray, who could teach her English until she felt ready to go out on her own. Marina, however, must have been missing Lee, for she gave him the new number to call.

McMillan: Within minutes of her arrival, he telephoned and begged her to see him. "I'm lonely," he said. "I want to see Junie and talk to you about Thanksgiving."
Marina caved in. "All right," she said, "come over."[23]

At this point, it is necessary to quote close to a full page from *Marina and Lee.* If it is ungracious to enter a cavil, it may nonetheless be necessary, for their dialogue has obviously been composed by Mrs. McMillan. Marina was speaking in Russian when she gave her account to Priscilla Johnson McMillan in 1964, and the author's translation could be more responsive to her own sense of romantic dialogue than to Lee and Marina's way of conversing with each other—at least if we have obtained any notion of how they spoke from the KGB transcripts.
Nonetheless, this uneasiness admitted, it is also true that scenes of reconciliation between knotty, anger-filled people tend to be moving, and the author does not fail to produce:

McMillan: Marina's heart jumped when she saw her husband. They went into a room by themselves.
"Forgive me," he said. "I'm sorry. Why do you torture me so? I come home and there's nobody there. No you, no Junie."
"*I* didn't chase *you* out," Marina said. "*You* wanted it. You gave me no choice."
He loved her, he said. It wasn't much, he knew, but he loved her the best he knew how. He begged her to come back to him. Robert, he added, had invited them for Thanksgiving and it would be terrible to show up without her.
Marina realized that Lee needed her. He had no friends, no one to count on but her. Harsh as his treatment was, she knew he loved her. But she brushed him away when he tried to kiss her. He went down on his knees and kissed her ankles and feet. His eyes were filled with tears and he begged her

forgiveness again. He would try to change, he said. He had a "terrible character" and he could not change overnight. But change he would, bit by bit. He could not go on living without her. And the baby needed a father.

"Why are you playing Romeo?" Marina said, embarrassed at his being at her feet. "Get up or someone will come in the door." Her voice was severe, but she felt herself melting inside.

He got up, protesting as he did so that he refused to get up until she forgave him. Both of them were in tears.

"My little fool," she said.

"You're my fool, too," he said.

Suddenly Lee was all smiles. He covered the baby with kisses and said to her: "We're all three going to live together again. Mama's not going to take Junie away from Papa any more."[24]

In the written narrative that Marina would prepare for the FBI, she says, "We talked alone in the room, and I saw him cry for the first time."

By other accounts she has already provided, we know that she must have seen him weep on at least eight or ten occasions, yet she is still seeing him burst into tears for the first time. Is one entitled to think that such a reaction may be characteristically Russian? An adult's open sorrow is, after all, a signal occasion. Just as each act of sex for blissfully accommodated lovers always seems to be a magical first event, so too would Marina react each time to his weeping. She waxes eloquent here:

From Marina's narrative: What woman's heart can resist this, especially if she is in love? [Lee] asked my forgiveness, and promised me he would try to improve, if only I would come back. Do not think I am boasting—as if to say, Look how he loves her, and he is even crying. But . . . I felt that this man is very unhappy, and that he cannot love in any other way. All of this, including quarrels, mean love in his language. I saw that if I did not go back to him, things would be very hard for him [and] I felt for the first time that this person was not born to live among people, that among them he was alone. I was sorry for him and frightened. I was afraid that if I did not go back to him something might happen. I didn't have anything concrete in mind, but my intuition told me that I couldn't do this, [because] he needed me . . . What can you do when a person has been this way all his life? You can't reform him at once. But I decided that if I had enough patience, everything would be better and that this would help him . . .[25]

A little later that night, after supper, Marina, Lee, and June were driven by their host, Frank Ray, back to their apartment on Elsbeth St. It did not take long for the other émigrés to hear. As one would expect, they decided that they had had quite enough of the Oswalds.

MRS. DE MOHRENSCHILDT. . . . really furious. We wasted the whole day, so much aggravation, go through all that trying to do something for them and then she dropped the whole thing. So, why bother, you know? So, from then on, we were really disgusted . . .[26]

To the other émigrés it was an unmitigated disgrace. Bouhe announced that he was washing his hands of both of them. A story made the rounds among the émigrés, and suggests the tenor of their collective humor:

McMillan: No sooner had the couple made up, the story went, than Lee plucked the cigarette from his wife's lips and snuffed it out on her shoulder. The Russians recalled that in the early days of the Bolshevik régime, officers of the Cheka, as the secret police were called, used to extinguish a cigarette on human flesh when they were trying to break a prisoner. Marina denies that her husband did any such thing to her ever. But the Russians believed that he did—stunning testimony as to how they felt about Oswald.[27]

It is indeed stunning testimony, but it attests to no more than the essential nastiness of the émigrés. Lee may not have been off target in his assessment of them.

From Marina's narrative: For Thanksgiving we went to Robert's house in Fort Worth. I liked this good American holiday, it is very agreeable to celebrate it. In the station Lee asked me if I wanted to hear the music from the movie *Exodus*. I did not know this movie but I liked the music very much. Lee paid a lot for this record, played it several times, and said that it was one of his favorite melodies. Now that Lee is no longer alive, I like this melody even more since it is associated with happy memories. Lee was in a very gay mood, we joked a lot, fooled around, photographed one another in the station and laughed at how silly we were getting. At Robert's house everything was also gay and in a holiday mood.[28]

We can quote here from Robert Oswald's book *Lee*. His account is bland, but give him the benefit of the doubt: Some families cannot have a decent time if anything of consequence is discussed.

John [Pic] and Lee had a lot to talk about, after ten years. They exchanged stories about their experiences in Japan, but Lee didn't mention Russia. We didn't bring it up either. It just seemed better to wait for Lee to volunteer whatever he wanted to say about it. He said nothing.

We didn't mention Mother, either . . .[29]

4

Christmas and Red Caviar

We do well to keep reminding ourselves: Everything that De Mohrenschildt tells the Warren Commission has a subtext. To maintain his profitable situation in Haiti depends on George convincing Papa Doc Duvalier that he was never seriously associated with any alleged Marxist assassin. De Mohrenschildt could ingratiate himself with Duvalier if he were ready to explain that he did a debriefing on Oswald for the CIA, but even one hint of that would be anathema to the Agency.

MR. DE MOHRENSCHILDT. You know, this affair actually is hurting me quite a lot, particularly right now in Haiti, because President Duvalier—I have a contract with the government.

MR. JENNER. Yes; I want to inquire on that.

MR. DE MOHRENSCHILDT. They got wind I am called by the Warren Committee. Nobody knows how it happened. And now he associates me, being very scared of assassination, with a staff of international assassins, and I am about to be expelled from [his] country. My contract may be broken.[1]

We know, therefore, why he and Jeanne speak of Lee and Marina in pejorative terms. Yet it is a delicate game. Being an old hand, George comprehends that it is not safe to toady too much to professionals in intelligence, for then they will demand more and more of you. Rather, it is better to suggest that one is not without one's own strengths if pushed. So we do get contradictory bits of testimony:

MR. DE MOHRENSCHILDT. Unless a man is . . . proven to be guilty by the court, I will not be his judge, and there will always be a doubt in my mind, and throughout my testimony I explained sufficiently why I have those doubts. And mainly because he did not have any permanent animosity for President Kennedy. That is why I have the doubts.[2]

It is a way of serving notice on the CIA: De Mohrenschildt, who is a study in self-interest, is not likely to defend Oswald without a motive, and here it is to keep alive for the CIA his awareness that they need Oswald to be seen as a lone demented killer without any connection to them. In effect, De Mohrenschildt is saying: I can help you or hurt you on this point.

For the most part, however, George maintained his covert CIA stance: Oswald was insignificant; he felt sorry for him; he saw very little of him. Only in the last year of De Mohrenschildt's life (troubled by intermittent spells of insanity, haunted by hideous visions— De Mohrenschildt may be worthy of an opera bearing his name) did George write *I'm a Patsy.* It was as if, coming closer to eternity, he had to redress the balance. When free of these bouts of madness, he was, in his last year, still sane, shrewd, and practical. So, he calculated that the American reading public by 1977 was looking for a sympathetic portrait of Oswald, and in his manuscript, he not only gives us his agreeable picture of Lee but reveals how much he was actually seeing of the Oswalds after their reconciliation.

One day we visited them in their apartment on Elsbeth Street in Oak Cliff . . . the atmosphere of the house and the neighborhood conducive to suicide. The living room was dark and smelly, the bedroom and kitchen facing bleak walls. But Lee was proud of his own place and showed me his books and magazines as well as some letters from Russia which we read together. The place was spruced up by lovely photographs of the Russian countryside taken by Lee and later enlarged by him. Trees and fields, charming peasant huts and cloudy skies contrasted strangely with the dreary walls and the lugubrious atmosphere. Some pictures were framed by Lee, others unframed were carefully assembled in an album . . . "Look at these churches, look at these statues," he exclaimed proudly. Indeed, almost all his pictures had a professional touch, he was justly proud of them.[3]

The month between Thanksgiving and Christmas may be the closest that the Oswalds will come to a peaceful time together.

From Marina's narrative: When we were not quarreling, I was very happy with my Lee. He helped me with the housework and . . . devoted a great deal of time to June. He also . . . used to bring home dozens of books from the library and just swallowed them down, even reading at night. Sometimes it seemed to me that he was living in another world and [would only go] to work to earn money for his family, to eat and to sleep. Perhaps this is not true, but in my opinion he had two lives, spending most of his time in his own separate life. Previously, in Russia, I had not noticed this, since he was not so withdrawn.[4]

On the other hand, Lee was also becoming quite a housekeeper, for he would vacuum the apartment, dispose of the garbage, even turn down the bedcovers at night. Priscilla Johnson McMillan describes "periods when he would follow Marina around all day. At such times, she said, he literally 'wore me out with his kisses.' "[5]

He also allowed her to sleep in the morning, and would make his own breakfast and leave coffee for her to be warmed. On weekends, this paragon would even serve Marina breakfast in bed.

McMillan: . . . most evenings, it was he who gave the baby her bath. He did not trust Marina and was afraid she would drown the child. He drew the water and tested its temperature with great care . . . Then, to Marina's horror, he would step in himself, utterly naked, with the exception of a wash-cloth over his private parts. Then he would splash June and play with her as if he longed to be a little child himself.

"Mama," he would shout to Marina, "we got water on the floor." Marina would tell him to mop it up himself. "I can't," he would shout back to her. "I'm in the bathtub with Junie."

"Mama," he would call out again, "bring us our toys." And she would bring them.

"Mama," came the call a third time, "you forgot our rubber ball." And, to the baby's delight, he would splash the rubber ball in the water.

"Mama," he would call out one last time, "bring us a towel, quick. We have water on our ear."[6]

Has he entered the warm, welcoming territory of the infantile return? We all do it. The unspoken notion seems to be that if you can get yourself into a state of pre-verbal sentience where in effect your breath, yourself, and the universe are no longer whole categories apart but instead are languorously related, then something lovely occurs. You have gone back far enough into your early years to remake your personality, or commence to. You can feel as if you are not necessarily doomed to drive down some pre-ordained road to dull, slow extinction. The trouble is that most routes back to an infantile state are judged harshly by others. You can, for instance, get very drunk, or loll like a couch potato in front of the TV, space out on pot, play solitaire, sleep endlessly, or linger for hours in a rocking chair; but there is a bad name for each of these activities—alcoholic, slug, druggie, solitaire-player, slug-a-bed, or too old to do anything—so one's ego suffers, even as one's infantile return brings its touch of beatitude. Oswald would have been slammed and damned by our prescriptive culture—child seducer, he would have been called for taking a bath with his baby when all he was trying to accomplish was to become a baby himself, and so be able to substitute Marina for Marguerite as a mommy in that old fold of the psyche where some of the trouble was stored.

Yet, how close husband and wife were for a little while:

McMillan: Around this time, Marina lost a purse containing $10 he had given her for groceries and she expected to be scolded or even beaten. When he hardly responded at all, Marina broke into tears. Lee tried to cheer her up by talking baby talk and then talking like a Japanese. He played games on the way to the grocery store, where he bought her red caviar, smoked herring, and other treats.[7]

Marina has no recollection of Lee buying her red caviar, but then, she will admit that her memory now bears resemblance to a city under siege for years. So much has been flattened.

No matter. Red caviar or no, there were happy days through Christmas. One evening, since Lee was not prepared to lay out money for a Christmas tree, Marina took care of that:

McMillan: . . . [She] slipped out on the street, found an evergreen branch, propped it up on their bureau in front of the mirror, and spread cotton around it for snow. The next day she gathered up 19 cents which Lee had left lying about and . . . bought colored paper and miniature decorations. She shredded the colored paper into tinsel; the decorations went on the branch. Lee was proud and surprised. "I never thought you could make a Christmas tree for only nineteen cents," he said.[8]

They are not fated to put their trust in happiness, however. Disruption comes with a Christmas party. De Mohrenschildt bears down on Katya Ford to invite the Oswalds to a post-Christmas gathering. That De Mohrenschildt may have more in mind than merely catering to his client can be deduced from the extra strides he takes after Marina declines the invitation because she can hardly bring June with them.

Not at all, De Mohrenschildt assures her; he will take care of that as well—a nice lady who speaks Russian is lined up to be a baby-sitter at the De Mohrenschildt apartment. So off they went, Oswalds and De Mohrenschildts, to the party. The Fords lived in a large modern house with a large stone fireplace offering its full blaze on this festive evening. Lots of lights. The other guests, needless to say, were all but shocked at the sight of the Oswalds.

MRS. DE MOHRENSCHILDT. There were quite a lot of people from the Russian colony and among them was a little Japanese girl . . . I don't remember her last name because we always called her Yaeko . . . She is supposed to be from a very fine Japanese family. She was wealthy . . . she did some work with

Neiman Marcus . . . Then she was a musician . . . playing with the Dallas Symphony,[9] . . . To tell you frankly, I never trusted Yaeko. I thought there was something fishy, maybe because I was brought up with the Japanese, you know, and I know what treachery is, you know. [She was] very strange to me that way, she was floating around, you know, and everything. There is another strange thing happened, too, with that Yaeko.

MR. JENNER. Involving the Oswalds?

MRS. DE MOHRENSCHILDT. Yes . . . That was very funny because [Yaeko and Lee] practically spent all evening together at that party, and Marina was furious, of course, about it. And the party that brought Yaeko to the party was furious about it, too, and I don't blame him for it. And from what I understand, Marina told me that Oswald saw Yaeko after, which was very unusual, because I don't think Oswald wanted to see anyone, let's put it that way . . .

MR. JENNER. How, otherwise, did Oswald act at this Christmas party?

MRS. DE MOHRENSCHILDT. Yes; what did they talk about, I don't have the slightest idea. But everybody remarked and we were laughing about it. We were teasing Marina how he had a little Japanese girl now, you know. That was just as fun, of course, you know. But evidently they not only talked because she said he saw her later and he liked her. That is what she told me. He really liked Yaeko.[10]

Priscilla Johnson McMillan lets us know what they were talking about:

> . . . Japanese and American customs, and about Ikebana, the Japanese art of flower arrangement, which Miss Okui was certified to teach. But Marina noticed that [Yaeko] spoke Russian and was drinking only Coca-Cola, nothing stronger. It occurred to her that Miss Okui might work for American Intelligence. During an interval in the kitchen, she cautioned Lee against talking politics and especially against praising Khrushchev. "Watch out," she said. "That girl is pretty and very charming. Only, she may be a spy. Don't be too frank with her." Never before, and never again, was she to feel prompted to warn her secretive husband to keep his mouth shut.

One other person reacted to Miss Okui exactly as she did—George de Mohrenschildt. To all appearances he was busy chasing a couple of girls, but his antennae were out and he remarked to Marina: "That Japanese girl—I don't trust her. I think she works for some government or other, but which one, I don't know."[11]

We can take it for granted that De Mohrenschildt, in the course of debriefing Oswald, would have had many conversations with him about sex and would have known of his considerable regard for Japanese women. In *Legend,* Edward Epstein explores the matter further:

> George De Mohrenschildt subsequently testified that ... [Oswald] had made some "contacts with Communists in Japan" and that these "contacts" had induced him to go to the Soviet Union. At least this was what Oswald had confided to him. Now, as he watched them talk across the room, he wondered whether [Yaeko] might be trying to find out about this earlier period in Oswald's life. In any case, [George] didn't trust her.
>
> Yaeko herself never fully divulged the contents of this long conversation with Oswald ... She would later say when questioned by the FBI in 1964 that she and Oswald had discussed "flower arrangements."
>
> At about midnight, De Mohrenschildt suggested to Oswald that they leave ... Oswald wrote down a number that Yaeko gave him, as Marina observed; then he followed De Mohrenschildt out the door.[12]

As happens over and over in attempting to find a credible route through Oswald's adventures, the trail forks, then divides again: 1) It is all as it seems on the surface; Oswald has found an attractive girl who likes him. 2) De Mohrenschildt is not, in fact, prepared for Miss Okui, since she is working for Japanese intelligence. 3) As Marina believes, Yaeko Okui is connected to the CIA, only it is for a section that is not connected to George's operation. Or, 4) De Mohrenschildt has been given instructions, and the meeting with the young lady has been arranged in advance—Miss Okui is there to become friends with Oswald and debrief him in depth to see whether deeper use can be made of him. Indeed, Miss Okui is exactly the reason that George brought the Oswalds to the party; he and Jeanne are only pretending to be distrustful.

5

Grubs for the Organism

If one would ask why the CIA would now be interested to this degree in Lee Harvey Oswald, it may be worth offering one insight on the complex nature of the Agency. Of all government bureaucracies, the CIA probably bears the greatest resemblance to an organism: that is, its analogical stomach, mind, lungs, and limbs, while capable of communicating with each other, often need to do so no more than minimally—large parts of the CIA function almost entirely out of communication with other large parts. To assume that the CIA as a whole was interested in Oswald is to alienate oneself from understanding more likely possibilities. It is safer to suppose that word-of-mouth concerning Oswald, as it slowly seeped through certain parts of the CIA, made him a figure of interest to particular operatives in a few enclaves of the Agency who, by December 1962, were no longer welcome in the Director's office.

It will not come as shocking information to most readers that through the Bay of Pigs, and then for the year and a half that followed, there had been a working agreement between the CIA and the Mafia to assassinate Fidel Castro. It had been perhaps the most important and secret aspect of a large effort, called Operation Mongoose, that worked out of the most powerful CIA base in the world, JM/WAVE, stationed in Miami and southern Florida for the purpose of harassing Cuba through a variety of raids, bombings, and other means of sabotage. Following the missile crisis of October 1962, however, an agreement was worked out with Khrushchev to avert further nuclear confrontation, and as a by-product of that endeavor, Kennedy gave orders to cut down on Operation Mongoose. Soon after, the FBI began to disarm various anti-Castro Cuban groups that had until then been in special training in covert camps along the Gulf of Mexico from Texas to Florida.

This shift in Kennedy's direction opened a schism in the CIA. Small groups of officers, feeling betrayed by the President's new policy, began to function in concealed enclaves. To them, Oswald could certainly have been of interest. Of course, his real sympathies had to be plumbed, his character estimated, and his willingness to take risks measured. Since Mongoose had been downgraded, the full resources of the CIA were hardly to be brought to bear, but it is possible that De Mohrenschildt, in his debriefings on Oswald, had passed along a favorable verdict: "This fellow is essentially desperate enough to pull off quite a few things."

Naturally, no evidence of any of this was reported by the CIA to the Warren Commission, but the House Select Committee on Assassinations did succeed in obtaining the 144-volume Agency file on Oswald and was able to interview some of the CIA personnel involved, among them J. Walton Moore. Epstein's researches are more than pithy here:

> . . . although Moore had previously "recalled" meeting De Mohrenschildt only twice in his life—once in 1958 and once in 1961—the documents found in De Mohrenschildt's CIA file showed that there was far "more contact between Moore and De Mohrenschildt than was stated." In fact, they revealed that Moore had interviewed him numerous times over a course of years and prepared reports based on this information. Moore himself testified that he had "periodic" contact with De Mohrenschildt for "debriefing purposes" and, although maintaining he could not recall any discussion about Oswald, acknowledged that these contacts may have extended to 1962.[1]

Given such meetings, there would have been contact reports passing from Dallas to the CIA in Langley.

> *Epstein:* Since the committee's investigators found no trace of [such contact reports], they would have had to have been systematically purged from the files. But why would the CIA, which in those days legally debriefed some twenty-five thousand U.S. citizens a year through its Domestic Contacts Service, go to such dangerous lengths to conceal this debriefing?[2]

Epstein has opened a velvet-lined gun case. If he has not come upon a smoking gun, he has certainly succeeded in pointing out the hollow impression left in the velvet by the removal of that gun. When he asks, Why are they going to such lengths, we are pointed toward an assassination attempt on a prominent right-wing figure in the John Birch Society named General Walker. It will take place in Dallas in April 1963, but J. Walton Moore, having confessed belatedly to "periodic" meetings with De Mohrenschildt, will not acknowledge that any could have taken place as late as April of 1963. That would be a line he could not have crossed; it might have been equal to testifying sooner or later that he and De Mohrenschildt had conversations about Oswald and Walker, which would have opened disclosures the CIA could never afford. It was better to make an error on the date, and claim that he had not seen De Mohrenschildt since 1962. They can't hang you for mixing up your dates.

There is another curious piece of business that took place between De Mohrenschildt and Moore. Sometime in September or October of 1962, during that period when De Mohrenschildt must have just acquired Oswald's fifty-page manuscript about the Soviet Union, George went to Houston on a business trip and, on his return, discovered that someone had been looking over a travel journal that he had been writing about that two-thousand-mile walking trip he and Jeanne had taken through Mexico and Central America. Since he had spent a considerable amount of time in Guatemala during those winter months when the CIA was training its anti-Castro brigades in local jungles for the invasion of April 1961, and since George was now performing a function for the Agency, it might have been deemed prudent by some of his superiors to take a look at what he was writing. The act, however, as De Mohrenschildt describes it for the Warren Commission, makes no immediate sense:

MR. DE MOHRENSCHILDT. . . . I left all my typewritten pages, some 150 typewritten pages, in my closet. When I returned from the trip and started looking through the pages . . . I noticed small marks on the pages . . . small marks with a pencil . . .

I told my wife, "Jeanne, have you fiddled around with my book?" She said, "Of course not." I said, "That's impossible." And I forgot it for a while.

In the evening . . . the idea came back to me that somebody must have been in my apartment and . . . took photographs.

And it was such a horrible idea that Jeanne and I just could not sleep all night. And the next morning we both of us went to see Walter Moore and [I asked] "Have you Government people . . . looked through my book?" He said, "Do you consider us such fools as to leave marks on your book if we had? But we haven't." . . . I never could figure out who it was. And it is still a mystery to me.[3]

Of course, the marks on De Mohrenschildt's papers may have been a diversion and the real interest have been in photographing Oswald's manuscript and any additional notes that De Mohrenschildt might have written on the debriefing of Oswald. Information in the CIA, as in all intelligence organizations, is cloistered department by department, desk by desk, officer by officer, and considerable effort must sometimes be exercised to obtain information that is just across the hall.

By the beginning of December there is a likelihood that Oswald is being paid either by De Mohrenschildt or by an associate (unless, of course—always the speculative trail divides—Oswald's phantom boyfriend is giving him gifts of cash), but whatever the source, the fact is that Oswald, in debt since May of 1962 to the State Department to the sum of $435.71 for family transportation from Moscow to New York, first begins to repay that debt on August 13, 1962. At that time he sends $10 in cash from Mercedes Street and follows it with a money order for $9.71 on September 5, and another money order for $10 on October 10, and still another $10 on November 19, 1962, a picayune total of $39.71 eked out over fourteen weeks. Suddenly, he is able to pay off the rest of his debt—ten times as much—$396.00!—in the interval from December 11, 1962, to January 29, 1963—that is, in seven weeks: $190.00 in a money order purchased on December 11 (just twenty-three days after he sent $10), another $100 on January 9, and a last money order, purchased on January 29, for $106.00.

There were balance sheets drawn up by the Warren Commission to attempt to explain how Oswald could have accomplished such a financial feat. His earnings at Jaggars-Chiles-Stovall were never more than $70 a week and often ten or fifteen dollars less. His rent on Elsbeth Street was $69.50 a month, his family's expenditures for food and other materials had to be calculated at $15 a week, and every small extra disbursement noted in various persons' testimony was added to the figures, but it is one of those balance sheets that would fall apart with the loss of one pocketbook containing even ten dollars.

Oswald earned $305, $240, and $247 in November, December, and January, and for living disbursed $182, $165, and $190 in those same months (both sets of figures from Warren Commission findings).[4] So, for that period, Oswald has $805 in income, and expenses of $527, or a net gain of $278. As soon, however, as we take away $396 for the State Department debt, he is now $118 in arrears, and even this figure depends on there being no other expenditures than those that were noted by the Warren Commission. It is highly unlikely that every cent he spent in those three months was recorded.

Perhaps it is worth taking a look again at Harlot's precepts: The first step taken by the handler is to gain the confidence of the target. The second is to offer him money for his services.

"It is easier," said Harlot, "than you would suppose . . . Pay off, for instance, some old nagging debt of the client . . . Sooner than you would believe, our novice agent is ready for a more orderly arrangement. If he senses that he is entering into a deeper stage of the illicit, money can relieve some of his anxiety . . . a weekly stipend can be arranged . . . Questions?"

"Can you afford to let the agent become witting of who he is working for?"

"Never . . . the true purpose of the stipend is to give a sense of participation, even if the agent does not know exactly who we are . . ."[5]

We have crossed over wholly into speculation, but the question remains vital: Was Oswald being groomed to become some sort of provocateur in left-wing organizations? That he was reasonably sincere in his Marxism would not have deterred him. Not Oswald. He would have been contemptuous of officials in the American Communist Party, seeing them as peons of the Soviets, and he would hardly be impressed by the Socialist Workers Party, which was Trotskyite and had no power. He would have seen his own role as double-edged. While working as a provocateur for U.S. intelligence, he could also learn much about the intelligence establishment, much that might be of use in some future time of upheavals and new revolutionary governments. Having negotiated his own double passage between the U.S. and the USSR, he had the confidence that he was not an ordinary mortal. Work as a provocateur could open many avenues.

Let it be understood that after Kennedy curtailed Operation Mongoose and the most gung-ho anti-Castro forces were in disarray, an unspecified zone developed. Militant but now covert enclaves began to bivouac on the borders of the American intelligence establishment, and we may even obtain glimpses of such a presence when Oswald gets to New Orleans.

For now, we can try to answer one question. Why was Oswald so intent on discharging his debt to the State Department? More than once in KGB surveillance reports he is described as slipping off a Minsk bus without paying. A man who would cheat on a petty fare is not likely to honor a State Department loan unless he has a reason. He does. It is to acquire a new passport. He cannot travel out of America until he pays off his loan. So he pays it off. Perhaps others are also encouraging him to travel.

6

Trouble at Work

In the narrative Marina wrote for the FBI, she remarks that "New Year's was very dull for us and we stayed home. Lee went to bed early."[1]

The Russian community was having parties, she knew, and it was New Year's Eve, but the Oswalds had not been invited to anything. She had done her best to be witty at the Fords' house, and she had succeeded. People had been charmed by her. No returns. She recalled the animation she had seen on Lee's face when he had been speaking to Yaeko. He did not show happiness like that when he spoke to her:

> . . . I sat up and thought about Russia and my friends there. It was very depressing, especially when I thought of my home, my relatives, who were making merry and I was not with them, but sitting alone and unhappy.[2]

In the depths of a mood such as this, she began to think of her old boyfriend Anatoly, who was tall but not good-looking and wore outlandish clothes. In Minsk she had been so ashamed of his lack of elegance that she used to steer him along back streets when they were out on a date so that her girlfriends would not see him. But then they would stop to kiss in empty courtyards on winter nights, and there had never been anyone like him when it came to that.

She wrote a letter on this New Year's Eve of 1963:

> Anatoly dear,
>   . . . I want to wish you a Happy New Year.
>   It is not for this I am writing, however, but because I feel very much alone. My husband does not love me and our relationship here in America is not what it was in Russia. I am sad that there is an ocean between us and that I have no way back. . . .
>   I regret that I did not appreciate the happy times we had together and your goodness to me. Why did you hold yourself back that time? You did it for me, I know, and now I regret that, too. Everything might have turned out differently. But maybe, after the way I hurt you, you would not have me back . . .
>   I kiss you as we kissed before.
>
> Marina
> P.S. I remember the snow, the frost, the opera building—and your kisses. Isn't it funny how we never even felt the cold?[3]

She obviously debated the propriety of her act, because she did not mail her letter for several days. Then it came back for lack of postage. Lee read it to her aloud.

McMillan: He slumped on the sofa and sat there, his head in his hands, for a long time. Finally he straightened up. "Not a word of it is true," he said. "You did it on purpose. You knew they changed the postage and that the letter would come back to me. You were trying to make me jealous. I know your woman's tricks. I won't give you any more stamps. And I'm going to read all your letters. I'll send them myself from now on. I'll never, ever trust you again." He made her get the letter and tear it up under his eyes.[4]

One night in bed, in the middle of January, there on Elsbeth Street, Lee asked her if she had been with any other man since their marriage. And she said yes. She told him how she had seen Leonid Gelfant when Lee had gone to Moscow, and how she ran home and felt dirty. Lee kept saying, "You're putting me on." He didn't believe her. She was young and no expert on life, but she didn't understand why he would not believe her.

By the end of January, their marriage was not as affectionate as it had been in December. He was preoccupied. Soon he began to be away from home for an hour or two every evening—he had signed up, he told her, for a course in typing that he took after work.

There is nothing he does in January that would prove he is some kind of petty provocateur-in-training, and if not for his sudden ability to pay off the State Department, one could even be comfortable with the notion that everything he does is on his own; but still, there is that mysterious money, never accounted for, and now he goes on a spree of purchasing left-wing pamphlets and magazine subscriptions as if to establish a radical name for himself on a few lists.

> *Epstein:* From Pioneer Publishers . . . connected with the *Militant* (to which he was a subscriber), he ordered these political tracts: *The Coming American Revolution, The End of the Comintern,* and the *Manifesto of the Fourth International,* [plus] the English words to the song "The Internationale." From the Washington Book Store in Washington, D.C., he asked for subscriptions to . . . *Ogonek, Sovietskaya Byelorussia, Krokodil* and *Agitator.* From the Dallas library . . . he took out books about Marxism, Trotskyism and American imperialism in Latin America, particularly Cuba.[5]

It is a flurry but not an isolated burst of activity. In late November and in December he had already written to the Communist Party headquarters in New York and volunteered to help them on their publications, presenting samples of his output at Jaggars-Chiles-Stovall, including a poster: "Read The Worker If You Want to Know about Peace, Democracy, Unemployment, Economic Trends," a printing job done with company equipment. He had received friendly answers. He was being treated like a responsible man. From *The Worker,* on December 19, he had been told, "Your kind offer is most welcome and from time to time we shall call on you. These poster-like blow-ups are most useful at newsstands and other public places . . ."[6]

From Bob Chester at the Socialist Workers Party came a comradely letter full of technical questions:

> 116 University Place
> New York 3, New York
> Dec. 9, 1962

Mr. Lee H. Oswald
Box 2915
Dallas, Texas

Dear Mr. Oswald:

 . . . I am familiar with reproductions and offset printing processes. It is clear from your work that you are skilled at blow-ups, reversals, and reproduction work generally. Do you do any other phases of the process as well as photography? What about layout and art work?

We have access to a small offset shop here in New York. Generally, when we need any copy work done we have taken it there directly. However there might very well be occasions when we could utilize your skill for some printing project. It would, of course, necessarily have to be a project in which we would have flexibility as to time . . .

I would like to know what size camera you have; how large a paper print you can make; how large a negative; and any other technical information that you can give us that would help us judge how your aid would be most effective . . .

> With best wishes for a year of progress,
> Bob Chester[7]

Who can calculate the fresh energy released by being taken seriously? Yes, December was a good month. January, however, is plagued by thoughts of Anatoly plus other distractions.

De Mohrenschildt weighs in on this in his manuscript:

> . . . I wouldn't have known about it had it not been for Marina who came over one day furious and told me: "I found in Lee's pocket this Japanese girl's address. What a bastard, he is having an affair with her."

I did not say anything but just smiled and thought: "good for him."

"That Japanese bitch," she cried bitterly, "we had a fight over her—and look at the result."

She sported a new black eye.[8]

By the end of January, he was also having trouble at work. If he liked his job at Jaggars-Chiles-Stovall more than any other he had ever had, that was back in the fall. For three months he had been essentially a trainee, learning new techniques as well as enjoying unofficial perks: On company time he could make enlargements from his negatives of his own photographic work. If, in his boyhood, *I Led Three Lives for the FBI* had been his favorite TV show, now he had the capacity, so invaluable for anyone who has a taste for living with more than one identity, to produce calling cards, birth certificates, and other varieties of I.D.

By the middle of January, however, inexplicable tensions have come into his job. In the narrow corridors of the darkroom, he has begun to push past other workers, jostling them as they adjusted delicate enlarging machines:

MR. JENNER. . . . he was inconsiderate? . . . and selfish and aggressive?

MR. OFSTEIN. Yes; I think he thought he had the right of way in any case, either that or he was just in a hurry to get through, [but] through his hurrying he made no regard for anyone else's well-being . . .[9]

MR. JENNER. What about his aptitudes with respect to the work for which he was being trained?

MR. OFSTEIN. . . . he was fast, but I noticed that quite a few of his jobs [came] back within a normal working day . . . he was turning out a lot of work [which] had to be redone.[10]

Oswald's floor boss offers a similar appraisal:

MR. GRAEF. . . . Whenever he was asked to do a job over, he would do it willingly for me, [and was] perturbed at himself that he had made an error . . . It wasn't that he wasn't trying or didn't work hard to do the job, but . . . there were too many times that these things had to be made over.[11]

Perhaps he has a good deal on his mind. On January 27, two days after he pays off the State Department debt, he fills out a coupon, using the name Alik Hidell, and sends $10 in cash as down payment on a $29.95 purchase to Seaport Traders, Inc., in Los Angeles. It is for a .38 special caliber Smith & Wesson revolver with a five-inch barrel cut down to 2¼ inches.

Sawed-off pistols are tailored for very close range—one is looking into the eye of the enemy as one squeezes the trigger. So, such a weapon has more impact upon the owner's imagination than a long-barreled pistol or a rifle.

Probably he had already decided to kill General Edwin A. Walker. Or—let us bear the full existential weight of such a resolution—he was going to try. Head-on and at close range with a pistol. How could he know that he had the will to do it? He had never fired a shot in anger at a human being whom he could see (unless he was indeed the man who had killed Marine Private Martin Schrand.) So, by all odds, he was facing the largest gamble of his life. Then he waited all through February for the pistol to arrive C.O.D., but it never did, not in February. He was on edge. Of course he was on edge, and bumping into people while at work.

7

——————

In Order to Feel a Little Love

On February 13, De Mohrenschildt arranged an evening in his home between Oswald and a young geologist named Volkmar Schmidt, who had studied psychology at Heidelberg. The two men, having been brought together, talked for hours over the kitchen table.

> *Epstein:* Schmidt . . . tried to win his confidence by appearing to be in sympathy with his political views and making even more extreme statements . . .
>
> In an intentionally melodramatic way Schmidt brought up the subject of General Edwin A. Walker, who had been forced to

resign from the Army because of his open support for the John Birch Society . . . He suggested that Walker's hate-mongering activities at the University of Mississippi, which the federal government was then trying to desegregate, were directly responsible for the riots and bloodshed—including the deaths of two reporters—on that campus. He compared Walker with Hitler and said that both should be treated as murderers at large.

Oswald instantly seized on the analogy between Hitler and Walker to argue that America was moving toward fascism. As he spoke, he seemed to grow more and more excited about the subject.

Schmidt could see that he had finally got through to Oswald. As he listened to Oswald define more closely his political ideas, he began to work out his "psychological profile," as he called it. Oswald seemed to be a "totally alienated individual," obsessed with political ideology and bent on self-destruction . . . a Dostoyevskian character impelled by his own reasoning toward a "logical suicide."[1]

Like most psychological judgments, it is too comfortable for the judge. Oswald's aim in life was to achieve greatness. For that, he believed, he was uniquely destined. If he had to take a few enormous chances to arrive at his goal and those chances would result in his death, well, that was one logical outcome of serious danger, but he had not chosen suicide.

All through February and March he prepares himself to strike at Walker. The notion that the General was a Hitler in the making was key to choosing him for a target. The soft underbelly, however, of so lofty a notion—stop the second Hitler before he arises—comes in large degree because of Oswald's concealed sense of himself—even from himself!—of also being a putative Hitler. A physical resemblance between the two men had to be, consciously or unconsciously, in Oswald's mind. One need only pencil in a mustache on any photograph of Oswald in profile to feel the force of the resemblance. In his fantasies, would Oswald have refused a Faustian pact? Allow him to steal Hitler's powers of ascendancy, and he could convert them to his own vastly more idealistic vision. But first he must kill a minor god. When it came to available deities, General Edwin A. Walker was the nearest one to be found.

So each night in his dreams Oswald must have entered that chimerical castle of high intent where our most dangerous scenarios are played out in nocturnal dungeons and moats. He would have been testing himself. Would he find the courage to repel each terror that leaped out at him from every unexpected corner of his psyche?

The verdict of his dreams must have been negative; through all of February, he was, according to Marina, in a foul mood and grew progressively more violent. There is a logic to small acts of physical abuse in marriage—at least, if one is ready to advance the ignoble proposition that most people contain more meanness than they can express with friends or strangers. So, for cowards, marriage is an ideal solution, since quarrels are permitted to become ritual: Each mate's psychic excrement can be evacuated with full mutual understanding that the process, like all acts of elimination, is healthful, a veritable zero-sum economy of aggression.

In Minsk, Oswald's quarrels with Marina were classics of this fashion. They quarreled constantly, but at a temperature that was all but thermostatically regulated for them to regain quickly a little love for each other. In America, however, Oswald no longer enjoyed the curious respect that many Russians had felt for him as a special case. In Texas he was, to the contrary, seen as a deadbeat. Worse! He was anti-patriotic. So, the ante went up in the daily wars of their marriage. "Quantity changes quality," Engels once wrote, three words to capture the nature of process, and they apply here. Oswald was beginning to beat her up regularly:

> *McMillan:* No longer did he strike her once across the face with the flat of his hand. Now he hit her five or six times— and with his fists. The second he got angry, he turned pale and pressed his lips tightly together. His eyes were filled with hate. His voice dropped to a murmur and she could not understand what he was saying. When he started to strike her, his face became red and his voice grew angry and loud. He wore a look of concentration, as if Marina were the author of every slight he had ever suffered and he was bent on wiping her out . . .
>
> Marina could defend herself only with words. "Your beating me shows your upbringing," she said on one occasion.
>
> "Leave my mother out of this!" Lee cried, and struck her harder than before.[2]

In Fort Worth, at the beginning of such marital violence, there had been no more than two slaps, a very formal two slaps, as if a mother were punishing a child by saying: "There, you've done it again, two slaps for you!" Now, she was in legitimate fear of what he might do next. Sex became abrupt as well. He had come a distance from the patient swain who never made a pass at Ella Germann. Now he would "bark at her, 'Stop washing the dishes. Lee's hot!' and try to force himself upon her. He insisted on having sex any time he felt like it . . ."[3] He has acquired the athlete's externality. He speaks of himself in the third person—"Lee's hot!"—a force. It is further proof, if we need it, that he has become his own project.

By the middle of the month she knows she is pregnant again, but the beatings do not cease. He obviously feels trapped. He tells Marina that she must go back to the Soviet Union. She is consumed with suspicions that it is not typing lessons but an affair that keeps him from getting home until eight o'clock each night.

Indeed, he is taking typing lessons at Crozier Tech High School—there are witnesses to confirm that he comes in for class sessions three evenings a week after work, but then he is late getting home all five nights each week. Odds are that he cannot forgive Marina for her abortive message to Anatoly. The fathomless rage of the future leader of legions of humankind is in his heart—such a leader must have absolute fealty. They can quarrel in the privacy of the home, even be violent, but she must not have another fellow on her mind. He has the right to dispense with her if need be, but not she with him.

If authoritarianism is the cohort to murder, that is underlined here. The average man of mild demeanor—which is how Oswald was generally perceived in Minsk—can reach the state of murder, and continue to live in its livid high focus, only by pumping up the authoritarian in himself. To add to the turn of the screw, he does not even have a weapon. The pistol he has ordered still refuses to arrive. Nearly every day he goes to his post office box, but the notice is not there. It is like getting ready to make love without knowing if your phallus is in accord. His irritability carries over to work:

MR. GRAEF. . . . I began to hear vague rumors of friction between him and the other employees . . . Flareups of temper or an ugly word . . . very few people liked him. He was very difficult to get along with.[4]

The *Dallas Morning News* features General Walker on February 17. The John Birch Society is becoming respectable; it has a human face, and that face belongs to General Walker. And Oswald learns as well that Walker is now going away on a five-week tour beginning February 28. Oswald has but eleven days to get him and still no pistol.

A letter from Valya, written on January 24, 1963, but weeks late, arrives around this time:

> My dear Marinochka, we received your letter and greeting card. Thank you very very much for not forgetting us. I wept wholeheartedly when I received your letter, the way you did when you received mine . . . We are very pleased that Alik is such a decent fellow. You know we liked him and now I liked him twice as much as before in my thoughts. The photograph is beautiful. You look fine; little Marishka has grown a lot. I wanted so much to hold her in my arms. She does not look like you; she seems to be the very image of Alik.
>
> We were very glad to get your photograph. I look at it every day and it seems to me that you are here, next to me. I will preserve it. You know that I love you too, although I did scold you sometimes; but in my heart I was sincere. For me you took the place of a daughter and a friend. We are very sorry that you went so far away, but what can one do? Now we wish you only the best in life. Now you have an heiress growing up; someone to live and work for . . .
>
> During the school vacation, we had Aunt Musya's [daughter]. She spent about four days with us; she is growing into a very interesting girl—intelligent and determined. She asked me, "Aunt Valya, show me the picture of Marina; I will look at it again and remember it forever." . . .
>
> We hug and kiss you.
> Kiss my "granddaughter" for me.
>
> Aunt Valya and Uncle Ilya[5]

On February 17, at Oswald's insistent urging, Marina writes to the Russian Embassy. It is a flat letter and will break no bureaucratic hearts, but if she was determined not to go back to Russia, Valya's letter may have softened some of that resolve:

> Dear Comrade Reznichenko!
> I beg your assistance to help me to return to the Homeland in the USSR where I will again feel myself a full-fledged

citizen. Please let me know what I should do for this, i.e., perhaps it will be necessary to fill out a special application form. Since I am not working at present (because of my lack of knowledge of the English language and a small child), I am requesting to you to extend to me a possible material aid for the trip. My husband remains here, since he is an American by nationality. I beg you once more not to refuse my request.

Respectfully,
Marina Oswald[6]

MR. LIEBELER. The Commission has been advised that some time in the spring of 1963, you, yourself, either threatened or actually tried to commit suicide. Can you tell us about that?

MARINA OSWALD. Do I have the right now not to discuss that?

MR. LIEBELER. If you don't want to discuss that, certainly, but I really would like to have Lee's reaction to the whole thing. But if you don't want to tell us about it, all right.

MARINA OSWALD. At my attempt at suicide, Lee struck me in the face and told me to go to bed and that I should never attempt to do that—only foolish people would do it.

MR. LIEBELER. Did you tell him that you were going to do it, or did you actually try?

MARINA OSWALD. No; I didn't tell him, but I tried.

MR. LIEBELER. But you didn't want to discuss it any further?

MARINA OSWALD. No.[7]

She had thrown a wooden box at him. It contained, such as they were, pins and cuff links and jewelry. When it struck him, he threw her on the bed, took her by the throat, and said, "I won't let you out of this alive,"[8] at which point the baby began to cry, and he let go of her and took June into the next room while Marina lay on the bed alone.

It was then she went into the bathroom, stood on the john, tied a clothesline to a rod high on the wall, and wound the other end around her neck. She had been depressed for a very long time and now she felt abandoned. She was not wanted, and there was no way back. She was so depressed that she did not even think about June. If Lee loved the baby, he would take care of her. It was very selfish, she knew, but she wasn't worth anything to anyone.

Suicide was best. It was certainly easier than the road back to Minsk.

At that moment, before she could jump, he came in, slapped her, and made her get down. She was surprised that he had come in. She could not believe that someone wanted to care about her:

> *McMillan:* They both began to cry like babies. "Try to understand," he begged. "You're wrong sometimes, too. Try to be quiet when you can." He started kissing her as though he were in a frenzy. "For God's sake, forgive me. I'll never, ever do it again. I'll try and change if only you will help me." . . .
>
> They made love the whole night long, and Lee told Marina again and again that she was "the best woman" for him, sexually and in every other way. For Marina, it was one of their best nights sexually. And for the next few days, Lee seemed calmer . . .[9]

By the end of the month, Walker left on his tour, and Lee was calmer. That lasted for a few days.

Then their fights started up again. Mr. and Mrs. Tobias present the community reaction in this small brick building of poor apartments on Elsbeth Street.

> **MR. TOBIAS.** . . . I tried to talk to him several times and all I could get out of him was a grunt. He was the kind of a guy that wouldn't talk to you at all . . .
>
> **MR. JENNER.** How did your other tenants feel toward Oswald?
>
> **MR. TOBIAS.** . . . They didn't like the way he beat her all the time. [One tenant] told me, he said, "I think that man over there is going to kill that girl," and I said, "I can't do a darn thing about it." I says, "That's domestic troubles . . ."[10]

Mrs. Tobias amplifies her mate's comments:

> **MRS. TOBIAS.** . . . they always kept their blinds down, you know, the shades was always pulled.
>
> **MR. JENNER.** They were?
>
> **MRS. TOBIAS.** Oh, yes—day and night, you never seen any shades up over there, their shades was always down . . . they fought so much . . . and the tenants would come and tell my husband that

they kept them awake and the baby cried so much and he could hear them falling down as if Mrs. Oswald was hitting the floor . . . and we had one tenant over him . . . and she came over and she said, "Mr. Tobias, I think he has made a new opening down there." She said, "I think he's put her right through there." And he did break a window, my husband had to fix that . . . they knocked it out—I guess from fighting—we don't know.

MR. JENNER. You weren't there?

MRS. TOBIAS. No, [the tenants] said they could hear glass falling and evidently [Oswald] had put a baby blanket there—a baby blanket was over it, tacked down over the window . . . so my husband told them if they didn't straighten up . . . other people had to rest too, that he was sorry, but they would have to find another place.

MR. JENNER. And it was shortly after that that they left?

MRS. TOBIAS. Yes; shortly after that they moved in over on Neely.[11]

The apartment on Neely Street, just three blocks away, is on the second floor, has several small rooms and a scabby old wooden balcony. It also contains a very small room that Oswald appropriates for himself as a closet-sized studio. In it, through the month of March, he will do the writing and complete the research that will accompany his now developing effort to terminate Edwin A. Walker on the General's return to Dallas early in April.

8

Hunter of Fascists

McMillan: . . . Lee devoted his first two evenings on Neely Street to fixing up the apartment. He was handy at carpentry, building window boxes for the balcony and painting them green. He also built shelves for his special room and moved in a chair and a table, creating his own tiny office . . . "Look," he said to her . . . "I've never had my own room before. I'll do all my work here, make a lab and do my photography . . . But you're not to come in and clean. If I ever come in and find one single thing has been touched, I'll beat you."[1]

Having his own workplace seemed to be conducive to the sybaritic:

McMillan: When he took a bath, he would ask her to wash him. First he stretched one leg in the air. When she had finished and was ready to do the other leg, he would say No, the right one wasn't clean yet. He made her wash one leg four or five times before he would consent to raise the other. "Now I feel like a king," he would say beatifically. But he cautioned her to be more gentle. "I have sensitive skin, while you have rough, Russian ways."

Next, he would refuse to get out of the tub, his complaint being that the floor was cold, and he told her to put a towel down for him. When she had done as he asked, she would say, "Okay, prince, you can get out now."[2]

By March 10, he takes the equivalent of a deep breath and goes out on reconnaissance. He scouts the alley behind Walker's home, which is a two-story house on 4011 Turtle Creek Boulevard, and with his Imperial Reflex camera he photographs the backyard and rear wall of the place, presumably to familiarize himself with its windows, then proceeds to take snapshots of some railroad tracks seven hundred yards away. His motive here would hardly be comprehensible if one does not assume that already he is planning to bury his weapon in some particular clump of bushes near the tracks and needs the photographs to orient himself. One more advantage of working at Jaggars-Chiles-Stovall—he need be the only one who develops his negatives and prints.

Two days later, having estimated the possibilities, he comes to the conclusion that he needs a rifle, not a pistol, and so orders a Mannlicher-Carcano 6.5 mm carbine from Klein's Sporting Goods Company in Chicago—can he have any idea that this will become the most notorious rifle in history? The gun costs a total of $22.95, with a four-power scope mounted, postage and handling included. A few days later, on March 15, he writes to his brother Robert, who has just been promoted and is going to buy a larger house: "It's always better to take advantage of your chances as they come along, so I'm glad for you."[3]

It is the basic maxim of the man of action. He has been following it, sometimes well, sometimes badly, for a good part of his life. It certainly gives us one more understanding of his readiness to lie: Mistruths tilt the given and create openings—one can dart through them. "Take advantage of your chances as they come along . . ."

The second quality of the man of action—the ability to see his situation in the round—is sadly lacking. When it comes to assessing his own situation, Lee has tunnel vision. In the same letter to Robert he writes: "My work is very nice; I will get a rise in pay next month and I have become rather adept at my photographic work."

> MR. GRAEF. . . . I was working at my own desk one time and I looked over and . . . Lee was reading a newspaper, and I could see it—it was . . . not a usual newspaper and I asked him what he was reading and he said, "A Russian newspaper." . . . and I said, "Well, Lee, I wouldn't bring anything like that down here again, because some people might not take kindly to your reading anything like that." . . . of course, I know how people are and [him] causing suspicion and so forth, by having that newspaper or at least running around with it, flaunting it, we'll say.[4]

Meanwhile, at home, he is setting down in a blue-covered journal, a gift from George Bouhe in more generous times, the results of each reconnaissance he makes to Walker's house. The timetables of various bus routes within a mile of his target are included with his photographs, and he also puts in his estimate of the distance to various rear windows and doors from various sites of aim in the back alley. His joy as a young adolescent in studying the Marine Corps manual is being exercised again. He has dedication to detail. If it takes a General to kill a General, there is going to be balance in this event. Needless to add, the other half of himself, the enlisted man who despised all officers, can be a populist now: It takes a Private to shoot a General! That kicks off more in the scheme of things. So, Private-General Oswald, serving as his own staff, elaborates his plans. On his nocturnal missions, he even takes a nine-power hand telescope that he has brought back with him from Russia to aid in his estimates of distance. Like any good

General, he knows that the more you prepare, the more inevitable it becomes that you will actually go into battle and thereby commence that semi-unbelievable activity of killing your fellow man.

The Mannlicher-Carcano carbine arrives some two weeks after it has been ordered, and the Smith & Wesson revolver with the sawed-off barrel, delayed for nearly two months, also comes in on the same day, March 25. One is at the post office, the other at REA Express near Love Field. How can he not see it as a sign? Having arrived on the same day, perhaps they will be used on the same day. Perhaps they were.

A fellow employee, Jack Bowen, recalls that Oswald, having brought the rifle over to Jaggars-Chiles-Stovall after he picked it up at the post office, showed it to him.[5] Oswald is even acting like a man from Texas, which place, after all, is not one of the fifty states so much as a separate nation with specific customs: An offering of friendship is to show your neighbor the rifle you have just acquired.

Now came the cleaning of his weapon. To the degree that one sees one's rifle as a loyal servant—if treated properly—cleaning one's gun becomes a sacramental act. One is imbuing the wood of the stock and the metal of the barrel with nothing less than an infusion of one's own dedication. The axiom is basic: The more one cleans a piece, the more accurately it will shoot; but then, every gun lover is a closet mystic. It is one reason that congressmen are terrified of the National Rifle Association. Not many politicians understand mystics, and not many politicians like what they do not understand.

> *From an FBI report:* MARINA . . . said she can now recall that OSWALD cleaned his rifle on about four or five occasions during the short period of time which elapsed from the time he acquired the rifle in March, 1963, until his attempted assassination of General WALKER. [She also] said it would have been entirely possible for him to have practiced on any of the times he was away from the house ostensibly attending school and if he had practiced on such occasions, it would have been without her knowledge.[6]

From April 1 on, Oswald attended no more typing classes, but did not inform Marina.[7]

> *From an FBI report:* . . . He had his rifle wrapped in a raincoat and told MARINA he was going to practice firing with the

rifle. She remonstrated with him. She said the police would get him. He replied he was going anyway and it was none of her business. He did not say where he was going to practice firing the rifle, other than he was going to a vacant spot . . .[8]

To Marina, he looked so suspicious. Every time he took his rifle out of the house, he would wear a dark green military overcoat even if the weather in Dallas was unseasonably warm. That was because he could walk along carrying the rifle under his green coat.

At night he would call out in his sleep, and say things in English she could not understand; then he would mumble and seem frightened. He was certainly afraid of something. She never did know where and how he practiced. Afterward, people would say it had to be at the Trinity River, which had a levee thirty-five feet high that you could use as a backstop for bullets.

In fact, she tried to keep her distance from the rifle and never went near it when she cleaned. Who knew? It could go off![9]

On the last day in March, a Sunday, Lee had Marina photograph him in their backyard. He was dressed in a black shirt and black pants and dark cowboy boots. He held his rifle in his left hand, his pistol in a holster on his hip and he had *The Worker* and *The Militant* in his right hand. For years, those famous photographs Marina took on that day were under suspicion by Warren Commission critics. They looked to be doctored. His head sits at an odd angle to his neck, and the shadow under his nose is vertical while the shadow of his body slants away at an angle. These anomalies are so evident that in 1964, a good lawyer could have created real doubt in a jury's mind whether the body of the man holding the gun belonged to Oswald. By now, simulated photographs taken at the same time of day and year in Dallas have been able to produce the identical discrepancies in the shadows. Even though only one of the original negatives was ever found, microscopic analysis of the grain in this negative shows that head and body belong to the same man. Moreover, grain analysis of the prints for which no negatives were found indicates that they were printed from the same roll that contained the negative that was found. The prevailing conclusion is, then, that the photographs are real, and Marina took them. The most novel supposition left to us now is that some instinct which had developed in Oswald from working all those months in an enlarging room at Jaggars-Chiles-Stovall now told him to cant his neck at an odd angle. Who can know how much filigree he puts, consciously and/or unconsciously, into his scenarios?

Marina's reactions, thirty years later, to this odd Sunday morning of taking photographs are still of interest. There was Lee! Dressed all in black—an idiot! When she was asked how many times she pressed her shutter, she said, "Three at least," but then, when she was asked if it might have been five or six times, she added, "I don't know." After she took two pictures, he said, "Once again," then he said, "Wait, it's not finished yet," and changed his position so that the outside stairs of their apartment would now be to his left. She asked him, "Why are you wearing that stupid outfit?" and he said, "For posterity." She told him, "Yes, it will be very nice for children to remember all that, standing there with all those guns," and he just mumbled some stupid excuse. His voice was embarrassed even, so obviously dumb.

Still, he'd been very careful to choose a good hour when they took pictures. He didn't want any neighbors to see him standing in the backyard with a rifle and a pistol. So he listened and waited until their neighbors left for church—then he said, "Okay, let's do it now before they return."

It was probably on the Monday following this Sunday that he lost his job:

MR. GRAEF. . . . I said, "Lee, come on back, I would like to talk to you." So, we went back, and I said, "Lee, I think this is as good a time as any to cut it short." I said, "Business is pretty slow at this time, but the point is that you haven't been turning the work out like you should. There has been friction with other people," and so on.

MR. JENNER. What did he say when you said that?

MR. GRAEF. Nothing. And I said, "This is, I think, the best time to just make a break of it." I believe I gave him a few days . . .

And there was no outburst on his part. He took this the whole time looking at the floor, I believe, and after I was through, he said, "Well, thank you." And he turned around and walked off.[10]

He might even have seen it as one more favorable sign. Free of his job, he would have more time to prepare for Walker.

Graef's best recollection is that Oswald was given this notice on Friday, March 29, or on April 1, a Monday, and Lee continued to work through Saturday, April 6, which is a perfect example of how essential chronology is to motive. For if Oswald was fired on March 29, he might well have reacted by asking Marina to take the photographs of himself with rifle and revolver on March 31, whereas if he was given notice on Monday, April 1, the two events are considerably less well connected, and all we can assume is that there was a glint in Oswald's eye while he was listening to Graef: To hell with being fired—just let me get back to the darkroom and develop those negatives. In his last week at Jaggars-Chiles-Stovall, he still puts in overtime, but then, he probably wants to leave a little money for Marina if all goes wrong.

General Walker was also a romantic. He had called his five-week lecture tour Operation Midnight Ride. Since he was coming back to Dallas on Monday, April 8, Oswald, a day or two before the General's return, took his rifle and went out to the area near Walker's house on Turtle Creek Boulevard and, presumably, buried it close to some railroad tracks a half mile away. Scouting the Mormon church next to Walker's house, he then saw a notice of services on Wednesday night and most probably concluded that the presence of a stranger on Turtle Creek Boulevard, or in the alley parallel to it, would seem less suspicious if he made his attempt on that same night, Wednesday, April 10.

We have to assume that Oswald has found some kind of blind among the bushes in the alley behind Walker's house so that he can look across the backyard from his concealed post and see into Walker's windows. Presumably, the General, obligingly, will come into view.

> *McMillan:* On the morning of Wednesday, April 10, Marina thought Lee looked pensive and rather sad. With tears in his eyes, he confessed at last that he had lost his job. "I don't know why," he said. "I tried. I liked that work so much. But probably the FBI came and asked about me, and the boss just didn't want to keep someone the FBI was interested in. When *will* they leave me alone?"
>
> Marina ached with sympathy. She had no idea how to comfort him; and when he went out for the day she supposed he was looking for work. He was dressed in his good gray suit and a clean white shirt.[11]

On the night of April 10, when Oswald arrives in the alley, we do not know how long he has to wait, but he is able to draw a bead on

General Walker, who, conveniently, is sitting at a desk in a well-lit room with no drapes drawn, no shades down. Of course, we cannot know whether Oswald went for nervous walks and came back, having concealed his rifle in shrubbery each time, or, indeed, whether his blind was so well concealed that he could sit and wait for the half hour or hour it took until Walker happened to come to his desk. Of course, if one wishes to see Oswald's actions on this night as a piece of choreography inspired by Destiny, it is not impossible that Walker was at his desk as Oswald arrived. There he sat, an impeccable model for the crosshairs on Oswald's scope.

Lee fired and took off without stopping to see whether he had hit his target or not. That alone can give us a sense of how much caterwauling anxiety had come pouring in on him with the pull of the trigger.

Thirty years later, Marina can no longer remember whether or not he came home for supper on April 10—she seems to think he did not—but in any event, she very much remembers being alone at 8:00 P.M. and putting June to bed. By nine and ten o'clock, her ears preternaturally sensitive to every passing sound outside on lonely, shabby Neely Street, Marina's condition at that hour deserves a name; *mate-dread,* one is tempted to call it. Nearness to a person gives all the intimations we don't wish to have of how unstable he or she is, especially since he or she is not at home and yet feels so near to one's senses as to make it certain that something is wrong, fearfully wrong.

By ten, she can no longer bear it. She invades his oversized closet, his *sanctum sanctorum.* On the writing table is a sheet of paper with a key placed on top of it. "Farewell!" says the mute presence of the key. As she would later tell the FBI, "[My] hair stood on end."[12] She picked up the paper and read what he had written. It comes down to us in good stiff English furnished by Secret Service translators, who straightened out whatever was ungrammatical in the suspect's Russian.

> This is the key to the mailbox which is located in the main post office in the city on Ervay Street. This is the same street where the drugstore, in which you always waited, is located. You will find the mailbox in the post office which is located 4 blocks from the drugstore on that street. I paid for the box last month so don't worry about it.

2. Send the information as to what happened to me to the [Russian] Embassy and include newspaper clippings (should there be anything about me in the newspapers.) I believe the Embassy will come quickly to your assistance on learning everything.

3. I paid the house rent on the 2nd so don't worry about it.

4. Recently I also paid for water and gas.

5. The money from work will possibly be coming. The money will be sent to our post office box. Go to the bank and cash the check.

6. You can either throw out or give my clothing, etc., away. Do not keep these. However, I prefer that you hold onto my personal papers (military, civil, etc.).

7. Certain of my documents are in the small blue valise.

8. The address book can be found on my table in the study should you need same.

9. We have friends here. The Red Cross also will help you.

10. I left you as much money as I could, $60 . . . You and [June] can live for another 2 months using $10 per week.

11. If I am alive and taken prisoner, the city jail is located at the end of the bridge through which we always passed on going to the city . . .[13]

9

Stoicism, Majestic in Purpose

In the depths of Oswald's logic lies an equation: Any man who is possessed of enough political passion to reach murderous intensity in his deeds is entitled to a seat at the high table of world leaders. Such may have been Oswald's measure. The route to becoming a great political leader—given his own poor beginnings—might have to pass through acts of assassination.

As we can see by his note to Marina, he was more or less prepared to be captured or to die. So, he had not only assembled the integument of his art—the plans, photographs, bus schedules, and his farewell letter—but had also attempted to give a presentation of his political thought. He was not only possessor of a unique rank, Private-General, but looked to hold the desk of Philosopher-General.

Under the burden of not knowing whether his social ideas would soon be read with the respect one gives to the last words of a dead man or used as a text in his trial—his defense would be political!—or, meanest option of them all, would end as no more than a few more notes written to himself (especially if he had no opportunity to fix his sights on Walker, or, worse, lost his nerve), he chose to print his message out by hand, and it appears with relatively few errors among his other papers.

What follows is a good portion of the several parts of this credo. He was but five years ahead of his time—which is to say that by 1968 he would not have felt so prodigiously alone. By then, in Haight-Ashbury, many of his formulations would have seemed reasonable. Hippies were moving up into Northern California and Oregon to found small societies on principles much like his. Indeed, what Oswald offers seems more a libertarian pronouncement than a radical call to arms, a menu of fifteen one-sentence programs large and small for the free man of the future.

The Atheian system

A system opposed to Communism, Socialism, and capitalism.

1. Democracy at a local level with no centralized State.
    A. That the right of free enterprise and collective enterprise be guaranteed.
    B. That Fascism be abolished.
    C. That nationalism be excluded from every-day life.
    D. That racial segregation or discrimination be abolished by law.
    E. the right of the free, uninhibited action of religious institutions of any type or denomination to freely function
    G. Universal Suffrage for all persons over 18 years of age.
    H. Freedom of dissemination of opinions through press or declaration or speech.
    I. that the dissemination of war propaganda be forbidden as well as the manufacture of weapons of mass destruction.

J. that Free compulsory education be universal till 18.

K. nationalization or communizing of private enterprise or collective enterprise be forbidden.

L. that monopoly practices be considered as capitalistic.

M. That combining of separate collective or private enterprises into single collective units be considered as communistic.

N. That no taxes be levied against individuals.

O. That heavy graduated taxes of from 30% to 90% be leveled against surplus profit gains.

R. that taxes be collected by a single ministry subordinate to individual communities. that taxes be used solely for the building or improvement of public projects.[1]

He is mounting a pincers attack on the status quo. With his Atheian system, he will look to reach the mass of Americans—that is one arm of the attack. He is also looking to abolish the largest obstacle to a new and powerful party of the left in America, nothing less than the Communist Party.

Only by declaring itself to be, not only not dependent upon, but *opposed* to, Soviet domination and influence, can dormant and disillusioned persons hope to unite to free the radical movement from its inertia.

Through the refusal of the Communist Party U.S.A. to give a clear cut condemnation of Soviet piratical acts, progressives have been weakened into a stale class of fifth columnists of the Russians.

In order to free the hesitating and justifiably uncertain, future activist for the work ahead we must remove that obstacle which has so efficiently retarded him, namely the devotion of the Communist Party U.S.A., to the Soviet Union, Soviet Government, and Soviet Communist International Movement.

It is readily foreseeable that a coming economic, political or military crisis, internal or external, will bring about the final destruction of the capitalist system, assuming this, we can see how preparation in a special party could safeguard an independent course of action after the debacle, an American course . . .[2]

It is time to speak of larger purposes and awesome requirements:

No man, having known, having lived, under the Russian Communist and American capitalist system, could possibly make a choice between them, there is no choice. One offers oppression, the other poverty. Both offer imperialistic injustice, tinted with two brands of slavery.

But no rational man can take the attitude of "a curse on both your houses." There *are* two world systems, one twisted beyond recognition by its misuse, the other decadent and dying in its final evolution.

A truly democratic system would combine the better qualities of the two upon an American foundation, opposed to both world systems as they are now.

This then is our goal.[3]

Yet, Oswald does not wish to frighten everybody away. It is time for a disclaimer. Since he has learned (the hard way) that very few human beings will rush to take up arms against both world systems, one must hint that there will be help from the cosmos.

We have no interest in violently opposing the U.S. Government, why should we manifest opposition when there are far greater forces at work to bring about the fall of the United States Government than we could ever possibly muster.

We do not have any interest in directly assuming the head of Government in the event of such an all-finishing crisis.[4]

Has there ever been a dictator who did not issue comparable statements in the early years of his revolution?

Lee Harvey Oswald will, however, underline the dedication necessary for those who would choose to be part of the Atheian system:

. . . only the intellectually fearless could even be remotely attracted to our doctrine, yet this doctrine requires the utmost restraint, a state of being in itself majestic in power.

This is stoicism, and yet stoicism has not been effected for many years, and never for such a purpose.[5]

And then, because he is Oswald, and cannot be content unless he can even cheat on his own system, he adds a coda to these presentations:

sale of arms   pistols should not be sold
in any case, rifles only
with police permission,
shotguns free.[6]

Yes, these have been his writings in his time of preparation for
terminating the life of Edwin A. Walker.

10

Waiting for the Police

From an FBI report: She advised that about midnight that
night, OSWALD came rushing into the house in a very agitated
and excited state and his face was very pale. As soon as he
entered the house, he turned on the radio. Later he laid
down on the bed and MARINA again noticed how pale he was.
She asked him what was wrong and he confessed to her that
he had tried to kill General WALKER by shooting at him with a
rifle but didn't know whether he had hit him or not. He said
he wanted to find out on the radio . . . MARINA said she became angry with OSWALD for shooting at General WALKER and
he replied to her that General WALKER was the leader of the
fascist organization here and it was best to remove him . . .
   She stated OSWALD did not have the rifle with him when he
returned to the house . . .[1]

Thirty years later, this is the way she recalls his return to their
apartment on Neely Street:
   He was out of breath. He was back—yet he was not. Still somewhere else. She showed him the note he had left, and he said,
"Don't ask me about that." He turned on their radio. Nothing was
there for him. She kept asking questions, and he kept saying,
"Don't bother me." She went to bed and lay waiting for him, and
now she can't remember what time it was—but he was still in the

other room, still waiting to hear something on that radio. Then he turned it off. He looked shocked. "I missed."

She said, "What are you talking about?"

He told her, "I thought I'd shot General Walker."

Of course, she jumped out of bed. "Are you crazy? What right do you have? Who is General Walker?"

He said, "Look how many people would have been spared if somebody had eliminated Hitler."

He told her that General Walker was a pro-Nazi kind of person. A fascist.

She said he had no right to eliminate anybody.

He repeated himself. He said, "Look how many people would have been spared if that had been done to Hitler."

She said, "Maybe it was good for Hitler's time, but not right now. Not in America. Change your system."

It is an odd, near-improbable conversation. He has just found out that he missed. An unlikely miss. He had been thirty-five yards away. He had been looking at Walker through a four-power scope. In the crosshairs, Walker's head was large. One could not miss. As soon as he had squeezed the trigger, Lee had been off and running. And with what fear! Walker's bodyguards might catch him if he remained long enough to take a second shot. So he had run— exaltation must have accompanied his fear.

Then he buried the rifle—in what a fever!—came home, and waited for confirmation. Now, the radio had told him that he missed. His anguish has to be intense: Once again he is the sorriest Marine in the training platoon. At that moment, he blurts out the truth. He has to tell someone that he has taken a shot at Walker. And missed!

The conversation about Hitler is not as easy to believe. Not for that moment. Perhaps Marina misremembers and it took place next day. Since we cannot know, let us go back to her account:

According to Marina, he soon fell asleep. He looked exhausted. Like a dead man. She began to walk around, just as she had been pacing for hours before he came home. Once again, she was listening to the night outside. Such a quiet street. She remembers thinking that at any minute police would be banging on their door. She had no idea if he had done it alone or with others—he never gave her one detail. She did ask him where his rifle was now, and he answered, "I left it where it will not be found."

She looked at him asleep and got in beside him, but he took up all the bed. He was spread out, arms and legs extended, his bare bottom up, his backside open to the night air.

GENERAL WALKER. . . . It was right at 9 o'clock and most of the lights were on in the house and the shades were up. I was sitting down behind a desk facing out from a corner, with my head over a pencil and paper working on my income tax when I heard a blast and a crack right over my head.

MR. LIEBELER. What did you do then?

GENERAL WALKER. I thought—we had been fooling with the screens on the house and I thought that possibly somebody had thrown a firecracker . . . Then I looked around and saw that the screen was not out, but was in the window, and . . . I noticed there was a hole in the wall, so I went upstairs and got a pistol and came back down and went out the back door, taking a look to see what might have happened.

MR. LIEBELER. Did you find anything outside that you could relate to this attack on you?

GENERAL WALKER. No, sir; I couldn't. As I crossed a window coming downstairs in front, I saw a car at the bottom of the church alley just making a turn onto Turtle Creek. The car was unidentifiable. I could see the two back lights, and you have to look through trees there, and I could see it moving out. This car would have been about at the right time for anybody that was making a getaway.[2]

When Walker had discussed it with the police, one of them said, "He couldn't have missed you."

GENERAL WALKER. . . . But as I later was analyzing the thing, [that rifleman] couldn't see from his position any of the lattice work either in the window or in the screens because of the light. It would have looked [to him] like one big lighted area, and he could have been a very good shot and just by chance he hit the woodwork.

MR. LIEBELER. Which he did in fact?

GENERAL WALKER. Which he did, and there was enough deflection in it to miss me, except for slivers of the bullet, the casing of the bullet, that went into my arm laying on the desk—slivers of the shell jacket.[3]

Walker had seen a car go down the alley, and a fourteen-year-old neighbor, Kirk Coleman, was reported to have seen two cars. Having heard the shot, he went out to a fence in the back of his house, looked down the alley, and "saw one man putting something in the trunk of a Ford sedan and a few feet away, a second man getting into another car. Both cars then raced away."[4]

From a Secret Service interview with Marina: . . . Lee Oswald told her, after reading in the papers that some young man saw an automobile containing three men pulling away from the scene of the shooting, that the Americans always think they [need] a car to get away from the scene of a crime and that he would rather use his feet to do so than to have a car. He also told her that he took buses to go to the Walker residence and that he took a different bus to return home after the shooting.[5]

On the following night, Lee had anxiety attacks. He never did wake up, but two times, even three times an hour, he would begin to shake and to tremble beside her.

McMillan: . . . She was afraid, terrified, that he would take another shot . . .
   Marina immediately began to beg Lee . . . [never to] do such a thing again. She told him that . . . it had been a sign from fate. "If God saved him this time, He will save him again. It is not fated for this man to die. Promise me you'll never, ever do it again."
   "I promise."[6]

With her good Russian soul, how could she not believe that Providence showed itself most clearly in those awesome moments when no one had any idea how things would turn out? "Promise me," she had asked, and if Marina's memory is correct, he did reply, "I promise." Perhaps it was his belief as well.
   Providence is Providence, but we have not accounted for the cars. Gerald Posner in *Case Closed* comes close to disposing of the issue:

Contrary to press reports that [the fourteen-year-old] saw two men get into separate cars and race away, he told the FBI that he only saw one car leave, and it moved at a normal rate of speed. At least six other cars were in the parking lot at the same time. Other neighbors contradicted Coleman's story, saying no cars left after the noise.[7]

It is the fundamental principle of evidence. If one witness says "A," you can always find another to say "Z."

Still, the odds are that Oswald made his attempt on Walker with no confederates. Indeed, the essay into his motive for shooting at Walker would be seriously flawed if Oswald did not do it alone. Yet, it is just as well to recognize that this narrative is an exploration into the possibilities of his character rather than a conviction that one holds the solution.

There is, after all, a possibility that other people besides Oswald had a motive to kill Walker. There are puzzling aspects to Oswald's attempt. Unless someone inside Walker's house was ready to steer the General at a given moment to a chair in front of a lighted window with no shades, how long would Oswald have had to wait until by chance Walker came into view? If it had taken hours, how could Oswald have remained unnoticed for so long? (Of course, hiding in a parked car while waiting does serve such a purpose.) The police did find a nick in the freshly painted fence that separated the alley from Walker's backyard, and concluded that the gunman had rested his rifle there—the position conformed to the trajectory of the shot—but, of course, firing from one side of a fence, back exposed to passing onlookers in the alley, hardly sounds like a concealed blind.[8]

It can be argued that in the course of his preparations, Oswald had scouted the house and knew Walker's habits, but that is not likely. Walker was away on his tour until Monday, April 8, two days before the attempt. The only conclusion, if Oswald managed it by himself, running entirely on his own schedule, is that he went to Walker's house on Wednesday night to shoot him, and there was the General in full collaboration. As stated earlier: Luck! Of course, luck may be the product of extra-sensory perception in crucial areas, and Oswald may be an unhappy example of a man with extraordinary luck.

Let us not banish, however, the possibility that certain extreme right-wingers had come to the conclusion that General Edwin A.

Walker was not only eminently expendable but would be of much more use to his movement as a dead martyr than as a live embarrassment whose secret homosexual life was bound sooner or later to be exposed. Life, however, moves on a more dilatory schedule than paranoia, and it was only in the eighties that Walker, by then close to eighty himself, solicited a vice-squad cop in a men's room, was arrested, and his lifelong homosexuality became common knowledge. Yet, his closet life was no secret in the circles close to Walker. The John Birch Society obviously had a problem.

Add one more observation: If the dedicated spirit of the Cold War encouraged the CIA to enter serious relations with the Mafia in order to assassinate Fidel Castro, why not assume that fantastical operations, if on a smaller scale, were being developed all over the Sun Belt? In the mountains, caves, and swamps of America, and in big cities like Miami, New Orleans, and Dallas, the warriors-for-liberty were gathering. A decision to assassinate Walker might have been one step in a serious set of moves to take over the John Birch Society.

MR. JENNER. Now, Mr. Surrey, was there an occasion preceding April 10, 1963, that you noticed an automobile and some people in the automobile in and about General Walker's premises?

MR. SURREY. . . . April 8; yes, sir . . . the gist of the matter is that two nights before the assassination attempt, I saw two men around the house peeking in windows and so forth, and reported this to the General the following morning, and he, in turn, reported it to the police on Tuesday, and it was Wednesday night that he was shot at. So that is really the gist of the whole thing.[9]

It is, of course, a huge jump in our comprehension of Oswald to believe he is now part of a right-wing conspiracy; we have no trace of connections to such people in that period of his life. On the other hand, from October 1962 to April 1963, there have to be a hundred, if not two hundred, hours that no one (certainly not Marina) can account for. Who knows what he did and whom he met in that time? We have, for example, no idea whether Lee and Yaeko Okui were having a romance or were cooperating in one or another intelligence function; or, for all we know, Yaeko saw him but once, at the Christmas party, and that was all there was to it. Still, one would add a footnote from Edward Epstein:

When interviewed in Tokyo in 1976, Okui said that she did not remember the subject of her conversation with Oswald, but that the one brief contact with him "ruined her life." She would not elaborate further.[10]

We have constructed a portrait of Oswald as a solitary man, but he has his sides—as we shall see in New Orleans. In any event, a man who can have congress with Stalinist and Trotskyite organizations at the same time when they have been implacable enemies for close to three decades, may be ready to deal with any political contradiction if it will advance his purpose. Moreover, some ultra-right-wingers do not sound like reactionaries but libertarians; that, on the evidence of the Atheian credo, appealed to Oswald. It is certainly safe to believe he did wish to kill Walker, but it does not follow automatically that he thought he could do it without help.

There is a famous photograph Lee took of Walker's backyard that shows a parked car with a hole in the print large enough to obliterate the license plate. Posner points out:

> A photo of evidence taken from Oswald's flat after the assassination shows the hole was in the print at that time. Also, the photo was taken from such a distance that the license plate of the car would not have been legible in any case, and it was later determined that the car belonged to a Walker aide . . .[11]

It is a large assumption that the "license plate would not have been legible in any case." Oswald worked at Jaggars-Chiles-Stovall, where high-quality lenses that maintained image detail in extreme enlargements were used every day. It is not impossible that he recognized the car in the photograph as one he had been riding in with a confederate: In a moment of anxiety, he could have cut out the license plate. It is also possible that he did it for no reason at all—just, in case he was caught, to confound the authorities, wear them out, send them off on false leads. He was a veteran in wars against bureaucracy and knew that the way to win was to exhaust the foe. Bureaucracies, after all, exercised power by wearing their adversaries out, and Oswald understood that rare is the sadist who is ready to receive the kind of punishment he is ready to mete out—a spiritual fact!—so, fatigue the authorities. It is worth remembering that in life, as in other mysteries, there are no answers, only questions, but part of the pleasure of intellection is to refine the question, or discover a new one. It is analogous to the fact that there are no facts—only the mode of our approach to what we call facts.

The only conclusion we can come to here is that Oswald almost certainly did shoot at Walker, and was probably alone, but there are bits of puzzling and conflicting evidence which make it impossible to decide definitively that he made the attempt without confederates.

11

Telescopic Sight

From an FBI report: MARINA said she had asked OSWALD . . . what he had done with the rifle because she was worried lest he had left it somewhere where it would be found. OSWALD said he had buried the rifle in the ground far from the actual spot of the shooting. He then mentioned a field and the fact that the field was near a railroad track.

She . . . recalls OSWALD returned to the NEELY Street home with the rifle wrapped in a raincoat on the Sunday following the [Wednesday] night of the assassination attempt.[1]

Having hidden his farewell letter in her Russian cookbook, she was now in a position to warn him that if he ever wanted to play games again with his rifle, she would go to the police. Until such a terrible time, the letter, she assumed, would be safe.

She did not feel as secure about his notes on General Walker's house and the accompanying bus schedules.

MARINA OSWALD. . . . I was so afraid after this attempt on Walker's life that . . . there would be evidence in the house such as this book.

MR. LIEBELER. Did you talk to Lee about it?

MARINA OSWALD. Oh, yes . . . I suggested to him that it would be awfully bad to keep a thing like that in the house.[2]

It appears that this is one time when he did listen to his wife.

McMillan: . . . next thing she knew he was standing by the toilet with some sheets of paper in his hand and a box of matches. Slowly he tore the sheets in half, crumpled them into balls, and one by one touched a match to them. As each ball of paper caught the flames, he dropped it into the toilet. He did this thoughtfully, with great reluctance, as if it were the funeral pyre of his ideas. But . . . [he] did not burn the handwritten pages which contained his political philosophy and program . . . Marina had seen how reluctant he had been to burn his papers. "I wonder if he burned them," she asked herself, "because he does not trust *me?*"[3]

A few days earlier, however, he had been in a manic mood:

McMillan: The Dallas papers of Thursday, April 11, ran front-page stories about the attempt on Walker's life. Lee left the apartment to buy both morning and afternoon editions . . .

Reading [them], Lee roared with laughter. "Americans are so spoiled!" he said, proud of his escape. "It never occurs to them that you might use your own two legs . . ."[4]

. . . Lee was astonished at how easily he got off and at the ineptness of the police. They had the bullet, yet they identified it wrongly and wrongly identified the rifle from which it was fired.[5]

Here, Patricia Johnson McMillan offers a salient perception:

He had tried something cataclysmic—and he had not been caught. He had not even been touched.

Thus by far the greatest legacy Lee carried out of the Walker attempt was the conviction that he was invulnerable, that he stood at the center of a magic circle swathed in a cloak of immunity. It was a feeling which fitted dangerously with the feeling he already had that he was special, that he had particular prerogatives. He and he alone was entitled to that which was forbidden to everybody else.[6]

McMillan seems to assume that such beliefs, once arrived at, are as permanent as concrete, whereas the likelihood is that Oswald frequently wavered in his idea of himself, prey at any given moment to puncture or depression. Those of his actions that seem most irrational or needlessly ugly have to be attempts to defend his faith in his powers. He would slap Marina for a small remark because if he accepted her last reductive statement—whatever it was; it could be no more than "You are stupid" or "You are a baby"—his ego would be punctured. Depression would come in a flood. We have to keep reminding ourselves of the great weight he bore. He believed he was the only man alive who could make a profound difference in how the future would be shaped; yet he was dyslexic and half in love with a woman who did not respect him; worse, she was ready, as he saw it, to go over to the enemy. On top of that, he had just lost the only job he ever liked.

Yes, he is in a most changeable state in the first few days after the attempt on Walker, and into the middle of this come the De Mohrenschildts again. An odd little business occurs:

> *From an FBI report:* MARINA said that a few days after the assassination [attempt,] GEORGE DE MOHRENSCHILDT was in their home on NEELY Street and made a joking remark to OSWALD to the effect, "How is it that you missed General WALKER?"[7]

Naturally, the Warren Commission had to take this up. To their question on this point came the following answer:

> MARINA OSWALD. De Mohrenschildt—as soon as he opened the door—he said to Lee, "How could you have missed, how could you have missed him?" . . . Lee could not speak that evening. [Later he] asked me if I had told De Mohrenschildt about it and when I said I didn't, he said, "How did he guess it?"[8]

Even thirteen years later, George was still counting his losses on that particular statement by Marina. In his Warren Commission testimony, he would go so far as to admit that he had said, "Did you take a pot shot at General Walker, Lee?" but that is not quite the same as "How could you have missed?" In 1977, De Mohrenschildt would write, "This innocuous remark of mine influenced our lives."

It is enough to account for his animus toward Marina. By 1967, he would lose his sinecure in Haiti, and would attribute part of the damage to her.

Let us try to follow it through. We can begin with George's testimony in 1964:

MR. DE MOHRENSCHILDT. And Jeanne told me that day, "Let's go and take a rabbit for Oswald's baby."

MR. JENNER. This was on Easter Sunday?

MR. DE MOHRENSCHILDT. . . . I don't remember if it was Easter Sunday . . . Maybe my wife will remember the date exactly. And so we drove over quite late in the evening and walked up—I think they were asleep. They were asleep and we knocked at the door and shouted, and Lee Oswald came down undressed, half undressed, you see, maybe in shorts, and opened the door and we told him that we have the rabbit for the child. And it was a very short visit, you know. We just gave the rabbit to the baby and I was talking to Lee while Jeanne was talking to Marina . . . Oswald and I were standing near the window looking outside and I was asking him, "How is your job?" or "Are you making any money? Are you happy?" some question of that type. All of a sudden, Jeanne who was with Marina in the other room told me, "Look, George, they have a gun here." And Marina opened the closet and showed it to Jeanne, a gun that belonged obviously to Oswald.

MR. JENNER. This was a weapon? Did you go in and look?

MR. DE MOHRENSCHILDT. No . . . Jeanne was looking at it, the gun, and . . . Marina said, "That crazy idiot is target shooting all the time." So frankly I thought it was ridiculous to [go] target shooting in Dallas, you see, right in town. I asked him, "Why do you do that?" [and he said,] "I like target shooting." So out of the pure, really jokingly, I told him, "Are you then the guy who took a pot shot at General Walker?" And he . . . sort of shriveled, you see, when I asked this question . . . and didn't answer anything, smiled, you know, made a sarcastic—not sarcastic, made a peculiar face . . . Changed the expression on his face.

MR. JENNER. [Do you recall that] as soon as you opened the door, you said, "Lee, how is it possible that you missed?"

MR. DE MOHRENSCHILDT. Never. I don't recall that incident . . . I remember very distinctly saying, "Did you take the pot shot at General Walker?"[9]

The likelihood is that he and Jeanne have prepared a story. As Jeanne will establish, their visit was at ten o'clock on Saturday night, April 13, three days after the attempt. The gun, however, was not in the closet at that time.

According to Marina, the rifle was only retrieved from Lee's hiding place near the railroad tracks on Sunday, but if, indeed, the weapon was back by Saturday night, it was still not in the closet because, according to Marina, Lee hid it again after he brought it back. Saturday, after all, was the day when Marina, in panic, had convinced him to destroy his Walker papers. But even if Marina's testimony is incorrect and the gun was in the closet, would Marina, of all people, have been so careless as to offer Jeanne a look at it so soon after the shooting?

The larger possibility is that Jeanne De Mohrenschildt had paid another, and earlier, visit to Marina, on April 5, five days before the attack on Walker. On that occasion, George was in New York, working out some final details concerning their trip to Haiti, and Jeanne, having quit her job in preparation for departure, had enough free time in the afternoon to drive over to Neely Street and drop in on Marina. While she was in the Oswalds' apartment, Marina, according to McMillan, opened a clothes closet and showed Lee's rifle to Jeanne:

> *McMillan:* "Look at that!" Marina said. "We have barely enough to eat and my crazy husband goes and buys a rifle." She told Jeanne that Lee had been practicing with it.
>
> Jeanne's father had been a gun collector . . . Instantly she spotted something: . . . Lee's gun had a telescopic sight . . . [When] George got back from New York, she seems to have told him that poor as the Oswalds were, Lee had bought a rifle with a scope and had been practicing.[10]

McMillan's description of the event, since it offers no citation, had to have come from Marina. During Jeanne's Warren Commission testimony, she claims not to be able to recognize a telescopic sight, but then her story is hardly convincing, since she admits she loves skeet shooting. While that is hardly the same as target practice with a rifle and scope, still the likely supposition is that after the visit on April 5, Jeanne has decided to admit neither to this visit nor to the telescopic sight. For if she did, it would then seem logical to any interrogator to ask whether she did not tell George all about it when he returned from New York, and that would mean that George knew before there was an attempt on General Walker that Oswald was in possession of a high-powered rifle with scope. Such knowledge would almost certainly have to be imparted quickly to his case officer.

Let us look at Jeanne's testimony and see if we can locate the lies and the blurring of detail that she is obliged to offer up in order to conceal her visit on April 5 to Marina. It is crucial that the Warren Commission not discover that she and George knew about the rifle in advance:

MR. JENNER. Now, something occurred in Easter, 1963, when you went to visit them?

MRS. DE MOHRENSCHILDT. Yes.

MR. JENNER. Was this Easter Sunday or the day after?

MRS. DE MOHRENSCHILDT. No, to my best recollection it was Saturday before Easter. By the way, the first time [the FBI] talked to us about it, I completely mixed all the dates. I thought it was in the fall. But it was the day I [now] remember when we came over with the big pink rabbit for the baby.

MR. JENNER. Did you arrive there during the day?

MRS. DE MOHRENSCHILDT. No; it was in the evening. I think we were playing tennis, and then we were somewhere, and then I decided we will be busy tomorrow, and I wanted to take the rabbit to the baby . . .[11]

Already she has established that her memory is so poor that she cannot separate fall from spring. Yet she also recalls that it was Saturday night before Easter Sunday. Her difficulty is that she does not know how much Jenner or the Warren Commission knows, or how precise Marina has been in her testimony. Given such doubt, it is best to blur her recollections wherever she can:

MRS. DE MOHRENSCHILDT. . . . and we came over late at night. It was 10 o'clock or maybe later. And I remember they gave us something to drink.

MR. JENNER. You arrived there. Were they—had they retired for the night?

MRS. DE MOHRENSCHILDT. I think they were halfway in bed already, because the house was dark. I remember we banged on the door. It was dark.

MR. JENNER. And Lee came to the door?

MRS. DE MOHRENSCHILDT. I don't remember who came to the door, Marina or Lee . . .[12]

It is more likely that the De Mohrenschildts are arriving late on purpose. They wish to wake the Oswalds up. They want to catch them by surprise. If De Mohrenschildt knows already that Lee has a rifle and scope, then we can assume there may have been a directive from George's case officer to find out, if he could, whether Oswald had taken a shot at Walker.

So, when the question of an earlier visit comes up, Jeanne does her best to deny that she was there on Neely Street before April 13, yet she is careful not to commit herself altogether.

MR. JENNER. Had you been there before?

MRS. DE MOHRENSCHILDT. No.

MR. JENNER. That is the first time you had ever been there?

MRS. DE MOHRENSCHILDT. I don't remember. Maybe I was. I don't think so.

MR. JENNER. All right.

MRS. DE MOHRENSCHILDT. I don't think so.

MR. JENNER. You got there. No, just relax—

MRS. DE MOHRENSCHILDT. I am trying to think hard because every little fact could be important.

MR. JENNER. But you are excited. Relax, and tell me everything that occurred, chronologically, as best you can on that occasion. You came to the door and either Marina or Oswald came to the door, and you and your husband went in the home?

MRS. DE MOHRENSCHILDT. That is right.

MR. JENNER. Then, go on. Tell me about it.

MRS. DE MOHRENSCHILDT. And I believe from what I remember George sat down on the sofa and started talking to Lee, and Marina was showing me the house—that is why I said it looks like it was the first time, because why would she show me the house if I had been there before? Then we went to another room and she opens the closet, and I see the gun standing there. I said, what is the gun doing over there?[13]

Now come the disclaimers on the telescopic sight. She admits to shooting skeet and loving to use a rifle in an amusement park, because she knows that one of the émigrés might mention as much, yet she maintains her fiction concerning the telescopic sight:

MR. JENNER. And then other things that arrested your attention, as I gather from what you have said, is that you saw a telescopic sight?

MRS. DE MOHRENSCHILDT. Yes; but I didn't know what it was . . . It was not a smooth, plain rifle. That is for sure.

MR. JENNER. . . . were you concerned about it?

MRS. DE MOHRENSCHILDT. I just asked what on earth is he doing with a rifle?

MR. JENNER. What did she say?

MRS. DE MOHRENSCHILDT. She said, "Oh, he just loves to shoot . . . he goes in the park and he shoots at leaves and things like that." But it didn't strike me too funny, because I personally love skeet shooting . . .

MR. JENNER. Didn't you think it was strange to have someone say he is going in a public park and shooting leaves?

MRS. DE MOHRENSCHILDT. But he was taking the baby out. He goes with her, and that was his amusement . . .[14]

Not only has Marina led her to the gun, but now Lee is using it to shoot leaves! In a public park! If June is with him, presumably other children are in the park as well! Jeanne is doing her best to diminish Oswald's potential for violence in her eyes and, collaterally, in her husband's eyes. Indeed, she will go further than George. She pretends that Oswald did not have a large reaction to her husband's now embattled remark:

MRS. DE MOHRENSCHILDT. . . . George, of course, with his sense of humor . . . said, "Did you take a pot shot at Walker by any chance?" And we started laughing our heads off, big joke, big George's joke . . .

MR. JENNER. Were you looking to see whether [Oswald] had a change of expression?

MRS. DE MOHRENSCHILDT. No; none at all. It was just a joke . . .

MR. JENNER. But did you not look at him to see if he reacted?

MRS. DE MOHRENSCHILDT. No; I didn't take it seriously enough to look at him.[15]

The De Mohrenschildts would leave Dallas on April 19 for New York, Philadelphia, and Washington. In the capital, George would shepherd his patron, Clemard Charles, president of the Banque

Commerciale de Haiti, into a meeting with CIA staff officer Tony
Czaikowski on May 7, 1963. The indication from a CIA liaison officer named Sam Kail was that "Charles might prove useful in ongoing efforts aimed at overthrowing Castro . . ."[16]

> **MR. JENNER.** You returned to Dallas in May?
>
> **MRS. DE MOHRENSCHILDT.** End of May.
>
> **MR. JENNER.** Did you call the Oswalds?
>
> **MRS. DE MOHRENSCHILDT.** No; we didn't. We heard that they were
> already gone . . . we had a card from them in New Orleans with
> their address. But I don't think we ever wrote to them . . . We
> were going to send them a Christmas card.[17]

From Marina's narrative: . . . In the meantime, I decided that
if Lee did not have a job, it would be better to go to a different city. I was also afraid that in Dallas Lee would be very
tempted to repeat his attempt on Walker. I suggested that we
leave for New Orleans—Lee's home town. There he had relatives. I thought he would be ashamed to do the same things
there as he had done in Dallas. I wanted to get as far as possible from the occasion of sin.[18]

George gives one more disclaimer:

> **MR. DE MOHRENSCHILDT.** I repeat again that they were out of my
> mind completely—after the last time we saw them.[19]

It is worth repeating: The nearest we have come to a smoking
gun is Edward Epstein's discovery that the CIA contact reports on
De Mohrenschildt for April and May of 1963 were removed from
the file. Would those contact reports have failed to mention De
Mohrenschildt's probable conclusion that Oswald was the man
who shot at Walker?

In the notes to his book *Legend,* Edward J. Epstein gives us, without citation, this terse piece of information:

> . . . in 1964, George De Mohrenschildt told a friend in
> Houston, Jim Savage, that he had inadvertently given Marina
> the money Oswald used to buy the rifle. Marina said to him
> that spring, "Remember the twenty-five dollars you gave me?
> Well, that fool husband of mine used it to buy a rifle."[20]

Let us add up the damage from the CIA's point of view:

1. A contract agent, George De Mohrenschildt, serving as handler for Oswald, knew in advance that Oswald had a rifle with scope and notified the Agency before April 10.

2. After the Walker episode, De Mohrenschildt was all but convinced that Oswald had been involved in the shooting, and he so notified the Agency. His handlers at Langley now possessed the knowledge that a man in Dallas who had once defected to the Soviet Union had probably taken a shot at General Walker.

3. If De Mohrenschildt also admitted to his case officer that he had given Oswald the money to purchase a rifle with a telescopic sight, then the Agency, in the event this was disclosed, would be damned in the eyes of the media for doing nothing about a putative assassin in Dallas whom they were, at one remove, responsible for arming.

4. If ever confirmed, points 1, 2, and 3 would be small but containable disasters in public relations. Harder to measure was the potential for damage in those missing contact reports. If those papers were ever to be exposed, their routing symbols would reveal which CIA desks had become privy to the knowledge that Oswald was a putative assassin. If the CIA had any suspicions that a few of its people might have been involved in the assassination of JFK—and, indeed, how could they not, given the boiling disaffection at JM/WAVE in Miami over Kennedy's withdrawal of support from Operation Mongoose?—then the routing of De Mohrenschildt's contact reports could show that inside knowledge on Oswald and Walker had reached some of the most unaccountable and hair-trigger of the Agency's enclaves.

Given such fears, how could the contact reports not be removed from the file? If there is real ground to point 4, then the CIA had a great deal more to be concerned about than a spell of bad public relations.

We must leave it here. If there is any connection between these speculative matters and Oswald's adventures in New Orleans, it may well be located in some undefined species of Bermuda Triangle then forming among right-wing money, CIA malcontents, and ex-FBI men. The question, for which there will not be one answer but two, is whether Oswald's activities in New Orleans must then be comprehended on these two different levels: 1) Was everything he did done simply because he was Oswald? Or, 2) to the contrary, was he functioning as a provocateur? Of course, as he would have seen it, he was using the people who were using him.

PART IV

THE BIG EASY

1

"A Terrifically Sad Life"

From an unpublished interview with Marguerite Oswald in 1976:

INTERVIEWER: They said you were very pretty.

MARGUERITE: I was. Very pretty. . . . My hair was absolutely gorgeous. And my teeth . . . Oh, I had pearl teeth. They were just beautiful. They really were. I was very nice looking, like, uh, I have to say it because I really was. . . . My complexion was good and my eyes changed with the color of my clothes, you know, blue, they got blue, green, they got green. And my hair was nice and curly and wavy. I was a very popular young lady.

INTERVIEWER: How much education did you have?

MARGUERITE: None. I only went to high school one year.

INTERVIEWER: Was your husband, Robert E. Lee Oswald, interested in General Robert E. Lee?

MARGUERITE: His mother was.

INTERVIEWER: His mother?

MARGUERITE: [She] was very much in love with him.[1]

An old acquaintance of Lillian Murret and Marguerite Oswald named Myrtle Evans was paid a visit mid-morning on Thursday, May 9, 1963, at her real estate office in New Orleans. It was one day less than a month following the attempt on General Walker's life.

> MRS. EVANS. . . . this young man was at the door and . . . did I have an apartment to rent? . . . I told him I might be able to find something for him, and he told me he had a wife and child over in Texas, and that he was going to bring them over here as soon as he could find something . . .

When we were walking down the steps I looked at him real hardlike, and I didn't recognize him, but something made me ask, "I know you, don't I?" and he said, "Sure; I am Lee Oswald; I was just waiting to see when you were going to recognize me." I said, "Lee Oswald, what are you doing in this country? I thought you were in Russia. I thought you had given up your American citizenship . . ." and he said, "No," he said, "I went over there, but I didn't give up any citizenship." He said he had been back in the States for quite a while, and that he had brought his Russian wife back with him . . . and so I said, "Well, come on, Lee, I don't know anybody that will take children," I said, "but we will just ride up and down the streets and see what we can find." So we rode in and out and all around Baronne and Napoleon and Louisiana Avenue, and Carondelet, you know, just weaving in and out the streets, and looking for any signs of apartments for rent, so we finally rode down Magazine Street . . . and all of a sudden he said, "Oh, there's a sign," and . . . we went up and rang the doorbell, and . . . one apartment was very good for the money . . .

I said, "Lee . . . this is the best you can do" . . . it had a living room that was a tremendous room. . . . and it had a front screened porch, and a yard, and . . . an iron fence, like they use around New Orleans . . . I told Lee to give her the deposit, so she could get the electricity turned on, because he wanted his wife to come for Saturday [two days later. Then we] got in the car and rode on home, and I think I . . . ran to the grocery store too and got a pound of ham and some stuff, and we sat and ate lunch, and he drank a Coke, I think, and we talked, and I asked him, I said, "Well, how does it feel to be back in New Orleans?" and he said, "I have wanted to move back to New Orleans."

He said, "New Orleans is my home."[2]

That conversation brought back quite a bit of the past, and Myrtle Evans thought of how she had not even heard of Lee Oswald's being in Russia until she learned about it by running into Lillian Murret:

MRS. EVANS. . . . . I hadn't seen her in years. I am Catholic and she is Catholic, [and] they had this card party . . . over at the Fontainebleau Motel, and a number of ladies was present, and it was for charity, and we played bingo and canasta . . . and so she said, "Oh, Myrtle, did you hear about Lee, he gave up his American citizenship and went to Russia, behind the Iron Curtain," and I said, "My God, no," and she said, "Yes." . . .

MR. JENNER. Was this the first you knew or had become aware of the fact that Lee Harvey Oswald was living in Russia?

MRS. EVANS. Yes; now, it was undoubtedly in the newspapers and on TV but I sometimes get to doing a million things and I don't get a chance to read a newspaper. . . . So a lot of times I don't know what's going on, but she said . . . "Lee has done gone and given up his United States citizenship," and I said, "Poor Marguerite, that's terrible; I feel so sorry for her."[3]

Myrtle did. She spoke to Mr. Jenner about Marguerite Oswald for as long as he wished to hear.

MRS. EVANS. Yes; Marguerite has a terrifically sad life, and she was just a wonderful, gorgeous wife. She married this John Pic and had his boy, and he didn't want any children at all, so she left him and went to live with her sister and [her next husband] Oswald . . . was a Virginia Life Insurance salesman [who] started taking her out . . . and then she married him, and . . . had the two boys, and they were very happy, and then one day he was out mowing the lawn, and he had this terrific pain, and she was several months pregnant with Lee . . .

Now, he left her with $10,000, I think, in insurance, so she sold her home, and by that time her two boys were old enough, so she put them in this home . . . and went to work [and] she had got this couple to come and stay with Lee . . . some young couple. I don't know their names. She said people told her that when Lee was in the high chair, that he used to cry a lot and they thought they were whipping little Lee, so she came home unexpectedly one night, and the child had welts on his legs, and she told them to get out and get out now . . . all her love, I think, she dumped on Lee after her husband died. . . . she always sort of felt sorry for Lee for that reason, I think, and sort of leaned toward Lee.[4]

Well, Mr. Jenner was patient. He listened. Now he wanted to know how mother and son had comported themselves years later, when they came back from New York because at that time Myrtle

Evans had rented an apartment to them in a building she lived in and managed:

MR. JENNER. What kind of housekeeper was Margie?

MRS. EVANS. A very good housekeeper; very tasty; she . . . had a lot of natural talent that way and she was not lazy. . . . she kept a very neat house, and she was always so lovely herself. That's why, when I saw her on TV, after all this happened, she looked so old and haggard, and I said, "That couldn't be Margie," but of course it was, but if you had known Margie before all this happened, you would see what I mean. She was beautiful. She had beautiful wavy hair.

MR. JENNER. What about Lee?

MRS. EVANS. Well . . . when he wanted supper, or something to eat, he would scream like a bull. He would holler, "Maw, where's my supper?" Some of the time Margie would be downstairs talking to me or something, and when he would holler at her, she would jump up right away and go and get him something to eat. Her whole life was wrapped up in that boy and she spoiled him to death. [If you go back earlier] it's my opinion that Lee . . . demanded so much of his mother's attention that they didn't get along—I mean her and Ekdahl, because of Lee . . .

MR. JENNER. That's just your surmise?

MRS. EVANS. Yes, sir; I can't help feeling that if she had put Lee in a boarding school, she might have hung onto her meal ticket, and considering Mr. Ekdahl's condition and everything, if all that hadn't happened, she would have been sitting on top of the world. She wouldn't have had another worry in her life, as far as money goes, but instead her children came first, I mean, Lee. She just poured out all her love on him, it seemed like.[5]

"He Walks and Talks Like a Man"

The Big Easy—a.k.a. New Orleans—may be the only American city where the middle levels of the Mafia are all but indistinguishable from the middle class, but then New Orleans may be more tolerant than other places. Perhaps it is the permissiveness offered by sub-tropical heat; to own a strip-joint and also be a dedicated churchgoer offers little inner contradiction. It is as if people in the Big Easy take it for granted that humankind is a spiritual house of cards built on flimsy, and therefore is full of contradiction and ready to collapse. Opposites in oneself, consequently, are given equal welcome.

It could also be said that Lee had unfinished business in New Orleans, having spent part of his adolescence (once Marguerite could no longer afford the rent at Myrtle Evans' apartment) living in an apartment over a pool hall on a street on the edge of the French Quarter, Exchange Alley, which had its share of whores, small-time hoods, and petty gamblers. Rare is the adolescent who listens to such nocturnal action from a second-story window without expectations building up in him of a dramatic street life to come.

One cannot say, however, that he was drawn back to New Orleans entirely by old memories. Marina, as we know, wanted to get him out of Dallas as quickly as possible. So, she encouraged him to go and promised she would follow as soon as he found a job. In the meantime, she would live with a new friend, Ruth Paine. On April 24, therefore, Lee had gotten on a bus to New Orleans, where, on arrival, he telephoned his aunt, Lillian Murret, and asked if he could be put up for a few days. Actually, it turned out to be a couple of weeks before he and Myrtle Evans found the apartment on Magazine Street.

McMillan: [The Murrets] were extremely conservative, they disapproved of his going to Russia, and he was afraid they might not welcome him to New Orleans. Anticipating this, Lee had confided to Marina that he suspected the Murrets lived beyond what his uncle's earnings would support. Lillian's husband, Charles Ferdinand, or "Dutz," Murret, as he had been known since his prizefight days, was a steamship clerk, and Lee thought that his uncle might be engaged in some other activity on the side, like bookmaking. There is no evidence that this was so . . .[1]

On the contrary, there is some. The House Select Committee on Assassinations (HSCA) probed Dutz Murret's activities and decided he was well connected to

significant organized crime figures associated with the Marcello organization. . . . an associate of Dutz Murret reportedly served as a personal aide or driver to Marcello at one time. In another instance, the committee found that an individual connected to Dutz Murret, the person who arranged bail for Oswald following his arrest in August 1963 for a street disturbance, was an associate of two of Marcello's syndicate deputies.[2]

MR. JENNER. What kind of boy was Lee Harvey Oswald?

MR. MURRET. Well, I'll tell you, I didn't take that much interest in him. I couldn't tell you anything about that, because I didn't pay attention to all that. I do think he was a loud kid, you know what I mean; he was always raising his voice when he wanted something from his mother, I know that, but I think a lot of times he was just the opposite. He liked to read, and he stuck by himself pretty much in the apartment.

MR. JENNER. Did you and Marguerite get along all right?

MR. MURRET. Not too well . . .

MR. JENNER. What was your impression of Lee then, after he appeared at your house after all those years?

MR. MURRET. . . . . I just couldn't warm up to him, but he said he wanted to find a job and get an apartment and then send for his wife in Texas, so I wasn't going to stand in his way.[3]

Murret would have spoken in much the same manner if he had had a good deal to do with Oswald in New Orleans in 1963, but we do have Lillian Murret's testimony for corroboration, and it gives a clue: Murret may have had his Mob relations, but he and his wife cherished their hard-won respectability and the college education they had been able to provide for their children. Oswald, given his stint in Russia, would not have been Murret's first choice for a houseguest. Like just about every other semi-respectable figure on the periphery of the Mafia, Dutz was an ardent patriot.

Because of Murret, much has been made of Oswald's possible connections to the Mob, but no evidence has arisen that uncle and nephew did anything but keep their relations at a good arm's length. Lee's blood tie was with Lillian; indeed, it may have been Lee's good fortune that it was his aunt, not his uncle, who picked up the phone when he called from the bus station. She told him to come right over.

MRS. MURRET. . . . he was trying to find a job, he told me, and then he said he would send for Marina, his wife, and the child, and I asked him . . . to describe her, and he said, "Well, she's just like any other American housewife." He said, "She wears shorts."

. . . He said he would have to have a newspaper to scan the want ads and try to find himself a job and [then] he would go out every morning with his newspaper . . . and he wouldn't come back until the afternoon, till supper time. I had supper anywhere from 5:30 to 6:00 o'clock, and he was there on time every day for supper, and after supper he didn't leave the house. He would sit down about 6:30 o'clock or 7:00 o'clock and look at some television programs and then he would go right to bed, and he did that every day while he was at the house, and so then on the first Sunday he was there, he was talking—we were talking about relatives and he said to me, "Do you know anything about the Oswalds?" and I [told him] "I don't know any of them other than your father," . . . Now what he didn't tell me was that on Sunday he must have gone to the cemetery where his father was buried . . . I guess he went to ask the person in charge about the grave.[4]

One morning, his older cousin John Murret gave him the white short-sleeved shirt and tie that he would be wearing ten weeks later, when he would distribute pamphlets on Canal Street for the Fair Play for Cuba Committee:

MRS. MURRET. Yes, Lee was getting ready . . . and John was in the back getting dressed to go to work, I think, and he didn't think Lee looked presentable. John . . . said it in such a nice way—he can do it, you know, but he asked Lee, he said, "Lee, here's a shirt; take it; it doesn't fit me. You put it on and here's a nice tie to go with it." He said, "Come on, kid, you want to look good when you go for that job, you know," and so he gave the white shirt and the tie to Lee to go after the job, and Lee took them.[5]

On May 9, the same day in which he will later find his apartment, he manages to get hired by the Reily Coffee Company.

MRS. MURRET. . . . he came home waving the newspaper, and he grabbed me around the neck and he even kissed me and he said, "I got it; I got it!" . . . I said, "Well, Lee, how much does it pay?" and he said . . . "It don't pay very much, but I will get along on it."

I said, "Well, you know, Lee, you are really not qualified to do anything too much. If you don't like this job, why don't you try to go back to school at night time and see if you can't learn a trade . . ." And he said, "No, I don't have to go back to school. I don't have to learn anything. I know everything." So that's the way it was. I couldn't tell him any more . . .

MR. JENNER. Did you get the impression when you were talking along those lines that he really believed he was that smart?

MRS. MURRET. He believed he was smart; yes, sir.[6]

The William B. Reily Company distributed a product called Luzianne Coffee, and Oswald was taken on as a greaser for the large grinding machines.

McMillan: On his brief application there, he may have set his own record for lies. He said that he had been living at 757 French Street (the Murrets') for three years; that he had graduated from a high school that he had attended for only a few weeks; and he gave as references his cousin John Murret, whose permission he did not ask; Sergeant Robert Hidell (a composite of his brother Robert and his own alias "Hidell"), "on active duty with the U.S. Marine Corps" (a fiction from beginning to end); and "Lieutenant J. Evans, active duty U.S. Marine Corps" (the surname and first initial of [Myrtle Evans' husband], combined with a fictitious Marine Corps rank and identification).[7]

He understands how to give job references. At low levels of employment, who will spend the time to check? Yet what a creative liar is Oswald! Every name he offers is taken from a different sector of his experience. Past, present, and future, family, Marines, and Myrtle Evans' husband, whom he has not even met, are drawn upon to shape his lies. He is comfortable with a wealth of sources. If only he had been a poet instead of a liar.

With it all, the false facts have a purpose. He never knows when he will be on the lam, and so he likes to leave a trail with a plethora of offshoots to befuddle future pursuers.

Besides, he is now obliged to come down from the monumental high of knowing that he had taken a shot at a General. Now, he will only be lubricating big-bellied machines.

He may also be losing the freedom of his daylight hours. It is possible he had been having a lively time for himself in New Orleans until he found work. There is certainly some testimony from Dean Adams Andrews to contemplate. How true it may be is another matter. As described by Gerald Posner, Andrews was a "three-hundred-pound, forty-four-year-old jive-talking attorney with a reputation for exaggeration and showmanship."[8]

MR. LIEBELER. I am advised by the FBI that . . . Lee Harvey Oswald came into your office . . .

MR. ANDREWS. I don't recall the dates, but briefly, it is this: Oswald came in the office accompanied by some gay kids. They were Mexicanos. He wanted to find out what could be done in connection with a discharge, a yellow paper discharge, so I explained [that] when he brought the money, I would do the work . . .

MR. LIEBELER. The first time he came in he was with these . . . gay kids. By that, of course, you mean people that appeared to you to be homosexuals?

MR. ANDREWS. Well, they swish. What they are, I don't know. We call them gay kids. . . .

MR. LIEBELER. Have you seen any of them since? . . .

MR. ANDREWS. Yes. . . . First district precinct. Police picked them up for wearing clothes of the opposite sex.

MR. LIEBELER. How many of them were there?

MR. ANDREWS. About 50. . . . I went down for the ones I represented. They were in the holding pavilion. I paroled them and got them out. . . .

MR. LIEBELER. You say that some of the gay kids [that] the police arrested . . . were the ones that had been with Oswald?

MR. ANDREWS. Yes. . . .

MR. LIEBELER. Let me try and pin down how long it was after the first time Oswald came in that these kids all got arrested. . . . Was it a month? . . .

MR. ANDREWS. . . . Ten days at the most.

MR. LIEBELER. I suppose the New Orleans police department files would reflect the dates these people were picked up?

MR. ANDREWS. I checked the first district's blotter [and] they wear names just like you and I wear clothes. Today their name is Candy; tomorrow it is Butsie; next day it is Mary. . . . Names are a very improbable method of identification. . . . You know them by sight mostly.

MR. LIEBELER. Do you remember what date it was that that large arrest was made?

MR. ANDREWS. No; every Friday is arrest day in New Orleans. . . .

MR. LIEBELER. In May of 1963?

MR. ANDREWS. Yes . . .[9]

MR. LIEBELER. Did Oswald appear to you to be gay?

MR. ANDREWS. You can't tell. I couldn't say. He swang with the kids. He didn't swish, but birds of a feather flock together. . . .

MR. LIEBELER. When you say he didn't swish, what do you mean by that?

MR. ANDREWS. He is not effeminate; his voice isn't squeaky; he didn't walk like or talk like a girl; he walks and talks like a man.

MR. LIEBELER. . . . Was there anything striking about the way he carried himself?

MR. ANDREWS. I never paid attention. I never watched him walk other than into and out of the office. There's nothing that would draw my attention to anything out of the ordinary, but I just assumed that he knew these people and was running with them. They had no reason to come. The three gay kids he was with, they were ostentatious. They were what we call swishers. You can just look at them. All they had to do was open their mouth. . . . With those pronounced ones, you never know what the relationship is with anyone else with them, but I have no way of telling whether he is gay or not, other than he came in with what we call here queens. That's about it.[10]

The enigma of Oswald's homosexuality might now be clarified to a degree, except that we are being told all this by a man whose word, according to Posner, is not considered reliable. We have, then, no more than another question to add to our understanding of Lee's relation to Marina now that she is arriving and his vacation from marriage is over.

It is worth reminding ourselves, however, of a paradox concerning Oswald. If to some degree he will always remain mysterious, that contributes nonetheless to our developing sense of him. He is a man we can never understand with comfort, yet the small mysteries surrounding him give resonance to our comprehension. An echo is less defined than the note that created it, but our ear can be enriched by its reverberation. If he is homosexual at all, if the inner drama of his marriage is that he is only half connected to Marina and the other half of him is drawn toward having sex with men, and if this need has been intermittently expressed in his adolescence, his Marine Corps years and, covertly, in Russia and perhaps in Dallas, then the picture offered by Dean Adams Andrews takes on credibility. It certainly helps to explain those periods of desire for Marina that alternate in him with a lack of interest in Marina so complete that she complains aloud about it to people she does not even know well. In the sexual sense, it could be said that he seems married to her no more than fifteen weeks in the year.

Forbidden Strings

One of those weeks begins on the night of May 11, when Ruth Paine arrives in her station wagon with her two children and Marina and June. According to McMillan, that night Lee and his wife

> were happy to be together again—"I've missed you so," Lee said again and again—and they made love three times that night and the next morning. It was the first time they had made love since March 29 or 30, the weekend when Marina had taken Lee's photograph with the rifle.[1]

Since we are speaking of Lee and Marina, it was not necessarily so loving as that. The groundwork for new disagreements in New Orleans was established as soon as Marina saw the apartment.

> **MRS. PAINE.** . . . Lee showed her, of course, all the virtues of the [place] he had rented . . . He was pleased . . . it was large enough that he could invite me to stay . . . And he pointed out this little courtyard with grass, and fresh strawberries ready to pick, where June could play. And a screened porch entryway. And quite a large living room. And he was pleased with the furniture and with how the landlady said this was early New Orleans style. And Marina was definitely not as pleased as he had hoped. I think he felt—he wanted to please her. This showed in him.
>
> **MR. JENNER.** Tell us what she said. What led you to this conclusion?
>
> **MRS. PAINE.** She said it is dark, and it is not very clean. She thought the courtyard was nice, a grass spot where June could play, fenced in, but there was very little ventilation. We were immediately aware there were a lot of cockroaches.
>
> **MR. JENNER.** Was she aware of this and did she comment on that?
>
> **MRS. PAINE.** I don't know as anything was said. He was pretty busy explaining. He was doing his best to get rid of them. But they didn't subside. I remember noticing that he was tender and vulnerable on this point, when she arrived.
>
> **MR. JENNER.** He was tender?

MRS. PAINE. . . . hoping for approval from her, which she didn't give.[2]

Priscilla Johnson McMillan remarks: ". . . it occurred to Ruth that Lee might or might not care about Marina, but he certainly cared about her opinion."[3]

Indeed he did. In Russia he had promised that he would provide for them in America; he had not done too well. Now, he was hoping that she would love the new apartment. Once again, fresh hope for his marriage was corroded by the acid animosity of Marina's equally deep but equally contrary heart.

MRS. PAINE. . . . they argued most of that weekend. I was very uncomfortable in that situation, and he would tell her to shut up, tell her, "I said it, and that is all the discussion on the subject."

REPRESENTATIVE FORD. What were the kinds of discussions that prompted this?

MRS. PAINE. I . . . I do recall feeling that the immediate things they were talking about were insufficient reason for that much feeling being passed back and forth, and I wondered if I wasn't adding to the strain in the situation, and did my best to get back to Texas directly.[4]

Ruth Paine had arrived on Saturday and was gone by Monday, and we can only surmise the inner range of her feelings. Thirty years later, Marina was asked by the interviewers whether she had ever suspected Lee of homosexual activity, and she replied that she had never seen evidence of it. Yet, it was also true of Marina that she wished to accommodate whoever was questioning her, and so after some thought, she remarked that when Ruth Paine had stayed over in New Orleans those two nights in May, Lee had been making love in a new way. With some embarrassment, Marina implied that he had mounted from the rear, an act which he had never initiated before, and at that moment, their door ajar, Ruth Paine had passed. Probably, thinks Marina, Ruth saw them. "Lee," Marina recalled, "was not embarrassed at all," and that to her now seemed some small evidence, perhaps, of homosexual behavior (as if his lack of dismay at being glimpsed in the act was not to be seen as natural heterosexual behavior.)

In any event, it may have been uncomfortable for Ruth Paine.

Perhaps it is time to describe her: She was tall, she was thin, she had a long narrow freckled face and was a converted Quaker. She and her husband, Michael, were devoted to madrigal singing and folk dancing. It had helped to bring them together.

Ruth wore rimless glasses. She was serious. In the hundreds of pages of her testimony before the Warren Commission, there are not a great many humorous remarks. Much the same can be said of Michael Paine. A highly respected helicopter engineer, dry, tall, slim man, quite as serious as Ruth in his testimony—one does get a picture of two exceptionally decent people living under the curse of true gentry: They have been brought up to be so decent to others, so firm and uncompromising about not allowing the greedy little human animal within ever to speak, that one can almost hear strings snapping. Needless to say, it was not a happy marriage. They were respectful of each other, always respectful of each other, but their personal relations, by the time they encountered the Oswalds, had gone cold in the water.

Marina had met Ruth Paine at a party in Dallas given the previous February by a geologist named Everett Glover. De Mohrenschildt, small surprise, had managed the meeting. This would later cause considerable suspicion of Ruth Paine until the nature of her careful open testimony, so responsible to the need for certifying, then fortifying, the smallest detail, made it evident that she could not possibly be an agent in American or Soviet intelligence: She had no instincts for prevarication. Indeed, we would have to put her up in lights as a great actress if the person she presented to the Warren Commission was no more than a role she was playing.

The emotional facts she offered to explain the friendship were not complex. Ruth had responded to Marina as only a woman who loves her husband and is not loved in return would respond to an attractive waif of a girl who spoke no English inasmuch as her husband did not wish her to learn the language because then—so Marina explained—he might lose his Russian.

Such sentiment was an outrage to Ruth. So was the pressure that Lee regularly put upon Marina to return alone to Russia. Michael Paine, whose attitude toward Lee and Marina was much the same as his wife's, thought it was next door to a crime that Lee was actually serious about sending Marina back to the USSR:

MR. PAINE. . . . I felt that he was keeping her a vassal and since I was more eager to hear her opinions of Russia than his opinions of Russia, I was eager that she should learn English, and when—

Ruth told me that Marina thought she might have to go back to the Soviet Union, and I thought out of the largesse of this country it should be possible for her to stay here if she wanted to stay here, and she quite apparently did, she struck me as a somewhat apolitical person and yet true, just and conscientious . . .[5]

The Paines might not be living together, but they still thought as one. Ruth loved the Russian language, and had been studying it devotedly. She quickly concluded that if Marina lived with her in that husbandless house in Irving, Texas, where Ruth now dwelt with her children, it might be good for both women. Michael Paine agreed entirely: ". . . it was agreeable to me to look forward to financing her stay until she could make her own way here."[6]

It is interesting that on April 7, three days before Lee would make his attempt on Walker, Ruth Paine, with considerable difficulty, wrote a long letter in Russian to Marina. From its tone, we can be certain that Marina had already confided many a private corner of her marriage to Ruth; and quite likely, given the secret agenda of such confessions (which is to clear the bile out of one's system so that one can love again), Marina had probably painted a portrait of her relations with Lee that was even more miserable than the reality.

Dear Marina,

I want to invite you to move here and live with me both now and later when the baby is born. I don't know how things are for you at home with your husband. I don't know what would be better for you, June and Lee—to live together or apart. It is, of course, your affair, and you have to decide what is better and what you wish to do. But I want to say that you have a choice. When you wish, for days, weeks, months, you could move here. I have already thought about this invitation a lot. It is not a quick thought.

It seems to me that it would be pleasant and useful for us both to live together. We can easily help one another. When you converse, it helps me. If you sometimes correct my mistakes in conversation or letters, I would be very happy. It is so helpful to me that I would consider it proper to buy all which we need from the grocery store, food, soap, etc. Lee would need to give you enough money to pay for clothes and medical expenses.

You can get rest here such as you need during pregnancy. During the day it is quiet here, but not so quiet as at
your place. You and June would be by yourselves in the
room which fronts the street. There you would find privacy.

Here, I think, it would not be difficult to learn English.
From me and from my children, you would learn words.

In the course of two weeks you could learn all I know
about cooking. I'm bad at housecleaning. Perhaps you
could help me with this a bit.

I don't want to hurt Lee. Of course I don't know what he
wants. Perhaps he feels like Michael, who at one time
wants and doesn't want to live with me. You know, you
could live here workdays and return home weekends. You
would only need to carry back and forth clothes, diapers,
etc. The other things necessary for June and you are here
all the time: beds, sheets, towels, a highchair for June, etc.

Please think about this invitation and tell me (now or
later) what you think. If you are interested . . . I want to
write an official letter to you and Lee, and I want him to
know all I have said to you. Where you and June live—that
is of course a matter which touches him deeply. Therefore
I want to speak directly with him about it.

> Your
> Ruth[7]

It gives a turn in our sense of Ruth that, in fact, she never did
send this letter. Her conscience debated whether one had a right,
no matter one's good intentions, to come between a husband and
wife.

Then, three weeks after she did not mail the letter, Lee was off
to New Orleans. By mutual agreement of all, Paines and Oswalds,
Marina and Lee vacated the Neely Street apartment, and Marina
lived with Ruth in Irving, Texas, for the next two weeks and
enjoyed it. Her life was tranquil, and Ruth respected her.

Now, on Magazine Street, Ruth, passing their open doorway,
catches a glimpse of husband and wife in the act, and Marina is
evidently not as unhappy with Lee as she has pretended. Small surprise if Ruth leaves next day and, with her dutiful conscience, tries
to hope for the best for both of them.

4

Love, Heat, and Grease

McMillan: Marina made no secret of her interest in sex. At the newsstands, where they fairly often found themselves at night, she would pick out the most unwholesome-looking magazines she could find and pore over the photographs of nude men and women. Lee affected to be above it all . . . But more than once she spied him flicking through a girlie magazine.

Aside from June . . . sex was again the brightest feature of their marriage. For all his Puritanism, Lee enjoyed making love. After intercourse, he would go into the bathroom to wash off, emerge singing one of his arias, and lie down with his back to Marina.

"Don't touch me," he would say. "And don't say a word. I'm in paradise now. I don't want my good mood spoiled."

There was a mirror at the foot of their bed, and Lee would pile up pillows at the head of the bed so he could watch them making love. Marina did not like it. She pulled the pillows down or turned her head away. She was hurt that the mirror seemed to excite Lee more than she did . . .

"Who are you kissing me for—me or the mirror?"

"You mean you don't like it?"

"Of course not," she would answer, and give him a little rap on the rear end.[1]

It was infuriating. Her husband, Lee Harvey Oswald, was more stimulated by the sight of himself than by her. But then, Marina had not had a mother like Marguerite to keep telling her how wonderful she was. Since his interior often felt considerably less extraordinary than Marguerite's description of him, he was naturally eager to encounter that other person, described as so wonderful by his mother—occasionally, the mirror would be kind enough to offer agreeable sights. What an attractive fellow!

Sometimes, in the New Orleans heat, he could get sexy. "He liked to take this pose, that pose, in front of the mirror," Marina said, "and then he would ask, 'Don't you think I'm gorgeous?' He liked to walk naked. Never ashamed of his body. It was hot and, you know, he would strip everything and sit on the screened-in porch in the air. He just liked it."

And, of course, they fought. From the moment Ruth left, they fought even more. Ruth Paine had hardly been aware that they had been on their best behavior with her.

McMillan: Marina sometimes got up at night and went to the kitchen for something cold to drink. The place would be swarming with cockroaches.

"Come in and admire your handiwork," she would call out toward the bedroom—it was "his" handiwork because Lee did not allow her to use the spray.

He would run in naked from the bedroom, brandishing a can of roach spray and squirting it everywhere. Marina laughed, because he was too stingy to buy decent spray, too stingy to use enough of it, and because he put it in the wrong places.

"You woke me up and now you're laughing at me." He was hurt.[2]

During the day, he squirted grease on his machines; at night it was bug-killer on Magazine Street. He stank of oil; he stank of insect poison. He festered in the heat. Nor had he told her he was working in a coffee factory. He had pretended it was a photographic shop, but he couldn't explain why he smelled of coffee. Finally, he told her. He had to. He not only reeked from his job, but it affected his personal habits. He went around in sandals, old work pants, and a soiled T-shirt he hardly ever changed. Marina could bedevil herself with the thought that she had been ashamed of the way Anatoly dressed in Minsk, and now Lee walked around in outright filthy condition.

McMillan: "My work isn't worth getting dressed for," he told Marina.

"Do it for yourself, then," she said. "Or if you won't do it for yourself, do it for me."

"I simply don't care," he replied.[3]

The grunge at work—the grease from coffee beans and the grease from the machines, the heat, the sense of sliding into new kinds of trouble. His temper is on edge.

MRS. GARNER. . . . I said, "Lee, why don't you talk English to your little girl and your wife? That way she could learn to talk English and when the little girl goes to school it wouldn't be so hard on her."

He said, "She has time enough to learn that," and he never had a nice word to say to me after that. . . .

MR. LIEBELER. Did you have any other contact with Oswald yourself, personally?

MRS. GARNER. Yes. One time I went for my rent. It was a few days past due, the rent, and I mean, you know, when you let them go they wait too long and they don't ever get it. . . . he was starting out the drive to catch a bus on the corner, and when he saw me he turned around and . . . I said, "Oswald, you got the rent?" . . . He said, "Yes, I have it."

He was fixing to go to the bus, [but] he turned around . . . and he just pushed me aside and went by me and went and got the money and handed it to me. . . .

MR. LIEBELER. He actually laid his hands on you?

MRS. GARNER. Put his hands on me just like that and pushed me. . . . He didn't say a thing. Came back and gave me the money and that was it.

MR. LIEBELER. When was the next time you had any—

MRS. GARNER. Well, I didn't talk to him any more than that because [he] wouldn't answer you when you say good morning or good evening . . . The only thing was at night he used to come past behind the house and always wore trunks, yellow trunks with thongs, no top shirt, and he used to stuff all my garbage cans and all the cans on the street, and never would talk to anybody, pass right by the door of the apartment of the other people and never did talk to anybody.[4]

Usually, he is just as unresponsive at work:

MR. LE BLANC. . . . I put him on the fifth floor and told him to take care of everything on the fifth floor and I would be back shortly to check. . . . and about a half hour or 45 minutes or so, I would go back up . . . and I wouldn't find him., So I asked the fellows that would be working on the floor had they seen him and they said yes, he squirted the oil can a couple of times around different things and they don't know where he went. So I would start hunting all over the building. There is five stories on one side and four on the other. I would cover from the roof on down and I wouldn't locate him, and I asked him, I said, "Well, where have you been?" And all he would give me was that he was around. I asked him, "Around where?" He says, "Just around," and he would turn around and walk off.[5]

If he stays in dirty clothes once he gets home, that might be related to sitting in dirty diapers as a child. There had been so many hours when he was two and three years old and Marguerite had been away at work and the young couple she had hired did not take much care of him. Now, the dirt and grease in which he works seem to be turning him on to guns. Is it possible that the dirt and the grease—like the torpor induced by sitting in packed diapers—stimulates him to low dirty impulses?

MR. ALBA. . . . employees at Reily told [the FBI] after the assassination, of course, that Lee Oswald spent as much time "Over at Alba's Garage as he did over here at the plant." . . .

MR. LIEBELER. You said that he was called from your place to go back to the coffee company from time to time?

MR. ALBA. There were anywhere from two to four different occasions that I can remember that someone would come in there and tell him, "Now, Lee Oswald, they are looking for you over there. If you keep this up, you are going to get canned." And Oswald would say, "I'm coming. I'm coming."[6]

But Oswald and Adrian Alba did have interesting conversations in the front office of the garage:

MR. ALBA. Well, we have a coffee urn and a Coke machine . . . and on the coffee table I would say that I had approximately anywhere from 80 to 120 magazines. [Oswald] requested permission to take one or two off at a time, and kept them anywhere from 3 days to a week, and would make the point of letting me know he was returning them. And then a few days later he would ask that he borrow another magazine or two magazines. . . .

MR. LIEBELER. Did he strike you as being peculiar in any way?

MR. ALBA. Yes; he did. He was quiet . . . You could ask Lee Oswald two or three questions, and if Lee Oswald wasn't apparently interested in the course of the conversation, he would just remain paging through the book and look up and say, "Did you say something to me?" . . . but all you had to do was mention guns and gun magazines and Lee was very free with the conversation . . .[7]

MR. LIEBELER. I am looking at an FBI report. [Did Oswald mention] that a small calibre bullet was more deadly than the larger one, to which point you agreed.

MR. ALBA. . . . We went into the discussion of basing the thing on the ice pick versus the bread knife—I don't think I mentioned this part to the FBI—reflecting the whole picture that you would be better off receiving a wound from a 10-inch bread knife than you would be being gigged once with a 2- or 3-inch ice pick, and that reflecting the difference between the large calibre wound and the small calibre wound.

MR. LIEBELER. What led you and Oswald to agree that you would be better off being hit with a bread knife than with an ice pick?

MR. ALBA. Internal bleeding.[8]

About this time, Marina wrote a letter in Russian to Ruth which the Warren Commission would translate into English.

25 May 1963
New Orleans

Dear Ruth! Hello!

Here it is already a week since I received your letter. I can't produce any excuses as there are no valid reasons. I'm ashamed to confess that I am a person of moods. And my mood currently is such that I don't feel much like anything. As soon as you left all "love" stopped and I am very hurt that Lee's attitude toward me is such that I feel each minute that I bind him. He insists that I leave America, which I don't want to do at all. I like America very much and think that even without Lee I would not be lost here. What do you think?

This is the basic question which doesn't leave me day or night. And again Lee has said that he doesn't love me, so you see we came to mistaken conclusions. It is hard for you and me to live without the return of our love—interesting, how will it all end? . . .[9]

MRS. MURRET. Now, what he did at home—how he acted around Marina there, I don't know, but when he was in my presence he was very attentive to her and very well-mannered. He would, I mean, open the car door for her and so forth—very attentive. He would pull the chair out for her and things like that. He was very well-mannered. I have to say that for him.

MR. JENNER. What was her attitude toward him?

MRS. MURRET. Well, she seemed the same way. They seemed to get along very nicely together, I thought, when they were here in New Orleans. They would take a ride out to the French Market and buy some crabs and some shrimp and come home and boil and cook them. They got a big bang out of doing things like that.[10]

5

Fair Play for Cuba

As Lee and Marina come together and draw apart, the question of whether she should return to Russia has become one of the recurring elements in their marriage. Whenever he is most vexed, he threatens to dispatch her back. In October of 1962, hardly three months after they have returned to America, the theme is introduced, and on Elsbeth Street, he has her applying to the Soviet Consulate in Washington for permission to return home. It so depressed her that she even flirted with suicide, yet all the same, a correspondence did ensue between Marina and the Soviets in Washington.

She can read between the bureaucratic lines, however. Soviet officials, Marina can see, are not in a hurry to take her back. Processing her application, they indicate, will require half a year. Even by June 4, after several exchanges of letters over the months between, little has gone forward—here, for example, is a letter of June 4, 1963, from V. Gerasimov of the Consulate Section of the Soviet Embassy:

June 4, 1963

Dear Marina Nicolaevna,

In connection with your request for entrance to the Soviet Union for permanent residence, in our letter of April 18th we requested you if possible to come to Washington and visit the Consulate Section of our Embassy.

If it is difficult for you to visit us we request you to advise us by letter concerning reasons which made you request this permission . . .[1]

She made no rush to answer. A pot such as this could be kept simmering for years.

It is no small matter for Lee, however. If she hates his absorption in politics, he hates the mill-stone of his marriage. It is inhibiting to his political career. The attack on General Walker had been a species of shakedown cruise to test his capacities. Was he sufficiently ruthless to kill for political purposes? Since he had missed, the answer could only be a qualified yes. Moreover, he had had to withdraw altogether from Marina in the weeks preceding that attempt. It was as if his murderous impulses could only be gathered if he was without sexual release. To continue his marriage was to condemn himself, therefore, to a life of mediocrity, yet—there is no other explanation for so many of his actions—a sizable part of him adored Marina, and this quite apart from his full affection for June. For that matter, devotion to June was like an open display of his infatuation with himself. But Marina he loved as his woman, his difficult, caustic, contrary, and often wholly attractive wife—even if he could hardly tolerate her for most of the month. Are half of the young husbands in existence all that much unlike him? Or young wives?

Ruthlessness! He must have whipped himself with the thought that he lacked the cruelty to be a revolutionary, stern and disciplined. Now, in New Orleans, on May 23, the first book he takes out from the public library is *Portrait of a Revolutionary: Mao Tse Tung*. The author, Robert Payne, says of Mao, "He represented even in those days a new kind of man; one of those who single-handedly construct whole civilizations."[2] If that was the noble role Mao had sculpted from history, how could Oswald not have decided—indeed, can we doubt it?—that it is not enough to be a leader; one has to fashion a new kind of existence.

First, however, is the little matter of playing an active role in history. If he had been a warlock, he would have consulted his runes, but he was, as he saw it, a twenty-three-year-old master of new revolutionary politics on the road to future glory—and the road went straight through Cuba. As Edward Epstein puts it, "Once he got to Havana, he could no doubt find contacts and connections with the Castro government. He even at one point bragged to Marina that he would become a 'minister' in the government."[3] No, he would not have found it hard to believe that if he could get there and reach the ear of those who counted, he could become an intimate adviser on what was going on in the USSR. (Indeed, in retrospect, we can ask ourselves—it is a fair question—whether Castro's advisers knew as much about Soviet reality as Oswald.)

Epstein: The problem for Oswald was getting there. Since it was illegal at the time for a United States citizen to travel to Cuba, he would have to obtain his visa at a Cuban Embassy outside the country, and to do that, he would need some credentials to prove that he was a supporter of the Cuban government. His game in New Orleans involved creating just such a record for himself.[4]

May 26

Dear Sirs,

I am requesting formal membership in your organization. . . .

Now that I live in New Orleans I have been thinking about renting a small office at my own expense for the purpose of forming a F.P.C.C. branch here in New Orleans. Could you give me a charter?

Also, I would like information on buying pamphlets, etc., in large lots, as well as blank F.P.C.C. applications, etc.

Also, a picture of Fidel, suitable for framing, would be a welcome touch.

Offices down here rent for $30 a month and if I had a steady flow of literature I would be glad to take the expense.

Of course I work and could not supervise the office at all times but I'm sure I could get some volunteers to do it.

Could you add some advice or recommendations?

I am not saying this project would be a roaring success *but I am willing to try* an office, literature, and getting people to know you. [You] are the fundamentals of the F.P.C.C. as far as I can see so here's hoping to hear from you.

Yours respectfully,
Lee H. Oswald[5]

Three days later, well before he could receive a reply, he went into the Jones Printing Company on Girod Street with an eight-by-ten sheet of paper on which he had written out the final draft of a handbill:

HANDS
OFF
CUBA!
Join the Fair Play for
Cuba Committee
New Orleans Charter
Member Branch
Free Literature, Lectures
Location:
Everyone Welcome![6]

Early in June, he would receive a letter from the National Director of FPCC, V. T. Lee, and would probably have seen it as considerably more than coincidence that the man's last name was the same as his own first name. V. T. Lee was, however, cautionary, and advised Oswald not to take an office. The American public, if polled, would probably have come out 95 percent against Castro in that late spring of 1963, or at least 95 out of 100 people were not going to be caught saying anything positive about Fidel to a pollster. V. T. Lee's letter gives a small hint of a siege mentality:

May 29, 1963

Lee H. Oswald
1907 Magazine Street
New Orleans, Louisiana

Dear Friend:
. . . Your interest in helping to form an FPCC Chapter in New Orleans is gratefully received. I shall try to give you . . . a better picture of what this entails [since we] know from experience it . . . requires some sacrifice on the part of those involved.
You must realize that you will come under tremendous pressures . . . and you will not be able to operate in the manner which is conventional here in the north-east. Even most of our big-city Chapters have been forced to abandon the idea of operating an office in public. The national office in

New York is the only one in the country today . . . Most Chapters have discovered it is easier to operate semi-privately out of a home and maintain a P.O. Box for all mailings and public notices. . . . We do have a serious and often violent opposition and this [gives rise to] many unnecessary incidents which frighten away prospective supporters. I definitely would not recommend an office, at least not one that will be easily identifiable to the lunatic fringe in your community. Certainly, I would not recommend that you engage one in the very beginning but wait and see how you can operate in the community through several public experiences . . . [We] have learned a great deal over the last three years through some bitter experiences . . .

We hope to hear from you very soon in this regard and are looking forward to a good working relationship for the future. Please feel free to discuss this matter quite thoroughly with me.

Fraternally,
V. T. Lee[7]

Oswald would follow none of this advice. His real purpose, after all, was not to create a functioning branch of the FPCC but to build as quickly as possible a record that would impress Castro's officials. So, Oswald's first need was to assemble a dossier of official FPCC letters, to which he could add such documents as handbills and, even more important, news clippings. He would have to select actions that would attract media attention. A first step would be to create other officials besides himself in the New Orleans chapter of the FPCC:

MR. RANKIN. Were the words "A. J. Hidell, Chapter President" . . . in your handwriting?

MARINA OSWALD. Yes. . . . Lee wrote this down on a piece of paper and told me to sign it on this card, and said that he would beat me if I didn't . . . I said, "You have selected this name because it sounds like Fidel" and he blushed and said, "Shut up, it is none of your business."

MR. RANKIN. Was there any discussion about who Hidell, as signed on the bottom of that card, was?

MARINA OSWALD. He said . . . there is no Hidell [and] I taunted him about this and . . . said how shameful it is that a person who has his own perfectly good name should take another name, and he said, ". . . I have to do it this way, people will think I have big organization . . ."[8] After he became busy with his pro-Cuban activity, he received a letter from somebody in New York . . . from some Communist leader and he was very happy, he felt that this was a great man that he had received a letter from.

You see, when I would make fun of him, of his activity to some extent, he said that I didn't understand him and here, you see, was proof that someone else did, that there were people who understood his activity.[9]

From Marina's narrative: . . . To tell the truth, I sympathized with Cuba. I have a good opinion of this new Cuba, since when I was living in Russia I saw lots of excellent movies about the new life in Cuba [and] I came to think that the people were satisfied . . . and that the revolution had given to many work, land, and a better life than they had had before. When I came to the United States and people told me that they did not love Fidel Castro, I did not believe them. . . .

But I did not support Lee since I felt that he was too small a person to take so much on himself. He became conceited about doing such an important job and helping Cuba. But I saw that no one here agreed with him. So why do it? . . . Cuba will get along by itself, without Lee Oswald's help. I thought it was better for him to take care of his family.[10]

Of course, Marina's grandmother used to tell her, "Politics is poop!" How Russian is such an attitude: My private life is my only wealth! She was in this sense the worst possible wife for Oswald.

McMillan: She believed it was his family, June and herself, whom he loved in his heart, but that in accordance with his lofty ideas about himself, he . . . forced himself to put politics above everything. It seemed to her that Lee was not being true to himself. Marina longed to cry out to him: "Why do you torture us so? You know you don't believe half of what you are saying."[11]

We come back to his basic dilemma: To which half of himself will he be faithful—his need for love, or his need for power and fame? What is never taken seriously enough in Oswald is the force of his confidence that he has the makings of a great leader. If his living conditions are mean and his role is not viewed solemnly by anyone but himself, he can still fortify his belief in the future of Lee Harvey Oswald by contemplating those anonymous early years spent by Lenin and Hitler. So his ideas are at least as real to him as the family that he does indeed care for—in his fashion.

Public events, however, may have been tipping the balance. On June 11, Kennedy broadcast a nationwide speech that called for a new civil rights bill, and on that same night, Medgar Evers of the NAACP was fatally shot on the doorstep of his home in Jackson, Mississippi.

Jackson was but two hundred miles from New Orleans, and the air was boiling in the Deep South. Oswald may have seen it as his personal duty to face into such heat. On June 16, the day after Medgar Evers' funeral, he went to the Dumaine Street wharf, where the USS *Wasp,* an aircraft carrier, was docked.

Oswald started passing out his newly acquired Fair Play for Cuba leaflets. Here is part of the text:

> On January 16, 1961, the United States Government issued a ban on travel by U.S. citizens to Cuba. Failure to abide by the ban is punishable by a fine of $5,000 or 5 years in jail or both. . . .
>
> What mysterious features exist on this tiny island of 6-½ million people to become so taboo for American eyes? Although the policy of the Castro government is to promote tourism everywhere in Cuba, our government innocently explains that the travel ban is to safeguard our welfare. . . .
>
> #Why then do other Western countries such as Canada, Mexico, England, France, West Germany, etc., find that the safety of their nationals does not require restrictions on travel to Cuba? . . .
>
> #Why then is travel allowed and even encouraged to *admittedly* Communist countries such as Poland, Yugoslavia and even the Soviet Union?
>
> In short, WHAT IS THE GOVERNMENT HIDING?
>
> #Can it be that the new schools, homes, and hospitals of revolutionary Cuba might contrast severely with the Cuba that served as a U.S. plantation and might weigh heavily on the American conscience? . . .

WE MAINTAIN THAT THE TRUTH ABOUT CUBA IS IN CUBA AND THAT WE HAVE THE RIGHT TO OBSERVE AND JUDGE FOR OURSELVES WHAT IS HAPPENING THERE![12]

There were a few consequences to handing out the leaflets. From a report by a Special Agent of the FBI on July 21, 1963:

Patrolman Ray stated that late in the afternoon, possibly between 3:00 pm and 5:00 pm, he was approached by an unknown enlisted man from the "USS Wasp" who told him that the Officer of the Deck of the "USS Wasp" desired Patrolman Ray to seek out the individual who was passing out leaflets regarding Cuba and to request the individual to stop passing out these leaflets. Patrolman Ray . . . immediately went to the Dumaine Street Wharf where he saw an unknown white male . . . age late 20's, 5'9" tall, 150 pounds and slender build. He said this individual was distributing these leaflets to U.S. Naval personnel in the area and also to civilians who were leaving the USS Wasp. Patrolman Ray stated that he approached this person and asked if he had permission to distribute the leaflets. This person replied that he . . . was within his rights to distribute leaflets in any area he desired to do so. Patrolman Ray stated that he told this individual that the wharves and buildings along the Mississippi River . . . are operated by the Board of Commissioners of the Port of New Orleans, and that if this individual received permission from the Board of Commissioners, he could distribute these leaflets. Patrolman Ray stated that . . . this person kept insisting that he did not see why he would need anyone's permission and thereafter, Patrolman Ray informed this individual that if he did not leave the Dumaine Street Wharf, Patrolman Ray would arrest him. Upon hearing this, this person left the Dumaine Street Wharf. . . .

Patrolman Ray stated that he feels this unknown individual who was distributing the leaflets was Lee Harvey Oswald.[13]

It is not hard to feel the suppressed intensity of that confrontation! He may be frequently hysterical at home, but is a model of emotional austerity on the street: calm, firm, quiet-voiced, formal, unbending. He is even—his own favorite word—stoic. We can only guess how much it costs him to conceal his emotions. All the same, he moves ahead. In the following week, on June 24, he will apply successfully for a passport—his belated reward for paying off the State Department loan. Now, he will be able to leave the United States once more, and as a political adventurer in a game of high stakes. His anxiety erupts:

> *McMillan:* . . . one night toward the very end of June he had four anxiety attacks during which he shook from head to toe at intervals of half an hour and never once woke up. Just as in the period when he was making up his mind to shoot General Walker, these attacks appear to have presaged a decision that was causing him pain.[14]

On the following night, Marina was watching him read and he looked up at her:

> *McMillan:* . . . she saw a look of sadness in his eyes. He put his book down and went into the kitchen by himself. Marina waited a few minutes. Then she put the baby down and followed him. Lee was sitting in the dark with his arms and legs wrapped around the back of a chair and his head resting on top. He was staring down at the floor. Marina put her arms around him, stroked his head, and could feel him shaking with sobs . . .
>
> Finally she said: "Everything is going to be all right. I understand."
>
> Marina held him for about a quarter of an hour and he told her between sobs that he was lost. He didn't know what he ought to do. At last he stood up and returned to the living room.[15]

Recalling that night thirty years later, she said that if he had wanted to tell her about his problem he would have, but it was better not to ask. She could still feel his burden. There was something so heavy he had been carrying, and she didn't know what it was. She never knew. It was sad, she said. When they were a little hungry, he would offer meat from his plate to give to her; she would offer meat from her plate to give to him. "Save it for yourself later," each of them would say.

That night, they felt so close.

McMillan: . . . he said suddenly, "Would you like me to come to Russia, too?"

"You're kidding."

"No," he said. . . . "I'll go with my girls . . . We'll be together, you and me and Junie and the baby [when she is born]. There is nothing to hold me here. I'd rather have less but not have to worry about the future . . ."

A while later they were in the kitchen together. Lee held her by the shoulders and told her to write the Soviet Embassy that he would be coming too. He would add his visa request to her letter . . .

That weekend, the 29th or 30th of June, Marina wrote her longest, warmest, and so far her only uncoerced letter to Nikolai Reznichenko, head of the consular section of the Soviet Embassy in Washington.[16]

Dear Comrade Reznichenko!

I received two letters from you in which you requested me to indicate the reason for my wish to return to the USSR.

But first of all, permit me to apologize for such a long silence on my part and to thank you for a considerate attitude toward me on the part of the Embassy. The reasons for my silence were certainly family "problems" which is also one of the reasons I wish to return to the Homeland. The main reason, "of course" is homesickness, regarding which much is written and spoken, but one learns it only in a foreign land.

I count among family "problems" the fact that . . . my relatives were against my going to America and, therefore, I would be ashamed to appeal to them. That is why I had to weigh everything once more before replying to your letter.

But things are improving due to the fact that my husband expresses a sincere wish to return together with me to the USSR. I earnestly beg you to help him in this. There is not much that is encouraging for us here and nothing to hold us. I would not be able to work for the time being, even if I did find work. And my husband is unemployed. It is very difficult for us to live here. We have no money to enable me to come to the Embassy, not even to pay for hospital and other expenses connected with the birth of a child. We both urgently solicit your assistance to enable us to return and work in the USSR.

In my application I did not specify the place in which I would like to live in the Soviet Union. I earnestly beg you to help us to obtain permission to live in Leningrad where I grew up and went to school. I have a sister and a brother of my mother's second marriage there. I know that I do not have to explain to you the reason for my wish to live precisely in that city. It speaks for itself. I permit myself to write this without any desire to belittle the merits of our other cities . . .

These are the basic reasons why I and my husband wish to return to the USSR. Please do not deny our request. Make us happy again, help us to return to that which we lost because of our foolishness. I would like to have my second child, too, to be born in the USSR.

Sincerely and respectfully,
M. Oswald[17]

By morning, he had changed his mind. His strength was restored. In his own note, which he enclosed with Marina's letter, he wrote:

Dear Sirs,

Please *rush* the entrance visa for the return of Soviet citizen Marina N. Oswald.

She is going to have a baby in *October,* therefore you must grant the entrance visa and make the transportation arrangements before then.

As for my return entrance visa please consider it *separately.*
Thank You
Lee H. Oswald
(husband of Marina Nicholeyev)[18]

To commit his mind to one action sometimes meant no more than that he was constructing a mental platform which would enable him to spring off in the opposite direction. He was the living embodiment of the dialectic—where was the thesis in him that would fail to create its antithesis? But then, that is the nature of narcissists, locked forever into an inner dialogue with themselves. Half of the self captures the argument for a night; the other half takes over in the morning.

Their letters to the Soviet Embassy are sent off on June 30. The next day, he takes out from the public library William Manchester's biography of John F. Kennedy, *Portrait of a President*. Maybe he is looking to see what he might be giving up by leaving America. Five days later, he takes out Solzhenitsyn's *One Day in the Life of Ivan Denisovich*. If an outspoken book about a prisoner in a gulag can actually be published under Khrushchev, then Soviet life is becoming more liberal. Five days later, he reads Alexander Werth's *Russia Under Khrushchev*. He must be looking for reinforcement of the idea that it is worth going back. Of course, this is just one theme among several. The following week, he will peruse JFK's *Profiles in Courage*, and for that matter, he takes out C. S. Forester's *Hornblower and the Hotspur* on the same day as *Ivan Denisovich*. We have to keep reminding ourselves that he is only twenty-three years old, and there are days when thrillers and naval battles are closer to him than politics. On July 18, he took out *Five Spy Novels* selected by Howard Haycraft.

We can recall that the first book he took out from the New Orleans Public Library was Robert Payne's biography of Mao, and in it he must have come across the following passage. What reassurance it must have offered to such a devoted reader and individual thinker (by his own measure) as Oswald:

> Mao could read twice or three times as fast as any other man. In libraries he surrounded himself with a wall of books. No one Hsiao San had ever known had ever hungered for such a vast quantity of knowledge on so many different levels. [However, said Mao,] it was perfectly easy to read but that something more was necessary—an understanding of the laws of civilization.[19]

Exploring these "laws of civilization" was a quest for Oswald as intense as any fifteenth-century navigator's belief that he could find a westward passage to India. Oswald was dyslexic, yet how much he reads. It is altogether uncharacteristic for those afflicted with dyslexia to go out of their way to read, but once again, Oswald does not fit a category, no more than would any man who leads an expedition. The obvious pain that Oswald suffers from, however, is that on his expedition he has no support team, no equipment, no funds, no goal that others can recognize, and his first mate is his most constant critic.

Atheism and Morality

Unaware of Lee's proposal to Marina that the Oswald family go back to Russia, Ruth Paine, on July 11, wrote a letter in Russian to Marina with a wholly different suggestion:

> If Lee doesn't wish to live with you any more, and prefers that you go to the Soviet Union, think about the possibility of living with me. It would be necessary, of course, to live dependent on me for a year or two, while the babies are small, but please do not be embarrassed. You are an able girl. Later, after a year or two, you could find work in America. . . .
>
> You know, I have long received [financial support] from my parents. I lived "dependent" a long time. I would be happy to be an aunt to you. And I can. We have sufficient money. Michael would be glad. This I know. He just gave me $500.00 extra for the vacation or something necessary. With this money it is possible to pay the doctor and hospital in October when the baby is born. Believe God. All will be well for you and the children. I confess that I think this opportunity for me to know you, came from God. Perhaps it is not so, but I think and believe so. . . .
>
> Marina, come to my home the last part of September without fail. Either for two months or two years. And don't be worried about money.
>
> I don't want to hurt Lee with this invitation to you. Only I think that it would be better if you and he do not live together if you do not receive happiness. I understand how Michael feels—he doesn't love me, and wants the chance to look for another life and another wife. He must do this, it seems, and so it is better for us not to live together. I don't know how Lee feels, I would like to know. Surely things are hard for him now, too. I hope that he would be glad to see you with me where he can know that you and the children will receive everything that is necessary, and he would not need to worry about it. Then he could start life again.
>
> Write, please . . .[1]

By the time this letter arrived, two weeks must have gone by since the night when Lee had cried in her arms so, doubtless, matters had shifted again. At the least, Marina must have given much private consideration to the possibility offered by Ruth.

Soon enough, new and depressing events came over the mood of the Oswalds' household:

MR. LE BLANC. He was standing there by me and watching me, [so] I says, "Are you finished all your greasing?" He said yes . . . he stood there a few minutes and all of a sudden, he said, "You like it here?" I said, "What do you mean?" He says, "Do you like it here?" I said, "Well, sure I like it here. I have been here a long time, about 8½ years or so." He said, "Oh, hell, I didn't mean this place." I said, "Well, what do you mean?" He says, "This damn country." I said, "Why, certainly, I love it. After all, this is my country." He turned around and walked off. He didn't say any more.[2]

MR. LIEBELER. Did [his absences] get worse as he stayed there?

MR. LE BLANC. Well, toward the last it began to get pretty regular, and that is when I think they decided to let him go. . . . he had this habit, every time he would walk past you . . . just like a kid playing cowboys or something—you know, he used his finger like a gun. He would go "Pow!" and I used to look at him, and I said, "Boy, what a crackpot this guy is!"[3]

On July 17, his employment was terminated.

MR. ALBA. When he did leave, he came in the office and he says . . . "Well, I will be seeing you." I said, "Where are you headed?" He said, "Out there, where the gold is." I said, "Where is that?" He said, "I told you I was going to Michaud [the NASA space center]." He said, "Well, I have heard from them and I have just wound up things next door at the coffee company, and I am on my way out there now."[4]

He had spent many grave hours conversing with Mr. Alba on such matters as the mortality of wounds and the merits of guns. Oswald was not about to tell him now that he had been fired. Serious riflemen take farewell of one another in a golden light—"Out there, where the gold is."

McMillan: Marina was to be twenty-two on July 17, and Lee had promised her something special, a dress or a new pair of shoes. He . . . returned home as usual, oblivious of the date. Over supper Marina looked morose, and he asked her why. "Today was my birthday," she said.

A few minutes later, Lee said, "Come on. Let's go out."

"The stores are closed now anyway," she answered without enthusiasm.

He took her to the drugstore across the street and bought her face powder and a Coca-Cola.

The next day he gave her his news . . .[5]

After he lost his job at the coffee factory, Lee stopped shaving on weekends. Sometimes he would not even shave on a weekday. Sometimes he brushed his teeth only at night. He didn't wash his face in the morning. He would sit in a chair for three days melting away. One night he began to talk in his sleep again.

McMillan: . . . when he took a bath, he even stopped using soap. He just sat listlessly in the bathtub until he could stir himself to get out. "I'm not dirty," he would say . . . He would burp at meals without excusing himself . . . His breath got bad and Marina used to beg him to brush his teeth, especially if he was going to kiss her. "You're my wife. You're supposed to love me any way I am," and he would come at her, his mouth open, breathing as hard as he could.[6]

It is possible that part of Lee's anxiety was that he was going to give a lecture on July 27 at a Jesuit seminary in Mobile, Alabama, and this could prove to be a severe test. He would be speaking before college seminarians who were, at the least, not sympathetic to his ideas.

On July 6, a letter had been sent to him by his cousin Gene Murret, who was studying to enter the priesthood.

Dear Lee and Marina,

Here at the House of Studies during the summer months we have a series of lectures [that] deal with art, literature, economics, religion, politics, etc. We usually have a speaker every one or two weeks on a Saturday or Sunday night. Since we are studying philosophy, most of us are interested in the various phases of Communism, as this is a very timely and practical subject.

We were hoping you might come over to talk to us about contemporary Russia and the practice of Communism there. [Our best time] to have you speak, if you are willing, is on Saturday night, July 27. The talk usually begins at 7 and lasts for about an hour. Then there is a five minute intermission and the speaker returns for a question period which may last a half-hour or so . . . be assured we want you to feel at home talking to us . . .[7]

On July 27, Dutz and Lillian Murret drove Lee and Marina to the House of Studies at Spring Hill College, Mobile. Since the women were not allowed to be part of the seminarians' audience, they were given instead a tour of the grounds.

Before they separated, Aunt Lillian asked Lee if he had prepared any notes in order to leave himself less prone to be nervous, and he, whether ready to lie or feeling confident, said, "Oh, don't worry about me. I give talks all the time."[8] In his daydreams, he had certainly given many public talks.

The only record we have of Lee's performance comes from FBI interviews in 1964 with two of the priests who were present:

Father MULLEN said that OSWALD conducted himself very well [and] spoke very well and he at the time thought he was a college graduate.

He further recalled that whenever the subject of religion came up, OSWALD passed it off and would not comment on it. He said he definitely received the impression OSWALD was an atheist.[9]

Father JOHN F. MOORE, S.J., Professor of Logic and Epistemology, Jesuit House of Studies . . . advised that OSWALD was not an outstanding speaker but in his opinion was just fair. He said OSWALD used no notes whatsoever during his talk, but handled himself very well. He said he definitely received the impression OSWALD had at least a college education. He also said OSWALD did not appear to be prosperous, but was casually dressed in sports clothing. He further informed that to the best of his recollection OSWALD made no statements indicating he was in favor of a revolution and he did not receive the impression OSWALD was a violent individual.[10]

The FBI report goes on to give a summary of the question-and-answer period that followed Oswald's lecture:

Q: What does atheism do to morality? How can you have morality without God?

A: No matter whether people believe in God or not, they will do what they want to do. The Russian people don't need a god for morality; they are naturally very moral, honest, faithful in marriage.

Q: What is the sexual morality in comparison with the United States?

A: It is better in Russia than in the United States. Its foundation there is the good of the state.

Q: What impressed you most about Russia? What did you like most?

A: The care that the state provides for everyone. If a man gets sick, no matter what his status is, how poor he is, the state will take care of him.

Q: What impresses you most about the United States?

A: The material prosperity. In Russia it is very hard to buy even a suit or a pair of shoes, and even when you can get them, they are very expensive.

Q: What do the Russian people think of Khrushchev? Do they like him better than Stalin?

A: They like Khrushchev much better. He is a working man, a peasant. An example of the kind of things he does: Once at a party broadcast over the radio he had had a little too much to drink and he began to swear over the radio. That's the kind of thing he does.

Q: What about religion among the young people in Russia?

A: Religion is dead among the youth of Russia.

Q: Why did you return to the United States? (The question was not asked in exactly this way, but this is its content.)

A: When he saw that Russia was lacking, he wanted to come back to the United States, which is so much better off materially. He still held the ideals of the Soviets, was still a Marxist, but did not like the widespread lack of material goods that the Russians had to endure. [He also] praised the Soviets for rebuilding so much and for concentrating on heavy industry. He said at one point that if the Negroes in the United States knew it was so good in Russia, they'd want to go there.

Another question:

Q: Why don't the Russians see they are being indoctrinated and they are being denied the truth by these jamming stations?

A: They are convinced that such contact would harm them and would be dangerous. They are convinced that the state is doing them a favor by denying them access to Western radio broadcasts.[11]

While Marina does not recall his mood on their return from Mobile, odds are that Oswald had to be a bit impressed with himself, for when they began to talk about the new baby who would be born in October, he was not only convinced that it would be a boy but that he would know just how to bring him up.

> *McMillan:* "I'll make a President out of my son." He had spoken this way before the birth of his first child, and again . . . before he tried to shoot General Walker. But now, he went a step further. He said that in twenty years' time, *he* would be President or prime minister. It did not seem to matter that America has no prime minister.[12]

Perhaps he was thinking of an entirely new structure of government. The Atheian system was going to produce great changes in America.

7

Out of Omens Come Events

Somewhere around the end of July, Oswald sent the following letter to FPCC headquarters in New York:

> Dear Mr. Lee,
>   I was glad to receive your advice concerning my try at starting a New Orleans FPCC Chapter. I hope you won't be too disapproving at my innovations, but I do think they are necessary for this area.

As per your advice, I have taken a P.O. box (no. 30061).

Against your advice, I have decided to take an office from the very beginning.

As you see from the circular, I had jumped the gun on the charter business but I don't think it is too important; you may think the circular is too provocative, but I want it to attract attention, even if it's the attention of the lunatic fringe. I had 2,000 of them run off. . . .

In any event, I will keep you posted, and even if the office only stays open for one month, more people will find out about the FPCC than if there had never been any office at all . . .[1]

As he told the Warren Commission, V. T. Lee was sufficiently dismayed by this letter to cease corresponding with Oswald:

MR. LEE. . . . he had gone ahead and acted on his own without any authorization . . . when somebody writes to you and says they would like to help you, your immediate response is, "Well, wonderful. Here is a new contact in a new part of the hinterlands and, gee, I hope things work out." And then, when somebody goes off like this, violating all the rules that you send him, it comes as quite a disappointment because you had hopes. Obviously, this man was not operating in an official capacity for the organization.[2]

Oswald, however, was as yet unaware that his last letter had ruptured relations:

Dear Mr. Lee,

In regards to my efforts to start a branch of FPCC in New Orleans.

I rented an office as I planned and was promptly closed three days later for some obscure reasons by the renters, they said something about remodeling, etc; I'm sure you understand. After that I worked out of a post office box and by using street demonstrations and some circular work have sustained a great deal of interest but no new members.

Through the efforts of some Cuban-exile "gusanos," a street demonstration was attacked and we were officially cautioned by the police. The incident robbed me of what support I had, leaving me alone.

Nevertheless, thousands of circulars were distributed and many, many pamphlets which your office supplied.

We also managed to picket the fleet when it came in and I was surprised in the number of officers who were interested on our literature.

I continue to receive through my post office box inquiries and questions which I shall endeavor to keep answering to the best of my ability.

Thank you,

Lee H. Oswald[3]

McMillan: The letter was dated August 1 and postmarked August 4 and it contains not a single true fact apart from the reference to picketing the fleet, which had occurred a month and a half before.

The uncanny thing . . . is that on Monday, August 5, the day after he mailed it, Lee started to bring [into being some of the] events he had just described.[4]

The essence of magic is to exist in a state of consciousness where past and future seem interchangeable. Classical Hebrew, for example, has only two tenses: There is the present, and then there is another tense which barely distinguishes between past and future. To indicate a past action, it is enough to say, "I went"; yet, to speak of the future, one need only add the word "and" as in, "and I went," and it becomes equal to "I will go." A primitive sense of existence is suggested—one that would transgress our modern separation between the real and the imaginary. In such an ancient grammar, yesterday's events are not seen as facts which have already occurred so much as intimations of the future, that is, omens received from a dream. In that primitive world, the events of yesterday mix in one's memory with the portents of last night's dream. To say, therefore, that you have done something which you have not yet done becomes the first and essential step in shaping the future. Out of omens come events. It is as if the future cannot exist without an *a priori* delineation of it. God conceives of the world, then makes it. The cabalistic sense is that in His act of conceiving the world, God has already made it. (The rest is details!)

Let us repeat one sentence from Oswald's letter to V. T. Lee. "Through the efforts of some Cuban-exile 'gusanos,' a street demonstration was attacked and we were officially cautioned by the police." That was written on August 1.

MR. BRINGUIER. Well, the first day that I saw Lee Harvey Oswald was on August 5, 1963, but before we go any deeper in this matter about Oswald, I think that I would like to explain to you . . . my feeling at the moment.

MR. LIEBELER. That is perfectly all right. Go ahead.

MR. BRINGUIER. . . . you see, in August 24, 1962, my organization, the Cuban Student Directorate, carry on a shelling of Havana, and a few days later a person from the FBI contacted me here in New Orleans—his name was Warren C. deBrueys. Mr. deBrueys was talking to me in the Thompson Cafeteria. At that moment I was the only one from the Cuban Student Directorate here in the city and he was asking me about my activities . . . and when I told him that I was the only one, he didn't believe it, and he advised me—and I quote, "We could infiltrate your organization and find out what you are doing here." My answer to him was, "Well, you will have to infiltrate myself, because I am the only one." . . .

After that, after my conversation with deBrueys, I was always waiting that maybe someone will come to infiltrate my organization from the FBI [so] when Oswald came to me on August 5 [1963], I had inside myself the feeling, well, maybe this is from the FBI, or maybe this is a Communist, [but] I only had that [as a] feeling on August 5 because 4 days later I was convinced that Oswald was not an FBI agent but that he was a pro-Castro agent.

. . . Now that day, on August 5, I was talking in the store with one young American—the name of him is Philip Geraci—and 5 minutes later Mr. Oswald came inside the store [while] I was explaining to Geraci that . . . he was too young, that if he want to distribute literature against Castro, I would give him the literature but not admit him to the fight.

At that moment also . . . Oswald start to agree with my point of view and he show real interest in the fight against Castro. He told me that he was against Castro and that he was against communism [and] he asked me first for some English literature against Castro . . .

After that, Oswald told me that he had been in the Marine Corps and that he had been training in guerrilla warfare and that he was willing to train Cubans to fight against Castro. Even more, he told me that he was willing to go himself. . . . That was on August 5.

I turned down his offer. I told him that . . . my only duties here in New Orleans are propaganda and information and not military activities. That was my answer to him [but] before he left the store, he put his hand in the pocket and he offered me money.

MR. LIEBELER. Oswald did?

MR. BRINGUIER. Yes.

MR. LIEBELER. How much did he offer you?

MR. BRINGUIER. Well, I don't know. As soon as he put the hand in the pocket and he told me, "Well, at least let me contribute to your group with some money," at that moment I didn't have the permit from the city hall here in New Orleans to collect money in the city, and I told him that I could not accept . . . he could send the money directly to the headquarters . . . and I gave him the number of the post office box . . . in Miami.[5]

The youth, Philip Geraci, who Bringuier had decided was too young to join the active fight, offers in his testimony a closer account of the conversation with Oswald:

MR. GERACI. . . . he came in and said, "Excuse me," and you know, he acted a little nervous and things like that. He asked, "Is this the Cuban headquarters, Cuban exile headquarters?" . . . And Carlos said yes; . . . and then Oswald said something like, "It is kind of exciting meeting . . . somebody who is a real Cuban exile, you know, someone who is really trying to do something to help free Cuba and all that." . . . Carlos just answered real simply [and] didn't go into any big speeches, [then Carlos had to go] and that left Oswald, me, and Vance [my friend] by ourselves.

Then, well, we asked—you know, we were a little interested in guerrilla warfare . . . and he said, well, he was an ex-Marine . . . He said he learned a little bit about that stuff . . . I remember, like he said the way to derail a train was to wrap chain around the ties of the track and then lock it with a padlock and the train would derail. He said the thing he liked best of all was learning how to blow up the Huey P. Long Bridge. He said you put explosive at each end on the banks and blow it up, and that leaves the one column standing. And he said how to make a homemade gun and how to make gunpowder, homemade gunpowder . . .

He didn't really go into detail or anything. We didn't ask him. And by this time, Carlos came back . . . and he was listening, and, well, that is about all.

Oh, there was one important thing. Oswald said something like that he had a military manual from when he was in the Marines, and he said he would give it to me, and I said, "That is all right. You don't have to. You can give it to Carlos." He said, "Well, OK, he will give it to Carlos next time he comes."[6]

Four days later, this scene would take on considerable significance for Carlos Bringuier:

MR. BRINGUIER. . . . Next day, on August 6, Oswald came back to the store . . . and he left with my brother-in-law a Guidebook for Marines for me with the name "L. H. Oswald" in the top of the first page. When I came back to the store. . . . I found interest in it and I keep it, and later . . . on August 9 I was coming back to the store at 2 o'clock in the afternoon, and one friend of mine with the name of Celso Hernandez came in to me and told me that in Canal Street there was a young man carrying a sign telling "Viva Fidel" in Spanish . . . At that moment was in the store another Cuban with the name of Miguel Cruz, and we went all three . . . to Canal Street to find the guy . . . but we could not [so] I went back to the store [and then] Miguel Cruz came running and told me that the guy was another time in Canal Street and that Celso was watching him over there.

I went over [again] and I was surprised when I recognized that the guy . . . was Lee Harvey Oswald [and when] he recognized me, he was also surprised, but just for a few seconds. Immediately he smiled to me and he offered the hand to shake hands with me. I became more angry and I start to tell him that he don't have any face to do that, with what face he was doing that? . . . He was a Castro agent . . .

That was a Friday around 3 o'clock at this moment, and many people start to gather around us to see what was going on over there. I start to explain to the people what Oswald did to me, because I wanted to move the American people against him, not to take the fight for myself as a Cuban but to move the American people to fight him, and I told them that he was a Castro agent, that he was a pro-Communist, and that he was trying to do to them exactly what he did to us in Cuba, kill them and send their children to the execution wall. Those were my phrases at the moment.

The people in the street became angry and started to shout to him, "Traitor! Communist! Go to Cuba! Kill him!" and some other phrases . . . bad phrases, bad words.[7]

At that moment, a policeman arrived and told Bringuier to keep walking:

MR. BRINGUIER. [The policeman said] to let Oswald distribute his literature that he was handing out—yellow leaflets of the Fair Play for Cuba Committee, New Orleans Chapter—and I told to the policeman that I was a Cuban, I explained to him what Oswald did to me, and I told him . . . that I will not leave that place until Oswald left and that I will make some trouble.

The policeman left, I believe going to some place to call the headquarters, and at that moment my friend Celso took the literature from Oswald, the yellow sheets, and broke it and threw it on the air. There were a lot of yellow sheets flying. And I was more angry, and . . . I took my glasses off and I went near to him to hit him, but when he sensed my intention, he put his arm down as an X, like this here (demonstrating).

MR. LIEBELER. He crossed his arms in front of him?

MR. BRINGUIER. That is right, put his face and told me, "OK, Carlos, if you want to hit me, hit me."

At that moment, that made me to reaction that he was trying to appear as a martyr if I will hit him, and I decide not to hit him, and just a few seconds later arrive two police cars, and . . . they put Oswald and my two friends in one of the police cars, and I went . . . in the other police car to the First District of Police here in New Orleans [and now] we were in the same room, one small room over there, and some of the policemen start to question Oswald if he was a communist . . . and Oswald at that moment [was] really cold blood. He was answering the questions that he would like to answer, and he was not nervous, he was not out of control, he was confident in himself at that moment over there.[8]

MR. LIEBELER. Now it doesn't seem likely, does it, that Oswald would go around handing out literature in the streets like he did if he was actually attempting to infiltrate the anti-Castro movement?

MR. BRINGUIER. Remember that that was after I turned down his offer and after I told him that I don't have nothing to do with military activities and here there is nothing, and that I turned down completely him . . . he went openly to do that after he was turned down . . .[9]

Oswald had landed in jail late on Friday afternoon—not the easiest time to get out. Dutz Murret was away on a three-day religious retreat, Lillian Murret was in the hospital for an eye operation, and the only person available to help him was his cousin Joyce Murret O'Brien, one of Lillian's daughters. She certainly did not get her cousin out on Friday night, but Joyce did stay at the jail long enough to tell the authorities that Lee Harvey Oswald had been in Russia.

MRS. MURRET. . . . she had been there twice with the money in her hand, and each time she came back out again . . . She told me she had talked to this officer there and [that] the man told her not to be foolish and give her money up like that, because she might not get it back. . . . He said, "Have somebody parole him." So Joyce didn't know what to do. She had been out of New Orleans a long time. . . . This officer showed her the sign they said Lee was carrying . . . "Viva El Castro," so when Joyce saw that . . . "Oh, my God," she said, "I am not about to get him out of here if he's like that," so she didn't . . . give up her money. She said, "Here he was supposed to be out looking for a job, and he was doing things like that, walking up and down Canal Street all day long with signs and everything."[10]

Next morning, Oswald was the center of attention. That seems to be equal to saying that he was calm and cool. The officer questioning him was Lieutenant Francis Martello of the Intelligence Division of the New Orleans police force, and he compiled a report of their meeting.

. . . I then asked him if he was a communist and he said he was not, I asked him if he was a socialist and he said 'guilty.' We then spoke at length concerning the philosophies of communism, socialism, and America. He said he was in full accord with the book Das Kapital, which book was written by KARL MARX. I know that this book condemns the American

way of government in entirety. I asked him if he thought that
the communist way of life was better than the American way
of life and he replied there was not true communism in Russia. He said that MARX . . . was not a communist but a socialist. He stated this was the reason he did not consider himself
to be a communist. I asked him what was his opinion of the
form of communism in Russia since he had lived there for
two years and he replied, 'It stunk.' He said they have 'fat
stinking politicians over there just like we have over here,'
. . . I asked him what he thought about President JOHN F.
KENNEDY and NIKITA KHRUSHCHEV. He said he thought they got
along very well together. I then asked him if he had to place
allegiance or make a decision between Russia or America,
which he would choose and he said, 'I would place my allegiance at the foot of democracy.'[11]

MR. LIEBELER. Now, your memorandum indicates that you asked
Oswald what he thought about President Kennedy and Premier
Khrushchev . . .

MR. MARTELLO. . . . . all of his thoughts seemed to go in the direction of the Socialist or Russian way of life, but he showed in his
manner of speaking that he liked the President, the impression
I got, or if he didn't like him, of the two he disliked the President the least. He is a very peculiar type of an individual, which
is typical of quite a few of the many demonstrators that I have
handled during the period of 2 years while in the Intelligence
Division. They seemed to be trying to find themselves or something. I am not expert in the field or anything, not trying to go
out of my bounds, but quite a few of them, after lengthy interviews you find that they have some peculiarities about their
thinking that does not follow logically with their movements or
their action.

MR. LIEBELER. Did he indicate which [country] in his opinion,
was the lesser of the two evils?

MR. MARTELLO. From the way he spoke, the impression I received,
it appeared to me that he felt Russia was the lesser of the two
evils.

MR. LIEBELER. Did he express this idea with great forcefulness, or
just sort of a "pox on both your houses" fashion, that really it
was just too ridiculous, and that sort of thing?

MR. MARTELLO. With a nonchalant attitude. He was a very cool speaker . . . no aggressiveness or emotional outbursts in any way, shape, or form. It was just a very calm conversation we had, and there was no emotion involved whatsoever.

MR. LIEBELER. Did he show any hesitancy about expressing these ideas to you as a member of the police department?

MR. MARTELLO. None whatsoever, sir.[12]

Oswald is thirsty for conversation. He will speak to anyone. He wishes to establish himself as a unique figure in the political, social, and police theatre of New Orleans. Since we have yet to steal up to the question of whether he was doing all this entirely for himself or was receiving a stipend from some official, semi-official, or impromptu group, a few sinister possibilities have to be kept in mind. Yet not unduly so. We have not grasped anything of Oswald if we assume that if he is being paid by the FBI to perform their left-wing activities, we are obliged to change all our ideas of him. Even if he was doing a little work for the FBI, there is no need to assume he was loyal to them. His fealty would be to himself and to his own ideas. Any actions he performed for others—if indeed he did—would be adapted to his personal agenda, which was to get to Cuba with impressive credentials. Creating attention for FPCC in New Orleans would not only serve the aim of the FBI to enhance a few Red-baiting possibilities, but would increase his own importance.

Stimulated to the hilt, therefore, by police interest in him, he now informs Lieutenant Martello that he wishes to be interviewed by somebody from the FBI. He has obviously enjoyed talking to Martello, and must be in a state of high adrenaline. He is ready for ultimates—so why not test his wits with an FBI man? If we need a more self-serving motive, it is fair to assume he was also afraid—what with the virulence of local anti-Castro sentiments—of getting roughed up and/or raped in that jail; given the shilly-shallying of cousin Joyce, he might have to spend another night in the can. Requesting the presence of an FBI man would give the prison personnel and the prison population a few second thoughts about taking him on.

Special Agent John Quigley's testimony on their meeting is a model demonstration of how the FBI can reduce an uncommon event to a common one:

MR. QUIGLEY. . . . . At one point of the interview he told me that he had held one of the Fair Play for Cuba Committee meetings at his home. I asked him, "Well, how did you get in touch with the other people?" "Well, I don't care to discuss that." "Who were the persons at the meeting?" "I don't know." "Did you know any names at all?" "Yes. They were introduced to me by first names only." "What were their first names?" "I cannot remember." So it was apparent to me that he was certainly not going to furnish anything . . . for example, I asked him about A. J. Hidell . . . "Well, Mr. Hidell had a telephone." "What was Mr. Hidell's telephone number?" "Mr. Hidell's telephone has been disconnected." "What was the number?" "I can't remember."[13]

MR. STERN. Would it be usual, or had it occurred before that someone would ask for an interview and then refuse to respond to your questions? Didn't that seem strange?

MR. QUIGLEY. Not necessarily; not necessarily. Frequently people will have a problem and want to talk to an FBI agent and they want to tell them what their problem is, but then when you start probing into it then they don't want to talk to you. I think that is just human nature. If you are probing too deep it gets a little touchy.[14]

After Joyce had come back without Lee, Lillian Murret called a friend of the family, Emile Bruneau, a state boxing commissioner who got Oswald out on his own recognizance until his trial, Monday, August 12. Lee came home from jail late that Saturday morning, August 10.

On Friday night, Marina had not fallen asleep until three in the morning, but she had not felt anything like the dread she had known on the night of April 10 in Dallas. Here on Magazine Street, his rifle was still in the closet, and so she assumed correctly that he had been arrested for distributing his pamphlets.

McMillan: Lee arrived home in scapegrace good spirits, dirty, rumpled, unshaven, with a glint of humor in his eye and an air of gaiety about him. "I've been to the police station."

"I thought so," said Marina. "So that's the way it turned out."

She wanted to know where he slept. He explained that the beds had no mattresses, so he had taken off all his clothes and made a mattress of them.

"You slept without any pants on?"

"It was hot. And it was just men, anyway. If they didn't like it, they could have let me out sooner."[15]

Oswald was taking his pants off, and to hell with what every hungry con thought of his ass. Or so he claimed. But we know that he knew better. One doesn't take one's pants off on a one-night stand in jail.

McMillan: That evening, Dutz Murret, home from the retreat, went immediately to the Oswalds'. He noticed with horror Castro's photograph pinned to the wall, and asked Lee straight out if he was part of any "Commie" group. Lee answered that he was not. Dutz told him in no uncertain terms to show up in court the next day and, after that, go out, get a job, and support his family.[16]

MR. BRINGUIER. On August 12, we appear in the second municipal court in New Orleans. I came first with my friends, and there were some other Cubans there, and I saw when Oswald came inside . . . See, here in the court you have two sides, one for the white people and one for the colored people, and . . . he sat directly among [the colored people] in the middle, and that made me angry too, because I saw that he was trying to win the colored people for his side. When he will appear in the court, he will defend Fidel Castro, he will defend the Fair Play for Cuba, and the colored people will feel good for him, and that is a tremendous work of propaganda for his cause. This is one of the things that made me to think that he was really a smart guy and not a nut.[17]

Oswald pled guilty to "disturbing the peace," paid a $10 fine, and left. His coup of sitting among the blacks may have balanced his annoyance at having to accept the fine, but then, his feelings for blacks could have been genuine. Moreover, it was hardly a cheap gesture. Only two months had passed since Medgar Evers had been gunned down in Mississippi.

Was Oswald oblivious of the irony that Emile Bruneau, a big-time gambler, had helped to get him out of jail? That had been fitting. He had been gambling all his life for the largest personal stakes. Like his brethren, he had runs of luck, and doubtless he believed that you had to run with your luck and bet double with your winnings.

Since the lecture at the Jesuit House of Studies had gone well and his arrest had just established his credentials to speak for Castro's Cuba, it was now time to search out the media.

McMillan: On Friday, August 16 . . . Lee waited with unaccustomed patience for Marina to iron his favorite shirt. He had already called the local TV stations to tell them that there would be a Fair Play for Cuba demonstration that day in front of the Trade Mart building in downtown New Orleans.

Lee hired two recruits . . . to help him hand out his leaflets. The fifteen- or twenty-minute demonstration went off without trouble, and pictures of Lee were shown on the televised news that night.[18]

The media arrived next day at 8:00 A.M. in the form of a thin, bearded man named William Kirk Stuckey, who had a radio program on WDSU called "Latin Listening Post."

8

Fair Play

MR. STUCKEY. . . . I went early because I wanted to get him before he left.

MR. JENNER. This was a Saturday?

MR. STUCKEY. It is a Saturday. I knocked on the door, and this young fellow came out, without a shirt. He had a pair of Marine Corps fatigue trousers on. I asked him, "Are you Lee Oswald?" And he said, "Yes."

I introduced myself and I told him I would like to have him on my program that night. . . . He said he would ask me in for some coffee but that his wife and baby were sleeping so we had better talk on the porch.[1]

Oswald showed him a pamphlet of a speech by Fidel Castro translated into English—"The Revolution Must Be a School of Unfettered Thought"—and another by Sartre, "Ideology and Revolution."

> **MR. STUCKEY.** . . . I asked him about the membership of this organization, and he said there were quite a few . . . members. The figure 12 or 13 sticks in my head, I don't really recall why now.[2]

Oswald and twelve apostles. An ideologue dreaming of world-shaking action, he takes it for granted that he can find points of identification with everyone from Jesus to Hitler.

> **MR. JENNER.** Just give your best recollection of what he said on that occasion.
>
> **MR. STUCKEY.** . . . he was very vehement, insisting he was not the president, but was the secretary, and that was the occasion in which he pulled out his card showing that . . . this other gentleman, Hidell, was the president . . . He appeared to be a very logical, intelligent fellow, and the only strange thing about him was his organization. [It seemed incongruous that] he should associate with a group of this type . . . he did not seem the type at all . . . I was arrested by his cleancutness . . . I expected a folksinger type . . . somebody with a beard and sandals and . . . instead I found a fellow who was neat and clean, [and] seemed to be very conscious about all of his words, all of his movements, sort of very deliberate . . . He was the type of person you would say would inspire confidence. This was the incongruity that struck me, the fact that this type of person should be with this organization . . .
>
> I asked him to meet me at the radio station that afternoon about 5 o'clock . . . and he agreed [to give] a recorded interview prior to the broadcast.
>
> **MR. JENNER.** Why would you do that?
>
> **MR. STUCKEY.** To avoid the possibility of errors. It is a risky business going on live. You know, you never know when you are going to slip up and, particularly, with somebody as controversial as a representative of the Fair Play for Cuba Committee you want to know what you have in hand before you put it on.[3]

The excerpt that follows is taken from the full thirty-seven-minute interview. This passage and the debate Oswald will have with anti-Castro spokesmen a few days later are two of the best examples of his style of speaking and his skill in argument. If he had not been dyslexic, it is more than likely that he would have been able to write at least as well as he spoke, and that would have been not unimpressive for a twenty-three-year-old polemicist.

STUCKEY: Tonight we have with us a representative of probably the most controversial organization connected with Cuba in this country. The organization is the Fair Play for Cuba Committee. The person, Lee Oswald, secretary of the New Orleans Chapter for the Fair Play for Cuba Committee. This organization has long been on the Justice Department's blacklist and is a group generally considered to be the leading pro-Castro body in the nation. As a reporter of Latin American affairs in this city for several years now, your columnist has kept a lookout for representatives of this pro-Castro group. None appeared in public view until this week, when young Lee Oswald was arrested and convicted for disturbing the peace. He was arrested passing out pro-Castro literature to a crowd which included several violently anti-Castro Cuban refugees. When we finally tracked Mr. Oswald down today and asked him to participate in "Latin Listening Post," he told us frankly that he would because it may help his organization to attract more members in this area . . . And knowing that Mr. Oswald must have had to demonstrate a great skill in dialectics before he was entrusted with his present post, we now proceed on the course of random questioning of Mr. Oswald.[4]

With such an introduction, how could Oswald not be near to heaven? He is, however, no longer in the world of manners but in the media. His host moves quickly to the attack:

STUCKEY: Mr. Oswald, there are many commentators in the journalistic field in this country that equate the Fair Play for Cuba Committee with the American Communist Party. What is your feeling about this and are you a member of the American Communist Party?

OSWALD: Well, the Fair Play for Cuba Committee with its headquarters at 799 Broadway in New York has been investigated by the Senate sub-committees who are occupied with this sort of thing.

They have investigated our organization from the viewpoint of taxes, subversion, allegiance and in general, where and how and why we exist. They have found absolutely nothing to connect us with the Communist Party of the United States. In regards to your question as to whether I myself am a Communist, as I said, I do not belong to any other organization. . . .

STUCKEY: Does your group believe that the Castro regime is not actually a front for a Soviet colony in the Western Hemisphere?

OSWALD: Very definitely. Castro is an independent leader of an independent country. He has ties with the Soviet Union . . . That does not mean, however, that he is dependent on Russia. He receives trade from many countries, including Great Britain to a certain extent, France, certain other powers in the Western Hemisphere. He is even trading with several of the more independent African states, so that you cannot point at Castro and say that he is a Russian puppet. . . . I believe that was pointed out very well during the October crisis, when Castro definitely said that although Premier Khrushchev had urged him to have on-site inspection of his rocket bases in Cuba, that Fidel Castro refused.

STUCKEY: Do you feel that the Fair Play for Cuba Committee would maintain its present line as far as supporting Premier Castro if the Soviet Union broke relations with the Castro regime in Cuba?

OSWALD: We do not support the man. We do not support the individual. We support the idea of an independent revolution in the Western Hemisphere, free from American intervention. . . . If the Cuban people destroy Castro, or if he is otherwise proven to have betrayed his own revolution, that will not have any bearing upon this committee. . . .

STUCKEY: Do you believe that the Castro regime is a Communist regime?

OSWALD: They have said . . . that they are a Marxist country. On the other hand, so is Ghana, so is several other countries in Africa. Every country which emerges from a sort of feudal state, as Cuba did, experiments, usually, in socialism, in Marxism. For that matter, Great Britain has socialized medicine. You cannot say that Castro is a Communist at this time, because he has not developed his country, his system, this far. He has not had the chance to become a Communist. He is an experimenter, a person who is trying to find the best way for his country. If he chooses a socialist or a

Marxist or a Communist way of life, that is something upon which only the Cuban people can pass. We do not have the right to pass on that. . . .

STUCKEY: Mr. Oswald, does it make any difference to you if any of the activities of the local branch of the Fair Play for Cuba Committee benefit the Communist Party or the goals of international Communism?

OSWALD: Well, that is what I believe you would term a loaded question. However, I will attempt to answer it. It is inconsistent with my ideals to support Communism, my personal ideals. It is inconsistent with the ideals of the Fair Play for Cuba Committee to support ideals of international Communism. We are not occupied with that problem. We are occupied with the problem of Cuba. We do not believe under any circumstances that in supporting our ideals about Cuba, our pro-Castro ideals, we do not believe that is inconsistent with believing in democracy. Quite the contrary. . . .[5]

They began to speak of other countries in Latin America. Oswald remarked: "Who will be able to find any official or any person who knows about Latin America who will say that Nicaragua does not have a dictatorship?" They had come to the crux of the discussion. Stuckey may have thought that Oswald was now in trouble:

STUCKEY: Very interesting. [We] have heard about these dictatorships for many, many years, but it is curious to me why no Nicaraguans fled to the United States last year, whereas we had possibly 50,000 to 60,000 Cubans fleeing from Cuba to the United States. What is the Fair Play for Cuba Committee's official reply to this?

OSWALD: Well, a good question. Nicaragua's situation is considerably different from Castro's Cuba. People are inclined not to flee their countries unless some new system, new factor, enters into their lives. I must say that very surely no new factors have entered into Nicaragua for about 300 years, in fact, the people live exactly as they have always lived in Nicaragua. I am referring to the overwhelming majority of the people in Nicaragua, which is a feudal dictatorship with 90 percent of the people engaged in agriculture. These peasants are uneducated. They have one of the lowest living standards in all of the Western Hemisphere [so] no new factor, no liberating factor has entered into their lives, they remain in Nicaragua. Now the people who have fled Cuba, that is the interesting situation. Needless to say, there are classes of criminals; there are classes of people who are wanted in Cuba for crimes against humanity and most of those people are the same people who are in New Orleans and have set themselves up in stores with blood money and who engage in day to day trade with New Orleanians. Those are the people who would certainly not want to go back to Cuba and who would certainly want to flee Cuba. There are other classes. There are peasants who do not like the collectivization in Cuban agriculture. There are others who have one reason or another . . . for fleeing Cuba. Most of these people . . . are allowed to leave after requesting the Cuban government for exit visas. Some of these people for some reasons or another do not like to apply for these visas or they feel they cannot get them; they flee, they flee Cuba in boats, they flee any way they can go, and I think that the opinion and the attitude of the Cuban government to this is good riddance.

STUCKEY: Mr. Oswald, this is very interesting because as a reporter in the field for some time I have been interviewing refugees now for about three years and I'd say that the last Batista man, officially, that I talked to left Cuba about two and a half years ago and the rest of them that I've talked to have been taxicab drivers, laborers, cane cutters, and that sort of thing. I thought this revolution was supposed to benefit these people . . .

OSWALD: . . . You know, it's very funny about revolutions. Revolutions require work, revolutions require sacrifice, [and] people who have fled Cuba have not been able to adapt themselves to the new factors which have entered these peoples' lives. These people are the uneducated. These people are the people who do not remain in Cuba to be educated by young people, who are afraid of the alphabet, who are afraid of these new things which are occurring, who are afraid that they would lose something by collectivization. They are afraid that they would lose something by seeing their sugar crops taken away and in place of sugar crops, some other vegetable, some other product, planted, because Cuba has always been a one-product country, more or less. These are the people who have not been able to adapt.

STUCKEY: Mr. Oswald, you say their sugar crops. Most of the Cubans I have talked to that have had anything to do with agriculture in the last year and a half have not owned one single acre of ground, they were cane cutters.[6]

If Stuckey has made a telling point, it will hardly stop Oswald. Potentially, he has debater's reflexes worthy of Richard Nixon—he treads water for the duration of three sentences, gathers his reply, and proceeds to give it:

OSWALD: That is correct and they are the ones who are fleeing the Castro regime. That is correct, sir. That is very, very true and I am very glad you brought that point up. You know, it used to be that these people worked for the United Fruit Company or American companies engaged in sugar refining, oil refining in Cuba. They worked a few months every year during the cane cutting or sugar refining season. They never owned anything, and they feel now that . . . the right to work for five months a year has been taken away from them. They feel that now they have to work all year round to plant new crops, to make a new economy, and so they feel that they have been robbed, . . . of the right to do as they please . . . What they do not realize is that they have been robbed of the right to be exploited, robbed of the right to be cheated, robbed of the right of New Orleanian companies to take away what was rightfully theirs. Of course, they have to share now. Everybody gets an equal portion. This is collectivization and this is very hard on some people, on people preferring the dog-eat-dog economy.[7]

MR. JENNER. . . . you supplied the FBI with [a radio] transcript?

MR. STUCKEY. No, as a matter of fact I gave the tape to the FBI the Monday following the interview, which would have been August 20, 1963. I told them I thought it was very interesting, and if they would like to have a transcript they could copy it, which they did. They made a copy and then they gave me a copy of their transcript and returned the tape to me. . . .

MR. JENNER. . . . would you tell us about that broadcast?

MR. STUCKEY. Yes.

As I said, this was a 37-minute rambling interview between Oswald and myself and following the interview, first we played it back to hear it. He was satisfied . . . I think he thought he had scored quite a coup.

Then I went back over it in his presence and with an engineer's help excerpted a couple . . . of his comments in which he said Castro was a free and independent leader of a free and independent state, and the rest of it, as I recall, was largely my summarizing of the other principal points of the 37-minute interview, and it was broadcast on schedule that night.

MR. JENNER. You had watered it down in length to how many minutes?

MR. STUCKEY. Five minutes.

MR. JENNER. Five minutes?

MR. STUCKEY. Actually 4 and a half.

MR. JENNER. . . . Was that your last contact with Mr. Oswald?

MR. STUCKEY. No, it was not. . . . I told him that I was going to talk to the news director to see if [he] was interested in running the entire 37-minute tape later, [but] the news director [said] there would be more public interest if we did not run this tape at all but instead arranged a second program, a debate panel show, with some local anti-Communists on there to refute some of his arguments . . .

I picked Mr. Edward S. Butler [who] is the Executive Director of the Information Council of the Americas in New Orleans . . . an anti-Communist propaganda organization. Their principal activity is to [distribute] strongly anti-Communist . . . tapes to radio stations throughout Latin America . . .

MR. JENNER. [Mr. Butler] was an articulate and knowledgeable man in this area to which he directs his attention?

MR. STUCKEY. Yes; so I asked him to be one of the panelists on the show, which he accepted, and incidentally, I let him hear the 37-minute tape in advance; and for the other panelist, I asked Mr. Carlos Bringuier [in order] to give it a little Cuban flavor.

And then Oswald called me . . . and I told him we were going to arrange the show and would he be interested, and he said, yes, indeed, and then he said, "How many of you am I going to have to fight?" That was his version of saying how many are on the panel.

MR. JENNER. He said this to you?

MR. STUCKEY. Yes; in a jocular way . . . He said he thought that would be interesting.[8]

Lee is ready to believe that he may just be as good as he has been telling himself he is ever since he started dominating political discussions in the Marine Corps.

Of course, his estimate of the power of the machine he opposes is not nearly so keen as his recognition of his own capacities when he is at his best.

McMillan: While he was talking to an FBI source over the telephone that day, Stuckey, as he remembers it, was put through to the chief or deputy chief of the New Orleans bureau, and this man read aloud to him over the phone portions of Oswald's FBI file, including the facts that he had been to Russia, tried to renounce his U.S. citizenship, stayed there nearly three years, and married a Russian woman. Stuckey went to the FBI office and was permitted to examine the file, as well as newspaper clippings from Moscow at the time of Oswald's defection.[9]

MR. JENNER. And was he unaware when he came in at 5:30 on the afternoon of Wednesday that you had done this, and received this information and had done some research?

MR. STUCKEY. He was unaware of that fact. During the day . . . Mr. Butler called and said he too had found out the same thing . . . his source apparently was the House Un-American Activities Committee [and] we agreed together to produce this information on the program that night.

MR. JENNER. . . . You thought it might be a bombshell and be unaware to him?

MR. STUCKEY. Exactly.

MR. JENNER. All right.

MR. STUCKEY. . . . So at about 5:30 that afternoon I arrived at the studio alone. Oswald appeared, and in a very heavy gray flannel suit, and this is August in New Orleans, it is extremely hot, but he appears in [this] very bulky, badly cut suit, and looking very hot and uncomfortable. He had a blue shirt on and a dark tie, and a black looseleaf notebook . . . then Mr. Butler came in with Mr. Bringuier. Both looked as if they had pounds and pounds of literature with them, and statistics . . .

MR. JENNER. Had Oswald met Mr. Butler before?

MR. STUCKEY. . . . I think he knew who he was. Oswald asked me something about the organization, and I told him, I said, "Well, it is just like your organization; it is a propaganda outfit, just on the other side of the fence," and that satisfied his curiosity.

I think he immediately kissed it off as a hopeless rightist organization . . .[10]

Carlos Bringuier and Oswald had a conversation before the show began:

MR. BRINGUIER. . . . I was. . . . trying to be as friendly to him as I could. I really believe that the best thing I could do is get one Communist out of the Communist Party and put him to work against communism, because [then] he know what communism mean, and I told to Oswald that I don't have nothing against him in the personal way, just the ideologic way. I told him that for me it was impossible to see one American being a communist, because communism is trying to destroy the United States, and that if any moment . . . he will start to think that he can do something good for his country, for his family, and for himself, he could come to me, because I would receive him, because I repeat to him that I didn't have nothing against him in the personal way. He smiled to me. He told me—he answered me that he was in the right side, the correct side, and that I was in the wrong side, and that he was doing his best. That were his words at that moment.

Before we went inside the room of the debate, he saw my guidebook for Marines that I was carrying with me, because I did not know what will happen in the debate and I will have to have that weapon with me to destroy him personally as a traitor if he is doing something wrong in the debate. When he saw the guidebook for Marines, he smiled to me, and he told me, "Well, listen, Carlos, don't try to do an invasion with that guidebook for Marines, because that is an old one and that will be a failure." That was his joke in that moment . . ."[11]

They began—Oswald against Bringuier and Butler and Stuckey and a moderator named Slatter. After the introductions, no time was wasted:

BILL STUCKEY: . . . Mr. Butler brought some newspaper clippings to my attention . . . that Mr. Oswald had attempted to renounce his

American citizenship in 1959 and become a Soviet citizen. There was another clipping dated 1962 saying that Mr. Oswald had returned from the Soviet Union with his wife and child after having lived there three years. Mr. Oswald, are these correct?

OSWALD: That is correct. Correct, yeah.

BILL STUCKEY: You did live in Russia for three years?

OSWALD: That is correct, and I think that the fact that I did live for a time in the Soviet Union gives me excellent qualifications to repudiate charges that Cuba and the Fair Play for Cuba Committee is communist-controlled.

SLATTER: Mr. Oswald, [is it correct] that you at one time asked to renounce your American citizenship and become a Soviet citizen . . . ?

OSWALD: Well, I don't think that has particular import to this discussion. We are discussing Cuban-American relations.

SLATTER: Well, I think it has a bearing to this extent, Mr. Oswald: You say apparently that Cuba is not dominated by Russia and yet you apparently, by your own past actions, have shown that you have an affinity for Russia and perhaps communism, although I don't know that you admit that you either are a communist or have been, could you straighten out that part? Are you or have you been a communist?

OSWALD: Well, I answered that prior to this program, on another radio program.

STUCKEY: Are you a Marxist?

OSWALD: Yes, I am a Marxist.

BUTLER: What's the difference?

OSWALD: The difference is primarily the difference between a country like Guinea, Ghana, Yugoslavia, China, or Russia. Very, very great differences. Differences which we appreciate by giving aid, let's say, to Yugoslavia in the sum of a hundred million or so dollars a year.

BUTLER: That's extraneous. What's the difference?

OSWALD: The difference is, as I have said, a very great difference. Many parties, many countries, are based on Marxism. Many countries such as Great Britain display very socialistic aspects or characteristics. I might point to the socialized medicine of Britain.

BUTLER: I was speaking of—

SLATTER: Gentlemen, I'll have to interrupt and we'll be back in a moment to continue this kind of lively discussion after this message.

COMMERCIAL

STUCKEY: Mr. Oswald, I believe you said in a reply to a question of Mr. Butler's that any questions about your background were extraneous to the discussion tonight. I disagree because of the fact that you're refusing to reveal any of the other members of your organization, so you are the face of the Fair Play for Cuba Committee in New Orleans. Therefore, anybody who might be interested in this organization ought to know more about you. For this reason, I'm curious to know just how you supported yourself during the three years that you lived in the Soviet Union. Did you have a government subsidy?

OSWALD: Well, as I, er, well—I will answer that question directly then, as you will not rest until you get your answer. I worked in Russia . . . At no time, as I say, did I renounce my citizenship or attempt to renounce my citizenship, and at no time was I out of contact with the American Embassy.

BUTLER: Excuse me, may I interrupt just one second. Either one of these two statements is wrong. The *Washington Evening Star* of October 31, 1959, page 1, reported that Lee Harvey Oswald, a former Marine, 4936 Connally Street, Ft. Worth, Texas, had turned in his passport at the American Embassy in Moscow [and] had applied for Soviet citizenship. Now it seems to me that you've renounced your citizenship if you've turned in your passport.

OSWALD: Well, the obvious answer to that is that I am back in the United States. A person who renounces his citizenship becomes legally disqualified for return to the U.S. [but] as I have already stated, of course, this whole conversation, and we don't have too much time left, is getting away from Cuban-American problems. However, I am quite willing to discuss myself for the remainder of the program . . .

SLATTER: Excuse me. Let me interrupt here. I think Mr. Oswald is right to this extent. We shouldn't get to lose sight of the organization of which he is the head in New Orleans, the Fair Play for Cuba.

OSWALD: The Fair Play for Cuba Committee.

SLATTER: As a practical matter, knowing as I'm sure you do, the sentiment in America against Cuba, we, of course, severed diplomatic relations some time ago. I would say Castro is about as unpopular as anybody in the world in this country. As a practical matter, what do you hope to gain for your work? How do you hope to bring about what you call "Fair Play for Cuba," knowing the sentiment?

OSWALD: The principles of thought of the Fair Play for Cuba consist of restoration of diplomatic, trade and tourist relations with Cuba. That is one of our main points. We are for that. I disagree that this situation regarding American-Cuban relations is very unpopular. We are in the minority, surely[, but] we are striving to get the United States to adopt measures which would be more friendly toward the Cuban people and the new Cuban regime in that country. We are not at all communist-controlled regardless of the fact that I had the experience of living in Russia, regardless of the fact that we have been investigated, regardless of any of those facts, the Fair Play for Cuba Committee is an independent organization not affiliated with any other organization. Our aims and our ideals are very clear and in the best keeping with American traditions of democracy.

BRINGUIER: Do you agree with Fidel Castro when in his last speech of July 16th of this year he qualified President John F. Kennedy of the United States as a ruffian and a thief? Do you agree with Mr. Castro?

OSWALD: I would not agree with that particular wording. However, I and the Fair Play for Cuba Committee do think that the United States government, through certain agencies, mainly the State Department and the CIA, has made monumental mistakes in its relations with Cuba. Mistakes which are pushing Cuba into the sphere of activity of, let's say, a very dogmatic communist country such as China is . . .[12]

The show ended soon after.

MR. STUCKEY. . . . I think that after that program, the Fair Play for Cuba Committee, if there ever was one in New Orleans, had no future there, because we had publicly linked the Fair Play for Cuba Committee with a fellow who had lived in Russia for 3 years and who was an admitted Marxist.

The interesting thing, or rather the danger involved, was the fact that Oswald seemed like such a nice, bright boy and was extremely believable before this. We thought the fellow could probably get quite a few members if he was really indeed serious about getting members. We figured after this broadcast of August 21, why, that was no longer possible . . .

MR. JENNER. And after the broadcast broke up, was that the last of your contacts with Oswald?

MR. STUCKEY. No; . . . the others left, and Oswald looked a little dejected, and I said, "Well, let's go out and have a beer," and he says, "All right." So we left the studio and went to a bar called Comeaux's Bar. It is about a half-block from the studio and this was the first time that his manner kind of changed from the quasi-legal position, and he relaxed a little bit. This was the first time I ever saw him relaxed and off his guard. We had about an hour's conversation . . . and by the way . . . he told me afterward [this] suit was purchased in Russia, and they didn't know much about making clothes over there . . .

I asked him at that time how he became interested in Marxism and [whether] his family was an influence on him in any way. He says, "No," and he kind of looked a little amused. "No," he says. "They are pretty typical New Orleans types," and that was about all he said . . .

MR. JENNER. Was he comfortable in the sense—was he eager, was he pleased—

MR. STUCKEY. He was relaxed, he was friendly. He seemed to be relieved it was all over. My impression was he was relieved that he did not have to hide the bit over the Russian residence any more, and that it had been a strain doing so . . .

MR. JENNER. Following that tete-a-tete in Comeaux's Bar for about an hour, did you ever see Oswald after that?

MR. STUCKEY. That was the last time I ever saw him . . .[13]

Stuckey's reactions to Oswald are not unusual for a media man. On the one hand, Oswald is the opponent of the day, and therefore all means at hand are fair to use against him—stack four against one in the debate, shift the ground of the argument—Russia, not Cuba—and do it all without a backward glance. Yet, media people have to be endlessly curious (if only for so long as it takes to satisfy their curiosity), and they are without rancor—should they screw you, they are nice enough not to have hard feelings afterward, just curiosity and a detached kind of sympathy for one more interesting specimen under the glass.

Stuckey sums it up:

MR. STUCKEY. . . . It was my impression Oswald regarded himself as living in a world of intellectual inferiors.

MR. JENNER. Please elaborate on that.

MR. STUCKEY. . . . I had paid some attention to Oswald, nobody else had particularly, and he seemed to enjoy talking with somebody he didn't regard as a stupid person . . . I don't mean to say that there was any arrogance in his manner. There was just—well, you can spot intelligence, or at least I can, I think, and this was a man who was intelligent . . . and who would like to have an opportunity to express his intelligence—that was my impression.[14]

The show left its lacerations, however.

McMillan: Marina had no idea what he was reading, but from indoors she could see that sometimes Lee was not reading at all. He was just sitting on the porch looking out on the street . . .

One evening during the last week of August, she and June went for a stroll. Arriving home about twilight, they found Lee on the porch perched on one knee, pointing his rifle toward the street. It was the first time she had seen him with his rifle in months—and she was horrified.

"What are you doing?" she asked.

"Get the heck out of here," he said. "Don't talk to me . . ."

A few evenings later, she again found him on the porch with his rifle.

"Playing with your gun again, are you," she said, sarcastically.

"Fidel Castro needs defenders," Lee said. "I'm going to join his army of volunteers . . ."

After that, busy indoors, Marina frequently heard a clicking sound out on the porch while Lee was sitting there at dusk. She heard it three times a week, maybe more often, until the middle of September.[15]

Picking Up the Pieces

A week after his radio debate, Oswald wrote a letter to the Central Committee of the Communist Party of the United States. It is interesting for its modesty and apparent sincerity. Is he for the first time in his life looking for advice? Or is the letter written on instructions from others—its aim to ingratiate Oswald with the leadership of the CP-USA?

August 28, 1963

Comrades:

Please advise me upon a problem of personal tactics. . . .

I had, in 1959, in Moscow, tried to legally dissolve my United States citizenship in favor of Soviet citizenship, however, I did not complete the legal formalities for this.

Having come back to the U.S. in 1962 and thrown myself into the struggle for progress and freedom in the United States, I would like to know *whether*, in your *opinion*, I can continue to fight handicapped as it were, by my past record, can I still, under these circumstances, compete with anti-progressive forces, above ground, or *whether* in your *opinion*, I should always remain in the background, i.e., underground.

Our opponents could use my background of residence in the USSR against any cause which I join, they could say the organization of which I am a member is Russian *controlled, etc.* I am sure you see my point.

I could of course openly proclaim, (if pressed on the subject) that I wanted to dissolve my American citizenship as a personal protest against the policy of the U.S. government in supporting dictatorship *etc.* But what do you think I should do? Which is the best tactic in general?

Should I dissociate myself from all progressive activities?

Here in New Orleans, I am secretary of the local *branch* of the "Fair Play for Cuba Committee," a position which, frankly, I have used to foster communist ideals. On a local radio show, I was attacked by Cuban exile organization representatives for my residence *etc.*, in the Soviet Union.

I feel I may have compromised the FPCC, so you see that
I need the advice of trusted, long time fighters for progress.
Please advise.

> With *Fraternal* Greeting
> Sincerely,
> Lee H. Oswald[1]

His letter was answered by Arnold Johnson, who was one of the
leaders of the Communist Party in America.

> September 19, 1963

Dear Mr. Oswald:
 . . . While the point you make about your residence in
the Soviet Union may be utilized by some people, I think
you have to recognize that as an American citizen who is
now in this country, you have a right to participate in such
organizations as you want, including possibly Fair Play,
which are of a very broad character, and often it is advisable for some people to remain in the background, not
underground. I assume this is pretty much of an academic
question now, and we can discuss it later.

> Sincerely yours,
> Arnold Johnson[2]

In any event, whether he was working alone or as a paid provocateur, his activities for the FPCC have ground to a halt; the thousand handbills were distributed and the flurry on radio had not
brought in even one member.

He is discovering the great gap between publicity and its tangi-
ble results. Oswald, too, had bought the American dream of
bonanza—with publicity you become rich and/or famous and/or
powerful. The dirty little secret that is not passed on to good Americans in quest of this bonanza is that a burst of publicity makes one
neither rich, famous, nor powerful—just Queen for a Day.

In the gap between his concerted efforts and their empty outcome, only one bold course of action remained—move to Havana.
He could be of great use to Castro.

McMillan: The obstacles were formidable. Lee had saved a
little money, but possibly not enough to get to Cuba. Moreover, the State Department had banned travel to Cuba by

American citizens, and all that summer *The Militant* had been filled with stories about Americans who faced imprisonment and fines on their return. That was only a minor deterrent, however, for Lee did not intend to return. He hoped to stay . . . Or, if he did not like it there, he would go to China, or else seek readmission to Russia, where he would rejoin Marina. But the problem was how to get [there] in the first place.[3]

Of course, he has already been thinking in bold terms. His offer to join any group of Carlos Bringuier's that was ready to invade Cuba would have been one extreme means of getting there. Presumably, Oswald planned on arrival to abandon the exile group and offer whatever information he had about them to the pro-Castro cadres he would meet soon enough.

What dangerous means he was contemplating! It is a scenario so fraught with peril that it bears the same relation to reasonable danger as kinky sex to the more compassionate varieties.

Marina recalls one hot night when they were sitting in their living room, and it was so hot and they were so poor. No air conditioner. It was New Orleans in summer. Husband and wife both sweating. All of a sudden, he said, "What if we hijack a plane?" She said, "Who is we?"

"You and me," he told her.

"You are joking?"

"No," he said.

"In Russia," she said, "it wasn't good, now America's no good—so it's Cuba."

He said, "I am serious."

She said, "All right, I will have to listen to you and your stupid idea."

He said, "You don't have to kill anybody."

She repeated that as a question: "Kill anybody?"

"You will need a gun," he said, "and I will have a gun, but you will not have to kill anybody. Just be there to threaten people."

She said, "Yes, everybody will be scared of me—a pregnant woman holding a gun, and she doesn't know how to hold it."

He kept saying, "Repeat after me—" That's when he tried to get her to say in English: "Stick 'em up." She couldn't even repeat it. She began laughing. He tried to persuade her. "Repeat after me . . ." but it was fiasco, just a fiasco.

She was pregnant with Rachel, and Lee was trying to teach her what she was supposed to say to passengers in English. She couldn't even pronounce those words: "Stick 'em up." Everybody was going to drop dead laughing. She said, "You really are a kook. My God, you and I have nothing to eat and you are cooking up dumb things." It wasn't that she was a bitchy wife and always after him to make money. She didn't want him to make a *lot* of money; she wanted him to be glad for what he had.

She was telling the story thirty years later, and the interviewer said: "You don't have a criminal mind. In those years, it wasn't a bad way to hijack a plane. With a pregnant woman. He had it all figured out. You would hide the gun beneath your belly. You were indispensable to him."

MARINA: I said, "I'm sorry, I refuse."

INTERVIEWER: At that point he probably said to himself, "I'm married to the wrong woman."

MARINA: He probably said that from day one.

She wished to shrug this conversation away:

MARINA: It was so long ago. I'm fifty-two years old. Put it behind me. I don't have to report what I did when I was twelve years old, thirteen, or twenty. I'm going to heaven. I already made my reservation.

INTERVIEWER: Wherever you go, they are going to sit you down and they will say, "Tell us about Lee Harvey Oswald."

MARINA: Where, in heaven?

INTERVIEWER: They'll say, "We were waiting, Marina, for you to tell us."

MARINA: Isn't the wife last to know?

We can take note of Oswald's frustration: to be wed to a woman who has no appreciation of the beauty of a brilliant criminal idea. He had had it all figured out: a pregnant woman—who would take a second look when they boarded the plane?

Right around that time back then, a mirror broke, just fell off the wall and broke, and she was unhappy because that was certainly an omen. One morning, she took a look at the amber heart she kept in a locket, and it was cracked—she thought somebody was going to die.

From an FBI report: . . . He said it would be better to hijack a plane that was going inward from the coastal region of the United States because it would be less suspicious than boarding a plane on an international flight. OSWALD's plans were to take a plane leaving New Orleans for another point in the United States and thereafter transfer to another plane which would be the one he would hijack . . .

He told MARINA that he, OSWALD, would sit at the front of the airplane with the pistol which he owned and MARINA would sit at the back of the plane with a pistol which he would buy for her. They would have their daughter, JUNE, with them. They would force the crew to fly the plane to Cuba. OSWALD told MARINA that she was to stand up at the back of the airplane at the appointed time and yell out "Hands up" in English. She told OSWALD she could not say that in English. He replied for her to say it in Russian and stick the gun out and everybody would know what she meant . . .

OSWALD said he would buy MARINA a light-weight pistol for her to use in the hijack scheme [but she] told him not to buy one because she would not participate in the scheme. OSWALD had said he had wanted her to at least learn how to hold a pistol but she refused. . . .

She said OSWALD tried to talk her into participating in the hijack scheme on at least four occasions. . . .

During the time he was planning to hijack the plane, OSWALD began taking physical exercises at home for the purpose of increasing his physical strength.[4]

McMillan: Lee kept up his exercises for a couple of weeks, causing much merriment in the household. Afterward he rubbed himself all over with a strong-smelling liniment, took a cold shower, and came out of the bathroom as red as a lobster.

Meanwhile, he had brought home airline schedules and a large map of the world which he tacked up inside the porch. He started measuring distances on the map with a ruler . . .[5]

To commemorate so apocalyptic an action, and to ensure good reception in Cuba, he told her that the new child—it could only be a boy—ought to be called Fidel. She told him that there was going to be no Fidel in her body.

He did not argue. He was putting together a résumé of his life. Once again, determined to go to Cuba, he is also contemplating a move of his family to Washington, Baltimore, or New York. Either way, he needs to prepare his papers. In New York, he can show them to officers in the Communist Party or the Socialist Workers Party. If he makes it to Cuba, he can present his dossier.

All this while, a part of him has to feel as shattered as if a grenade had gone off in his guts. The radio debate had destroyed so much; now, there is the prodigious concern of finding a way to get to Cuba, and the wholly separate option of going east to New York, Washington, or Baltimore and joining the Communist Party.

It spews over into his writing. If we may speak of dyslexia as a species of spiritual eruption, this is the worst case we see in all the samples of his writing in all the eleven volumes of Warren Commission Exhibits.

Here is an uncorrected example of what he will either bring to Cuba or use to seek entrance into the Communist Party:

> I first read the communist manifesto and 1st volume of capital in 1954 when I was 15 I have study 18th century plosipers works by Lein after 1959 and attened numerous marxist reading circle and groups at the factory where I worked some of which were compulsory and other which were not. also in Russia through newspapers, radio and T.V. I leared much of Marx Engels and Lenins works. such articles are given very good coverage daliy in the USSR.[6]

What a contrast to the Stuckey interview! It is Oswald at his worst. How huge is his anxiety: His ambition is always leading him to worlds where his experience is small—he does not even speak Spanish—and this anxiety wells up in every misspelled syllable as he goes on to describe his abilities as "Street Agitator," and "Radio Specker."

Since his letters to officials are usually far more accurate in spelling, we can presume that he usually takes the time to correct his first draft with a dictionary, yet here, where the dossier might be most important for him, he has made no corrections. It is powerful evidence of what must be close to overwhelming inner panic.

Yet all of this is gone by the time of a visit from Ruth Paine. She had written to Marina on August 24 that she would be coming back from visiting her relatives in the East and Midwest by September and would stop off in New Orleans for a quick visit.

On September 20, true to her promise, Ruth arrived in New Orleans and was greeted warmly by Lee. He was in a very good mood, Ruth would say afterward, the best mood she had ever seen him in. If his bouts of anxiety were as deep as immersions in a pit, he could, given the wide spectrum of his swings of mood, pass all the way over to blue sky and high noon. He had made up his mind: He would choose Cuba. A large problem had been resolved. In addition, all the details of Marina's delivery of their second child, perhaps a month away, would be taken care of by Ruth. She would now make all the arrangements at Parkland Hospital in Dallas, and he would have to pay very little for it since he had worked for six months at Jaggars-Chiles-Stovall and so could show a Texas residency. Now, as far as Ruth knew, which is to say as far as he allowed Marina to tell her, he was on his way to Houston to look for work. He would come for his wife and children once he was reestablished.

Marina took Ruth to see the sights in the French Quarter. They would peek through the swinging doors of the strip-tease bars, one tall woman and one tiny woman holding the hands of three children. Meanwhile, Lee was at home packing. In the course of it, he wrapped and tied his gun in a blanket that he would stow in Ruth's car before the two women departed on Monday.

McMillan: No sooner had they said their goodbyes and driven off than Ruth noticed a rumbling in one of her tires. She pulled up at a gas station one block from the apartment to have it changed. Lee, in his sandals, followed them there. Marina took him to one side and they parted all over again. She was tender to him, telling him to be careful and eat properly.

"Stop," he said. "I can't stand it. Do you want me to cry in front of Ruth?"

For him, too, the hardest thing was to conceal from Ruth that the parting might be forever. And so, while the two of them fought back their tears, Lee held Junie in front of the Coke machines to help them regain their composure. "Come on, Junie," he said. "Show me with your fingers what you want." . . . [When] he had a grip on himself, he warned Marina that, above all, she was not to tell Ruth he was going to Cuba.[7]

He stayed in the apartment for another night or two. Just when he left New Orleans is in doubt, but he managed to depart without paying the landlady, Mrs. Garner, the last two weeks of rent. She had seen him packing Ruth's car on Sunday night, but he told her that Marina was going to Texas to have the baby and he would stay on. He didn't. He decamped.

PART V

PROTAGONISTS AND
PROVOCATEURS

1

Protagonists and Provocateurs

Oswald is leaving New Orleans, yet we do not know if he has had a secret life or not. If now and again we have had intimations of as much, others did too. A formidable number of books have been written by conspiracy theorists examining many a possibility of intelligence activity by and around Oswald. Yet, after all this time, there is no overruling evidence that he was definitely associated with the FBI, the CIA, Army or Navy Intelligence, or any Cuban groups. It is still possible to believe that Oswald was simply an over-ambitious yet much henpecked husband, with an unbalanced psyche, a vein of brutality toward his wife, and that was the sad sum of him.

Such an interpretation has been given by Priscilla Johnson McMillan in *Marina and Lee,* by Jean Davison in *Oswald's Game,* and most recently by Gerald Posner in *Case Closed,* a work which provided great joy to every element of the media that had been antipathetic to Oliver Stone's *JFK* and was generally offended by conspiracy theorists.

This book, however, was undertaken without a fixed conclusion in either direction; indeed, it began with a prejudice in favor of the conspiracy theorists. All the same, one's plan for the work was to take Oswald on his own terms as long as that was possible—that is, try to comprehend his deeds as arising from nothing more than himself until such a premise lost all headway. To study his life in this manner produces a hypothesis: Oswald was a protagonist, a prime mover, a man who made things happen—in short, a fig-ure larger than others would credit him for being. Indeed, this point of view has by now taken hold to a point where the writer would not like to relinquish it for too little. *There* is the danger! Hypotheses commence as our servant—they enable us to keep our facts in order while we attempt to learn more about a partially obscured subject. Once the profits of such a method accumulate, however, one is morally obliged (like a man who has just grown rich) to be scrupulously on guard against one's own corruption. Otherwise, the hitherto useful hypothesis will insist on prevailing over everything that comes in and so will take over the integrity of the project.

One can feel such a tendency stirring. It is possible that the working hypothesis has become more important to the author than trying to discover the truth. For if Oswald remains intact as an important if dark protagonist, one has served a purpose: The burden of a prodigious American obsession has been lessened, and the air cleared of an historic scourge—absurdity. So long as Oswald is a petty figure, a lone twisted pathetic killer who happened to be in a position to kill a potentially great President, then, as has been argued earlier in this work, America is cursed with an absurdity. There was no logic to the event and no sense of balance in the universe. Historical absurdity (like the war in Vietnam) breeds social disease.

We have, of course, an alternative posed by the movie *JFK* There, our President was killed by the architects of a vast plot embracing the most powerful officers of our armed forces, our intelligence, and our Mafia, a massive array of establishment evil that is thrilling to our need to live imaginatively with great stakes in great wars, but such a thesis also leaves us with horror: We are small, and the forces of evil are huge.

Of course, the odds that a huge conspiracy can succeed and remain hidden are also small. And Oswald would have been the last man that a leader of such a vast conspiracy would have selected to be in on the action. While *JFK* satisfies our growing and gloomy sense that nine tenths of our freedom has been pre-empted by forces vastly larger than ourselves (and Stone's hypothesis gives great power to the film), it does not come near to solving the immediate question: Did Lee Harvey Oswald kill JFK, and if he did, was he a lone gunman or a participant in a conspiracy?

Given the yeast-like propensities of conspiracy to expand and expand as one looks to buttress each explanation, it can hardly be difficult for the reader to understand why it is more agreeable to keep to one's developing concept of Oswald as a protagonist, a man to whom, grudgingly, we must give a bit of stature when we take into account the modesty of his origins. That, to repeat, can provide us with a sense of the tragic rather than of the absurd. If a figure as large as Kennedy is cheated abruptly of his life, we feel better, inexplicably better, if his killer is also not without size. Then, to some degree, we can also mourn the loss of possibility in the man who did the deed. Tragedy is vastly preferable to absurdity. Such is the vested interest that adheres to perceiving Oswald as a tragic and infuriating hero (or, if you will, anti-hero) rather than as a snarling little wife abuser or a patsy.

Still, one has to remain aware of the danger of bypassing those interesting leads that do point to a conspiracy. Mysteries are kin to mammoth caves. One can hardly take pride for what has already been reconnoitered without remaining open to the labyrinth that still remains unexplored. Before we quit New Orleans, then, let us take some measure of the events that do not fit the picture we have so far obtained of Oswald through these heat-filled months of May, June, July, August, and the greater part of September down in the Big Easy.

We can commence with a minor testimony by a young Cuban bartender named Evaristo Rodriguez, who worked in the Habana Bar, at 117 Decatur Street in the French Quarter. His remarks, while of no great importance, have the virtue of reminding us that the prose of Ernest Hemingway, as he was the first to admit, was not foreign to Spanish notions of syntax and sequence:

MR. RODRIGUEZ. . . . these men came into the bar . . . the one who spoke Spanish ordered the tequila, so I told him the price . . . was 50 cents. I brought him the tequila and a little water. The man protested at the price . . . and he made some statement to the effect that . . . the owner of this bar must be a capitalist, and we had a little debate about the price, but that passed over. Then the man who I later learned was Oswald ordered a lemonade. Now I didn't know what to give him because we don't have lemonades in the bar. So I asked Orest Pena how I should fix [one.] Orest told me to take a little of this lemon flavoring, squirt in some water, and charge him 25 cents . . .

MR. LIEBELER. What time of day did this happen?

MR. RODRIGUEZ. This happened . . . between 2:30 and 3 in the morning. I am not certain of the exact hour but that's the best of my recollection.

MR. LIEBELER. Were either of these men drunk?

MR. RODRIGUEZ. The man I later learned to be Oswald had his arm around the Latin-appearing man and Oswald appeared to be somewhat drunk . . .

MR. LIEBELER. Are you able to say the nationality of the man who was with Oswald?

MR. RODRIGUEZ. . . . He could have been a Mexican; he could have been a Cuban, but at this point, I don't recall.

MR. LIEBELER. What did this [other] man look like? . . .

MR. RODRIGUEZ. . . . about 28 years old, very hairy arms, . . . He was a stocky man with broad shoulders, about 5 feet, 8 inches . . . He probably hit around 155 . . .

MR. LIEBELER. Now how tall would you estimate Oswald was?

MR. RODRIGUEZ. I didn't get a good look . . . because Oswald was drunk and he was more or less in a sagging position most of the time . . .

MR. LIEBELER. Did Oswald become sick?

MR. RODRIGUEZ. He became sick on the table and on the floor.

MR. LIEBELER. Then did he go in the street and continue being sick?

MR. RODRIGUEZ. The Latin-appearing man helped him to the street where he continued to be sick.

MR. LIEBELER. What was Oswald wearing?

MR. RODRIGUEZ. Oswald, as I recall, had on a dark pair of pants and a short-sleeved white shirt.

MR. LIEBELER. Did he have a tie on?

MR. RODRIGUEZ. Oswald had what appeared to be a small bow tie.

MR. LIEBELER. Are you sure?

MR. RODRIGUEZ. . . . Oswald's collar was open and this thing was hanging from one side of it.

MR. LIEBELER. It was a clip-on bow tie?

MR. RODRIGUEZ. It was a clip-on thing . . .

MR. LIEBELER. When did this happen? What month?

MR. RODRIGUEZ. I can't remember exactly, but I know it was just about 1 year ago, and I presume it was in August.[1]

Could he have mistaken August for May? New Orleans can be as hot in May as in mid-summer, and the man with Oswald may have been one of the Mexicans who went with Lee to see the lawyer Dean Adams Andrews about rectifying his Marine Corps discharge.

On the other hand, if it was August or September, then the bartender could be referring to the same Mexican or Cuban who, conceivably, will go to Dallas with Oswald and a man named Leopoldo two mysterious individuals we are going to encounter in the next chapter. Either way, Evaristo Rodriguez has given us the record of a small event that does not fit into our framework. To the best of Marina's recollection, Lee, but for the exception of the afternoon he was arrested, spent every night in New Orleans at home with her. So, her memory is betraying her or the event took place in early May (or on Monday or Tuesday night, September 23 or 24, after Marina had left with Ruth Paine for Irving, Texas). Or: the man was not Oswald.

Yet, the story rings true in at least one detail. Oswald, terribly drunk early in the morning and there with his arm around another man, would probably be ready to throw up.

The episode also introduces us to Orest Pena, the boss of the bar. Pena is macho to a reasonable degree. That is, he is prudently macho, but then, how can you be a Cuban presiding over a Cuban establishment with the proud name of Habana Bar without settling for oxymoronic faculties—prudent and macho?

> **MR. PENA.** . . . they asked my bartender, Evaristo, why I charge so much for the drinks and I was a capitalist charging too much for the drinks. He went and came to me and told me about it. I said, "Don't worry about it. They pay you already?" "Yes." "Don't worry about it. If you are going to worry about all the customers, you are going to go crazy."[2]

Soon, Orest Pena is talking about the FBI and his relation to them:

> **MR. PENA.** . . . when I joined the organization against Castro in New Orleans, one of the agents of the FBI, de Brueys, started going to my place very, very often asking me about many different people, Spanish people, what I knew, what I thought. I told him what I knew; that some people was for Castro and some people was against. I told him what I saw. I never did ask him what he found out about those people.

MR. LIEBELER. Sometimes you would call the FBI and give them information [which] you picked up from conversations that took place at your bar? . . .

MR. PENA. Yes . . . Then de Brueys came to the organization . . .

MR. LIEBELER. He joined it?

MR. PENA. No, he didn't join it, but he was sticking with the organization very, very close . . . we knew he was an FBI agent. So from time to time he [came] to my place and was asking me about this guy and that guy, different people here in New Orleans. So I told him . . . about people that I am for sure they are for Castro here in New Orleans. So one way or the other, he was interfering with me somehow, Mr. de Brueys, so—

MR. LIEBELER. De Brueys was interfering with you?

MR. PENA. Yes. Somehow. So one day I went to the FBI. They called me to the FBI. I don't remember exactly for what they called me. So I told . . . de Brueys' boss . . . that I don't talk to de Brueys. I don't trust him as an American.

MR. LIEBELER. Did you tell them the reasons why you didn't?

MR. PENA. Because he was interfering very close with the organization against Castro . . . So 2 days later he went to my place of business. He said to me at the table, "I want to talk to you." I said, "Okay, let's go." He said not to talk about him any more because what he could do is get me in big trouble. He said, "I am an FBI man. I can get you in big trouble."[3]

The House Select Committee on Assassinations gives its assessment of this matter:

[De Brueys] acknowledged that he did use Pena informally as an occasional source of information because of his position as a bar owner in New Orleans, but he declined to characterize Pena as an informant because of the absence of any systematic reporting relationship.[4]

The HSCA then adds: ". . . there is no Bureau record of Pena ever having served as an informant. This, too, supported de Brueys testimony that Pena was never used on any systematic basis as a source of information . . ."[5]

. . .

Semantics to the side, we now know that Pena was, at the least, a minor informant, a source of information. Since de Brueys did not keep a file on him, it is reasonable to assume that any FBI man who was using Oswald as a similar source would also eschew a file.

There are other idications of FBI men working with Oswald:

From the HSCA Report: Adrian Alba testified before the committee that . . . one day an FBI agent entered the garage and requested to use one of the Secret Service cars garaged there. The FBI agent showed his credentials, and Alba allowed him to take a Secret Service car, a dark green Studebaker. Later that day or the next day, Alba observed the FBI agent in the car handing a white envelope to Oswald in front of the Reily Coffee Company. There was no exchange of words. Oswald, in a bent position, turned away from the car window and held the envelope close to his chest as he walked toward the Reily Coffee Co. Alba believed that he had observed a similar transaction a day or so later as he was returning from lunch, but on this occasion he failed to see what was handed to Oswald . . .

Alba did not relate his account of the transactions between Oswald and the FBI agent when he testified before the Warren Commission. He told the committee in 1978 that he first remembered these incidents in 1970, when his memory was triggered by a television commercial showing a merchant running to and from a taxi to assist a customer.

The committee examined Alba's records for possible corroboration. These records indicated that in 1963 several Secret Service agents had signed out two Studebakers, a Ford and a Chevrolet at various times, but the records did not indicate that any FBI agents had signed out any of these cars.[6]

Precisely. Alba could hardly show a Secret Service auditor that someone in his garage had charged out a car to an FBI man. Such a transaction could, however, have been easily taken care of by a cash payment. That would not have shown on the books.

The HSCA was then being asked to choose between a man whose memory was jogged six years after his Warren Commission Testimony by a TV commercial and the testimony of a number of FBI men. Unless the Committee was ready to take on the FBI, their agents would have had to be seen as too full of integrity to engage in cover-ups.

Given Hoover's conclusion in the first twenty-four hours after JFK's assassination that Oswald did it all by himself, the word passed down the line quickly: FBI men would prosper best by arriving at pre-ordained results. The process was guaranteed to produce flattening of evidence, destruction of evidence and, if it came to it, creation of evidence. All of those were incidental vices, however, compared to the prevailing mind-set: Avoid leads that go in the wrong direction.

Hoover's one-day solution of the murder was probably reflexive: There was enough awful stuff under enough official rugs—FBI and CIA both!—to dictate the avoidance of anything resembling an all-out investigation. The next best thing, therefore, was accomplished—the appearance of a thorough investigation. The FBI went to great lengths, for example, to obtain basic information on every bus passenger who traveled with Oswald from Laredo to Mexico City, an inquiry that had to have consumed hundreds of man-hours in order to come up with two dozen people whose only link to Oswald was that they had all traveled on the same public vehicle. A full exploration into the pro- and anti-Castro movements in New Orleans, however, was never attempted. A very wide inquiry without search in depth was the unspoken directive behind FBI labors on the Oswald case. So, the cardinal suspects in any small-scale conspiracy—the pro- and anti-Castro Cubans who were on the scene in Miami, New Orleans, Houston, and Dallas—were never studied too closely in 1964, when the leads were still warm and alive and electric. Yet, in that covert world of putative terrorists, secret agents, and provocateurs, what was more to be expected than a pro-Castro conspiracy manipulated secretly by anti-Castro Cubans, or the reverse? An attempt to assassinate Kennedy would be catastrophic for any group that did it if such a group was uncovered after the event. To the eternal shame of the FBI, they did not choose to explore such possibilities. Of course, Hoover was not about to let them cross certain lines, because if they did, the close working relation of such criminal figures as Sam Giancana and John Rosselli with a few of the highest officers in the CIA in a mutual mission to kill Castro might have been disclosed.

Hoover was, of course, considerably less worried about the CIA than about the Bureau. The FBI had its own bare buttocks to cover. Acres of bare buttocks! More than a decade later, some activities of COINTELPRO (short for Counter-Intelligence Program), the FBI's own undercover group, would be revealed.

It is worth quoting here from David Wise's *The American Police State:*

> The most outrageous of the FBI's activities was its COINTELPRO operation which the Bureau admitted it had conducted for fifteen years, between 1956 and 1971. Under this program, a secret arm of the United States government, using taxpayers' funds, harassed American citizens and disrupted their organizations, using a wide variety of covert techniques. As the House intelligence committee concluded in its own study of COINTELPRO, "Careers were ruined, friendships severed, reputations sullied, businesses bankrupted, and, in some cases, lives endangered." . . . A secret and powerful government hand moved behind the scenes . . . to break up marriages, to cause people to be fired from their jobs, and even to foment violence . . . In case after case, it was disclosed that many an FBI informant was playing the role of *agent provocateur,* often teaching activist groups how to use explosives, and urging that the members commit specific crimes.[7]

COINTELPRO had a mode of operation that left its signature. Sometimes the most violent, irrational, embarrassing, and/or crazy member of a left-wing, student, or Black Panther group was an FBI provocateur inciting other members into more and more ill-conceived acts. Under the inspiration of COINTELPRO agents, students at Berkeley were hearing some wild adjurations: Let's burn a dog on campus to show the American public what it's really like in Vietnam, or some equivalent, would have been the likely gambit. As late as 1971, we learn by way of David Wise, that "Robert Hardy, an FBI informant, testified that he actually led a group of thirty antiwar activists in a raid on the Camden, New Jersey, draft board . . . 'I taught them everything they knew,' he said, 'how to cut glass and open windows without making any noise . . . how to open file cabinets without a key.' "[8]

No evidence has surfaced that COINTELPRO, as such, had relations with Oswald in the early Sixties, but some of his activities bear the mark. Of the seven programs in COINTELPRO, two offered scope to Oswald's abilities—specifically, boring within the Communist Party and the Socialist Workers Party. For a man in his early twenties, Oswald was relatively sophisticated about left-wing activities. He would almost certainly have known that Stalin in the late 1930s gave the order to murder Leon Trotsky and that this act, committed successfully by the killer driving a mountain ax into Trotsky's brain, had reverberated in left-wing movements through the Forties and Fifties. These warring factions of the Communist Party and the Socialist Workers Party were still at whole odds with each other in the early Sixties, yet on August 31, 1963, Oswald wrote a letter to the Socialist Workers Party and on the next day a letter to the Communist Party, advising both New York groups that he was planning to move soon to the Baltimore-Washington area and would like to contact Party members there.

If Oswald was receiving a stipend from COINTELPRO or some equivalent organization, there is no need to assume he had been given precise goals and a master plan. Sabotage of American left-wing organizations, since they are small, does not depend upon carrying out specific activities so much as on creating general trouble and waste. To become a member of both the Communist Party and the Socialist Workers Party would guarantee disruption further down the line, particularly should such a member be exposed as belonging to both.

All the while, other agents in the FBI and their informants are observing him:

> A confidential source advised our New York Office on June 26, 1963, that one Lee Oswald, Post Office Box 30061, New Orleans, Louisiana, had directed a letter to "The Worker," New York City. Our New Orleans office checked this post office box and determined it was rented to L. H. Oswald . . . [and] further inquiries showed Oswald was residing at 4905 Magazine Street, New Orleans . . . [and] verified on August 5, 1963, by Mrs. Jessie James Garner, 4909 Magazine Street, New Orleans. On the same date his employment at the William B. Reily Coffee Company, 640 Magazine Street, New Orleans, was terminated.[9]

We can recall that when John Fain, the FBI man who first interrogated Oswald on his return to America, asked whether Lee was in American intelligence, he had received for an answer, "Don't you know?"

Of course, Fain didn't know. COINTELPRO was a special arm of the FBI and so its provocateurs would be revealed neither to agents like Fain nor to run-of-the-mill FBI informants in the Communist Party. Intelligence organizations are not unskilled at maintaining secret echelons above, below, and to the side of their official operatives. Often, the work of those in the concealed enclaves is at cross-purposes with their own organization's methods and activities.

From Lee's point of view, however, being a closet provocateur offered the possibility of playing his own game within the larger game. Oswald, if he was on a secret FBI stipend, might have been breaking the rules when he asked for an FBI man to come to the New Orleans jail. Perhaps he was not even aware that the agent who would arrive was not witting of his case and so he turned uncommunicative as soon as he realized that Quigley was not there to lift him out of incarceration.

In fact, we are wandering in the dark. Quigley might have known that Oswald was a special case, or Oswald might have told him. As a professional, Quigley was hardly about to pass such information on to the Warren Commission.

Still, the thought of Oswald working for the FBI does not fit our sense of him as someone who could not be easily bought. His hatred of American capitalism was too deep. On reflection, however, it is not inconceivable that he did entertain a relationship with the FBI. He would have loved a role in which he could pretend to serve the forces he would yet manage to overthrow. And, of course, he could have written those letters to the Communist Party and the Socialist Workers Party in the knowledge that he was gulling his handlers in the FBI while he was in fact getting ready to make a big move in the opposite direction—not to the northeast, but to Cuba. On the other hand, if he was also feeling recurring uncertainty before the real difficulties of getting to Havana, he may have seriously considered the idea that he would lead a family life while working as a radical in Baltimore or Philadelphia. It is not impossible that after his impressive performance under pressure on Stuckey's two radio shows, his COINTELPRO handlers had decided he could be employed on more advanced ventures with top-level radical officials in the East.

What is even more likely, and adds to our frustrated sense that several trails could be crossing each other, is that if Oswald was a provocateur, the people taking care of his stipend may not have been officially associated with the FBI.

We have to remind ourselves still one more time of the underground atmosphere of that period. Following the missile crisis in October 1962, the detestation of Communism among right-wing Americans was at its most intense. Kennedy was hated virulently by the more passionate cohorts of the right.

When we take into account that the FBI and the CIA, not to mention Army and Navy Intelligence, also had their share of extreme right-wing zealots, it is more than likely that such patriots in official organizations had linked up with individuals outside their ranks who were cooking up all kinds of semi-legal and illegal capers that even went beyond the loose limits of COINTELPRO.

Two of the most prominent of such men in New Orleans were W. Guy Banister and David Ferrie.

2

Right-wing Adventurers

One can wonder which movie star Guy Banister would have chosen to play his part—Edward G. Robinson, James Cagney, Victor McLaglen, Humphrey Bogart. It is a fair question.

Banister had been in on the capture and kill of John Dillinger, and became Special Agent in Charge for Chicago; he had a commendation from J. Edgar Hoover. Serving as a G-man for the FBI when it still made a romantic impression on the public, Banister is reputed to have worked in Naval Intelligence during World War II, and was subsequently hired by the Mayor of New Orleans to become Deputy Chief of Police.

Anthony Summers, in his book *Conspiracy,* gives a concise and nicely written summary of Banister's career in the Big Easy:

> In 1957, at the age of fifty-eight, Banister was pushed into retirement after an incident in New Orleans' Old Absinthe House, when he allegedly threatened a waiter with a pistol. By all accounts Banister was a choleric man and a heavy drinker [but he] stayed on in New Orleans to start Guy Banister Asso-

ciates, nominally a detective agency. In fact, Banister's intelligence background, coupled with a vision of himself as a superpatriot, led him into a personal crusade against Communism. He was a member of the fervently right-wing John Birch Society, of Louisiana's "Committee on Un-American Activities," of the paramilitary Minutemen, and . . . [even in] 1963, say former members of Banister's staff, the offices of the "detective agency" were littered with guns of every description. It was no coincidence that the exiles' government in exile, the Cuban Revolutionary Council, made its New Orleans base in the same building as Guy Banister. For Banister and his Cuban protégés the building was well located—close to the local offices of both the CIA and the FBI . . .[1]

His offices also happened to be around the block from the Reily Coffee Company and Adrian Alba's garage. For that matter, 544 Camp Street, Banister's address, was stamped inside the cover of a forty-page FPCC pamphlet similar to the ones Oswald was passing out on Canal Street when he got into his altercation with Carlos Bringuier.

Since then, long chapters in many a volume about the assassination have been devoted to a possible relationship between Oswald and Banister, but the evidence is never firm. By stamping 544 Camp Street onto FPCC pamphlets, Oswald was implicitly making a claim that he rented office space there; however, the landlord, Sam Newman, says the building had three empty offices all summer and Oswald never rented. There are certainly no receipts.

Of course, if Oswald was being paid a stipend by Banister to do some kind of undercover work, it would hardly have made sense for them to be seen together or to have established any paper trail. On the other hand, Banister, given his connections, could hardly have failed to be aware of Oswald and his potential.

Moreover, we do well not to lose sight of the contact reports missing from the CIA files for the period when Oswald tried to kill Walker. The assumption, we can recall, was that such reports were missing because their routing symbols would indicate who within the Agency knew what, and when: They would have revealed, for example, that information about Oswald's failed attempt might have been transmitted to the sort of CIA officer who would have contact with right-wing activists like Banister. Of course, nothing is more seductive than an interesting speculation that is built upon another interesting speculation, so if there is no hard evidence connecting Banister to Oswald, that can be used to claim that their relations were serious enough for them to take pains to conceal the evidence after the assassination, but then, we are only speaking of a cloud of possibility, not even the shadow of a certitude.

Matters are a little better with David Ferrie. Oswald, at fifteen, had been a cadet in the Civil Air Patrol, and since Ferrie was one of the key New Orleans figures in that group, there has always been controversy about whether they knew each other.

> *Summers:* . . . He denied ever having any sort of relationship with Oswald. Since he also denied knowing that the Cuban Revolutionary Council [had] ever operated from Camp Street, a fact he certainly did know about, Ferrie's denials should have raised suspicions. The FBI, however, conducted a mockery of an inquiry into Oswald's membership in the Civil Air Patrol and the matter was dropped [. However,] the Assassinations Committee noted . . . that Ferrie's "appeal to several young men may have been related to his taking an extraordinary interest in them. . . . He often gave parties at his residence where liquor flowed freely . . ."
>
> Ferrie's homosexuality, and his weakness for young boys in particular, is a matter of record. [Eventually] Ferrie's misconduct with youths in the Air Patrol led to scandal. There were reports of drunken orgies, of boys capering about in the nude, and in the end it was this that ended Ferrie's tenure with the New Orleans unit. There is not yet any evidence that Oswald was involved in such goings-on, but—at the age of sixteen and the threshold of an adult sexual life—he was certainly vulnerable to the likes of Ferrie. The Assassinations Committee noted that—homosexuality aside—Ferrie exerted "tremendous influence" through his close associations with his pupils in the Patrol. A Committee analysis adds that he "urged several boys to join the armed forces."[2]

There is also, for what it is worth, one unexplained fact about Oswald's first year in the Marine Corps. Stationed at Keesler Air Force Base in Mississippi, which was only a couple of hours by bus from New Orleans, Oswald would go to the Big Easy every weekend on pass. Daniel Powers, who reported this to the Warren Commission, assumed that he was visiting relatives, but Lillian

Murret testified that she only had one phone call from him in this period, and Marguerite was living then in Fort Worth. So, another unsupported speculation arises that Oswald was seeing Ferrie.

It should be noted that Ferrie could have been the most striking figure Oswald had met up to that time. Strange in appearance, in later years he suffered from alopecia, a disease that left him hairless, and thus wore mohair for false eyebrows (which has left Ferrie as a comic figure in assassination mythology); he was, at the time Oswald first knew him in 1955, an airplane pilot of legendary skills (he could bring a light plane down on a postage stamp of a clearing in the jungle) as well as a serious hypnotist, a cancer researcher assertive enough to believe he would find a cure, a self-appointed Catholic bishop in a theology that he had evolved himself, and to keep his options open, was also private pilot to the godfather of New Orleans, Carlos Marcello. All in all, Ferrie was enough of a local genius to have attracted a young bruised Marine like Oswald looking for a weekend away from the base.

Ferrie and Banister were associated with one another by way of Carlos Marcello, since Banister did a good deal of investigative work for G. Wray Gill, a leading attorney for the Don. All those who believe in guilt by association had a rich time with the possibility that Banister and Ferrie could be the link among the CIA, the FBI, and the Mafia. Oswald is then connected, if tenuously, to all of them, but there is, unfortunately, no sighting of any sort. No one has come forward who even glimpsed Ferrie and Oswald together in New Orleans during the summer of 1963.

There is, however, the famous morning in September when, ninety miles north of New Orleans, a big black limousine drove into a modest-sized town, Clinton, Louisiana, and parked ostentatiously near the registrar's office. On that morning, a long line of blacks were waiting to be registered as voters, an action organized by the Congress of Racial Equality (CORE). A young man came out of the limousine, leaving a driver and another passenger behind, and joined the black people on line. This young man was later identified as Lee Harvey Oswald, and the passenger as David Ferrie. The District Attorney in New Orleans, Jim Garrison, who brought Clay Shaw to trial for conspiracy in the assassination of JFK, had the driver pegged as the same Clay Shaw. Subsequently, after Garrison lost much of his credibility, some conspiracy theorists would decide that the driver, generally described as a good-looking middle-aged man with gray hair, was Guy Banister.

Anthony Summers decided that the story never did make a great deal of sense with Shaw as a principal, and indeed, why would one of the wealthiest and most powerful men in New Orleans drive ninety miles out of the city to sit in a car all day and watch blacks register to vote? Banister made more sense. He saw CORE as a left-wing organization ready to befoul and disrupt everything in the South as part of a larger Communist strategy set up to destroy the United States. Indeed, the CORE organizer who was in Clinton that day assumed the car was there to suggest an unfriendly FBI presence. CORE had been withstanding many attempts to intimidate them that summer.

The young white man who stepped out of the car and joined the blacks on line had to wait three hours before he reached the desk of the registrar of voters, Henry Palmer. At that point, he "pulled out a U.S. Navy I.D. card [and] . . . the name on it . . . was Lee H. Oswald with a New Orleans address."[3]

Summers: According to Palmer, Oswald's story was that he wanted a job at the nearby East Louisiana State Hospital [and] had more chance of getting it if he registered [in Clinton]. To Palmer it was an odd request, out of context with the black registration drive. He finally told Oswald he had not been in the area long enough to qualify for registration. Oswald thanked him and departed.[4]

This Clinton episode seems to tie Oswald to David Ferrie, who by then had alopecia, and with his red wig, mohair eyebrows, and extremely white skin, was identified as one of the three men in the limousine. The story, therefore, had to be disproved by Gerald Posner if he was to prove his case that Oswald was a lone killer, since, from Posner's point of view, a connection between Ferrie and Oswald was a most unattractive loose end; but then, he had a few other enigmas to dispose of as well.

Posner: The first problem arises over the time of the purported visit. Summers says the episode took place "in early September." It is imperative that the alleged visit not have taken place later because Oswald permanently left New Orleans and Louisiana on September 24 . . . [But] Reeves Morgan, the state representative for the parish, said Oswald visited him at his home to inquire about obtaining the hospital job. There was a chill in the air, and Morgan recalled lighting the fireplace. Review of U.S. Weather Bureau records for the period through September 24 show daily temperatures above 90 degrees, with only a few days dipping into the eighties, with high humidity. There was certainly no day that was "cool" or required a burning fireplace. The registrar of voters, Henry Palmer, felt very strongly that the visit was the "first week of October, possibly around the 6th or 7th." Oswald was in Dallas then.[5]

Let us not give up on September too easily, however. Posner speaks of daily temperatures above 90 degrees, "with only a few days dipping into the eighties . . ." Of course, such temperatures are given for the high point of the day. It so happens that on September 23 and September 24, the two days when Oswald was alone in New Orleans after Marina left with Ruth Paine, the weather report shows the low temperatures to be, respectively, 62 degrees and 56 degrees.[6] Certainly, for older people used to living in 90-degree temperatures, early morning or evening might offer the kind of chill one does light a fire for. Even if one came by at 10:00 A.M., there might be enough of that early-morning cold left in the old house and the old bones to keep a few coals alive.

Posner also had to deal with the House Select Committee on Assassination's conclusion in 1979 that the six witnesses they interviewed who had been in Clinton that day in 1963 offered "credible and significant testimony."[7] Posner, however, managed somehow to obtain access to the files of Edward Wagmann, one of Clay Shaw's defense lawyers. That, indubitably, was a feat. Lawyers for rich men in the South are not generally in a hurry to give privileged material to investigators from the North, not unless they come very well recommended. In any event, Posner did obtain the original reactions of the witnesses in Clinton, materials that had been submitted in the beginning to Jim Garrison, and Posner set out to demolish the possibility that Oswald, Ferrie, and Banister (and/or Shaw) were in that car and made that visit together to Clinton, Louisiana. He was certainly able to demonstrate how very much the original statements of the witnesses diverge from the later ones submitted to the HSCA. One person saw only a woman and a man in the car and they had a baby in a bassinet. Other witnesses saw four men, or two men, or one man. The only trouble with all this is that Oswald, as pointed out by James DiEugenio in the newsletter *Back Channels,* September 1994, was in Jackson, Louisiana, about fifteen miles from Clinton, the night before, and Posner is combining testimony from witnesses in two towns and mixing them together as one.

So, his strongest remaining card (although he did not see that it could eventually prove to be his weakest) was his insistence that the event could not have taken place in September because it was not cool enough. Of course, if the visit had taken place in October, then the young man who presented an I.D. card to the registrar, Henry Palmer, was not Oswald. But in that case, who were the people who had come to Clinton in October, and why had they gone to the trouble of obtaining false credentials for Oswald? The difficulty with closing the case on Oswald is that every time one shuts the door, a crack opens in the wall.

It would be a great relief to terminate the case on the assassination of John Fitzgerald Kennedy, but one has to be certain the job is actually being accomplished. For example, Posner is too positive that Oswald and Ferrie never met at all:

> *Posner:* Ferrie was interviewed by the FBI on November 27, 1963, and denied ever knowing Oswald in the Civil Air Patrol. CAP records show that while Ferrie was a member through 1954, he was disciplined because he gave unauthorized political lectures to the cadets. When he submitted his 1955 renewal, he was rejected. Ferrie was not reinstated until December 1958. He was not even in the Civil Air Patrol when Oswald was a member in 1955.[8]

In November 1993, however, the TV program *Frontline* showed a group photograph taken in 1955 of some sixteen men and boys on a picnic. Since Ferrie and Oswald are visible at opposite ends of the group, the most that Posner can now claim is that Ferrie may have believed he was telling the truth when he said that they never met.

In fact, the odds are great that, at the least, they were introduced to each other on the occasion. Since the pilot was having many sexual relations with teenagers in that period, he might (in the manner that a heterosexual who makes love to many women will often have difficulty bringing to mind every encounter) have had no recollection of sleeping with Oswald. Of course, if Ferrie did recall such an event, he would have denied it after the assassination. Posner, trying to seal everything, writes: ". . . he told the truth." A very large assumption.

This executive tendency to chop off nuances as if they are profitless distractions can be seen at its most dramatic in Posner's treatment of Sylvia Odio, whom we will encounter in the next chapter. First, however, we have to deal with how Oswald gets out of the Big Easy. No literary vice is more damnable in a writer than needlessly irritating the reader, yet not even Lee Harvey's departure from New Orleans is free of complications.

3

An Inexplicable Visit

After Marina left New Orleans to go to live in Irving, Texas, with Ruth Paine, Lee may or may not have remained at the apartment on Magazine Street for the next couple of days. Neighbors did see him, but their testimonies do not agree. He could have left on Monday or Tuesday evening. Come Wednesday, when Mrs. Garner looked into the apartment, Lee was gone.

By Wednesday morning, his $33 unemployment compensation check had been cashed at the Winn-Dixie store on Magazine Street, but it is possible some unknown person endorsed the check for him since the FBI could not authenticate the signature. Nor was anyone found who observed Oswald getting on any bus that left New Orleans on Wednesday for Houston—which was the most logical stop on the way to Mexico City, where he hoped to obtain a visa for Cuba.

We cannot be certain of his whereabouts until 2:35 A.M. on Thursday. There, in the shank of the early morning hours, he did get on Continental Trailways bus no. 5133, which departed from Houston for Nuevo Laredo, then traveled south through Mexico all day Thursday, and by ten on Friday morning, September 27, he was in Mexico City, a bus trip of thirty-one and a half hours.

Still, the question poses itself: Did Oswald on Wednesday go directly from New Orleans to Houston? Or, did he leave New

Orleans with one or two unidentified associates and drive with them all the way to Dallas, where he would become one of the three men who, about 9:00 P.M. on Wednesday night, would knock on the door of an attractive Cuban lady named Sylvia Odio?

According to Sylvia Odio's testimony, she was at that time getting dressed to go out on a date. Since, as she declares, she felt highly suspicious of her visitors, she kept her door on the latch. She had cause. Her father, once the trucking tycoon of Cuba, was now in jail on the Isle of Pines, imprisoned as a conspirator in a plot to kill Fidel Castro. Sylvia Odio had suffered the trauma of his arrest, then a divorce from her husband in Puerto Rico, and now she was under the care of a psychiatrist. Small surprise if her travails had left her naturally distrustful of strangers. The spokesman for these three men told her, however, that they were members of JURE (Junta Revolucionaria), an anti-Castro group formed in part by her father.

The stranger who did most of the talking was tall and thin and called himself Leopoldo. The second man was squat and "greasy"—and by her description, both were "kind of low Cubans," although the short one could have been Mexican. The third man was American and he "said just a few little words in Spanish, trying to be cute."[1]

MR. LIEBELER. Was the chain [on your door] fastened?

MRS. ODIO. No; I unfastened it after a little while when they told me they were members of JURE, and . . . one of them said, "We are very good friends of your father." This struck me, because I didn't think my father would have such kind of friends unless he knew them from anti-Castro activities. He [Leopoldo] gave me so many details about where he saw my father and what kind of activities he was in. I mean, they gave me almost incredible details about things that [only] somebody . . . informed well knows . . . And he said, "We wanted you to meet this American. His name is Leon Oswald." He repeated it twice. Then my sister Annie by that time was standing near the door. She had come [back] to see what was going on . . . And [Leopoldo] said, "We have just come from New Orleans and we have been trying to get this movement organized down there, and . . . we think we could do some kind of work." This was all talked very fast, not slow as I am saying it now. You know how fast Cubans talk . . . And then I think I asked something to the American, trying to be nice,

"Have you ever been to Cuba?" And he said, "No, I have never been to Cuba."

And I said, "Are you interested in our movement?" And he said, "Yes."

. . . I said, "If you will excuse me, I have to leave," and I repeated, "I am going to write to my father and tell him you have come to visit me." . . . And I think that was the extent of the conversation. They left, and I saw them through the window leaving in a car. I don't recall the car. I have been trying to.

MR. LIEBELER. Do you know which one of the men was driving?

MRS. ODIO. The tall one, Leopoldo.

MR. LIEBELER. Leopoldo?

MRS. ODIO. Yes; oh, excuse me, I forgot something very important. They kept mentioning that they had to come to visit me at such a time of night, it was almost 9 o'clock, because they were leaving on a trip. And two or three times they said the same thing . . . The next day Leopoldo called me. I had gotten home from work, so I imagine it might have been Friday. And they had come on Thursday. I have been trying to establish that. He was trying to get fresh with me that [second time]. He was trying to be too nice, telling me that I was pretty . . . That is the way he started the conversation. Then he said, "What do you think of the American?" And I said, "I didn't think anything."

And he said, "You know, our idea is to introduce him to the underground in Cuba because he is great, he is kind of nuts." . . . [Leon] told us [that we] don't have any guts . . . because President Kennedy should have been assassinated after the Bay of Pigs, and . . . I started getting a little upset with the conversation.

And [Leopoldo] repeated again that they were leaving for a trip and they would very much like to see me on their return to Dallas. Then he mentioned something more about Oswald. [Leopoldo] said he had been a Marine and he was so interested in helping the Cubans, and he was terrific. That is the words [Leopoldo] more or less used in Spanish, that he was terrific . . . Three days later I wrote to my father after they came, and mentioned the fact that two men had called themselves friends of his. And later in December, because the letter takes a long time to get here, he writes me back, "I do not know any of these men. Do not get involved with any of them . . ."[2]

At the end of the interview, Sylvia Odio is asked:

MR. LIEBELER. Well, do you have any doubts in your mind after looking at these pictures that the man that was in your apartment was the same man as Lee Harvey Oswald?

MRS. ODIO. I don't have any doubts.[3]

Sylvia Odio thinks the visit of those three men could have come no earlier than 9:00 P.M., Thursday, September 26, but by that hour Oswald had already been on his Mexico City bus for hours. There are any number of witnesses to testify to that. So, Sylvia Odio either misremembered a visit on Wednesday night and substituted Thursday or, once again, the American, whoever he was, was not Oswald. Indeed, he could have been Oswald only if he had been driven all the way (possibly by Leopoldo) from New Orleans on Wednesday to the Odio apartment in Dallas (which is at least a ten-hour drive). From there, either someone drove him south to catch a bus leaving Houston in the early morning, 2:35 A.M., Thursday, September 26 (which would arrive in Laredo, Texas, in time for an early-afternoon departure for Mexico City, twenty hours further down the road), or else he caught an 11:00 P.M. bus in Dallas on Wednesday night that connected with the bus from Houston to Laredo in Alice, Texas, at 10:25 the following morning. The likelihood is that he was driven to Houston, since an English couple from Liverpool, Mr. and Mrs. McFarland, recollect seeing him on the trip from Houston to Laredo:

> A: We changed buses at Houston, Texas at 2:00 A.M. September 26th and it was probably about 6:00 A.M. after it became light that we first saw him [and] the last we saw of him was waiting at the luggage check-out place obviously to collect some luggage [in Mexico City].
> Q: When did it first occur to you that Lee Harvey Oswald was the man you had met on the bus?
> A: When we saw his pictures in the newspapers.[4]

If Sylvia Odio was mistaken in her dates, then Oswald could have been at her door on Wednesday night at 9:00 P.M. But if it was Thursday or Friday night, then the American who Leopoldo said was ready to fire at Castro or at Kennedy had to be an impostor familiar with Oswald's name after Lee's radio appearances on

Stuckey's show in New Orleans that summer. In which case, why was Sylvia Odio insisting the man was Oswald unless the resemblance was so close that Lee Harvey might indeed be some kind of patsy?

Odio was first interviewed on December 18, 1963, by FBI men James P. Hosty and Bardwell D. Odum, and they hardly had to have it underlined for them that her testimony, if verified, would seriously injure the unspoken Warren-Hoover-Dulles concordat that Oswald had done the job all by himself. The Warren Commission's energies would then have to be directed toward exploring who Oswald's associates were on this occasion—which was equal to investigating the pro-Castro and anti-Castro underground in Miami, New Orleans, Houston, and Dallas. The unspoken anxiety of the elders was that by the end of such an exploration, there would be sheer hell to pay for all the attendant discoveries: COINTELPRO, Giancana, Rosselli, and the numerous attempts to assassinate Castro.

By dint of adroit juggling, which we will have an opportunity to observe, the FBI was able to resolve a double dilemma. Indeed, which was worse for them: Oswald-at-the-door, or someone-impersonating-Oswald-at-the-door?

4

A Nimble Solution

In his book *The Last Investigation,* Gaeton Fonzi offers the following:

> ... On August 23rd, 1964, with the first drafts of the Warren Commission Report being written, Chief Counsel J. Lee Rankin wrote to J. Edgar Hoover: "It is a matter of some importance to the Commission that Mrs. Odio's allegations either be proved or disproved."
>
> One month later, with the Report already in galleys, the Odio incident was still a critical concern for staffers. In a memo to his boss, Staff Counsel Wesley Liebeler wrote:

". . . Odio may well be right. The Commission will look bad if it turns out she is. There is no need to look foolish by grasping at straws to avoid admitting that there is a problem."[1]

Fifteen years later, the House Select Committee on Assassinations would *virtually* contradict the Warren Commission by declaring that Odio's "testimony is essentially credible . . . there is a strong probability that one of the men was or appeared to be Lee Harvey Oswald."[2]

The investigator for the HSCA (the same Gaeton Fonzi just quoted) had been assigned to interview Odio and her sister Annie, but the HSCA was not prepared to follow his conclusions too far. They were going to declare that the assassination had probably been a conspiracy brought off by the Mafia. Odio, therefore, was still in the way, since her testimony pointed toward Cubans and their CIA handlers.

So the matter rested until *Case Closed* was published in 1993. Posner's book is so concerted a validation of FBI work that it could not have served the Bureau's need to dispose of conspiracy theories more if a committee of skilled FBI men had written it for him.

Since the key to closing the case on Oswald is to discredit Odio, Posner sets out to accomplish this by eroding her credentials as a witness:

> *Posner:* By the time of her Oswald story, she had a history of emotional problems. In Puerto Rico, where she had lived before moving to Dallas in March 1963, she had seen a psychiatrist over her fractious marriage. According to FBI reports, he decided she was unstable and unable, mentally or physically, to care for her children.[41] A doctor who was called to treat her once for an "attack of nerves" discovered she had made it up to get the attention of her neighbors. He described her as a very mixed-up young lady, and was told by others that she had also been under psychiatric care while living in Miami, when she moved to the States in 1961.[42]
>
> In her divorce proceedings of 1963, she lost custody of her four children, because of charges of neglect and abandonment.[43] [3]

The three endnotes, (41), (42), (43), all refer to FBI memoranda concerning her condition *before* coming to Dallas. But Odio was not neglecting or abandoning her offspring on the night that she spoke to the three visitors. Indeed, all four of her children were living with her in a small apartment. Posner could have detected as much from such references in her Warren Commission testimony as: "my sister Annie . . . had come over . . . to babysit for me."[4] Or, one page earlier, "I told them at the time I was very busy with my four children."[5] But then, Posner would have had to give as much attention to her testimony as to FBI memoranda. Later, in one more section attributed to FBI sources, Posner writes that Silvia Herrera, her mother-in-law, "went so far as to say that Odio was an excellent actress who could intelligently fabricate such an episode if she wished."[6] Posner is not even calling on a mother-in-law to make his case but an *ex*-mother-in-law!

Or, again: "By the time of the assassination, she had been seeing [her psychiatrist] for more than seven months, at least weekly, sometimes more frequently."[7]

Once a week or, as Posner adds hopefully, "sometimes more frequently," would suggest a woman who is looking for mental and emotional support; what Posner really needs to make his case is a patient who is closeted with her doctor five times a week.

In an interview that Posner conducted with Carlos Bringuier (Oswald's old foe), a telling accusation against Odio is brought in. "I believe it is possible," says Bringuier,

> that she was visited by someone—there were a lot of people with different organizations out there. But after the assassination, I believe her immediate reaction would have been the same as mine, to have jumped up and called the FBI and say, "Hey, that guy visited me!" Instead [after being released from the hospital], she casually told a neighbor, and that neighbor told the FBI, and that's the only reason it came out. That makes me suspicious of her story. It doesn't sound right, and I know from my own personal experience on what I did and how I felt when I realized I had some contact with the man who killed the President of the United States. I heard the name Lee Harvey Oswald and I jumped from my seat. I didn't finish my lunch—I called the FBI immediately. Maybe with all the news after the assassination she became confused and put Oswald's face and name onto the person she actually met. I have seen this as a lawyer in criminal cases. There is an accident with four witnesses and they give four different ver-

sions and they all believe they are telling the truth, and could even pass a lie detector. She thinks she is telling the truth. I hate to say she is lying, but she is mistaken.[8]

What Bringuier leaves out of his otherwise convincing analysis is that while he felt full of virtue and vindication as he leapt out of his chair to call the FBI, Odio was terrified. She didn't know the men who had been at her doorway or whether they might come back if she called attention to herself. In fact, twelve years later, when Fonzi located her in Miami, she was still afraid.

Case Closed, however, keeps going back to the FBI reports rather than taking a look at the Warren Commission testimony:

Posner: Odio insists that she told at least two people, before the assassination, that three men, including Oswald, had visited her apartment. One of the people she told was Lucille Connell. But when the FBI questioned her in 1964, Connell said that Odio only told her about Oswald after the assassination, and then said she not only knew about Oswald, but he had given talks to groups of Cuban refugees in Dallas.[9]

That last sentence, if true, is wholly damaging to Odio. But Posner does not let Sylvia Odio speak for herself:

MR. LIEBELER. Did you tell Mrs. Connell that you had seen Oswald at some anti-Castro meetings, and that he had made some talks to these groups of refugees, and that he was very brilliant and clever and captivated the people to whom he had spoken?

MRS. ODIO. No.

MR. LIEBELER. You are sure you never told her that?

MRS. ODIO. No.

MR. LIEBELER. Have you ever seen Oswald at any meetings?

MRS. ODIO. Never . . . she probably was referring [to] John Martino [who] was in Isle of Pines for 3 years . . . [Mrs. Connell] did go to that meeting. I did not go, [but Martino] came to Dallas and gave a talk to the Cubans about conditions in Cuba, and she was one of the ones that went to the meeting.

MR. LIEBELER. Mrs. Connell?

MRS. ODIO. Yes. And my sister Annie went too . . .[10]

Gaeton Fonzi interviewed Annie Odio in 1975 about her meeting with Sylvia a few hours after the assassination of the President. In the next passage, Fonzi is quoting Annie:

"The first thing I remember when I walked into the room was that Sylvia started crying and crying. I think I told her, 'You know this guy on TV who shot President Kennedy? I think I know him.' And she said, 'You don't remember where you know him from?' I said, 'No, I cannot recall, but I know I've seen him before.' And then she told me, 'Do you remember those three guys who came to the house?' " That's when, Annie said, she suddenly knew where she had seen Lee Harvey Oswald before.[11]

We can continue with Fonzi's account:

Both Sylvia and Annie . . . decided not to say anything to anyone about it. "We were so frightened, we were absolutely terrified," Sylvia remembered. "We were both very young and yet we had so much responsibility, with so many brothers and sisters and our mother and father in prison, we were so afraid and not knowing what was happening. We made a vow to each other not to tell anyone." [Of course, they did tell Lucille Connell, who] told a trusted friend and soon the FBI was knocking on Sylvia Odio's door. She says it was the last thing in the world she wanted, but when they came she felt she had a responsibility to tell the truth.[12]

Gaeton Fonzi's interviews with the Odio sisters took place between 1975 and 1979, but back in 1964, the FBI was looking for and found a way to discredit Odio's testimony.

Posner: The FBI thought it had solved the Odio mystery when it found three men who might have visited her apartment near the end of September. Loran Hall, a prominent anti-Castroite, bore a marked resemblance to the man Odio described as the leader, Leopoldo. Hall told the FBI on September 16, 1964, that he was in Dallas soliciting funds during September 1963 and had been to the Odio apartment. He named his two companions as Lawrence Howard and William Seymour.[13]

Let us move over to Fonzi for the rest of this account:

> . . . Hall claimed he had been . . . trying to raise anti-Castro funds with two companions, one of whom might have looked like Oswald. The Warren Commission grasped at that straw and detailed that interview in its final report, giving the impression that Hall and his companions were Odio's visitors . . .
>
> Neither did the Warren Commission [however] note in its final Report—even though it *knew*—that the subsequent FBI interviews revealed that Hall's two companions denied being in Dallas; that neither looked at all like Oswald; that Sylvia Odio, shown their photographs, did not recognize them; and that Loran Eugene Hall, when questioned again by the FBI, admitted he had fabricated the story. (Still later, when questioned by the Assassinations Committee, Hall denied he had ever told the FBI he had been to Odio's apartment.)[14]

The timing, however, had been serviceable. Loran Hall visited the FBI on September 16, 1964, and the Warren Report came out eight days later. Apprised of Hall's contributions, the Warren Commission rushed to include Hall's first interview in the final Report, and it supplied their definitive conclusion: "Lee Harvey Oswald was not at Mrs. Odio's apartment in September of 1963."[15]

Four days later, on September 20, Hall recanted his story, and the rest of his tale fell apart. However, the Warren Commission, having stopped the presses on September 16, was not about to stop them again. The Warren Commission did not call attention to the error.

There is a maneuver in rock climbing that only the most skillful can employ. It consists of using several tenuous grips in a quick continuous set of moves. Not one of the grips will support your hands or your feet for more than a moment, but in that interval you can gain a crucial few feet, and reach the next halfgrip, then the next, until your momentum has carried you to a place where you can stop in safety. Let us give credit to a master. If J. Edgar Hoover did not have the body of such a rock climber, he had the mind.

On to Mexico. We may never learn definitively how much or how little Lee Harvey Oswald had to do with the visit to Sylvia Odio's apartment, but there is new material available on what happened to him at the Russian Embassy in Mexico, and it comes from a book written by a KGB man who was on the premises.

5

———————

Mexico

The bus on which Oswald was traveling from Laredo to Mexico City arrived, we can remind the reader, at 10:00 A.M. on Friday, September 27, 1963, and Oswald, carrying his duffle bag and a small hand bag with all his valuable papers, looked into the rates at a number of hotels before settling on the Hotel del Comercio, which cost, room with bath, $1.28 a day.

Then he went over to the Cuban Embassy. There is every reason to believe he was confident the Cubans would give him a visa, since he had certainly established his credentials as a supporter of Castro. He had newspaper clippings to show his arrest, he had the stationery of the FPCC chapter he had formed in New Orleans, receipts for the money he had spent on pamphlets to distribute, and if any Castro supporters had heard him on the radio with Bill Stuckey, he would obtain the advantage of having his claims confirmed by other parties.

The first person he met at the Cuban Embassy was a woman named Silvia Duran, who spoke English. She listened to Oswald for a full fifteen minutes. Posner gives a good description based on the testimony of the Consul, Eusebio Azcue, before the HSCA:

> . . . [Oswald] proceeded to tell her he was going to the USSR but that on the way he wanted a transit visa to stop in Cuba, for at least two weeks. He then began placing documents on her desk, each accompanied with a short explanation . . . [and said] that he wanted to leave by September 30, only three days later . . . Duran, an admitted Marxist, took a liking to Oswald . . . [and she] called on Eusebio Azcue to see if he might expedite the process for the young American.[1]

Azcue told him that he could not rush matters since he had to get authorization from the Cuban government in Havana. Moreover, Oswald would have to fill out an application and obtain five passport-size photographs. When Lee came back from that errand and completed his application, he learned that the best way to expedite his visa was to obtain permission at the Russian Embassy to visit the USSR.

Oswald was visibly upset at the hurdles looming before him and began to protest. As a friend of Cuba, he ought to be able to obtain a visa immediately. Azcue replied that he could be given a fifteen-day permission for visiting Cuba, but only after obtaining a Soviet visa. Or he could go through the normal channels, which would take several weeks in Mexico. Oswald replied that he did not have several weeks, and soon they were in a dispute that grew so loud that another official, Alfredo Mirabel Diaz, came out of his office to witness it.

Oswald then took off for the first of his two visits to the Soviet Embassy, which, conveniently, was no more than a couple of blocks away. For years, these two visits to the Russians have been a source of confusion or of obfuscation: The CIA kept a camera watch in a building across from the entry gate to the Soviet compound, yet CIA files have never produced a picture of Oswald entering or leaving the gate. The unadmitted likelihood is that the CIA certainly did have surveillance photos of Oswald entering the Russian Embassy and they were lifted from the Agency file after the assassination; indeed, this is to be expected if Oswald had attracted CIA attention after the Walker affair.

In any event, we can now be all but certain that it was Oswald who did visit the Russian Embassy and spoke there to three KGB agents who were doubling as consular officials. One of them, Oleg Nechiporenko, has written a book, *Passport to Assassination,* which tells of the two meetings in considerable detail.

Oswald arrived at the Soviet Embassy gate at twelve-thirty that afternoon, and waited in the reception area until one of the consulate employees, Valery Vladimirovich Kostikov, came out, listened to his request for a visa, glanced at the man's papers, and heard him say "that he was under constant surveillance in the United States by the FBI and . . . wanted to return to the USSR."[2]

Kostikov had a meeting to take care of, and this fellow was hardly a run-of-the-mill subject. His visit was obviously going to take time. So, Kostikov called his colleague Oleg Maximovich Nechiporenko to the phone.

Listen, some gringo is here, Kostikov said . . . He's asking for a visa to the Soviet Union. Supposedly he already lived there, married one of our girls. They live in the States, but the FBI is harassing them. Come over here and get to the bottom of this. It seems to be more in your line of work. I'm in a hurry.[3]

Nechiporenko then adds:

As I approached the small building that housed the consular division, I saw a stranger, apparently twenty-five to twenty-seven years old, standing on the steps and leaning against the doorpost . . . He seemed to be looking beyond me, absorbed in his thoughts, and did not even react as I approached him. He was clad in a light jacket, a sport shirt with an unbuttoned collar, and either gray or brown slacks that were wrinkled. I greeted the stranger with a nod. He responded in kind.[4]

Kostikov, who shared an office with Nechiporenko, made the introductions and left. Oswald and Oleg were now in the same room, and the American, being invited to sit down, did so and began to talk in a state of considerable agitation. He looked exhausted.

Once again, Oswald took out his papers, complained about the FBI, and said he had come to Mexico to obtain visas to two countries—Cuba, to visit, and then the USSR, for a permanent return.

I silently cursed Valery for "transferring" him to me and decided that it was time to bring this meeting to a close. I had more important items in my agenda. I explained to Oswald that, in accordance with our rules, all matters dealing with travel to the USSR were handled by our embassies or consulates in the country in which a person lived. As far as his case was concerned, we could make an exception and give him the necessary papers to fill out, which we would then send on to Moscow, but the answer would still be sent to his permanent residence, and it would take, at the very least, four months.

Oswald listened intently to my explanation, but it was clear from his gestures and the expression on his face that he was disappointed and growing increasingly annoyed. When I had finished speaking, he slowly leaned forward and, barely able to restrain himself, practically shouted in my face, "This won't do for me! This is not my case! For me, it's all going to end in tragedy!"

I shrugged my shoulders and stood up, signaling the end of our meeting. Oswald's hands shook as he put the documents back into his jacket. I led Oswald through the reception area and showed him the way out of the compound. He departed, obviously dissatisfied with the results of our talk. He appeared to be extremely agitated. This was how Oswald's first visit to our embassy in Mexico ended.[5]

Later that day, however, Nechiporenko began to think about the American who had come by that morning in such a state of tension about the FBI.

What guided us most of all—and I do not think I am mistaken in assuming it was the same for all intelligence services—in working with such foreigners was the principle of "fifty-fifty." This meant that the probability of obtaining a source of good, possibly even valuable, information was equal to the probability that the source was a "plant," that is, a trap set by the enemy with unpredictable consequences.

As I thought about that day's visitor and weighed the criteria of one "fifty" against another, I came to the conclusion that he fit neither category, meaning that he did not have any interest for us . . . It was perfectly clear that our internal counterintelligence back home had already studied him. Now that he was under FBI surveillance, let him be their headache, I thought.[6]

In the evening, Nechiporenko, relaxing with Kostikov at a Mexican cantina, was told by him of a call from Silvia Duran. Oswald had gone back to see the Cubans and told them that the Soviets had promised him a visa, so Silvia Duran was interested in checking. Kostikov had corrected her impression. Now, for a little while, over their mugs of beer, they discussed Oswald. Being young themselves and in fine shape physically, they found it agreeable to debate whether the man was schizoid in personality or merely neurotic.

It is probably fair to say that the physical appearance of Kostikov and Nechiporenko was Mexican. They had been serving in Mexico City long enough to have grown full mustaches, and both men were dark. Perhaps they had cultivated their appearance. It is an advantage for an intelligence officer to look like a native, and to some degree they may even have begun to think like Mexicans— which will have its bearing on an extraordinary episode that takes place the following morning, Saturday, when Oswald returns to the Soviet Embassy.

Kostikov, Nechiporenko, and their immediate superior, Yatskov, were stars of the Soviet diplomats' volleyball team. A "serious match" was scheduled for that same Saturday morning against a team composed of military intelligence personnel—GRU.[7]

It is one of the ironies surrounding Oswald's trip to Mexico that on this important day in his life, when he reenters the Soviet Embassy to attempt to convince these Soviet officials that he should, given his qualifications, be granted a quick visa, their minds are elsewhere. His presence in their office only serves to make them late for the game.

Pavel Yatskov, who was first to arrive at his desk that Saturday morning, was relieved when Kostikov joined him inasmuch as the stranger who had just come in for an interview was speaking in English—which Yatskov barely understood. Kostikov would later describe the scene to Nechiporenko. It is worth following at some length:

> I flung open the door to the first office, and there I saw Pavel sitting at his desk, and at the attached desk to his right, his back to the window, was the American who visited us the previous day. He was disheveled, rumpled, and unshaven. He had the look of someone who was hounded and he was much more anxious than the day before. I greeted him, and he nodded in response. Pavel also seemed tense. He turned to me and said, "Listen, help me out. I don't fully understand what it is he wants." . . . At this point, Oswald, on his own initiative . . . reported that he had . . . traveled to the Soviet Union as a tourist, where he had remained for political reasons, and had lived for a while in Belorussia, where he married a Russian and returned to the United States. He even dropped some hints that he had supposedly carried out a secret mission. He announced that he was a Communist and a member of an organization that defended Cuba. Pavel interrupted his monologue and said, since he had been in the Soviet Union, lived and worked there, that he could probably explain himself in Russian and looked at him disapprovingly. Without

answering, he switched over to broken Russian, in which the rest of the conversation was conducted . . .

While telling his story, Oswald again, as he had the day before, tried to support it by showing various documents . . . [and] repeated his desire to quickly obtain a visa to the USSR . . . He said he was motivated by the fact that it was very difficult for him to live in the United States, that he was constantly under surveillance, even persecuted, and that his personal life was being invaded and his wife and neighbors interrogated. He lost his job because the FBI had been around his place of employment asking questions. In recounting all this, he continually expressed concern for his life.

In his words, he dreamed of returning to his former job in the Soviet Union and living quietly there with his family. He spoke with noticeable warmth about his wife and child.

Throughout his story, Oswald was extremely agitated and clearly nervous, especially whenever he mentioned the FBI, but he suddenly became hysterical, began to sob, and through his tears cried, "I am afraid . . . they'll kill me. Let me in!" Repeating over and over that he was being persecuted and that he was being followed even here in Mexico, he stuck his right hand into the left pocket of his jacket and pulled out a revolver, saying, "See? This is what I must now carry to protect my life," and placed the revolver on the desk where we were sitting opposite one another.

I was dumbfounded, and looked at Pavel, who had turned slightly pale but then quickly said to me, "Here, give me that piece." I took the revolver from the table and handed it to Pavel. Oswald, sobbing, wiped away the tears. He did not respond to my movements. Pavel, who had grabbed the revolver, opened the chamber, shook the bullets into his hand, and put them in a desk drawer. He then handed the revolver to me, and I put it back on the desk. Oswald continued to sob, then pulled himself together and seemed indifferent to what we had done with his weapon. Pavel poured Oswald a glass of water and handed it to him. Oswald took a sip and placed the glass in front of him.[8]

At this point, Oleg Nechiporenko, suited up in shorts for volleyball, knocked on the door to summon the others and then opened it to come in. They were already late for the game.

But now, of course, there was no question of that. Not with the revolver on the table. Nechiporenko closed the door again. Afterward, Yatskov would tell Nechiporenko:

> . . . his eyes were wet with tears, and his hands shook . . . I began to console him, saying that it might seem terrible to him, [but] the reasons for his being victimized were not immediately evident [to us]. Valery repeated a few of my sentences in English. Regarding his visa to the Soviet Union, we explained our rules once again, but in view of his condition, I offered him the necessary forms to be filled out. [Then in] response to his persistent requests that we recommend that the Cubans give him a visa, as an alternative to obtaining our visa, we told him that Cuba was a sovereign nation and decided visa questions for itself . . .
>
> Oswald gradually calmed down . . . [and] did not take the forms we offered him. His state of extreme agitation had now been replaced by depression. He looked disappointed and extremely frustrated. Valery and I exchanged glances and let it be known that the subject of this conversation had been exhausted and that it was time to break it up. I rose from the table. Oswald got up from his chair, and simultaneously grabbed the revolver and stuck it somewhere under his jacket, either in a pocket or in his belt. Turning to Valery, he once again said something about being followed. I bent down to get the bullets from the desk drawer. I then handed them to Oswald, who dropped them into a pocket of his jacket. We said good-bye with a nod of our heads. Valery also stood, calmly opened the door leading into the reception area, and after letting him go first, followed right behind him . . .[9]

Here, Oleg, who has apparently opened the door again, now overlaps Yatskov's account with his own:

> At that moment I distinctly heard Oswald say that he was afraid to return to the United States—where he would be killed. "But if they don't leave me alone, I'm going to defend myself." Valery confirms these were Oswald's words.
>
> It was said without mentioning anyone in particular. At the time this phrase meant nothing to us. What happened to him in his own country was his problem. We recalled these words

only on that fateful November twenty-second. When I led Oswald out of the reception area into the courtyard and showed him the way to the gate, he pulled his head down, and raised the collar of his jacket to conceal his face and thus attempt to avoid being clearly photographed . . .[10]

Recently, Nechiporenko was asked by this book's interviewers how it was possible that a responsible KGB man would give back not only a gun but its bullets to someone as disturbed in appearance as Oswald. Nechiporenko shrugged. It had happened, he said. He could not speak for why. Yatskov had done it, but it did not seem exceptional at the time.

"If this same episode had taken place in London, would any of you have returned the bullets?"

"Never," said Nechiporenko.

That gave some purchase for believing this story. It could be proposed that these three KGB men had served in Mexico long enough to feel that it was wrong to deprive a man of his gun. That, by the Mexican logic of the *cantinas*, was equal to emasculation, and to a Mexican no act could be considered more heinous.

"All right," he was asked, "one can understand giving back the gun. But the bullets! What if Oswald had reloaded his gun on the way out and shot the first person he encountered on the street? And then said, 'The Russians gave me the bullets'?"

Nechiporenko shook his head. It had happened the way it happened, he said, and perhaps you had to be there to believe it. They just had not been afraid that this man Oswald would go out in the street and cause trouble with his gun.

They would never admit it, but perhaps they did think that he might need a weapon to defend himself against the FBI. After all, how many FBI men in the same situation would not believe that a Russian defector would need his bullets returned in order to defend himself against the KGB?

Or, if we are to muse upon Yatskov's motive, perhaps he did not wish to create a situation where Oswald could go to the American Embassy in Mexico City and claim that the Soviets were holding some of his property. The fellow might be a skilled provocateur.

In any event, the three officers never got to the volleyball game that day against the GRU. Yatskov, Kostikov, and Nechiporenko were busy filing a coded cable to Moscow Center that described the meeting with Oswald. Since their team lost to the GRU, they felt guilty.

. . .

On that wholly frustrating Saturday morning, Oswald next went from the Soviet compound down the street to the Cuban Embassy and ran into another quarrel with the Consul, Eusebio Azcue:

Posner: Oswald again demanded that he be issued a visa because of his political credentials, but the consul repeated it was impossible without a Russian visa . . . "I hear him make statements that are directed against us," recalled Azcue, "and he accuses us of being bureaucrats, and in a very discourteous manner. At that point I also become upset and I tell him to leave the consulate, maybe somewhat violently or emotionally." He told Oswald that "a person like him, instead of aiding the Cuban revolution, was doing it harm." Azcue moved toward Oswald, prepared to force him physically out of the embassy. "Then he leaves the consulate," recalled Azcue, "and he seems to be mumbling to himself, and slams the door, also in a very discourteous mood. That was the last time we saw him around."[11]

It is painful to think of Oswald walking down the street, his documents in his ditty bag. All his striving had gone into collecting those documents, yet no one had been stirred by his deeds.

On Sunday, he went to a bullfight and on Monday he called Nechiporenko one more time. Had there been any affirmative word from Moscow on his application for a visa? None, replied Nechiporenko.

Oswald went to the bus terminal and bought a ticket home. If, once in 1959 and again in 1962, he had prevailed against the giant bureaucracies of the Soviet Union and the United States, he could no longer maintain the luster of that achievement.

On Wednesday, he departed from Mexico City at eight-thirty in the morning. In something like thirty hours, he was back in Dallas. He did not call Marina at Ruth Paine's house in Irving, but instead took a room at the Y and, presumably, he slept alone with his arms around the ash-heap of his plans.

PART VI

DENOUEMENT

1

The Road to Domesticity

On the bus returning from Mexico, there is a revealing moment. As they cross the border into Texas, Oswald is eating a banana. Since there are signs displayed not to bring fresh produce into the U.S., he is gobbling his food down as they enter the Customs shed in Laredo. Or so the official remembers it. That's all right, Oswald is told, take your time, you can finish your banana.[1]

It is a small episode, but it speaks of changes in him. After the ravages of Mexico, he is going to be law-abiding for a time. If the conflict in his adult life has been between fame and family, this last trip has turned the balance. He left in the belief that he might never see Marina again, but on his return, he is prepared to be loving.

First, however, having arrived in Dallas at mid-day, he spends the afternoon at the Texas Employment Commission, where he files his claim for the last of his series of unemployment compensation checks, and registers for work. Then he puts up at the Y that night and in the morning applies for a job as a typesetter. It is equal to Buster Keaton becoming a banker. Dyslexic Oswald will set type! Or does he see it as a major opportunity to print his own materials?

He certainly does well on the interview: "Oswald was well-dressed and neat. He made a favorable impression on the foreman of the department . . . Since Oswald had worked in a trade plant, I was interested in him as a possible employee . . ."[2]

Unfortunately, Lee had listed Jaggars-Chiles-Stovall as a place of previous employment, and so, on the back of his application, Theodore F. Gangl, the plant superintendent who interviewed him, later adds: "Bob Stovall does not recommend this man. He was released because of his record as a troublemaker—*Has communistic tendencies.*"[3]

Feeling confident that he would get the job, Oswald called Marina and hitchhiked up to Irving, where she was staying with Ruth.

McMillan: He followed her like a puppydog around the house, kissed her again and again, and kept saying, "I've missed you so."

Lee spent the weekend at the Paines'. Ruth left them alone as much as she could, and even tried to keep June out of their way. Carefree as children, they sat on swings in the back yard . . . All weekend he showed the greatest solicitude toward her, trying to get her to eat more, especially bananas and apples, to drink juices and milk, things that would strengthen her before the baby came. But Marina saw that he was distracted—worried about finding a job. As Ruth drove him to the bus station at noon on Monday, Lee asked if Marina could stay until he found work. Ruth answered that Marina was welcome to stay as long as she liked.[4]

Back in Dallas, he rented a room from a lady named Mary Bledsoe, and it takes no more than a bit of her testimony to recognize that she is so classic a landlady, one can even visualize the pucker of her not-so-generous lips.

MR. BALL. Did you talk to him about the use of the refrigerator?

MRS. BLEDSOE. Well, he said he was going to put something in there, and I said—I didn't have anything to say, and I hemmed-and-hawed, I said, "Well, no; I don't have a very big refrigerator."

Well, he said, "I won't use it after this time." He was very, very congenial.

MR. BALL. Did he go down to the grocery store?

MRS. BLEDSOE. He bought some peanut butter and some sardines, and some bananas and put it all in his room, except the milk, and he ate there, ate in his room. I didn't like that either . . . Then he talked to somebody on the phone and he talked in a foreign language . . . I was in my room, and the telephone is over there [indicating], and I didn't like that, so I told my girlfriend, I said, "I don't like anybody talking in a foreign language."[5]

Oswald is a prodigious snob, but given some of the people he meets, who would not be?

He was paying seven dollars a week, and on Friday, ready to go back to Irving again, he spoke to Mrs. Bledsoe about a few house-keeping details:

MRS. BLEDSOE. . . . he said, "And I want my room cleaned and clean sheets put on the bed."

And I said, "Well, I will after you move because you are going to move."

He said, "Why?"

I says, "Because I am not going to rent to you any more."

. . . He said, "Give me back my money." Now, $2.

I said, "Well, I don't have it."

So, he left Saturday morning . . .[6]

Without the two dollars. It was just after his first week back. Having lost a room for no evident reason, and a job he thought he had, Oswald could have come to the conclusion that the FBI was alerting people to his presence. So, for the next room he rented after his return to Dallas from the second weekend in Irving, Oswald gave his name as O. H. Lee to Earlene Roberts, who was taking care of the rooming house for the landlady, Mrs. Johnson. It was this alias, O. H. Lee, that may have brought him to the end of the drama that was his life.

His relations with Earlene Roberts were marginally better than his encounters with Mrs. Bledsoe.

MR. BALL. Did you ever talk to him about anything?

MRS. ROBERTS. No; because he wouldn't talk.

MR. BALL. Did he say hello?

MRS. ROBERTS. No.

MR. BALL. Or goodbye?

MRS. ROBERTS. No.

MR. BALL. Or anything?

MRS. ROBERTS. He wouldn't say nothing.

MR. BALL. Did you ever speak to him?

MRS. ROBERTS. Well, yes—I would say, "Good afternoon," and he would maybe just look at me—give me a dirty look and keep walking and go on to his room.[7]

Over the next forty days, he will see a great deal of Ruth Paine and her estranged husband, Michael, on weekends in Irving. Ruth, as indicated earlier, is an apostle of reason and decency, as archetypical a liberal as Mrs. Bledsoe is a landlady.

While Ruth Paine has no great comprehension of Lee, it is hardly fair to ask her to have divined the secret thoughts of a young man who draws his spiritual sustenance equally from authoritarians and anarchists.

Ruth Paine became, nonetheless, one of the stand-bys of the Warren Commission even if the FBI started with great distrust of her—could she be a KGB agent hooked into Marina? Then they found out that her husband, Michael, was the son of Lyman Paine, an American radical who had gone to Norway in the Thirties to visit Leon Trotsky, who was there in exile from Russia.

On questioning her, the Warren Commission discovered that Ruth had written numerous letters to her mother about Marina and Lee. In the course of having such letters read into her testimony, and indeed the letters are full of Ruth Paine's gifts at fine-tuning her reactions to Lee and Marina, she ends up with the greatest number of pages of testimony—more than De Mohrenschildt, or Marina, or Marguerite, or Robert Oswald, or Captain Fritz of the Dallas police, a feat marred only by the fact that we don't really learn a great deal more than we knew before. It is no great surprise to us that Oswald is, already by half, a most domesticated husband:

MRS. PAINE. I disliked him actively in the spring when I thought he just wanted to get rid of his wife and wasn't caring about her . . . I then found him much nicer, I thought, when I saw him next in New Orleans in late September, and this would be a perfectly good time to admit the rest of the pertinent part of this letter to my mother written October 14, because it shows something that I think should be part of the public record, and I am one of the few people who can give it, that presents Lee Oswald as a human person, a person really rather ordinary, not an ogre that was out to leave his wife and be harsh and hostile to all that he knew.

But in this brief period during the times he came out on weekends, I saw him as a person who cared for his wife and child, tried to make himself helpful in my home, tried to make himself welcome although he really preferred to stay to himself.

He wasn't much to take up a conversation. This [letter] says, "Dear Mom—He arrived a week and a half ago and has been looking for work since. It is a very depressing business for him, I am sure. He spent last weekend and the one before with us here and was a happy addition to our expanded family. He played with Chris"—my 3-year-old, then 2—"watched football on the TV, planed down the doors that wouldn't fit . . . And generally added a needed masculine flavor. From a poor first impression I have come to like him."[8]

The next excerpt may give a glimpse of Michael Paine, who was not without concern for the shadings of moral nicety:

MR. LIEBELER. When did you have this discussion with your wife concerning whether or not you should let Marina live with you? Was that before they came back from New Orleans?

MR. PAINE. Yes, it was.

MR. LIEBELER. And you concluded at the time there was no reason why Marina should not come here; is that right?

MR. PAINE. That is right. Of course, Ruth went in and sounded them out rather cautiously and reported to me also [Oswald's] facial expressions and what-not when she was suggesting this, and he seemed to be glad of that rather than worried.

MR. LIEBELER. Now, after Marina came and lived at your house, Oswald was there during parts of the months October and November . . . was [your opinion] reinforced on the basis of his activities and your observation of him during that period?

MR. PAINE. It was reinforced.

MR. LIEBELER. You did not think him to be a violent person or one who would be likely to commit an act such as assassinating the President?

MR. PAINE. I didn't—I saw he was a bitter person, [with] quite a lot of very negative views of people in the world around him, very little charity in his view toward anybody, but I thought he was harmless.

REPRESENTATIVE FORD. Was this a different reaction from the one you had had at your first meeting or first acquaintance?

MR. PAINE. When we first became acquainted I was somewhat shocked, especially that he would speak so harshly to his wife in front of a complete stranger, and it was at that point . . . that I was persuaded I would like to free Marina from her bondage and servitude to this man [so] I became interested in helping her escape from him. Of course, I was not going to try to force that. I didn't want to be separating a family that could get along.

MR. LIEBELER. This bitterness you detected following his return from Mexico, was that a new reaction?

MR. PAINE. No. That bitterness had existed all along [but] when Marina came to our house, she gained in health and weight. She started to look better and it looked to me as if the strain was off the family relationship. They were not quarreling. They billed and cooed. She sat on his lap and he said sweet things in her ear.[9]

Back in Dallas after the weekend in Irving, Lee would call every night, and each night he had the same sad story to recount: no job yet.

Later, many conspiracy theorists would find his employment at the Texas School Book Depository to be suspicious in the extreme, but on the face of it, he got the job through one of Ruth Paine's neighbors, who remarked that "her brother worked in the School Book Depository and there was apparently an opening there."[10] That Ruth would be instrumental in getting him hired was, naturally, one of the elements in the FBI's early suspicion of her.

MR. TRULY. I received a phone call from a lady in Irving who said her name was Mrs. Paine [and she said,] "Mr. Truly, you don't know who I am but I have a neighbor whose brother [Wesley Frazier] works for you [and] he tells his sister that you are very busy. And I am just wondering if you can use another man . . . I have a fine young man living here with his wife and baby, and his wife is expecting a baby—another baby—in a few days and he needs work desperately."

. . . I told Mrs. Paine to send him down, and I would talk to him—that I didn't have anything in mind for him of a permanent nature, but if he was suited we could possibly use him for a brief time . . .

So he came in, introduced himself to me, and I took him in my office and interviewed him. He seemed to be quiet and well mannered.

I gave him an application to fill out, which he did. . . . I asked him about experience that he had had, or where he had worked, and he said he had just served his term in the Marine Corps and had an honorable discharge . . .[11]

He did not give Jaggars-Chiles-Stovall as a reference.

MR. TRULY. . . . thinking that he was just out of the Marines, I didn't check any further back. I didn't have anything of a permanent nature in mind for him. He looked like a nice young fellow to me—he was quiet and well mannered. He used the word "sir," you know—which a lot of them don't do at this time.

So I told him [to] come in to work on the morning of the 16th . . .

MR. BELIN. Well, could you describe how his work progressed as he was working for you?

MR. TRULY. [For] the time he was there, the work that he did was a bit above average . . . he did a good day's work.

MR. BELIN. What was his pay?

MR. TRULY. $1.25 an hour . . . he worked by himself. His job was something that he needed no help with, other than to ask occasionally for stock . . . Consequently, he didn't have much occasion to talk with the other boys.

I thought it was a pretty good trait at the time, because occasionally you have to spread your boys out and say, "Quit talking so much, let's get to work."

And it seemed to me like he paid attention to his job.[12]

That Friday, the eighteenth of October, was his twenty-fourth birthday. He had a new job three days old, Marina's pregnancy was close to term, and there was a surprise birthday party with decorations on the table. As Marina told Priscilla Johnson McMillan, Lee "could not hold back the tears."[13] It is a touching moment until we realize it is one more thundering contradiction between the two halves of his nature—the stoic and the man who has wept for us a score of times already. Of course, tears are near to tenderness, and he is thoughtful of Marina's condition—he massages her ankles and props her back with pillows. Yet, he is still Marguerite's son, a perfectionist:

> *McMillan:* He brought his dirty laundry to the house each weekend for Marina to wash and iron, and he often refused to wear a shirt she had just ironed on the grounds that she had failed to do it exactly right. No sooner would they sit down at the dinner table than he would snap at Marina: "Why don't you fix me iced tea? You knew I was coming out." Or he would put on a baby face and complain in baby talk that he couldn't eat because Marina had forgotten to give him a fork and a spoon. He never once got up to fetch for himself or help a wife in the final stages of pregnancy . . .[14]

Still, he did cradle her head while they watched television that night.

By the end of the weekend, October 20, Marina went into labor. Lee, however, had to let Ruth take her to Parkland Hospital in Dallas and he was obliged to stay back in Irving baby-sitting Ruth's two children and June. He did not know how to drive.

After no more than two hours of labor, Marina gave birth to a girl, while Lee, having gone to sleep, found out only on Monday morning before he went off to work.

> *McMillan:* He returned to Irving that afternoon with Wesley Frazier, but for some reason seemed reluctant to visit the hospital. Puzzled, Ruth guessed he was afraid to go lest someone [there] find out that he had a job and charge him with the expenses of the birth. And so Ruth told him that the hospital already knew he had a job; she had been asked the night before at the admissions office and had told the truth. But it did not make any difference. The delivery and maternity care still were free. After learning that, Lee agreed to go.
>
> Marina never knew of his reluctance. "Oh, Mama, you're wonderful," he said, as he sat down on her bed. "Only two hours. You have them so easily." He had tears in his eyes.[15]

From Marina's narrative: He was very happy at the birth of another daughter and even wept a little. He said that two daughters were better for each other—two sisters . . . In his happiness he said a lot of silly things and was very tender with me, and I was very happy to see that Lee had improved a little, i.e., that he was thinking more about his family.[16]

By the following weekend in Irving, he had become the model of a loving father:

McMillan: He held the baby to his shoulder and stroked her head. "She's the prettiest, strongest baby in the world," he boasted. "Only a week old and already she can hold up her head. We're strong because Mama gives us milk and not a bottle that's either too hot or too cold. Mama gives us only the very best." He studied her fingers, her "tender little mouth," and her yawn. He was delighted with them all and pronounced that his baby was getting prettier every day. "She looks just like her mama," he said.[17]

The baby's full name is Audrey Marina Rachel Oswald. She will be called Rachel.

Meanwhile, fatherhood brings out the conservative in Lee. Marina tries to enlarge his understanding of Ruth's marital situation, but he is censorious of Michael's behavior.

McMillan: Lee thought it was a man's obligation once married to want his wife and want children. He was indignant at Michael for having married without wanting children. And he condemned Michael for coming home, eating supper, and seeing his children just like a married man, and then leaving . . . Lee was not ordinarily interested in other people's private affairs. But now he regularly asked Marina, over the telephone and on his arrival for the weekend, how Ruth and Michael were getting along. For the first time, he seemed aware of the Paines as human beings. He even gave signs of awareness that he and his family might be in the way in the modest one-story ranch house . . .[18]

Now a letter comes to Marina in Irving from her younger sister, Galina, in Leningrad:

September 29, 1963
Leningrad

Hello, dear Marinochka!

. . . I dream very often about mother; it is even unpleasant, somehow, for, after all, she is dead. And when I wake up, I feel rather frightened . . .

Marinochka, how nice it would be if you could come here to the Homeland; you could find a job for yourself and your husband would have work and the children could be sent to a public nursery, and everything would be all right. But would they allow you to return again? If you adopted American citizenship, they may not permit it, and generally, it seems to me, that it would be very difficult for you to leave. But, honestly speaking, I would like it better if you would live here. The unemployment is the most vicious scourge in life. We do not have it here; we do not even know what *unemployment* is. You know it yourself. There is a crying need for pharmacists in Leningrad. Come, I am always waiting for you. If things get hard—we will help you . . .

Come, Marina. We will walk together, you and I, and recollect our youth. It was nice then, and even then you, too, could have gotten married and we would have been together in Leningrad. But we were fools.

Marinochka, my dear, write to me about everything in detail. I, too, am always glad to receive your letters . . .

Galka[19]

While this letter stands for itself, it has collateral effects. Certainly, it has been perused by both the Soviet and the American mail-intercept programs. So, it has enabled the FBI, which had lost sight of Oswald's whereabouts once he left New Orleans, to pick up his address in America again.

2

The Shadow of the FBI

On Friday afternoon, November 1, while Marina was setting her hair in preparation for Lee's arrival, an FBI man came to Ruth's house in Irving. A dark, strong, pleasant-looking man with a dark mustache, his name was James P. Hosty, and as he would later tell the Warren Commission, he had a revolving load of about forty cases to take care of around Dallas and environs. Lee Harvey Oswald was one of those cases. Back in April, he had located Oswald on Neely Street, but before he could interview him, Oswald had moved. Now, Hosty had not only picked up the address in Irving, but knew that Oswald had been in Mexico City visiting the Cuban and Soviet embassies. Since the FBI had a source installed in the Russian compound, they now knew that Oswald had been closeted with Valery Kostikov, who was categorized by FBI and CIA as a functioning officer in the Thirteenth Department of KGB, precisely the cadre that took care, from time to time, of those bloodletting actions described euphemistically as "wet jobs." The FBI, we can recognize, had a colder view of Kostikov than Oleg Nechiporenko's portrayal of him as a star volleyball player.

> *McMillan:* . . . Ruth was doing work around the house when [Hosty] reappeared . . . She greeted him cordially, asked him in, and the two sat in the living room talking pleasantries. Hosty said that, unlike the House Un-American Activities Committee, the FBI was not a witch-hunting organization.
>
> Gradually, Hosty switched the conversation to Lee. Was he living at Ruth's house? Ruth answered that he was not. Did she know where he was living? Once again the answer was a surprising "No." Ruth did not know where Lee was living, but it was in Dallas somewhere and she thought it might be Oak Cliff. Did Ruth know where he was working? She explained that Lee thought he had been having job trouble on account of the FBI. Hosty assured her that it was not the FBI's way to approach an employer directly. At this Ruth softened, told him where Lee was working, and together they looked up the address of the book depository in the telephone book. Lee worked at 411 Elm Street.[1]

About this time, Marina came into the room:

McMillan: Before Hosty left, Marina begged him not to interfere with Lee at work. She explained that he had had trouble keeping his jobs and thought he lost them "because the FBI is interested in him." . . .

"I don't think he has lost any of his jobs on account of the FBI," Hosty said softly.

Ruth and Marina urged the visitor to stay. If he wanted to see Lee, they said, he would be there at 5:30. But Hosty had to get back to the office; and . . . he asked Ruth to find out where he was living. Ruth thought that would be no problem; she would simply ask Lee.[2]

MRS. PAINE. I said to Agent Hosty that if in the future Marina and Lee are living together, and I know, or I have correspondence with them, I would give him his address if he wished it. Then it was the next day or that evening or sometime shortly thereafter Marina said to me while we were doing dishes that she felt their address was their business . . . This surprised me. She had never spoken in this way to me before, and I didn't see that it made any difference.[3]

We can only speculate on the kind of contained wrath Oswald would feel at Ruth Paine's obeisance to authority in the name of being aboveboard, forthright, keeping her word, and having nothing to hide.

Lee had been in a fine mood on arrival, but the moment he heard of Hosty's visit, it was obvious that he was upset. At supper, he descended into depths of silence. He went through the motions all weekend, hung up the diapers on the clothesline in the backyard, played with the children under a tree in that same yard, watched football, which was his greatest diversion each Saturday and Sunday afternoon, but his mind was on the FBI. He gave Marina specific instructions: The next time *they* came, he wanted her to be able to describe the car, note how many doors it had and what color it was, and, most important, take down the license number.[4] He even told her that if the car was not in front of Ruth's house, it would still be there on the street, next door probably. He was in one of those moods she had come to know all too well on

Neely Street, and was silent again all Sunday afternoon as he watched football.

> *McMillan:* Michael was at home and had occasion to step over Lee while he was lying stretched out on the floor. Michael felt a pang of self-reproach. He thought he was being rude, stepping over Lee that way without even trying to make small talk . . . He did not resent Lee lying on his floor, watching his television, and crowding his house a bit. But he did feel that for a man who professed to be a revolutionary, Lee had an awful lot of time on his hands . . . To lie around watching television all day, Michael said to himself, "is one hell of a way for a revolutionary to be spending his time."
>
> Late in the afternoon Ruth gave Lee his third driving lesson—backing, parking, and a right-angle turn. She thought Lee really got the feel of parking that day.[5]

Two days later, on November 5, a Tuesday, Hosty came again. His second visit with Ruth was even friendlier than the first:

> **MR. JENNER.** . . . Have you now exhausted your recollection on the subject?
>
> **MRS. PAINE.** I think one other thing. Agent Hosty asked me . . . if I thought this was a mental problem, his words referring to Lee Oswald, and I said I didn't understand the mental processes of anyone who could espouse the Marxist philosophy, but that this was far different from saying he was mentally unstable or unable to conduct himself in normal society.
>
> I did tell Lee that this question had been asked. He gave no reply, but more a scoffing laugh, barely voiced.[6]

There is some question whether Marina spoke to Hosty that second time or not. The FBI man has no recollection of that, but Marina insists she did and had a nice conversation with Hosty.

Since Marina, like Lee, was not incapable of going in opposite directions at once, she had also managed to slip outside long enough to memorize the color and shape of Hosty's car, and the license-plate number, which details she proceeded to jot down on a paper as soon as she got back to her bedroom.

> *McMillan:* Later, she and Ruth discussed whether to tell Lee about the visit. Ruth thought it might be better to wait until

the weekend and Marina agreed. Each time he called that week (he called twice a day, during his lunch break and at 5:30 in the afternoon), he started by asking: "Has the FBI been there?" Each time Marina said No.

No sooner had he arrived on Friday than Lee went outside where Marina was hanging diapers and asked: "Have they been here again?"

Marina said Yes . . .

"How on earth could you forget?"

"Well, it upset you last time . . ."

"It upsets me worse if you keep it from me. Why must you hide things all the time? I never can count on you . . ."[7]

"I never can count on you!" It is the barbaric yawp of every husband and wife who have half of a good marriage and can't begin to gain a foothold up the wall that separates them from the other half.

McMillan: "He's such a nice man, Lee. Don't be frightened. All he did was explain my rights and promise to protect them."

"You fool," said Lee . . . "He doesn't care about your rights. He comes because it's his job . . . I trust you didn't give your consent to having him defend your 'rights'?"

"Of course not," said Marina, "but I agreed with him."

"Fool," he said again. "As a result of these 'rights,' they'll ask you ten times as many questions as before. If the Soviet Embassy gets wind of it and you agreed to let this man protect your 'rights,' then you'll really be in for it . . ."[8]

The only item that ameliorated his mood was that she had taken down the license-plate number. First thing Saturday morning, November 9, he asked to borrow Ruth's typewriter. Then, in a highly secretive posture, covering up a page of handwriting that he was now copying, he worked away on something of obvious importance to him—nothing less than a letter to the Soviet Embassy in Washington:

Dear Sirs:
    This is to inform you of events since my interview with Comrade Kostine in the Embassy of the Soviet Union, Mexico City, Mexico.

I was unable to remain in Mexico City indefinitely because of my Mexican visa restrictions which was for 15 days only. I could not take a chance on applying for an extension unless I used my real name so I returned to the U.S.

I and Marina Nicholeyeva are now living in Dallas, Texas.

The FBI is not now interested in my activities in the progressive organization FPCC of which I was secretary in New Orleans, Louisiana, since I no longer live in that state.

The FBI has visited us here in Texas. On Nov. 1st agent of the FBI James P. Hosty warned me that if I attempt to engage in FPCC activities in Texas the FBI will again take an "interest" in me. This agent also "suggested" that my wife could "remain in the U.S. under FBI protection," that is, she could defect from the Soviet Union.

Of course I and my wife strongly protested these tactics by the notorious FBI.

I had not planned to contact the Mexico City Embassy at all so, of course, they were unprepared for me. Had I been able to reach Havana as planned, the Soviet Embassy there would have had time to assist me. But of course the stupid Cuban Consul was at fault here. I am glad he has since been replaced by another.[9]

It was a bizarre letter and could serve no conceivable purpose with the Soviets in Washington. They would have to be wholly mistrustful. Either Oswald was out of his normal, manipulative powers of mind—such as they were!—or he wrote the letter on the assumption that it would be read by the FBI and so would cause havoc between its formal and covert echelons—a COINTELPRO action improvised in this case by Oswald. Let us remind ourselves that it was not Ian Fleming but the FBI that chose the name COINTELPRO.

The question we have to ask once more is whether Oswald was indeed working with COINTELPRO or some analogous group. To ask this much, however, is to encourage another question: Was Oswald trying to escape from such a group, or was he looking to embarrass it? Or had he begun to go mad from the pressure of trying to live like other people?

In any case, his extreme reaction to Hosty may reflect the pressure he was being subjected to by any group that was paying him a stipend. If, by hiding in Dallas, he has felt free for a little while, Hosty's arrival, even if it is in the relatively innocent line of duty as an FBI professional, could kick off Oswald's somewhat justifiable paranoia. He would, after all, not know who was communicating with whom in the FBI.

There is, of course, a rational explanation for why he is so upset. It is that if he agreed to be a working provocateur for what he considered to be an FBI group, then he had been promised that there would be no FBI visits at home or at work. Now the rules of the game had changed.

In any event, two days later, on November 12, during his midday break, he went up to the main FBI office on Commerce Street, which was not far from his job at the Book Depository, and with "a wild look in his eye," as described by the receptionist,[10] he gave her a note in an unsealed envelope for Hosty. The FBI man was out to lunch.

We are left with no more than Hosty's recollection of the contents. That is hardly certified to be trustworthy inasmuch as Hosty was told to destroy the note on the orders of his superior, Gordon Shanklin. According to Hosty, for what such testimony is worth under the circumstances, Oswald's note told Hosty not to visit or bother his wife, and then suggested that if Hosty did not desist, he, Oswald, was ready to take action against the FBI. Whether that action would be legal or was a personal threat could not be determined.

According to Hosty, he received comparable unsigned notes all the time, so he did not even know whether this had come from Oswald or someone else. He just filed it in his work box. Such indifference, however, does not square very well with the fact that Hosty knew Oswald had been in Mexico City and had visited the Russian Embassy twice and had been in conversation there twice with a KGB agent who was conversant, according to the FBI, with "wet jobs."

In the meantime, Ruth was having her own flight of paranoia. On Sunday, November 10, while Lee was typing the letter to the Russian Embassy, he left his handwritten copy on Ruth's desk. She, inflamed with curiosity she could not quite admit, finally read the first couple of lines and was so agitated by them—"Comrade Kostine" indeed!—that:

MRS. PAINE. I then proceeded to read the whole note, wondering, knowing this to be false, wondering why he was saying it. I was irritated to have him writing a falsehood on my typewriter, I may say, too. I felt I had some cause to look at it.[11]

Her buried sense of property is coming out. This is one of the very few remarks that Ruth Paine makes in hundreds of pages of testimony which suggests there may be other forces at work in the universe than reason, sweet reason.

> MR. JENNER. Did you ever have any conversation with him about [the letter]?
>
> MRS. PAINE. No. I came close to it . . . He was sitting up watching a late spy story, if you will, on the TV, and I got up and sat there on the sofa with him saying, "I can't sleep," wanting to confront him with this . . . But on the other hand, I was somewhat fearful, and I didn't know what to do.
>
> REPRESENTATIVE FORD. Fearful in what way?
>
> MRS. PAINE. Well, if he was an agent, I would rather just give it to the FBI . . .
>
> MR. JENNER. Were you fearful of any physical harm?
>
> MRS. PAINE. No, I was not . . . though I don't think I defined my fears. I sat down and said I couldn't sleep and he said, "I guess you are real upset about going to the lawyer tomorrow."
>
> He knew I had an appointment with my lawyer to discuss the possibility of divorce the next day, and that didn't happen to be what was keeping me up that night, but . . . it was thoughtful for him to think of it. But I let it rest there, and . . . then I excused myself and went to bed.[12]

On Friday the fifteenth, when Lee called at mid-day to talk about his next weekend trip to Irving, Marina suggested that Ruth and Michael might need some time to themselves. Of course, Marina might also have been seeking a little rest from Lee. His intense reaction to Hosty's second visit had left her exhausted, and that could hardly be good for her milk. She did not say as much, but then, he readily accepted her suggestion, said that it was all right; he had things to do over the weekend in Dallas.

No one knows what, other than work, he did do in Dallas between Monday, November 11, and Wednesday, November 20. On the twenty-first, a Thursday, the night before President Kennedy would come to Dallas, Oswald went out one night early to Irving, and his time is accounted for that evening, but the gap of those ten days from November 11 to November 20 is marked only by his unsuccessful visit to FBI headquarters on November 12 to see Hosty.

Gerald Posner made a large point of quoting Earlene Roberts' statement that she never saw Oswald go out at night, but omits her subsequent remark to the Warren Commission: "If he did, it was after I went to bed, and I never knew it."[13]

His room, small and narrow, was on the ground floor, but it had low windows on the outside wall, so he could have slipped out whenever he wished. This is not to insist that he kept late hours but to point out—one can never do it too often—that many a hard fact cited with authority is about as hard and as longstanding as an eggshell.

Certainly, by Sunday night, November 17, after Lee, as agreed, had not come to Irving for the weekend but had not called either, Marina was feeling uneasy:

> *McMillan:* . . . when she saw Junie playing with the telephone dial, saying, "Papa, Papa," she decided impulsively, "Let's call Papa."
>
> Marina was helpless with a telephone dial, so it was Ruth who made the call . . . and a man answered.
>
> "Is Lee Oswald there?" Ruth asked.
>
> "There is no Lee Oswald living here." . . .
>
> The next day, Monday, November 18, Lee called as usual at lunchtime. "We phoned you last evening," Marina said. "Where were you?" . . .
>
> There was a long silence on the other end. "Oh, damn. I don't live there under my real name."
>
> Why not? Marina asked . . .
>
> "You don't understand a thing," Lee said. "I don't want the FBI to know where I live, either." He ordered her not to tell Ruth . . .
>
> Marina was frightened and shocked. "Starting your old foolishness again," she scolded. "All these comedies. First one, then another. And now this fictitious name. Where will it all end?"
>
> Lee had to get back to work. He would call later, he said.[14]

Marina was now feeling no small rage that he was using a false name. To her, it was equal to concluding that he would never give up his larger ideas; with considerable justice from her point of view, she saw his political commitment as poison to their marriage. His ideas were equal to his need to lie.

She would not forgive him for this alias—O. H. Lee. She kept refusing to forgive him. It would even ruin their last night together. Her timing, as is true of most mates' in marriages that work by half, is, at the least, askew.

Then Lee made the mistake of calling her later that Monday evening, November 18, and getting into a fight. He commanded her to take his number out of Ruth Paine's telephone book. She was to do this so that the FBI could not get hold of it. Marina told him she would not touch Ruth's property.

"I order you to cross it out," said Lee. His voice was so ugly that she said, "I won't," and hung up on him.

He did not call her Tuesday or Wednesday. On Thursday, November 21, he approached Wesley Frazier during work hours:

> MR. FRAZIER. . . . I was standing there getting the orders in and he said, "Could I ride home with you this afternoon?"
>
> And I said, "Sure. You know, like I told you, you can go home with me anytime you want to, like I say, anytime you want to go see your wife that is all right with me." [Then] I come to think it wasn't Friday and I said, "Why are you going home today?"
>
> And he says, "I am going home to get some curtain rods." He said, "You know, put in an apartment."
>
> . . . I said, "Very well." And I never thought more about it . . ."[15]

Oswald has come, by now, to a serious decision. It is still preliminary to his final determination, but he has decided to take his rifle to the School Book Depository on Friday, November 22. All week, the talk at work has been concerned with President Kennedy's visit. The route has been published in the newspapers. The official motorcade will pass by the Texas School Book Depository on Elm Street. Our man, who has spent half of his life reading books and now works in a place that ships out textbooks to the children and college youth of America, may be preparing to engage in an act that some huge majority of the people who read books devotedly would be ready to condemn.

MR. RANKIN. Did he tell you he was coming Thursday, [the 21st]?

MARINA OSWALD. No . . .

MR. RANKIN. And the assassination was on the 22nd.

MARINA OSWALD. This is very hard to forget.

MR. RANKIN. Did your husband give any reason for coming home on Thursday?

MARINA OSWALD. He said that he was lonely because he hadn't come the preceding weekend and he wanted to make his peace with me . . .

MR. RANKIN. Were you upset with him?

MARINA OSWALD. I was angry, of course [and] he was upset . . . He tried very hard to please me. He spent quite a bit of time putting away diapers and playing with the children on the street.

MR. RANKIN. How did you indicate you were angry with him?

MARINA OSWALD. By not talking to him.

MR. RANKIN. And how did he show he was upset?

MARINA OSWALD. . . . He tried to start a conversation with me several times, but I would not answer and he said that he didn't want me to be angry with him because this upsets him [and] he suggested that we rent an apartment in Dallas. He said that he was tired of living alone and that perhaps the reason for my being so angry was the fact that we were not living together, that if I want to, he would rent an apartment in Dallas tomorrow . . . He repeated this not once, but several times, but I refused. And he said that once again I was preferring my friends to him and I didn't need him.

MR. RANKIN. What did you say to that?

MARINA OSWALD. I said it would be better if I remained with Ruth until the holidays . . . because while he was living alone and I stayed with Ruth, we were spending less money, and I told him to buy me a washing machine, because with two children it became too difficult to wash by hand.

MR. RANKIN. What did he say to that?

MARINA OSWALD. He said he would buy me a washing machine.

MR. RANKIN. What did you say to that?

MARINA OSWALD. Thank you, that it would be better if he bought something for himself, that I would manage . . .

MR. RANKIN. Did this seem to make him more upset . . . ?

MARINA OSWALD. Yes. He then stopped talking and sat down and watched television and then went to bed. I went to bed later. It was about 9 o'clock when he went to sleep. I went to sleep at about 11:30, [and] it seemed to me that he was not really asleep, but I didn't talk to him.[16]

He has gone from demoralization in Mexico to a subtler set of defeats. Marina, living with Ruth, is now relatively liberated. She no longer needs him to survive. We can deduce from the petty tyrannies he has exercised upon her since their marriage just how deep is his lonely and fearful conviction that if she did not need him, she would never have anything to do with him. So his need for love (as opposed to his ability to love) was profound. Love was a safeguard against physically attacking the human species itself. If Kennedy was at the moment the finest specimen of the American species available, Lee's anxiety over Marina's love or lack of it was bound to be large on the night before Kennedy arrived. Kennedy was the kind of man any woman (most certainly Marina) would find more attractive than himself. So, yes, he was agitated by whether she had any real love for him. No pit was so deep for Oswald as the abyss of unrequited love.

That evening as the twilight deepened, it was still warm enough in Texas in November to fool around outside:

> *McMillan:*   Lee went out on the front lawn and played with the children until dark—the Paine children, the neighbors' children, and June. He hoisted June to his shoulders and the two of them reached out to catch a butterfly in the air. Then Lee tried to catch falling oak wings for June.[17]

One can have a sense of final moments—the last time we catch oak wings together.

> *McMillan:*   The evening was a peaceful one. Lee told Ruth, as he had Marina, that he had been to FBI headquarters, tried to see the agents, and left a note telling them in no uncertain terms what he thought about their visits. Marina did not believe him. She thought that he was "a brave rabbit," and this was just another instance of his bravado. After that,

the conversation at supper was so ordinary that no one remembers it; but Ruth had the impression that relations between the young Oswalds were "cordial," "friendly," "warm"—"like a couple making up after a small spat."[18]

Ruth is right on the nose again, right on the nose of total error. Oswald has reached that zone of serenity that some men attain before combat, when anxiety is deep enough to feel like quiet exaltation: You are finally going into an action that will be equal in dimension to the importance of your life.

McMillan: Marina was still at the sink when Lee turned off the television set, poked his head in the kitchen, and asked if he could help. Marina thought he looked sad.
   "I'm going to bed," he said. "I probably won't be out this weekend."
   "Why not?"
   "It's too often. I was here today."
   "Okay," Marina said.[19]

MR. JENNER. What did you do that evening? Did you have occasion to note what he did?

MRS. PAINE. We had dinner as usual, and then I sort of bathed my children, putting them to bed and reading them a story, which put me in one part of the house. When that was done I realized he had already gone to bed, this being now about 9 o'clock. I went out to the garage to paint some children's blocks and worked in the garage for half an hour or so. I noticed when I went out [to the garage] that the light was on . . .

MR. JENNER. Was this unusual?

MRS. PAINE. Oh, it was unusual . . . I realized that [Lee] had gone out to the garage [before me.] They were getting things out from time to time, warmer things for the cold weather, so it was not at all remarkable . . . but I thought it careless of him to have left the light on.[20]

Possibly, he had gone out there to break down his gun and put the stock and barrel in the long paper bag he had glued and taped together at the Book Depository and had brought back with him to Irving this evening.

McMillan: Marina was as usual the last to bed. She sat in the tub for an hour, "warming her bones" and thinking about nothing in particular, not even Lee's request that she move in to Dallas. Lee was lying on his stomach with his eyes closed when she crept into bed. Marina still had pregnancy privileges; that is, she was allowed to sleep with her feet on whatever part of his anatomy they came to rest. About three in the morning, she thinks, she put a foot on his leg. Lee was not asleep and suddenly, with a sort of wordless vehemence, he lifted his leg, shoved her foot hard, then pulled his leg away.

"My, he's in a mean mood," Marina thought.[21]

The domestic intimacy of her foot must have felt suffocating to Lee at that instant—a false promise designed to divert him from any kind of daring project.

McMillan: Lee usually woke up before the alarm rang and shut it off so as not to disturb the children. On the morning of Friday, November 22, the alarm rang and he did not wake up.

Marina was awake, and after about ten minutes she said, "Time to get up, Alka."

"Okay."[22]

He did not kiss her when he left. He merely told her that he had left some money on the bureau.

When she did get up, she discovered that the sum was nothing less than $170. If we know with hindsight that it left him with only a few dollars for a getaway, it was also his way of suggesting that she could still call him at work. But she was not about to. Her warning system was not on alert. She did not even discover that he had left his wedding ring in a cup on the dresser, and that was something he had never done before.

Pigeons Flew Up from the Roof

From an FBI report: On the morning of November 22, 1963, at approximately 7:10 A.M., LINNIE MAE RANDLE was standing at her sink in the kitchen looking out the window when she saw LEE HARVEY OSWALD walking . . . toward the carport which adjoins the kitchen. She opened the back door a slight bit to see what he was doing and saw him go to the far side of her brother's car [where] OSWALD opened the right rear door of the car . . . [and she] called to her brother, BUELL WESLEY FRAZIER, that OSWALD was waiting . . .

Mrs. RANDLE stated that at the time she saw OSWALD . . . he was carrying a long package wrapped in brown paper [which] appeared to contain something heavy . . .[1]

FRAZIER went to his car, entered the left front door while OSWALD entered the right front door, both getting into the front seat. As he started to drive out of the yard, FRAZIER glanced back and noticed a long package, light brown in color, lying on the back of the rear seat [and] OSWALD explained that it was curtain rods. FRAZIER then remarked to OSWALD, "Oh, yes, you said you going to get some curtain rods yesterday." . . .

FRAZIER stated that he and OSWALD drove to work and he parked the car about two blocks north of the [Texas School Book Depository] building. OSWALD got out of the car first and FRAZIER . . . observed that OSWALD had . . . the one end of the package . . . under his armpit and the other end [was] apparently held with his right fingers. OSWALD then walked toward the building with his back to FRAZIER and continued in front of FRAZIER for the entire distance, possibly 200 or 300 yards . . . By the time OSWALD reached the Texas School Book Depository building, he was at least 50 feet ahead of FRAZIER, and when FRAZIER entered the building, he did not see OSWALD and does not know where he went. He did not subsequently see him with the package again.[2]

Ruth Paine awakened after Lee left.

MRS. PAINE. . . . the house was extremely quiet and the thought occurred to me that Lee might have overslept [but] I looked about and found a plastic coffee cup in the sink that had clearly been used and judged he had had a cup of coffee and left . . .

MR. JENNER. A plastic cup with some remains in it of coffee?

MRS. PAINE. Instant coffee; yes.[3]

When Roy Truly, superintendent of the School Book Depository, arrived at 8:00 A.M., he could see that Lee was already working, clipboard in hand.

McMillan: Knowing Marina's fascination with the President and Mrs. Kennedy, Ruth had left the television on when she went out . . . [and Marina] settled down on the sofa to watch . . . a rerun of a breakfast Mr. Kennedy had attended in Fort Worth. Somebody gave him a ten-gallon hat and he seemed to enjoy it.[4]

After the breakfast, Jack Kennedy had gone back to his hotel room for a few minutes of relaxation before he and his entourage would get into *Air Force One* for the brief flight from Fort Worth to Love Field in Dallas. In this passage taken from William Manchester's book *Death of a President,* the First Lady is speaking:

"Isn't this sweet, Jack?" she said. . . . "They've just stripped their whole museum of all their treasures to brighten this dingy hotel suite." . . . Taking the catalogue, he said, "Let's see who did it." There were several names at the end. The first was Mrs. J. Lee Johnson III. "Why don't we call her?" he suggested. "She must be in the phone book." Thus Ruth Carter Johnson, the wife of a Fort Worth newspaper executive, became the surprised recipient of John Kennedy's last telephone call. She was home nursing a sick daughter. She had watched the ballroom breakfast on WBAP-TV, and when she heard the President's voice she was speechless.[5]

Mrs. J. Lee Johnson III! One has to observe that her married name bears the first initial of J. Edgar Hoover, has Lee in the middle, and ends with the last name of the President who will succeed Jack Kennedy. (As a bonus, her maiden name is Carter.) Perhaps the cosmos likes to strew coincidences around the rim of the funnel into which large events are converging.

Manchester: [Kennedy] apologized for not phoning earlier, explaining that they hadn't reached the hotel until midnight. Then Mrs. Kennedy came on. To Mrs. Johnson she sounded thrilled and vivacious. "They're going to have a dreadful time getting me out of here with all these wonderful works of art," she said. "We're both touched—thank you so much."[6]

Ken O'Donnell, the President's assistant, now carried in an unpleasant item. There was a full-page ad in the *Dallas Morning News* with a black border of the sort that accompanies the announcement of a death. It welcomed the President in one breath and then proceeded to accuse him of being a Communist tool. The people who had paid for the ad called themselves "The American Fact-Finding Committee."

Kennedy was not amused by what he read. His face showed as much when he passed the *Dallas Morning News* over to Jackie:

Manchester: Her vivacity disappeared; she felt sick. The President shook his head. In a low voice he asked Ken, "Can you imagine a paper doing a thing like that?" Then, slowly, he said to her, ". . . You know, last night would have been a hell of a night to assassinate a President." . . . He said it casually, and she took it lightly; it was his way of shaking off the ad. . . . "I mean it," he said now . . . "There was the rain, and the night, and we were all getting jostled. Suppose a man had a pistol in a briefcase." He gestured vividly, pointing his rigid index finger at the wall and jerking his thumb twice to show the action of the hammer. "Then he could have dropped the gun and briefcase—" in pantomime he dropped them and whirled in a tense crouch—"and melted away in the crowd."[7]

The flight to Dallas took less than twenty minutes, and Vice-President Johnson was there at Love Field to head up the welcoming committee. The Kennedys got into the rear seat of the presidential limousine and Governor and Mrs. Connally took the jump seats. They would ride to the Trade Mart for a lunch scheduled to begin at twelve-thirty.

On the sixth floor of the Book Depository, a large part of the floor had been ripped up, and five men were laying plywood all morning. Lee had been around the sixth floor from time to time, but they had paid no particular attention to him since he had been busy filling orders from stacks of books some fifty or sixty feet away. Besides, they could not see him much of the time—there were walls of cartons from floor to ceiling all over that warehouse space on the sixth floor.

McMillan: At 11:45 or 11:50, the five men who were laying the floor broke for lunch. [They] got on the freight elevators, and raced each other to the ground floor. On the way down, they saw Lee standing by the fifth-floor gate.
    Once he was on the ground floor, [one of them], Givens, realized that he had left his jacket, with his cigarettes in it, on the sixth floor. He rode back up and once again saw Lee.[8]

Another one of the men, Bonnie Ray Williams, had been planning to watch the President drive by. From the sixth floor there would be a good view of his motorcade as it came down toward the building from Houston Street. Then it would take a sharp left on Elm Street to pass right beneath them; in fact, the left turn from Houston to Elm was so sharp that the motorcade would have to slow down. So it would offer a boss view of Kennedy. Bonnie Ray Williams did not go down in the freight elevator, therefore, with the others, but ate his lunch on the sixth floor. Since none of the others came back up, he had to eat his food alone, and then he went down to look for them.
    Even if Oswald was ensconced behind book cartons at the other end of the sixth floor, he must still have been put into a state at all these comings and goings. How could he know whether he would be alone when the time came? There might be a crowd of workers hooting and hollering on just the other side of all those cartons.

In Dealey Plaza, people had collected on the grassy knoll and on the two triangular islands of grass formed by the convergence of Elm Street, Main Street in the middle, and Commerce Street into side-by-side routes through the triple underpass. Hundreds of people had gathered, most of them on both sides of Elm Street, and the atmosphere had a hint of that agreeable mood which comes on a sunny day to a county fair. A big event is coming, a man is going to be shot out of a cannon, but it will all be over by the time you hear the boom. Even so, people on Elm Street can feel the excitement of that crowd half a mile away who are lining the sidewalk on Main Street as the motorcade comes toward Dealey Plaza like a slow tide rolling in. Time is there to burn. It is like a little money you will never see again. Not every day does the President come to Texas, not even to Dallas, insurance capital of the world.

Forrest Sorrels, the Secret Service man in charge of the Dallas office, was in the lead car of the motorcade. He was perhaps thirty feet in front of the presidential limousine:

MR. STERN. Do you recall remarking on anything you observed in the windows as you drove along Main Street?

MR. SORRELS. Yes, I do; there was a tremendous crowd on Main Street. The street was full of people. I made the remark, "My God, look . . . They are even hanging out the windows." . . .

MR. STERN. Now, as you made the right turn from Main Street onto Houston Street, did you observe anything about the windows of any building in your view?

MR. SORRELS. Yes, I did . . . The Book Depository, as we turned to the right on Houston Street, was right directly in front of us . . . I saw that building [and] I remember distinctly there were a couple of colored men that were in windows almost not quite to the center of the building, probably two floors down from the top . . . But I did not see any activity—no one moving around or anything like that . . . I do not, of course, remember seeing any object or anything like that in the windows such as a rifle or anything pointing out the windows . . . No activity, no one moving around that I saw at all.[9]

Let us put ourselves in the mind of a rifleman who has set himself up in a nest of book cartons on the sixth floor. As the motorcade on Houston Street approaches the Depository building, there is an open view of the face and body of the President in the rear seat of his open convertible. It is a direct head-on shot with the target steadily growing in size through the eyepiece of the telescopic sight.

On the other hand, trained professionals are staring at the Book Depository windows from the lead car in the motorcade, and police on motorcycles are scouring the building with their eyes. A sniper's instinct would probably pull him back into relative darkness a few feet from the window.

If the sniper is, in addition, an amateur and not certain whether he will or will not have the stuff to cross the irrevocable bridge that leads to squeezing off his shot, if he should choke on the trigger and not shoot, will he ever trust himself again?

The motorcade slows down and turns to the left on Elm Street and the first large opportunity has been lost.

From an FBI deposition: I, BONNIE RAY WILLIAMS, freely furnish the following voluntary statement . . .

I am a Negro male and I was born September 3, 1943 at Carthage, Texas . . .

On November 22, 1963, I, along with HAROLD "HANK" NORMAN and JAMES EARL JARMAN, JR., both of whom are also employed by the Texas School Book Depository, were on the fifth floor of the Depository Building looking out the windows waiting for the presidential motorcade . . .[10]

Finally, the limousine with JFK in it passed under their window:

MR. WILLIAMS. The last thing I saw him do was he pushed his hand up like this. I assumed he was brushing his hair back. And then the thing that happened then was a loud shot—first I thought they were saluting the President, somebody—maybe even a motorcycle backfire . . . I really did not pay any attention to it, because I did not know what was happening. The second shot, it sounded like it was right in the building, the second and third shot. And it sounded—it even shook the building, the side we were on. Cement fell on my head.

MR. BALL. You say cement fell on your head?

MR. WILLIAMS. Cement, gravel, dirt, or something . . . because it shook the windows and everything. Harold [Norman] was sitting next to me and he said it came right from over our head. If you want to know my exact words, I could tell you.

MR. BALL. Tell us.

MR. WILLIAMS. My exact words were, "No bullshit."[11]

This was for keeps. Something big had just happened. "No bullshit." Hank Norman agreed.

MR. MCCLOY. . . . after you heard the shots, did you have any thought that you might run upstairs [to the sixth floor] and see if anybody was up there . . . ?

MR. NORMAN. No, sir.

MR. MCCLOY. Did you feel it might be dangerous to go upstairs?

MR. NORMAN. Yes, sir.[12]

Unarmed, he would not feel all that inclined to mount a flight of stairs and face a gunman. Not at those wages. James Earl Jarman decided it was time for them to "get the hell away from there."[13]

Secret Service agent Forrest Sorrels was unable to see from which window the shots came because his car was by then on Elm Street in front of the President's Lincoln and the angle from his rear window was too great. The sound, however, was engraved upon his ear.

MR. STERN. Can you estimate the overall time from the first shot to the third shot?

MR. SORRELS. Yes. I have called it out to myself, I have timed it, and I would say it was very, very close to 6 seconds.

MR. STERN. It sounds like you can still hear the shots.

MR. SORRELS. I will hear them forever—it is something I cannot wipe from my mind ever.[14]

Equally was it engraved upon the memory of Lady Bird Johnson:

It all began so beautifully. After a drizzle in the morning the sun came out bright and beautiful. We were going into Dallas . . . The streets were lined with people—lots and lots of people—the children all smiling; placards, confetti; people waving from windows . . .

Then . . . suddenly there was a sharp loud report—a shot . . . Then a moment and two more shots in rapid succession. There had been such a gala air that I thought it must be firecrackers or some sort of celebration . . . I heard over the radio system "Let's get out of here," and our Secret Service man who was with us, [Rufus] Youngblood, I believe it was, vaulted over the front seat on top of Lyndon, threw him to the floor, and said, "Get down."

Senator Yarborough and I ducked our heads. The car accelerated terrifically fast—faster and faster . . .[15]

A motorcycle officer, Marrion Baker, would tell the Warren Commission of the immediate experiences of other motorcycle officers flanking the open convertible that held the Kennedys and the Connallys:

MR. BELIN. All right. [This officer] was on the front and to the left of the President's car?

MR. BAKER. Yes, sir; that is right.

MR. BELIN. What did he say to you about blood or something?

MR. BAKER. . . . he said the first shot he couldn't figure out where it came from. He turned his head backward, reflex, you know, and then he turned back and the second shot came off, and then the third shot is when the blood and everything hit his helmet and his windshield.

MR. BELIN. Did it hit the inside or the outside of his windshield, did he say?

MR. BAKER. . . . Now, as far as the inside or the outside of the windshield, I don't know about that. But it was all on the right-hand side of his helmet.

MR. BELIN. Of his helmet?

MR. BAKER. On his uniform also.[16]

Baker will be the first policeman to enter the Book Depository building, and there he will encounter Oswald.

First, however, let us take him back to Main Street, where he is trundling along on his motorcycle a number of vehicles back from the President:

MR. BAKER. As we approached the corner there of Main and Houston we were making a right turn, and [a] strong wind hit me and I almost lost my balance.

MR. BELIN. How fast would you estimate the speed of your motorcycle, if you know?

MR. BAKER. . . . we were creeping along real slowly.

MR. BELIN. . . . Now, tell us what happened after you turned onto Houston Street.

MR. BAKER. As I got myself straightened up there, I guess it took me some 20, 30 feet, something like that, and it was about that time that I heard those shots come out . . . It hit me all at once it was a rifle shot because I had just got back from deer hunting and [so] it sounded to me like it was a high-powered rifle.

MR. BELIN. All right . . . what did you do and what did you see?

MR. BAKER. . . . I immediately kind of looked up, and I had a feeling it came from the building . . . in front of me . . . this Book Depository Building [because] as I was looking, all these pigeons began to fly up . . . and start flying around . . .

MR. BELIN. . . . After the third shot, then, what did you do?

MR. BAKER. Well, I revved that motorcycle up and I went down to the corner which would be approximately 180 to 200 feet from the point where . . . we heard the shots . . . You see, it looked to me like there were maybe 500 or 600 people in this area here [who] started running, you know, every direction, just trying to get back out of the way . . .

MR. BELIN. You then ran into the building, is that correct?

MR. BAKER. That is correct, sir.

MR. BELIN. What did you see and what did you do as you ran into the building?

MR. BAKER. As I entered this building . . . I just spoke out and asked where the stairs or elevator was, and this man, Mr. Truly, spoke up and said, it seems to me like he says, "I am a building manager. Follow me, officer, and I will show you." So . . . we kind of all ran, not real fast but, you know, a good trot, to the back of the building . . . and he was trying to get that service elevator . . . He hollered for it, said, "Bring that elevator down here."

MR. BELIN. How many times did he holler, to the best of your recollection?

MR. BAKER. It seemed like he did it twice . . . I said let's take the stairs . . .

MR. BELIN. . . . what was your intention at that time?

MR. BAKER. . . . to go all the way to the top where I thought the shots had come from, to see if I could find something there . . .

MR. BELIN. And did you go all the way up to the top of the stairs right away?

MR. BAKER. No, sir, we didn't . . . As I came out to the second floor there, Mr. Truly was ahead of me and . . . I caught a glimpse of this man walking away . . . about 20 feet away from me in the lunchroom.

MR. BELIN. What did you do?

MR. BAKER. I hollered at him at that time and said, "Come here." He turned and walked straight back to me . . .

MR. BELIN. He walked back toward you then?

MR. BAKER. Yes, sir . . .

MR. BELIN. Was he carrying anything in his hands?

MR. BAKER. He had nothing at that time.

MR. BELIN. All right. Were you carrying anything in either of your hands?

MR. BAKER. Yes, sir; I was . . . I had my revolver out.

MR. BELIN. When did you take your revolver out?

MR. BAKER. As I was starting up the stairway . . . I assumed that I was suspicious of everybody because I had my pistol out.

REPRESENTATIVE BOGGS. Right.

MR. BAKER. . . . Mr. Truly had come up to my side here, and I turned to Mr. Truly and I says, "Do you know this man? Does he work here?" And he said yes, and I turned immediately and went on out up the stairs . . .

REPRESENTATIVE BOGGS. When you saw him, was he out of breath, did he appear to have been running or what?

MR. BAKER. It didn't appear that to me. He appeared normal, you know.

REPRESENTATIVE BOGGS. Was he calm and collected?

MR. BAKER. Yes, sir. He never did say a word or nothing. In fact, he didn't change his expression one bit.

MR. BELIN. Did he flinch in any way when you put the gun up to his face?

MR. BAKER. No, sir . . .

MR. BELIN. . . . was there any expression after Mr. Truly said he worked there?

MR. BAKER. At that time I never did look back toward him . . . I turned immediately and run on up.[17]

4

An Afternoon at the Movies

Innocent or guilty, the average man would be bound to flinch looking into the implacable eye of a pistol barrel. Oswald had to be in a remarkable state at this point, a calm beneath agitation, as if at rest in the vibrationless center of a dream. This, of course, assumes that he was the man who shot at Kennedy from the sixth floor. For some, however, there is no greater evidence of his innocence than that he was so cool. How could a man aim and fire three times at a moving target, see that there was impact, and yet have been able to spring up, hide his gun between other cartons in another end of the room, race silently down four flights of stairs, and be standing there in the lunchroom, unwinded, gazing passively at Officer Baker and his gun? For many critics, this seems impossible unless Oswald was not on the sixth floor when the shooting took place. The only reply if one supposes that he did shoot Kennedy is that he had passed through the mightiest of the psychic barriers—he had killed the king. It was equal psychologically to breaking through the sound barrier. All the controls were reversed. If such a transcendent calm was his state facing into Baker's gun, it must have lasted for only a little while. In the following minute, he slipped out of the Texas School Book Depository, and this remarkable if short-lived grasp on such powers of control began to come apart. The next time we see him, and it will be through the eyes of a highly biased witness—his former landlady Mrs. Bledsoe!—he looks demented.

First, however, we must conceive of the impact of Elm Street and Dealey Plaza upon his senses in that instant he steps outside. If he is the killer, then we know enough about him to understand that he has been living within a spiritual caul all morning, and the voices of others have seemed as far away as echoes heard from the other side of a hill. He has been centered on his mission, balanced on his own heartbeat, living in a sense of dread and expectation so intense that it is beyond agitation. He possesses the kind of inner silence some can know when ultimates are coming to a moment of decision: Will he have the courage to fire his rifle and will he shoot well? Everything else, including the mounting tempo of excitement in the crowds outside the Book Depository, has no more presence for him than the murmur of a passer-by. Stationed within himself, he has now descended to those depths where one waits for final judgment.

He must still have been in such a state when Officer Baker confronted him.

Stepping out into Dealey Plaza, therefore, must have been not unlike being hurled through a plate-glass window. Hundreds of people were milling around in disconnected hysteria. Men and women were weeping. Police sirens from every street and avenue in the area were screaming their way toward Dealey Plaza.

If the act of firing upon Kennedy had taken place as an event staged between himself and his vision of a great and thunderous stroke that would lift him at once from the mediocre to the immortal, this vision would not have included anyone else. Not even the victim.

Now, however, everybody around him is distraught. It is as if, all alone, he has set off an explosion in a mine-shaft. Then, having climbed to the surface, he has come suddenly upon a crowd of the bereaved. It is a scene alien to him. He hurries down the street away from the Book Depository until, several blocks away, he catches a bus.

On it is Mrs. Bledsoe, the same landlady who had cheated him of $2 in the first week he was back in Dallas after Mexico:

MRS. BLEDSOE. . . . Oswald got on. He looks like a maniac. His sleeve was out here [indicating]. His shirt was undone . . . a hole in it, and he was dirty, and I didn't look at him. I didn't want to know I even seen him, and I just looked off, and then about that time the motorman said the President had been shot.[1]

She may have been recollecting the inner light in Lee's eye when she told him that he would have to leave her rooming house.

The bus moves a block and stops. It is jammed in the gridlock around Dealey Plaza. Oswald goes up to the driver, asks for a transfer and gets off, then walks to the Greyhound bus station, where he can pick up a taxi.

MR. WHALEY. He said, "May I have the cab?"

I said, "You sure can. Get in." And instead of opening the back door, he opened the front door, which is allowable there, and got in . . . the front seat. And about that time an old lady, I think she was an old lady, I don't remember nothing but her sticking her head down past him in the door and said, "Driver, will you call me a cab down here?"

. . . he opened the door a little bit like he was going to get out and he said, "I will let you have this one," and she says, "No, the driver can call me one."

I didn't call one because I knew before I could call one, one would come around the block and keep it pretty well covered [so] I asked him where he wanted to go and he said, "500 North Beckley."

Well, I started up . . . to that address, and the police cars, the sirens was going, running, crisscrossing everywhere, just a big uproar in that end of town and I said, "What the hell. I wonder what the hell is the uproar?"

And he never said anything. So I figured he was one of those people that don't like to talk so I never said any more to him.

But when I got pretty close to the 500 block at Neches and North Beckley which is the 500 block, he said, "This will do fine," and I pulled over to the curb right there. He gave me a dollar bill, the trip was 95 cents. He gave me a dollar bill and didn't say anything, just got out and closed the door and walked around the front of the cab over to the other side of the street. Of course, traffic was moving through there and I put it in gear and moved on . . .[2]

Oswald walked a quick five blocks to his rooming house. Officer Baker, standing inside the Book Depository with his pistol out, must have proved a sufficiently electrifying sight to propel him back to to his rented room for his own revolver.

MRS. ROBERTS. . . . he came home that Friday in an unusual hurry.

MR. BALL. And what time was this?

MRS. ROBERTS. Well, it was after President Kennedy had been shot and I had a friend that said, "Roberts, President Kennedy has been shot," and I said, "Oh, no." She said, "Turn on your television," and I [did] but I couldn't get the picture and he come in and I just looked up and I said, "Oh, you are in a hurry." He never said a thing, not nothing. He went on to his room and stayed about 3 or 4 minutes.[3]

When he came out, he had changed his windbreaker for another. Perhaps he had intimations that details on what he was wearing that morning had already been given. He did not know it, but a witness in Dealey Plaza, Howard Brennan, who claimed to have exceptionally good vision, had already given a description of a man with a rifle that he saw in a sixth-floor window. The description is general, but can fit Oswald, and it has gone out at 12:45 P.M., fifteen minutes after the three shots were fired, and something like fifteen minutes before Oswald left his rooming house forever.

From Howard Brennan's deposition to the Dallas County Sheriff's Department: . . . I had seen him before the President's car arrived. He was just sitting up there looking down apparently waiting . . . to see the President. I did not notice anything unusual about this man. He was a white man in his early 30s, slender, nice looking, slender and would weigh about 167 to 175 pounds. He had on light colored clothing but definitely not a suit. I proceeded to watch the President's car as it turned left at the corner [and] I then saw this man I have described in the window and he was taking aim with a high-powered rifle . . . Then this man let the gun down to his side and stepped down out of sight. He did not seem to be in any hurry . . .[4]

Nobody saw Oswald in the ten minutes between his departure from the rooming house and his arrival at the corner of Tenth Street and Dalton, a trip of ten or twelve blocks along residential streets of small houses. Near the intersection of Tenth and Dalton, however, Oswald—or a man who fit his general description (there were witnesses with enough disagreement over identification to offer opportunities to a defense lawyer)—was stopped by Officer J. D. Tippit, who had been cruising by slowly in a police car. Presumably, Tippit had heard the description of the suspect. It had been broadcast four times on police radio since 12:45 P.M. Now, the man he had stopped was obeying Tippit's order to place his hands on the right front window of the police car, or so witnesses later described it. Officer Tippit got out slowly from his side of the car, his pistol still in its holster, and started to go around the front of his car, but he was then shot four times and killed by that man who had had his hands up properly on the right front window but took them off long enough to pull out a revolver and shoot. The man was heard by one witness to say, "Poor dumb cop," as he ran off. He was emptying his spent cartridges even as he ran.

There is a good deal of evidence that it was Oswald who shot Tippit, but since the approach of this work is not legal, technical, or evidentiary but novelistic—that is, we are trying to understand Oswald—let us judge that if he killed Kennedy, then it is well within the range of our expectations of him that he would be frantic enough after seeing that pistol in his face, descending into Dealey Plaza, and fleeing to his rooming house and out again to be, yes, frantic enough to kill Tippit as well. If, however, he did not shoot at Kennedy, then small but confusing details in this second murder take on much more prominence. For if Oswald was innocent of shooting Kennedy, why would he have fired at Tippit?

In any event, a man who most certainly is Oswald is walking west on Jefferson Street, a few blocks away, just a few minutes later. John Calvin Brewer, the young manager of a shoe store on Jefferson Street, notices that this man now ducks into the long entryway between the shoe store's twin front windows just as some police cars go screaming by toward the scene of the Tippit murder. As they do, the stranger puts his back to the street so the police won't see his face, but the store manager decides that the fellow looks "scared" and "messed up," and indeed, as soon as the police are out of sight, Brewer sees the man sneak into the Texas Theatre a few doors down without paying, so Brewer goes up to the cashier, informs her, and she calls the police.[5]

What comes next is a concise description offered by the one-volume Warren Commission Report:

Patrol cars bearing at least 15 officers converged on the Texas Theatre. Patrolman M. N. McDonald, with Patrolmen R. Hawkins, T. A. Hutson, and C. T. Walker, entered the theatre from the rear. Other policemen entered the front door and searched the balcony. Detective Paul L. Bentley rushed to the balcony and told the projectionist to turn up the house lights. Brewer met McDonald and the other policemen at the alley exit door, stepped out onto the stage with them and pointed out the man who had come into the theatre without paying. The man was Oswald. He was sitting alone in the rear of the main floor of the theatre near the right center aisle. About six or seven people were seated on the theatre's main floor and an equal number in the balcony.

McDonald first searched two men in the center of the main floor, about 10 rows from the front. He walked out of the row up the right center aisle. When he reached the row where the suspect was sitting, McDonald stopped abruptly and told the man to get on his feet. Oswald rose from his seat, bringing up both hands. As McDonald started to search Oswald's waist for a gun, he heard him say, "Well, it's all over now." Oswald then struck McDonald between the eyes with his left fist.[6]

MR. BELIN. Who hit who first?

MR. BREWER. Oswald hit McDonald first and he . . . knocked McDonald down. McDonald fell against one of the seats. And then real quick he was back up . . . and I saw this gun come up— in Oswald's hand . . . And somebody hollered, "He's got a gun."

And there were a couple of officers fighting him and taking [it] away from him, and he was fighting, still fighting, and I heard some of the police holler, I don't know who it was, "Kill the President, will you." And I saw fists flying and they were hitting him.

MR. BELIN. Was he fighting back at the time?

MR. BREWER. Yes; he was fighting back.

MR. BELIN. Then what happened?

MR. BREWER. Well, in a short time they put the handcuffs on him and they took him out . . .

MR. BELIN. Did you hear Oswald say anything?

MR. BREWER. As they were taking him out, he stopped and turned around and hollered, "I am not resisting arrest," about twice. "I am not resisting arrest." And they took him outside.[7]

In all of Oswald's history, through all of his mishaps, this is the only account we have, since his fracas with the Neumeyer brothers in high school, where he throws a punch at another man.

McMillan: He was driven to police headquarters and arrived in the basement about 2:00 P.M. There were reporters milling around in case a suspect in the President's murder should be brought in. He was asked if he would like to cover his face as he was taken inside. "Why should I cover my face?" he replied. "I haven't done anything to be ashamed of."[8]

5

The Hour of Panic

Lady Bird Johnson has been last left in the vice-presidential car with a Secret Service agent covering her husband's body even as she and the other occupants hunch down below the level of the windows while the car accelerates down the road and away.

> Suddenly they put on the brakes so hard that I wondered if they were going to make it as we wheeled left and went around the corner. We pulled up to a building. I looked and saw it said "Hospital" . . . Secret Service men began to pull, lead, guide and hustle us out. I cast one last look over my shoulder and saw, in the President's car, a bundle of pink, just like a drift of blossoms, lying on the back seat.[1]

It was Mrs. Kennedy, huddled over the body of her husband.

Perhaps half an hour later, Lady Bird encountered Jackie Kennedy again. She had been in and out of the operating room where they were trying to keep Jack Kennedy alive, that is, working to keep his heart still beating even if a sizable portion of his brain had been lost. Jackie Kennedy had found a large piece in the rear seat of the presidential limousine and had been holding it ever since in her white-gloved hand until, numbly, silently, nudging the head surgeon with her elbow, she had given it over to him.

Lady Bird knew none of this.

> . . . Suddenly I found myself face to face with Jackie in a small hall. I think it was right outside the operating room. You always think of her—or someone like her—as being insulated, protected; she was quite alone. I don't think I ever saw anyone so much alone in my life. I went up to her, put my arms around her, and said something to her. I'm sure it was something like "God help us all," because my feelings for her were too tumultuous to put into words.[2]

Out in Irving, Ruth and Marina are still in a state of relative innocence.

MRS. PAINE. . . . I had only just begun to prepare the lunch [when] the announcement was made that the President had been shot and I translated this to Marina. She had not caught it from the television statement. And I was crying as I did the translation. And then we sat down and waited at the television set, no longer interested in the preparing of lunch, and waited to hear further word.

I got out some candles and lit them, and my little girl also lighted a candle, and Marina said to me, "Is that a way of praying?" and I said, "Yes, it is, just my own way."[3]

Marina is the first to recognize that the event may concern them directly.

MR. RANKIN. Did Mrs. Paine say anything about the possibility of your husband being involved?

MARINA OSWALD. . . . she only said, "By the way, they fired from the building in which Lee is working."

My heart dropped. I then went to the garage to see whether the rifle was there, and I saw that the blanket was still there, and I said, "Thank God." I thought, "Can there really be such a stupid man in the world that could do something like that?" But I was already rather upset at that time . . .[4]

It has been Marina's dirty little secret. She has not told Ruth that Lee owns a rifle and that Lee had wrapped it up in a green blanket and sent it along with the luggage in Ruth Paine's station wagon when the two women drove up from New Orleans to Irving. Now, the rolled-up green blanket lay on the floor of the garage. The Paines had assumed it was camping equipment.

When Marina came back to the living room, she was informed by Ruth that President Kennedy was dead.

From Marina's narrative: I was so shocked by this that I wept freely. I do not know why, but I cried for the President as though I had lost a close friend, although I am from a completely different country and know very little about him.[5]

Ruth is still not worrying about Lee's presence in the Texas School Book Depository.

SENATOR COOPER. Did you have any thought at all that Lee Oswald might have been the man who fired the shot?

MRS. PAINE. Absolutely none; no.

MR. JENNER. Why was that, Mrs. Paine?

MRS. PAINE. I had never thought of him as a violent man. He had never said anything against President Kennedy, [and] I had no idea that he had a gun . . . I do recall then sitting on the sofa when the announcement was definitely made that the President was dead. And she said to me . . . "Now the two children will have to grow up without the father." . . .

MR. MCCLOY. Just take a little time to compose yourself.

SENATOR COOPER. Why don't you rest a few minutes?

MRS. PAINE. I can proceed. I recall [that] I cried after I had heard that the President was dead, and my little girl was upset too, always taking it from me more than from any understanding of the situation. And she cried herself to sleep on the sofa, and I moved her to her bed, and Christopher was already asleep in his crib. June was in bed asleep.

MR. JENNER. Was Marina emotional at all? Did she cry?

MRS. PAINE. No. She said to me, "I feel very badly also, but we seem to show that we are upset in different ways." She did not actually cry.[6]

Then there was a very loud knocking on the door. When Ruth Paine opened it, six officers were on her threshold. They announced themselves as being from the sheriff's office in Irving and from the Dallas police:

MR. JENNER. Did you say anything?

MRS. PAINE. I said nothing. I think I just dropped my jaw. And the man in front said by way of explanation, "We have Lee Oswald in custody. He is charged with shooting an officer." That is the first I had any idea that Lee might be . . . in any way involved in the day's events. I asked them to come in. They said they wanted to search the house. I asked if they had a warrant. They said they didn't. They said they could get the sheriff out here right away with one if I insisted. And I said no, that was all right, they could be my guests.[7]

Marina would characterize the behavior of the police as "not very polite."

MARINA OSWALD. . . . They kept on following me. I wanted to change clothes because I was dressed in a manner fitting to the house. And they would not even let me go into the dressing room to change . . . They were rather rough. They kept on saying, hurry up.[8]

MR. RANKIN. When did you learn that the rifle was not in the blanket?

MARINA OSWALD. When the police arrived and asked whether my husband had a rifle, and I said, "Yes."

MR. RANKIN. Then what happened?

MARINA OSWALD. They began to search the apartment. When they came to the garage . . . I thought, "Well, now, they will find it."[9]

Ruth Paine had been standing on the blanket when Marina told her the rifle was under her feet. Ruth translated this for the officers, and they told her to get off the blanket.

MRS. PAINE. I then stepped off it and the officer picked it up in the middle, and it bent so.

MR. JENNER. It hung limp just as it now hangs limp in your hand?

MRS. PAINE. And at this moment I felt this man was in very deep trouble . . .[10]

The reaction of the police was that these women were highly suspicious. They spoke Russian to each other and one, at least, had known about the gun. It was decided that they would have to come down to the police station.

MRS. PAINE. . . . Marina wanted to change from slacks as I had already done to a dress. They would not permit her to do that. I said, "She has a right to, she is a woman, to dress as she wishes before going down." And I directed her to the bathroom to change. The officer opened the bathroom door and said no, she had no time to change. I was still making arrangements with the babysitters, arranging for our leaving the children there, and one of the officers made a statement to the effect of "we'd better get this straight in a hurry, Mrs. Paine, or we'll just take the children down and leave them in juvenile while we talk to you."

And I said, "Lynn, you may come too," in reply to this. I don't like being threatened. And then Christopher was still sleeping so I left him in the house, and took Lynn my daughter, and Marina took her daughter and her baby with her to the police station, so we were quite a group going into town in the car . . . The [police officer] in the front seat turned to me and said, "Are you a Communist," and I said, "No, I am not, and I don't even feel the need of a Fifth Amendment." And he was satisfied with that. We went on then to the police station and waited until such time as they could interview us.[11]

Back at Parkland Hospital, there had been more than a few confusions. In the operating room, the President had been declared dead at 1:00 P.M. Lyndon Johnson, however, was more than a little concerned that the former presidential entourage and/or the new one might be in one or another form of dire peril and so he decided that they should both hasten back to Love Field, where they could board *Air Force One* and be out of Dallas before the death was publicly announced. Who knew what was behind this fatally successful attack on the Presidency? The sound of the shots in Dealey Plaza had had such authority. It could have been a manifestation of the John Birch Society, the Mafia, the Castro Cubans, the anti-Castro Cubans or, most fearful and dangerous of all, it could—God willing that the answer be no—prove to be a plot in a series of steps by the Russians to set off World War III.

Lyndon Johnson was hardly voicing these hypotheses, but his instincts as a good Texan told him to get the hell out of Texas before the news broke that Kennedy was dead. Having been, by the judgment of his peers, the best or one of the best Majority Leaders the Senate ever had, Lyndon Johnson did trust his own powerful gifts of anticipation, but in the face of an event as horrific as this, anticipation can turn to paranoia—let's tear ass and run.

Jacqueline Kennedy, however, proved to be immovable. She would not leave Jack's body behind. Lyndon Johnson's contingent, which had already boarded *Air Force One* by the time John F. Kennedy's death was announced to the world at 1:33 P.M. Central Time, still sat on the tarmac, therefore, surrounded by guards, while a gruesome comedy went through its turns. Dallas city officials argued with grief-stricken, maddened members of the JFK traveling party. The question was whether the body could be released. The crime had taken place in Texas, and there the autopsy must be held. Texas was a sovereign state. Before it was all over, some were saying that Secret Service men had drawn their weapons and pulled the body out of Texas jurisdiction. In any event, it was not until a little after 2:00 P.M. that Jacqueline Kennedy and a Brigadier General and four Secret Service agents were able to place the coffin in an ambulance and set out for the airport, where they boarded *Air Force One* at 2:18. Lyndon Johnson, having had the courtesy and/or the political wisdom not to leave without Jackie Kennedy and the body, also took the time to be sworn in by a local judge—don't abuse Texas sentiments altogether!—before they took off. Jackie Kennedy sat by the casket all the way home.

Lady Bird testifies to this hour in Jacqueline Kennedy's existence:

> We had at first been ushered into the main private Presidential cabin on the plane—but Lyndon quickly said, "No, no," and immediately led us out of there; we felt that is where Mrs. Kennedy should be . . . I went in to see Mrs. Kennedy and, though it was a very hard thing to do, she made it as easy as possible. She said things like, "Oh Lady Bird, it's good that we've always liked you two so much." She said, "Oh, what if I had not been there? I'm so glad I was there." I looked at her. Mrs. Kennedy's dress was stained with blood. Her right glove was caked—that immaculate woman—with blood, her husband's blood. She always wore gloves like that because she was used to them. I never could. Somehow that was one of the most poignant sights—exquisitely dressed and caked in blood. I asked her if I couldn't get someone in to help her change, and she said, "Oh, no. Perhaps later . . . but not right now." . . .
>
> I said, "Oh, Mrs. Kennedy, you know we never even wanted to be Vice-President and now, dear God, it's come to this." I would have done anything to help her, but there was nothing I could do . . . so rather quickly I left and went back to the main part of the airplane where everyone was seated.[12]

The Return of Marguerite Oswald

At headquarters, the police showed Marina the Mannlicher-Carcano, and she told them she could not identify it because she hated guns. They all looked the same to her.

Her fear at this moment was not that Lee had killed Kennedy but that they might start thinking of her husband in connection with the shooting of General Walker. She asked to see Lee, and they told her he was being questioned and the interrogation was likely to go on all day. Perhaps she could see him tomorrow.

At that point, Marguerite Oswald appeared. She had been getting ready to go to work when she heard the news that Lee had been arrested.

> MARGUERITE OSWALD. I had a 3 to 11 shift . . . I had my lunch, and I dressed with my nurse's uniform on . . . I have to leave home at 2:30. So I had a little time to watch the Presidential procession.
>
> And while sitting on the sofa, the news came that the President was shot . . . However, I could not continue to watch it. I had to report to work.
>
> So I went in the car and approximately seven blocks away I turned the radio on in the car. I heard that Lee Harvey Oswald was picked up as a suspect.
>
> I immediately turned the car around and came back home, got on the telephone, [and] called the *Star Telegram* and asked if they could possibly have someone escort me, because I realized I could not drive to Dallas. And they did. They sent two . . . *Star Telegram* reporters . . .[1]

While she is waiting, she receives a call from the nurse she is supposed to replace on duty. In an interview with Lawrence Schiller in 1976 (where she speaks in virtually the same voice, cadence, and idiom she was using for the Warren Commission in 1964), we are told:

> . . . it was about five after three and I hadn't showed up, and she said, "How come you're home? Why, why haven't you come to relieve me?" I said, "Oh, my boy has been picked up in the

assassination of President Kennedy." . . . And, I'll never forget this . . . she scolded me. She said in a terrible tone of voice, "Well, the least you could have done is pick up the phone and let me know so I could have made some arrangements in your place." At a time, uh, I, well, I've been scolded through all of this. Nobody ever sympathized with me to the extent that I'm a human being and I have my emotions and my tears.[2]

It is interesting to note how seamless are her transitions over these twelve years:

MARGUERITE OSWALD. Now, upon arriving . . . I asked specifically to talk to FBI agents. My wish was granted. I was sent into a room . . .

MR. RANKIN. What time of day is this?

MARGUERITE OSWALD. This is approximately 3:30. So I am escorted into an office and two Brown FBI agents, they are brothers, I understand . . .

MR. RANKIN. By that you mean their names were Brown?

MARGUERITE OSWALD. Their names were Brown . . . and I told them who I was. And I said, "I want to talk with you gentlemen because I feel like my son is an agent of the government, and for the security of my country, I don't want this to get out . . . I want this kept perfectly quiet until you investigate. I happen to know that the State Department furnished the money for my son to return to the United States, and I don't know if that would be made public what that would involve, and so please will you investigate this and keep this quiet?"

Of course that was news to them.

They left me sitting in the office . . . you see, I was worried about the security of my country . . .

MR. RANKIN. Did you know anything else that you told them about why you thought he was an agent?

MARGUERITE OSWALD. No, I didn't tell them anything. But [one] of them said, "You know a lot about your son. When was the last time you were in touch with him?" . . .

I said, "I have not seen my son in a year."

He said sarcastically, "Now, Mrs. Oswald, are we to believe you have not been in touch . . . ? You are a mother."

I said, "Believe what you want [but] my son did not want me involved. He has kept me out of his activities. That is the truth, God's truth, that I have not seen my son in a year."

And the gentlemen left, and I did not see them after that.

And they sent the stenographer that was in the outer office to sit with me, and she started to question me.

I said, "Young lady, I am not going to be questioned. You may just as well make up your mind that I am just going to sit here."[3]

Once more, no twelve-year interval is apparent as she speaks to Schiller in 1976:

She said, "Uh, well, Mrs. Oswald, I'm here to be with you," [and] she didn't try to question me or anything. I'm going to say something that is beneath my dignity, but we live in a world, I mean, it's not beneath my dignity. I told her I wanted to go to the bathroom. But I couldn't even leave the room, I was under wraps. She put a lot of newspaper in the wastebasket and let me urinate in it. I was indignant and furious [but] I didn't say too much because I sensed she was, you know, an officer of the court.[4]

MARGUERITE OSWALD: I sat in the office approximately 2 or 3 hours alone, gentlemen, with this woman who came in and out [before] I was escorted into the office where Marina and Mrs. Paine was. And, of course, I started crying right away and hugged Marina. And Marina gave me Rachel, whom I had never seen. I did not know I had a second grandchild until this very moment. So I started to cry. Marina started to cry. And Mrs. Paine said, "Oh, Mrs. Oswald, I am so glad to meet you. Marina has often expressed the desire to contact you, especially when the baby was being born. But Lee didn't want her to."

And I said, "Mrs. Paine, you spoke English. Why didn't you contact me?"[5]

McMillan: Marina has no idea how long they were at police headquarters, but eventually she, Ruth, Michael, and the four children were allowed to go back to the Paines'. She does not remember whether they ate, or what they ate, or who did the cooking. But the house was in an uproar. It was overrun by reporters who wanted to talk to Marina, Ruth, and Marguerite. Suddenly there were angry words between Ruth and Marguerite.[6]

MARGUERITE OSWALD. Why I am bringing this up was because after I was in [Mrs. Paine's] home about 5 minutes, there was a knock on the door, and these two *Life* representatives entered the home.

The name of the men, one is Allan Grant, and the other is Tommy Thompson.

And I was not introduced . . .

MR. RANKIN. What time of day was this?

MRS. OSWALD. This was approximately 6:30. We had just arrived . . . We are home 5 minutes when they knocked on the door.

Mrs. Paine immediately says, "I hope you have colored film so we will have some good pictures."

I didn't know who they were.

But then I knew they were newsmen, because of her statement and the camera.

So Tommy Thompson started to interview Mrs. Paine. He said, "Mrs. Paine, tell me, are Marina and Lee separated since Lee lives in Dallas?"

She said, "No, they are a happy family. Lee lives in Dallas because of necessity. He works in Dallas, and this is Irving, and he has no transportation, and he comes every weekend to see his family."

"Well," he said, "what type of family man is he?"

She said, "A normal family man. He plays with his children. Last night he fed June. He watches television and just normal things." . . .

Now, while this little episode went on, I was fuming, gentlemen, because I didn't want this type of publicity. I thought it was uncalled for, immediately after the assassination, and the consequent arrest of my son.

But I was in Mrs. Paine's home.

Now I had an opportunity to be gracious. I spoke up . . . and I said, "Now, Mrs. Paine, I am sorry. I am in your home. And I appreciate the fact that I am a guest in your home. But I will not have you making statements that are incorrect. Because I happen to know you have made an incorrect statement. To begin with, I do not approve of this publicity. And if we are going to have the life story with *Life* magazine"—by that time I knew what it was—"I would like to get paid. Here is my daughter-in-law with two small children and I, myself, am penniless, and if we are going to give this information, I believe we should get paid for it." . . .

Then with that, the *Life* representative got up and said, "Mrs. Oswald, I will call my office and see what they think about an arrangement of your life story."

. . . He closed the door and called in private. And nothing was said—in the living room . . .

He came out from the telephone conversation and said no, that the company would not allow him to pay for the story. What they would do—they would pay our expenses while in Dallas, our food and expenses, hotel accommodation.

So I told him that I would think about it.

Now, they continued to hang around. And they were taking pictures continuously, all the while this was going on—the photographer, Mr. Allen, was continuously taking pictures. I was awfully tired and upset. I rolled my stockings down, and the picture is in *Life* magazine . . . So I got up and said, "I am not having this invasion of privacy. I realize that I am in Mrs. Paine's home. But you are taking my picture without my consent and a picture that I certainly don't want made public." It is the worst—with me rolling my hose. I wanted to get comfortable.

He followed Marina around in the bedroom. She was undressing June. He took pictures of everything. And Mrs. Paine was in her glory—I will say this. Mrs. Paine was very happy all these pictures were taken . . . until finally I became indignant and said, "I have had it. Now, find out what accommodations you can make for us, for my daughter-in-law and I so that we can be in Dallas to help Lee, and let me know in the morning."

So they left.[7]

MRS. PAINE. . . . It was by this time dark, and I think it was about 9 o'clock in the evening. I asked Michael to go out and buy hamburgers at a drive-in so we wouldn't have to cook, and we ate these as best we could, and began to prepare to retire . . .

Just close to the time of retiring Marina told me that just the night before Lee had said to her he hoped they could get an apartment together again soon. As she said this, I felt she was hurt and confused, wondering how he could have said such a thing which indicated wanting to be together with her when he must have already been planning something that would inevitably cause separation. I asked her did she think that Lee had killed the President and she said, "I don't know."[8]

McMillan: Marina later made a terrible discovery. She happened to glance at the bureau and saw that, again by a miracle of oversight, the police had left another of her possessions behind. It was a delicate little demi-tasse cup of pale blue-green with violets and a slender golden rim that had belonged to her grandmother. It was so thin that the light glowed through it as if it were parchment. Marina looked inside. There lay Lee's wedding ring.[9]

Since the ring was loose on his finger, sometimes at work he would put it in his pocket for safekeeping. But he had never failed to have it with him. Now, this morning, he had left it behind.

There were other discoveries. In a baby book they were keeping for June, she found two photographs of Lee holding his rifle and his revolver, those same stupid pictures he had made her take of him that stupid Sunday on Neely Street.

McMillan: She took them out of the baby book carefully and, in the privacy of the bedroom, showed them to her mother-in-law. "Mama," she said, pointing to the photographs and explaining as best she could in English, "Walker—this is Lee." "Oh, no," Marguerite moaned, [and] put her finger to her mouth, pointed toward Ruth's room, and said, "Ruth, no." She shook her head, meaning Marina was not to show the photographs to Ruth, or tell her anything about them.[10]

This compact to hide evidence takes us, however, well into Friday night. Where is Lee by now? We last saw him about two o'clock in the afternoon. What has been happening since he entered police headquarters in City Hall after informing the police that he would not cover his face since he had done nothing to be ashamed of?

The Octopus Outside

The pandemonium on the third floor of police headquarters in the City Hall of Dallas began to increase an hour after Lee's arrest and it would mount day and night (with small respites in the early hours of the morning), through Friday afternoon and evening, all of Saturday, and Sunday morning. The press of America, of the Western world, and much of the rest of the world, as well as every scout and stringer of TV and radio able to get a ticket to Dallas, crowded onto that third floor, and the descriptions given by Captain Will Fritz, who led the intermittent interrogation of Oswald during those forty-four hours, and by Forrest Sorrels, the Secret Service chief in Dallas, manage to depict the scene.

> **MR. HUBERT.** [Was it] your concern that the position and closeness and mass of the news media there presented a threat . . . ?
>
> **MR. FRITZ.** We didn't know many of these people. We knew very few. We knew the local people. Many people were there from foreign countries and some of them looked unkempt. We didn't know anything about who they were.
>
> For that reason, we wouldn't want them up there with us at all if we could avoid it, plus the fact that the camera lights were blinding, and if you couldn't see where you were going or what you were doing, anything could happen.
>
> We didn't think we would have lights in our eyes but we were blinded by the lights. Just about the time we left the jail office, the lights came on and were blinding.
>
> We got along all right with the press here in Dallas. They do what we ask. [Our] people didn't act that way. [But the other] people were excited and acted more like a mob.[1]
>
> **MR. SORRELS.** . . . You would have to elbow your way through, and step over cables and tripods and wires, and every time almost that I would come out of Captain Fritz's office, the minute the door opened, they would flash on these bright lights, and I got where I just shadowed my eyes when I walked down there to keep the light from shining in my eyes. They had cables run through one deputy sheriff's office, right through the windows from the street up the side of the building, across

the floor, out to the boxes where they could get power—they had wires running out of that, had the wires taped down to keep people from actually falling or stumbling over the wires. And it was just a condition that you can hardly explain.[2]

Like an octopus, the media seized the event with its limbs and suffocated movement with its body. The media had become a new force in human existence; it was on the way to taking over everything, as Nixon would learn at Watergate, and as Oswald would find out in a thunderclap on Sunday at 11:22 in the morning after two days of gathering in some vast multiple of all the attention he had been denied for most of his life.

But let us go back and take the events of those days in order, even if there was very little order.

MR. BALL. . . . Now, what time was it that you heard the President had been shot?

MR. FRITZ. . . . one of the Secret Service men that was assigned to [our] location . . . got a call on his little transistor radio and Chief Stevenson . . . asked me to go to the hospital [but] I felt we were going to the wrong place, we should go to the scene of the crime and he said, "Well, go ahead," . . .[3]

Arriving at the Book Depository at 12:58 P.M., Captain Fritz ordered the building sealed and began searching the floors methodically.

MR. FRITZ. We started at the bottom; yes, sir. And of course . . . different people would call me when they would find something that looked like something I should know about and I ran back and forth from floor to floor as we were searching, and it wasn't very long until someone . . . wanted me to come to the front window, the corner window, they had found some empty cartridges [in] the sixth floor corner . . .

MR. BALL. What did you do?

MR. FRITZ. I told them not to . . . touch anything until we could get the crime lab to take pictures of them just as they were lying there . . .[4]

MR. MCCLOY. . . . Was there anything in the nature of a gun rest there or anything that could be used as a gun rest?

MR. FRITZ. Yes, sir; [one box] was in the window, and another box was on the floor. There were some boxes stacked to his right that more or less blinded him from the rest of the floor. If anyone else had been [there] I doubt if they could have seen where he was sitting.[5]

. . . A few minutes later some officer called me and said they had found the rifle over near the back stairway . . .

MR. BALL. While you were there, Mr. Truly came up to you?

MR. FRITZ. Yes, sir . . . Mr. Truly came and told me that one of his employees had left the building, and . . . he gave me the name, Lee Harvey Oswald, and . . . the Irving address.[6]

Truly's testimony offers the impression of a decent man in an indecent situation.

MR. TRULY. . . . I noticed that Lee Oswald was not among these boys . . . I asked Bill Shelley if he had seen him, he looked around and said no . . . So Mr. Campbell is standing there and I said, "I have a boy over here missing. I don't know whether to report it or not." . . . [and he] said, "Well, we better do it anyway." It was so quick after that.

So I picked the phone up then . . . and got the boy's name and general description and telephone number and address at Irving . . .

MR. BELIN. Why didn't you ask for any other employees?

MR. TRULY. That is the only one that I could be certain . . . was missing. [Then] I told Chief Lumpkin that I had a boy missing over here—"I don't know whether it amounts to anything or not." And he says, "Just a moment. We will go tell Captain Fritz."

[And Captain Fritz] says, "Thank you, Mr. Truly. We will take care of it."

And I went back downstairs in a few minutes.

There was a reporter followed me away from that spot, and asked me who Oswald was. I told the reporter, "You must have ears like a bird or something. I don't want to say anything about a boy I don't know anything about. This is a terrible thing." Or words to that effect.

I said, "Don't bother me. Don't mention the name. Let's find something out."[7]

Captain Fritz now drove over to City Hall to ascertain whether the missing employee had a criminal record, but when he got there

> . . . we heard that our officer had been killed, [and] I asked . . . who shot [Tippit], and they told me his name was Oswald, and I said, "His full name?" And they told me and I said, "This is the suspect we are looking for in the President's killing."[8]

At that point, Fritz started to send some men to the house in Irving, but an officer told him, "Captain, we can save you a trip. There he sits."

Yes, there he sat in an interrogation room in City Hall.

> **MR. FRITZ.** So then I . . . asked them about how much evidence we had on the officer's killing and they told me they had several eye witnesses . . . and I instructed them to get those witnesses over for identification just as soon as they could, and for us to prepare a real good case on the officer's killing so we would have a case to hold [Oswald] without bond while we investigated the President's killing where we didn't have so many witnesses.[9]

Now that he had a suspect who could be held, he was ready to begin questioning:

> **MR. BALL.** Will you describe the interrogation room . . . ?
>
> **MR. FRITZ.** . . . room 317, on the third floor of the courts building . . . I believe it is 9½ feet by 14 feet . . . Glass all around, and it has a door leading out into a hallway . . .[10]
>
> My office is badly arranged for a thing of this kind. We never had anything like this before, of course. I don't have a back door and I don't have a door to the jail elevator without having to go through that hall for 20 feet, and each time we went through the hallway to and from the jail we had to pull him through all those [press and TV] people and they, of course, would holler at him and say things to him, and some of them were bad things, and some were things that seemed to please him and some seemed to aggravate him, and I don't think that helped at all in questioning him. I think that all of that had a tendency to keep him upset.

MR. BALL. What about the interview itself?

MR. FRITZ. . . . we did have a lot of people in the office there to be interviewing a man. It is much better, and you can keep a man's attention and his thoughts on what you are talking about to him better, I think, if there are not more than two or three people.

But in a case of this nature . . . we certainly couldn't tell the Secret Service and the FBI we didn't want them to work on it . . . so we, of course, invited them in too but it did make a pretty big crowd.

MR. BALL. Did you have any tape recorder?

MR. FRITZ. No, sir; I didn't have a tape recorder. We need one; if we had one at this time we could have handled these conversations far better.

MR. BALL. The Dallas Police Department doesn't have one?

MR. FRITZ. No, sir; I have requested one several times but so far they haven't gotten me one.[11]

MR. BALL. And you had quite a few interruptions, too, during the questioning, didn't you?

MR. FRITZ. Yes, sir; we had quite a lot of interruptions . . . I don't think there was a lot that could have been done other than move that crowd out of there, but I think it would have been more apt to get a confession out of it or get more true facts from him if I could have got him to sit down and quietly talked with him.[12]

Yes, there was Captain Fritz without a tape recorder, taking notes on a pad when Oswald would answer a question; pleasant, almost friendly was Fritz, a short man, built like a bull, and he wore thick-lensed glasses. He was famed in Dallas for his powers of interrogation, which were considered both very good and yet not good at all by the same man, Henry Wade, the District Attorney.

MR. WADE. . . . Fritz runs a kind of one-man operation where nobody else knows what he is doing. Even me, for instance, he is reluctant to tell me, either, but I don't mean that disparagingly. I will say Captain Fritz is about as good a man at solving a crime as I ever saw, to find out who did it, but he is the poorest in the getting evidence that I know, and I am more interested in getting evidence, and there is where our major conflict comes in.[13]

The solution to a crime and the evidence to prosecute the perpetrator are often at odds. The laws of evidence are strict, and full of pitfalls. An improper question by the policeman conducting the investigation can result in the inadmissibility of the answer as evidence or even in a reversal on appeal.

Rigid procedures in questioning get, however, in the way of the interrogator. He is seeking to find rapport with a suspect, looking to relax him, even carry him companionably into a confession. That is at odds with a district attorney's approach. A prosecutor looks to keep the evidence pristine.

Whether an interrogator is more interested in the solution of a crime or in gathering enough evidence to make a conviction stick, the need in both cases is, however, not to have a tape recorder. The machine, after all, will reveal every step in the questioning that might be in arguable violation of the prisoner's rights: Given the tricks, threats, and traps through which an interrogation progresses, a transcript is a breeding ground for appeals.

In Russia, KGB officers found it impossible to believe that the police department of a city as large as Dallas would function without a tape recorder, but then, the KGB had never had to contend with *Miranda* (or with its precursors before 1966) and so did not understand that one mistake in phrasing, visible there in a transcript, could overturn a conviction.

Captain Fritz might have paid lip service to the department's need for a recording instrument, but odds are he had no use for one until this exceptional weekend in November, when there was not only Lee Harvey Oswald to deal with, but the gathering suspicion of the world community that the police in Dallas had been up to no good with this man Oswald.

By now, it is possible to believe that Fritz, under the circumstances, was simply doing his best, or so it appears.

In any event, he began with quiet, relatively easy questions:

MR. FRITZ. I asked Oswald about why he was registered under that other name . . . of O. H. Lee. He said, well, the lady didn't understand him, she put it down there and he just left it that way.[14]

When Fritz asked him why he had his pistol with him while seeing a movie, Oswald replied, " 'Well, you know about a pistol. I just carried it.' "[15]

MR. BALL. Before you questioned Oswald the first time, did you warn him?

MR. FRITZ. Yes, sir . . . I told him that any evidence that he gave me would be used against him . . .

MR. BALL. Did he reply to that?

MR. FRITZ. He told me that he didn't want a lawyer and he told me once or twice that he didn't want to answer any questions at all . . . and I told him each time he didn't have to if he didn't want to. So later he sometimes would start talking to me again.[16]

After a while, given the impatience created by the number of people in the room, some of the questions had to get downright personal:

MR. BALL. Did you ask him if he shot Tippit?

MR. FRITZ. Oh, yes.

MR. BALL. What did he say?

MR. FRITZ. He denied it . . . "The only law I violated was in the [movie] show; I hit the officer in the show; he hit me in the eye and I guess I deserved it." He said, "That is the only law I violated." He said, "That is the only thing I have done wrong."[17]

MR. BALL. Did you ever ask him if he had kept a rifle in the garage at Irving?

MR. FRITZ. Yes, sir; I did. I asked him, and I asked him if he had brought one from New Orleans. He said he didn't.

MR. BALL. He did not.

MR. FRITZ. That is right.

I told him the people at the Paine residence said he did have a rifle out there, and he kept it out there and he kept it wrapped in a blanket and he said that wasn't true.[18]

Oswald was not about to open any door. So long as he didn't admit to having a rifle, he could claim that others were framing him.

All the same, his vanity keeps him from staying silent for too long. If it is a battle of wits, he wants to best his interrogators. When the cost of this indulgence mounts, he becomes cautious again. But he is on a high, and full of combat insanity.

They show him the photograph where he is holding the rifle, and he disavows it:

MR. FRITZ. . . . he said that wasn't his picture. ". . . that is my face and [somebody] put a different body on it." He said, "I know all about photography, I worked with photography for a long time. That is a picture that someone else has made. I never saw that picture in my life."[19]

On occasion, he was coy. And sometimes he was so cynical that his answer sounded sacrilegious.

MR. FRITZ. . . . I told him, I said, "You know, you have killed the President and this is a very serious charge."

He denied it and said he hadn't killed the President.

I said he had been killed. He said people will forget that in a few days and there will be another President . . .[20]

MR. DULLES. What was Oswald's attitude toward the police and police authority?

MR. FRITZ. You know, I didn't have any trouble with him. If we would just talk to him quietly like we are talking right now, we talked all right until I asked him a question that meant something, that would produce evidence, he immediately told me he wouldn't tell me about it and he seemed to anticipate what I was going to ask. In fact, he got so good at it one time, I asked him if he had had any training, if he hadn't been questioned before.

MR. DULLES. Questioned before?[21]

It is Allen Dulles who is asking the question: Questioned by whom? At this point, Allen Dulles may have come wide awake!

MR. FRITZ. [He said] the FBI had questioned him when he came back from Russia for a long time and they tried different methods. He said they tried the buddy boy method, and the thorough method, and let me see some other method he told me and he said, "I understand that."[22]

There had been one verbal fracas, however. Not too long after serious questioning began, a call had come in from Gordon Shanklin, the FBI Special Agent in Charge for Dallas:

MR. FRITZ. . . . Mr. Shanklin asked that Mr. Hosty be in on that questioning, he said he wanted him in there because of Mr. Hosty knowing these people . . .[23]

... and [Shanklin] said some other things that I don't want to repeat, about what to do if [my assistant] didn't do it right quick. So I ... walked out there and called [Hosty] in.[24]

We have to recall the note that Oswald had left for Hosty at FBI headquarters. Shanklin may, by now, have become aware of the existence of that piece of paper.

As soon as Hosty came into the interrogation room and Oswald heard his name, everything changed:

MR. FRITZ. ... Mr. Hosty spoke up and asked him ... if he had been to Russia, and he asked him if he had been to Mexico City, and this irritated Oswald a great deal and he beat on the desk and he went into kind of a tantrum [and] he said he had not been. He did say he had been to Russia, he was in Russia, I believe he said, for some time ...

MR. BALL. Was there anything said about Oswald's wife?

MR. FRITZ. Yes, sir. He said, he told Hosty, he said, "I know you." He said, "You accosted my wife on two occasions," and he was getting pretty irritable and so I wanted to quiet him down a little bit because I noticed if I talked to him in a calm, easy manner it wasn't very hard to get him to settle down, and I asked him what he meant by accosting, I thought maybe he meant some physical abuse or something and he said, "Well, he threatened her." And he said, "He practically told her she would have to go back to Russia." And he said, "He accosted her on two different occasions."[25]

Oswald beat the table again. Since his wrists were handcuffed in front of him, the impact must have resounded through the room. In effect, Oswald has succeeded in confusing his interrogators by the intimacy of his attack on the FBI man. Nor are Special Agent Hosty's troubles due to cease quickly.

McMillan: ... on his return from interviewing Oswald in the Dallas County Jail, Hosty was confronted at the FBI office by Special Agent in Charge J. Gordon Shanklin with the note which Oswald had left several days earlier. Shanklin, who appeared "agitated and upset," asked Hosty about the circumstances in which he had received the note and about his visits to Ruth Paine and Marina Oswald. On Shanklin's orders, Hosty dictated a two- to four-page memorandum setting forth all he knew and he gave the memorandum, in duplicate, to Shanklin.[26]

Following this episode, there are breaks in the interrogation on Friday afternoon for line-ups (or, as they called it in Dallas, showups). The taxicab driver, William Whaley, was one of the people asked to look at Oswald. The means were conventional. Whaley sat behind a one-way window and stared out at the group assembled for him:

MR. WHALEY. . . . six men, young teenagers, and they were all hand-cuffed together. Well, they wanted me to pick out my passenger.
    At that time he had on a pair of black pants and a white T-shirt, that is all he had on. But you could have picked him out without identifying him by just listening to him because he was bawling out the policemen, telling them it wasn't right to put him in line with these teenagers and all of that . . .

MR. BALL. They had him in line with men much younger?

MR. WHALEY. With five others . . . young kids, they might have got them in jail.

MR. BALL. Did he look older than those other boys?

MR. WHALEY. Yes.

MR. BALL. And he was talking, was he?

MR. WHALEY. He showed no respect for the policemen [running the show-up], he told them what he thought about them . . . they were trying to railroad him and he wanted his lawyer.

MR. BALL. Did that aid you in the identification of the man?

MR. WHALEY. . . . anybody who wasn't sure could have picked out the right one just for that. It didn't aid me because I knew he was the right one as soon as I saw him . . . When you drive a taxi that long, you learn to judge people and what I actually thought of the man when he got in was that he was a wino who had been off his bottle for about two days, that is the way he looked, sir, that was my opinion of him . . .[27]

At 7:10 on Friday evening Oswald was arraigned for the murder of Officer Tippit. Then, he was brought back to interrogation again. Later that night he would be taken out once more through the cables and the TV lights to another showup, with Howard Brennan, the eyewitness who had seen a rifleman on the sixth floor. Brennan, however, refused to make an absolute identification that night.

> MR. BALL. . . . there were two officers of the vice squad and an officer and a clerk from the jail that were in the showup with Oswald?
>
> MR. FRITZ. That is true. I borrowed those officers. I was a little bit afraid some prisoner might hurt him, there was a lot of . . . feeling right about that time, [and] we didn't have an officer in my office the right size to show with him so I asked two of the special service officers if they would help me and they said they would be glad to, so they took off their coats and neckties and fixed themselves where they would look like prisoners and they were good enough to stand on each side of him in the showup, and we used a man who works in the jail office, a civilian employee, as a third man.
>
> MR. BALL. Now, were they dressed a little better than Oswald, do you think, these three people?
>
> MR. FRITZ. Well, I don't think there was a great deal of difference. They had on their regular working clothes and after they opened their shirts and took off their ties, why, they looked very much like anyone else.[28]

Of course, Oswald was the only one who had bruises on his face. On the other hand, Brennan had his own reasons for not picking Oswald out:

> MR. BRENNAN. I believe at that time, and I still believe it was a Communist activity, and I felt like there hadn't been more than one eyewitness, [myself], and if it got to be a known fact that I was an eyewitness, my family or I, either one, might not be safe.
>
> MR. BELIN. Well, if you wouldn't have identified him, mightn't he have been released by the police? . . .
>
> MR. BRENNAN. No. [A] greater contributing factor than my personal reasons was that I already knew they had the man for murder and I knew he would not be released.

MR. BELIN. The murder of whom?

MR. BRENNAN. Of Officer Tippit.

MR. BELIN. Well, what happened in between to change your mind . . . ?

MR. BRENNAN. After Oswald was killed, I was relieved quite a bit . . . there was no longer that immediate danger.[29]

After Brennan refused to identify him that night, Oswald was put back into interrogation. On they went through half of the night.

It is worth hearing the reaction of a police officer who was present with Captain Fritz while Oswald was being questioned by the Dallas police, the Secret Service, and the FBI.

MR. BOYD. I tell you, I've never saw another man just exactly like him.

MR. STERN. In what way?

MR. BOYD. Well, you know, he acted like he was intelligent; just as soon as you would ask him a question, he would just give you the answer right back—he didn't hesitate . . . I never saw a man that could answer questions like he did . . .

MR. STERN. Of course, this was a long day for everybody—did he seem by the end of the day still to be in command of himself, or did he appear tired or particularly worn out?

MR. BOYD. Well, he didn't appear to be tired . . . I imagine he could have been [but] he didn't show it.

MR. STERN. This is quite unnatural—really rather exceptional; this is, of course, why you say somewhat unusual, a man accused of killing two people, one of them the President of the United States, and at the end of the day he is pretty well in command?[30]

Yes, Mr. Stern really has a good question.

MR. BOYD. Yes, sir; I'll tell you— Oswald, he answered his questions until [he finally] got up and said, "What started out to be a short interrogation turned out to be rather lengthy," and he said, "I believe I have answered all the questions I have cared to answer, and I don't care to say anything else."

And sat back down.[31]

They even returned him to his jail cell for a time. Then they brought him out to be arraigned for the murder of President Kennedy. A justice of the peace, David Johnston, conducted the proceedings in a small room filled with file cabinets. On the bottom of the form that the judge filled out was written: "No Bond— Capital Offense."

So ended the longest day of that year, Friday, November 22, 1963, which only came to its conclusion early Saturday morning. Later on that Saturday, in the afternoon, Lee would get to see his brother Robert, and Marina, and Marguerite.

8

A Black Pullover Sweater with Jagged Holes in It

Since *Life* magazine had agreed to pay for their rooms at the Adolphus, the move was made from Ruth Paine's house in Irving early next day.

MARGUERITE OSWALD. We arrived at the Adolphus Hotel between 9:30 and 10:00.

MR. RANKIN. This was what day?

MARGUERITE OSWALD. . . . the morning of Saturday, November 23.

While we were there, an FBI agent, Mr. Hart Odum, entered the room with another agent and wanted Marina to accompany him to be questioned . . . And I said, "No, we are going to see Lee." We were all eating breakfast when he came in . . .

So, he said, "Well, will you tell Mrs. Oswald, please"—to the interpreter, "I would like to question her . . ."

I said, "It is no good. You don't need to tell the interpreter that because my daughter-in-law is not going with you . . . any further statements that Marina will make will be through counsel."

Mr. Odum said to the interpreter . . . "Will you tell Mrs. Oswald to decide what she would like to do and not listen to her mother-in-law." . . .

Just then my son Robert entered the room and Mr. Odum said, "Robert, we would like to take Marina and question her."

He said, "No, I am sorry, we are going to try and get lawyers for both she and Lee."

So he left.

We went to the courthouse and we sat and sat, and while at the courthouse my son, Robert, was being interviewed by—I don't know whether it was Secret Service or FBI agents—in a glass enclosure . . . So we waited quite a while . . . in the afternoon before we got to see Lee.

MR. RANKIN. Was anyone else present . . . ?

MARGUERITE OSWALD. No. Marina and I were escorted back [to] where they had an enclosure and telephones. So Marina got on the telephone and talked to Lee in Russian. That is my handicap. I don't know what was said. And Lee seemed very severely composed and assured. He was well-beaten up. He had black eyes, and his face was all bruised, and everything. But he was very calm. He smiled with his wife, and talked with her, and then I got on the phone and I said, "Honey, you are so bruised up, your face. What are they doing?"

He said, "Mother, don't worry. I got that in a scuffle." . . . So I talked and said, "Is there anything I can do to help you?"

He said, "No, Mother, everything is fine. I know my rights and I will have an attorney . . . Don't worry about a thing." . . . That was my entire conversation to him.

Gentlemen, you must realize this. I had heard over the television my son say, "I did not do it. I did not do it." . . . I think by now you know my temperament, gentlemen. I would not insult my son and ask him if he had shot at President Kennedy. Why? Because I myself heard him say, "I didn't do it, I didn't do it."

So, that was enough for me. I would not ask that question.[1]

Marina's conversation with Lee is almost as brief:

MR. RANKIN. . . . did you ask him if he had killed President Kennedy? . . .

MARINA OSWALD. No. I said, "I don't believe you did that, and everything will turn out well."

After all, I couldn't accuse him—after all, he was my husband.

MR. RANKIN. And what did he say to that?

MARINA OSWALD. He said that I should not worry . . . But I could see by his eyes that he was guilty. Rather he tried to appear to be brave. However, by his eyes I could tell that he was afraid.

This was just a feeling. It is hard to describe.

MR. RANKIN. Would you help us a little bit by telling us what you saw in his eyes that caused you to think that?

MARINA OSWALD. He said goodbye to me with his eyes. I knew that. He said that everything would turn out well but he did not believe it himself.[2]

Marguerite Oswald has an ability to get a good deal out of the given when it comes to defending Lee:

MR. RANKIN. About how long did you and Marina spend with your son?

MARGUERITE OSWALD. I would say I spent about 3 or 4 minutes on the telephone, and then Marina came back to the telephone and talked with Lee [and after that] we left . . . So Marina started crying. Marina says, "Mama, I tell Lee I love Lee and Lee says he love me very much. And Lee tell me to make sure I buy shoes for June."

Now, here is a man who is accused of the murder of a President. This is the next day, or let's say about 24 hours that he has been questioned. His composure is good. And he is thinking about his young daughter wearing shoes.

Now June was wearing shoes belonging to Mrs. Paine's little girl, Marina told me—they were little red tennis shoes and the top was worn [and] the boy is concerned about shoes for the baby, [even if] he is in this awful predicament. So he must feel innocent, or sure that everything is going to be all right, as he told me.[3]

Then it is Robert's turn to visit with Lee. It is a year since they have been together at Thanksgiving, but they are brothers, and so their conversation has a tendency to stay inside brotherly parameters. What follows is from Robert Oswald's book, *Lee.*

After a little more talk about the baby and Marina, I finally asked him bluntly, "Lee, what the Sam Hill is going on?"

"I don't know," he said.

"You don't know? Look, they've got your pistol, they've got your rifle, they've got you charged with shooting the President and a police officer. And you tell me you don't know. Now, I want to know just what's going on."

He stiffened and straightened up, his facial expression was suddenly very tight.

"I just don't know what they're talking about," he said very firmly and deliberately. "Don't believe all this so-called evidence."

I was studying his face closely, trying to find the answer to my question in his eyes or his expression. He realized that, and as I stared into his eyes, he said to me quietly, "Brother, you won't find anything there."[4]

Robert is not about to give up that easily. He asks about the attorney in New York whom Lee has tried to contact. Lee sloughs the question by suggesting that he is no more than the man Lee desires to have for representation. He is not about to tell Robert that his choice, John Abt, was the lawyer who had defended the leaders of the Communist Party, Gus Hall and Benjamin Davis, against charges of conspiracy to overthrow the U.S. government. It would provoke a quarrel stronger than the bonds of their brotherhood.

Robert, however, knows Lee well enough to sense that something large is amiss. He says:

"I'll get you an attorney down here."
"No," he said, "you stay out of it."
"Stay out of it? It looks like I've been dragged into it."
"I'm not going to have anybody from down here," he said very firmly. "I want this one."
"Well, all right."[5]

The gift Southerners receive with their mother's milk is not to push a family disagreement too far. They are all aware of old family histories of relatives who brooded on a minor insult for twenty years and then came to their cousin's door with a loaded shotgun and blew his head off.

McMillan: . . . just after his visit with Marina, Oswald tried to reach Abt. He succeeded in obtaining Abt's home and office numbers from the New York operator, but he failed to find him at either place . . .

Fritz later asked whether Oswald had succeeded in reaching Abt. He answered that he had not, then courteously thanked Fritz for allowing him to use the prison phone.[6]

We can picture the consternation of the Communist Party in New York when Oswald's desire to retain Abt is announced in the newspapers. If Oswald had been working for COINTELPRO, it would seem he has not yet resigned!

Or, perhaps, he is being doggedly simple. Abt will know how to give him a political defense and dramatize his trial. The Communist Party will have to pay a heavy price for that, but by Oswald's balance sheet, the personal plus will more than compensate for the Party's gaping minus.

MRS. PAINE. Then about 3:30 or 4 [in the afternoon] I got a telephone call . . .

MR. JENNER. Did you recognize the voice? . . .

MRS. PAINE. The voice said, "This is Lee."

MR. JENNER. Give your best recollection of everything you said and, if you can, please, of everything he said, and exactly what you said.

MRS. PAINE. I said, "Well, hi."[7]

Lee instructed her to call Abt as soon as the long-distance rates went down that evening. "Ruth was stunned—stunned by his gall . . . [but] appalled and angry as she was, Ruth did try to reach Abt and . . . failed."[8] The lawyer was in a cabin in Connecticut and not reachable.

MR. BALL. You asked him about the gun again, didn't you?

MR. FRITZ. I asked him about a lot of things that [Saturday] morning, I sure did . . .

MR. BALL. And you asked him the size and shape of the [paper] sack, didn't you?

MR. FRITZ. He never admitted bringing the sack . . . He said his lunch was all he brought . . .[9]

The lie has been Oswald's tool all his life. But now it is different. Where once he could muster five quick lies to confuse one person, now five practical experts in the study of mendacity are examining each one of his lies. His cutting tool is being called upon to work against the most obdurate human materials.

> **MR. FRITZ.** I asked him [again] about the photograph and he said . . . It wasn't his picture at all . . .
>
> **MR. BALL.** . . . the picture was made by somebody superimposing his face?
>
> **MR. FRITZ.** That is right; yes.[10]

McMillan: Shortly after 5:00 P.M. on Saturday, Louis H. Nichols, president of the Dallas Bar Association, [was led] to Oswald's maximum security cell on the fifth floor. Oswald was at the center of three cells with no one on either side. He was lying on his cot. He stood up to greet Nichols and the two men talked on a pair of bunks 3 or 4 feet apart. Nichols explained that he had come to see if he wanted an attorney.

Did he, Oswald asked, know a lawyer in New York City named John Abt?

Nichols said that he did not.

Well, Oswald said, that was the man he would like to have represent him. Failing that, Oswald said he belonged to the A.C.L.U. and would like someone from that organization to represent him. But if that should fall through, he added, "and I can find a lawyer here [in Dallas] who believes in anything I believe in, and believes as I believe, and believes in my innocence"—here Oswald hesitated—"as much as he can, I might let him represent me."[11]

About an hour later, at six on Saturday evening, Marina and Marguerite and June and Rachel were moved by Secret Service men from the Hotel Adolphus (where there were too many people around for good security) over to the Executive Inn near Love Field. By the time they had settled into the new rooms, they had also come to the decision to burn the photograph of Lee that showed his pistol in his belt and his rifle in his upraised hand.

> **MR. RANKIN.** Had you said anything to her about burning it before that?
>
> **MARGUERITE OSWALD.** No, sir. The last time I had seen the picture was . . . when she was trying to tell me the picture was in her shoe. I state here now that . . . she tore up the picture and struck a match to it. Then I took it and flushed it down the toilet . . .

MR. RANKIN. What day?

MARGUERITE OSWALD. On Saturday, November 23. Now, I flushed the torn bits and the half-burned thing down the commode. And nothing was said. There was nothing said.[12]

They did not know that the picture they were destroying was not crucial evidence but merely one more print of material already in the hands of the police who had found other copies of those same photographs among Oswald's effects in the Paines' garage.[13]

Marguerite, however, awoke on Sunday morning with an attack of anxiety. It was as if one more trouble, still unfocused, was close at hand to meet all her other troubles, which were many. Where were she and Marina going to live, and how were they going to pay for it? They were two women alone and in need of assistance. They also needed to be able to speak to one another in greater privacy without some official translator from the FBI or the Secret Service hovering between them.

It was not long that morning before she thought of a possible Russian translator. That would be Peter Paul Gregory, the man who gave language lessons in his native tongue at the Fort Worth Library; yes, that must be meant to be because Marguerite had taken language lessons with Peter Paul Gregory earlier in this year of 1963 with the idea that when Lee was in the mood to see her again, she would be able to converse with her granddaughter in Russian. It had been a dream. She gave up after two lessons. Mr. Gregory had given no sign at all that her name was familiar to him, and besides, Russian was very difficult to learn.

Still, it was meant to be. Peter Paul Gregory was the first important person outside the family that Lee had met when he came to Fort Worth fifteen months ago from Soviet Russia.

MARGUERITE OSWALD. So I called . . . I said, "Mr. Gregory, I won't say who I am, but you know my son and you know my daughter-in-law, and I am in trouble, sir. I am over here."

He said, "I am sorry, but I won't talk to anybody I don't know."

MR. RANKIN. What name did you give him?

MARGUERITE OSWALD. I didn't give him any name.

He said, "I am sorry, but I won't talk to anyone I don't know."

And I said again, "Well, you know my son real well."

He said, "Oh, you are Mrs. Oswald."

I said, "Yes, sir, this is Mrs. Oswald. We are at the Executive Inn in Dallas, stranded. And do you know of anyone who would give my daughter-in-law and I a home, and put us up for the time this is going on, so we can be near Lee at the courthouse? I need help, Mr. Gregory."

He said, "Mrs. Oswald, what is your room number? I will help you. Hold still. Help will be coming."

And so that was the end of my conversation with Mr. Gregory.[14]

Marguerite could not know, but at City Hall they were ready to transfer Oswald to the County Jail, where he would be under the custody of the sheriff's office and security would be easier to enforce. There had been plans to move him to that County Jail since three o'clock yesterday, Saturday afternoon, and different procedures for a safe passage had been discussed and then rearranged, and the time had been altered as well.

MR. BALL. Did you consider transferring him at night? . . .

MR. FRITZ. . . . on Saturday night, I had a call at my home from a uniformed captain, Captain Frazier I believe is his name, [who] told me they had some threats and he had to transfer Oswald.

And I said, well, I don't know. I said there has been no security setup . . . He called me back then in a few minutes and he told me . . . to leave him where he was.[15]

Next, they decided on a scheduled move at 10:00 A.M. on Sunday, but even then, they were late.

MR. FRITZ. I did do one thing here I should tell you about. When the chief came back and asked me if I was ready to transfer him, I told him I had already complained . . . about the big cameras set up in the jail office and I was afraid we couldn't get out of the jail with him with all those cameras and all those people in the jail office.

So when the chief came back he asked if we were ready to transfer and I said, "We are ready when security is ready," and he said, "It is all set up." He said, "The people are across the street, and the newsmen are all well back in the garage," and he said, "It is all set . . . We have got the money wagon up there to transfer him in," and I said, "Well, I don't like the idea, chief, of transferring him in a money wagon." We, of course, didn't know the driver, nor who he was, nor anything about the money wagon, and he said, "Well, that is all right. Transfer him in your car if you want to, and we will use the money wagon for a decoy . . ."[16]

Actually, Fritz, who knew he would lose custody of Oswald as soon as he was transferred over to the sheriff, had been talking to the prisoner for most of Sunday morning. Finally, at 11:10 A.M., after this last interrogation had gone on for an hour longer than expected, Oswald was made ready for the transfer:

McMillan: But the shirt he had been wearing when he was arrested had been sent to a crime lab in Washington, and he had on only a T-shirt. Some hangers with his clothing were handed in to Fritz's office, and the officers selected what they considered his best-looking shirt for him to wear. Oswald was adamant. No, he said, and insisted on wearing a black pullover sweater with jagged holes in it. He was now dressed, as he had been in the photographs taken by Marina, all in black—black trousers and a black sweater. Fritz then suggested that he wear a hat to camouflage his looks. Once again, as he had done on entering the jail two days earlier, Oswald refused. He would let the world see who he was.
  Accompanied by Captain Fritz and four detectives, Oswald [reached] the basement of the police station [at 11:20 A.M.,] where he was to step into a waiting car . . .[17]

MR. BALL. How far behind Oswald were you . . . ? Oswald was behind you?

MR. FRITZ. Behind me.

MR. BALL. How many feet would you say?

MR. FRITZ. In feet, I would probably say 8 feet . . . We first called down and they told us everything was all right . . . I kept my officers back in the jail [and] I asked two officers outside the jail if security was good, and they said it was all right. But when we walked out . . . we met the crowd and the officers coming forward . . .[18]

It could be said without undue exaggeration that Dallas, the corporate soul of Texas, has not yet recovered altogether from what transpired in the next few seconds, when a man stepped out of the crowd and, in front of everyone, killed Lee Harvey Oswald.

9

"He Cry; He Eye Wet"

Let us, at least, bury Lee before we look to comprehend what intent might have lived in the mind of Jack Ruby.

MARGUERITE OSWALD. At 11:30 A.M., Sunday . . . my son [Robert] and Mr. Gregory came to the Executive Inn, all excited. We had diapers strung all over the place. My uniform was washed. I had no clothes with me.

I went with the [wet] uniform.

"Hurry up, we have to get you out of here."

I am not one to be told what to do, and you gentlemen know that by this time. I said, "What's your hurry? We have diapers and all. I want to tell you what happened."

"Mother, Mother, stop talking. We have to get you out of here."

Mr. Gregory said, "Mrs. Oswald, will you listen and get things together? We have to get you out of here." . . .

I said, "That is all we have been doing since yesterday, running from one place to another. Give us just a minute. We are coming, but we have to pack things." . . .

"Mrs. Oswald, we will talk later. We have to get you out of here."

MR. RANKIN. Did you have television in this room?

MARGUERITE OSWALD. Yes, sir.

Now here is another Godsend. We watched the television, Marina and I. She watched more than I did. We were very busy, Mr. Rankin. The babies had diarrhea and everything. I was very busy with the babies and the Russian girl . . . we were just getting snatches of it. But Marina wanted to know. "Mama, I want to see Lee." She was hoping Lee would come on the picture, like he did. So this morning, Sunday morning, I said, "Oh, honey, let's turn the television off. The same thing over and over."

And I turned the television off. So Marina and I did not see what happened to my son.

We turned the television off.

So we did not know.

But frantically Robert and Mr. Gregory kept insisting that we pack and run.

So when we get downstairs, there was Secret Service men all over.[1]

You could count on one reaction: Marguerite Oswald would bristle at the sight of authority.

MARGUERITE OSWALD. . . . . as soon as we got in the car Mr. Gregory says, "We are taking you to Robert's mother-in-law's house."

Now . . . [they] are dairy people—Robert's in-laws. And they wanted to take us there, which would have been approximately 45 miles from Dallas.

And I said, "No, you are not taking me out in the sticks . . . I want to be in Dallas where I can help Lee."

"Well for security reasons, this is the best place. Nobody would ever find it."

I said, "Security reasons? You can give me security in a hotel room in town. I am not going out in this little country town. I want to be in Dallas where I can help Lee."

And so I am not being well liked, because all the arrangements were made that we were going to go to this little farmhouse. But I would not go.

I could not survive if I was 40 or 50 miles away and my son was picked up as a murderer. I had to be right there in Dallas [but] we needed clothes—Marina and the baby needed clothes. So then they decided that they should go to Irving . . .

When we reached there, they brought us to the chief of police's home. And there were cars all around.

As soon as the car stopped, the Secret Service agent said, "Lee has been shot."

And I said, "How badly?"

He said, "In the shoulder." . . .

I cried, and said, "Marina, Lee has been shot."

So Marina went into the chief of police's home at Irving, to call Mrs. Paine to get the diapers and things ready . . .

So I am sitting in the car with the agent. Marina is in the home now . . .

So something comes over the mike and the Secret Service agent says, "Do not repeat. Do not repeat."

I said, "My son is gone, isn't he?"

And he didn't answer.

I said, "Answer me. I want to know. If my son is gone, I want to meditate."

He said, "Yes, Mrs. Oswald, your son has just expired." . . .

As a matter of fact, when I got the news, I went into the home and I said, "Marina, our boy is gone."

We both cried. And they were all watching the sequence on television. The television was turned to the back, where Marina and I could not see it. They sat us on the sofa and his wife gave us coffee. And the back of the television was to us. And the men and all, a lot of men were looking at the television. It probably just happened, because the man said, "Do not repeat." And I insisted.

They gave us coffee . . .[2]

Later on that Sunday, the Secret Service decided to move Marina and Marguerite and June and Rachel to the Inn of the Six Flags, a motel between Dallas and Fort Worth that would be just about empty now in November, but first there was the question of whether the wife and mother would be allowed to see Lee's body.

MARGUERITE OSWALD. . . . Immediately I said, "I want to see Lee." And Marina said, "I want to see Lee, too."

And the chief of police and Mr. Gregory said, "Well, it would be better to wait until he was at the funeral home and fixed up."

I said, "No, I want to see Lee now."

Marina said, "Me too, me want to see Lee." . . .

They didn't want us to . . . from the ugliness of it, evidently. But I insisted, and so did Marina . . .

On the way to the car they are trying to get us to change our minds. And he said, Mr. Mike Howard—he was driving the car—"Mrs. Oswald, for security reasons it would be much better if you would wait until later on to see Lee . . ."

I said, "For security reasons, I want you to know I am an American citizen, and even though I am poor I have as much right as any other human being, and Mrs. Kennedy was escorted to the hospital to see her husband. And I insist upon being escorted, and enough security to take me to the hospital to see my son."

Gentlemen, I require the same privilege.

So Mr. Mike Howard said . . . "I want you to know when we get there we will not be able to protect you. Our security measures end right there. The police will then have you under protection . . ."

I said, "That is fine. If I am to die, I will die that way. But I am going to see my son."

Mr. Gregory says—and in the most awful tone of voice, I will always remember this—remember, gentlemen, my son has been accused, I have just lost a son.

He said, "Mrs. Oswald, you are being so selfish. You are endangering this girl's life and the lives of these two children."

I want to elaborate on this. He is not thinking about me. He is thinking about the Russian girl. I am going to bring this up over and over—that these Russian people are always considering this Russian girl. He snapped at me.

I said, "Mr. Gregory, I am not speaking for my daughter-in-law. She can do what she wants. I am saying I want to see my son."

And so they brought us to the hospital . . .

MR. RANKIN. And then what happened?

MARGUERITE OSWALD. Then Mr. Perry, the doctor, came down . . . And he said, "Now, I will do whatever you ladies wish . . . However, I will say this. It will not be pleasant. All the blood has been drained from him and it would be much better if you would see him after he was fixed up."

I said, "I am a nurse. I have seen death before. I want to see my son now."

[Marina] said, "I want to see Lee too." So she knew what the doctor was saying.

We were escorted upstairs into a room. They said it was a morgue, but it wasn't. Lee's body was on a hospital . . . table like you take into an operating room. And there were a lot of policemen standing around, guarding the body. And, of course, his face was showing. And Marina went first. She opened his eyelids. Now, to me—I am a nurse, and I don't think I could have done that. This is a very, very strong girl, that she can open a dead man's eyelids. And she says, "He cry. He eye wet." To the doctor. And the doctor says, "Yes."

Well, I know that the fluid leaves, and you do have moisture. So I didn't even touch Lee. I just wanted to . . . make sure it was my son.

So while leaving the room I said to the police—"I think some day you will hang your heads in shame."

I said, "I happen to know, and know some facts, that maybe this is the unsung hero of this episode . . ."

And with that, I left the room.

Then we were . . . introduced to the chaplain . . . at Parkland Hospital [and I] told him that I thought my son was an agent [and] I wanted my son buried in the Arlington Cemetery.

Now, gentlemen, I didn't know that President Kennedy was going to be buried [there]. All I know is that my son is an agent, and that he deserves to be buried in Arlington Cemetery. So I talked to the chaplain about this [and] I asked him if he would talk to Robert because . . . as soon as I started to say something, he would say, "Oh, Mother, forget it." . . .[3]

From the hospital they are driven to the Inn of the Six Flags. Robert comments that "within an hour after our arrival, the inn was like an armed camp":

Robert Oswald: "All we need is to have one more of you killed or injured and we're in real trouble," one of the agents said to me.

We felt completely cut off from the outside world. We were not allowed to see newspapers, listen to the radio, or watch television that Sunday afternoon or Sunday night.[4]

Robert was busy all evening trying to make arrangements for Lee's funeral on Monday. The first step was to hire an undertaker (known even thirty years ago in the Dallas–Fort Worth area as a funeral director).

Robert Oswald: The funeral director began telephoning various cemeteries to prepare the way for me to buy a burial plot for Lee. One cemetery after another refused even to discuss the possibility of accepting Lee's body . . .

While the funeral director was kind enough to continue to search, I began telephoning various ministers in the Dallas-Fort Worth area to request that they officiate at the burial services [and] I was astonished by the reactions. . . . The first one, the second one, the third one, and the fourth one flatly refused even to consider my request.

One of the ministers, a prominent member of the Greater Dallas Council of Churches, listened impatiently . . . and then said sharply, "No, we just can't do that."

"Why not?" I asked.

. . . "Your brother was a sinner."

I hung up. The question of who would officiate at Lee's funeral was still unsettled when I went to bed Sunday night, although the time of the funeral had been set for four o'clock Monday afternoon.[5]

It would hang over him all of Monday morning. His stress is painful to contemplate. Robert is on his way to becoming a successful corporate executive. Yet, like many another straight arrow, he assumes that he must restrain all personal deviations from the approved pattern and to hell with the psychic cost. That psychic cost can be measured by the intensity of the plots one sees everywhere. Robert now exhibits a share of his mother's gift for strong scenarios. He has, for instance, needed but one look on meeting Ruth and Michael Paine early Friday afternoon in the company of Marina and the police to decide that the Paine couple are highly suspicious and could be linked conceivably in some plot with the Russians. Perhaps it was their faintly patrician air. Robert, after all, must have seen a good deal of Alger Hiss in the early days of TV.

He is also more than alert to the growing friction between Secret Service and FBI. He hears the Secret Service agents talking:

Robert Oswald: As early as Friday night I had heard some speculation about the possibility of a conspiracy behind the assassination of the President, and . . . I had wondered if Marina herself might be a part of such a conspiracy. On Saturday and Sunday there were rumors in Dallas that the "conspiracy" might involve some government agency. By Sunday night I realized that the agency under greatest suspicion was the FBI.[6]

Given the covert existence of COINTELPRO in the early Sixties, there may have been reason for suspicion—we shall eventually get an inkling of how distrustful J. Edgar Hoover was of his own people—but in this setting, the rumors had probably been started by police gossip after Oswald's tirade on encountering Hosty in Captain Fritz's office. Of course, it is quintessentially American to love situations that raise suspicions, and who are more American than the Dallas police?

Still, to say that Americans are somewhat enamored of paranoia requires at least this much explanation: Our country was built on the expansive imaginations of people who kept dreaming about the lands to the west—many Americans moved into the wild with no more personal wealth than the strength of their imaginations. When the frontier was finally closed, imagination inevitably turned into paranoia (which can be described, after all, as the enforced enclosure of imagination—its artistic form is a scenario) and, lo, there where the westward expansion stopped on the shores of the Pacific grew Hollywood. It would send its reels of film back to the rest of America, where imagination, now land-locked, had need of scenarios. By the late Fifties and early Sixties, a good many of these scenarios had chosen anti-Communism for their theme—the American imagination saw a Red menace under every bed including Marina Oswald's.

Now, in addition to Robert Oswald's grief over the death of his brother, the horror of the assassination, and his own fear that Lee did it, he could include his suspicions of Marina and the Paines, plus his new look askance at the FBI, only to be faced at the end of all these scenarios with the recognition that it would have been easier to arrange a funeral for a leper than for his brother Lee Harvey Oswald.

Robert Oswald: Finally, two Lutheran ministers who seemed sympathetic appeared at the Inn of the Six Flags about eleven o'clock Monday morning. One stayed in the lobby, but the other came back to see us. The National Council of Churches office in Dallas had asked the ministers to come out and offer to serve at the funeral service, which was now scheduled for 4 P.M. that day at the Rose Hill Cemetery.

The minister did not seem at all eager to officiate, but he did say, rather reluctantly, that he would be at the cemetery at four.[7]

Why were all these ministers being so un-Christian? Well, in Dallas–Fort Worth, it might cost a minister his future assignment to a more prestigious church if he officiated at Oswald's last rites. Soon enough, word arrived that the Lutheran minister who had given his assent to conduct the service had now rescinded it.

While these unhappy negotiations continue, Marguerite finally convinced one of the Secret Service agents to record her on tape—she wanted to set down for posterity why Lee, in her opinion, should, by all rights, be interred in Arlington; but before she had been speaking for long, Robert came out of the bedroom and he was crying and so Marguerite said to the tape recorder, "I'm sorry, but my thoughts have left me because my son is crying."

> MARGUERITE OSWALD. . . . I thought for a moment that Robert was crying because of what I was saying, and he was sorry he had not listened to me before, because I tried to tell him about the defection and my trip to Washington. But Robert was crying because he received a telephone call that we could not get a minister at my son's grave.[8]

Recalling this blow, she informs the Warren Commission of her personal credo, which she is proud to deliver:

> MARGUERITE OSWALD. . . . I have no church affiliation. I have learned since my trouble that my heart is my church. [In that sense] I go to church all day long, I meditate. [Besides] I am working on Sunday most of the time, taking care of the sick, and the people that go to church that I work for, . . . have never once said, "Well, I will stay home and take care of my mother and let you go to church, Mrs. Oswald, today."
>
> You see, I am expected to work on a Sunday.
>
> So that is why—I have my own church. And sometimes I think it is better than a wooden structure . . .[9]

It is a credo for lonely people: My heart is my church.

Meanwhile, the complications continue. At some point, another minister appears:

> MARGUERITE OSWALD. . . . Well, a Reverend French from Dallas came out to Six Flags and we sat on the sofa. [Robert] was crying bitterly and talking to Reverend French and trying to get him to let Lee's body go to church. And he was quoting why he could not.
>
> So then I intervened and said, "Well, if Lee is a lost sheep and that is why you don't want him to go to church, he is [exactly] the one that should go into church . . ."
>
> And that agent [who up until now] had the decency to stay at the far end of the room . . . said, "Mrs. Oswald, be quiet. You are making matters worse."
>
> Now, the nerve of him—[and then] Reverend French [told us] that he could not take the body into the church. And we compromised for chapel services.[10]

The agent who had told Marguerite that she was making matters worse soon reappears in her narrative:

MARGUERITE OSWALD. . . . He was very, very rude to me. Anything that I said, he snapped. At this particular time, they showed the gun on television. I said, "How can they say Lee shot the President? Even though they would prove it is his gun doesn't mean he used it—nobody saw him use it."

He snapped back and he said, "Mrs. Oswald, we know that he shot the President."

I then walked over to Mr. Mike Howard and I said, "What's wrong with that agent? That agent is about to crack. All he has done is taunt me ever since he has been here."

He said, "Mrs. Oswald, he was the personal bodyguard to Mrs. Kennedy for 30 months and maybe he has a little opinion against you."

I said, "Let him keep his personal opinions to himself. He is on a job."[11]

When it comes to circling the wagons around her ego, she is the equal of any FBI or Secret Service man.

Her complaints at the unfeeling deportment of everyone around her will not abate. It is difficult for Marguerite to grieve because she must first pass through the round of her discontents, and they are numerous enough to seal her off from her sorrow:

MARGUERITE OSWALD. Marina was very unhappy with the dress—they brought her two dresses. "Mama, too long." "Mama, no fit." And it looked lovely on her. You can see I know how to dress properly. I am in the business world as merchandise manager. And the dress looked lovely on Marina. But she was not happy with it.

I said, "Oh, honey, put your coat on. We are going to Lee's funeral. It will be all right."

And we had one hour in order to get ready for the funeral.

I said, "We will never make it. Marina is so slow."

She said, "I no slow. I have things to do."[12]

While Marina was complaining about her dress, my little grandbaby, two years old—she is a very precious little baby, they are good children—was standing by her mother. And Marina was very nervous by this time. She was not happy with the dress. And Marina was combing her hair. She took the comb and she hit June on the head. I said, "Marina, don't do that." And this agent—I wish I knew his name—snapped at me and said, "Mrs. Oswald, you let her alone." I said, "Don't tell me what to say to my daughter-in-law when she was hitting my grandbaby on the head with a comb." . . .

Now, why did this man do these things?

MR. RANKIN. Are you saying that the agent did anything improper, as far as Marina was concerned? . . .

MARGUERITE OSWALD. No. I am saying—and I am going to say it as strongly as I can—and I have stated this from the beginning—that I think our trouble in this is in our own Government. And I suspect these two agents of conspiracy with my daughter-in-law in this plot . . .

MR. RANKIN. What kind of a conspiracy are you describing that these men were engaged in?

MARGUERITE OSWALD. The assassination of President Kennedy.

MR. RANKIN. You think that two Secret Service agents and Marina and Mrs. Paine were involved in the conspiracy?

MARGUERITE OSWALD. Yes, I do. Besides another high official.[13]

Grief, fear, rage, woe, and growing detestation of Marguerite are a few of the emotions circulating in the car that goes out to the cemetery that has agreed to accept Lee's body. There, the last rites will be held:

Robert Oswald: Marina, Mother and the children went into the chapel first. I followed, accompanied by Mike Howard and Charlie Kunkel.

The chapel was completely empty. I saw no sign of any preparation for the funeral service.

"I don't understand," I said to Mike and Charlie, and they were obviously puzzled too. They said they would try to find out what had happened.

Two or three minutes later, one of them came back into the chapel, where I had been waiting.

"Well, we were a few minutes late," he said. "There's been some misunderstanding, and they've already carried the casket down to the grave site. We'll have a graveside service down there."[14]

To which Marguerite adds in her testimony, "Robert cried bitterly."[15] She had to know how much he would detest these numerous descriptions of him in tears that she freely offers to the Warren Commission.

Every few yards along the cemetery fence, uniformed officers were on guard.

The coffin was covered in moleskin, and supposedly, the gravediggers did not know that its occupant was Lee Harvey Oswald. They were told that the dead man's name was William Bobo.[16]

Of course, they soon found out. A horde of newsmen had arrived at the cemetery.

Robert Oswald: We drove down a curved road to the grave site. Just before we reached it, one of the Secret Service men turned to Bob Parsons and said, "All right, now. You stay in the car with the carbine. If anything happens, come out shooting."

   "Nothing would give me greater pleasure than to mow down fifteen or twenty reporters," Bob said.

   The Lutheran minister who had promised to be there at four had not appeared, and the Secret Service received word that he would not be coming out. The Reverend Louis Saunders, of the Fort Worth Council of Churches, had driven out to Rose Hill by himself just to see if he could be of any help to Marina and the family. When he was told that the other minister would not be there, the Reverend Mr. Saunders spoke the simple words of the burial service . . .

   I motioned to Mike Howard, and when he came over I told him that I planned to have the coffin opened and would like to have all reporters and spectators moved back some distance from the grave site. He nodded, and almost immediately six or eight plainclothesmen from the Fort Worth police department formed a kind of protective semicircle between us and the crowd, insuring a certain amount of privacy.

   Mother, Marina, the children and I then got up and walked toward the open coffin. After I had taken a last, long look at my brother's face, I turned to go back to the place where we had been sitting. I then noticed the semicircle of plainclothesmen standing guard, solemn and stony-faced. . . .[17]

They are stony-faced, and Robert has been weeping. For two days now he has been unable to control himself. His emotions seem to be the most poignant among the assembled, but then, the love of an older brother for a younger one is rarely without its paradox, since the kid brother is the first human being one has been able to control, scorn, bully, scold, tease, and torment, while beneath, sometimes wholly concealed from oneself, a reservoir of love can well up through the years. Lee wrote a long letter to Robert one month after coming to Moscow in 1959, and one can wonder whether Robert was recalling its contents now in the hours after Lee was shot. The letter was certainly at a distance from recent events, and it could hardly have been a communication Robert enjoyed—indeed, it denied everything he believed—but yet, its tone suggests a bond between the brothers. Is that now part of Robert's grief? Written in a lonely hotel room by a young man just turned twenty, the sentiments are so steeped in the passion, innocence, and idealism of a very young man that the words could have rested silently in the very center of Robert's feelings for his kid brother. Now, even as Lee is buried, it may be worth going back to this letter to note how much has changed in four years:

Nov. 16, 1959

Dear Robert,

. . . I will ask you a question, Robert: What do you support the American government for? What is the ideal you put forward? Do not say "freedom" because freedom is a word used by all peoples through all of time. Ask me and I will tell you I fight for *communism*. This word brings to your mind slaves or injustice, this is because of American propaganda . . . you speak of advantages. Do you think that is why I am here? For personal, material advantage? Happiness is not based on oneself, it does not consist of a small home, of taking and getting. Happiness is taking part in the struggle where there is no borderline between one's own personal world and the world in general. I never believed I would find more material advantages at *this* stage of development in the Soviet Union than I might have had in the U.S. . . .

You probably know little about this country so I will tell you about it. I did find, as I suspected I would, that most of what is written about the Soviet Union in America is for the better part fabrication. The people here have a seven

hour work day now and only work till three o'clock on Saturdays with Sundays off. They have socialization which
means they do not pay for their apartments or for medical
care. The money for this comes from the profit they help
to create in their labor, which in the U.S. goes to capital-
ists . . . Most important [here] is the fact they do not work
for employers at all, a milkman or a factory supervisor are
both socially equal. This does not mean they have the
same salary, of course. This just means their work goes for
[the] common good of all.

These people are a good, warm, alive people. They wish
to see all peoples live in peace, but at the same time, they
wish to see the economically enslaved people of the West
free. They believe in their ideals and they support their
government and country to the full limit.

You say you have not renounced me. Good, I am glad,
but I will tell you on what terms I want this arrangement.

I want you to understand what I say now, I do not say
lightly or unknowingly, since I have been in the military as
you know, and I know what war is like.

1. In the event of war I would kill *any* American who put
a uniform on in defense of the American government—
any American.

2. That in my own mind I have no attachments of any
kind in the U.S.

3. That I want to, and I shall, live a normal, happy and
peaceful life here in the Soviet Union *for the rest of my life.*

4. That my mother and you are (in spite of what the
newspapers said) *not* objects of affection, but only examples of workers in the U.S.

You should not try to remember me in any way I used to
be since I am only now showing you how I am. I am not all
bitterness or hate, I came here only to find freedom. In
truth, I feel I am at last with my own people. But do not let
me give you the impression I am in another world. These
people are so much like Americans and people the world
over. They simply have an economic system and the ideal
of communism which the U.S. does not have. I would
never have been personally happy in the U.S. . . .

It is snowing here in Moscow now, which makes everything look very nice. I can see the Kremlin and Red Square

and I have just finished a dinner of *mjaso i kartoshka,* meat and potatoes. So you see the Russians are not so different from you and I.

Lee[18]

Doubtless, he had not only written the letter for Robert but for Soviet eyes as well. Certainly, he had wanted to impress his new country with his desire to serve. He did not know that he was orating into the face of general agreement among Soviet authorities that this young American was essentially ignorant of Marxism. Indeed, he was—his knowledge of Marxism was pre–World War I. He had no idea of the ponderous immensity of the new system or of the elephantiasis of that bureaucracy which had burgeoned out of Lenin's vaulting confidence that human nature was a river like any other, there to be dammed and channeled by the foresight of social engineers imbued with the correct revolutionary spirit.

So, that earlier letter to Robert now sits on the page with all the irony of a repudiated testament, equal in its romantic excess to a declaration of love to a former mate. We can measure the hardening of Oswald's spirit in the journey he has taken from that impassioned outburst to where he presently rests in a grave bought in the name of William Bobo.

PART VII

THE AMATEUR
HIT MAN

1

The Amateur Hit Man

The mystery of Oswald subsumes the enigma of Jack Ruby. Yet, if the first mystery has haunted the American intelligence establishment with the fear that it is implicated, Jack Ruby buggers reasonable comprehension for the rest of us. A minor thug from the streets of Chicago with a mentally unbalanced and often hospitalized mother, he has Mob connections. While they are no more impressive than those cherished by a hundred thousand other petty hoodlums in fifty American cities—which is to say, connections so tenuous and yet so familial that one can make a whole case or no case out of the same material—he has grown up among the Mob, and is on a first-name basis with Mob figures of the middle ranks. He is of the Mob in the specific values of his code, and yet never a formal member in any way—too wacky, too eager, too obsessed with himself, too Jewish even for the Jewish Mob. All the same, he is pure Mafia in one part of his spirit—he wants to be known as a patriot in love with his country and his people. He is loyal. Select him and you will not make a mistake.

We all know his famous story or cover story. He was grief-stricken by the death of JFK, so bereaved that he shut down his strip-joints for the weekend, and was so appalled at the possibility that Jacqueline Kennedy might have to come to Dallas to testify in Oswald's trial that he decided to shoot the accused—"the creep," as he would call him. But only at the last moment did he so decide. No premeditation. At 11:17 on Sunday morning, after waiting on line at a Western Union office to send $25 to one of his strippers who was desperately in need of money, he crossed the street, went down the ramp into police headquarters, and ran smack into Oswald, who was being filmed by TV cameras in the basement as he walked with his police escort to a car that would take him to the

County Jail. There, imprinting the American mind forever with the open-mouthed expression of the victim and the squint-eyed disbelief of his guards, Ruby killed Oswald. Never before in history was a death witnessed by so many people giving full attention to their television sets. Much of the world now believed that Ruby was a Mafia hit man. The logic of such an inference suggested a conspiracy not only to kill Kennedy but Oswald as well, because he knew too much.

The concept, clear as a good movie scenario, ran into one confusion that has never been resolved: Why was Ruby standing on line in Western Union waiting his turn to send $25 to a stripper while time kept floating away and Oswald might be moved at any moment? The question could not be answered. How many confederates—and most of them had to be police—would be necessary to coordinate such a move? No one who is the key figure in a careful schedule that will reach its climax just as the target is being transferred is going to be found dawdling across the street at a Western Union office with only a few minutes to go. It would take hours for a stage director to begin to choreograph such a scene for an opera.

Ruby himself would say in the last interview he gave before he died of cancer that there was no way he could have been part of any calculation to bring him there at just the instant Oswald passed unless "it was the most perfect conspiracy in the history of the world . . . the difference in meeting this fate was thirty seconds one way or the other."[1]

So, the death of Oswald is filled with the groans of thwarted logic. Yet never on the face of it has a crime seemed to belong more to the Mafia.

In a brilliant book exploring the rifts within the American establishment, *The Yankee and Cowboy War,* Carl Oglesby was the first to advance the notion that Ruby was trying to tell Earl Warren that the Mafia certainly did order him to commit the deed. If Warren would just fly him, Jack Ruby, back to Washington on that same day, he, Jack Ruby, could furnish Warren with all the truth and, to prove it, would take a lie detector test on the spot.

As one reads these declarations in Jack Ruby's testimony, it is difficult not to believe that Oglesby is right. In the course of a half hour, Ruby repeats his request five times.

MR. RUBY. Is there any way to get me to Washington?

CHIEF JUSTICE WARREN. I beg your pardon?

MR. RUBY. Is there any way of you getting me to Washington?

CHIEF JUSTICE WARREN. I don't know of any. I will be glad to talk to your counsel about what the situation is, Mr. Ruby, when we get an opportunity to talk.

MR. RUBY. I don't think I will get a fair representation with my counsel, Joe Tonahill. I don't think so . . .[2]

He disavows Joe Tonahill. He is all but saying that he cannot know whom his lawyer is working for.

In another minute, he repeats himself:

MR. RUBY. . . . Gentlemen, unless you get me to Washington, you can't get a fair shake out of me.

If you understand my way of talking, you have got to bring me to Washington to get the tests.

Do I sound dramatic? Off the beam?

CHIEF JUSTICE WARREN. No; you are speaking very rationally, and I am really surprised that you can remember as much as you have remembered up to the present time.

You have given it to us in detail.

MR. RUBY. Unless you can get me to Washington, and I am not a crackpot, I have all my senses—I don't want to evade any crime I am guilty of.[3]

Five minutes go by. They speak of other matters.

Then Ruby pushes his request again, even takes it another step:

MR. RUBY. . . . Gentlemen, if you want to hear any further testimony, you will have to get me to Washington soon, because it has something to do with you, Chief Warren.

Do I sound sober enough to tell you this?

CHIEF JUSTICE WARREN. Yes; go right ahead.

MR. RUBY. I want to tell the truth, and I can't tell it here. I can't tell it here. Does that make sense to you?

CHIEF JUSTICE WARREN. Well, let's not talk about sense. But I really can't see why you can't tell this Commission.[4]

Well, he can't. Not in Dallas. Ruby all but shrieks at them: You dummies!—can't you see that I can't tell it here? You people don't run this town. You can't protect me in Dallas. I'll get knifed in my cell, and the guards will be looking the other way.

MR. RUBY. . . . My reluctance to talk—you haven't had any witness in telling the story, in finding so many problems?

CHIEF JUSTICE WARREN. You have a greater problem than any witness we ever had.

MR. RUBY. I have a lot of reasons for having those problems . . . If you request me to go back to Washington with you right now, that couldn't be done, could it?

CHIEF JUSTICE WARREN. No; it could not be done. It could not be done. There are a good many things involved in that, Mr. Ruby.

MR. RUBY. What are they?

CHIEF JUSTICE WARREN. Well, the public attention that it would attract, and the people who would be around. We have no place there for you to be safe when we take you out, and there are not law enforcement officers, and it isn't our responsibility to go into anything of that kind . . .[5]

Ruby tries to explain it to them in the simplest terms. "Gentlemen, my life is in danger." Then he adds, "Not with my guilty plea of execution." (He has been sentenced to death by a jury in Dallas.) No, he is trying to tell them: I will be killed a lot sooner than that.

MR. RUBY. . . . Do I sound sober enough to you as I say this?

CHIEF JUSTICE WARREN. You do. You sound entirely sober.

MR. RUBY. From the moment I started my testimony, have I sounded as though, with the exception of becoming emotional, have I sounded as though I made sense, what I was speaking about?

CHIEF JUSTICE WARREN. You have indeed. I understood everything you have said. If I haven't, it is my fault.

MR. RUBY. Then I follow this up. I may not live tomorrow to give any further testimony . . . the only thing I want to get out to the public, and I can't say it here, is with authenticity, with sincerity of the truth of everything and why my act was committed, but it can't be said here . . .

Chairman Warren, if you felt that your life was in danger at the moment, how would you feel? Wouldn't you be reluctant to go on speaking, even though you request me to do so?

CHIEF JUSTICE WARREN. I think I might have some reluctance if I was in your position, yes; I should think I would. I think I would figure it out very carefully as to whether it would endanger me or not.

If you think that anything that I am doing or anything that I am asking you is endangering you in any way, shape, or form, I want you to feel absolutely free to say that when the interview is over.

MR. RUBY. What happens then? I didn't accomplish anything.

CHIEF JUSTICE WARREN. No; nothing has been accomplished.

MR. RUBY. Well, then you won't follow up with anything further?

CHIEF JUSTICE WARREN. There wouldn't be anything to follow up if you hadn't completed your statement.

MR. RUBY. You said you have the power to do what you want to do, is that correct?

CHIEF JUSTICE WARREN. Exactly.

MR. RUBY. Without any limitations?

CHIEF JUSTICE WARREN. . . . We have the right to take testimony of anyone we want in this whole situation, and we have the right . . . to verify that statement in any way that we wish to do it.

MR. RUBY. But you don't have a right to take a prisoner back with you when you want to?

CHIEF JUSTICE WARREN. No; we have the power to subpoena witnesses to Washington if we want to do it, but we have taken the testimony of 200 or 300 people, I would imagine, here in Dallas without going to Washington.

MR. RUBY. Yes; but those people aren't Jack Ruby.

CHIEF JUSTICE WARREN. No; they weren't.

MR. RUBY. They weren't.[6]

In the pause, Ruby tries to inform them of the incalculable depth of the peril he feels:

MR. RUBY. I tell you, gentlemen, my whole family is in jeopardy. My sisters, as to their lives.

CHIEF JUSTICE WARREN. Yes?

MR. RUBY. Naturally, I am a foregone conclusion. My sisters Eva, Eileen, and Mary . . .

My brothers Sam, Earl, Hyman, and myself naturally—my in-laws, Harold Kaminsky, Marge Ruby, the wife of Earl, and Phyllis, the wife of Sam Ruby, they are in jeopardy of loss of their lives . . . just because they are blood related to myself—does that sound serious enough for you, Chief Justice Warren?

CHIEF JUSTICE WARREN. Nothing could be more serious, if that is the fact . . .[7]

At this point, Ruby begins to despair of reaching Warren with his message. He cannot know how great the odds are that Lyndon Johnson has already reached Earl Warren more than half a year earlier with an even more secret message—*lone gunman; no conspiracy; the calm and well-being of our country is asking for nothing less.* So Ruby, in all the lacerated but still functioning wounds of his sensibility, is beginning to recognize that his own agenda is hopeless. If he keeps talking this way and Warren does not listen to him, then the record of this testimony could open him and his family to Mafia reprisal. So he returns—he reverts—to the sound of his own music, his operatic cover story: He invokes the name of Jackie Kennedy.

MR. RUBY. . . . I felt very emotional and very carried away for Mrs. Kennedy, that with all the strife she had gone through—I had been following it pretty well—that someone owed it to our beloved President that she shouldn't be expected to come back to face trial of this heinous crime.

And I have never had the chance to tell that, to back it up, to prove it.[8]

Since he has already spoken of threats to his life and to his brothers and sisters and Warren will not take him back to Washington, he now has to remove all onus from the Mafia. So he brings in the John Birch Society, but vaguely . . . vaguely . . . No one can follow him now.

MR. RUBY. . . . there is a John Birch Society right now in activity, and Edwin Walker is one of the top men of this organization—take it for what it is worth, Chief Justice Warren.

Unfortunately for me, for me giving the people the opportunity to get in power, because of the act I committed, has put a lot of people in jeopardy with their lives.

Don't register with you, does it?

CHIEF JUSTICE WARREN. No; I don't understand that.[9]

Back goes Ruby to Jackie Kennedy. It may not be very convincing, but at least it is a story that cannot be disproven. What with the way he has learned to talk, back and forth, in and out, about and around, nobody is going to get into his head and refute his tale.

MR. RUBY. Yes . . . a small comment in the newspaper that . . . Mrs. Kennedy may have to come back for the trial of Lee Harvey Oswald.

That caused me to go like I did; that caused me to go like I did.

I don't know, Chief Justice, but I got so carried away. And I remember prior to that thought, there has never been another thought in my mind; I was never malicious toward this person. No one else requested me to do anything.[10]

"No one . . . requested me to do anything."

If a copy of this transcript gets out—and there are lawyers and lawyers' clerks abounding in the halls of Ruby's paranoia ready to rush to the wrong people with just such a text—he can always point to this line: "No one else requested me to do anything."

It is so serious to him, and so godawful. He, Jack Ruby—a good and generous man who fought his way up from the Chicago streets into a decent existence, a semi-decent existence, anyway—is now going to be executed by the government, or else he will be killed by some Mafia minion, some prison guard or convict, in a jail he knows is not safe, because of a crime he did not wish to commit in the first place.

It is monstrously unfair to Ruby, thinks Ruby, and more unfair to his family. The people outside who will punish him if he rats on them are evil. And evil has no bounds, as Hitler proved. So, if Jack Ruby tries to explain to the Warren Commission that he was only an agent in the death of Oswald, a pawn for the Mafia leaders who passed the order down the line to the man who gave him the order, then there will be Mafia leaders rabid with rage because he tried to rat on them. In retaliation, they will yet kill all the Jews. The safety of the Jews always hangs by a hair, anyway.

Let us try to assimilate the reasoning. It is not that Ruby is insane. He is, however, all but insane: He has an even larger sense of the importance of his own life than did Oswald. If they kill Ruby, feels Ruby, then all of his immediate family and his larger family, world Jewry, is in peril.

So he rallies for one more attempt:

> MR. RUBY. . . . it is pretty haphazard to tell you the things I should tell you . . . I am in a tough spot and I do not know what the solution can be to save me . . . I want to say this to you . . . The Jewish people are being exterminated at this moment. Consequently, a whole new form of government is going to take over our country, and I know I won't live to see you another time.
>
> Do I sound sort of screwy in telling you these things?
>
> CHIEF JUSTICE WARREN. No; I think that is what you believe, or you wouldn't tell it under your oath.
>
> MR. RUBY. But it is a very serious situation. I guess it is too late to stop it, isn't it?[11]

If he cannot save himself, then he cannot save humanity. He is, unknowingly, a spiritual brother to Oswald. The fate of mankind, so each reasoned separately, rested on his shoulders.

He makes his very last attempt. How many times will he have to spell it out? Can't they comprehend why he must get to Washington for these lie detector tests?

> MR. RUBY. I have been used for a purpose, and there will be a certain tragic occurrence happening if you don't take my testimony and somehow vindicate me so my people don't suffer because of what I have done.[12]

Yes, if I am killed, my people will be killed.

> MR. RUBY. . . . Because when you leave here, I am finished. My family is finished.
>
> REPRESENTATIVE FORD. Isn't it true, Mr. Chief Justice, that the same maximum protection and security Mr. Ruby has been given in the past will be continued?
>
> MR. RUBY. But now that I have divulged certain information . . .[13]

He has spoken too much on this day, he is trying to tell Gerry Ford. His security will be affected. "I want to take a polygraph test," he tells them, but "maybe certain people don't want to know the truth that may come out of me. Is that plausible?"[14]

If Ruby is not out of his mind, merely all-but-insane—that is, highly disturbed but sane—then he really does seem to be saying that he acted as a hit man. Yet there is still the odd wait on line in the Western Union office. How to explain that?

We had better take a look at a few Mafia sentiments concerning Kennedy. Indeed, we are obliged to.

For months, through all of 1963, there had been low sounds rumbling down from the summits. "Who will remove this stone from my shoe?" asked Carlos Marcello, referring to Jack Kennedy as the stone, and Santos Trafficante had said worse. Jimmy Hoffa was livid on the subject of the Kennedys. Not only was there a host of rumors after November 22 that Trafficante, Marcello, and Hoffa had given the order to kill Jack Kennedy, but indeed the House Select Committee on Assassinations, so far as it came to a conclusion, decided in 1979 that the Mafia probably had done it (although, certainly, no smoking gun was found).

Recently a book, *Mob Lawyer,* by Frank Ragano, Trafficante's legal counselor, was a bit more specific, although no more can be claimed for such a work in relation to the assassination than that it is a teaser; but Ragano does make it clear that Marcello and Trafficante certainly wanted Jimmy Hoffa to believe they were responsible for the act. "You tell him he owes me, and he owes me big," said Marcello to Ragano,[15] passing a message to Hoffa in impeccable Sicilian metaphor that a proper repayment for such a coup might be to receive a loan of $3.5 million from the Teamsters' pension fund for investment in a lavish French Quarter hotel that Marcello and Trafficante wished to open. Ragano's disclosure supplies no witness to their conversation but Trafficante (now dead).

Nonetheless, it stimulates one's own imagination toward two hypotheses, each of which, for our purposes, can point in the same direction. An hypothesis, no matter how uncomfortable or bizarre on its first presentation, will thrive or wither by its ability to explain the facts available: These two hypotheses are able not only to live but to nourish themselves on the numerous details Gerald Posner gathered from various sources in his long and careful delineation of Jack Ruby's movements during the three days, Friday, Saturday, and Sunday, of Oswald's incarceration. Indeed, Posner's chapter on Ruby may be the most careful and well-written section in his book.

Posner amasses these details to prove that Ruby was not acting under orders but was mentally unbalanced, and he gives us more than thirty pages of text as he follows Ruby's behavior after the President's death.

It will be interesting, however, to use Posner's carefully collected details to support an opposite point—that Ruby killed Oswald under orders from above.

Let us take up our two hypotheses. The first, and larger, one is that Marcello and/or Trafficante did give an order sometime in September, October, or November to assassinate Jack Kennedy. Given, however, the solemnity of such a deed and the dangers surrounding such an attempt, the precautions employed to wall themselves off from the act would have been so thoroughgoing that the order had to pass through a number of cut-outs, and each cut-out would only be able to identify the man who had given him his order. Be it said that the executive details of the assassination were left to people at the other end of the line—those who would do the deed. So great was the separation, in fact, that Marcello and/or Trafficante would not know the killer (or killers) or the date or the place. It could happen anywhere—Miami, Texas, Washington, New York—it would not matter. They would not be near any of the immediate details.

Immediately after the assassination of Kennedy occurred, they assumed—how would they not?—that it was the fulfillment of their order. When they learned, therefore, in the first hour that Oswald was calling himself a patsy, his fate was sealed. A patsy talks—Oswald had to be removed. That he was the nephew of Dutz Murret and so could be connected, no matter how indirectly, to Marcello doubled the need to get rid of him. That he had not been one of their killers and had nothing to do with them might never have occurred to Marcello or Trafficante. They were hardly going to be in conference with their cut-outs. Instead, a quick order was sent out: Put a hit on Oswald. This time they were in a rush, so there were probably not as many cut-outs; and more than one candidate for hit man in Dallas may have been selected, either in the way of locals or out-of-state professionals quickly dispatched there on Friday afternoon. Ruby—so this hypothesis would go—was one of the putative hit men. He was an amateur, a flake, and might be lacking enough dedication to pull off the job.

But Ruby did present two positive factors: He was, when all was said, a part of their culture—he would be afraid to talk—and he had the huge and unique advantage of access. For every soldier they made, the Mafia knew the characters and habits of a thousand men. So they also knew that Ruby was on good, friendly terms with at least a hundred Dallas cops. Ergo, Ruby could get to Oswald. He might not be the best man for the job, but he was certainly the one who would have the best chance of doing it in the shortest possible time.

Word, therefore, was passed to him by somebody he saw on Friday afternoon. It would be rank speculation to fix on Ralph Paul, Ruby's oldest friend, a man then in his sixties, for Paul was gentle and had no more known relations to the Mafia than that he ran a restaurant in Dallas. Of course, it can be said that big-city restaurant owners are rarely without liaison to the Mob. Ralph Paul was also one of Ruby's closest friends and was owed tens of thousands of dollars by Ruby—which the Mob would also have known. Ralph Paul could have delivered a message: "Kill Oswald and *they* will take care of you."

If the question was how could Ruby do the deed and get away with it, the answer was that with the right lawyer, Ruby would only receive a few years or, with a defense on grounds of insanity, might get away with no time at all. His financial condition could certainly be alleviated. His deep debts would be rearranged, and the money he owed to the IRS could be paid off. And for motive Ruby was furnished with a beautiful if crazy reason, or came up with the reason himself—which is even more likely—because the reason existed already as a kind of minor motive within him, a small infatuation: He was the kind of exceedingly sentimental man who would indeed have detested the pain it would cause Jackie Kennedy to testify in Dallas. An actor can play a killer, or a lover, or a policeman, or a thief if even 5 percent of such a possibility exists within him. Ruby was an actor manqué: He had the first requirement for good stage performance—his emotions were quickly available, so available indeed that they kept intruding on his syntax, which is why his speeches are sometimes so hard to follow.

The above is the first hypothesis. The second is simpler. Marcello and Trafficante had made their noises back and forth with Hoffa about getting a hit on the President, but they had issued no orders. They had merely fumed, and been afraid to make such a move. Yet when the President was killed, they had an opportunity to rake in some huge profits with Teamster funds, so they took pains to let Hoffa know that they had been the masterminds behind the deed. Indeed, Ragano hints at this likelihood in *Mob Lawyer:* "If there was a possibility of making big money, Santo and Carlos were capable of conning Jimmy into believing they had arranged the assassination solely for his benefit."[16] Now Jimmy could show his appreciation by diverting those Teamster pension monies into a loan for their hotel. The problem was Oswald. When he talked, assuming he would, Hoffa would be able to see that Marcello and Trafficante had had nothing to do with the death in Dealey Plaza. So Oswald had to be marked for extinction.

Hypothesis One and Hypothesis Two may be at great variance, but they come to the same conclusion—given the need to move quickly: Jack Ruby is anointed to be a hit man.

That he did not see it as an honor is evident in his behavior. The assignment is equal to the total disruption of his life. Ralph Paul, if he was the last cut-out to Ruby, would have issued no personal threats, but then, he would not have had to. To disobey that kind of order would prove considerably more damaging than the cost of doing the deed. Ruby could only guess who might have initiated such a project, but whoever the top man was, he would not be sitting far from the devil's right hand.

If we are now in position to see whether the details collected by Posner conflict or agree with the common point of these two hypotheses, the first question to pose is when Ruby might have been given such an order: The earliest time that one can reasonably suggest is when he talked to Ralph Paul, at about 2:45 that Friday afternoon. It was only an hour and a quarter after the announcement of the death, but then, the move from above could have been quick. Marcello and Trafficante may have been renowned not only for their caution but for their speed.

Posner: The Carousel's records show a call to the Bullpen [Paul's] restaurant at 2:42 for less than a minute. When Ruby discovered Paul was not at his restaurant but instead at home, he telephoned him there. The phone record shows he called Paul at 2:43.[17]

MR. PAUL. . . . when I got home Jack called me and he said, "Did you hear what happened?" I said, "Yes; I heard it on the air." He says, "Isn't that a terrible thing?" I said, "Yes; Jack." He said, "I made up my mind. I'm going to close it down." . . .

MR. HUBERT. Did he discuss with you whether he should close down?

MR. PAUL. No; he didn't discuss it. He told me he was going to close down.[18]

Unless it was Paul who told him to. Ralph Paul, as the message bearer, could well have said: "Jack, you've got to close down for the next couple of days. You are going to need all your free time to find a way to bring this off."

Posner presents evidence that would oppose such an assumption. Ruby is very emotional in the office of the *Dallas Morning News* after he first hears of the attack, and speaks already of how awful it is for Jackie Kennedy and her children. He is crying when he leaves the newspaper office. This, however, is only by Ruby's own account to the Warren Commission: "I left the building and I went down and got my car, and I couldn't stop crying . . ."[19] But he may have been lying, particularly if he did not start crying until later that day.

In any event, he visits his sister twice that afternoon, and by then must certainly have been given the word. His sister was ill in bed, having just returned to her home a few days before from an abdominal operation, and he had gone out to shop for her.

Posner: Ruby was back at Eva's by 5:30 and stayed for two hours.

Eva said he returned with "enough groceries for 20 people . . . but he didn't know what he was doing then." He told her that he wanted to close the clubs. "And he said, 'Listen, we are broke anyway, so I will be a broken millionaire. I am going to close for three days.' " In dire financial straits, and barely breaking even with both clubs open seven days a week, his decision to close was an important gesture . . .

But his sister Eva witnessed the real depth of his anguish, and unwittingly contributed to it. "He was sitting on this chair and crying. . . . He was sick to his stomach . . . and went into the bathroom . . . He looked terrible."[20]

As she says to the Warren Commission:

MRS. GRANT. . . . he just wasn't himself, and truthfully, so help me, [he said] "Somebody tore my heart out," and he says, "I didn't even feel so bad when pops died because poppa was an old man."[21]

This, she indicates, is the worst state she has ever seen him in. That he has brought more food than anyone can eat is natural. Food is life, and his life may soon be over. It is all very well to take a shot at Oswald, but what if he, Jack Ruby, is mowed down in the process?

Once he left his sister's house, he went over to police headquarters at City Hall, where Oswald was being interrogated. He never had had trouble getting in before, and now, given the exceptional influx of newsmen, there was no difficulty at all. From 6:00 P.M. on, he was there, expecting, but not knowing whether he would have, an opportunity to get near enough to Oswald to do the job.

> *Posner:* John Rutledge, the night police reporter for the *Dallas Morning News,* knew Ruby. He saw him step off the elevator, hunched between two out-of-state reporters with press identifications on their coats. "The three of them just walked past policemen, around the corner, past those cameras and lights, and on down the hall," recalled Rutledge. The next time Rutledge saw him, he was standing outside room 317, where Oswald was being interrogated, and "he was explaining to members of the out-of-state press who everybody was that came in and out of the door. . . . There would be a thousand questions shot at him at once, and Jack would straighten them all out. . . ." Soon several detectives walked by, and one recognized him. "Hey, Jack, what are you doing here?" "I am helping all these fellows," Ruby said, pointing to the pack of reporters . . .
>
> Victor Robertson, a WFAA Radio reporter, also knew Ruby. He saw him approach the door to the office where Oswald was being interrogated and start to open it. "He had the door open a few inches," recalled Robertson, "and began to step into the room, and the two officers stopped him. . . . One of them said, 'You can't go in there, Jack.' "
>
> Ruby probably left police headquarters shortly after 8:30 . . .[22]

He had failed in his first attempt. Now he made a quick trip to his apartment, where he found George Senator, his roommate, at home. Senator later stated in an affidavit that it happened to be the "first time I ever saw tears in his eyes."[23] Then Ruby went on to his synagogue. No surprise if he was ready to pray.

> *Posner:* He cried openly at the synagogue. "They didn't believe a guy like Jack would ever cry," said his brother Hyman. "Jack never cried in his life. He is not that kind of a guy . . ."[24]

Yes, he will tell people, he simply cannot bear the thought of that beautiful woman, the former First Lady, Jacqueline Kennedy, being obliged to return to Dallas and testify. You pay your money and you take your choice, but as a betting proposition—with all due respect to Jacqueline Kennedy—it must be 18 to 5 that Ruby is thinking of himself. And if it were anyone but Jacqueline Kennedy, the odds might be 99 to 1 that he is brooding about no one but himself. All he has is his life, and it is being taken away from him. A precious gem, a ruby, is about to be thrown into the crapper.

After the synagogue, he went right back to police headquarters.

> *Posner:* When he arrived at the third floor of the station, he encountered a uniformed officer who did not recognize him. Ruby saw several detectives he knew, shouted to them, and they helped him get inside. Once there, he said he was "carried away with the excitement of history." Detective A. M. Eberhardt, who knew Ruby and had been at his club, was in the burglary-and-theft section when Jack "stuck his head in our door and hollered at us. . . . He came in and said hello to me, shook hands with me. I asked him what he was doing. He told me he was a translator for the newspapers. . . . He said, 'I am here as a reporter' and he took the notebook and hit it."[25]

He has taken cognizance of the situation. He has not been a vendor in ball parks and burlesque houses and a street hustler for too little: He is laying the groundwork to become indispensable to any number of reporters. He never knows when the right door will open and the opportunity will be there. This is the field of operations, and he may have a chance to try again before midnight.

> *Posner:* In less than half an hour, Oswald was brought out of room 317 on the way to the basement assembly room for the

midnight press conference. Ruby recalled that as Oswald walked past, "I was standing about two or three feet away."[26]

The challenge has to be equivalent to jumping for the first time into a quarry pool from a height of forty or fifty feet. And Ruby cannot take the step. All he has to do is pull out his gun and finish Oswald off, but he cannot make the move. It is, after all, a vertiginous leap.

He is sick at his own cowardice, even as all of us are when we fail to take that daring little jump which some higher instinct, or a bully, or a parent, or a brother, is commanding us to take.

Posner: In his first statement to the FBI, Ruby admitted he had his .38 caliber revolver with him on Friday night (Commission Document 1252.9). Later, when he realized that carrying his pistol might be construed as evidence of premeditation, he said he did not have his gun on Friday. However, a photo of the rear of Ruby, taken in the third-floor corridor that night, shows a lump under the right rear of his jacket. If he was a mob-hired killer with a contract on Oswald, he would have shot him at the first opportunity. Certainly, any contract to kill Oswald would not have been one Ruby could fulfill at his leisure. Yet when he had the perfect opportunity, with Oswald only a couple of feet away, Ruby did not shoot him.[27]

Posner may lack empathy here. Just because you are told to kill Oswald doesn't mean you can do it. Indeed, Ruby may still be looking for some way to perform the act and yet get out scot-free. That is a fantasy, but then, he is not a professional killer. What he cannot stomach is that there seems no way he will be able to follow orders without paying a prohibitive price.

In the meantime, to cut the losses to his ego, he continues networking.

MR. PAPPAS. It was at this point that I ran into Ruby—the first time that I recall. He came up to me as I was waiting for Wade and he said . . . "Are you a reporter?" I said, "Yes." . . . And he reached into his pocket, and he pulled out a card. It said the Carousel Club on it. And I was amazed. I didn't know who he was or what he was. My immediate impression of him was that he was a detective. He was well dressed, nattily dressed, I imag-

ine. [A little later] he said, "What's the matter?" I said, "I am trying to get Henry Wade over to the telephone." He said, "Do you
want me to get him?" . . . I said, "Yes, I would like to have him
over here." And he went around the desk, over to Henry Wade
on the telephone . . ."[28]

Ruby is investing more and more of himself in a role that
enables him to hang around the third floor, waiting to pick up a
better opportunity. It helps that he loves the role. As long as he
can live within it, he can, like an actor, feel vital and alive; he can
keep the dread of his real mission apart from himself.

Once he leaves police headquarters, however, he has to pass
through a *Walpurgisnacht*. He wanders back and forth to newspaper offices and takes sandwiches to the people working at KLIF. In
between, he spends an hour in a car talking to a couple, Kathy
Kay, a former stripper at the Carousel, and Harry Olsen,[29] a
policeman, and all three are talking in Olsen's car about how terrible it must be for Jackie Kennedy. The stripper begins to weep
and the men join her with a few tears. In the moil and meld of
such mutual compassion for Jackie Kennedy, all three feel respect
for each other, deep respect, and each expresses it so.

After more wandering through the Dallas night, Ruby goes back
to his apartment and wakes up George Senator.

MR. SENATOR. Yes; it was different. It was different; the way he
looked at you . . .

MR. HUBERT. Had you seen him in that condition before?

MR. SENATOR. . . . I have seen him hollering, things like I told
you in the past, but this here, he had sort of a stare look in his
eye . . .

MR. GRIFFIN. I didn't catch that. What kind of a look?

MR. SENATOR. A stare look; I don't know . . . I don't know how to
put it into words.

MR. HUBERT. But it was different from anything you had ever
seen on Jack Ruby before?

MR. SENATOR. Yes.

MR. HUBERT. And it was noticeably so?

MR. SENATOR. Oh yes.[30]

Ruby then calls up his handyman, Larry Crafard, at the Carousel, wakes him up, and drives the youth and George Senator out to a billboard in Dallas that says: IMPEACH EARL WARREN. Ruby had been very upset earlier that day when he saw an ad, taken out by a man named Bernard Weissman, in the *Dallas Morning News* alluding to Jack Kennedy as a Communist supporter. He is now convinced that the John Birch Society invented the name Weissman in order to blame the Jews.

Now he, Jack Ruby, will soon be one of the Jews being blamed for the death of Kennedy, even if he will only be blamed in the secondary sense that *they* have selected him to be the one to kill Oswald. So Jack Ruby, a Jew, will pay the second heaviest price. He is a scapegoat, just like the Jews in the Holocaust, and just like all Jews who will soon be blamed for the Weissman ad.

In his distraught state, he takes photographs of the billboard—IMPEACH EARL WARREN—as if this is not only evidential material of some sort but may even prove sacramental for someone in his position. If he is acting a little loopy, well, very few hit men out on a mission are reputed to comport themselves as one hundred percent sane.

It is daybreak on Saturday before he drops Larry Crafard off at the Carousel and the handyman promptly goes back to sleep on the sofa in Ruby's office.

Crafard has his revenge, however, by telephoning Ruby at eight-thirty in the morning. There is no food for the dogs at the Carousel, he tells his boss. Ruby flies into a rage for having had his sleep disturbed and proceeds to chew Crafard out as he never has before. Indeed, his language is so personal that Crafard packs his stuff and takes off. He is angry enough or uneasy enough to hitch-hike back home to Michigan.

Somewhat later that morning, we learn from Posner,

Ruby turned on the television and saw a memorial service broadcast from New York. "I watched Rabbi Seligman," he recalled. "He eulogized that here is a man [JFK] that fought in every battle, went to every country, and had to come back to his own country to be shot in the back. That created a tremendous emotional feeling for me, the way he said that."[31]

Doubtless, Ruby is trying to find impressive reasons for his intended act. He is too big a man to do such a job just because the

Mob has ordered it; no, he is potentially an honorable Jewish patriot who wishes to redress a wrong in the universe. We have to recognize that Ruby, now that he has been given his assignment, does not have to justify it with Mob motivations or by Mob professionalism—"I'm there to do the hit, that's it"—no, Ruby, being an amateur, would look to ennoble his task.

In any case, he seems to move without large purpose until midafternoon, when he goes to Dealey Plaza. As he sees the multitude of wreaths laid out for Jack Kennedy in the plaza, he weeps in his car, or so he testifies.

> *Posner:* When he left Dealey Plaza, it appears Ruby once more went to the third floor of the police headquarters, expecting an Oswald transfer that never took place. He later denied being there Saturday because, again, he probably feared it might be interpreted as evidence of premeditation. The Warren Commission said it "reached no firm conclusion as to whether or not Ruby visited the Dallas Police Department on Saturday." Yet credible eyewitness testimony shows he was there.[32]

He is still looking and he is still weeping. Ruby must have wept and/or had tears in his eyes ten to twenty times from Friday to Sunday. But, we can remind ourselves once more, he is crying for himself. His life is slipping away from him. Nevertheless, to maintain some finer sense of himself, he is also weeping for Jack, Jackie, and the children.

Soon enough, he begins to prowl again:

> *Posner:* . . . Later in the afternoon [TV reporters in their van] saw him on their monitors wandering the third floor of police headquarters and approaching Wade in an office, from which regular reporters were barred.[33]

Indeed, he is hyperactive:

> *Posner:* Thayer Waldo, a reporter with the *Fort Worth Star-Telegram,* watched Ruby giving out Carousel cards to reporters between 4:00 and 5:00 P.M. He was aggressive in getting the reporters' attention, pulling the sleeves of some and slapping others on the back or arms. When he got to Waldo, Ruby said,

"... Here's my card with both my clubs on it. Everybody around here knows me.... As soon as you get a chance, I want all of you boys to come over to my place ... and have a drink on me ..."[34]

Half of the time he is even behaving as he would if his life were to go on just as it used to. He seems to have forgotten that he has closed the Carousel. He is living in two states of being. He is in his own skin and he is also playing the lead in a film full of significance and future heartbreak.

That Saturday night, with Oswald locked in his jail cell on an inaccessible floor, begins another long dark journey. Ruby has failed to produce, and it is a reasonable assumption that *they* will soon be letting him know about it.

Posner: By 9:30 Ruby had returned to his apartment. There, he received a call from one of his strippers, Karen Bennett Carlin, whose stage name was Little Lynn. She had driven into Dallas from Fort Worth with her husband and wondered if the Carousel was going to open over the weekend, because she needed money. "He got very angry and was very short with me," Carlin recalled. "He said, 'Don't you have any respect for the President? Don't you know the President is dead? ... I don't know when I will open. I don't know if I will ever open back up.' "[35]

How can he? If he does not kill Oswald, the Mob, after breaking his nose, his chin, and his kneecaps, will proceed to take his clubs away. But if he succeeds, the government will take the Carousel. At ten o'clock, he telephones his sister Eva to complain about how depressed he is.

An hour goes by, and then he calls Ralph Paul. No answer.

Posner: Ruby telephoned [Paul's] restaurant again at 11:18 and discovered Paul had gone home. He then telephoned Paul three times at home, at 11:19 for three minutes, at 11:36 for two minutes, and at 11:47 for one minute. Paul said he did not feel well, and told Ruby "I was sick and I was going to bed and not to call me."[36]

That night, the Dallas jail received anonymous phone threats on Oswald's life. On later reflection, Captain Fritz thought the calls might have come from Ruby. Perhaps they did. Ruby would have been looking for excuses—I had it all set up for Sunday, but they moved Oswald on Saturday night.

Now, he calls an old friend, Lawrence Meyers, who is in Dallas for a couple of days:

> MR. MEYERS. . . . he was obviously very upset . . . he seemed far more incoherent than I have ever listened to him. The guy sounded absolutely like he had flipped his lid, I guess . . .
>
> I said, Jack, where are you . . . He said come have a drink with me or a cup of coffee with me . . . I said, Jack, that is silly. I am undressed. I have bathed. I am in bed. I want to go to sleep but, I said, if you want a cup of coffee you come on over here and come on up to my room . . . He said, no, no, he had things to do. He couldn't come over . . . This went on for a little while and the last thing I said, Jack, why don't you go ahead and get a good night's sleep and forget this thing. And you call me about 6 o'clock tomorrow night . . . and we will have dinner together and he said okay . . .
>
> MR. GRIFFIN. . . . the FBI has quoted you as saying that one of the things that Ruby told you in the conversation was, "I have got to do something about this." Do you remember that?
>
> MR. MEYERS. Definitely.[37]

We can interpret that remark in two ways: I, on my own, have to do something about this; or, I have been told to do something about this.

He slept in one or another fashion that night and awoke in a terrible mood:

> MR. SENATOR. . . . He made himself a couple of scrambled eggs and coffee for himself, and he still had this look which didn't look good . . . how can I express it? The look in his eyes? . . .
>
> MR. HUBERT. The way he talked or what he said?
>
> MR. SENATOR. The way he talked. He was even mumbling, which I didn't understand. And right after breakfast he got dressed. Then after he got dressed he was pacing the floor from the living room to the bedroom, from the bedroom to the living room, and his lips were going. What he was jabbering I didn't know. But he was really pacing.[38]

In the telephone conversation the night before, Meyers, referring to Jackie Kennedy, had said: "Life goes on. She will make a
life for herself . . ."[39]

It was the worst thing Meyers could have said. By now, Jack Ruby
and Jackie Kennedy are one—two suffering souls who have
merged. Ruby does not want to make a new life for himself—he
wants his old one back.

It is so painful. Ruby cannot ask directly for sympathy, but his
self-love is pouring out of him. He is bleeding for Jackie Kennedy
as if she is that beautiful element in his soul that no one else
knows about, and soon it will all be lost.

He is distraught in still another fashion. When he woke up on
Sunday morning, he must have been living with what he had
learned the night before—Oswald was scheduled to be transferred at 10:00 A.M. If he wasn't at City Hall for the transfer, he
might never have as good an opportunity at the County Jail.

Ruby, however, had decided not to be present. During the
night, he had made up his mind. He would take whatever consequences would come from the Mob. Fuck them. He would not be
their hit man.

Events, however, intervened.

Posner: At 10:19, while still lounging in the apartment in his
underwear, he received a telephone call from his dancer
Karen Carlin . . . "I have called, Jack, to try to get some money,
because the rent is due and I need some money for groceries
and you told me to call." Ruby asked how much she needed,
and she said $25. He offered to go downtown and send it to
her by Western Union, but told her it would "take a little while
to get dressed . . ."[40]

Then he went out. It was a little before 11:00 A.M., and on his
way he drove past Dealey Plaza and began to cry once more.

Of course, if you have been debating with yourself for close to
forty-eight hours whether you are or are not going to pull a trigger, and either way death or utter ruin stands before you, you
might cry too at every reminder of where you are. Which is that
you didn't take your last opportunity at 10:00 A.M.

Oswald, however, has not yet been transferred. Fritz has
decided to let the press have one more look at him. A photo
opportunity!

Meantime, Ruby is at the Western Union office sending $25 to his stripper. If his life is going to be smashed, he can at least do one last good deed.

Posner: . . . he patiently waited in line while another customer completed her business . . . When he got to the counter, the cost for sending the moneygram totaled $26.87. He handed over $30 and waited for his change while the clerk finished filling out the forms . . . Ruby's receipt was stamped 11:17. When he left Western Union, he was less than two hundred steps from the entrance to police headquarters.[41]

And about two hundred and fifty steps from dubious immortality.

MR. RUBY. [I] walked the distance from the Western Union to the ramp. I didn't sneak in. I didn't linger in there.
 I didn't crouch or hide behind anyone, unless the television camera can make it seem that way . . .[42]

Posner: On the third floor of the headquarters, police had informed Oswald shortly after 11:00 A.M. that they would immediately take him downstairs . . . He asked if he could change his clothes. Captain Fritz sent for some sweaters . . . If Oswald had not decided at the last moment to get a sweater, he would have left the jail almost five minutes earlier, while Ruby was still inside the Western Union office.[43]

MR. RUBY. . . . I did not mingle with the crowd. There was no one near me when I walked down that ramp . . .[44]

It is worth hearing the account of a plainclothesman named Archer, a detective on the Dallas force:

MR. ARCHER. . . . I could see the detectives on each side of Oswald leading him towards the ramp . . . I did have some bright lights shining into my eyes, and [it was hard] for me to recognize someone on the opposite side of the ramp [but] I caught a figure of a man. . . . I had been watching Oswald and the detectives . . . and my first thought was, as I started moving—well, my first thought was that somebody jumped out of the crowd, maybe to take a sock at him. Someone got emotionally upset and jumped out to take a sock at him, [but] as I moved forward, I saw the man reach Oswald, raise up, and then the shot was fired.[45]

MR. RUBY. . . . I realize it is a terrible thing I have done, and it was a stupid thing, but I just was carried away emotionally. Do you follow that?

CHIEF JUSTICE WARREN. Yes; I do indeed, every word.

MR. RUBY. I had the gun in my right hip pocket, and impulsively, if that is the correct word here, I saw him, and that is all I can say. And I didn't care what happened to me.[46]

The irony is that he was indeed impulsive. He has meditated upon the act since Friday; he has had his opportunities and not taken them. Now that he has lost his opportunity, or so he sees it, he has gravitated back to the police station. It has been the center of his activities for the last two days, after all. Yet, to his surprise, here and now is Oswald! It was as if God had put the man there. God was now giving the message: Jack Ruby was supposed to do it after all. So he fulfilled his contract. Let us say that he fulfilled two contracts. He did his job for the Mob, but since he had been talking about it so much that he had come to believe it, he did it as well for Jack, Jackie, the children, and the Jewish people. He fused himself into his all but unbelievable cover story and did it for Jackie Kennedy, after all.

To the Warren Commission, he describes his feelings with considerable style. Nothing is more difficult than to combine elegance with piety, but Jack has had seven months in jail to prepare this speech for Earl Warren:

. . . I wanted to show my love for our faith, being of the Jewish faith, and I never used the term and I don't want to go into that—suddenly the feeling, the emotional feeling came within me that someone owed this debt to our beloved President to save her the ordeal of coming back. I don't know why that came through my mind.[47]

He had been less sanctimonious, however, right after his gun was seized on that terminal Sunday:

MR. ARCHER. . . . we took him on into the jail office and I assisted in keeping his left arm behind him and someone got his right. I couldn't say who it was that had his other arm. Laid him down on the floor, his head and face were away from me at that particular time. But that is when I said, "Who is he?" [He answered] "You all know me. I'm Jack Ruby." . . . And he said at that particular point, "I hope I killed the son of a bitch." . . . I said to Ruby at that time, "Jack, I think you killed him," and he just looked at me right straight in the eye and said, "Well, I intended to shoot him three times."[48]

Posner: When they got to the third floor, Ruby, who was excited from the shooting, talked to anybody who came by. "If I had planned this I couldn't have had my timing better," he bragged. "It was one chance in a million. . . . I guess I just had to show the world that a Jew has guts." . . .[49]

For forty and more hours before that, awake and asleep, he must have been castigating himself: You Jew, you do not have the guts to be a hit man—only Italians are that good. So he wanted to give the Mafia a real signature, his own—three shots—wanted to show the world that a Mob-style execution was not out of reach for him, a Jew.

The Parkland surgeons were not able to save Oswald:

Posner: "It's pretty hard to imagine one bullet doing more damage than that," says Dr. John Lattimer. "It perforated the chest cavity, went through the diaphragm, spleen, and stomach. It cut off the main intestinal artery, and the aorta, and the body's main vein, as well as breaking up the right kidney. That wound was definitely fatal."[50]

Jack Ruby would wear brass knuckles when he got into a fight in his nightclub. He would brag to his handyman, Larry Crafard, that he had been with every girl in his club, and yet . . . and yet . . . As with Oswald, there is always more to Ruby.

MRS. CARLIN. . . . He was always asking the question, "Do you think I am a queer? Do you think I look like a queer? Or have you ever known a queer to look like me?" Everytime I saw him he would ask it.

MR. JACKSON. Do you mean he would bring up the subject himself?

MRS. CARLIN. Yes; he would say, "Do you think I look like one or act like one?"[51]

A man of many sides—he loved his animals:

Posner: His favorite dog, Sheba, was left in the car. "People that didn't know Jack will never understand this," Bill Alexander told the author, "but Ruby would never have taken that dog with him and left it in the car if he knew he was going to shoot Oswald and end up in jail. He would have made sure that dog was at home with Senator and was well taken care of."[52]

Yes, Posner must be absolutely right that Ruby was not planning to kill Oswald on Sunday at 11:21 A.M. But that does not take care of why Ruby finally—for reasons considerably closer to his heart than the pain and turmoil awaiting Jacqueline Kennedy—did the deed and threw the cloak of a thousand putative conspiracies over the mystery of Lee Harvey Oswald, his life and his death.

PART VIII

OSWALD'S GHOST

—◀○▶—

1

The Punishment of Hosty and the
Death of the Handler

De Mohrenschildt has figured prominently in our account; FBI Special Agent Hosty has been a passing figure. Yet, of all the men in security and intelligence whose careers would be blighted in the aftermath of Kennedy's assassination, no others stand out so prominently, and so a quiver of insight may be obtained by learning what happened to them.

The memorandum to which Priscilla Johnson McMillan will soon make reference is the "two- to four-page document" mentioned earlier that was dictated by Hosty at Special Agent in Charge J. Gordon Shanklin's suggestion after Oswald's angry encounter with Hosty in Captain Fritz's office.

> *McMillan:* Between two and four hours after Oswald's [demise] on November 24, Shanklin summoned Hosty. Hosty recalls that Shanklin was standing in front of his desk and . . . took out both the memorandum and Oswald's note. "Oswald is dead now," he said. "There can be no trial. Here, get rid of this." Hosty started to tear up the documents in Shanklin's presence. "No," Shanklin shouted. "Get it out of here. I don't even want it in this office. Get rid of it." Hosty then took the note and memorandum out of Shanklin's office, tore them up, and flushed them down a toilet at the FBI. A few days later, Shanklin asked Hosty whether he had destroyed Oswald's note and the memorandum and Hosty assured him that he had.[1]

The HSCA reported that Shanklin, in 1963, denied he had any knowledge of the note. In fact until 1975, the Dallas FBI office kept secret the destruction of the note.[2]

McMillan: Hosty's . . . answers on an internal FBI questionnaire were subsequently falsified either by Shanklin or by
someone in FBI headquarters in Washington to admit "poor
investigative work" in the Oswald case. Hosty received letters
of censure from J. Edgar Hoover, was placed on proba-
tion . . . and demoted to Kansas City. Years later, a promotion
that was recommended for him was blocked by Clyde Tolson,
chief deputy of J. Edgar Hoover. Except for Shanklin and two
others, every FBI agent who had anything to do with the
Oswald case in 1962 or 1963 was censured, transferred,
demoted, or barred from promotion, while Shanklin received several letters of commendation from Hoover.[3]

It is very hard to believe that the note was as simple and direct
in its contents as Hosty says it was. The irony, of course, is that
Hosty was part of the legitimate FBI, as opposed to COINTEL-
PRO, and so may have had almost as little to do with Oswald as he
claims; but Hoover could not have known that to a certainty, since
the working boundaries between daily FBI work and COINTEL-
PRO adventures were not going to be defined with high clarity in
inter-office memos—and besides, the evidence had been destroyed. That made Hosty a part of the detritus that J. Edgar
Hoover had to hide under bureaucratic sanctity. So Hosty was chosen as Hoover's patsy.

More is available when we look at the Baron. Recounting how he
heard the news in Haiti that someone had killed Kennedy, he is
pleased with his own acumen:

MR. DE MOHRENSCHILDT. Now I do not consider myself . . . a
genius. But the very first thought after we heard . . . [the news
from] an employee of the American Embassy in Port au Prince,
and he mentioned that the name of the presumable assassin is
something Lee, Lee, Lee—and I said, "Could it be Lee Oswald?"
    And he said, "I guess that is the name."

MR. JENNER. That occurred to you?

MR. DE MOHRENSCHILDT. That occurred to me.

MR. JENNER. As soon as you heard the name Lee?

MR. DE MOHRENSCHILDT. As soon as I heard the name Lee. Now,
why it occurred to me—because he was a crazy lunatic.[4]

The Haitian government must have gone through quite a few changes of mind over the next weeks concerning its relation to De Mohrenschildt. We obtain more than a clue in George's manuscript *I'm a Patsy.*

> . . . We learned that a letter was sent by someone influential in Washington to the officials of the Haitian government to drop me from the payroll and to exile me as fast as possible. Fortunately I had good friends and the latter did not happen. And later, little by little, we were ostracized by the United States Ambassador Timmons, then by the American businessmen and government employees with whom we had been on very good terms, and, finally, came the news of the investigation of all our friends and even acquaintances in the United States.
>
> . . . At last, after a good long time, we were officially invited to come to Washington and help the Warren Commission in their investigation. Although we could contribute very little, we still accepted to go to Washington to testify. Although our depositions were supposed to remain confidential, all three hundred pages of irrelevant conversation were printed and promiscuously distributed.[5]

Toward the end of his manuscript, he gives a more candid explanation of the process:

> As the atmosphere of Port-au-Prince became oppressive . . . we were considering abandoning my survey . . . and returning to the States. But President Duvalier found himself a solution to this situation. He asked Dr. Herve Boyer, Minister of Finance, Secretary of Treasury, and a good friend of mine who had helped me get the survey contract, to invite me to his office and to have a chat with me. [Boyer] said decisively: "You are in the hot water. Everyone is talking about you and your wife. Do not abandon your survey but go back to the States and clear your name somehow. If you cannot, come back, wind up your work and leave the country."
>
> It so happened that on the same day our Embassy received a letter, addressed to me and my wife, from Mr. J. Lee Rankin, General Counsel of the Warren Commission. Mr. Rankin invited us to come to Washington, D.C., if we wished, and to

testify . . . Of course, we were most anxious to cooperate as much as we could to solve this crime. But Jeanne refused to travel without our two dogs—Manchester terriers—and, after the exchange of wires, Mr. Rankin accepted this additional "dog expense." . . .

I was the first to testify. The man who took my deposition was Albert Jenner, a lawyer from Chicago, who much later became well known in connection with the Watergate case . . . I have to admit that either he was much cleverer than I or that I was impressed by the whole setting and situation as it unfolded in Washington at the time. Anyway, Jenner played with me as if I were a baby.[6]

In fact, it was a trial of nerves. He had to protect the CIA and he had to protect himself, and as we can recall, his *modus operandi* was to remind the Agency that he could certainly pull them in with him if they should be so rash as to disown him completely and thereby destroy his shaky purchase on a sinecure in Haiti.

At the conclusion of his stay in Washington, De Mohrenschildt may have looked to better his situation at a small dinner party:

Very tired by our testimonies, we were invited after our ordeal to the luxurious house of Jacqueline Kennedy's mother and her stepfather, Mr. Hugh Auchincloss. This luxurious house was located in Georgetown and Auchincloss' money originated out of some association of Hugh's family with John D. Rockefeller, Sr., of the oil fame . . .[7]

Almost in passing, De Mohrenschildt mentions that Allen Dulles was also there. Is it fair to suspect that Dulles asked the Auchinclosses to arrange the dinner? Dulles, having been all but forcibly retired from the CIA after the Bay of Pigs, would still have been in contact with many a CIA loop; Dulles was bound to have questions concerning Agency connections with De Mohrenschildt. Even an active director of the CIA will have a good deal of sensitive information concealed from him, and in this situation, relegated to the sidelines for more than two years, Dulles must have had his own share of concern about how closely CIA was involved, since it was on his watch, after all, that the Agency had tried to kill Castro.

Of course, if he and George had any private conversation that night, there would be no record of it. De Mohrenschildt contents himself with remarking that Allen Dulles "asked me a few questions about Lee."

> One of them was, I remember, did Lee have a reason of hating President Kennedy? However, when I answered that he was rather an admirer of the dead President, everyone took my answer with a grain of salt. Again, the overwhelming opinion was that Lee was the sole assassin.[8]

De Mohrenschildt is, as ever, ready to divert us from the point:

> I was still thinking of poor Lee, comparing his life with the life of these multi-millionaires. I tried to reason—to no avail. It seemed to me that I was facing a conspiracy, a conspiracy of stubbornness and silence. Finally, both Jeanne and Janet (Mrs. Auchincloss) got very emotional, embraced each other, and cried together, one over the loss of her son-in-law, the other over the loss of a great president she admired so much.
> "Janet," I said before leaving, "you were Jack Kennedy's mother-in-law, and I am a complete stranger. I would spend my own money and lots of my time to find out who were the real assassins and the conspirators. Don't you want any further investigation? You have infinite resources."
> "Jack is dead and nothing will bring him back," replied she decisively.[9]

As usual, there is no emotional sequence to De Mohrenschildt's account. One thing happens, and then another, and each little matter seems to have very little to do with the next. The best way to forestall the development of a scenario is to keep your events episodic:

> But we were still in the Auchincloss' luxurious mansion, about ready to leave. "Incidentally," said Mrs. Auchincloss coldly, "my daughter Jacqueline never wants to see you again because you were close to her husband's assassin."
> "It's her privilege," I answered.
> Hugh, who was a very silent man, asked me suddenly: "And how is Marina fixed financially?"
> "I do not know. I just read that she received quite a lot of money from the charitable American people—maybe eighty thousand dollars."

"That won't last her long," he said thoughtfully and, almost without transition, pointed to an extraordinary chess set: "This is early Persian valued at sixty thousand dollars."

We said goodbyes amicably to the Auchinclosses and drove off back to our hotel. "That son of a gun Hugh has an income running into millions," I told Jeanne thoughtfully.

"Such figures are beyond my comprehension," she said sadly.[10]

For his testimony before the Warren Commission, De Mohrenschildt was reimbursed with job security. Or, to be precise, he was and he was not. Forces were in play with counterforce.

> Fortunately, the Haitian Ambassador in Washington was reassured by the Warren Commission that we were decent people. The Ambassador transmitted this message to President Duvalier and we could return safely to Haiti. But my contract became hopelessly harmed by the intervening publicity and by the peculiar attitude taken by the American Embassy toward us. And President Duvalier, the astute Papa Doc, knew through his informants, that our Embassy would not protect my rights any more. And the old fox was absolutely right; the payments for my survey began drying up and in later years I never received any cooperation from anyone in our Embassy or in the State Department in trying to recover the large balance of my contract still due to me.[11]

Still, he was able to hang on in Haiti until 1966, after which he and Jeanne came back to Dallas.

> *McMillan:* . . . his life had changed once again for the worse. He had failed to pull off the big coup in sisal or oil that he had counted on. His book on his Central American adventures had been refused by several publishers. And, as always, George was feeling financial pressure. Having spent his life among tycoons, he had never been able to earn as much as he felt he needed. His relations with Jeanne became bitter. They divorced, but then went on living together, estranged from everyone they knew. Jeanne had a job, while George taught French at a small black college in Dallas . . . A decade or so after the assassination . . . his spirits sank into depression . . .[12]

Posner, picking up on this deterioration in De Mohrenschildt, does his best to render him permanently incompetent:

Posner: . . . de Mohrenschildt was quite mad by the time he gave his final [Epstein] interview. For nearly a year before his death, he was paranoid, fearful that the "FBI and Jewish mafia" were out to kill him. He twice tried to kill himself with drug overdoses, and another time cut his wrists and submerged himself in a bathtub. After he began waking in the middle of every night, screaming and beating himself, his wife finally committed him to Parkland Hospital psychiatric unit, where he was diagnosed as psychotic and given two months of intensive shock therapy. After his treatment he said he had been with Oswald on the day of the assassination, though he was actually with dozens of guests at the Bulgarian embassy in Haiti the day JFK was killed. Despite de Morenschildt's imbalance, Epstein and others still quote the final interview as though it were an uncontested fact.[13]

De Morenschildt does not deserve the label "quite mad" at the time he gave his final interview. Once again, Posner is not including those sources who would indicate that De Mohrenschildt in the last month of his life was depressed but not delusional.

McMillan: Sam Ballen, who saw him in Dallas only one month before he died, found George "beating himself pretty hard." He berated himself for friendships he had lost and opportunities he had tossed aside and said that his life had been a failure . . .
    Ballen, who had not seen De Mohrenschildt in years, came away from their meeting feeling sad. For all his faults, of which the greatest was his "utter irresponsibility," George was, Ballen believed, "one of the world's great people." . . . He invited him to come to Santa Fe and offered him the kind of rough, outdoor work that seemed likely to help George the most. Afterwards Ballen looked back with the feeling that he had been dining with "Hemingway before the suicide."[14]

Yes, De Mohrenschildt was in the grip of that grim appraisal of self that weighs so heavily upon older men of once large personal resources who no longer have the energy to improve their lives or their careers and so are left to brood on all that went wrong; but, given Sam Ballen's assessment, it seems excessive for Posner to decide that De Mohrenschildt was completely out of his mind when he spoke to Edward Epstein about his CIA connections with J. Walton Moore.

We can take leave of George with this passage from Gaeton Fonzi's book *The Last Investigation*. Fonzi has just located the oceanfront mansion in Palm Beach where De Morenschildt is living in 1977.

> The house was hidden behind a barrier of high hedges . . . a strangely grim house for that narrow, monied stretch of Florida coastline, where the mansions are usually chic pastel modern or classy traditional white . . .
>
> As I got out of the car, a young woman emerged unexpectedly from behind the building. She was strikingly beautiful, tall and dark with a smooth sculpted face, long raven hair and deep brown eyes. She wore a tight black leotard and moved with the supple, sensuous ease of a dancer. Her tan body glowed with a sheen of perspiration; she had obviously been exercising. She wiped her brow and arms with a small towel.
>
> "Excuse me," I said as I approached her . . . "I'm looking for George de Mohrenschildt."
>
> She hesitated a moment, her eyes cautious, probing.
>
> "He's not in at the moment. I'm his daughter, Alexandra. May I help you?"
>
> I told her my name and why I was there . . . "I'd appreciate it," I said, "if you would tell him that I'll be calling and would like to see him." We hadn't yet been issued official identification so my only credentials were old business cards which identified me as a staff investigator for U.S. Senator Richard Schweiker. I crossed out Schweiker's name on one and wrote above it "House Select Committee on Assassinations." She took it and said she would tell her father to expect my call . . .
>
> About 6:30 that evening I received a call from . . . Palm Beach State Attorney Dave Bludworth [who] said my card had been found in de Mohrenschildt's shirt pocket. About four hours after I had been there, de Mohrenschildt had returned to Nancy Tilton's house. His daughter told him of my visit and gave him my card. He put the card in his pocket and, according to Alexandra, did not seem upset, but shortly afterwards he said he was going upstairs to rest. What de

Mohrenschildt then apparently did was take a .20-gauge shotgun that Mrs. Tilton kept beside her bed for protection. He sat down in a soft chair, put the stock of the shotgun on the floor and the end of the barrel in his mouth, leaned forward and pulled the trigger.[15]

2

In the Rubble of the Aftermath

As long as Lee was alive, for all of those forty and more hours in which Marguerite was anticipating a long drawn-out trial, the problem as she saw it was how she, Marina, and the children would live. She knew she could cash in her insurance policy for $836, and that would provide a base for her new family.

> MARGUERITE OSWALD. . . . I am not interested in material things, gentlemen . . . I thought, as a family, Marina and I should stick together and face our future together. . . . I thought it would be [best] to live in my apartment and do the best we can. And I even said ". . . give us a chance as a family. Don't put the girl in a strange home, a Russian girl, a foreign girl, taken away from her mama."[1]

Yes, for the less than forty-eight hours that Lee would be alive after the death of JFK, Marina may also have been contemplating a life with Marguerite; they could work together on some kind of defense of Lee. After he was killed, however, everything worked to separate them. Marina, after all, did not like her mother-in-law that much; the Secret Service, on whom Marina was depending more and more, certainly detested Marguerite; and the business manager Marina soon took on was looking at a cash-cow in her future: The lonely Soviet widow of the President's assassin was already receiving small contributions with every mail—some good Americans don't mind paying a tithe to their sentimental responses. Marguerite, whether she was first or last to sense it, was on the way out.

> MARGUERITE OSWALD. . . . One of the other Secret Service men had gone to talk to Robert's boss, because Robert was worried about his job [and] he patted Robert on the shoulder and said, "Now, Robert, I have talked to your boss and you are all right. I assured him you are not involved in this in any way."
>
> So, gentlemen, Marina is taken care of; Robert is taken care of—I am not feeling sorry for myself, believe me, because I can take care of myself. But here is a mother who has come to the rescue, lost her job, offered her good love and insurance money and nobody has wondered what is going to become of me.
>
> MR. RANKIN. Well, did you think it was improper that the Secret Service man would go to Robert's boss and tell him he was not involved, and there was nothing improper?
>
> MARGUERITE OSWALD. No, sir, I do not. I think it was a fine gesture. And that is the point I am trying to make . . . Why are these fine gestures to see that Marina is going to have a home and be taken care of, and Robert's job is secure—but I am nothing. I was not included in the plans. And what is going to become of me? I have no income. I have no job. I lost my job. And nobody thought about me.
>
> I don't mean to imply I'm sorry for myself. I am trying to bring out a point that through all of this, that I have not been considered, even as much as to testify. I want to know why. I don't understand why.
>
> It is very strange.[2]

The embitterment is on the way to becoming colossal.

> MARGUERITE OSWALD. This is the 28th. So [I told] the agent that was taking me home . . . that I wanted to tell Marina that I was going. He knocked on the door. The Russian interpreter from the State Department, Mr. Gopadze, came to the door and the agent said, "Mrs. Oswald is going home and wants to tell Marina and the children goodbye."
>
> He said, "Well, we are interviewing her and she is on tape. She will get in touch with you."
>
> So I never saw Marina after that time.[3]

Well, she would see her on television:

MARGUERITE OSWALD. The first time Marina ever made any statement or public appearance was approximately two weeks ago, or maybe not that long. She was on an exclusive television program, Channel 4 in Fort Worth, Texas, when she stated publicly that in her mind she thought that Lee shot President Kennedy. What an awful thing for this 22-year-old foreign girl to think . . . She doesn't know. But she thinks, gentlemen . . . "In my mind I think Lee shot President Kennedy." . . . She is a Russian girl, and maybe they do this in Russia. But what I am going to say is that Marina Oswald was brainwashed by the Secret Service, who have kept her in seclusion for eight weeks—eight weeks, gentlemen, with no one talking to Marina.

Marina does not read English. Marina knows none of the facts from newspaper accounts. The only way Marina can get facts is through what the FBI and the Secret Service probably are telling her, or some of the facts that Marina has manufactured since.[4]

By the end of winter 1964, Marina would break relations with her business manager, Jim Martin—she grew suspicious of everyone who had commercial relations with her—and she bought a home of her own in Richardson, Texas. It would take her testimony before the Warren Commission and the better part of a year before Marina lost her fear of imprisonment and of deportation. By then, she saw Marguerite as an irritant—Marina's knowledge of English increased, and she could pick out items in the newspapers concerning her former mother-in-law's latest conclusions about just how Lee had been framed.

MR. RANKIN. Will you describe to us your relationship with your mother-in-law now?

MARINA OSWALD. . . . I understood her motherly concern. But in view of the fact of everything that happened later, her appearances in the radio, in the press, I do not think that she is a very sound-thinking woman, and I think that part of the guilt is hers. I do not accuse her, but I think that part of the guilt in connection with what happened with Lee lies with her . . . If she were in contact with my children now, I do not want her to cripple them.

MR. RANKIN. Has she tried to see you since the assassination?

MARINA OSWALD. Yes, all the time.

MR. RANKIN. And have you seen her since that time?

MARINA OSWALD. Accidentally we met at the cemetery on a Sunday when I visited there, but I didn't want to meet with her, and I left.[5]

A little later in this day before the Warren Commission, Rankin had to steer close to a touchy matter. Marguerite had been making public claims that Marina had been brainwashed, and so it was necessary to reconnoiter the subject:

MR. RANKIN. After the assassination, did the police and the FBI and the Secret Service ask you many questions?

MARINA OSWALD. In the police station there was a regular routine questioning. And then . . . the Secret Service and the FBI, they asked me many questions of course—many questions. Sometimes the FBI . . . told me that if I wanted to live in this country, I would have to help in this matter, even though they were often irrelevant. That is the FBI . . .

MR. RANKIN. Did you see anyone from the Immigration Service during this time?

MARINA OSWALD. Yes . . .

MR. RANKIN. What did he say to you?

MARINA OSWALD. That if I was not guilty of anything, if I had not committed any crime against this Government, then I had every right to live in this country. This was a type of introduction before the questioning by the FBI. He even said that it would be better for me if I would help them . . .

MR. RANKIN. Did you understand that you were being threatened with deportation if you didn't answer those questions?

MARINA OSWALD. No, I did not understand it that way.

You see, it was presented in such a delicate form, but there was a clear implicaton that it would be better if I were to help.[6]

The Secret Service had had suspicions of Michael and Ruth Paine. Michael was active in the ACLU, and that was a radical activity as far as the authorities in Texas were concerned. Then, the Dallas police had come up with the letter which Lee had written to Marina in Russian back in April on Neely Street before he took a shot at Walker. Marina had hidden that letter in a Russian-language cookbook, and the police had the letter translated and even assumed at first that it had been written by Ruth. Indeed, on its discovery, Marina had not only been confronted with the letter but with the fear that she could conceivably be imprisoned or deported if she persisted in withholding information about Lee.

Somewhere around this time, Marina began to cooperate with the authorities. Her friendship with Ruth was over. Both women had their grievances. Marina had not told Ruth about the rifle, or about General Walker, or of Lee's trip to Mexico; Marina, in turn, felt that Ruth had been careless in handing over the cookbook to the police, and so had left her in a position where she had to defend herself at the expense of exposing Lee. June and Rachel would be known as the children of an assassin.

These are hard equations! Yet, it is not easy to break relations entirely with a generous friend because of a few lapses in her protection of you. One looks to find a definitive breach of taste.

> **MR. RANKIN.** You said that . . . Ruth Paine . . . wanted to see you for her own interests. Will you tell us what you meant by that?
>
> **MARINA OSWALD.** . . . She likes to be well known, popular, and I think that anything I should write her, for example, would wind up in the press.
>
> The reason that I think so is that the first time that we were in jail to see Lee, she was with me and with her children, and she was trying to get in front of the cameras, and to push her children, and instructed her children to look this way and look that way. And the first photographs that appeared were of me and her children.[7]

Marina is as responsive as Henry James might have been to this brief crack in the Quaker-like goodness of Ruth Paine. A small flaw that one cannot forgive is, by the measure of Jamesian percipience, equal in size to an unsightly hole in the firmament.

In any event, Ruth Paine is out, and Marguerite is out. Marina has two children she wishes to rear, and for that she must survive. She must wall herself away from the past. Marina, given her powerful sense of roots and her deep pools of guilt, can hardly be unaware of the cost of cauterizing her past for a third time—once on leaving Leningrad, once on leaving Russia, and now again saying farewell to Lee.

She could not do it successfully. By her Russian lights, she was his wife. So she was responsible for his acts. To her, it was not always certain that she held no blame for the deaths of the President and the policeman, Tippit. What a burden their children, now fatherless, would have as they suffered in common with the burden of her own two children. She might cry out in conversation that if Lee came back to earth and she could talk to him, "I'd give him such a scolding that he would die all over again,"[8] but that was merely a sentiment. To cauterize the past was her real goal.

McMillan: . . . Marina became a little wild, taking only fitful care of her children and spending as many waking hours as she could on escapades with boyfriends and neighbors, on all-night bowling sprees, and on well-publicized sorties to a Dallas nightclub called the Music Box, where she was soon a favorite. Aware of her self-destructiveness, Marina calls 1964 "her second Leningrad period."[9]

By 1965, after rejecting numerous marriage proposals (with the suspicion that she might be loved less for the complex composition of herself than for her newfound money—when it came to receiving compliments, she possessed as many quills as a porcupine), she decided to marry a man for whom she could feel some trust, a tall, gentlemanly Texan with fine, laid-back manners.

McMillan: Today she lives outside Dallas on a seventeen-acre farm, with cattle on it, with Kenneth Porter, whom she married in 1965. They were divorced in 1974, but they continue to live together as man and wife. Kenneth loves life on the farm, and he is an expert mechanic, "one of the best," Marina says. He is a handsome man, and a devoted stepfather, a fact which Marina, after her own difficult childhood, values greatly.[10]

She was still there in 1993. There was talk of interviewing June and Rachel and Mark, her son with Kenneth Porter, children now just over thirty-one, twenty-nine, and twenty-seven, but Marina would have none of that, and who could argue against the legitimacy of such a refusal?

The thought that there would be one more book about Lee and herself was painful in the extreme. Ghosts seeped into her mind like poison vapors in a horror film. She did not want to talk about the past. She can hardly remember her old testimony. Rather, she would declare that she now believes Lee was innocent. Or, if not innocent, then part of a conspiracy. But, she would say, he was not the man who fired the gun. Since evidence is a blur to her, she soon will say that she cannot be certain what she believes. If only she knew whether he did it or not. What a great weight would be lifted from June and Rachel if he did not commit the deed. What do you think? she asks. We are trying to find out, say the interviewers.

3

Evidence

Did Oswald do it?

If one's answer is to come out of anything larger than an opinion, it is necessary to contend with questions of evidence. In that direction, however, one encounters a jungle of conflicting expert estimates as to whether Oswald could fire the shots in time, was a good enough marksman, was the only gunman in Dealey Plaza, and on one can go, trying to explore into every last reach of possibility, only to encounter a disheartening truth: Evidence, by itself, will never provide the answer to a mystery. For it is in the nature of evidence to produce, sooner or later, a counterinterpretation to itself in the form of a contending expert in a court of law.

It will be obvious to the reader that one does not (and should not) respect evidence with the religious intensity that others bring to it:

MR. SPECTER. Would the use of a four-power scope be a real advantage . . . ?

SERGEANT ZAHM. . . . particularly at the range of 100 yards . . . It allows you to see your target clearly, and it is still of a minimum amount of power that it doesn't exaggerate your own body movements . . .

MR. SPECTER. . . . would a man with Oswald's marksmanship capabilities be able to complete such a shot and strike the target on the white mark there?

SERGEANT ZAHM. Very definitely . . . With the equipment he had and with his ability, I consider it a very easy shot.

MR. SPECTER. . . . would a marksman of Mr. Oswald's capabilities using such a rifle with a 4-power scope be able to strike the President in the back of the head? . . .

SERGEANT ZAHM. . . . This would have been a little more difficult and probably be to the top of his ability, aiming and striking the President in the head. But assuming that he aimed at the mass of the center portion of the President's body, he would have hit him very definitely someplace . . .[1]

One can envision the scene in court if Oswald had lived. The defense would have brought in their expert to testify to the opposite of Sergeant Zahm's opinion, and much would have been made of the dubious setting of the scope on the Mannlicher-Carcano, since the first riflemen who did tests with that gun for the Warren Commission had to correct the alignment before their shots could even hit a stationary target.

MR. FRAZIER. . . . I think I must say here that this mount was loose on this rifle when we received it. And apparently the scope had even been taken off of the rifle, in searching for fingerprints on the rifle. So that actually the way it was sighted-in when we got it does not necessarily mean it was sighted-in that way when it was abandoned.[2]

A technical discussion followed. In the tests, shims had had to be used in the mounting of the scope and then the elevation crosshair could not be adjusted all the way, but enough, Frazier concluded, "to accurately sight-in the rifle."[3]

Arguments in court about that scope would have produced a classic dispute between experts.

These are, however, relatively simple matters. But when we come to the Warren Commission's theory of the magic bullet, we are entering the technology of ballistics, and that is a wasteland for those who are not forensic experts, and the best people in forensics—it is a foregone conclusion—will also disagree.

So this work is not going to concern itself with ballistics. If one were a lawyer, one would wish to demonstrate that the odds against a single bullet passing through both Kennedy's and Connally's bodies (thereupon to emerge long enough to smash Connally's wrist before finally coming to rest in his thigh, and be the same bullet that was found, on examination, to be hardly deformed by its journey) must be, as odds, a 500-to-1, or even a 5,000-to-1, shot. One could probably assemble a dozen experts to say as much. Then, it would be up to the prosecutor to advance the counterargument, supported by his experts, that each bullet, and the wound it causes, has an inter-relation as unique as a fingerprint or a signature; indeed, it is recorded that on one occasion a bullet struck a man's brow at such an angle that the bullet traveled completely around his head between scalp and skull, making a full circle before it chose to exit near the entry point.[4] One can try repeating that shot! By the logic of such an argument, the proof of the magic bullet is that it happened. One cannot introduce the odds after the fact. So would go the rebuttal.

It is the same with Oswald's marksmanship. He is judged by various people, depending on the needs of the ax they grind, to be a poor rifleman, a fair one, a good one, or virtually an expert. Much the same has been stated about the difficulty of the shot itself. It has been estimated to be everything from as easy as Sergeant Zahm has testified to nearly impossible.

Such a debate is, however, moot. A rifleman can fire with accuracy one day and be far off target on another. Why should we ascribe any more consistency to a man with a gun (in the equivalent of combat conditions) than we would expect from a professional basketball player whose accuracy often varies dramatically from night to night?

Moreover, we are dealing with Oswald. We have seen him become hysterical on one occasion and, on another, be the coolest man in the room. If we have come through the turnings of this book without comprehending that the distance between his best and worst performance is enacted over a wide spectrum, then we have not gained much. The point is that Oswald, at his best, was certainly capable of hitting a moving target at eighty-eight yards on two out of three shots over five and a half seconds even if in Russia he could not drop a rabbit with a shotgun from ten feet away. We need only compare his performance in New Orleans on the radio with Stuckey to the incapacities demonstrated by his worst dyslexia two weeks later—or, for that matter, his hysteria before the KGB in Mexico to his calm during interrogation by Captain Fritz in Dallas at police headquarters.

So, the real question is not whether Oswald had the skills to bring off the deed but whether he had the soul of a killer. Yet, the formulation is too simple. It could be said that everybody alive is, potentially, under sufficient stress, a murderer, a suicide, or capable of both. Phrased more closely, the question becomes: Would Oswald, pushed to such an extreme, have the soul of a killer?

We know a great deal about Oswald by now. Assuming that the facts chosen by the author have been salient—a sizable assumption when dealing with Lee Harvey—it is still difficult not to believe that he pulled the trigger. For one thing, it violates our understanding of Oswald that he would allow his Mannlicher-Carcano to be fired by another man on the sixth floor while he lingers in the lunchroom four landings below. To what end? What purpose would that serve for him? If he has allowed his rifle to be used in such fashion by others, he is still deeply implicated. Yet the conspiracy allows him to amount to no more than a cog in the machine. That could hardly be enough for the man who has been depicted over the length of this book. If one misperceives his character on this point, then one has misunderstood him entirely.[5]

If one's personal inclinations would find Oswald innocent, or at least part of a conspiracy, one's gloomy verdict, nonetheless, is that Lee had the character to kill Kennedy, and that he probably did it alone. This conclusion now stated, one must rush to add that a good lawyer in a trial venue outside of Dallas might well have gotten him off—ridicule of the magic bullet would have drilled many a hole through the body of evidence amassed by the prosecution. Besides, no one can be certain that our protagonist was not only the killer but was alone. The odds in favor of one's personal conclusion can be no better than, let us say, 3 out of 4 that he is definitively guilty and the sole actor in the assassination. Too much is still unknown about CIA and FBI involvement with Oswald to offer any greater conviction. There are, for example, other possibilities to be remarked upon. While one is certainly not going to enter the near-impenetrable controversy in acoustics that would prove or disprove whether a fourth shot was fired from the grassy knoll—delineation of character, not exposition of sound-wave charts, is the aim of this work!—one would not be surprised that if there was indeed another shot, it was not necessarily fired by a conspirator of Oswald's. Such a gun could have belonged to another lone killer or to a conspirator working for some other group altogether. When the kings and political leaders of great nations appear in public on charged occasions, we can even antic-ipate a special property of the cosmos—coincidences accumulate: All variety of happenings race toward the core of the event. It is not inconceivable that two gunmen with wholly separate purposes both fired in the same few lacerated seconds of time.

All the same, none of that conflicts with the premise that Oswald—so far as he knew—was a lone gunman. Every insight we have gained of him suggests the solitary nature of his act. Besides, it is too difficult, no matter how one searches for a viable scenario, to believe that others could have chosen him to be the rifleman in a conspiracy. Other amateurs, conceivably. But not professionals. Who would trust him to hit the target? Any concerted plan that placed Oswald in the gunner's seat would have had to have been built on the calculation that he would miss. That, indeed, was the thesis of the CIA men in Don DeLillo's fine novel *Libra*. Indeed, it is not wholly implausible: Great damage will be done to your polit-ical enemies if the deed you designed appears to be their conspir-acy. Still! It is even more difficult to organize the aftermath of a planned failure than to do the deed and escape.

We have come then, to the last set of questions: Why did Oswald choose Kennedy?

Every account of his sentiments by every witness who recalls his occasional remarks about Jack Kennedy agrees—that rarest of phenomena for evidence—agreement! There is whole consensus that he saw JFK as, relatively speaking, a good President, and he liked him. Or so he professed. Given Oswald's reflexive impulse to lie at the drop of a hat, one could question whether he was not paying lip service precisely to conceal any hint, especially to Marina, that he had such a project of assassination already in his mind. Given the absence, however, of any opportunity in Dallas or New Orleans to be close enough to the throne to commit such an act until the last couple of weeks in November, the more reason-able assumption is that he probably did like Kennedy as much as he could approve of a conventional politician but that, finally, such sentiments had very little to do with his act. He would not be shooting at Kennedy because he liked him or disliked him—that would be irrelevant to the depth of his deed.

The focus has then shifted. Recognizing that one only argues this point in the likelihood that Oswald is guilty rather than as a found conclusion, what then happened to be the real intent of his deed?

4

Character

The answer speaks out of our understanding of him: It was the largest opportunity he had ever been offered.

The assassination of a President would be seismographic in its effect. For Americans, the aftershocks would not cease for the rest of the century or more. Yet he would also be punishing the Russians and the Cubans. They would suffer side effects for decades to come. But then, he was above capitalism and he was above Communism. Both! He had, as he would have seen it, a superior dedication, and the potential of a man like Lenin. If we know that he had none of Lenin's capacity to achieve large goals both philosophically and organizationally, Oswald did hold an equally intense belief in that fabulous end which would justify all his quotidian means. His deepest despair had to arise in those moments when he could not see himself any longer as the key protagonist in forging a new world.

Given his humiliation in Mexico and his lack of stature on weekends in Irving, the odds are that Oswald's political ideology had finally come to rest in the live nerve of nihilism—things had to get vastly worse before they could get better. We can refer ourselves back to that note he wrote on Holland-America Line stationery even as he may have been returning to America:

> I wonder what would happen if someone would stand up and say he was utterly opposed not only to the governments, but to the people, to the entire land and complete foundation of his society.[1]

All the motivation for shooting Kennedy is in that sentence. It may be worth quoting from *Mein Kampf* again:

> Even then I saw that only a twofold road could lead to the goal of improving these conditions:
> *The deepest sense of social responsibility for the creation of better foundations for our development coupled with brutal determination in breaking down incurable tumors.* [Hitler's italics][2]

Kennedy had the ability to give hope to the American ethos. That was, therefore, cause enough to call upon "brutal determination in breaking down incurable tumors." Kennedy was not, as American Presidents went, a bad President; therefore, he was too good. In the profoundest sense, as Oswald saw it, he had located the tumor—it was that Kennedy was too good. The world was in crisis and the social need was to create conditions for recognizing that there had to be a new kind of society. Otherwise, the malignant effects of capitalism, added to the Soviet degradation of Communism, were going to reduce people to the point where they lost all will to create a better world.

An explosion at the heart of the American establishment's complacency would be exactly the shock therapy needed to awaken the world.

It is doubtful that Oswald wanted to debate such a question with himself. He may well have possessed an instinct that told him he had to do something enormous and do it quickly, do it for his own physical well-being. The murderer kills in order to cure himself—which is why murder is properly repudiated. It is the most selfish of acts.

> *McMillan:* ... the uncanny selection of a route that would carry the President right under his window could mean only one thing. Fate had singled him out to do the dangerous but necessary task which had been his destiny all along and which would cause him to go down in history.[3]

Back in March, living on Neely Street, he had said in a letter to Robert Oswald, "It's always better to take advantage of your chances as they come along."[4]

Which may have been Oswald's way of saying that the intent of the universe is ready to reveal itself to us by the chances we are offered. Since the President would pass beneath his Book Depository windows, he did not have the right to violate such a monumental opportunity. Could there be another person in the universe who had been more uniquely designed to take advantage of such a situation, "vouchsafed to *him*," writes McMillan,

> to deal capitalism that final, mortal blow[?] And he would strike it not at the right nor at the left, but, quite simply, at the top. It had become his fate to decapitate the American political process. *He* was history's chosen instrument.[5]

The point absent here from Priscilla Johnson McMillan's interpretation is that after the assassination, Oswald had a choice. He might not only be the instrument but the leading man. That presented a new conflict—to be the instrument of history *or* the leading man? The latter could occur only if he was captured and stood trial. If he succeeded in the act but managed to remain undiscovered, obscurity would be his lot again. He had learned as much from his attempt on Walker.

Capture, however, would guarantee him a very high level of attention. And if he was convicted, he had the temperament to live alone in a cell; he was more than half habituated to that already. He could even view his life up to this point as a preparation for spending many years in prison.

Indeed, it may even have been the thought of his trial that fired him on. What a podium! Such a trial could alter history, stimulate the stupid, rouse the lethargic, confound the powerful. So he had to feel divided between his desire to escape and his recognition that capture, trial, and incarceration might generate a vastly larger destiny.

His personal attitude toward Kennedy had little to do, therefore, with his act. In war, one may execute a man for whom one feels respect or even personal affection; Oswald saw it as an execution. One mighty leader was going to be dispatched by another high and mighty personage—of the future. The future would preempt the present.

If he failed to escape, well, he could tell his story. He could becloud the issue and possibly be acquitted, and if it came to twenty years of prison, he would be able to forge his political agenda—even as Hitler, Stalin, and Lenin had done. Should he face capital punishment, then, at the least, he would be immortal. He would take care of that at his trial. He would expound his ideas.

What he may never have taken into account is that the furies he set loose would devour him before he could utter one idea. The first element in the loss of an heroic trial became the four shots he fired into Tippit. There can be little doubt that he panicked. As soon as he killed Tippit, the mighty architecture of his ideology, hundreds of levels high and built with no more than the game cards of his political imagination, came tumbling down. He knew Americans well enough to recognize that some might listen to his ideas if he killed a President, but nearly all would be repelled by any gunman who would mow down a cop, a family man—that act was small enough to void interest in every large idea he wished to introduce. By killing Tippit he had wrecked his grand plan to be one of the oracles of history. Now he had to improvise a defense: I'm a patsy.

It may never have occurred to Oswald that the obfuscation and paranoia which followed the assassination of Kennedy would contribute immensely to the sludge and smog of the world's spirit.

Oswald may never have read Emerson, but the following passage from "Heroism" gives us luminous insight into what had to be Oswald's opinion of himself as he sat on the sixth floor waiting for the Kennedy motorcade—he was committing himself to the most heroic deed of which he was capable.

> Self-trust is the essence of heroism. It is the state of the soul at war, and its ultimate objects are the last defiance of falsehood and wrong, and the power to bear all that can be inflicted by evil agents. [Heroism is] scornful of petty calculations and scornful of being scorned. It persists; it is of an undaunted boldness and of a fortitude not to be wearied out. Its jest is the littleness of common life. [Heroism] works in contradiction to the voice of mankind and in contradiction, for a time, to the voice of the great and good. Heroism is obedience to a secret impulse of an individual's character. Now to no other man can wisdom appear as it does to him, for every man must be supposed to see a little farther on his own proper path than anyone else [so] every heroic act measures itself by its contempt of some external good . . .[6]

It would have wounded Oswald to the quick if he had known that history would not see him as a hero but as an anti-hero. He went off to work that last morning, leaving the dregs of instant coffee in a plastic cup, and in two days he ascended to the summit of our national obsessions—he became our First Ghost.

Oswald owned all the properties that belong to a ghost—ambition, deceit, a sense of mission, and the untold frustration of an abrupt death just as a long-held dream of personal prominence is about to unfold. Can there be any American of our century who, having failed to gain stature while he was alive, now haunts us more?

Let us give a word to Lee's brother John, whom he saw so seldom:

> **MR. PIC.** Well, sir, ever since I was born and I was old enough to remember, I always had a feeling that some great tragedy was going to strike Lee in some way or another . . . In fact, on the very day of the assassination I was thinking about it when I was getting ready to go to work . . . and I figured well, when he defected and came back—that was his big tragedy. I found out it wasn't.[7]

5

—————————

The Widow's Elegy

First, Jacqueline Kennedy was a widow, and then Marina. As the second widow, she can no longer know what it is she knows. She has passed through thirty years of interviews, more than a thousand hours of interviews, and the questions never cease. She may be the last living smoker to consume four packs a day. How can it be otherwise? The past is filled with guilt—the future is full of dread. Only the present is clear; she always suspects the motives of the new people to whom she speaks. How innocent can be their motive for approaching? These days she feels that the walls are coming closer. If she starts thinking about what has happened to her, not with pity, she will say, or sorrow for herself, but just hop-

ing to lessen stress, she feels she is choking. She still thinks of the
night Lee sat in the dark on their porch in New Orleans and he
was weeping. It was such a heavy burden for him. Something, and
she does not know what it was.

It is hard for her to remember details. After her Warren Commission testimony, everybody accused her of lying, but she was just
a human being and if she was lying, it was honestly—because she
was floating through a foggy world. Memories kept coming, going.
Maybe it was some self-protective mechanism. To keep her psyche
from collapsing. People were saying to her, "You're so strong"—
but it was not heroic effort. "It is in every one of us—you just
decide not to die, that's all. You dare not to die."

Now that she is fifty-two, Marina would agree that one doesn't
need to approach her with such labels as good woman, bad
woman, villainess, heroine, someone-who's-been-treated-unfairly,
someone-treated-too-well. "You can be all of that in one person,"
said Marina. "One can be a villain, and next time a hero.

"If we go through Lee's character, I myself would like to find
out: Who is he? Was he really that mean of a person?—which I
think he was—but it's a hard road for me to take because I do not
want to understand him. I have to tell you in advance that, as far
as Lee is concerned—I don't like him. I'm mad at him. Very mad
at him, yes. When a person dies, people have such anger. They
loved their husband or wife for a long time so they say, 'How dare
you die on me?' Okay, but that's not my reason. For me, it's, 'How
dare you abandon me? In circumstances like that? I mean, *you* die
but I'm still here licking my wounds.'

"All the same, I'm definitely sure he didn't do it, even if I'm still
mad at him. Because he shouldn't involve a wife and family if he
was playing those kinds of games. Yes, I do believe he was on a mission, maybe even when he went to Russia, but first I have to figure
out what he was doing here. It wasn't just happening here all of a
sudden in America. It was a continuation. In my mind, I'm not trying to convince you or the American public—I have to resolve it
for myself. But I think he was sent over to Russia, maybe. I think
so. I have no proof. I have nothing. I do think he was more human
than has been portrayed. I'm not trying to make an angel out of
him, but I was interested in him because he was different, he
would broaden my horizon, and all the other men I wanted had
been taken or didn't want me."

Every time she watches a film and sees an actor playing Lee, the actor is nothing like him. He turns his head like Lee or waves his hair the same way, but, she says, your American public knows Lee only from a few photographs, and that is what this actor is copying. She sees another Lee, and she does not know the psyche of that fellow. She still has it to discover.

Her interviewers asked how she would have felt if a truck had hit Alik in Minsk—if she had been his widow then, would she have thought of him fondly? She said yes. She would have thought it was just a stormy beginning but they were breaking ground that they would later stand on in their marriage. After all, she took a chance. She had crossed the ocean for him. Of course, she was afraid of him already, even if little by little she had been learning that she did not know, never knew, where she stood. Not with him. But at least you could hope.

She will never forget that on their last night in Irving, he had kept making advances to her until he went to bed, and she had refused. She had said to herself, "No, if I don't teach him this lesson right now, this lying will continue. O. H. Lee will continue. Don't butter up to me." She tried to discipline him.

Afterward, she had to think, What if he really wanted to be close to me? What if I put him in a bad mood? It torments her. What if they had made love that last night? But she is the wrong person to talk to about this, she would say, because she is not a sexual person. Sensuous but not sensual. She didn't like sex, she would say. She was not expert, nor could she tell you how grandiose something had been, because she had never experienced that. No Beethoven or Tchaikovsky for her, not in bed, no grand finale.

MARINA: In Texas, sun is very intense for me and very harsh, very bright. I love moon. It's cool and it's shiny and that's my melancholy period. And some people are shining and they are bright and they burn. You know what I mean? I'm not sun. I'm a moon . . .

I look at America, it's all wonderful. But you go to the damn grocery store and it's 200 varieties of cereal. And basically it's only oats, corn, how many things . . . Just so somebody going to make extra million off that. It's so unnecessary. If that's progress, if that's abundance, how stupid for us to want it. 300 bags of poison, maybe only two or three good [well,] that kind of progress I don't think we should strive for . . . Do I make any sense to you? Or I'm just complaining?

INTERVIEWER: No, I agree with you.

After the assassination, there were times when she was close to ending her life. She wondered when her breaking point would come. She had crossed that ocean for nothing. Still, she tried to survive. It was a lonely life. Every day. The worst of the pain was that maybe she loved him more by the end than in their beginning. Maybe grieving was just starting to happen now! Maybe! Because she had never really had such a process. Just numb, with pain always there.

She doesn't know whether they would have stayed married, but still, Lee was the person she would have liked to have been able to make it with. Through life. There was some goodness in him to hold on to, and on that last unexpected Thursday when he came to visit, he was kind of sheepish because of that big lie, O. H. Lee.

And when he came in, he said, "Hi," nice and everything, and she said, "What are you doing here?"—cold and rude.

Later, she couldn't understand. Maybe he didn't love her, maybe he cared less for her, but he loved his little girls enormously, and even thirty years later she heard a story about how in those last days, when he lived on North Beckley, he was playing with the grandchildren of the woman who ran his last rooming house. These children called him Mr. Lee. He asked one of those boys, "Are you a good boy?" and that kid shook his head in the negative, said, "Uh-unh," and Lee said, "Never be so bad that you hurt somebody." This kid was now grown-up, but he still remembered that, still told that story.

The morning when Lee left, Friday morning, November 22, 1963, she did not get up with him when he arose very early. She tried to, but he said, "Don't worry. Go back to sleep." And he left quietly.

She had gone to bed after him the night before. He was already asleep or pretended to be. Then, when she woke up in the middle of the night to check on baby Rachel, she took a look at him. The only illumination was by nightlight, very low. But Lee scared her. She touched him with her foot and he kicked it away. Then he lay so still that it was like he had died. He didn't move for the next hour. She said to herself, "Is he alive?" He looked so still. Absolutely gone. She couldn't hear his breath. She had to bend over very close to feel his breathing—she thought he had died on her. Isn't that funny? For all these years she remembered saying, "Thank goodness he's alive." And he made no sound all night and never moved again.

In the morning, he made himself instant coffee, drank it in a plastic cup, and went off to work.

She sits in a chair, a tiny woman in her early fifties, her thin shoulders hunched forward in such pain of spirit under such a mass of guilt that one would comfort her as one would hug a child. What is left of what was once her beauty are her extraordinary eyes, blue as diamonds, and they blaze with light as if, in divine compensation for the dead weight of all that will not cease to haunt her, she has been granted a spark from the hour of an apocalypse others have not seen. Perhaps it is the light offered to victims who have suffered like the gods.

6

The Third Widow

MARGUERITE OSWALD. I don't believe this letter belongs with the letters. May I see it, please? Is that a letter from Russia? I don't think so from what I can see from here.

MR. RANKIN. It purports to be, Mrs. Oswald. I hand it to you. Is it Exhibit 198 you are speaking of?

MARGUERITE OSWALD. Yes. I'm sorry. There was another very important letter of this size that I thought maybe had become confused with the Russian letters. You will have to forgive me, Chief Justice Warren, but this is quite a big undertaking.[1]

All day long, throughout her testimony, she has been fumbling through her file of letters, bringing forth "documents, gentlemen," that prove nothing but that she has had her share of lonely nights filled with intolerable scenarios of suspicion. Her letters prove of little use in the lawyerly air of the Warren Commission Hearings. She is wasting their time with trivia, and all the while her possession of these letters remains as important to her as tombstones. Who is moving the tombstones in the family graveyard?

The interlocutors grow testy:

REPRESENTATIVE BOGGS. Why did your son defect to Russia?

MARGUERITE OSWALD. I cannot answer that yes or no sir. I am going to go through the whole story or it is no good. And that is what I have been doing for this Commission all day long—giving a story.

REPRESENTATIVE BOGGS. Suppose you just make it very brief.

MARGUERITE OSWALD. I cannot make it brief. I will say I am unable to make it brief. This is my life and my son's life going down in history.[2]

Marguerite has taken sufficient blame, scorn, and ridicule from other people (including the barely concealed animus of the Warren Commission) that there is no need to depict her in one more unfavorable light—it seems certain at the least that every malformation, or just about, of Lee Harvey Oswald's character had its roots in her. That much granted, it is also difficult not to feel some guarded sympathy for Marguerite Claverie Oswald. As with Lee, the internal workings of her psyche were always condemned to hard labor, and so much of what she tried, and with the best intentions, would fail—especially her obvious desire to receive some love from her sons, enough love at least to match her harsh pride. It is not agreeable to see Marguerite's life through her eyes. The boys are always leaving her as quickly as they can, and their willful wives—willful as she sees them—have no belief in her desire to be a decent mother-in-law. Her sacrifices are many and real—but no love comes back. Merely banishment from her children, and icy silence. And then her favorite is accused of killing the President.

In her heart of hearts she has to wonder whether indeed he did it—she knows how far he can go.

Denigrators of Marguerite Oswald will remark on how much she loved the limelight after he was gone, and it is true: His love of attention was equaled by hers—she spoke to large audiences for the first time in her life, and it was a great step forward from that sales job in New York where she was fired because of intractable body odor.

Yet, for all her latter-day notoriety, we have to recall that she died alone and full of a literal cancer to follow upon the bottomless cancer of those endless wounds within personal wounds—no, she had her life, and one would not want it, but somewhere in the bureaucratic corridors of Karmic Reassignment she is probably arguing now with one of the monitors, dissatisfied with the low station, by her lights, of her next placement. "I gave birth to one of the most famous and important Americans who ever lived!" she will tell the clerk-angel who is recording her story.

INTERVIEWER: Do you have any family here at all?

MARGUERITE: I have no family, period. I brought three children into the world, and I have sisters, I have nieces, I have nephews, I have grandchildren, and I'm all alone. That answers that question and I don't want to hear another word about it.[3]

There she stands with her outrageous ego and her self-deceit, her bold loneliness and cold bones, those endless humiliations that burn like sores.

Yet, she is worthy of Dickens. Marguerite Oswald can stand for literary office with Micawber and Uriah Heep. No word she utters will be false to her character; her stamp will be on every phrase. Few people without a literary motive would seek her company for long, but a novelist can esteem Marguerite. She does all his work for him.

Given such modest thoughts, it is time to conclude one's sad tale of a young American who lived abroad and returned to a grave in Texas. Let us, then, say farewell to Lee Harvey Oswald's long and determined dream of political triumph, wifely approbation, and high destiny. Who among us can say that he is in no way related to our own dream? If it had not been for Theodore Dreiser and his last great work, one would like to have used "An American Tragedy" as the title for this journey through Oswald's beleaguered life.

THE END

APPENDIX

Worth quoting here are a few passages from Dr. Howard P. Rome of the Mayo Clinic, whose report on dyslexia is buried in Volume XXVI of the Warren Commission papers, Exhibit No. 3134, pp. 812–817.

I think that this disability and its consequential effect upon him, while a minor point in the total array of evidence accumulated by the Commission, is relevant since it amplifies the impression from many sources about the nature of Oswald's estrangement from people, his diffident truculence during school years and his unwarranted estimation of his literary capacities.

Such traits as these are not uncommon sequelae of a life-experience which has been marked by repeated thwarting in almost every sphere of endeavor. For a bright person to be handicapped in the use of language is an especially galling experience. It seems to me that in Oswald's instance this frustration gave an added impetus to his need to prove to the world that he was an unrecognized "great man."

... handicapped by an inability to read and spell at a level of efficiency which could otherwise be attended by rewards, a person with this handicap is at a great premium to maintain sustained attention and interest in activity where he is a consistent poor performer.

The high social value placed upon adequate literate performance by our culture invokes sanctions of considerable significance upon these persons. Inasmuch as they tend to lose status in the eyes of their peers as well as superiors (teachers, parents, and adults), they are prone to develop a range of alternative ways of coping with their disadvantaged state: apparent indifference, truculent resistance, and other displacement activities by which they hope to cover up their deficiency and appear in a more commendable light. . . .

There are many examples of his typical efforts at a crude approximation of proper spelling: "enorgies" for "energies," "compulusory" for "compulsory," "patrioct" for "patriotic," "opions" for "opinions," "esspicialy" for "especially," "disire" for "desire," "unsuraen" for "insurance," "indepence" for "independence," "negleck" for "neglect," "immeanly" for "immediately," "abanded" for "abandoned," "nuclus" for "nucleus," "triditionall" for "traditional," "imperilistic" for "imperialistic," "alturnative" for "alternative," "traiditions" for "traditions," "neccary" for "necessary," "trations" for "traditions," "prefered" for "preferred," . . . [and the list continues for another page].

Very few people have patience to read a writer who spells badly, but since I was obliged to go over Oswald's writings for this book, I was able to discover that our protagonist, cleansed of the grime of his misspellings and poor punctuation, was not only an intelligent man but had, doubtless, shielded himself from how his errors would affect others. So I thought that to understand Oswald's personal drama—that is to say, how he thought he was impressing himself on others—we ought to be able to read his thought at the level at which he thought he was presenting it. Ergo, what you have seen in this book is not the precise letter he composed but a more finished product. An editor and copy-editor (your author and his assistant) did the weeding. Those who wish to see what any particular letter or page of original manuscript was like need only refer to this book's citations from the twenty-six volumes of the Warren Commission Hearings and Exhibits.

It is worth repeating the point more than once: To show Oswald constantly in the toils of his dyslexia is to do no more than repeat society's low estimate of him, whereas to correct his spelling and punctuation brings us closer to his psychological reality—which is that he would yet be most important in the scheme of things. Be it said that if he had not distinguished himself verbally in the two radio debates with Stuckey, one would not have been nearly so inclined to dress up his literary appearance; but it was obvious from reading Stuckey's transcripts that Oswald had polemical gifts large enough to encourage a closer look at what he was saying.

To give readers an idea of the extent of the changes, a half page of some of the worst of his original text from his essay on Minsk will now be placed next to the copy-edited version.

Example of Oswald's uncorrected writing:

It may be explained that in the Eastern European custom all citizens upon reaching the age of 16 years are given a grey-green "passport" or identifecation papers. On the first page is a foto and personal information, on the following 4 pages , are places for registring address, this including rented rooms, on the next four pages are places for paticular remarks as to the conduct of the carier, a place better kept blank, the next three pages are for registering the places of work, then the next page is for marriage license and divorce stamps, these passprts are changed for a small chrage every five years, a lost passport can be replaced after a short investagation for 10 rubles, all persons regardless of nationality are required to carry these at all times in the Soviet Union nationalities are allso marked on the passport, for instance, a Urakranion is marked Urakrinuien, a Jew is marked Jew, no matter where he was born . . .

Oswald's writing as corrected:

It may be explained that in the Eastern European custom, all citizens upon reaching the age of 16 years are given a gray-green "passport" or identification papers. On the first page is a photo and personal information. On the following four pages are spaces for registering addresses, this including rented rooms. On the next four pages are places for particular remarks as to the conduct of the carrier—a place better kept blank. The next three pages are for registering the places of work; then the next page is for marriage licenses and divorce stamps. These passports are changed for a small charge every five years. A lost passport can be replaced after a short investigation for 10 rubles. All persons regardless of nationality are required to carry these at all times. In the Soviet Union, nationalities are also marked on passports. For instance, a Ukrainian is marked Ukrainian; a Jew is marked "Jew" no matter where he was born . . .

The excerpts that follow are corrected, and make up about half of those fifty-odd pages of Oswald's manuscript upon which George De Mohrenschildt offered his comments to the Warren Commission:

FROM THE COMMISSION EXHIBITS
VOL. XVI, PP. 287–336

The Minsk Radio and Television Plant is known throughout the Union as the major producer of electronic parts and sets. In this vast enterprise created in the early '50s, the Party Secretary is a 6' 4" man in his early forties [who] has a long history of service to the Party. He controls the activities of the 1,000 Communist Party members here and otherwise supervises the activities of the other 5,000 people employed at this major enterprise in Minsk, the capital of the third-ranking Republic, Byelorussia.

This factory manufactures 87,000 large and powerful radios and 60,000 television sets in various sizes and ranges, excluding pocket radios, which are not mass-produced anywhere in the USSR. It is this plant which manufactured several console model combination radio-phonograph-television sets which were shown as mass-produced items of commerce before several hundreds of thousands of Americans at the Soviet Exposition in New York in 1959. After the Exhibition, these sets were duly shipped back to Minsk and are now stored in a special storage room on the first floor of the Administrative Building—at this factory, ready for the next International Exhibit.

I worked for 23* months at this plant, a fine example of average and even slightly better than average working conditions. The plant covers an area of 25 acres in a district one block north of the main thoroughfare and only two miles from the center of the City with all facilities for the mass production of radios and televisions. It employs 5,000 full-time and 300 part-time workers, 58% women and girls.

Five hundred people during the day shift are employed on the huge stamp and pressing machines where sheet metal is turned into metal frames and cabinets for television sets and radios.

Another five hundred people are employed in an adjoining building for the cutting and finishing of rough wood into fine polished cabinets. A laborer's process, mostly done by hand, the cutting, trimming and the processes right up to hand-polishing are carried out here at the same plant. The plant also has its own stamp-making plant, employing 150 people at or assisting at 80 heavy machine lathes and grinders. The noise in this shop is almost deafening as metal grinds against metal and steel saws cut through iron ingots at the rate of an inch a

---

* This must be an error. He started in January of 1960 and quit in May 1962—twenty-eight months.

minute. The floor is covered with oil used to drain the heat of [the] metal being worked so one has to watch one's footing; here the workers' hands are as black as the floor and seem to be [so] eternally . . .

The plant has its electric shop where those who have finished long courses in electronics work over generators, television tubes, and testing experiments of all kinds. The green worktables are filled high here. Electric gadgets are not too reliable, mostly due to the poor quality of the wires, which keep burning out under the impact of the usual 220V voltage . . .

The plastics department is next. Here forty-seven women and three physically disabled persons keep the red-hot liquid plastic flowing into a store of odd presses, turning out their quotas of knobs, handles, non-conducting tube bases, and so forth. These workers suffer the worst conditions of work in the plant (an otherwise model factory for the Soviet Union) due to bad fumes and the hotness of the materials. These workers are awarded 30 days vacation a year, the maximum for workers. Automation is now employed at a fairly large number of factories, espcially in the war industry. However, for civilian use, their number is still small . . .

Factory meetings of the Kollectives are so numerous as to be staggering.

For instance, during one month, the following meetings and lectures are scheduled: 1 Professional Union, which discusses the work of the Professional Union in gathering dues, paying out receipts on vacation orders, etc.; 4 political information every Tuesday on the lunch hour; 2 Young Communist* meetings on the 6th and 21st of every month; 1 Production Committee made up of workers discussing ways of improving work; 2 Communist Party meetings a month called by the section Communist Party Secretary; 4 School of Communist Labor meetings, compulsory, every Wednesday; 1 sports meeting per month, non-compulsory—for a total of 15 meetings every month, 14 of which are compulsory for Communist Party members and 12 compulsory for all others. These meetings are always held after work or on the lunch hour. They are never held during working time. Absenteeism is by no means allowed. After long years of hard discipline, especially under the Stalin regime, no worker will invite the sure disciplinary action of the Party men, and inevitably the factory Party Committee, because of trying to slip out of the way or giving too little attention to what is being said.

A strange sight indeed is the picture of the local Party man delivering a political sermon to a group of usually robust, simple working men who through some strange process have been turned to stone. Turned to stone—all except the hard-faced Communists with roving eyes looking for any bonus-making catch of inattentiveness on the part of any worker. A sad sight for someone not used to it, but the Russians are philosophical. Who likes the lecture? "Nobody—but it's compulsory." . . .

For a good cross-section of the Russian working class, I suggest we examine the lives of some of the 58 workers and 5 foremen working in the experimental shop of the Minsk radio plant . . .

The shop itself is located in a two-story building with no particular noticeable mark on its red brick face. By 8:00 A.M. sharp all the workers have arrived and at the sound of a bell sounded by the duty orderly, who is a worker whose duty it is to see the workers don't slip out for too many smokes, they file upstairs, except

* Oswald uses Young Communist or Young Communist League or YCL interchangeably as a translation into English of Komsomol.

for 10 turners and lathe operators whose machines are located on the first floor. Work here is given out in the form of blueprints and drawings by the foreman Zonof and junior foreman Lavruk to workers whose various reliability and skills call for them, since each worker has with time acquired differing skills and knowledge. Work is given strictly according to so-called "pay levels," the levels being numbered 1 through 5 with the highest level [6, called] "master." For level 1, a worker receives approximately 68 rubles for work; level 2, a worker receives 79.50; level 3, 90 rubles; level 4, 105 rubles; for level 5, 125 rubles; and for "masters," about 150 . . . Except in instances of poor quality work, bonuses are always the same, giving rise to a more or less definite pay scale. A worker may demand to be tested for a higher pay level at any time [and] higher bonuses are awarded to the best shops by the factory committee for good production standards.

Our shop head Stephen Tarasavich is a stout, open-faced, well-skilled metalworker who, although he hasn't got a higher education (which is now a prime requisite for even a foreman's job) managed to finish a four-year specialty night school course . . . Stephen has an almost bald head except for a line of hair on the left side which he is forever combing across his shiny top. Aged 45, he is married, with two children aged 8 and 10. It may be explained that Russians seem to marry much older than their American counterparts. Perhaps that can be explained by the fact that in order to receive an apartment people often must wait for 5 or 6 years and since security is so unstable until a commonly desired goal is reached—that is, an apartment for oneself—most Russians do not choose to start families until later in life. Stephen is responsible to the Factory Committee and Director for the filling of quotas and production quality. His foreman Zonof is 38 years old, has a wife and 15-month-old baby. Not too long ago, [he] moved out of his one-room flat without kitchen or private toilet into a newly built apartment house and flat of two small rooms, kitchen and bath, a luxury not experienced by most Russians. A tall, thin man with dark creases in his face, his manner, nervous, spontaneous, and direct, betrays his calling. His job: keep the work on the premises going as quickly and efficiently as possible. His assistant, junior foreman Lavruk, is much younger, ten years younger, enigmatic, handsome, quick. He climbed to his post through a night school degree and a sort of rough charm which he instinctively uses in the presence of superiors. The shop's mainstay is composed of 17 "Shock Workers" whose pictures hang on a wall near the stairs so that all might strive to imitate them. Usually of the 5 level or "master" class of workers, they are experienced at work and politics.

Most Shock Workers are men of the older age groups, 40–50, and not always members of the Communist Party. They carry the production load and most of the responsibility of the inner life of the Kollective.

The remaining 41 workers are divided into about half 18–22 year olds, new metalworkers, trying to fulfill their obligatory two years at a factory before going on to full-time day studies at the local University or one of the specialized Institutes, and half [are] older workers who have been working at the plant for 4 to 6 years and occupy the middle number worker levels, 3 and 4; these workers are aged about 24–30 and form the mass of laborers at the factory. Seventy percent have families. Apartments are few. Most occupy rooms belonging to relatives or rooms to let by holders of two- and three-room apartments, often for rents as high as 20 rubles a month. The housing shortage is so critical that people count themselves lucky even to find a person willing to let his room. Room renting is also the most common form of speculation in the USSR. Often it reaches heights out of all proportion with reality, such as the man who derived 80 rubles a month from letting his rooms in the summer while he himself was living in a summer house or *dacha* in the country. Such speculation is forbidden and carries penalties including deportation to other economic areas of the USSR for terms of up to six months . . .

All plants and factories in the Soviet Union have Party Committees, headed by one graduate of a higher Party school whose function is to control discipline of members of the Communist Party, and who, working in conjunction with the Directors of the factory, control all factors pertaining to the work, alterations, and production of any given line. It must be noted that officially the Party man occupies a position exactly equal to the head of any factory. However, the facts point out that the Party man has, due to the fact that Communists hold the leading positions in plants, considerably more sway over the activities of the workers than anyone else. No suggestion of the Party man is ever turned down by the directors of our factory. That would be tantamount to treason. The Party man is appointed by the Headquarters of the Central Committee of the Communist Party. He designates who shall be Shop and Section Party Secretaries, a post well-coveted by employed Communists. These Communists, in reality, control every move of the Kollectives. They are responsible for the carrying out of directives pertaining to meetings, lectures, and Party activities in the local cells.

These meetings of *sabranias* are almost always held at the lunch hour or after working hours [and] meetings last anywhere from 10 minutes to two hours . . . An amazing thing in watching these political lectures is that there is taken on by the listeners a most phenomenal aspect, one impervious to outside interference or sounds. After long years of hard-fisted discipline, no worker will permit himself to be trapped and called out for inattentiveness by the ever-present and watchful Party Secretary and members of the Communist Party . . . At these times, it is best to curb one's naturally boisterous and lively nature. Under the 6′ by 6′ picture of Lenin, the Party Section Secretary stands, in our Section, a middle-aged pocked man by the name of Sobakin, an average-looking man wearing glasses. His wrinkled face and twinkling eyes give one the impression that at any moment he's going to tell a racy story or funny joke, but he never does. Behind this man stands twenty-five years of Party life. His high post, relatively speaking for him, is witness to his efficiency. He stands expounding from notes in front of him the week's "Information" with all the lack of enthusiasm and gusto of someone who knows that he has no worries about his audience or about someone getting up and going away.

In the same way, May Day and other "demonstrations" are arranged as well as spontaneous receptions for distinguished guests. I remember when I was in Moscow in 1959 I was just passing in front of the Metropole Restaurant when out of the side streets came a ten-man police unit which stopped all people on the street from passing in front of the entrance, surrounding the crowd and keeping them hemmed in (not detouring the flow of traffic, as would be expected) for three minutes until, right on schedule, an obviously distinguished foreign lady was driven up to the restaurant, where a meeting in her honor had been arranged. She was taken through the "spontaneous" welcoming crowd, after which the police were withdrawn, allowing the passers-by to continue.

Another instance of this was in 1961 when a Chinese delegation arrived in Minsk and was driven from the railway station to a house on the outskirts of the city. Even though it was 10:30 at night, all along the way members of the MVD (security) forces ran into apartment buildings and student dormitories ordering people out onto the street to welcome the arriving guests.

Although there was no prior notice of any delegation, another "spontaneous" welcoming committee met the cavalcade of black limousines and dutifully waved back to the darkened cars with their slightly protruding yellowish waving hands . . .

At the Minsk radio factory, holiday demonstrations (there are two a year, May Day and Revolution Day) are arranged in the following manner: Directives are passed down the Communist Party line until they reach the factory, shop, and mill Kollectives. Here they are implemented by the Communist Party Secretary, who issues instructions as to what time the demonstrators are to arrive. At the arrival point, names are taken well in advance of the march so that latecomers and absentees may be duly noted. Neither one is allowed. At the assembly point, signs, drums and flags are distributed and marchers formed in ranks. In the city of Minsk on such days, all roads are closed by driving trucks across them, except the prescribed route [of march]. This, as well as meticulous attention to attendance, ensures a 90% turnout of the entire population. Stragglers or late risers walking through the streets may be yanked into the steady stream of workers by the police or volunteer red-armbanded "people's militia." Anyone who argues may be subjected to close investigation later on—one thing to be avoided in any police state . . .

People have been known to do odd, even unlawful, things to get a little higher on the housing waiting list, such as faking the ownership of a baby or two to get special rating. The opening of [new] apartment houses is always done with a great deal of gusto and preparation. Indeed, for the lucky ones receiving their orders on rooms and flats, it is a big moment, a moment culminating years of waiting and often years of manipulation. The lucky few get the word to move out of their old quarters, usually one room in an oblong building built after the war which are mostly to be later torn down. As soon as a newly built [apartment] house is ready . . . it is opened—even though there may not be light fixtures or toilet seats just yet. What does that matter?! In 1960 there were 2,978,000 living places built in the USSR; in the USA 1,300,000, including Alaska and Hawaii . . .

The reconstruction of Minsk is an interesting story reflecting the courage of its builders. In a totalitarian system, great forces can be brought into play under rigid controls and support . . . The architectural planning may be anything but modern, but it is in the manner of almost all Russian cities.

With the airport serving as its eastern boundary, we find a large, spread-out township in appearance, one city only. The skyline pierced with factory booms and chimneys betrays its industrial background; I say "in appearance" because the tallest building here is the nine-story black apparatus house flanking the main street, Prospekt Stalinskaya, which is over two miles long and the only such boulevard in the Republic [of Byelorussia]. All other streets are narrow rock-laid streets, curving through the city like rivers of stone branching off the main street, ending at the other end in extensive parks. The design and content of this prospekt is very reflective of the sites of this city. From north to south, this straight-as-an-arrow vein of the city includes in the first two miles the central district of the city, the Hotel Minsk, and the Main Post Office. The hotel was built in 1957 on the direct orders of Khrushchev, who was grieved at the fact that only one old, dilapidated hotel existed at that time when he paid an official visit to this, the capital of Byelorussia. The hotel was built in three months, a record for the entire Soviet Union, and has over 500 rooms. A modern, well-built, well-serviced hotel, box-shaped, it serves many tourists traveling from Germany and Poland through Minsk to Moscow.

The Post Office handles all mail coming in and out of the city. Built in 1955, it has four columns at its entrance in the Greek style.

Next down the prospekt are a clothing store and children's store. The central movie house, the best one in Minsk, seats 400 people in a small unventilated hall. Next to it stands a shoe store, across from it the central beauty shop, the main drug store, and *orspranon* (Russian food store) and furniture store. Next is the Ministry of Internal Affairs, whose head is a tough military colonel, Nikoley Aksionov of the "people's militia." He holds the title Minister of Internal Affairs. Around the corner is his subsidiary, the KGB, Committee for Internal Security (Intelligence and Secret Police). Across from the Ministry is the ever-crowded Prospekt Book Shop, and across from this is the even more crowded restaurant, one of five in the city where for two rubles, a person can buy fried tongue or plates of chicken with potatoes and fried cabbage, instead of just *kotlets* (bread and ground meat patties) or *schnitzel* (with a little more meat and less bread) and beef steak (pure ground beef patties) served with potatoes and cabbage and sometimes macaroni. These are always served at workers' dining rooms and stand-up cafés for they open at night. And sometimes sweet rolls, coffee, fall fruits, salads and tomatoes can also be bought. Down from this café called "Springtime" is the bakery shop. Here for 13 kopecks a person can buy un-wrapped bread (white), for 7 kopecks, sweet rolls of different kinds, and for 20 kopecks black bread. (The black bread loaf is twice as large as the white, therefore cheaper per kilogram and more in demand. Also, black bread remains fresh for an exceptionally long time due to the hard crust.)

Across from this bakery shop is the confection place. Here is a kid's dreamland of sweets and chocolate, although owing to the climate, chocolate costs four times as much here as in the U.S. For four ounces one must pay 60 kopecks. Chocolate is much in demand since Russians have a vicious sweet tooth. Here there is always a crowd. Further down, we come to the only department store in Minsk, the GUM, which means "State Universal Store." Here one may buy anything sold in the smaller specialized stores and sign up on the list for refrigerators, vacuum cleaners, even cars (none of which can be bought anywhere outright). The waiting list for refrigerators (112 million sold from 1952 to 1958) is three months, and the same [length of time] for vacuum cleaners. For cars, the waiting list is anywhere from 6 months to a year, depending on which of the three existing types one puts a down payment on. The Moskvich, which costs 2,500 rubles, is presumed to be the best so the waiting list is almost a year for that; however, the Victory and Volga are a little cheaper and so one can expect it [delivery] after only a six or seven month wait. Cars are bought more or less to order here. The styles are not very impressive. The Moskvich looks like a box on wheels, while the Volga looks like a 1938 Studebaker, which, by the way, is what it is modeled after, "America's prewar aid."

Motorcycles and television sets can, however, be bought on the spot for ready cash. A good high-powered motorcycle costs 350 rubles and their quality is apt to be better that that of the more complex automobile. Television sets cost anywhere from 80 rubles for a 6-inch-by-6-inch screen to 350 rubles for a well-made television [with] a 22-inch screen. Other models (light table models) cost 190 and 145 rubles. Here ready-made suits of rough material can be bought. The cheaper style, a double-breasted blue for 110 rubles, or a better-made three-button suit for 250 rubles. [A] jacket costs 40 rubles and two pair of pants for not less than 15 rubles. There are a few cheap ones [jackets?] in stock. They usually cost 30 rubles.

Just before we come to Stalin Square, the end of the central district along the prospekt, we find the two automats, or stand-up cafés. These cafés are located across the prospekt from one another. The internal and external structure is exactly the same at each; both places serve the same dishes at the same prices. Why these were not built at opposite ends of the central district, or even at opposite ends of the square, is not known. Although it would, of course, be more convenient. The reason is [perhaps] that the architectural plans for all the cities in the Soviet Union come directly from Moscow which, as one can imagine, is a big responsibility for the architect. Since in the USSR one pays for a mistake with one's head, it seems that the logical reason for the standard architecture is that to build the street in [the simplest fashion] is therefore the safest way. Another characteristic and interesting structure in Minsk is the Trade Union Building. This houses an auditorium, offices for the training and costuming of the amateur groups who perform here periodically, and a small dance hall. There is not, as one might assume, the office of any trade union. They do not exist as we know them (since strikes or negotiations for higher pay or better working conditions are not allowed; of course, suggestions may be made by any worker but these are all handled through the local Communist Factory Committee and are passed along or shelved as it suits the Committee). An imposing structure, it looks like a Greek temple with figures atop the V-shaped roof supported by large white marble columns all around. However, a close look reveals not naked Greek gods but, from left to right, a surveyor complete with scope, a bricklayer holding a bucket, a sportswoman in a track suit, and a more symbolic structure of a man in a double-breasted suit holding a briefcase—either a bureaucrat or an intellectual, apparently.

It may be explained that in the Eastern European custom, all citizens upon reaching the age of 16 years are given a gray-green "passport" or identification papers. On the first page is a photo and personal information. On the following four pages are spaces for registering addresses, this including rented rooms. On the next four pages are places for particular remarks as to the conduct of the carrier—a place better kept blank. The next three pages are for registering places of work; then the next page is for marriage licenses and divorce stamps. These passports are changed for a small charge every five years. A lost passport can be replaced after a short investigation for 10 rubles. All persons regardless of nationality are required to carry these at all times. In the Soviet Union, nationalities are also marked on passports. For instance, a Ukrainian is marked Ukrainian; a Jew is marked "Jew" no matter where he was born. An immigrant is listed by place of birth, as is the case of the many immigrants in the USSR. Also on the pages for "special remarks" (usually of a criminal nature) immigrants have a short biography printed, such as: Carlos Ventura, born in Buenos Aires, 1934, resident of Buenos Aires till 1955, occupation student, immigrated to USSR 1956. This is enough to ensure that any and all who read this passport will give Carlos, along with any other of his fellow immigrants, the proper treatment and attention so that he never gets too far away from his registered address without a good reason or reaches too high a position at work. But otherwise, immigrants in the USSR, a relatively few French, Spanish, and Eastern Europeans, are treated with more respect than the Russians accord each other . . .

Twelve miles outside of Moscow is a "show" collective farm for foreign tourists who ask to see a genuine, average collective farm. On it is almost every imaginable help to man possible, including automatic milkers, feeders, even automatic floor cleaners. The collective farms at this place, along with their counterparts of the same sort south of Leningrad, have well-built apartment houses with food and clothing stores built right into the first floors.

For the benefit of everyone who doesn't want to be duped, I suggest you take the Moscow-to-Brest highway for 24 miles until you come to Uesteech, where by asking directions, you can, in five minutes, find a real collective farm, a village of the small black-mud-and-scrap-wood houses seen throughout the Soviet Union.

Although it's 50 minutes from the Kremlin, it doesn't have electricity or gas. Inside plumbing is unknown and the only automation is that done with a broom. There are 45,000 collective farms in the Soviet Union of this type, as well as 7,400 State farms run directly by the government. Collective farmers and their families number 65.5 million people, or 31.4% of the total population.

True, the collective farmer may own chickens or pigs or even a cow, as well as his own piece of land, usually a quarter of an acre, but the isolation and agonizingly hard work summer and fall offset these "advantages." Nowadays, although still without electricity, collective farms have wire-fed radio programs and speakers in every house. This is part of the propaganda system instituted by Stalin to "bring the cultural level of outlying collective farms up to the level of the city dweller." Therefore, although there are no lights, there is always the incessant roar of loudspeakers. School attendance for the children of collective farmers is compulsory, as it is for all children up to the age of maturity, that is, up to the age when they receive their passports, sixteen. Public schools are in general box-shaped 3-story affairs with no particular decoration. Teachers receive 80 rubles a month in these general educational institutions. Discipline, from the students' viewpoint, is strong. Starting school at the age of seven years, [a student] is taught to keep his Pioneer school costume, which all students must wear, neat in appearance, is taught to stand rigidly at attention when any adult enters the room or when the teacher asks a question. His studies, particularly foreign languages, are apt to be harder and more complex than their American counterparts'. Science is also stressed, as well as patriotism and Soviet history. An attitude toward his studies of complete seriousness is instilled in him at an early age. Young Russian students are apt to appear rather more bookish than Americans. . . .

Public care centers for young and old are an established principle in the USSR. Thousands of rest homes, sanatoria, and hospitals are scattered around the Black and Caspian seas, the "resort area" of the Soviet Union. For any worker to get a reservation to one of these places, he should apply to the factory committee for a *pitburov,* or ticket reservation, after showing that he has the right to his three weeks' vacation (thirty days for persons engaged in dangerous occupations or mining). He may buy the "Petrovkso" from Minsk to the Black Sea-Yalta resort area for three weeks at a cost of 70 to 100 rubles, depending on the class of service available. If [he is] a member of the trade unions (a worker pays 1% of his pay earnings as dues every month), he may only have to pay 50% of the total cost if [his vacation] is [booked] at a trade union-built house of rest. . . . Service at these places includes three good, balanced meals a day, the attention of doctors and nurses, sports and sailing facilities, private beaches, excursions, and all necessities.

More modest workers can, however, afford journeys to rest homes nearer home, in the case of Minsk, to Zhomovich, located in [a] pine forest three hours from Minsk. Here the same services, minus the beaches, fruit, and sun, can be had for as little as 25 rubles for two weeks.

The capital of Byelorussia has 12 institutions of higher learning including a university and Polytechnic Institute. These institutions are engaged in turning out highly trained specialists for the national economy. The city has many secondary schools, colleges, vocational, and factory schools. These schools teach a rigorous 5-year course of vocational and political subjects. Hostels for students are located near their respective Institutes, students non-resident in Minsk live here. Often these numbers exceed the rooms available and many have to rent rooms in the city. All rooms, 15 by 15 feet, house 5 to 6 students, with just enough room to allow metal beds to be placed around the walls and a table and chairs in the middle. There is not room enough for closets so clothing is kept in suitcases under beds. Here, except during the three-month summer vacation, students live and study for 5 years. Common rooms with stoves [for cooking] are also available at the rate of one common room per 8 student living-quarters. The cleanliness of linens, rooms, and the entire dormitory falls upon the students. The number of students in the USSR in 1960–61 was 2,396,000. [The] U.S. figure is 1,816,000 or 102 students per 10,000 [population]. All students in higher educational institutions receive stipends or grants of money at the rate of 40 rubles per month regardless of their chosen vocations. For excellent or outstanding grades, a student may receive a maximum of 50 rubles a month. Thus all students are paid to study in the Soviet Union, unlike the United States where students must pay tuition to learn. This is the reason why the Soviet Union turns out almost three times as many engineers (159,000 in 1959), twice as many agronomists, 477,200 technicians and other specialists. This is why the Soviet Union has more doctors per 10,000 population (18.5 in 1960) than any other country in the world. ([The] USA had 12.1 doctors [per 10,000 population] in 1960.) Regardless of the lack of dormitories and crowded living conditions of the students, . . . we could definitely learn from the rigorous and highly specialized educational system of the Soviet Union, a system which jointly and carefully instills political as well as vocational training into each and every student. Just as at the factories and plants, each and every Institute has its corps of Party chiefs, sectional and class, for teachers and professors as well as for students . . .

The radio and television station in Minsk is a four-story cement building located at No. 6 Kalinin Street near the small river Svishloch. Behind it stands the impressive 500-foot steel radio tower, the highest structure in Byelorussia. This radio tower and building are enclosed with high fences and patrolled by armed guards with dogs. Entrance into the courtyard must be through the building itself and persons cannot enter without a special pass shown to an armed guard. Performers are taken to a separate studio near the city center, where the productions and performances are fed back to the station and then to the broadcasting towers. In this way, the all-important communication system is guarded against sabotage or take-overs of the sort often achieved by Latin American counter-revolutionary or malcontent elements.

Near the television tower, 4 blocks east on Dolgabrodskaya Street, stand two more towers, approximately 200 feet each. They are not engaged in broadcasting. Quite the opposite, in fact. These very apparent landmarks with high-power cables strung between them are jamming towers, used to blank out high-frequency broadcasts from abroad. The main targets of these jamming towers are the Munich and Washington transmitters of the Voice of America programs, although they are also sometimes employed to disrupt the BBC and French broadcasts in Russian. These towers are likewise guarded by armed guards and entrance to the wire-enclosed blockhouse and tower area is forbidden except by passes. The amount of voltage used by these towers is known to be tremendous when one considers that necessary lighting at workplaces is only grudgingly turned on, even on cloudy days. It is ironic and sad to think of the tremendous waste, and [the] effort the Soviet Government goes to in order to keep other peoples' ideas out. But the jamming frequencies are only half those of the Radio Moscow propaganda programs which may be heard on any short-wave radio in the United States—and without jamming. These Radio Moscow programs assure people that the Iron Curtain no longer exists, never did exist, and is in general a fictitious slander against the Soviet Union thought up by reactionaries, *sic!!** . . .

---

* This "sic!!" is misspelled in the original manuscript as "sich!!"

Other means of distributing propaganda are through the *agitpunks* or, in English translation, "agitation points." These are located at desks or in small offices open 16 hours a day. They are manned by volunteer Communist or Young Communist Party members. They are [locations] for the distribution of pamphlets, bulletins, and other Party literature, and for the more or less informal meetings of groups of Communist Party members. Formed in the early 1920s, they were then "points" of armed workers located near each other who could down "White" uprisings or conveniently arrest anyone in the neighborhood. Now their functions have slightly changed but it's still known that any member may come in and report disloyal comments in an unguarded moment on the part of any citizen—there is always a telephone handy here. In Minsk there are only 12 movie houses but 58 *agitpunks* in the telephone book. They can be recognized at a distance by red flags and banners draped over the doors and windows of the respective buildings.

The Young Communist League or YCL embraces all young people from the age of 16, as soon as they outgrow the children's Pioneer League. Ninety percent of all persons between the ages of 16 to 26 belong to this organization, although they may attain Party membership as early as 19 or 20 years [of age]. Signed on as soon as they receive their passports at 16, they receive a YCL Party ticket and must pay small dues of 70 or 80 kopecks a month. After this, they are obliged to attend YCL meetings, go on harvesting trips on weekends during the fall to collective farms to help bring in the potatoes and grain, and to keep their studies up to high standards. A violation of conduct or refusal to toe the line will result in expulsion from the League and is a block to personal progress in the Soviet Union. Membership is considered a reference in hiring in factories or in institutions reviewing requests for a place at higher educational institutions, but expulsions are fairly common, about 20% being expelled before reaching the age where they may be chosen for Communist Party membership. A young student may become rather popular and powerful by being elected to the post of YCL secretary in his class at school or at work. A sure way to success is to remain at this post in one's local school or Institute, maintaining high standards of marks and discipline until chosen for Party membership. In this way, young people get a taste of what the Party can do for them if they have the right attitude. At our shop, the YCL secretary is Arkady _____ , a tall handsome lively Russian of 24 with a broad grin. He reminds one of a Texas or Oklahoma boy. His father is a minor bureaucrat, while his mother works as a nurse. Therefore, they have a full three-room apartment. His brother, also a YCL member, is the youngest and last member of this family group. Arkady has worked at this factory for 5 years after serving his 3 years in the navy in the Black Sea. He was only recently elected to the post of YCL secretary in our shop after the former person received CP membership. Usually an easy-going fellow if you don't get him riled, he takes his YCL duties seriously, collecting dues on every other payday (which are the 5th and 20th of the month) of 1% of the total paycheck, that is, 1% of 80 rubles, 80 kopecks. He checks off names and is responsible for turning in the cash to the factory YCL Committee and for helping to draw up the list of *drozhniks* who shall have the duty during the month. *Drozhniks* are "volunteer" civilians who patrol streets and parks as peace- and order-keepers. They are given a special card which they carry and when on duty wear red armbands . . . *Drozhniks* always walk in groups of threes and fours; often women and girls are seen in this capacity. This custom is relatively new and is not generally used except on Saturdays and Sundays, when there are boisterous groups of teenagers and a large number of drunks to be seen. Both these types of groups are on the downturn at least partly due to these "volunteer" efforts. Besides helping to draw up the list of *drozhniks* in their respective shops, the YCL secretaries are expected to set high examples of work and political "propriety" to their fellow workers and to help the shop and section leaders get to know their workers . . .

The headquarters of the Central Committee of the CP is located on Karl Marx Street, an eight-story yellow metal and brick structure. It is a rectangular-shaped [building] with almost none of the gaudy decorations seen on most buildings in the city. "The First Secretary of the Central Committee of the CP of the Republic of Byelorussia" is the imposing title carried by a short stocky man in his late 50's, K. T. Mazarof. Rarely seen on the streets, he and his family occupy a huge 8-room apartment on the top floor of a government apartment house on Prospekt Stalin. Entrance to this apartment building is guarded day and night by one uniformed policeman who checks passes and keeps unauthorized persons out. Here is also the residence of several ministers, such as Minister of Education K. S. Poroshebed, and Minister of Administration E. Zhezhel. Mazarof controls and directs all activities in his republic with authority no United States governor ever enjoyed, since his authority cannot be controlled or challenged by court orders or injunctions as it often is in the United States. Mazarof is responsible directly to Moscow and the Party Presidium chaired by Khrushchev. He appears in the reviewing box in the center of his cronies on the May 1st and November 7th holidays where he waves a congenial hand occasionally without the trace of a smile . . .

Corruption in the USSR takes [its] major form in embezzling and greasing of palms . . . In 1961, the death penalty for embezzlement of state funds in large sums was reenacted as an answer to widespread pilfering of goods, crops, and embezzlement of money and state bonds. On any collective farm, there is a certain percentage of state goods illegally appropriated by the collective farmers for their own private use to make up for low wages and therefore low living conditions. Often [these goods are] sold to private individuals, stores, or at open market types of bazaars. These goods may consist of only a pilfered lamp or piglet, or may run to scores of sheep or cows hidden in backwater swamps or thick pine forest and sold by the appropriator, [either] piecemeal or in wholesale lots, to crooked store supervisors, who are supposed to buy state meats and crops at government prices but pocket the difference in price from the black market without making entrance in their books that such merchandise was bought for state prices. Such practices are so common that without them, many stores would be almost empty if they had to rely on the sporadic poor-quality meat brought in from the state slaughterhouses at high prices. The directorship of even a small fruit or milk store opens up wide opportunities for lucrative enterprises by persons with even a slight business sense. It is almost impossible for the authorities to act on such goings-on because of difficulty in obtaining proof in acceptable amounts; such goings-on are usually in small amounts. Materials such as electrical appliances are often riddled with speculation, which often leads to poor goods or bad foods brought in and sold under the counter. Examples are horse meat used to supplement a "beef stew." Most of the bureaucratic apparatus can be detoured by a well-placed 10-spot. Persons occupying most of the housing ministry and passport office and visa offices expect remuneration for the life and death services which all Russians seek—namely—to receive permission for an apartment, and official visas to live in such an apartment. [By the] compulsory laws of the Soviet Union, without a city visa stamp, a person cannot work in that city. Once a position or work is decided upon or taken, it is a very difficult process to secure permission and work in order to receive an apartment in another city, therefore, to live in another city. In such instances, the administrator of an apartment house may expect 60–100 rubles for his stamp of approval on a request blank for an apartment, or to [approve] moving into an apartment already occupied by a family who is expecting to leave one city for another, the usual method of getting an apartment or room without having to wait on the so-called housing list, on which [it] may take 5–7 years to receive a one-room "apartment." . . .

On election day, all voters go to the polls (usually a school) and vote; they are given a ballot, which they drop into a box. On the ballot is the single name of the candidate for each post. That's all anybody ever does to "vote." This system ensures a 99% voter turnout and predetermined victory. In each polling place, there is a booth for secret balloting (crossing out the candidate and writing in your own). Under Soviet law, anyone can do this; nobody does for the obvious reason that anyone who enters the booth may be identified. There is a Soviet joke about the floor dropping out from under anyone stepping into the booth. But the fact is that if the entire population used the polling booth, they could beat the system. However, years of mass discipline and fear have made the people afraid to attempt any such demonstration. And with no means of communication in the hands of a would-be candidate, there is no way to communicate with the people and whip up support for a dark-horse candidate . . .

GLOSSARY OF NAMES

An asterisk indicates a pseudonym. Occasionally, by request, a person is identified only by his or her first name. A few women who testified before the Warren Commission were identified by married names only (i.e., Mrs. John Doe instead of Mary Doe) and are so listed in this glossary.

JOHN ABT: a New York lawyer whom Oswald tried to contact after his arrest in Dallas

ROSA AGAFONOVA: senior interpreter at Moscow's Hotel Berlin Intourist office

ADRIAN ALBA: proprietor of a garage next door to Reily Coffee Co.

ALBINA: friend of the Zigers'

ALIK: first name used most frequently for Oswald by his Russian friends and acquaintances

ALKA: variant of Alik

ALYOSHA: nickname given Oswald by Stellina

DEAN ADAMS ANDREWS: lawyer whose office was visited by Oswald

COLONEL ANDREYEV*: KGB officer who interrogated Yuri Merezhinsky

DON RAY ARCHER: Dallas police detective who was present at Oswald's murder and assisted in Ruby's arrest

EUSEBIO AZCUE: Consul at the Cuban Embassy in Mexico City in 1963

THOMAS BAGSHAW: Oswald's roommate at Atsugi airbase in Japan

MARRION BAKER: motorcycle police officer in the Kennedy motorcade

SAMUEL BALLEN: corporate executive who met with Oswald at George De Mohrenschildt's request

GUY BANISTER: retired FBI agent who was working as a private detective while Oswald was in New Orleans

TOMMY BARGAS: Oswald's supervisor at Leslie Welding

PAULINE VIRGINIA BATES: public stenographer who transcribed portions of Oswald's essay on life in the USSR

GALINA (GALYA) BELYANKIN: Yuri Belyankin's wife, a model who knew Marina and Lee

YURI BELYANKIN: Moscow-based cinematographer who met Marina and Lee while working in Minsk

MARY BLEDSOE: Oswald's first landlady when he returned to Dallas from Mexico City in October 1963

KONSTANTIN (KOSTYA) BONDARIN: student at Minsk Medical Institute; briefly one of Marina's boyfriends in 1961

PROFESSOR BONDARIN: faculty member of Minsk Medical Institute

GEORGE BOUHE: unofficial leader of the Russian émigré community in Dallas

JACK BOWEN: Oswald's co-worker at Jaggars-Chiles-Stovall

ELMER BOYD: Dallas police officer present during some of Oswald's questioning on November 22–24, 1963

HOWARD BRENNAN: a witness who saw a rifleman in a window of the Texas School Book Depository

JOHNNY BREWER: shoe store manager who saw Oswald enter the Texas Theatre without paying and had cashier call the police

CARLOS BRINGUIER: anti-Castro Cuban exile; one of Oswald's opponents in the New Orleans radio debate

EMILE BRUNEAU: friend of Charles Murret; arranged bail for Oswald after his arrest in New Orleans

EDWARD BUTLER: head of the anti-Communist Information Council of the Americas; one of Oswald's opponents in the New Orleans radio debate

RICHARD CALL: served with Oswald in USMC, California

DONALD CAMARATA: served with Oswald in USMC, Japan

JOHN CARRO: social worker who knew Oswald during his stay at Youth House in New York in 1953

GALI CLARK: Russian émigrée who knew the Oswalds in Dallas

MAX CLARK: Dallas lawyer, married to Gali Clark

LUCILLE CONNELL: Sylvia Odio's friend

PETER CONNOR: served with Oswald in USMC, Japan

SHERMAN COOLEY: served with Oswald in USMC boot camp

LARRY CRAFARD: handyman at Jack Ruby's nightclub

JESSE CURRY: Dallas Chief of Police

"GATOR" DANIELS: served with Oswald in USMC, Japan

NELSON DELGADO: served with Oswald in USMC, California

GEORGE DE MOHRENSCHILDT: Russian émigré; Oswald's best friend in Dallas

JEANNE DE MOHRENSCHILDT: George De Mohrenschildt's fourth and last wife

WILLIAM DONOVAN: Oswald's radar supervisor in USMC, California

SILVIA DURAN: secretary to the Cuban Consul at the Cuban Embassy in Mexico City in September 1963

LYDIA DYMITRUK: Russian émigrée who knew the Oswalds in Dallas

EDDIE DZHUGANIAN: a romantic interest of Marina's in Leningrad

MYRTLE EVANS: helped Oswald find an apartment when he returned to New Orleans in spring of 1963

JOHN FAIN: FBI agent who interviewed Oswald in Dallas after his return to the U.S.

DAVID FERRIE: associate of Guy Banister and adult leader of Civil Air Patrol in New Orleans when Oswald was a teenaged member

DECLAN FORD: Katya Ford's husband

KATYA FORD: Russian émigrée who knew the Oswalds in Dallas

WESLEY FRAZIER: Ruth Paine's neighbor and an employee at Texas School Book Depository

WILL FRITZ: Dallas Police Captain; Oswald's chief interrogator after his arrest

GALINA (GALYA): Marina's half-sister

MRS. JESSE GARNER: the Oswalds' New Orleans landlady on Magazine Street

JIM GARRISON: New Orleans District Attorney who brought Clay Shaw, a prominent businessman, to trial for conspiracy to assassinate Kennedy

PHILLIP GERACI: a teenager present in Carlos Bringuier's New Orleans store when Oswald initially approached the Cuban exile

ELLA GERMANN: Oswald's radio factory co-worker whom he courted for nine months

PAVEL GOLAVACHEV: Oswald's friend and KGB informant

JOHN GRAEF: Oswald's supervisor at Jaggars-Chiles-Stovall

EVA GRANT: Jack Ruby's sister
STEPAN VASILYEVICH GREGORIEFF*: KGB officer, Minsk; developer (analyst and administrator) on Oswald case
PETER PAUL GREGORY: Russian-born petroleum engineer who knew the Oswalds in Dallas
GURI: Valya Prusakova's father
ANNA HALL: Russian émigrée who knew the Oswalds in Fort Worth
LORAN HALL: anti-Castroite who claimed that he visited Sylvia Odio with a companion who resembled Oswald
JAMES HOSTY: FBI agent who twice visited Ruth Paine's home looking for Oswald
INESSA: Marina's girlfriend in Minsk
IRINA*: Marina's girlfriend in Leningrad
WILLIAM JARMAN: Oswald's co-worker at the Texas School Book Depository
KATYA: worker at Minsk radio factory
ALEX KLEINLERER: Russian émigré who knew the Oswalds in Dallas
NELLYA KORBINKA: student at the Foreign Languages Institute, Minsk, with whom Oswald claimed to have had an affair
LUDMILA KUZMICH: Larissa's older sister; wife of Mikhail Kuzmich and Valya and Ilya's neighbor
MIKHAIL KUZMICH: MVD medical officer, Ilya's co-worker and neighbor; Larissa's brother-in-law
VALERY KOSTIKOV: KGB officer attached to the Russian Embassy in Mexico City; saw Oswald during his visits to the Embassy
VLADIMIR (VOLODYA) KRUGLOV: student Marina met during a summer visit in 1957 to Ilya and Valya
IGOR IVANOVICH GUZMIN*: Chief of Counterintelligence, KGB, Byelorussia, at the time of Oswald's arrival in Minsk
LARISSA (LYALYA): Marina's best friend in Minsk; Valya and Ilya's neighbor
CHARLES LEBLANC: Oswald's co-worker at Reily Coffee Co.
LIBEZIN: Party Secretary at Minsk radio factory
LIKHOI: KGB nickname for Oswald used frequently in surveillance reports
LYUBA: Marina's aunt; Ilya's sister
MAGDA*: worker at Minsk radio factory
CARLOS MARCELLO: head of the Mafia in New Orleans
GENERAL MAROV*: composite character expressing the views of three high-ranking KGB officers in Moscow and Minsk, all of whom wished to remain anonymous
FRANCIS MARTELLO: New Orleans police lieutenant who interviewed Oswald after his arrest for the street altercation with Bringuier
PRISCILLA JOHNSON MCMILLAN: American writer who interviewed Oswald in Moscow; later, Marina's biographer
JOHN MCVICKAR: Snyder's assistant at the American Embassy, Moscow, at the time of Oswald's arrival
ALEXANDER MEDVEDEV: Marina's stepfather
KLAVDIA (KLAVA) MEDVEDEV (NÉE PRUSAKOVA): Marina's mother
PETYA MEDVEDEV: Marina's half-brother
YEVDOKIA MEDVEDEV: Marina's step-grandmother
ANNA MELLER: Russian émigrée who knew the Oswalds in Dallas
YURI MEREZHINSKY: student at Minsk Medical Institute, son of high-ranking scientists
LAWRENCE MEYERS: Jack Ruby's friend
ALINE MOSBY: UPI reporter who interviewed Oswald in Moscow
DAVID CHRISTIE MURRAY: served with Oswald in USMC
CHARLES (DUTZ) MURRET: Oswald's uncle; Lillian Murret's husband
DOROTHY MURRET: Oswald's cousin; Lillian Murret's daughter

JOHN MURRET: Lillian Murret's son; Oswald's cousin

LILLIAN MURRET: Oswald's aunt; Marguerite's sister

MUSYA: Marina's aunt; Ilya's sister

NALIM: KGB nickname (meaning "eel-like") for Oswald; used in some reports

OLEG NECHIPORENKO: KGB officer attached to the Russian Embassy in Mexico City as a consular officer, present during one of Oswald's visits to the Embassy

NIKOLAEV: engineer who worked with Ilya in Arkhangelsk, said by the Prusakov family to be Marina's natural father

HAROLD NORMAN: Oswald's co-worker at Texas School Book Depository

JOYCE MURRET O'BRIEN: Lillian Murret's daughter

ANNIE ODIO: Sylvia Odio's sister

SYLVIA (SILVIA) ODIO: Cuban exile living in Dallas who testified to the Warren Commission that Oswald, accompanied by three Cuban strangers claiming to be anti-Castro associates of her father, visited her home in late September 1963

HART ODUM: FBI agent who contacted Marina on several occasions after the assassination

DENNIS OFSTEIN: Oswald's co-worker at Jaggars-Chiles-Stovall

YAEKO OKUI: young Japanese woman with whom Oswald had an extended conversation at a party

MACK OSBORNE: served with Oswald in USMC, California

MARGUERITE CLAVERIE OSWALD: Oswald's mother

MARINA PRUSAKOVA OSWALD: wife of Lee Harvey Oswald

ROBERT OSWALD: Oswald's older brother

VADA OSWALD: Robert Oswald's wife

MICHAEL PAINE: Ruth Paine's estranged husband

RUTH PAINE: Marina's friend in whose home she, June, and Rachel lived after the Oswalds returned to Dallas from New Orleans

INNA PASENKO: student at Minsk Foreign Language Institute

OREST PENA: owner of the Habana Bar in New Orleans

JOHN PIC: Oswald's older half-brother

MARGERY (MARGY) PIC: John Pic's wife

SASHA PISKALEV: medical student; suitor to Marina in Minsk

JERRY PITTS: served with Oswald in USMC, Japan

DANIEL POWERS: served with Oswald in USMC

MAX PROKHORCHIK: worker at Minsk radio factory; married Ella Germann

ILYA PRUSAKOV: Marina's uncle and a colonel in the MVD

TATIANA PRUSAKOVA: Marina's grandmother; Ilya's mother

VALYA (VALENTINA) PRUSAKOVA: Marina's aunt; Ilya's wife

JOHN QUIGLEY: FBI agent who interviewed Oswald after his arrest in New Orleans

LINNIE MAE RANDLE: Ruth Paine's neighbor in Irving, Texas

EARLENE ROBERTS: live-in housekeeper at the boardinghouse in Dallas where Oswald was dwelling at the time of the assassination

EVARISTO RODRIGUEZ: bartender in the Habana Bar in New Orleans

MIGUEL RODRIGUEZ: served with Oswald in Japan; attacked by Oswald in incident that resulted in Oswald's second court-martial

JACK RUBY: Dallas nightclub owner who shot and killed Oswald

VOLKMAR SCHMIDT: German geologist introduced to Oswald by De Mohrenschildt

GEORGE SENATOR: Jack Ruby's friend; shared an apartment with him

GORDON SHANKLIN: Agent in Charge of the FBI's Dallas office

RIMMA SHIRAKOVA: Oswald's Intourist guide in Moscow

ALEXANDER SIMCHENKO: head of Moscow OVIR (Passport and Visa Office) in 1959

RICHARD SNYDER: Consul at the American Embassy, Moscow, at the time of Oswald's arrival

SONYA: worker at Minsk radio factory

FORREST SORRELS: Secret Service agent in Kennedy's motorcade

STELLINA: head of Intourist, Hotel Minsk

EVELYN STRICKMAN: social worker who interviewed both Oswald and his mother during Lee's stay at Youth House in New York in 1953

WILLIAM STUCKEY: radio journalist who broadcast one interview with Oswald after his arrest in New Orleans and arranged his radio debate.

ROBERT SURREY: member of General Walker's household staff

INNA TACHINA: student at the Foreign Languages Institute with whom Oswald claimed he had an affair

TAMARA: one of Marina's co-workers at Third Clinical Pharmacy, Minsk

TANYA*: Intourist guide at Hotel Minsk who dated Oswald for some months; KGB source

OLEG TARUSSIN: Marina's most serious suitor in Leningrad

ALEXANDRA TAYLOR: George De Mohrenschildt's daughter

GARY TAYLOR: George De Mohrenschildt's son-in-law

J. D. TIPPIT: Dallas policeman shot and killed an hour after JFK

MRS. MAHLON TOBIAS: the Oswalds' landlady on Elsbeth Street

KERRY THORNLEY: served with Oswald in USMC, California

ERICH (ERNST) TITOVETS: English-speaking student at Minsk Medical Institute, Oswald's closest friend in Minsk

SANTO TRAFFICANTE: Mafia don of Tampa

ROY TRULY: Oswald's supervisor at the Texas School Book Depository

EDWARD VOEBEL: Oswald's high school friend in New Orleans

IGOR VOSHININ: Russian émigré who knew the Oswalds in Dallas

MRS. IGOR VOSHININ: Russian émigrée who knew the Oswalds in Dallas

GENERAL EDWIN A. WALKER: controversial Dallas right-wing extremist crusader on whom an assassination attempt was made

WILLIAM WHALEY: Dallas taxi driver who drove Oswald to his boardinghouse after the assassination

BONNIE RAY WILLIAMS: Oswald's co-worker at Texas School Book Depository

WILLIAM WULF: high school acquaintance of Oswald's in New Orleans

PAVEL YATSKOV: KGB officer attached to the Russian Embassy in Mexico City who saw Oswald during his final visit to the Embassy

ALEXANDER ZIGER: engineer at Minsk radio factory and Oswald's friend

ANITA ZIGER: Alexander Ziger's daughter

ELEANORA ZIGER: Alexander Ziger's daughter

ACKNOWLEDGMENTS

Special acknowledgments are due:

—to Ludmila Peresvetova, who was our translator for more than nine tenths of these interviews and had so powerful and personal a point of view that her presence is also in this book.

—to Marina Oswald Porter, for subjecting herself to the pain of being interviewed for five consecutive days in Dallas and for her honesty, which was so notably severe upon herself that it kept her searching through many an old laceration to locate a shard of truth.

—to my good friend the private investigator William Majeski, for his percipient insights while we worked together in Dallas and New Orleans.

—to Mary McHughes Ferrell, for her boundless energy and for her generosity in making available her voluminous archives on the Kennedy assassination. In particular, the work of Mary Ferrell on Oswald's finances was of considerable help. A collateral acknowledgment goes to Gary Shaw, Mary Ferrell's friend and working partner.

—and to Jim Lesar of the Assassination Archive and Research Center, Washington, D.C., who kindly provided much research for this book with a full set of the twelve HSCA volumes concerned with the Kennedy assassination.

One is indebted to the following people for their willingness to be interviewed. Those with pseudonyms are in quotation marks: Rosa Agafonova, Lyuba Axyonova, Galina and Yuri Belyankin, Musya Berlova, Konstantin Bondarin, Valentin Borovtsov, the doctor from Botkin Hospital, Olga Dmovskaya, Leonid Bentzianovich Gelfant, Ella Germann, "Stepan Vasilyevich Gregorieff," Romanova Alexandra Gregoryevna, Pavel Golavachev, Ludmila and Misha Kuzmich, "Igor Ivanovich Guzmin," Nadazhda and Dementij Maknovets, Galina Makovskaya, "General Marov," Yuri Merezhinsky, Lidia Semenovna Merezhinsky, Valentin Yurivich Mikhailov, Oleg Nechiporenko, Stellina Pajaluista, Sasha Piskalev, Inna Andreyevna Pasenko (for whom further appreciation is due for her help as a translator on special projects), Galina Semenovna Prokapchuk, Max Prokhorchik, Polina Prusakova, Valentina (Valya) Prusakova, Yanina Sabela, Tamara Sankovskaya, Larissa (Lyalya) Sevostyanova, Albina Shalyakina, Rimma Semenova Shirakova, Anatoly Shpanko, Stanislav Shushkevich, Alexander Simchenko, Sonya Skopa, Misha Smolsky, Natasha Gregorievna Titovets, Leonid Stepanovich

Tzagiko, Raisa Maximova Vedeneeva, Inessa Yakhiel, Raisa Romanovna Zhinke-vich, Mrs. Alexander Ziger.

Two interviews, much desired, were not obtained. Don Alejandro Ziger was living in Argentina in 1992, and before we attempted to make contact, he had died. His widow was interviewed by Alex Levine, but Mrs. Ziger was now at that benignly advanced age where the prevailing desire is to initiate no difficulties for anyone. So, her remarks about Oswald were general—"He was a nice young man."

With Erich Titovets, the matter is more frustrating. Titovets was, by all accounts, Oswald's closest friend and associate in Minsk, and he kept sliding out of interviews with us. At present a doctor engaged in advanced research, Titovets met with us seven times, but never gave an interview. As he explained, he was going to write his own book on Oswald. Nonetheless, a game ensued. Often, he would agree to a meeting, but would change the date, or, once, was summoned out of his hospital office in the first few minutes by what had every appearance of being a pre-arranged call.

We had already interviewed his ex-wife, and she described him as immensely secretive, cold, and compartmented. While few men would wish to be measured by the judgments of a former spouse, it was obvious from meeting Titovets, a well-knit, well-built man who gives off a contradictory aura, prissy yet macho at once, that he was living in as sly and unique a manner as a much-pampered chee-tah. Our only consolation in not being able to interview him is that while he was obviously capable of talking to us for hours it was equally apparent that he would impart nothing he did not care to tell. The decision was made finally to approach him entirely from without and let him emerge as a character by way of his rela-tion to others.

One would also like to thank the following people for their assistance: Genrikh Borovik, Lenord Komarov, Anatoly Mikhailov, Sergei Pankovsky, Stanislav Shushkevich, Dmitri Volkogonov; as well as those members of the KGB in Minsk and Moscow who were in a position to give their names: Edward Ivanovich Shi-rakovsky, Ivan Chebrovski, Valentin Demidov, Yuri Kobaladze, Alexei Kondaurov.

One would also mention the aid offered by our staff in Minsk: Sasha Batanov, Tammy Beth Jackson, Robert Libermann, Keith Livers, Marat, Sasha Palchinkov.

And in the United States, one would acknowledge the help given by Lauren Agnelli, Henrietta Alves, Stephanie Chernikowski, Ingrid Finch, Tamara Gritsai, Boris Komorov, Alex Levine (in Buenos Aires), Maggie Mailer, Julianna Peresve-tova, Farris Rookstool III, Marc Schiller, Anatoly Valushkin, and from Random House, Jason Epstein, Harry Evans, Andrew Carpenter, Oksana Kushnir, Beth Pearson, Veronica Windholz, and in Los Angeles, Howard Schiller for his cover design.

After paying one's respects to the powerful insights and investigations of Edward Epstein, one would also offer a collegial salute to the following authors for the implicit assistance of their work: Jean Davison, Don DeLillo, Gaeton Fonzi, Oleg Nechiporenko, Carl Oglesby, Gerald Posner, Richard Russell, and Anthony Summers. While one can hardly offer an appreciation to Hitler, and there is only the shade of Ralph Waldo Emerson to thank, Robert Oswald, William Man-chester, Frank Ragano, Selwyn Raab, and David Wise should be cited.

Finally, a special statement is necessary to cover the contribution of Priscilla Johnson McMillan. Her book *Marina and Lee* was of obvious and considerable use to me in the composition of the second half of this work. While I have seri-ous disagreements on her interpretation of Lee's life and character (as indeed I would, or why else write my own book?), there is no work on Lee and Marina's married life in the United States as rich in detail as Mrs. McMillan's full treatment. Indeed, she spent months interviewing Marina and more than twelve years writing her book.

As already stated, Lawrence Schiller and I had the opportunity to interview Marina in Texas for five days, and used the greater part of such time for obtaining her latter-day narrative of her experiences in Leningrad and Minsk. Some of our effort went, however, into obtaining a corroboration of those passages I was preparing to choose from Mrs. McMillan's book. I think it fair to say that Marina, although no longer well disposed to her former friend, was usually ready to agree with the general truth of the examples chosen, although not inclined to accept as comfortable the tone of dialogue given to Lee and herself. Nonetheless, it is altogether to Mrs. McMillan's credit that she was not only the first but perhaps the only author to perceive the value of understanding Lee Harvey Oswald through his marriage.

NOTES

GENERAL NOTES:

1. All of Marina Oswald's recollections, unless otherwise attributed in the following notes, are from the author's and Lawrence Schiller's interviews with her that were done specifically for this book.

2. Lee Harvey Oswald was dyslexic, and this was apparent, to varying degrees, in virtually all of his writing. For the reader's convenience and in fairness to Oswald's ideas, his errors in spelling and punctuation have been corrected in all excerpts from his letters, Historic Diary, and other writings unless otherwise noted in the text.

3. Since the Warren Commission Hearings were published from direct transcript and were not edited closely, if at all, there are numerous small discrepancies—different spellings, for example, of the same Russian name. These occasional variations were dealt with on their merits, and where necessary, a note is appended.

ABBREVIATIONS USED IN CITATIONS:

WC TESTIMONY, VOL.: testimony given before the Warren Commission in the twenty-six volumes of Hearing and Exhibits accompanying the Warren Commission Report, referred to by volume and page number.

WC HEARINGS, VOL.: affidavits and other documents read into the Warren Commission record, referred to by volume and page number.

CE: Commission Exhibit (followed by exhibit, volume, and page number). Certain Exhibits were also assigned names by the Warren Commission, and this form has been followed where applicable, e.g., Paine Exhibit No. 1.

HSCA REPORT: House Select Committee Report on Assassinations (U.S. Government Printing Office edition).

HSCA, VOL.: The twelve Kennedy volumes of Hearings and Appendices of the House Select Committee on Assassinations, referred to by volume and page number.

VOLUME ONE: OSWALD IN MINSK WITH MARINA

PART II: OSWALD IN MOSCOW

Chapter 1: King's English
1. The Historic Diary, so named by Oswald, was found in his papers after his death, and was printed in the Warren Commission Exhibits, CE 24, Vol. XVI, pp. 94–105.

Chapter 3: Rosa, Rimma, and Richard Snyder
1. WC Testimony, Vol. V, p. 264.
2. Ibid., pp. 266–267.
3. Ibid., pp. 279–290.

Chapter 4: What's My News?
1. CE 943, Vol. XVIII, p. 157.
2. CE 942, Vol. XVIII, p. 156.
3. Priscilla Johnson McMillan, *Marina and Lee,* pp. 83–85.
4. In his Historic Diary, Oswald sometimes referred to old rubles, sometimes to new rubles. All figures provided here are in new rubles, which were each worth 10 old rubles. For example, the Red Cross gave him 5,000 rubles (old money), which was now worth 500 new rubles. His salary, commensurately, was worth 70 rubles a month in new money.
5. WC Testimony, Vol. V, p. 294.

PART III: OSWALD'S WORK, OSWALD'S SWEETHEART

Chapter 8: In Love with Ella
1. This diary extract is from what Oswald called "DIARY (extra page) not included in formal diary"; CE 2759, Vol. XXVI, p. 144.

Chapter 9: Ella and Lee
1. In his Historic Diary, Oswald spelled Inna Tachina's name "Ennatachina." The spelling has been corrected to avoid confusion.

Chapter 10: *Zdradstvy*
1. In his Historic Diary, Oswald spells Nellya Korbinka (referred to by Inna Pasenko on p. 126) as "Nell Korobka." To avoid confusion, the name has been corrected to Nellya Korbinka.
2. In the Diary text, Oswald again refers to Inna Tachina as "Enna." The name has been corrected to avoid confusion.

PART IV: MARINA'S FRIENDS, MARINA'S LOVES

Chapter 9: Anatoly
1. McMillan, op. cit, pp. 71–72.

PART V: COURTSHIP AND MARRIAGE

Chapter 1: Alik
1. In the transcripts of their testimony before the Warren Commission, both Marina and Marguerite Oswald (Lee's mother) are identified as "Mrs. Oswald." Similarly, Robert Oswald (Lee's brother) is always designated "Mr. Oswald." The author has added the first names of these three individuals wherever their testimony is quoted.
2. WC Testimony, Vol. I, pp. 90–92.
3. CE 994, Vol. XVIII, pp. 597–602. Marina's narrative was dated January 4, 1964; McMillan, op. cit., p. 583. In the Warren Commission translation of this document, the names Anatoly and Yuri were spelled Anatoli and Yuriy. The author has amended these to avoid confusion.

Chapter 2: A Little Bit of Conquering
1. CE 994, Vol. XVIII, p. 605.
2. CE 1401, Vol. XXII, p. 750.
3. CE 994, Vol. XVIII, p. 606.

Chapter 5: Early Married Days
1. CE 994, Vol. XVIII, pp. 606–607.
2. Ibid., p. 608.

PART VI: A COMMENCEMENT OF THE
LONG VOYAGE HOME

Chapter 2: Correspondence
1. CE 932, Vol. XVIII, p. 133.
2. Ibid., pp. 133–134
3. CE 1084, Vol. XXII, p. 31.
4. WC Testimony, Vol. V, p. 278.
5. CE 251, Vol. XVI, p. 251.
6. CE 1085, Vol. XXII, p. 33.

Chapter 3: Bureaucratic Soundings
1. CE 969, Vol. XVIII, p. 366.
2. CE 970, Vol. XVIII, p. 367.
3. CE 252, Vol. XVI, pp. 704–707.

Chapter 4: A Return to Moscow
1. CE 960, Vol. XVIII, pp. 340; 343.

Chapter 6: Traveler's Qualms
1. CE 977, Vol. XVIII, pp. 378–380.
2. CE 1122, Vol. XXII, p. 87.
3. CE 301, Vol. XVI, p. 833.
4. CE 1058, Vol. XXII, p. 9.

Chapter 9: The Queen of Spades
1. CE 305, Vol. XVI, p. 838.
2. CE 1122, Vol. XXII, p. 88.
3. CE 66–I, Vol. XVI, p. 226.
4. CE 53, Vol. XVI, p. 191.
5. CE 56, Vol. XVI, p. 196.
6. CE 55, Vol. XVI, p. 193.

PART VII: FATHERHOOD AND
MOTHERHOOD

Chapter 1: Cruel but Wise
1. CE 2744, Vol. XXVI, p. 120.
2. CE 309, Vol. XVI, p. 852.
3. CE 185, Vol. XVI, p. 544.

Chapter 2: A Bomb Scare
1. CE 985, Vol. XVIII, p. 433.
2. CE 311, Vol. XVI, pp. 857–858.

Chapter 4: On the Turn of the Year
1. CE 189, Vol. XVI, p. 554.
2. WC Testimony, Vol. I, pp.
193–194.

Chapter 5: Pen Pals
1. CE 1058, Vol. XXII, p. 9.
2. Ibid., p. 10.
3. CE 256, Vol. XVI, pp. 717–718.

4. CE 1101, Vol. XXII, p. 51.
5. CE 2743, Vol. XXVI, p. 117.
6. CE 190, Vol. XVI, p. 558.
7. CE 314, Vol XVI, p. 865.
8. CE 1081, Vol. XXII, p. 28.
9. CE 223, Vol. XVI, p. 613.
10. CE 192, Vol. XVI, p. 562.
11. CE 1082, Vol. XXII, p. 29.
12. CE 193, Vol. XVI, pp. 564–565.

Chapter 6: An Addition to the Family
1. McMillan, op. cit., p. 173.
2. CE 63, Vol. XVI, p. 212. In the
Warren Commission Exhibits,
variant spellings of the name
Alik—such as Aleck and Alek—
appear as transliterations from
the Russian by different
translators. The author has
amended these to avoid
confusion.
3. CE 37, Vol. XVI, p. 162.
4. CE 40, Vol. XVI, p. 169.
5. CE 60, Vol. XVI, p. 206.
6. CE 64, Vol. XVI, pp. 213–214.
7. CE 61, Vol. XVI, p. 207.
8. The KGB actually gave Oswald
two nicknames: "Likhoi," noted
above, used most often, and, less
frequently, "Nalim" (which means
"sly, eel-like"). This report uses
"Nalim" here; the author has
taken the liberty of substituting
the more familiar "Likhoi."

Chapter 7: "There Are Microbes in
Your Mouth"
1. CE 1086, Vol. XXII, p. 35.
2. CE 2687, Vol. XXVI, p. 47.
3. SOV is the State Department's
informal designation for its
Office of Soviet Union Affairs.
4. James Exhibit No. 2, Vol. XX, pp.
236–237.

Chapter 8: Second Thoughts
1. CE 2686, Vol. XXVI, p. 47.
2. CE 823, Vol. XVII, pp. 723–724.
3. CE 1315, Vol. XXII, p. 488.
4. CE 196, Vol. XVI, p. 573.
5. CE 317, Vol. XVI, pp. 877–878.

Chapter 9: "His Impertinence Knows No Bounds"
1. James Exhibit No. 5, Vol. XX, p. 242.
2. CE 2688, Vol. XXVI, p. 48.
3. James Exhibit No. 4, Vol. XX, p. 241.
4. James Exhibit No. 6, Vol. XX, p. 243.
5. CE 1105, Vol. XXII, p. 62.

Chapter 11: Leave-taking
1. CE 318, Vol. XVI, pp. 880–881.
2. From a report by FBI agents Anatole A. Boguslav and Wallace R. Heitman. CE 1401, Vol. XXII, p. 755.
3. CE 833, Vol. XVII, p. 790.

PART VIII: IN THE ANTEROOM OF HISTORY

Chapter 1: Across the Briny Deep
1. Oswald made two mistakes on the dates in Q. 6. In the left column, he had "spring of 1961," here corrected to "spring of 1962." In the right column his July 1962 was, in a similar vein, corrected to July 1961.
2. CE 100, Vol. XVI, pp. 436–439.
3. CE 25, Vol. XVI, pp. 106–122.

Chapter 2: Homecoming
1. WC Testimony, Vol. I, p. 318.
2. CE 994, Vol. XVIII, p. 616.
3. WC Testimony, Vol. I, pp. 313–314.
4. CE 994, Vol. XVIII, pp. 617–618.
5. WC Testimony, Vol. I, pp. 330–332.
6. Ibid., pp. 131–132.
7. WC Testimony, Vol. VIII, pp. 331–336.
8. CE 823, Vol. XVII, pp. 728–729.
9. WC Testimony, Vol. I, p. 689.

Chapter 3: A Visit to the Organs
1. CE 132, Vol. XVI, pp. 503–508.

VOLUME TWO: OSWALD IN AMERICA

PART I: EARLY YEARS, SOLDIER YEARS

Chapter 2: Mama's Boy
1. WC Testimony, Vol. I, p. 225.
2. WC Testimony, Vol. XI, pp. 11–12.

3. WC Testimony, Vol. VIII, pp. 106–107.
4. Ibid., p. 160.
5. Ibid., p. 103.
6. WC Testimony, Vol. XI, p. 17.
7. Ibid., Vol. XI, p. 27.
8. Ibid.
9. Ibid., p. 28.
10. WC Testimony, Vol. VIII, p. 112.
11. WC Testimony, Vol. XI, p. 29.
12. Ibid., p. 30.
13. WC Testimony, Vol. VIII, p. 119.
14. WC Testimony, Vol. XI, p. 75.

Chapter 3: Indian Summer, New York
1. WC Testimony, Vol. I, p. 226.
2. WC Testimony, Vol. XI, pp. 37–39.
3. WC Testimony, Vol. I, pp. 226–227.
4. WC Testimony, Vol. XI, pp. 39; 41–42.
5. WC Testimony, Vol. I, p. 227.

Chapter 4: Youth House
1. WC Testimony, Vol. VIII, p. 205.
2. Ibid., pp. 209–211.
3. Siegel Exhibit No. 2, Vol. XXI, pp. 497; 501.
4. Ibid., p. 485.
5. Ibid., pp. 497–499.
6. Ibid.
7. WC Testimony, Vol. XI, p. 43.
8. WC Testimony, Vol. I, p. 228.
9. Siegel Exhibit No. 2, Vol. XXI, pp. 503–505.
10. Ibid., p. 505.
11. WC Testimony, Vol. VIII, p. 207.
12. Ibid., p. 209.

Chapter 5: Macho Teenage Marxist
1. WC Testimony, Vol. VIII, p. 124.
2. Ibid., p. 127.
3. Ibid., p. 131.
4. Ibid., p. 125.
5. Ibid., p. 132.
6. WC Testimony, Vol. I, p. 200.
7. WC Testimony, Vol. VIII, pp. 2–7.
8. Ibid., pp. 7; 9–10.
9. Ibid., p. 19.
10. Ibid., p. 18.
11. CE 2240, Vol. XXV, pp. 140–141.
12. WC Testimony, Vol. XI, p. 4.
13. CE 1127, Vol. XXII, pp. 101–102.
14. WC Testimony, Vol. I, p. 256.

Chapter 6: The Loose End
1. WC Testimony, Vol. VIII, p. 319.
2. Ibid., p. 270.
3. Edward Jay Epstein, *Legend*, p. 352.
4. Ibid., p. 355.
5. Ibid., p. 357.
6. Ibid., p. 620, note 1.
7. Ibid., pp. 358–359.
8. Ibid., p. 621, note 7.
9. WC Testimony, Vol. VIII, p. 280.
10. WC Testimony, Vol. VIII, p. 316.
11. Epstein, op. cit., pp. 363–364.
12. Ibid., p. 621, note 11.
13. Ibid., p. 365.
14. Ibid., p. 359.
15. Ibid.
16. WC Testimony, Vol. VIII, p. 275.
17. Epstein, op. cit., p. 620, note 3.
18. Ibid., p. 366.
19. Folsom Exhibit No. 1, Vol. XIX, p. 683.
20. Epstein, op. cit., p. 367.
21. Ibid.
22. Ibid., p. 620, note 4.
23. Ibid., pp. 367–368.
24. Ibid., p. 360.
25. Ibid., p. 621, note 6.
26. Ibid., p. 368.
27. Ibid., p. 369.
28. Ibid., pp. 369–370.
29. Ibid., p. 370.

Chapter 7: The Man Who Would Take Over the Team
1. Epstein, op. cit., p. 373.
2. Ibid., p. 374.
3. WC Testimony, Vol. VIII, pp. 322–323.
4. Ibid., p. 321.
5. Ibid., pp. 233–234.
6. Ibid., pp. 240–241.
7. Ibid., pp. 291–292.
8. Ibid., p. 300.
9. Ibid., pp. 292–293.
10. Ibid., p. 295.
11. WC Testimony, Vol. XI, p. 87.
12. Ibid., pp. 89–94.
13. Ibid., pp. 94–95.
14. Epstein, op. cit., p. 624, notes 8–11.
15. Ibid., pp. 376–377.
16. WC Testimony, Vol. I, p. 214.
17. CE 200, Vol. XVI, p. 580.

18. WC Testimony, Vol. VIII, pp. 297–298.
19. WC Hearings, Vol. VIII, p. 317.

Chapter 8: Return to Moscow and Minsk
1. HSCA Report, p. 371.

Chapter 9: Maternity House
1. CE 1127, Vol. XXII, pp. 100–101.
2. CE 206, Vol. XVI, pp. 594–595.
3. WC Testimony, Vol. I, pp. 205–207.
4. Ibid.

PART II: CHARITY IN FORT WORTH

Chapter 1: Honeymoon
1. WC Testimony, Vol. I, p. 136.
2. McMillan, op. cit., p. 234.
3. WC Testimony, Vol. I, pp. 6; 5.
4. Ibid., p. 136.
5. CE 984, Vol. XVIII, p. 619.
6. WC Testimony, Vol. IV, pp. 416–426.
7. WC Testimony, Vol. I, pp. 133–135.

Chapter 2: In the China Closet
1. WC Testimony, Vol. II, pp. 338–339.
2. WC Testimony, Vol. VIII, pp. 351–352.
3. Ibid., pp. 363–364.
4. Ibid., pp. 371–372.
5. Ibid., p. 384.
6. WC Testimony, Vol. I, pp. 134–135.

Chapter 3: Deep in the Heart of Texas
1. McMillan, op. cit., p. 242.
2. WC Testimony, Vol. VIII, p. 380.
3. WC Hearings, Vol. XI, p. 122.
4. WC Testimony, Vol. II, p. 305.
5. WC Testimony, Vol. IX, p. 72.
6. WC Testimony, Vol. VIII, pp. 436–437.
7. WC Testimony, Vol. I, pp. 10–11.
8. Ibid., pp. 138–139.
9. WC Testimony, Vol. VIII, p. 383.
10. Ibid., p. 365.
11. Ibid., p. 397.
12. Ibid., p. 376.

Chapter 4: The Well-born Friend
1. De Mohrenschildt's name is spelled in various places as de Mohrenschildt and De Mohrenschildt. Since the Warren Commission chose the latter form, it was decided to go along with it even if the correct spelling is likely to be in the first form.
2. McMillan, op. cit., p. 265.
3. WC Testimony, Vol. IX, p. 99.
4. Ibid., p. 270.
5. Ibid., p. 222.
6. HSCA, Vol. XII, p. 75.
7. Ibid., p. 76.
8. Ibid., p. 153.
9. Ibid., p. 115.
10. Ibid., pp. 182–183.
11. Ibid., p. 97.
12. Ibid., p. 111.
13. WC Testimony, Vol. IX, p. 225.
14. Ibid., p. 228.
15. Ibid., p. 273.
16. Ibid., p. 282.
17. Ibid., p. 266.
18. Ibid., p. 241.
19. Ibid., p. 236.
20. Ibid., p. 237.
21. Ibid., p. 242.
22. Ibid., p. 243.

Chapter 5: Not in a Million Years
1. HSCA, Vol. XII, p. 116.
2. WC Testimony, Vol. IX, pp. 261–263.
3. Ibid., p. 235.
4. Ibid.
5. Ibid., pp. 253; 264.
6. Norman Mailer, *Harlot's Ghost,* pp. 414–417.
7. Epstein, op. cit., pp. 558–559.

PART III: DARK DAYS IN DALLAS

Chapter 1: Evenings in Dallas
1. HSCA, Vol. XII, p. 89.
2. WC Testimony, Vol. IX, p. 96.
3. Ibid., p. 78.
4. WC Testimony, Vol. I, p. 138.
5. WC Testimony, Vol. IX, pp. 82–83.
6. WC Testimony, Vol. X, p. 166.
7. Ibid., p. 165.

8. By the time she testified in 1964, Alexandra had divorced Gary Taylor and remarried. The transcript identifies her as "Mrs. Gibson"; her first name has been added for clarity.
9. WC Testimony, Vol. XI, p. 148.
10. Ibid., pp. 134–135.
11. WC Testimony, Vol. X, p. 178.
12. WC Testimony, Vol. IX, p. 86.
13. Ibid., p. 233.
14. WC Testimony, Vol. VIII, p. 366.
15. McMillan, op. cit., p. 254.

Chapter 2: Oswald's *Kampf*
1. McMillan, op cit., pp. 257–258.
2. Adolf Hitler, *Mein Kampf,* p. 25.
3. Ibid., p. 34.
4. Ibid., pp. 21–22.
5. Ibid., pp. 516–517.
6. WC Testimony, Vol. VIII, pp. 467–468.
7. WC Hearings, Vol. XI, p. 120.
8. Hitler, op cit., p. 435.
9. Ibid., p. 34.
10. WC Testimony, Vol. IX, p. 48.

Chapter 3: "I Refused to Tell a Lie"
1. WC Testimony, Vol. IX, pp. 323–324.
2. WC Testimony, Vol. XI, pp. 127–128.
3. WC Hearings, Vol. XI, pp. 121–122.
4. WC Testimony, Vol. XI, p. 143.
5. Ibid., p. 144.
6. Ibid., p. 147.
7. WC Hearings, Vol. XI, pp. 121–122.
8. McMillan, op. cit., p. 260.
9. WC Hearings, Vol. XI, p. 121.
10. WC Testimony, Vol. XI, pp. 140–141.
11. McMillan, op. cit., p. 262.
12. WC Testimony, Vol. X, pp. 239; 242–243.
13. WC Testimony, Vol. VIII, p. 386.
14. McMillan, op. cit., p. 263.
15. Ibid., pp. 280–281.
16. WC Testimony, Vol. IX, p. 238.
17. Ibid.
18. HSCA, Vol. XII, p. 138.
19. WC Testimony, Vol. I, p. 11.

20. WC Testimony, Vol. IX, p. 232.
21. HSCA, Vol. XII, pp. 138–141.
22. WC Testimony, Vol. II, pp. 302–303.
23. McMillan, op. cit., p. 284.
24. Ibid., p. 285.
25. CE 994, Vol. XVIII, p. 625.
26. WC Testimony, Vol. IX, p. 325.
27. McMillan, op. cit., p. 286.
28. CE 994, Vol. XVIII, p. 625.
29. Robert Oswald, with Myrick and Barbara Land, *Lee: A Portrait of Lee Harvey Oswald*, pp. 130–131.

Chapter 4: Christmas and Red Caviar
1. WC Testimony, Vol. IX, p. 167.
2. Ibid., p. 275.
3. HSCA, Vol. XII, p. 128.
4. CE 994, Vol. XVIII, p. 624.
5. McMillan, op. cit., p. 309.
6. Ibid., pp. 309–310.
7. Ibid., p. 306.
8. Ibid.
9. WC Testimony, Vol. IX, p. 319.
10. Ibid., p. 320.
11. McMillan, op. cit., p. 305.
12. Epstein, op. cit., pp. 481–482.

Chapter 5: Grubs for the Organism
1. Epstein, op. cit., p. 564.
2. Ibid., p. 565.
3. WC Testimony, Vol. IX, p. 235.
4. For these figures, the author is indebted to Mary McHughes Ferrell's compilation of financial data from Warren Commission Testimony and Exhibits. Her individual sums, which were calculated to the penny, are here rounded off to the nearest dollar.
5. Mailer, op. cit., pp. 418–419.

Chapter 6: Trouble at Work
1. CE 994, Vol. XVIII, p. 626.
2. Ibid.
3. McMillan, op. cit., p. 307.
4. Ibid., p. 308. In the course of interviewing Marina, Priscilla Johnson McMillan induced her to write the letter again from memory, perhaps a year and a half after it was first composed.
5. Epstein, op. cit., p. 482.

6. Weinstock Exhibit No. 1, Vol. XXI, p. 721.
7. Dibbs Exhibit No. 12, Vol. XIX, p. 579.
8. HSCA, Vol. XII, p. 172.
9. WC Testimony, Vol. X, p. 204.
10. Ibid., p. 206.
11. Ibid., p. 187.

Chapter 7: In Order to Feel a Little Love
1. Epstein, op. cit., pp. 484–485.
2. McMillan, op. cit., p. 317.
3. Ibid., p. 318.
4. WC Testimony, Vol. X, pp. 167–168.
5. CE 51, Vol. XVI, pp. 187–188.
6. CE 986, Vol. XVIII, p. 501; translated from the Russian by the Warren Commission.
7. WC Testimony, Vol. XI, p. 299.
8. McMillan, op. cit., p. 328.
9. Ibid., p. 329.
10. WC Testimony, Vol. X, p. 256.
11. Ibid., pp. 247; 242.

Chapter 8: Hunter of Fascists
1. McMillan, op. cit., p. 332.
2. Ibid., p. 333.
3. CE 322, Vol. XVI, p. 886.
4. WC Testimony, Vol. X, p. 189.
5. Epstein, op. cit., p. 488.
6. CE 2694, Vol. XXVI, p. 60.
7. Mary McHughes Ferrell, chronological compilation of Warren Commission Testimony and Exhibits.
8. CE 2694, Vol. XXVI, p. 60.
9. McMillan, op. cit., p. 349.
10. WC Testimony, Vol. X, p. 190.
11. McMillan, op. cit., p. 351.
12. CE 1403, Vol. XXII, p. 779.
13. CE 1, Vol. XVI, pp. 1–2.

Chapter 9: Stoicism, Majestic in Purpose
1. CE 98, Vol. XVI, p. 433.
2. CE 97, Vol. XVI, p. 424.
3. Ibid., pp. 429–430.
4. Ibid., pp. 425–426.
5. Ibid., pp. 426–427.
6. CE 98, Vol. XVI, p. 434.

Chapter 10: Waiting for the Police
1. CE 1401, Vol. XXII, p. 756.
2. WC Testimony, Vol. XI, p. 405.
3. Ibid., p. 410.
4. Epstein, op. cit., p. 491.
5. CE 2521, Vol. XXV, p. 730.
6. McMillan, op. cit., p. 359.
7. Gerald Posner, *Case Closed,* p. 116.
8. CE 2001, Vol. XXIV, p. 40.
9. WC Testimony, Vol. V, p. 446.
10. Epstein, op. cit., p. 647, note 1.
11. Posner, op. cit., pp. 116–117.

Chapter 11: Telescopic Sight
1. CE 1403, Vol. XXII, p. 777.
2. WC Testimony, Vol. XI, p. 293.
3. McMillan, op. cit., p. 358.
4. Ibid., p. 357.
5. Ibid., p. 373.
6. Ibid., p. 374.
7. CE 1403, Vol. XXII, p. 777.
8. WC Testimony, Vol. V, p. 619.
9. WC Testimony, Vol. IX, pp. 248–250.
10. McMillan, op. cit., p. 349.
11. WC Testimony, Vol. IX, p. 314.
12. Ibid., p. 315.
13. Ibid.
14. Ibid., p. 316.
15. Ibid., p. 317.
16. Epstein, op. cit., p. 564.
17. WC Testimony, Vol. IX, pp. 317–318.
18. CE 994, Vol. XVIII, pp. 629–630.
19. WC Testimony, Vol. IX, p. 234.
20. Epstein, op. cit., p. 648, note 10. In an interview with Lawrence Schiller, Marina confirmed that Lee bought the rifle with the $25 and that she did tell De Mohrenschildt about it and spoke of Lee as her "fool husband."

PART IV: THE BIG EASY

Chapter 1: "A Terrifically Sad Life"
1. Unpublished interview of Marguerite Oswald by Lawrence Schiller, conducted in 1976.
2. WC Testimony, Vol. VIII, pp. 58–59.
3. Ibid., p. 46.
4. Ibid., pp. 46–48.
5. Ibid., pp. 51–52; 55.

Chapter 2: "He Walks and Talks Like a Man"
1. McMillan, op. cit., p. 384.
2. HSCA, Vol. XII, p. 170.
3. WC Testimony, Vol. VIII, p. 183; 186.
4. Ibid., pp. 135–136.
5. Ibid., p. 151.
6. Ibid., p. 136.
7. McMillan, op. cit., p. 388.
8. Posner, op. cit., p. 427.
9. WC Testimony, Vol. XI, pp. 326–327.
10. Ibid., pp. 337–338.

Chapter 3: Forbidden Strings
1. McMillan, op. cit., pp. 396–397.
2. WC Testimony, Vol. II, p. 471.
3. McMillan, op. cit., p. 396.
4. WC Testimony, Vol. II, p. 470.
5. WC Testimony, Vol. IX, p. 460.
6. Ibid.
7. CE 422, Vol. XVII, pp. 140–144.

Chapter 4: Love, Heat, and Grease
1. McMillan, op. cit., pp. 398–399.
2. Ibid., p. 398.
3. Ibid., p. 415.
4. WC Testimony, Vol. X, pp. 267–268.
5. Ibid., pp. 214–215.
6. Ibid., p. 227.
7. Ibid., pp. 225–228.
8. Ibid., p. 223.
9. CE 408, Vol. XVII, pp. 88–91; translated by the Warren Commission.
10. WC Testimony, Vol. VIII, pp. 148–149.

Chapter 5: Fair Play for Cuba
1. CE 986, Vol. XVIII, p. 518.
2. Robert Payne, *Portrait of a Revolutionary,* p. 5.
3. Epstein, op. cit., p. 497.
4. Ibid.
5. Lee (Vincent T.) Exhibit No. 2, Vol. XX, pp. 512–513.
6. McMillan, op. cit., p. 400.
7. Lee (Vincent T.) Exhibit No. 3, Vol. XX, pp. 514–516.
8. WC Testimony, Vol. V, p. 401.
9. WC Testimony, Vol. I, p. 23.

10. CE 994, Vol. XVIII, pp. 631–632.
11. McMillan, op. cit., p. 411.
12. CE 1412, Vol. XXII, p. 807.
13. Ibid., pp. 805–806.
14. McMillan, op. cit., p. 417.
15. Ibid., p. 418.
16. Ibid.
17. CE 986, Vol. XVIII, pp. 521–522.
18. Ibid., p. 526.
19. Payne, op. cit., p. 40.

Chapter 6: Atheism and Morality
1. CE 410, Vol. XVII, pp. 102–104.
2. WC Testimony, Vol. X, p. 215.
3. Ibid., p. 216.
4. Ibid., p. 226.
5. McMillan, op. cit., p. 424.
6. Ibid., p. 416.
7. CE 2648, Vol. XXV, p. 919.
8. WC Testimony, Vol. VIII, p. 149.
9. CE 2648, Vol. XXV, p. 923.
10. CE 2649, Vol. XXV, pp. 923–924.
11. Ibid., pp. 927–928.
12. McMillan, op. cit., pp. 424–425.

Chapter 7: Out of Omens Come Events
1. Lee (Vincent T.) Exhibit No. 4, Vol. XX, pp. 518–521.
2. WC Testimony, Vol. X, p. 90.
3. Lee (Vincent T.) Exhibit No. 5, Vol. XX, pp. 524–525.
4. McMillan, op. cit., p. 430.
5. WC Testimony, Vol. X, pp. 34–36.
6. Ibid., p. 77.
7. Ibid., p. 37.
8. Ibid., p. 38.
9. Ibid., p. 45.
10. WC Testimony, Vol. VIII, p. 145.
11. WC Testimony, Vol. X, pp. 55–56.
12. Ibid., pp. 59–60.
13. WC Testimony, Vol. IV, p. 436.
14. Ibid., p. 438.
15. McMillan, op. cit., p. 433.
16. Ibid., p. 434.
17. WC Testimony, Vol. X, p. 39.
18. McMillan, op. cit., p. 438.

Chapter 8: Fair Play
1. WC Testimony, Vol. XI, p. 160.
2. Ibid., p. 162.
3. Ibid.

4. Stuckey Exhibit No. 2, Vol. XXI, p. 621.
5. Ibid., pp. 622–626.
6. Ibid., pp. 628–630.
7. Ibid., p. 630.
8. WC Testimony, Vol. XI, pp. 165–166.
9. McMillan, op. cit. p. 440.
10. WC Testimony, Vol. XI, p. 168.
11. WC Testimony, Vol. X, pp. 42–43.
12. Stuckey Exhibit No. 3, Vol. XXI, pp. 634; 637–641.
13. WC Testimony, Vol. XI, pp. 171–175.
14. Ibid., pp. 175–176.
15. McMillan, op. cit., pp. 451–452.

Chapter 9: Picking Up the Pieces
1. CE 1145, Vol. XXII, p. 168.
2. Johnson (Arnold) Exhibit 4–A, Vol. XX, p. 265.
3. McMillan, op. cit., p. 443.
4. CE 1404, Vol. XXII, p. 788.
5. McMillan, op. cit., p. 444.
6. CE 93, Vol. XVI, p. 339.
7. McMillan, op. cit., p. 463.

PART V: PROTAGONISTS AND PROVOCATEURS

Chapter 1: Protagonists and Provocateurs
1. WC Testimony, Vol. XI, pp. 341–342.
2. Ibid., pp. 350–351.
3. Ibid., pp. 361–362.
4. HSCA Report, p. 193.
5. Ibid.
6. Ibid., pp. 193–194.
7. Wise, David, *The American Police State*, pp. 314; 311.
8. Ibid., p. 311.
9. CE 833, Vol. XVII, p. 794.

Chapter 2: Right-wing Adventurers
1. Anthony Summers, *Conspiracy,* pp. 290–291.
2. Ibid., pp. 301–302.
3. Posner, op. cit., p. 146.
4. Summers, op. cit., p. 306.
5. Posner, op. cit., pp. 144–145.
6. National Oceanic and Atmospheric Administration, temperature records for Clinton,

Louisiana, September 1963;
NOAA Central Library, Silver
Spring, MD.
7. HSCA Report, p. 142.
8. Posner, op. cit., p. 142.

Chapter 3: An Inexplicable Visit
1. WC Testimony, Vol. XI, p. 370.
2. Ibid., pp. 370–374.
3. Ibid., p. 388.
4. Ibid., p. 214.

Chapter 4: A Nimble Solution
1. Gaeton Fonzi, *The Last
   Investigation*, p. 114.
2. HSCA, Vol. X, p. 29.
3. Posner, op. cit., p. 178.
4. WC Testimony, Vol. XI, p. 370.
5. Ibid., p. 369.
6. Posner, op. cit., p. 179.
7. Ibid., p. 177.
8. Ibid., p. 180.
9. Ibid., pp. 178–179.
10. WC Testimony, Vol. XI, pp.
    380–381.
11. Fonzi, op. cit., pp. 112–113. Fonzi
    uses the Spanish spelling Silvia
    for Mrs. Odio's name. The author
    has amended this to Sylvia, which
    was used by the Warren
    Commission.
12. Ibid., p. 113.
13. Posner, op. cit., p. 177.
14. Fonzi, op. cit., pp. 114–115.
15. Warren Report, p. 136.

Chapter 5: Mexico
1. Posner, op. cit., p. 181.
2. Oleg Nechiporenko, *Passport to
   Assassination*, p. 67.
3. Ibid., pp. 67–68.
4. Ibid., pp. 68–69.
5. Ibid., pp. 70–71.
6. Ibid., p. 72.
7. Ibid., p. 75.
8. Ibid., pp. 76–78.
9. Ibid., pp. 78–79.
10. Ibid., p. 80–81.
11. Posner, op. cit., pp. 185–186.

PART VI: DENOUEMENT

Chapter 1: The Road to Domesticity
1. McMillan, op. cit., p. 422.

2. WC Hearings, Vol. XIII, p. 479.
3. Gangl Exhibit No. 1, Vol. XX,
   p. 3.
4. McMillan, op. cit., p. 471.
5. WC Testimony, Vol. VI, pp.
   403–404.
6. Ibid., p. 406.
7. Ibid., p. 437.
8. WC Testimony, Vol. II, p. 509.
9. Ibid., p. 42.
10. CE 994, Vol. XVIII, p. 634.
11. WC Testimony, Vol. III, pp.
    213–214.
12. Ibid., pp. 210; 217–218.
13. McMillan, op. cit., p. 474.
14. Ibid., p. 489.
15. Ibid., p. 477.
16. CE 994, Vol. XVIII, p. 636.
17. McMillan, op. cit., p. 492.
18. Ibid., p. 491.
19. CE 75, Vol. XVI, pp. 237–240.

Chapter 2: The Shadow of the FBI
1. McMillan, op. cit., pp. 494–495.
2. Ibid., pp. 495–496.
3. WC Testimony, Vol. III, p. 100.
4. McMillan, op. cit., p. 497.
5. Ibid., pp. 504–505.
6. WC Testimony, Vol. III, p. 102.
7. McMillan, op. cit., pp. 498–499.
8. Ibid., p. 499.
9. CE 103, Vol. XVI, pp. 443–444.
10. McMillan, op. cit., p. 507.
11. WC Testimony, Vol. III, p. 14.
12. Ibid., p. 17.
13. WC Testimony, Vol. VI, p. 437.
14. McMillan, op. cit., pp. 515–516.
15. WC Testimony, Vol. II, p. 222.
16. WC Testimony, Vol. I, pp. 65–66.
17. McMillan, op. cit., p. 522.
18. Ibid., p. 523.
19. Ibid., p. 524.
20. WC Testimony, Vol. III, p. 47.
21. McMillan, op. cit., p. 524.
22. Ibid., pp. 524–525.

Chapter 3: Pigeons Flew Up from the
Roof
1. CE 2008, Vol. XXIV, p. 407.
2. CE 2009, Vol. XXIV, pp. 408–409.
3. WC Testimony, Vol. III, p. 68.
4. McMillan, op. cit., p. 537.
5. William Manchester, *Death of a
   President*, p. 121.

6. Ibid.
7. Ibid.
8. McMillan, op. cit., p. 528.
9. WC Testimony, Vol. VII, p. 342.
10. CE 1381, Vol. XXII, p. 681.
11. WC Testimony, Vol. III, p. 175.
12. Ibid., p. 197.
13. Ibid., p. 211.
14. Ibid., p. 345.
15. WC Hearings, Vol. V, p. 565.
16. WC Testimony, Vol. III, p. 265.
17. Ibid., pp. 245–252.

Chapter 4: An Afternoon at the Movies
1. WC Testimony, Vol. VI, p. 409.
2. WC Testimony, Vol. II, p. 256.
3. WC Testimony, Vol. VI, p. 438.
4. CE 2003, Vol. XXIV, p. 203.
5. McMillan, op. cit., p. 535.
6. Warren Report, pp. 71–72.
7. WC Testimony, Vol. VII, p. 6.
8. McMillan, op. cit., p. 536.

Chapter 5: The Hour of Panic
1. WC Hearings, Vol. V, p. 565.
2. Ibid., p. 566.
3. WC Testimony, Vol. III, p. 68.
4. WC Testimony, Vol. I, p. 74.
5. CE 994, Vol. XVIII, p. 639.
6. WC Testimony, Vol. III, p. 69.
7. Ibid., p. 79.
8. WC Testimony, Vol. I, p. 75.
9. Ibid., p. 74.
10. WC Testimony, Vol. III, p. 79.
11. Ibid., p. 81.
12. WC Hearings, Vol. V, p. 566.

Chapter 6: The Return of Marguerite
Oswald
1. WC Testimony, Vol. I, pp.
141–143.
2. Unpublished interview of
Marguerite Oswald by Lawrence
Schiller, 1976.
3. WC Testimony, Vol. I, pp.
141–143.
4. Unpublished interview of
Marguerite Oswald by Lawrence
Schiller, 1976.
5. WC Testimony, Vol. I, p. 143.
6. McMillan, op. cit., p. 543.
7. WC Testimony, Vol. I, pp.
144–146.
8. WC Testimony, Vol. III, p. 83.

9. McMillan, op. cit., p. 544.
10. Ibid.

Chapter 7: The Octopus Outside
1. WC Testimony, Vol. XV, p. 152.
2. WC Testimony, Vol. VII, p. 359.
3. WC Testimony, Vol. IV, p. 204.
4. Ibid., p. 205.
5. Ibid., p. 220.
6. Ibid., pp. 204–206.
7. WC Testimony, Vol. III, p. 230.
8. WC Testimony, Vol. IV, p. 206.
9. Ibid., p. 207.
10. Ibid.
11. Ibid., p. 232.
12. Ibid.
13. WC Testimony, Vol. V, p. 218.
14. WC Testimony, Vol. IV, p. 211.
15. Ibid., p. 214.
16. Ibid., p. 216.
17. Ibid., p. 214.
18. Ibid., p. 217.
19. Ibid., p. 226.
20. Ibid., p. 225.
21. Ibid., p. 239.
22. Ibid.
23. Ibid., p. 209.
24. Ibid., p. 238.
25. Ibid., p. 210.
26. McMillan, op. cit., p. 625, note
22.
27. WC Testimony, Vol. II, pp.
260–261.
28. WC Testimony, Vol. IV, p. 212.
29. WC Testimony, Vol. III, p. 148.
30. WC Testimony, Vol. VII, p. 135.
31. Ibid., p. 130.

Chapter 8: A Black Pullover Sweater
with Jagged Holes in It
1. WC Testimony, Vol. I, pp.
148–149.
2. Ibid., p. 78.
3. Ibid., p. 150.
4. Oswald, op. cit., p. 144.
5. Ibid., p. 145.
6. McMillan, op. cit., p. 551.
7. WC Testimony, Vol. III, p. 85.
8. McMillan, op. cit., p. 551.
9. WC Testimony, Vol. IV, pp.
228–229.
10. Ibid., p. 230.
11. McMillan, op. cit., p. 552.
12. WC Testimony, Vol. I, p. 152.

13. WC Testimony, Vol. IV, p. 226.
14. WC Testimony, Vol. I, p. 156.
15. WC Testimony, Vol. IV, p. 233.
16. Ibid., pp. 233–234.
17. McMillan, op. cit., p. 555.
18. WC Testimony, Vol. I, pp. 235; 150.

Chapter 9: "He Cry; He Eye Wet"
1. WC Testimony, Vol. I, pp. 156–157.
2. Ibid., pp. 158–160.
3. Ibid., pp. 161–163.
4. Oswald, op. cit., p. 155.
5. Ibid., pp. 158–159.
6. Ibid., p. 156.
7. Ibid., pp. 160–161.
8. WC Testimony, Vol. I, p. 166.
9. Ibid., p. 167.
10. Ibid., p. 167.
11. Ibid., p. 169.
12. Ibid.
13. Ibid., pp. 169–170.
14. Oswald, op. cit., p. 162.
15. WC Testimony, Vol. I, p. 168.
16. Epstein, op. cit., p. 532.
17. Oswald, op. cit., pp. 162–165.
18. CE 295, Vol. XVI, pp. 815–822.

PART VII: THE AMATEUR HIT MAN

Chapter 1: The Amateur Hit Man
1. Interview of Jack Ruby by Lawrence Schiller, 1966, © Alskog, Inc.
2. WC Testimony, Vol. V, p. 190.
3. Ibid., p. 191.
4. Ibid., p. 194.
5. Ibid., p. 195.
6. Ibid., p. 196.
7. Ibid., p. 197.
8. Ibid.
9. Ibid., p. 198.
10. Ibid., pp. 198–199.
11. Ibid., pp. 208–210.
12. Ibid., p. 211.
13. Ibid., p. 212.
14. Ibid.
15. Frank Ragano and Selwyn Raab, Mob Lawyer, p. 151.
16. Ibid., p. 152.
17. Posner, op. cit., p. 372, citing CE 2303, Vol. XXV, p. 27.
18. WC Testimony, Vol. XIV, p. 151.

19. WC Testimony, Vol. V, p. 185.
20. Posner, op. cit., p. 374.
21. WC Testimony, Vol. XIV, p. 468.
22. Posner, op. cit., pp. 375–376.
23. Ibid., p. 378, citing Affidavit of George Senator, November 24, 1963.
24. Posner, op. cit., p. 377.
25. Ibid.
26. Ibid., p. 378.
27. Ibid.
28. WC Testimony, Vol. XV, p. 364.
29. Harry Carlson's name is actually Harry Olsen, but since Ruby made the error in his testimony of calling him Carlson and the Warren Commission accepted that, it would have been confusing to correct their text.
30. WC Testimony, Vol. XIV, p. 221.
31. Posner, op. cit., pp. 382–383.
32. Ibid., p. 385.
33. Ibid.
34. Ibid., p. 386.
35. Ibid., p. 387.
36. Ibid., p. 389, citing WC Testimony, Vol. XV, pp. 672–673.
37. WC Testimony, Vol. XVI, pp. 632–633.
38. WC Testimony, Vol. XIV, p. 236.
39. Ibid.
40. Posner, op. cit., p. 391.
41. Ibid., pp. 392–393.
42. WC Testimony, Vol. V. p. 199.
43. Posner, op. cit., p. 393.
44. WC Testimony, Vol. V, p. 199.
45. WC Testimony, Vol. XII, p. 399.
46. WC Testimony, Vol. V, p. 199.
47. Ibid.
48. WC Testimony, Vol. XII, pp. 400–401.
49. Posner, op. cit., pp. 396–397.
50. Ibid., pp. 395–396.
51. WC Testimony, Vol. XIII, p. 215.
52. Posner, op. cit., p. 392.

PART VIII: OSWALD'S GHOST

Chapter 1: The Punishment of Hosty and the Death of the Handler
1. McMillan, op. cit., p. 625, note 22.
2. HSCA Report, p. 195.
3. McMillan, op. cit., p. 626, note 22.

4. WC Testimony, Vol. IX, p. 274.
5. HSCA, Vol. XII, p. 73.
6. Ibid., pp. 214–215.
7. Ibid., p. 225.
8. Ibid.
9. Ibid., pp. 225–227.
10. Ibid., pp. 228–229.
11. Ibid., pp. 229–230.
12. McMillan, op. cit., pp. 569–570.
13. Posner, op. cit., p. 118.
14. McMillan, op. cit., p. 570.
15. Fonzi, op. cit., pp. 189–192.

Chapter 2: In the Rubble of the Aftermath
1. WC Testimony, Vol. I, p. 172.
2. Ibid., pp. 173–174.
3. Ibid., p. 174.
4. Ibid., p. 175.
5. Ibid., pp. 60–61.
6. Ibid., pp. 79–80.
7. Ibid., p. 61.
8. McMillan, op. cit., p. 565.
9. Ibid., p. 563.
10. Ibid., p. 568.

Chapter 3: Evidence
1. WC Testimony, Vol. XI, pp. 308–309.
2. WC Testimony, Vol. III, p. 411.
3. Ibid., p. 412.
4. Author's November 1993 conversation with Dr. Robert Artwohl, head of Emergency Services, Union Memorial Hospital, Baltimore, Maryland.
5. One is, of course, assuming that it was Oswald's Mannlicher-Carcano that was used in the assassination. For, if it was not, then what did happen to his gun, and what was in the package he brought with him that morning to the Texas School Book Depository? Why indeed would he carry his gun to work if it was not going to be used? Would he take it there in order to allow others to implicate him? There are many arguments that would attempt to disprove the use of the Mannlicher-Carcano, but they all seem weak in the light of Ockham's Razor: The simplest explanation that covers all the facts is likely to be the correct explanation.

Chapter 4: Character
1. CE 25, Vol. XVI, p. 106.
2. Hitler, op. cit., p. 29.
3. McMillan, op. cit., p. 573.
4. CE 322, Vol. XVI, p. 886.
5. McMillan, op. cit., p. 518.
6. Ralph Waldo Emerson, The Complete Essays and Other Writings of Ralph Waldo Emerson, p. 253. One must apologize to Emerson, a great writer, for presuming to invert his second paragraph by placing it above the first.
7. WC Testimony, Vol. XI, pp. 49–50.

Chapter 6: The Third Widow
1. WC Testimony, Vol. I, p. 182.
2. Ibid.
3. Unpublished interview of Marguerite Oswald by Lawrence Schiller, 1976.

BIBLIOGRAPHY

NOTE: When more than one edition is listed, citations in the notes are from the starred edition.

GOVERNMENT REPORTS

Report of the President's Commission on the Assassination of President John F. Kennedy and 26 accompanying volumes of Hearings and Exhibits. Washington, D.C.: U.S. Government Printing Office, 1964. (Report, without accompanying volumes, also published by The Associated Press, 1964*; and by Doubleday, 1964.)

Report of the Select Committee on Assassinations, U.S. House of Representatives, with 12 accompanying volumes of Hearings and Appendices on the Kennedy investigation, Washington, D.C.: U.S. Government Printing Office, 1979. (Report, without supporting volumes, also published by Bantam, 1979.)

BOOKS

Emerson, Ralph Waldo. *The Complete Essays and Other Writings.* New York: Random House, Inc., 1940.

Epstein, Edward Jay. *Legend: The Secret World of Lee Harvey Oswald,* as printed in *The Assassination Chronicles.* New York: Carroll & Graf Publishers, Inc., 1992*. (Originally published as *Legend: The Secret World of Lee Harvey Oswald.* New York: Reader's Digest Press/McGraw-Hill, 1978.)

Fonzi, Gaeton. *The Last Investigation.* New York: Thunder's Mouth Press, 1993; first trade paperback edition, 1994*.

Hitler, Adolf. *Mein Kampf,* translated by Ralph Manheim. Boston: Houghton Mifflin, 1971.

McMillan, Priscilla Johnson. *Marina and Lee.* New York: Harper & Row, 1977.

Mailer, Norman. *Harlot's Ghost.* New York: Random House, 1991.

Manchester, William. *The Death of a President.* London: Michael Joseph, 1967.

Nechiporenko, Col. Oleg Maximovich. *Passport to Assassination.* New York: Birch Lane Press, 1993.

Oswald, Robert L., with Myrick and Barbara Land. *Lee: A Portrait of Lee Harvey Oswald.* New York: Coward-McCann, 1967.

Payne, Robert. *Portrait of a Revolutionary: Mao Tse-tung.* New York: Abelard-Schuman, 1961.

Posner, Gerald. *Case Closed: Lee Harvey Oswald and the Assassination of JFK.* New York: Random House, 1993; Anchor Books, 1994*.

Ragano, Frank, and Selwyn Raab. *Mob Lawyer.* New York: Charles Scribner's Sons, 1994.

Summers, Anthony. *Conspiracy.* New York: McGraw-Hill, 1980; Paragon House, 1989 and 1991*.

Wise, David. *The American Police State: The Government Against the People.* New York: Vintage Books, 1979.

UNPUBLISHED AND MISCELLANEOUS MATERIALS

Compilation of Oswald's earnings and expenditures from the Warren Commission Hearings and Exhibits, Mary McHughes Ferrell, 1993.

Interview of Marguerite Oswald by Lawrence Schiller, 1976, © New Ingot Company.

Interview of Jack Ruby by Lawrence Schiller, 1966, © Alskog, Inc.

National Oceanic and Atmospheric Administration, NOAA Central Library, Silver Spring, Md., temperature records for Clinton, Lousiana, September 1963.

Transcript of dialogue, *Frontline,* "Who Was Lee Harvey Oswald?" produced by WGBH, Boston, Mass., and broadcast on PBS stations, November (various dates) 1993.

ABOUT THE AUTHOR

NORMAN MAILER was born 1923 in Long Branch, New Jersey, and grew up in Brooklyn, New York. After graduating from Harvard, he served in the South Pacific during World War II. He published his first book, *The Naked and the Dead,* in 1948. *Oswald's Tale* is his twenty-eighth book. Mailer won the National Book Award and the Pulitzer Prize in 1968 for *Armies of the Night,* and was awarded the Pulitzer Prize again in 1980 for *The Executioner's Song.* He has directed four feature-length films, was a co-founder of *The Village Voice* in 1955, and was president of the American PEN from 1984 to 1986.

ABOUT THE TYPE

This book was set in Baskerville, a typeface that was designed by John Baskerville, an amateur printer and typefounder, and cut for him by John Handy in 1750. The type became popular again when the Lanston Monotype Corporation of London revived the classic Roman face in 1923. The Mergenthaler Linotype Company in England and the United States cut a version of Baskerville in 1931, making it one of the most widely used typefaces today.